THE CHANTS OF THE
VATICAN GRADUAL

By Dom Dominic Johner

Translated from the German
By Monks of
St. John's Abbey

GREGORIAN INSTITUTE OF AMERICA
Toledo 2, Ohio
1948

Imprimi potest:

✠ALCUINUS DEUTSCH, O.S.B.
Abbas S. Joannis Bapt.

Nihil obstat:

ALEXIUS HOFFMANN, O.S.B.
Censor Deputatus

November 22, 1934

Imprimatur:

C. THIEBAUT, V.G.
Adm. Dioec. S. Clodoaldi, Minn.

November 26, 1934

050707

Copyright, 1940
ST. JOHN'S ABBEY PRESS
Collegeville, Minnesota

CONTENTS

THE MASSES FOR SUNDAYS AND FEASTDAYS ACCORDING TO THE LITURGICAL SEASONS. (*Proprium De Tempore*).

SPECIAL FEASTS OF OUR LORD AND THE SAINTS
(*Proprium De Sanctis.*)

Contents

FOREWORD BY THE TRANSLATORS

In response to many requests for a book descriptive and explanatory of the Gregorian Mass chants, the monks of St. John's Abbey, Collegeville, Minn., undertook the translation from the German of Dom Johner's work: *Die Sonn- und Festtagslieder des Vatikanischen Graduale*, under the above title. In the foreword the author indicates the scope of his work. He writes: "The present work is intended chiefly to serve as an aid to the prayerful rendition of the variable chanted parts of the Mass. At the same time it aims to be a guide for the worthy and artistic rendition of those chants which have been handed down to us from an age of strong faith and noble taste." Chant is essentially a form of worship offered by the faithful and as such is an integral part of the liturgy. It is intimately connected with the very source of all Liturgy, the Eucharistic Sacrifice, and attempts to interpret and express in music the sentiments which the text expresses in words.

Individual consideration is given to the texts of the Introit, Gradual, Alleluia-verse, Tract, Sequence, Offertory, and Communion. These texts are given in Latin and in English, and are arranged in parallel columns. They are studied in their historical and liturgical setting, and their sentiments of joy and sorrow, hope and fear, gratitude and penance, are pointed out and developed. In this sense also the intimate relationship existing between these various texts is indicated; all are integrated into a unified whole and referred to the life of Christ and His Church. Following this short meditation, the author analyses the musical score accompanying the text, and attempts to show how Gregorian Chant interprets these various sentiments and gives adequate expression to them— in short, how Gregorian Chant is the prefect yet simple medium of tranlating religious emotion into the language of music.

An indispensable condition for the intelligent use of this book as a guide for interpretation is the simultaneous use of the Vatican Gradual, since musical notation has not been included in the present work. However, only a minimum and very elementary knowledge of Gregorian Chant is necessary for the fruitful use and understanding of the book. Further knowledge is given in a very significant Introduction, which describes the structure and expressiveness of the variable Mass Chants. The original German, as also the English manuscript, have been made the basis for a very successful summer school course in the study of Gregorian Chant. The book might adequately be described as "a study in the appreciation of Gregorian Chant."

ACKNOWLEDGMENT

The translators gratefully acknowledge their obligations to the following for the kind permission extended them to use copyrighted material: Msgr. H. T. Henry, for his translation of the *Lauda Sion*; Messrs. Burns, Oates and Washbourne, for the translations of the *Dies Irae* and the *Stabat Mater*, which appear in *Annus Sanctus*; P. J. Kenedy, for Abbot Cabrol's excellent version of the Roman Missal.

FOREWORD TO THE FIRST GERMAN EDITION

The present work is intended chiefly to serve as an aid to the prayerful rendition of the variable chanted parts of the Mass. At the same time it aims to be a guide for the worthy and artistic execution of those chants which have been handed down to us from an age of strong faith and noble taste. Choral music, or chant, is here considered not as a mere historic relic of the past, nor is worthy rendition to be understood in the sense of an elaborate concert interpretation of these monodic church compositions of the Middle Ages. Chant is more than this. It is an integral part of the liturgy, as much alive and inspiring today as ever. It is the praise of the living God by his people in union with Christ. Anyone, therefore, wishing to render chant properly must participate in the Christ-life of the Church, must seek spiritual nourishment at the heart of the liturgy, which is the Eucharistic Sacrifice. He must desire, as Christ did, to honor the Father with due reverence. These few thoughts have formed the guiding principles of the present work.

Questions of purely historical interest have been touched upon only as occasion offered. No attempt has been made to portray the historical development of the different Mass formulas, and still less has any critical study of the various readings of texts and melodies been attempted. Nor should the reader expect a systematic introduction to the liturgical year, although the author has made an effort to explain the texts in their proper liturgical setting in the Church year.

As the title states, the work has been limited to the Sundays and principal feasts of the year. Such feasts of the Saints, which according to the rubrics are to be celebrated even though they fall on a Sunday are included also. To these have been added Ash Wednesday, Holy Week, the feast of St. Joseph, and the Requiem Mass. The second Mass of Christmas has not been explained, since it is sung in few churches only. Historical sketches concerning the introduction of newer feasts have been given as occasion demanded. Where these sketches are wanting, there is question of feasts which belong to the more ancient liturgy and which with their chants are to be found in manuscripts dating from the ninth to the tenth century.

Purely theoretical questions were touched upon only lightly. These can be studied from textbooks treating of chant. The classic work of Professor P. Wagner; *Einfuehrung In Die Gregorianischen Melodien* (3 vols., Breitkopf and Haertel, Leipzig) is particularly recommended.

Outside of this one work few others proved to be of any great help for the scope of the present undertaking. *Betende Kirche* (Maria-Laach,

2nd ed., 1926); Reck, *Das Missale als Betrachtungsbuch* (Herder, Freiburg, 5 vols.), and similar excellent works devote little attention to the
texts that are chanted. Only occasional and very general remarks are
made concerning the melodies themselves. Periodicals of sacred music
in Germany, with few exceptions, lack a genuine appreciation of the
intrinsic value of the melodies of the Vatican Gradual. Periodicals in
other countries offer more on chant. A pertinent bibliography, as a guide
to further study of the subject, is subjoined. For the most part, however,
the author has had to rely on his own resources, and, for this reason,
feels keenly that his work is that of a pioneer in this particular field. He
knows well that our modern age listens to ancient melodies with some
misgivings. He realizes also that melodies have more than one signification and can therefore be interpreted in a manner different from that
which he has outlined in the following pages. The reader will find that
the author is not entirely alien to subjectivism, which often adapts more
than it explains. This fact, however, is not exactly a great misfortune.
Much greater is the danger that many choirs will sing the chant without
any feeling or art whatsoever. May this book lead them to the true
spirit of the chant and effect a more intimate understanding of the
melodies of Gregorian chant, to the end that these chants may be sung
as so many prayers by means of which the faithful soul may soar aloft
to God. May it also inspire the reader to strive after better technique,
so that he may express outwardly in a more perfect manner that which
he feels and understands inwardly.

An essential condition for understanding the content of the following pages is the simultaneous use of the Vatican Gradual. The musical
notation of the text has not been included in the book, although, without
doubt, it would have helped greatly for a better understanding of the
explanations given. Hence, whenever notes are indicated by the use of
their corresponding letters, the distinction of octaves $(G–g–g^1)$ is, as a
rule, not made.

Whenever reference is made to some other Sunday or feast for the
explanation of a designated text, there is always a question of similarity
of text and melody. If, for example, the explanation of a certain Introit
is referred to the Introit of another Mass, then the two are to be treated
alike in their rendition, unless, of course, something else to the contrary
has been expressly stated.

Here and there attention has been called to certain imperfections in
the melody. This has been done not in a spirit of criticism but out of
sincerity, and only to warn against the false notion that love and enthusiasm for chant must be artifically aroused. This is not at all required.

It would be astonishing, indeed, if only pearls of great value were to be found in its rich storehouse of treasures. These occasional imperfections give greater prominence to the beauty and sincerity of expression of the other melodies.

The sequence of the words in the Latin text has, as much as possible, been retained in the translation. Those unacquainted with Latin can in this way more easily compare the translation with the original text and its melody. For this reason, also, the division and phrasing indicated by the larger pause signs in the Vatican Gradual has been accurately retained and for the sake of clearness is shown here by numbers.

The present work is the outgrowth of the author's lecture course in the High School of Music in Cologne.

May God bless the work! May it be the means of ever more fully realizing the desire of the saintly Pope Pius X, and of teaching the Catholic world once more to sing as the chant of the Church sings, and to pray as it prays!

Feast of the Purification, 1928, Beuron.

THE AUTHOR

BIBLIOGRAPHY

Following are some works which might prove of interest to the readers of Johner, not because they will find any further and formal explanation of the Vatican Gradual and its melodies, but because these books should be of help towards a better understanding of the Graduale.

BOOKS

Benedictines of Stanbrook, *A Grammar of Plainsong*, 2nd Ed. (Worcester, 1926), 128 pp.

Benedictine Nuns of Stanbrook, *A Grammar of Plainsong* (Benziger Bros.), 80 pp.

Benedictines of Stanbrook, *Gregorian Music* (London, 1897), 97 pp.

Birkle, Dom S., *A Complete and Practical Method of the Solesmes Chant*, translated from the German by A. Lamaistre, (J. F. Wagner, New York, 1904), 150 pp.

Desroquettes, Dom J. Hebert, *L'Accompagnement Rhythmique d'apres les Principes de Solesmes* (Tournai), 73 pp.

Egerton, Clement C., *A Handbook of Church Music* (London, 1909), 218 pp.

Ferretti, Dom P., *Principii Teoretici e Practici di Canto Gregoriano*, 3rd Ed. (Rome, 1914), 24. pp.

Huegle, Dom Gregory, *Catechism of Gregorian Chant*, (J. Fischer and Bro., 1928), 115 pp.

Haberl, F. X., *Magister Choralis, A Theoretical and Practical Manual of Gregorian Chant*, Translated by Rev. N. Donnelly (Ratisbon), 283 pp.

Johner, Dom D., *A New School of Gregorian Chant*, Translated from the German, 3rd Ed., (Pustet, New York, 1925), 364 pp.

Johner, Dom D., *Erklaerung des Kyriale* (Pustet), 128 pp.

Laroche, Th., *Principes Traditionelles d' Execution du Chant Gregorien*, (Tournai, 1929), 331 pp.

Leone, Dom G., *Grammatica di Canto Gregoriano* (Badia di Cava, 1925), 91 pp.

Liturgical Movement, The (Liturgical Press, Collegeville, Minn.)

Missia, F. A., *A Church Music, A Brief Guide to its Meaning and Regulations for its Liturgical Observance.*

Mocquereau, Dom Andre, *Nombre Musical, Gregor., Le*, 2 Vols. (Tournai, 1908-1927).

Mocquereau, Dom Andre, *The Art of Gregorian Chant* (The Catholic Education Press, Washington, D.C.), 24 pp.

Mocquereau, Dom Andre and Cagin, Dom Paul, *Plain Chant and Solesmes*, (London, 1909), 71 pp.

Potiron, Henri, *Cours D'Accompagnement du Chant Gregorien*, New Edition (Paris, 1927), 134 pp.

Predmore, Geo. V., *Church Music in the Light of the Motu Proprio. A Guide for the Catholic Choir Director and Organist*, (Rochester, The Seminary Press), 82 pp.

Ravegnani, E., *Metodo Compilato di Canto Gregoriano*, 5th Ed. (Rome, 1926), 282 pp.

Ronan, J. E., *Catholic Church Music* (Toronto, St. Augustine's Seminary), 58 pp.

Schmidt, J. G., *Principal Texts of the Gregorian Authors concerning Rhythm*, (Buffalo Volksfreund Printing Co., Buffalo, N.Y.).

Schuster, Cardinal Ildephonse, *The Sacramentary* (Benziger Bros.).

Springer, Max, *The Art of Accompanying Gregorian Chant*, translated from the German (J. Fischer and Bro., New York), 238 pp.

Sunol, Dom Gregory, *A Textbook of Gregorian Chant*, translated from the Spanish by G. M. Dunford (Desclee & Cie., 1930), 221 pp.

Terry, Sir Richard, *The Music of the Roman Rite.*

Wagner, Peter, *Einfuehrung in Die Gregorianischen Melodien, Ein Handbuch der Choralkunde* (Freiburg, Switzerland, 1895), 311 pp.

Wagner, Peter, *Einfuerung in Die Gregorianischen Melodien, Ein Handbuch der Choralwissenschaft*, 3 Vols. (Leipzig, 1911-1921).

Ward, Mrs. Justine, *Gregorian Chant according to the Principles of Dom Andre Mocquereau of Solesmes* (Washginton, 1923), 262 pp.

White List, The, By the Musical Committee of the Society of St. Gregory of America, A Selection of Papal Documents and other information pertaining to Catholic Church Music. (J. Fischer and Bro., New York), 64 pp.

MAGAZINES

ENGLISH: *The Caecilia*, (100 Boylston Street, Boston, Mass.).
            The Catholic Choir Master (Niccola Montani, 1705 Rittenhouse Street, Philadelphia, Pa.).
GERMAN: *Musica Divina* (Vienna, Austria).
            Musica Sacra (Regensburg, Germany).

LITERATURE

With Abbreviations Used In Quoting

Betende, Kirche (Berlin, Augustinerverlag), 2nd Ed. [*B.K.*]

Caecilia, from 1883 (Strassburg).

Caecilienvereinsorgan, from 1856 (Regensburg, Pustet); from 1924 (M.-Gladbach, Volksvereinsverlag). [*C.O.*]

Choralblaetter (Beuron), Nos. 1-5.

David, L., O.S.B., *Analyses gregoriennes pratiques* (Grenoble, Bureaux de la Revue du chant greg.). [Analyses]

Grisar, H., *Das Missale im Lichte roemischer Stadtgeschichte* (Freiburg, Herder, 1925). [Missale]

Gregoriusblatt, from 1865 (Duesseldorf, Schwann).

Gregoriusbote (Duesseldorf, Schwann).

Johner, P. D., O.S.B., *A New School of Gregorian Chant* (N Y., Pustet, 1925), 3rd Ed. [*N. Sch.*]

   Der gregorianische Choral (Stuttgart, Engelhorn, 1924).

Jahrbuch fuer Liturgiewissenschaft, from 1920 (Muenster, Aschendorff).

Katholischer Kirchensaenger, 1910-1911 (Duesseldorf, Schwann). [*K.K.*]

Klosterneuburger Liturgiekalendar. [*K.L.*]

Kramp, J., S.J., *Messliturgie und Gottesreich* (Freiburg, Herder, 1921). Three parts, in the *Ecclesia orans* series.

Musica divina, from 1913 (Vienna, Universaledition).

Schuster, I., O.S.B., *The Sacramentary* (N.Y., Benziger, 1924-1931), 5 Vols.

Tippmann, R., *Die Messen der Fastenzeit* (Paderborn, Schoeningh, 1921).

Wagner, P., *Einfuehrung in die greg. Melodien* (Leipzig, Breitkopf und Haertel). I. *Ursprung und Entwicklung der liturgischen Gesangsformen,* 3rd Ed. 1910; II. *Neumenkunde,* 2nd Ed. 1912; III. *Gregorianische Formenkehre,* 1921.

Wiener Kirchenzeitung, Volume 8 contains excellent short explanations of Mass texts from the pen of P. Simon Stricker (Maria-Laach). [*W.K.*]

INTRODUCTION

Structure And Expressiveness Of The Variable Mass-Chants

The variable chants of the Mass (*Proprium Missae*—Proper of the Mass) show surprising diversity both in content and in mood. Unlike the inflexible sameness of the Oriental liturgy, which practically uses the same Mass, formulary day after day, the liturgy of the Western Church has since the fourth century witnessed a development so remarkable that it now has special texts and melodies for almost every Sunday and feast day of the year, including those for each day of Lent. Many of these selections are characterized by a joyful and sincere gratitude toward God; some are filled with the spirit of penance; still others are expressive of hopes and fears. As a preliminary to the study of each chant selection it is very helpful to determine: (1) whom do the words of the text represent as speaking—Christ, the Blessed Virgin, the saints, or the Church herself? (2) to whom are the words addressed—to Christ, to the saints, or to us?

There is no close relationship musically between the constituent parts of a Mass formulary. There is neither similarity of modes nor of motives to unify them. When songs which now immediately succeed one another, such as the Grual and the Alleluia (formerly this was not the case) have the same mode, it is purely a coincidence. The exclusive development of one thought or mood is likewise of infrequent occurrence.

The distinctive peculiarities of the chants are due entirely to the part they are destined to play in the liturgy of the Mass. On this basis they can be divided into two classes.

I.

The first class of chants embraces all those which are meant to accompany some liturgical action—in a broader sense one might call them "processionals." To this class belong the following: the Introit, which is to be sung during the solemn procession of the priest to the altar (*accedente sacerdote ad altare*, as the Rubrics of the Vatican Gradual have it) the Offertory, which formerly was sung during the Offertory procession of the faithful to the altar; the Communion, which was sung during the distribution of Holy Communion. These chants embody all those factors which make for a complete and artistic whole—word, song, and action. They express effectively the emotions of the soul, at the same time urging it on to still further activity. (Cf. Johner, *A New School of Gregorian Chant*, p. 120.)

A. THE INTROIT

The Introit is made up of an antiphon, a simple psalm-verse with the *Gloria Patri,* and the repetition of the antiphon. It has the schematic form A B A. Formerly the whole psalm was sung, or at least a goodly number of verses, and the antiphon was repeated after each verse. In fact, to arrive at a full understanding of most Introits, a thorough study of the entire psalm from which the Introit has been taken is necessary.

The verse has a distinctive melody for each of the eight modes. These typical melodies remain unchanged and therefore are not influenced by the subject matter or the spirit of the feast. The individual antiphons will be explained in their proper place. As regards the melody of the psalm-verse and its underlying text, however, a few remarks may be in place.

In the first, third, and seventh modes the middle cadence has two accents:

1.	*a*	*a*	*ác (a) a*	*(a)*	*ag ga*
3.	*c*	*c*	*d (c) c*	*(c)*	*ba ccc*
7.	*d*	*d*	*df (e) e*	*(e)*	*ed de*
Exsultáte	*Deo*	*adju-*	*tó ri*		*no-stro:*
Glória...	*et*	*Spí-*	*ri- tu- i*		*san-cto:*
Exsul-	*tá-*	*te*	*ju-sti in*	*Dó-mi - no:*	

In the sixth mode the middle cadence has two accents with a preparatory note:

$$\overset{\text{\tiny 1}}{}$$

aa a	*g*	*bb (a) a*	*ģ (f)*	*f*
Exsultáte Deo	*adju-*	*tó- ri*	*no- stro:*
Exsul-tá - te	*ju- sti in*	*Dómi-no:*

In the fifth mode the middle cadence has one accent with a preparatory note:

c c c d̄ | *d (c) c* *

c c c d̄	*d (c) c*
Exsultáte Deo adjutó- ri	*no- stro:*
justi in	*Dó-mi - no:*

In the second, fourth and eighth modes the middle cadence has one accent with three preparatory notes:

2.	*fe fg g* *f̄g (f) f*
Exsultáte Deo ad- ju- tó- ri	*no - stro:*
	Dó-mi - no:

In the first, second, third, sixth, seventh, and eighth modes, the final cadence begins with the fifth syllable from the end; in the fourth mode with the fourth syllable from the end.

		5	4	3	2	1
1.	*a*	*aca*	*g*	*f*	*fff*	*d*
2.	*f*	*g*	*fd*	*f*	*ec*	*ded*
3.	*c*	*cc b*	*ag*	*a*	*b*	*ga*
6.	*f*	*g*	*fd*	*f*	*g*	*f*
7.	*d*	*def*	*d*	*ċ*	*ccc*	*ag*
8.	*c*	*cc b*	*ga*	*cb*	*a*	*g*
4.	*a*	*a*	*gf*	*ga*	*g*	*e*

	5	4	3	2	1
jubi-lá - te		*De - o*		*Ja - cob*	

Here there is simple enumeration of syllables, with no reference to the word-accent. The text is subordinatd to the melodic rhythm, and according to Quintilian (*A.D.* 118), the syllables must then be lengthened or shortened to fit the pattern of the melody. Occasionally, in the Vatican edition, the sixth and eighth modes form exceptions when the verse closes with a dactylic rhythm, as is instanced in the Introit *In médio*:

			3	2	1		
f	*f*	*f*	*g*	*fd*	*f|ġ*	(*f*)	*f*

Dó- mi- ni tu- o Al\|tís- si- me;

and in the Introit of the Sunday after Christmas:

3		2	1		
cc	*b*	*ga*	*cb|á*	*a*	*g*

fortitúdinem et prae\|cín-xit se.

In both cases, therefore, there is one accent with three preparatory notes; this makes the rhythm of the eighth mode somewhat uneven.

Some modes have variant final cadences. These effect an artistic linking of the psalm-verse with the repetition of the antiphon. The ancients had a nice sense for the propriety of such a device. Occasionally the cadence suggests the beginning of the antiphon.

The eighth mode closes with the extended cadence *c cĉ b ga cb a gadffg* when the antiphon rises from a lower note, as for instance on Palm Sunday:

d	*fg*	*g*	*gag*

Dó- mi- ne.

The fourth mode has the final cadence *a gf ga g dgff* when the antiphon begins with *df*, as for instance on Maundy Thursday:

dfe

nos.

The first mode has the final cadence *fff dcdf*, when the antiphon begins with *cd*, as for instance on the feast of the Purification:

cd   dabb   a   a

Su- scé- pimus.

Otherwise it has the cadence *fga*, if the antiphon sets in on *a*, as, for instance, on the feast of the Conversion of St. Paul:

a   gag

Sci- o.

The fifth mode has the stirring and onward-urging cadence *c d b c ágágfg*, especially when the antiphon is defined within the tone range *f–a*, as, for instance, on Septuagesima Sunday:

fa   a   a   a   agga   f

Cir-cum-de - dé - runt me.

The sixth mode has the still more impelling cadence *f g f d f g f g a g* when the antiphon sets in on a low pitch, as, for instance, on Low Sunday:

c   d   d   d

Qua-si   mo-do

Evidently the need for contrast also comes into play here. The "*concors varietas*," as St. Augustine[1] has it; the "*suavis quaedam et concordabilis diversitas*—smooth and harmonious diversity," as Berno of Reichenau[2] (eleventh century) puts it. The same becomes apparent from the rule for the adaptation of individual phrases of the same composition: if one phrase closes on a low pitch, the following will have a tendency to rise. Thus in the Offertory of the second Sunday in Advent, the fourth phrase begins with *g–c*, while the foregoing one closes with *ff*. This is seen in various Graduals of the third mode, for example, the close and the beginning of the first and second phrases of Quinquagesima Sunday; three times on the feast of the Holy Name of Jesus; twice on the feast of St. Michael.

On the other hand, if one phrase begins in a high pitch, the following will have a tendency to begin with a low pitch. This is well exemplified in the Introit of the third Sunday of Advent, where the cadence over

---

1 *De Civitate Dei*, 1, 17, c. 14.
2 Gerbert, *Scriptores eccles. de musica*, II, 77.

hominibus closes on *gf* with reference to the following phrase, which begins in a higher pitch, while over *solliciti sitis* the same cadence becomes *fg* with reference to the following phrase, which begins with a lower pitch. For the same reason the cadence *e g f f e* of the fourth mode often becomes *e e f*; this, in fact, is the general rule whenever the following phrase begins with low *d* or low *c*. The rule for the adaptation of phrases, as will be pointed out later, effects a tension between the phrases and its various members.

B.   THE OFFERTORY

The Offertory is also called an antiphon, although in the oldest manuscripts it consisted of several verses with one or more refrains. It is, therefore, really a responsory, closely resembling the Gradual responsories in melodic richness. The Offertory of the Requiem Mass with its refrain *Quam olim* is the sole remaining example of this type of Offertory.

With truth it has been said that, to explain fully any given excerpt, it is best to adduce the entire selection from which the excerpt has been taken. In accordance with this, the setting for the Offertory as well as the Introit would become much more complete and the excerpted text much better understood, if the entire psalm from which the manuscript text as a rule is taken, would be subjoined. Such a procedure, however, would exceed the prupose and limits of the Gradual. Reference for such matter should there be made to commentaries on the psalms.[3]

The Introit and Offertory for the first Sunday of Advent have identical texts, albeit the melody of the Offertory is more quiet and severe. Similar observation can be made in regard to other Mass texts. This, however, would not permit us to generalize and to claim that the Offertory portrays to a higher degree the activities of the inner soul than does the Introit.

As Wagner (III, 418) has shown, Offertories avoid the lengthier syllabic element of chant. There are never more than five successive syllables on the same note. Melismas usually occur within the word, while at the end of the Offertory and particularly at the end of the last verse we find a rather ornate *vocalise*. The Offertories for the Vigil of Christmas and the twenty-second Sunday after Pentecost illustrate this well.

Some Offertories—Offertories alone—have text repetitions. These are introduced possibly for "artistic effect;" more probably, however, for a liturgical reason. They were necessitated formerly to occupy the

---

[3] The author refers to the German work *Heilige Gabe*, by P. Thomas Michels and Athanasius Wintersig.

time during which the faithful brought their gifts to the altar (Wagner, III, 429).

C. THE COMMUNION

The Communion, like the Introit, had at one time the form ABA, the sole remaining example of which we find in the Requiem Mass of today. In addition to the Communions that are practically syllabic and differ in nothing from ordinary antiphons, there are many which surpass the Introit in richness of melody, and others which are sung in extended responsorial form at the Night Office.

II.

In contrast to the above chants which originally accompanied some liturgical action, we might designate those chants which occur between the Epistle and Gospel as chants of rest, since they accompany no liturgical action. Historically this latter class is the older of the two. The early Church utilized these chants as a means to impress on the hearts of the faithful the lessons inculcated by the Epistle, and to make them the more readily susceptible for the Gospel. Clergy and laity should, without any further ado, be enabled to devote themselves entirely to the contemplation of the chant and its import.

"The Epistle and Gospel are chanted in simple, recitative style, generally monotone, with simple, stereotyped variations at the more important punctuation marks. And rightly so. Here the important feature is the word which leads to the comprehensive understanding of the text. Between the Epistle and Gospel, however, there are responsorial chants of the richest lyrical melodies. And this with wise forethought, for it accords with the laws of aesthetics in regard to contrast. These chants act as a counterpoise to the external musical simplicity of the Epistle and Gospel."[4]

D. THE GRADUAL RESPONSORIES

The Gradual responsories formerly had a refrain (hence the usual form ABA). Without this refrain, text and melody are at present sometimes unintelligible, as for instance, the Gradual on the feast of St. John the Baptist. Present usage, however, permits the addition of the refrain. According to the notation of the Vatican edition, the Gradual is divided into a *corpus* and a verse. The *corpus*, as a rule, is more quiet, simple, and reserved, and not infrequently assigned to a plagal mode. Accordingly, it may be well rendered by a small, choice choir. The verse is con-

---

4 *Gregoriusblatt*, 50, 18.

ceived as a solo, which moves upward brightly and joyfully. Generally a very extended melisma occurs after the first or second word.

The Graduals employ a series of typical melodies which are frequently adapted in their entirety to various other texts. Still more general is the use of about fifty typical formulas which in part may be assigned to various modes (shifting melismas[5]) and yet are combined in a pleasing manner. Some conclude a selection (final or codal melismas); others begin a selection (initial melismas), others again give prominence to the punctuation (caesural melismas), while others are found in the middle of a phrase (inner melismas), mostly over the accented syllable, at least in the verse. The favored mode of Graduals is the fifth. Only eighteen Graduals are assigned to the third mode and only three to the eighth mode.

At times the melody forms a recitative on the dominant, thus effecting a striking contrast to the preceding and subsequent melismas, which are interwoven in the chief parts of the text.

Combined with the subsequent Alleluia, technically the Gradual forms the artistic apex of the High Mass.

E. THE ALLELUIA

The Alleluia with its verse retains to the present time the form ABA, and hence belongs to the responsorial chants. A rich, jubilant melody (*jubilus*, neum, sequence) continues the melody over the word *Allelúia*.

Over the word *Allelúia* we generally find two motives. They are distributed in such a way that the first and lower-pitched comes over the first two syllables, while the second and higher-pitched comes over the last two syllables. In the ensuing *jubilus* plain chant displays its fine sense of form. It favors the repetition of a member, in such a manner, however, that a real development of the melody takes place. Thus, for instance, there would not simply be $a\ a$ but $a\ á^1$ (ninth Sunday after Pentecost), or $a\ b♭\ b♭^1$ (twelfth Sunday after Pentecost), or $a\ a\ a^1\ b♭^1$ (twenty-third Sunday after Pentecost), or $a\ a\ b♭\ c$ (eighteenth Sunday after Pentecost). Over and above repetition, plain chant also uses "the technique of motivation, which effects a more intimate connection between the various parts of the *jubilus*."[6]

No less than 170 *jubilus* precede their final note with a *pressus*; thus the third mode has $f\ e\ f\ g\ ff\ e$, the eighth mode has $g\ a\ c\ b\ aa\ g$. Of the remaining 64 closing melodies, 53 are assigned to the first and sec-

5 Wagner, III, 376 ff.
6 Wagner, III, 411 ff.

ond mode and have mostly the concluding form *d e f d* (= *a b c a*) or *c e f d*, six to the third and fourth mode, mostly with the concluding form *a b c g*. The *pressus* is thus most adaptable for concluding the *jubilus* melody.

The Alleluia-verse often bears the same relation to the preceding *Allelúia* and *jubilus* as do the variations of a theme to the theme itself. Seldom is every such relation absent. The first words of the verse frequently repeat the melody of the *Allelúia*. As in the Gradual verse, one syllable (which is, as a rule, the accented one) has a florid melisma and is finely membered, like that of the *jubilus*. Reference might be made to *odórem* in the Alleluia for the feast of St. Andrew.

It is proper to designate the systematical division of the various chants of the Gradual by *a a^1 b*, etc., and to designate identical and similar passages with a circumflex either above or below the neums. The singer is thus afforded a general view of the whole composition and acquires that self-confidence which is consonant with the spirit of prayer.

As a rule, the verse has the same rich closing melody, the same *jubilus* as the *Allelúia*. Only a few melodies, among them those of the three Christmas Masses, have a different ending. They were most likely composed at a time when the sense of the symmetrical rounding-off of phrases was not so well developed. Wagner (III, 398 ff.) assigns them to an older (archaic) form. Neither is the inner development of these melodies so clearly arranged as that which marks other melodies (cf. *Pal. mus.*, *III*, 53 ff).

F. THE TRACT

As a rule, the text of the Tract is taken from the Psalms or the Canticles. Its several verses have psalmodic structure. Tracts were invariably assigned either to the second or eighth mode. The first verse generally has an extended beginning and the last verse a rich closing melisma. The mediant divides each verse into two halves; in the following it is indicated by †.

The most frequently occurring form of mediant of the second mode is that which, for instance, is found in the first Tract of Good Friday over *tímui, cognoscéris, mea, véniet, eius*, and is characterized by the descent of a fourth with a *pressus* and close on *c*. A few other forms (in the same Tract over *innotescéris*) occur less frequently, but close on *c*. Between the beginning and the mediant, but more frequently the mediant and the closing cadence, a number of caesuras are now and then inserted, which as a rule have a melodic upward tendency and close on *f*, as, for instance, in the second Tract of Good Friday over *iníquo, die, áspidum*. In the following the caesura is indicated by (—).

The form of mediant of the eighth mode is similar to that of the second. We have an instance of it in the Tract *Sicut cervus* of Holy Saturday over *aquárum, vivum, nocte*. This form is also characterized by the descent of a fourth, *pressus*, and close on *f*, hence a whole step below the finale of the mode. A caesura is also inserted here, and that mostly after the mediant, as in the above Tract over *ad te Deus*. Thus melodic ornamentation is found where the text is set off by a punctuation mark, or where the singer finds it necessary to breathe. This melismatic punctuation is not proper to the Latin language. On account of its melodic structure, we must consider the Tract above all as the first fruits of Christian Mass chants.[7]

As a general rule, texts of a serious and pleading character prefer the second mode, which has a minor third over its tonic and as such gives us the effect of a modern minor key. On the other hand, texts of a joyful nature prefer the eighth mode which has a major third over its tonic, and as such gives us the effect of a modern major key. The sentiments expressed in the Tract of Laetare Sunday and in all the Tracts of Holy Saturday are well adapted to the eighth mode.

ARE THE VARIABLE MASS CHANTS EXPRESSIVE OF EMOTION?

The answer to this question is more than a matter of mere simple formula. Above all must be kept in mind the fact that in their essence the choral chants are liturgical chants. "Liturgy, however, directs all things to God and is governed by reverence for God. The goal of plain chant, therefore, must primarily be the glorification of God and not the reaction it has on man's ideas and sentiments. Hence it depicts reverential worship of the majesty of God, wonderment over His beauty, amazement over His divine deeds for us, trustful hope in Him whose impenetrable Wisdom guides all things—and then again a fervent, even joyful, gratitude for His love.

"Plain chant, therefore, knows no exuberance of sentiment, no predominance of mood in the face of quiet and serene reasoning. For this it is altogether too intimately connected with its text.

"It is prayer devoid of external manifestation and false pathos; it is direct as the words of a child to its father, plain and simple as the evening prayer of an innocent soul."[8]

Liturgical prayer and chant differ greatly from private devotion. Liturgy, according to its very name, presupposes a fellowship of spirit.

---

7 *Wagner*, III, 352 ff.; *Gregoriusblatt*, 50, 3 ff.; 42, 3 ff.

8 Johner, *Der greg. Choral*, 76 ff.

This naturally demands a restraint of the purely personal element and a renunciation of those traits which correspond to the inclinations and experiences of the individual.

The reverence for God and the attitude of the community often effect this community of sentiment, which is indicated rather than expressed. Religious activities are, in fact, less demonstrative.

This is especially noticeable in those chants which were designated above as "chants of rest," namely, Gradual (Alleluia-verse), Tract, and also the psalm-verse of the Introit. They are either composed entirely of typical melodies, which are adapted to different texts, moods, and feasts, or they make liberal use of typical forms. And it is precisely this that distinguishes religious and sacred art, that it rises above the natural propensities of the individual, and that it has a style of its own. All the forms of religious art—painting, sculpture, architecture, and also music and song—have these characteristics.

The melody in these cases does not serve as an interpretation, but rather as an embellishment of the text; it clothes the text with a more or less festal garb. Occasionally interesting attempts are made to sacrifice the typical form for individual expression.

Gregorian music, however, is not merely a music of embellishment; it does not describe the text in the manner in which a garland entwines itself about a pillar, effecting no inner connection with it. Chant can also make the text interpretative, expressive, and explanative. It often brings its gradations at the very point where a declamatory rendition of the text grows in warmth, and it emphasizes that word which marks its climax. Much would be gained for the proper understanding and rendition of the melody if we would first ask ourselves the question: How would I read or render this text according to its sense? It will become evident that chant unites text and melody well, and that there is an intimate relationship, a union of spirit, between them. Choral music, morevoer, makes prominent use of the esthetics of the interval.

The chants referred to above as processional hymns may be described as expressive of emotion. True, they make use of many typical forms, but the more these hymns are studied and analyzed the more apparent it becomes that they are more than mere feelers in the realm of emotionally expressive music. It is difficult to reconcile the opinion of Oswald Spengler[9] when, writing of the church music of the early Middle Ages, he says that its subjective emotions and sentiments are not conceivable by us. Indeed, plain chant with its limited means and devices to portray emotion and expression will not create the immediate reaction

---

[9] *Untergang des Abendlandes*, I, 224.

today that it did in bygone centuries. After all, those ages knew nothing of the enticing charms of modern harmony, chromatics, and rhythm, and were, therefore, more susceptible to the chaste allurements of monophonic melodies. Nevertheless, it still radiates today a warmth which effectively influences the religious life of the soul; it imparts faculties which enable us to soar over mundane things to the very Mystery of the altar, to union with God.

Plain chant like all vocal music utilizes two features or forms to render the melody expressive. The one endeavors to reproduce the single uniform mood as indicated by the liturgy. It does not center and concentrate itself on individual words but rather pervades the entire text; it pervades every phrase of the whole composition, just as the soul is found in every part of the body. This form of expressiveness is the one most frequently used in the so-called processional hymns.

Another form stresses the import of the individual words and is known as specific expressiveness of music. Plain chant, especially the Communion, knows many such rich *genre* pictures.

Let us endeavor to know and realize in our singing the spirit of each individual melody, but above all let us conceive it as prayer. Prayer is the raising of the heart and mind and the entire man to God. The objective in the liturgy should become our personal conviction, our personal property.

Pius X in his *Motu proprio* of November 22, 1903, says: "The proper aim of the melody is to add greater efficiency to the text, in order that through it the faithful may be the more easily moved to devotion and better disposed for the reception of the fruits of grace belonging to the celebration of the most holy mysteries." The same pertains also to the actual rendering of the melodies. We should penetrate deeply into the feeling of the liturgical chants. Our song rendered with reverence and love in the presence of God and of the faithful should portray that which we ourselves have experienced. The knowledge that we have imparted our own inward happiness to others and have been instrumental in leading them to the altar and closer union with God will then afford us a goodly measure of spiritual joy and delight.

The following observations should be noted in regard to the melody of newer feasts:

1.   Their text and melody as such are taken from an older Mass formulary (cf. what is noted concerning the Introit and Gradual of the feast of Corpus Christi).

2.   They adapt an older melody to a newly selected text (cf. Offertory and Communion of Corpus Christi). At times similarity of text or

word seems to have occasioned the choice of the melody: *Vidébunt* (Communion *Lánceae et Clavórum*) and *Vidérunt* (third Mass on Christmas); *Sta-(bant)* (Introit of feast of Seven Dolors) and *Stá-(tuit)* (Common of Martyr-Bishop); *qui vocátur Christus* (Communion for Solemnity of St. Joseph after Easter) and *qui dícitur Christus* (Vigil of St. Andrew); *in generatióne* (Introit for the Sacred Heart feast); and *a generatióne* (Tuesday after the first Sunday in Lent).

3.   They borrow individual phrases from various Mass formularies (Offertory and Communion on the feast of the Kingship of Christ).

4.   They employ an altogether new composition; this, however, is of rare occurrence (Offertory for the feast of the Immaculate Conception, and Sequence *Stabat Mater*).

Cf. *Revue*, 6, 158 ff.

The Masses For Sundays And Feastdays According To The Liturgical Seasons

(Proprium de Tempore)

FIRST SUNDAY OF ADVENT

INTROIT (Ps. 24: 1, 3)

1. *Ad te levavi animam meam: Deus meus in te confido, non erubescam:* 2. *neque irrideant me inimici mei:* 3. *etenim universi qui te exspectant, non confundentur. Ps. Vias tuas, Domine, demonstra mihi: * et semitas tuas edoce me.*

1. To thee have I lifted up my soul: in thee, O my God, I put my trust, let me not be ashamed: 2. neither let mine enemies laugh at me: 3. for none of them that wait on thee shall be confounded. Ps. Show, O Lord, thy ways to me: * and teach me thy paths.

"Lift up *(levate)* your heads, because your redemption is at hand." Thus the Lord consoles us in the Gospel for today, which, in the main, is intensely serious. He wishes to come as our Redeemer on Christmas night, and for this the Advent season, now beginning, is to prepare us. He wants to free our soul from the foes that press it from every side, from enemies who think they can already rejoice at our defeat. Although we may often have looked up *(leávi)* to some vain thing, considering its attainment our life's ambition, there has always come a time when we realized the nothingness of it all, realized that God alone can be our ideal, our goal. Only when we take cognizance of His ways *(vias tuas, Dómine)* and walk accordingly, can we find true happiness. God alone can guard the beauty and nobility of our soul against its every enemy. At the beginning of the liturgical year our soul strives, therefore, to elevate itself, definitely and decisively, to Him who by His incarnation becomes its God *(Deus meus)* and who wishes to be intimately united with it in Holy Communion. For this reason *Deus meus* sounds almost jubilant. For this reason, too, strong accents are placed over *in te confído;* and *non erubéscam* and *neque irrdíeant* sound more like a song of victory than a suppliant petition.

"Lift up your heads, for your redemption is at hand." Some time it will come, the perfected redemption, when the Son of Man will come in the clouds of heaven "with great power and majesty." Then all the world will see that no one who trusts in God is ever confounded. Then those who put their faith in men will stand abashed. Then the longing of all those *(univérsi)* who were turned toward God will be fulfilled and all the desires *(exspéctant)* of the human heart will find their complete satisfaction in God.

The antiphon is formed of the first verses of Psalm 24. In cases of this kind, the verse which immediately follows generally supplies the psalm-verse for the Introit. Here, however, the fourth has been chosen, the preceding verse having been passed by, most likely because it expresses the same thought as its predecessors.

According to the Vatican edition this virile melody is divided into three phrases, all having the same range and stressing the full step below the tonic. This gives added firmness to the chant. The first and third phrases have almost the same closing cadence. *Meam* and *mei* close on *f*. The most ancient reading, according to the German tradition of the Middle Ages, has this Introit rising from a low pitch *(d c f g)*, like other Introits of the eighth mode, e.g., those of Palm Sunday and of Whitsunday. *Amen* at the close of the psalm-verse has not the usual cadence, but *g a d f f g*, which acts as an introduction to the repetition of the antiphon. The fact that this cadence is given here indicates that in its original form this Introit began on low *d*, thus representing the lifting up of the soul to God in a more graphic manner. *Animam* seems like a reverent look at God, while *meam* is filled with childlike submission. We become more fully conscious of the force in *confido* if we first sing its half tone and full tone in the reverse order *c bb bb a*, and then sing the notes as given. After *b a*, *non* has a triumphant ring. The same spirit is retained in the following phrase, which sets in with an interval of a fourth and twice has a vibrating tristropha. Thus this prayer almost becomes a command: Lord, Thou canst not do otherwise than help me against my enemies.

Revue, 19, 69 ff.

As an antithesis to *g–c* over *ánimam* we have *c–g* over *(irríde) -ant me.*

Rhythmically the close over *(inimí)-ci mei* is related to *(con)-fído*. Now the song becomes more serene. The final phrase has no more large intervals, no more bistrophas or tristrophas. Characteristic of it are the thirds and the upward tendency of *f a g, g b a, g a c*, after *b c d*, which in the rendition should receive a powerful crescendo. Thus the Advent idea *(exspéctant)* is brought luminously into the foreground, and with the conviction that the preceding petition will be granted, the song comes to a close.

Our song should be a prayer, and our prayer a lifting of our whole being to God *(levávi ánimam meam)*. Such prayerful song will lift others, too, out of the shadowy valleys of this earth. Grace will then light up the way to the knowledge of Christ, to union with Him.

Revue, 19, 69 ff.; *Analyses*, II, 3 ff.; Johner, *N. Sch.* 54, 66; *C. O.*, 46, 136 ff.; Wagner, I, 219; III, 299.; *Gregoriusbote*, 43, 182 ff.

GRADUAL (Ps. 24: 3, 4)

Universi qui te exspectant, non confundentur, Domine. ℣. 1. *Vias tuas, Domine,* 2. *notas fac mihi:* 3. *et semitas tuas edoce me.*	*None of them that wait on thee shall be confounded, O Lord.* ℣. 1. *Thy ways, O Lord,* 2. *show thou to me:* 3. *and teach me thy paths.*

Few Graduals show such a clear and evident difference between the quiet, low-pitched *corpus* of the Gradual and the ornate, richly developed, and upward-surging verse with its change of clef. With its deep notes and emphasis on the dominant *f*, the *corpus* ought really to be ascribed to the second mode. The verse, on the contrary, is not satisfied with the dominant of the first mode *(a)*; its actual dominant is a third higher. In both parts the incisions are marked with elaborate melismas: *exspéctant, Dómine, mihi, mé*.

Perhaps the florid melody over *Univérsi*, rising from a low pitch, wishes to portray in tone-painting the large number, the multitude. With *exspéctant* the annotated manuscripts call for a broad rendition of all notes on the final syllable. This serves to augment the Advent spirit of longing and of expectancy, which is already expressed by the melody itself. An intense seriousness pervades the entire piece.

The very first notes of the verse show a combination of the tonic with the dominant *(d–a)*, the so-called chief repercussion, thereby introducing a change of sentiment. Ever more lively, more fervent, and more impressive the petition now becomes. The motive *f g a cc a*, striving upward and then sinking back again, is repeated with pleasant variations four times; *c* appears five times in the energetic form of the *pressus*.

The cadence at the close of *Dómine* might indicate something like weariness, but with unwonted power the melody again soars upward, as if to knock at the very gates of heaven and obtain a hearing. Only after this does it gradually sink to rest. "Modern music for a long time now has looked upon such repetition of motive as one of its most effective devices. The passage reminds us of Edward Grieg, the famous Norwegian lyrist (Op. 46, *Peer Gynt*, Suite I, '*Morgenstimmung*')."[1]

---

[1] Kreitmaier, *Dominantem*, 170.

Obviously, there must be a certain urgency running through the rendition. The annotated manuscripts give evidence of fine musical taste in indicating that all the notes of this motive are to be sung broadly. The close $b\flat$ $\widehat{gg}$ f of *Dómine* is answered by a $c\widehat{gg}$ f over *mihi.* Once again the abovementioned motive returns in a slightly different form over *et sémitas.* "The singer is reminded of the grace of Christ which mercifully descends upon man. With graceful condescension the melody bows down at *sémitas tuas,* as if to show how lovingly the grace of Christ is communicated to the suppliant."[2] The final *me* should be given a pronounced *ritardando.*

The text of the Gradual is already known to us from the close of the Introit and from its psalm-verse. But the Gradual, following the more ancient translation of the Scriptures, the Itala, has *notas fac* instead of *demónstra.* It seems that the ancient liturgy preferred to take the Introit and the Gradual from the same psalm. The preceding Epistle with its admonition: "It is now the hour for us to rise from sleep," sheds additional light on our present text. We must be of those who watch expectantly, otherwise understanding will come too late. We must "put on the Lord Jesus Christ," must become acquainted with His ways, His works, His manner of life. These we must learn to know and appreciate in all their awe-inspiring, adorable greatness. We sing therefore and pray with utmost fervor: "Show thy ways to me, O Lord!" And when we consider the many ways in which the human heart can go satray, the many paths not illumined by the light of truth, then shall we begin to share the motherly solicitude of the Church, and from the bottom of our hearts we shall sing and pray: "Lord, teach us to tread thy paths!"

ALLELUIA VERSE (Ps. 84: 8)

1. *Ostende nobis Domine misericordiam tuam*: 2. *et salutare tuum da nobis.*

1. *Show us, O Lord, thy mercy*: 2. *and grant us thy salvation.*

Ever since the first sin was committed, this cry has been ascending almost ceaselessly to heaven: "Show us, O Lord, thy mercy!" And never is it uttered in vain. The riches of divine mercy are infinite, inexhaustible. But men wish to *see* God's mercy, to feel it, to touch it bodily. Incarnate Mercy came to this earth when the only-begotten Son of God became man. His merciful love urges Him to seek that which was lost, to preach the Gospel to the poor, to heal wounded hearts, to speak that divinely

---

[2] *Gregoriusbote,* 43, 185.

effective word: "Thy sins are forgiven thee; go in peace." Lord, come Thou again into our hearts, into the hearts of all men, work the marvels of Thy forgiving love, and grant us Thy salvation! Such is the heartfelt supplication of this Advent song.

This melody with its archaic form has been thoroughly discussed by Dom Mocquereau in the second number of his *Monographies gregoriennes* (Tournai, Desclee). For much of what follows we are indebted to that excellent work; we are also allowing ourselves some additional observations. In the most ancient manuscripts this melody is found accommodated to various texts. In the present instance, however, text and melody fit so perfectly that one may without hesitation say that the verse *Osténde* is the original. Besides, in no manuscript has it a different melody than that assigned to it here, a fact which likewise testifies to its great age. *Allelúia* and *jubilus* are clearly joined by the final pressus on *a*. But they also show inner relationship. Compare, for instance:

```
            a g    a b c   b á   c
      Alle-              lú-   ia  and
  Allelúia.    g f   a b ćc  b ǵ  c
```

The verse has two parts with two large subdivisions. *Osténde* sets in lively and fervently with an interval of a fourth on the dominant of the eighth mode, as if to recall the words of St. James: "But let him ask in faith, nothing wavering" (1:6). However energetic this introduction should be, allowance must be made for a corresponding increase with *Dómine* and above all with *(miseri)-córdiam*. The cadence of *(Dómi)-ne* keeps the melody suspended; then before the next word-accent it sinks to *b a*. Now the word *misericórdiam* can shine forth in all its splendor. Upon this upward flight follows relaxation from *tuam* on, until the melody finally rests upon the tonic.

At its beginning the second phrase recites on the tonic, reminding us, with its *porrectus* on the word-accent, of the solemn psalm-intonation of the eighth mode. Corresponding to *c e d* over *(miseri)-córdiam* in the first phrase, everything here must be fitted to the principal accent of *tu-(um)*, which we should like to place on *d e c a* following the tristropha. According to the annotated manuscripts, however, only *c a* of this *pes subbipunctus* and the subsequent *torculus b d b* are to be sung with added emphasis and expression. Thus we have *d c b c g* and *b♭ a g a f* corresponding to one another. No one will experience much difficulty in discovering the similarity of *tuam* in the first phrase and *tuum* in the second:

```
ag      ccbg   a bb a f g bb a g
tu ..................... am
ca      c b g a c a f bb a g
tu ..................... um
```

The final member *(da nobis)* moves more quietly and prepares for the close. Its melody never goes above *c*; several times it rests upon low *f*. The resulting tritonic tone-sequences *f a b* and *b g f* are somewhat grating. But it is just this which makes them fit so well to the supplicating spirit of the whole. In the second last group of neums, *bb* is occasioned by the following *f*, just as *b* in the last group by the following *g*. The verses of Tracts in the eighth mode end on *a*. Compare:

Alleluia: *cc a g a bb g f   c c a g a b a a g*

Tract: *cc a g a bb g f   a c a b g g a a g*

The closing neum differs from that of the Alleluia jubilus; it has the archaic form. We find the richest melismas over *tuum* and *nobis*, as if the meldoy wished to say: Only *Thy* mercy, *Thy* salvation can help and heal us.

In its adaptation to other texts, the melody occasionally receives the character of a florid psalmody with intonation, dominant, and cadence. Compare, for example, the second phrase of this Alleluia with that of the feast of SS. Simon and Jude: *et salutáre* with *nimis confotátus est.*

Osténde! How often we pray to the Mother of God in the *Salve Regina* that after this exile she may show us her Son Jesus! Today, since at Rome the principal service (the *statio*) is being held in St. Mary Major, we cry out to her also, imploring her to show us here in our exile the incarnate Love which she once bore under her virgin heart.

OFFERTORY

This Offertory has the same text as the Introit. But it inserts "O Lord" among the words: "To thee have I lifted up my soul."

We sing this song while the priest is offering the sacrificial gifts and lifting his eyes heavenward. We also lift up our souls to Him who is fidelity unchanging. The heavenly bodies will one day be destroyed; terrible will be the roar of the ocean; cries of horror will escape from the terrified peoples; all worldly hopes will fail. One alone will remain ever the same. Therefore, O Christian soul—thus the Church admonishes again—let your confidence be unshakeable, even in the storms of the present life, even when you must bring also other than symbolic gifts to the altar, even when your vocation and your duties demand sacrifices from you which cut deeply into the heart, even when your fidelity results only in derision for yourself *(neque irrideant)*. Then pray and sing with your whole soul: "My God, I put my trust in Thee. I shall not be confounded." And behold, He for whom your heart longs will come to you in Holy Communion, to be your light and your strength!

Even more clearly than in the Introit does the melody here "lift" itself from the depths. *Erubéscam*, a heightened repetition of *(á)-nimam meam*, is much like the *erubéscam* of the Introit. The division of the phrases, moreover, is almost identical; in other respects, however, this Offertory travels its own path. The predilection of the second mode for the frequent combination of the tonic and dominant *(d–f)* determines the melodic line; in fact, the melody extends but a single tone above its dominant. The motive over *(Dó)-mine* is found again over *(confun)-déntur*, with a slight variation over *mei*, and, taking its rhythm into consideration $(2+4+2$ [4]), also over *te, á-(nimam), Deus meus*, and *confído*. All this assures the song a feeling of deep rest and unimpassioned reserve. But we must not forget that in early times the Offertory had two more verses, of which especially the last had a florid close. *Deus meus, non*, and *neque* set in on the dominant. The effect varies, however, depending on whether the preceding note rests on the same pitch, or a third or a fourth lower. As a result of its intonation, *non (erubéscam)* possesses special force, heightened by its pressus-like accent, the only one in the entire piece. While the Introit and the Gradual make *exspéctant* prominent, our present song stresses *univérsi* with its interval of a fourth. But the melody is more subdued and quiet than in the corresponding passage of the Introit. It would seem that the subsequent Secret already exerts its influence upon this song. According to the position it occupies liturgically, plain song knows how to give the same text its proper character, its own spirit. *Animam meam*, words and melody, is found also on the feast of St. Joseph of Cupertino. That song uses also the last phrase of today's Offertory, though with a different text.

Revue, 8, 49 ff.

COMMUNION (Ps. 84: 13).

1. *Dominus dabit benignitatem:*	1. *The Lord will give goodness:*
2. *et terra nostra dabit fructrum suum.*	2. *and our earth shall yield her fruit.*

All the chants of this Sunday are fervent and touching supplications. Here we have the answer to all these petitions, and especially to that of the Alleluia-verse, which is taken from the same psalm as the

Communion. Our prayer is not in vain. The Lord gives His blessing: a joyous animation runs through the melody with these words. What copious blessings has the Lord poured upon this earth, and what a plentitude of grace has He again placed in our souls in Holy Communion as seed for eternity! Wherever this seed falls upon rich soil, in souls who recognize that the one thing necessary is to do the will of God, there it bears rich fruit.

In the Blessed Virgin, however, this Communion finds its finest realization. Hitherto our earth had brought forth but thorns and thistles. We are, as Adam of St. Victor sang in the twelfth century, a thornhedge, lacerated by the thorns of sin; but Mary knows nothing of thorns. She is so richly blessed that the angel can greet her as "full of grace." The heart of this *ancílla Dómini* was fertile soil, moistened by the dew of heaven. Soon she will present us with the most beautiful flowerlet, the ripest and most luscious fruit which has ever graced the face of the earth, a fruit so precious that mankind, generation after generation, will never weary of calling out to her: "Blessed art thou amongst women, and blessed is the fruit of thy womb, Jesus!"

The first phrase has a range of a ninth; with *(benigni)-tátem* it lets the blessings drop gently from above. The second phrase, which treats of the fruits of the earth, does not extend above the dominant of the mode *(a)*. Both phrases descend in a gentle line to low *c* and begin the following member with an interval of a fourth. A fluent and bright rendition should characterize the whole piece.

This melody is sung also on the feast of St. Ignatius (July 31). "Lift up your heads;" in Holy Communion "your redemption is at hand."

*   *   *   *

SECOND SUNDAY OF ADVENT

Today the Introit, Gradual, and Communion speak of Sion, i.e., of Jerusalem. The Alleluia-verse also alludes to this. For at Rome the principal service was held in the Church of the Holy Cross in Jerusalem, close to the Lateran. Formerly it was a royal palace; now it shelters a most venerable relic of the holy cross. Our present Sion is the Catholic Church. It is also our individual soul, and likewise the church building in which we look for the Redeemer today. Here it is that we are being prepared for the heavenly Sion.

INTROIT (Is. 30: 30)

1. *Populus Sion, ecce Dominus veniet ad salvandas gentes: 2. et*

1. *People of Sion, behold the Lord shall come to save the nations:*

auditam faciet Dominus gloriam
vocis suae, 3. in laetitia cordis
vestri. Ps. Qui regis Israel, intende:
* qui deducis velut ovem Joseph.

2. and the Lord shall make the glory
of his voice to be heard, 3. in the joy
of your heart. Ps. Give ear, O thou
that rulest Israel: * thou that leadest Joseph like a sheep.

How different is the effect of the ascending fourth in today's Introit
from that of the descending fourth in last Sunday's! One seems to hear
a herald proclaiming to the people of Sion the most important news ever
told, the tidings which mankind had been awaiting for centuries. The
messenger commissioned by the Lord Himself, would have this message of joy penetrate into all hearts: "The Lord shall come to save the
nations." And you yourself may listen intently for the voice of the Lord.
For He will speak as one who has power; He will speak of His grace and
transcendent truth and glory. His voice will cause the heart to overflow
with joy.

Where such great things are promised, the petition of the psalm-
verse comes to mind spontaneously: "Give ear, O thou that rulest Israel."
Help us to live ourselves into this season of grace. For most lovingly
didst Thou lead Joseph from imprisonment to the regal throne.

The words of the antiphon were verified when the Lord came. Joy
filled the hearts of the shepherds when the Lord, through His angels,
announced to them the message of peace. And although the Child of
Bethlehem could not at that time speak a word, He has often conversed
secretly with our souls in laetitia cordis. A day will come when His voice
will resound majestically over the millions of men who have ever in-
habited the earth, announcing eternal joy to them who have listened to
it during their lifetime.

Three phrases are discernible in the melody, all beginning with the
same, or at least a similar, motive: Pópulus and et audítam g c c d and
in laetítia g g a c c d. Still more evident is the agreement of the closing
motives: gentes and vestri g a g g, and suae a fifth higher, d e d d. The real
dominant of the first and third phrases is c; that of the second, d.

Like Pópulus, Dóminus stresses c. Before this, however, the fifth over
ecce fixes the attention. And then it is as if the Lord Himself slowly and
solemnly came into view. Hitherto He had sent the prophets; now He
Himself appears. He comes not to judge, however, but to redeem; He
comes to bring redemption to all the nations. This thought is given a
more detailed treatment in the Epistle; and in the Gospel the Lord
speaks of His activity: "The blind see, the lame walk, the lepers are
cleansed, the deaf hear, the dead rise again, the poor have the gospel
preached to them." He comes to redeem the gentiles. At this gracious

manifestation of divine favor the melody bows down in gratitude. In the Sequence-like melody it is best to consider the torculus the points of support, and to rhythmize in a movement resembling five-eights time:

$$dd| \quad ćdb \quad ag| \quad ḃcb \quad ab \quad | \quad ġag \quad g$$
$$ad \qquad sal\text{-} \quad ván\text{-} \quad das \quad gen\text{-}tes.$$

Thus the word-accents are clearly brought to the fore.

The second phrase begins with the same motive as the first, but its span is greater. After the accented *c* and the following *d* it does not sink back to *c*, but establishes itself on *d*. However insignificant this small note may appear, it wields great power, urging up to the high *f*. After the ascent over *fáciet* comes a brief relaxation. But then follows a mighty cry (obviously the text has influenced the melody)—*glóriam vocis suae*.

The third phrase portrays the effects of this message. With full, round tones it soars upward from *g* to e^1, stressing this, as it afterwards does *c*. Then with an interval of a fourth it descends to the tonic and to the final cadence.

Revue, 19, 139 ff.; *Analyses*, II, 12 ff.

GRADUAL (Ps. 49:2-3, 5)

1. *Ex Sion species decoris ejus:*
2. *Deus manifeste veniet.* ℣. 1. *Congregate illi sanctos ejus,* 2. *qui ordinaverunt* 3. *testamentum ejus super sacrificia.*

1. *Out of Sion the loveliness of his beauty:* 2. *God shall come manifestly.* ℣. 1. *Gather ye together his saints to him,* 2. *who have set* 3. *his covenant before sacrifices.*

When the Lord will come, He will bring joy to the hearts of men: that is the promise of the Introit. The Epistle closed with similar words: "Now the God of hope fill you with all joy and peace in believing." This thought is prolonged by the Gradual. It speaks of the beauty of Him who is to come. All beauty, and especially that of the coming Messias, cannot but produce joy: that is the theme of this bright song. Not infrequently does it remind us of our modern major scale. In other passages the Psalmist has painted the beauty of the Messias in brilliant colors, describing Him as the most beautiful of the children of men. Now He is to come—and *maniféste*, in visible form. But this Ruler will not isolate Himself from His subjects, as is the custom of Oriental sovereigns. He will show Himself, and with the magic of His beauty He will capture all hearts.

But he does not come alone: a great host accompanies Him. Of this the Gradual-verse speaks, as we also read in one of the Advent antiphons: "Behold, the Lord cometh and all His saints with Him." When He comes at Christmastide, the saints who have sealed the covenant with the sacrifice of their blood will surround His cradle; St. Stephen, St. John, the Holy Innocents. But the full grandeur of these words of the Gradual will be realized only at the end of the world. When the angels' trumpets will sound—some persons will perhaps hear their echo in the notes of *Congregáte*—then will arise both the wicked and the just, the saints who sealed their covenant with God by sacrifice, by loyalty to the end, frequently by a martyr's bloody death. Now they all come to form the radiant retinue of the Saviour. However enchanting this prospect may be, God, the eternal Sun, infinite Beauty, of whom the saints are but reflections, will appear infinitely more glorious and resplendent.

We find the motive of *spécies* repeated over *(testaméntum) ejus*, in its second half over *(De)-us*, and in an enlarged form over the significant *vé-(niet)*. The repetition over *(ordinavé)-runt* becomes more intelligible from this motive. The melody over *(Si)-on* appears again over *(mani)-féste*; similarly *(il)-li sanctos*, *(te)-staméntum*, and *(su)-per sacri-(fícia)* sound much alike. This play of motives heightens the charm of the whole song.

The verse has the same range as the *corpus*, but surpasses it in the richness of its melismas. It begins, like the *corpus*, with *f a c*, which we may call a resolved major chord, and then toys with the third. Here one must distinguish well between what are only *clives* or bistrophas, and the accented *pressus*. In any case, the form *a c c é d c*, which occurs twice, must enliven the whole. In order to warn against any heaviness in the rendition of this passage, the annotated manuscripts give a light construction to all the neums over *Congregáte* except the last four notes; besides, they have "c" (—*celériter*, rapidly) marked over it in two places, the first one covering the first three thirds; and also "st" (—*statim*, continue immediately). The entire passage must therefore be light and airy, and not as if the angels had to drag the saints onto the scene. It is at the very beginning of the verse that we find the florid melisma: possibly this is a reference, in tone-painting, to the multitude of saints. In contrast to the tender neums over the first word, the annotated manuscripts demand a broad, serious, solemn rendition of *illi sanctos ejus*.

The second phrase *(qui ordinavérunt)* is somewhat difficult to sing properly. Here we also have an example of the small zigzag oscillations of imitative figures with short motives peculiar to the Dutch School. This, however, does not justify anyone in generalizing and saying that thereby "the ideal melody, the beautiful upward and downward line of movement, is essentially blotted out." The divisions of the melody are evident enough. First it descends three times to *g*, and then thrice down to *a*. Toward the end, *f* gains prominence and calls for *b♭* in place of *b*, which dominated the second phrase.

Hear the soft yet persistent undertone: Gather ye around Him, all ye His saints! Let us be mindful of our vocation to aspire to sanctity, since we are privileged to assist at the holy Sacrifice of the Mass. Here we should renew the covenant with Christ which He sealed with His bloody sacrifice. Perhaps *Congregáte* was intended to urge the early Christians to lead many of their pagan relatives and friends to Sion, to the Church (W. Dauffenbach).

N. Sch., 246.

ALLELUIA VERSE (Ps. 121: 1)

1. *Laetatus sum in his quae dicta sunt mihi*: 2. *in domum Domini ibimus.*

1. *I rejoiced at the things that were said to me*: 2. *We shall go into the house of the Lord.*

Allelúia with its two ascending fourths begins with an energetic swing, making one surmise that a greater development is to follow. In the *jubilus* and the verse, however, the melody rises but one full tone higher. The two members of the *jubilus* resemble each other: *b♭ c b♭ á b♭ g f̂ g a* and *f̂ a g é d̂ e c é f g*. The first part of the verse seems to have been formed from a typical antiphonal melody of the first mode, such as we find on Palm Sunday in the song *Púeri Hebraeórum*: *d̂ f d c f̂ a a á a c a ǵ f ǵ a*. *Dicta sunt mi-(hi)* exhibits a sort of sequence of thirds: *ga fg ef de*. *Domum* with its fifth, its *pressus*, and the broad *torculus*, possesses the greatest inner tension, the expression of sparkling joy. Such a melisma is also found on June 11, closing the word *fructus*, singing of the rich fruits of divine grace and vocation. A second higher *Dómini* has motives of the second member of the jubilus: *f éf̂d f̂gáag e⁼e d̂ec ef̂ĝfd*. *Allelúia, Laetátus sum*, and the beginning *of íbimus* show variations of the same motive.

The ancient plain-song manuscripts add a second verse to that given here: "Our feet were standing in thy courts, O Jerusalem." How brightly and spiritedly this song must have come from the lips of those who, arrayed in their festal robes, were making their pilgrimage to the Temple! Coming now from our hearts, it should have a still brighter ring. We are not obliged to make long pilgrimages to the house of the Lord; our Temple is our parish church, in which the true Emmanuel (God with us), He for whom the centuries longed, dwells and immolates Himself for us.

In olden times the neophytes used to sing this song during the procession of thanksgiving which each day during Easter Week led them to the baptismal font. There had they received grace, truth, and divine adoption. We also belong to the number of those fortunate ones. How happy we shall be when we can enter our celestial home, the heavenly Jerusalem whose streets re-echo with the cry of Alleluia!

OFFERTORY (Ps. 84: 7-8)

1. *Deus tu convertens vivifica-bis nos,* 2. *et plebs tua laetabitur in te:* 3. *ostende nobis, Domine, misericordiam tuam,* 4. *et salutare tuum da nobis.*

1. *O God, turning, thou wilt bring us life,* 2. *and thy people shall rejoice in thee:* 3. *show us, O Lord, thy mercy,* 4. *and grant us thy salvation.*

For a musician the change in the character of the melody at the beginning of the third phrase over *osténde* with the resolved chord *gb bdb* is obvious enough. Here and in the parallel sentence which follows we have the expression of the great Advent petition contained in Psalm 84, which last Sunday formed the Alleluia-verse. And today it is the only supplication found in the Mass chants. Hence it is well to leave the preceding *vivificábis* and *laetábitur* in their future forms; for this reason, also, we have purposely selected the translation given above. God Himself will again turn to us and bestow new life upon us; He it is who in the preceding Gospel Himself said: "The dead rise again." He alone can produce such an effect. This is forcibly brought out by the melody over *tu*. *Nobis* and *da*, as well as *(vivificá)-bis* and *(lae)-tábitur*, have either the same or a similar form of *pressus*. Care must be taken that these forms are not sung too hurriedly; the bistrophas and tristrophas on *c*, on the contrary, should be somewhat less prominent. Over *(vivifi)-cábis* the ascents *gc* and *ad* must not be overlooked. The second phrase rejoices in the fact that we are allowed to be God's people *(plebs tua)*, and that He so graciously takes us under His protection. All chants of this Sunday stress this joy, even more so than the chants of Gaudete Sunday. God wishes to enrich us with sure and lasting joy; hence the quiet seconds from *(laetá)-bitur* on. All this is not so much a supplication, but rather a happy experiencing. With *osténde* begins the petition, borne aloft by the joyous confidence of the first part. Tender half tones are heard over *misericórdiam*. In fact, it almost seems as if this feeling had already influenced the close of *Dómine*, so that the interval occurs five times in all. Compare with it the beginning of the Introit for the second Sunday after Easter, where the mercy of God is also expressed in half tones, as well as the passage *Dómine, suavis ac mitis es* from the Introit of the sixteenth Sunday after Pentecost with its semitones and minor thirds. These supply the small stones in the material necessary for the construction of an aesthetic of intervals in plain song.[1] In accordance with the rules for the adaptation of phrases, the beginning of *et salutáre (gc)* is preceded by the low-pitched *d e d*. From *et salutáre* on, with its introductory fourth and the fourth that follows it, the singer feels impelled to present his petition in an especially pleading manner. To this the pressus over *tuum* contributes considerably, and especially the development over *da*, which is to be sung with a marked *crescendo*. In case breath should not suffice, but only in that case, a brief pause may be made after the low *f*, after which the ascent from the prolonged *g* should be made slowly and prayerfully.

COMMUNION (Bar. 5: 5; 4: 36)

1. *Jerusalem surge, et sta in excelso:* 2. *et vide jucunditatem, quae veniet tibi a Deo tuo.*

1. *Arise, O Jerusalem, and stand on high:* 2. *and behold the joy that cometh to thee from thy God.*

Subdued joy, the quiet happiness of Advent, inspires this melody. It knows that the hopes of the soul are not in vain, that its expectation will surely be fulfilled. It has not that bright ring which is characteristic of the second mode for example in the second antiphon of Lauds at Christmas, which sings of the virgin motherhood of Our Lady; *gáudia matris habens cum virginitátis honóre.* But neither has it the seriousness of the Offertory of the first Advent Sunday, which never dared to rise above *g*. Here we have not that solemn jubilation with which the Gradual-verse for Epiphany sings its *Surge et illumináre*; nevertheless, *surge* of this Communion also penetrates deeply into the heart. Here we have a major third. It is a cry harking back to the spirit of today's Introit. Solemnly it continues—in accordance with the ancient annotated manuscripts, which give almost each note the broad form—"stand on high"; rise above your environment; despise what is earthly, as the Postcommunion puts it; view all things in their proper proportions. One thing alone can fill your heart with bliss—the salvation which comes to you from your God.

The Holy Communion which we receive lifts us to the heights of the other world, where eternal happiness awaits us in the possession and contemplation of God *(Kath. Kirchenzeitung,* Salzburg, 1927, 441).

The serious explanation offered by Oberhammer *(Im Lichte des Christkinds,* p. 28) hardly corresponds to the spirit of the melody. Ac-

---

[1] *N. Sch.* 247 ff.

cording to this commentator, the disciples return home to John and relate to him what they have seen and heard; and in his prison in the fortress Machairus, on the other side of the Dead Sea, John now rises up and for the last time calls to his people: *Jerúsalem, surge.* Otherwise the same fate awaits you as that to which the depths of the Dead Sea bear testimony.

The passage *f efd fa g* over *(Jerúsa)-lem surge* corresponds to *d cec ded* over *vide.* Now the melody becomes livelier. The endings over *(ex)-célso* and *(jucundi)-tátem, fg ed* and *fgfe,* sound almost alike. Over *véniet tibi* the melody shows the form of a melodic sequence. After the descent over *tibi,* we meet a bright major chord over *Deo.* Finally, the words *Deo tuo* should find an echo in our souls.

Jerusalem (thou ,O Christian soul), "behold the joy that cometh to thee" and listen intently to that which thy Saviour wishes to tell thee "to the joy of thy heart."

*   *   *   *

THIRD SUNDAY OF ADVENT

INTROIT (Philipp. 4: 4, 6)

1. *Gaudete in Domino semper; iterum dico, gaudete:* 2. *modestia vestra nota sit omnibus hominibus:* 3. *Dominus prope est. Nihil solliciti sitis:* 4. *sed in omni oratione petitiones vestrae innotescant apud Deum.* Ps. *Benedixisti, Domine, terram tuam: * avertisti captivitatem Jacob.*

1. *Rejoice in the Lord always: again I say, rejoice:* 2. *let your modesty be known to all men:* 3. *for the Lord is nigh. Be nothing solicitous:* 4. *but in every thing, by prayer let your petitions be made known unto God.* Ps. *Thou hast blessed thy land, O Lord: * thou hast turned away the captivity of Jacob.*

Some Sundays of the liturgical year sum up their character and spirit in the very first word of the Introit. Thus in today's Introit: *Gaudéte*—"Rejoice." The altars are decked with flowers as for a feast; rose-colored vestments are used; we again hear the organ. What is the meaning of all this? What kind of joy is to be expressed today? Someone has written (Feck, *Das Missale als Betrachtungsbuch,* I, 41): "The second Sunday of Advent already voiced joyous tones...On the present Sunday joy is to sound forth unrestrained." But is that really the case? He who lets the Introit *Gaudéte* work upon him will think differently. One will never come to a correct understanding of a liturgical text unlesss one views it in conjunction with the melody which proceeds from its inmost spirit. The praying and singing of plainsong, and therefore of the liturgy in general, express more shades of meaning and a richer gradation of feeling than is generally recognized. Advent and Christmas joy, for instance, differ greatly from the exultation of Easter time. There, indeed, one may speak of full-voiced rejoicing. The Introit *Laetáre*, with its extended intervals, already acclaims the victorious King who soon will enter in the fullness of His strength. But the Introit *Gaudéte* with its initial seconds and minor thirds has in mind the beautiful Babe of Bethlehem who "is near at hand," who out of pure love for us appeared in utter poverty and took on the weakness of an infant, though He is infinitely rich and mighty. The joy in this song, therefore, sinks into the heart slowly, sweetly, like gentle dew from heaven. The simplicity which the second phrase voices is already indicated by the melody of the first phrase.

The phrase *Dóminus prope est* occupies the central position in the piece, dominating the whole more by its florid neums than by its pitch. Since the Lord is nigh, we are exhorted to be: (1) joyous, (2) modest and friendly, (3) without solicitude, (4) persevering in confiding prayer —a veritable Advent program; a program, in fact, for the whole of life, including in itself our relations to God and to our fellowmen, and placing everything on the golden basis of true joy of heart.

It is surprising that the melody never employs the note *b*, which generally characterizes the Doric mode; the repeated *b♭* tends to make the melody tender and mild. The first and fourth phrases have almost the same close, but a different range. A pause on the dominant of the mode is made by the first three phrases. The first phrase may be taken as a model of phrase structure in chant: an ascent from the tonic to the dominant, a halting on the dominant, then a descent to the tonic. Each of its members moves within a different tetrachord: *c–f*, *f–b♭*, *d–g*. The continuous growth of the melody in the first half of the verse portrays gradations of feeling: Rejoice; then more: Rejoice in the Lord; then still more: Rejoice at all times. Here a crescendo is obviously demanded. What follows is somewhat surprising. Where we would sing *iterum dico* quietly, to give that feeling of expectation, and then *gaudéte* very emphatically, choral by its simple return to the tonic tells us: Let your Christmas joy be interior, heartfelt!

The ancients called for *ascensiones pudicas* in the melodic line: a modest, chaste rising upward. This is satisfied in the second phrase. There is some resemblance to *Dómino semper*; but here the melody does not reach high *b♭* by means of a third, but with ascending seconds. The prolongation of the dominant *a* over *ómnibus ho-(mínibus)* and the extension of *f* over *petitiónes* in the fourth phrase, according to some, portray the immense multitude of men, or perhaps their petitions. Then, all aglow with light, comes *Dóminus prope est*. A hidden urge must characterize the three *porrectus*; a note of joyful victory should resound in *Nihil solliciti sitis*. Here we find practically the same cadence as over *(ho)mínibus*.

Solemnity and impressiveness should mark the last phrase. Its low pitch and its emphasis on the dominant *f* puts it in marked contrast to the preceding. *Oratióne* alone seems to indicate that prayer is a lifting of the entire being to God. *Sed in omni* and *innotéscant* are similar. The *pressus* over *omni* effectively accents the thought that our prayer must be fervent. In free translation one might expand this to: everything in our lives should be transformed into prayer.

The psalm-verse stands out prominently, especially because several times it extends to high *c*, while the antiphon never went above *b♭*.

Revue, 20, 12 ff., *Analyses*, 2, 22 ff., *N. Sch.* 211 f.

GRADUAL (Ps. 79: 2, 3, 2)

1. *Qui sedes, Domine, super Cherubim*, 2. *excita potentiam, tuam et veni.* ℣. 1. *Qui regis Israel, intende:* 2. *qui deducis velut ovem 'Joseph.*

1. *Thou, O Lord, that sittest upon the Cherubim*, 2. *stir up thy might, and come.* ℣. 1. *Give ear, O thou that rulest Israel:* 2. *thou that leadest Joseph like a sheep.*

Gradual-responsories in general present many difficulties, and this is especially true of today's. It does not at all develop the way we should expect. We should undoubtedly have stressed the second phrase in the *corpus*, but we find it, in relation to the first, quite in the background. It supports itself on the tonic, not at all in the manner of the authentic mode, and even sinks below it four times. The descending fifth *a–d* over *tuam* acts as an antithesis to the high fifth over *super*. The second half of the second phrase is a more gratifying melody to sing than the first. Does the low-pitched melodic line perhaps aim at portraying the mysterious coming of God and His activity?

Perhaps the composer could not resist the temptation of showing, in tone-painting with the high *super*, how far God surpasses the Cherubim. Rightly does Wagner (III, 300) say: "Here the details are detrimental to the harmonic coherence of the single parts, thereby detracting from the artistic value of the whole. Such passagse, however, are exceptional." Some other pieces also show a predilection for tone-painting, much to the detriment of the leading thought; for example the *Allelúia* for the feast of St. Agnes. Here the confusion of voices at the announcement of the coming of the bridegroom is realistically indicated, but the leading idea: "Go ye forth to meet Christ the Lord," suffers thereby. The Communion *Quinque prudéntes Vírgines*, on the contrary, brings it into prominence in a most captivating manner. The antiphon on the feast of the Transfiguration portrays the Lord's going up to the summit of a hill, but the Transfiguration itself is given less attention. On the feast of the Ascension the Magnificat antiphon for second Vespers draws a picture of Christ's ascent; the accompnaying petition, however: "Leave us not orphans," which is less developed melodically, deserves more fervent expression. St. Peter's, where the liturgy is celebrated today, perhaps suggested tone-painting. There, gleaming from the mosaic above the altar, was a representation of the Lord ruling from His heavenly throne. Still, the composer may not have intended this as tone-painting so much as a development of the thought that God thrones above the Cherubim in absolute quiet, transcending all change and transitoriness, perfectly happy in Himself, needing nothing to add to His bliss. If we, notwithstanding His august majesty, are the recipients of untold favors at His hands, that but makes His goodness appear all the more brilliant before our eyes.

Owing to its abundance of melismas, the verse predominates over the *corpus*, although it has the same range. Its first phrase is the arsis, the rising, and closes on the dominant; its second phrase is the thesis, the relaxation, or rest, and closes on the tonic. In the verse we should have stressed the word *inténde*, as it is done, for instance, in the Gradual for the vigil of Christmas. The technique of Gradual-verses, however, calls for a florid melisma at the beginning. Today we have time to consider how God led His people, how long they wandered in the desert until they finally reached the Promised Land. The same florid melisma stands at the beginning of the verse on the twenty-third Sunday after Pentecost. Similarly prolonged passages occur in the Gradual for Wednesday after the third Sunday of Lent. The bending upward of the last note of a group is peculiar to the melisma over *regis*: *d c b g a, b̆ a g á g f g, á c á f g, d̆ e d c̆ b c d d.* A feeling of relaxation is introduced by the *clivis* over *inténde*, though not yet a feeling of perfect rest. The melody over *(de)-dúcis* merely repeats what was sung toward the end of the first member of *regis*.

ALLELUIA VERSE

1. *Excita, Domine, potentiam tuam,* 2. *et veni,* 3. *ut salvos facias nos.*

1. *Stir up thy might, O Lord,* 2. *and come,* 3. *that thou mayest save us.*

The initial motive of *Allelúia* (cf. *Caecilia*, 29, 69 ff.) is heard again over *Dómine*. In the latter case, however, the high *a* is strengthened by a *pressus*. The second motive over *Allelúia* is actually repeated four times in the *jubilus* in a motivated elaboration: *á b♭ a g g f, á b♭ a g g e, ǵ a g f e, f g f f e*, but with pleasing wave-like variations, fully corresponding to the great desire of the singer's heart. Over *(potén)-tiam tuam* the last groups are to be sung as two measures in two-fourths time: *á f é d é g f d d̂*. The second member must not be sung too rapidly; the first notes of each *clivis (a, g, f)* should be taken more broadly. By its *mora vocis* on *g, veni* is admirably divided. Thus we have the proportions *á b g e ǵ (g)* and *á b f d f̂ f* with their continuation. The avoidance of *b* gives the piece a tender, devout ring.

This melody is employed in several Masses; keeping within the limits of this book, we might, besides this Sunday, mention also the second Sunday after Epiphany, Ascension Day, and Pentecost. The Alleluia for the feast of Holy Innocents, which has been borrowed from the Saturday of Easter Week, has a similar verse. Several reasons support the contention that originally the melody belonged to the first Alleluia-verse of Pentecost. At Milan a similar melody has since early times accompanied the text *Emítte Spíritum*. One might also adduce a certain ancient Greek melody for comparisou (*Musica s.*, 44, 194).

The present verse with its fervent Advent petition which, incidentally, formed the first part of the Collect of the first Sunday of Advent, resembles most closely the suppliant character of the verse on Pentecost Sunday. A kind of daring, added to a deep faith, breathes from this supplication. Though it does not express the anxiety, akin to despondency, which seized the disciples when the Lord slept during that storm on the lake, it does state, with unmistakable conviction, that there is only One who can bring salvation and redemption: the Lord God with His all-powerful love.

OFFERTORY (Ps. 85: 2)

1. *Benedixisti, Domine, terram tuam: 2. avertisti captivitatem Jacob: 3. remisisti iniquitatem plebis tuae.*

1. *Thou hast blessed thy land, O Lord: 2. thou hast turned away the captivity of Jacob: 3. thou hast forgiven the iniquity of thy people.*

In the Gospel John the Baptist could announce that the Messias stood in the midst of His people. For faithful souls this was a message of great joy; now indeed God had sent His richest blessings upon this earth. The first phrase *(Benedixísti)* forms the theme of the Offertory; the two subsequent phrases but develop it. Gradually the melody grows:

Benedixísti has as range *d–a*; *Dómine, e–b*; *terram, d–c*. The *pressus* motive runs through this phrase; in the first word: *ǵ a g f̂ f d*, in the third word: *ĉ g f̂ f d* and *f g f̂ f d*. It even goes over to the second phrase; over the second word we have *a c á a f*, and over the third, *á c á a g*. The emphasis of the dominant *a* in the second phrase is no dout justified. If in Offertories we rarely find purely syllabic passages, in which each syllable carries but one note, it is still more rare to see passages which have the same note for a considerable length of time. Since we find a similar construction in the Introit for the twenty-third Sunday after Pentecost, and there, too, over the word *captivitátem*, we may well consider it a reference to the depressing fears and anxieties of captivity, to the bitter lot of a slave. But now all that affliction is gone. The hour has struck; sure and perfect liberty is come. For the soul has been freed from her load of sin, from the slavery of the passions; henceforth she is a child of God, and His peace will accompany her always. The follwoing verse therefore, goes on to say: "Thou hast covered all their sins: thou hast mitigated *(mitigásti)* all thy anger." Nevertheless, this Offertory does not forget that it still is an Advent petition. That this blessing may flow upon all men, it continues to pray: "Show us, O Lord, Thy mercy; and grant us Thy salvation." Our prayer is soon answered: the victim offered upon the altar will become for us the bread of eternal life, the font of joy unalloyed. It elevates us spiritually, transforms us to pure men, living in and with God. When the bell rings at the elevation, God again shows His merciful love; and in Holy Communion He grants us His salvation.

With artistic finesse the composer has succeeded in presenting the motive of the second phrase and the entire melodic line, in fact, in a more brilliant form in the third phrase. One need but compare the two phrases:

avertísti: *ḋg á g á bb a*   and

remisísti: *ḋgg á b á ǵ a b c*;   furthermore,

captivitátem Jacob: *a á a á a c áa f gag*   and

iniquitátem plebis: *ĉ c b̂ a ĉdc b̂ g á ǵ a g f*

Thus *remisísti* becomes the song of a soul that fully appreciates the dealings of God with her, who knows Him who stands in her midst, who gratefully acknowledges that this is "the freedom wherewith Christ has made us free."

COMMUNION (Isa. 35: 4)

1. *Dicite: Pusillanimes confortamini, et nolite timere:* 2. *ecce Deus noster veniet, et salvabit nos.*

1. *Say: Ye faint-hearted, take courage, and fear not:* 2. *behold, our God will come and save us.*

A mere glance at the melodic construction tells us that we are here treating of something out of the ordinary. If we first carefully recite the text alone and then sing the melody with it, we shall discover that the melody is not only a fine garment for the text, but that the text and melody form one whole, an entity as closely united as our intellect and will and feeling.

The song begins quitely, but soon with jubilant upward flight it strives to banish from the soul all fear and solicitude, tries to lift it above all things mundane and carry it up to that new world in which the angels sing a new canticle of peace and redemption. On Christmas night we shall hear them saying to the shepherds: *Nolíte timére*—"Fear not; for behold, I bring you good tidings of great joy...This day is born to you a Saviour" *(salvábit)*. Hence this Communion, in a way, introduces the feast of Christmas, just as in Matins for Gaudete Sunday the Invitatory ran: *Prope est jam Dóminus*—"Already the Lord is nigh." With all its jubilation, however, the melody follows a definite plan: *confortámini*, resting on the dominant of the mode, divides the first phrase into two halves. *Timére* repeats the motive of *nolíte*, and then closes a third lower, paralleling the final neums of *(confortámi)-ni*. These are formulas expressive of calm, but at the same time they advance the melodic thought. Now comes the joyful news: *ecce*, solemn and resolute, as one antiphon has it: *véniens véniet*—"He will surely come." Here the melody in a way makes a conclusion on the tonic; but it adds another very significant thought, and introduces it with a major second below the tonic and the F-major chord built on that note: "Behold, this God will be your Saviour."

What a magnificent ring the song must have had in the ancient basilicas, when the faithful, accompanied by this stirring melody, went up to the altar to receive the Holy Euchraist! Into him who approached, it instilled courage, for it said: *nolíte timére*. And to him who was returning from the altar it whispered: *ecce Deus noster*: He has come to you to free you from everything that hampers you, to heal you of every weakness, to make you cheerful and brave in your work, in your sufferings, in your vocation. For how many, likewise, was Holy Communion the source of supernatural strength *(confortámini)*, the Viaticum for martyrdom!

The song begins with *dícite*: a command to us singers. We are the privileged ones to bring this joyous message into the hearts of the faithful. Those who are bowed down, who scarcely dare to keep on hoping, those we can now console: Behold, God wishes to be also your Saviour; in your soul, too, there should be a Christmas.

FOURTH SUNDAY OF ADVENT

INTROIT (Is. 45: 8)

1. *Rorate caeli desuper, et nubes pluant justum*: 2. *aperiatur terra, et germinet Salvatorem. Ps. Caeli enarrant gloriam Dei*: * *et opera manuum ejus annuntiat firmamentum.*

1. *Drop down dew, ye heavens, from above, and let the clouds rain the just*: 2. *let the earth be opened and bud forth a Saviour. Ps. The heavens show forth the glory of God*: * *and the firmament declareth the work of his hands.*

Perhaps the word *caeli*, or the word *désuper*, which in late Latin was accented on the second syllable, necessitated the high pitch of the first half of the first phrase, just as *terra* influenced the low pitch of the second phrase (Wagner, III, 300). Be that as it may, the chant is not a description of the dew descending from heaven. The melody has a quite different intent. It has more sublime things to tell: it is the expression of a heart full of ardent desires, of intense longing; it would pierce the bleak lowering skies of December; it would take from thence Him for whom it yearns; it would bring the Just One down to this wicked, sinful, guilty world. The soul's emotions are expressed by the large intervals: *Roráte* has an ascending fifth; between *désuper* and *et* we have a descending fifth; between *nubes* and *pluant* occurs an ascending interval of a fourth. They are further manifested in the rapidly soaring melody and the powerful accents over *caeli*, *a é c a a g*, and *(nu)-bes pluant ju-(stum)*, *g éc a a gf agf f.*

Isaias, from whom these words have been culled, first of all cries for a liberator of the Israelites from their exile and slavery; Cyrus, whom he has seen in vision, is but a figure of the Saviour of all mankind. All the yearnings of the centuries have been compressed into this Introit.

What would this earth be without the Messias? A desert, an uncharted and arid waste scorched by the sun, having not one little flower or blade of grass. If new life is to spring forth, the ground must be cultivated, the clouds must send down their rain, the fructifying rain which is so valuable that the Portuguese say of the summer showers: "Gold pieces are now falling from heaven." Oh, that it might come, this rain, to penetrate into the hearts of men and awaken new life! Would that the clouds might have mercy! For the Israelites the concept of cloud was full of deep meaning: in the column of cloud God led His people through the desert; veiled by clouds He manifested Himself on Sinai; in a cloud the glory of the Most High descended upon the Temple which Solomon had built. Clouds are the symbol and the containers of life-giving rain, as well as of the grace of redemption which comes down to us from the heights of heaven, and of all the benefits and glories of the new kingdom of the Messias. When these clouds open, new life will bud forth *(gérminet)* about Nazareth, a life of unusual beauty, rich in blossoms and fruits.

The second phrase of the melody is more quiet. We hear the motive of *terra* repeated over *(gérmi)-net*. If we take the *f* on the first syllable of the first word as an upbeat, measured groups of two notes result. Contrast is effected by the three-note groups in the second part of this phrase. Since it is well to make a pause for breathing after *gérminet*, we have up to that point three groups of three notes and afterwards two more over *Salvatórem*—a symbol of energetic sprouting and blossoming. The group *a b c g* over *aperiátur* corresponds to *d e f c* over *Salvatórem*.

We implore the descent of the Just One from heaven. But His justice will not make His countenance the less benevolent, nor His eyes the less loving. He comes not to reproach, not to drive sin-laden man away in confusion; He comes as the Saviour, calling to Himself all who are weary or burdened.

Already a child of this earth is bearing the Just One in her virginal womb. From her will go forth the most beautiful flower *(gérminet)* that ever our earth has produced, the rose of sweetest odor. This earth will not be opened, for it will be from an intact virginal womb that the flower will proceed.

Upon his cry *Roráte* the prophet Isaias immediately received an answer from God: "I, the Lord, have created Him," that is, the Redeemer and Saviour. Our petition is answered in the psalm-verse: "The heavens show forth the glory of God." Already at the Annunciation the heavenly messenger spoke his *Ave, grátia plena;* soon heavenly messengers will descend in mighty array to sing their *Glória* to the Most High and to announce peace to mankind.

The ancient manuscripts assign today's entire Mass, with the exception of the Offertory and Alleluia, to Wednesday in the Ember Week of Advent. Formerly the grave Introit *Meménto nostri* was sung on the present Sunday.

Revue, 20, 79 ff.; *Analyses,* II, 30 ff.; *R. gr.,* 3, 145 ff.; *Musica s.,* 44, 214 f.

GRADUAL (Ps. 144: 18, 21)

1. *Prope est Dominus omnibus invocantibus eum:* 2. *omnibus qui inovcant eum in veritate.* ℣. 1. *Lau-*

1. *The Lord is nigh unto all them that call upon him:* 2. *to all that call upon him in truth.* ℣. 1.

dem Domini loquetur os meum: 2.   *My mouth shall speak the praise of*
et benedicat omnis caro nomen   *the Lord*: 2. *and let all flesh bless*
sanctum ejus.   *his holy name.*

The *corpus* of the Gradual supports itself on the tonic *f* and several
times descends below it. We find, however, that the closing words of
either phrase, *eum* and *-te*, have a higher pitch and a more florid melody.
Leaving these two passages out of consideration, we must ascribe the
piece to the sixth mode. The melodies over the double *eum* match quite
well: *ĉ b á c ǵg f̂ g ǵ f* and *f̂ g é f d̂d ĉ d d̂ c*. The verse is markedly different. Its lowest note is the tonic *f*, below which it never descends; its dominant is *c*, above which the melody soars several times to high *f*. We
here have an authentic mode, beyond all doubt. Hence this Gradual,
with the sixth mode in its *corpus* and the fifth mode in its verse, may well
be placed beside that of the first Sunday of Advent, where the *corpus*
and the verse exhibit first the second and then the first mode. The repeated accentuation of the *c* on *Dómini* gives the impression that it is
trying to resist the descent of the melody, but unsuccessfully. The melody
passes down to *a*, *g* and toward *f*. But as if to reassert itself, the *c* promptly sets in a fifth higher, and then the melody swings above it. The close
over *(e)-jus* corresponds to that of the *corpus* of the Gradual.

"The Lord is nigh." How consoling! That for which we hoped and
prayed so fervently is really coming true. He will come to us with all
His love. To all who pray to Him in truth He will reveal Himself and will
fulfill His word: "Even before ye call upon Me, behold, I am here." But
our prayer must be in truth; and our supplication must be straightforward, candid. Is my singing and praying all that it should be? Is it
true, sincere? So I unreservedly place all the powers of my soul, my
whole heart, in the service of God? How well today's Epistle stresses
the fact that when the Lord comes, He will disperse the darkness and
will draw all hidden things into the light!

The Lord's coming in the near future should evoke from us a song
of praise and thanksgiving. Would that we had a better appreciation of
Him and of the immense love that prompted Him to come down to this
earth! How the mere thought of His coming would then inspire us! The
Psalmist says: *benedicat omnis caro*—all mankind, the whole earth, ought
to join in this song of praise. But what is actually the case? Many do
not know that this is the time of Advent, that Christmas is at hand,
that the Christchild stands at the entrance of their hearts. Many do not
even want to know that today is Sunday; they do not want to come to
church. And of those who do come some intend merely to beg for this
favor or that; they seem to know almost nothing of praise or of thanks-

giving. All this should fire our zeal, should make this song of praise ascend from our inmost hearts, to help verify the closing thought of today's Epistle: "Then shall every man have praise from God."

ALLELUIA VERSE

1. *Veni, Domine, et noli tar-*   1. *Come, O Lord, and do not de-*
dare: 2. *relaxa facinora plebis tuae.*   *lay*: 2. *forgive the sins of thy people.*

Today's *Allelúia* begins like that of the Sunday after Epiphany. The *jubilus* has the form a a b. Its first member is formed from *g a b c c d b* of *Allelúia*. The relation of *Allelúia* to its verse is not readily apparent. We find the florid closing melisma of the verse in all its length at the close of many a verse in Gradual-responsories of the first mode. (Cf. All Saints, the twenty-second Sunday after Pentecost, or *Dómine praevenísti* in the Common of Abbots.) But here in the Alleluia after *f f e c* is inserted *g g f g a*, which is wanting in the previous melodies. Not only the close but the entire verse bears the impress of a piece of the first mode with its continued *b*. According to the present notation, the Alleluia belongs to the third mode, the verse to the first. Originally the verse closed on *e*. And since the melody goes a full tone over *e* (now *d e d*), it ran *e f♯ e*; thus the entire piece was sung with *f♯*, so that the verse began with *d e f♯ gg ga*. The melody not only had a frequent *f♯*, but in the passage over *et* which now runs *f a b c* it also had *c♯*. In order to write the *f♯* on lines according to the rules of the ancient notation it was necessary here, as in many other selections, to transpose the entire piece a fourth higher; then the piece began with *g a b c d* and closed with *a b a*, as, in fact, many of the early sources actually give it. Thus the entire piece could be written in the customary way, except for the passage over *et*, which even in the transposition retained an *f♯* (the original *c♯*). A second transposition of a fourth made it possible also to write this note; then the piece began with *c d e f g* and the passage in question became *f a b c*, the melody remaining intact. But now its relation to the *Allelúia* had been changed. Formerly closing with the same note as the *Allelúia*, on *e* (or a fourth higher on *a*), the verse now closed on *d* and the *Allelúia* on *e*. If originally, from a purely melodic standpoint (even if not theoretically), *e f♯ e* was sung, and afterwards *Allelúia* with *e f e* was added, this should not seem strange. Similar combinations can be found elsewhere in plain song. Thus in the Introit for the fourteenth Sunday after Pentecost the first phrase ends with *a g a b a b b a*, while the second begins with *a g a b a a*. With the present notation of *Allelúia* and verse a distinctive melodic finesse was lost. After the somewhat harsh ending on *e f♯ e*, *Allelúia* in the repetition entered gently and tenderly with *e e f d*.

· It is much simpler, of course, to say that *Allelúia* belongs to the third mode and the verse to the first.

These theoretical considerations should not cause us to overlook the delicately sensitive melody of the verse, so full of fervent Advent petitions and confiding trust. One cannot but join in with all one's heart.   ·

Using seconds only, the beginning of *Veni* seems almost timorous; *et* has the first interval of a third. The treatment of the motives *c d e f* then *f g a b♭*, and finally *f a b c* is obvious enough. As the motives develop, the expression must likewise grow and expand. Then the melody rises a fourth and soars above the previous melodic line over *tardáre*: "O Lord, for a long time now Thy people await Thee; leave us no longer in our darkness and impotence! Lord, do not delay!" It cannot be mere chance that only in this passage and only in this Alleluia-verse the melody exhibits such tenderness. On the twentieth Sunday after Pentecost and in the verse *Adducéntur* from the Mass *Loquébar* for a Virgin Martyr, which employs the same melody, this expansion is not found. It seems quite certain, nevertheless, that the verse *Parátum cor meum* for the twentieth Sunday after Pentecost must be regarded as the original composition. There also the second *parátum* with its increase is marvelously effective. The excessively florid melisma found here over *facínora* is there placed over *glória*: "I will sing, and will give praise to Thee, my glory." The singer, so the indication seems to be, cannot find sufficient outlet for his feelings. Whoever wants to resort to note-counting here has a real task. Nevertheless, two groups are quite easily distinguished. The one repeats the same motive thrice, but each time with a slightly different introduction; the other extends its motive, especially toward the end. Since the word *glória* frequently means "harp" in the psalms, one might also translate here: "I will play to Thee upon my many-stringed harp." Even if we did not know of the Alleluia for the twentieth Sunday after Pentecost, and that God is there lauded as our glory and our pride, the melody in itself would here not speak to us of the burden of sin, for it sounds more like the thanksgiving song of one from whose soul a great weight has been lifted.

We hear this melody likewise on the feast of St. John Damascene. *Revue*, 6, 33 ff., *Rev. gr.*, 3, 122 ff.; Wagner, III, 402.

OFFERTORY (Luke 1: 28)

1. *Ave Maria*, 2. *gratia plena*,   1. *Hail, Mary*, 2. *full of grace*,
3. *Dominus tecum*: 4. *benedicta tu*   3. *the Lord is with thee*: 4. *blessed*

in mulieribus, et benedictus fructus ventris tui.	art thou among women, and blessed is the fruit of thy womb.

This *Ave María* belongs to the most beautiful creations of plain song. Here we have reverence and wonderment, tenderness, astonishment, and love. The melody sinks into the deep with *grátia, tecum, fructus*; then it rises slowly with *Ave, grátia, ventris*; again it floats on high with *María*. It grows more ardent *(benedícta tu)*; then it expresses profound emotion and humble obeisance, while over all the song there hovers an ineffably sweet joy. Thus the Archangel Gabriel may have prayed the first *Ave María*; perhaps in his mind's eye he looked into the coming centuries, and perceived in millions of human hearts what Mary would mean to them, what blessings and what happiness the most blessed among women would bring upon this earth. No one can portray this adequately, but we get an inkling of it if we let the present melody penetrate into our hearts.

Over *Ave* the passage *f̆ a f ǵ f e* is soon followed by the very similar *f̆ a f ǵ a g*. After the upbeat over the first note of *María*, the grouping of the neums here given suggests a division into two-note groups: *a cc cc| c̆agf| ǵac̆a| f̆gg*; this, though serene in effect, resembles a trembling with holy joy. The two bistrophas, naturally, are to be sung with a very light swing. *Plena* is made prominent by its *pressus*, the first in this piece. We do not find the passage *Dóminus tecum* in the early manuscripts; its melody is found in the Offertory-verses *Posuísti* and *Angelus* over the words *glória* and *stetit* respectively (cf. Monday in Easter Week). With some variations, this tyle of singing the verses was adapted to the text of the Offertory *Beáta es*, which is now sung on September 8 and on some other feasts. Here the melody occurs over the word *virgo*. The second member is a repetition of the first. The brilliant phrase *benedícta* is characterized by its high pitch and by repeated and impressive accents: *c d é e–c d̆ d c–c d á a g–g c̆ c b*; then by the fourths *d–a, g–c, a–d*. These accents are still active in the last phrase: *f g á a g, g a f̆ f e*, and *g á a gg*.

We may not omit Mary, the Virgin Mother of God, from the liturgy of Advent. On the first Sunday of Advent we were led to her greatest shrine in Rome: Saint Mary Major. The vigil of Christmas will most appropriately find us there again, and in the Missal, heading the Midnight Mass, we find these words: "Station at Saint Mary Major, at the Crib." Almost every day during this season the second Collect is that of the Blessed Virgin. In the Divine Office for this time one finds many a delicate and charming allusion to her exalted dignity. And the closer we come to the feast of Christmas, the more frequently the chants of the Mass mention her. Thus today we sing to her the *Ave María*. How marvelously it scintillates in the light of Advent! This blessed one is bearing in her womb the Child that is God: *Dóminus tecum*. Just as mother and child form a unity, so the Son of God has become one with Mary. He is with her, in her, belongs to her, although He is the Lord whom she adores. But she wishes to present Him to us for the salvation of the world. Therefore do we call thee blessed, O glorious Virgin. Deborah and Judith were praised for delivering their people from dire distress; but thou hast turned mankind's curse into a blessing, and from thee flow streams of grace which shall carry us into a blissful eternity. *Ave Maria!*

COMMUNION (Isa. 7: 14)

1. *Ecce virgo concipiet, et pariet filium*: 2. *et vocabitur nomen ejus Emmanuel.*

1. *Behold a Virgin shall conceive, and bring forth a son,* 2. *and his name shall be called Emmanuel.*

This Communion has the same mode as that of the first Sunday of Advent, the same range, the same divisions, an arsis-movement in the first phrase resting on the dominant, then a thesis-movement in the second phrase. Both over *benignitátem* and *páriet* the pentatony, the use of a five-step scale with no semitones, is noticeable. But if we listen carefully, we find that the two Communions express quite different feelings. The Communion *Dóminus* breathes quiet confidence; hence the preference for seconds and thirds. There are, indeed, two intervals of fourths, but these occur in a low pitch, and the first one is not unexpected, since it returns to the *f* which occurred five times in the preceding word. Not so with the Communion *Ecce virgo*. This has descending fourths over *virgo, g–d*, and a fourth higher over *pá-(riet), d–a*; then ascending fourths over *et vo-(cábitur), g c c*. They are the expression of great astonishment over the marvel of the Incarnation wrought in the most pure womb of Mary. Behold, a *virgin* shall conceive: thus might we recite this passage; but there is even greater wonder: this virgin will become a *mother* and yet remain a *virgin: et páriet fílium*. After this great upward sweep we meet brighter and more tender notes over *et vocábitur*. At *Emmánuel* the melody is all reverence and amazement. O Wonder beyond human comprehension! The angel said to Mary: "The Lord is with Thee." We may now say: "The Lord is with us." And in His Name lies our guarantee of salvation and eternal peace and the inalienable possession of God.

When we receive the Saviour in Holy Communion our heart should be pure, virgin pure, like to the heart of the Mother of God. Then truly can we "put on the Lord Jesus," and make His thoughts and feelings,

His prayers and actions our own, so that that which beams forth in our souls through faith will, as the Collect for the second Mass of Christmas puts it, be reflected in our deeds.

Rass. gr., 7, col. 41 f.

*   *   *   *

VIGIL OF THE NATIVITY

INTROIT (Ex. 16: 6, 7)

1. *Hodie scietis, quia veniet Dominus, et salvabit nos:* 2. *et mane videbitis gloriam ejus.* Ps. *Domini est terra et plentitudo ejus:* * *orbis terrarum, et universi qui habitant in eo.*

1. *This day you shall know that the Lord will come, and save us:* 2. *and in the morning you shall see his glory.* Ps. *The earth is the Lord's and the fulness thereof:* * *the world and all they that dwell therein.*

With these words Moses announced to the people of Israel the manna from heaven during the journey through the desert. With these same words Mother Church heralds the true Manna, the Bread of Life, Jesus Christ, who is born at Bethlehem, the "house of bread" (Schott, *Messbuch.*)

The opening melody is arresting: it challenges our attention, for it augurs much. How will it be proclaimed, the message there so solemnly introduced? It is a message of mightiest import, spirit-stirring, enrapturing, than which nothing greater can be uttered: The Lord is coming as Redeemer; tomorrow He will come. The full meaning of the word *Dóminus* is explained by the Apostle in today's Lesson: the Lord comes as man, born of the tribe of David. But He is also God, eternal God, of the same essence as the Father. This God-man comes to redeem us. In spite of His humble condition, however, the spirit of holiness dwells within Him, and this leads Him in the end to the great wonder of His resurrection. The Lord is coming as Redeemer; tomorrow He will come. Tomorrow, after thousands of years of yearning and waiting; tomorrow, only a short while to wait, and the hour of deliverance will strike; tomorrow, and the glory will be revealed of Him whose rule extends over all the earth, as the psalm-verse says, and over all the inhabitants thereof.

And the melody? It is of the simplest style, foregoing all attempts at melismatic grouping. After the portentous introduction, it ranges itself unpretentiously around the tonic of the sixth mode, nor presuming to go more than a single tone above it, but several times sinking a fourth below it. And the significant *mane* ("tomorrow") only repeats what has already been sung over *et salvábit*. There are only allusions; nothing is definitely stated. The singer seems almost to regret that he spread his sails so broadly at the outset, for now he reefs them again. He fears that he has already divulged too much of that which is to be expected on the morrow. He lets fall the veil which he had scarce begun to lift. Even the enticing initial motive of the piece, once we have heard the psalm-verse, proves to be nothing else than a fine resume of the middle cadence: *(ple)-nitúdo ejus* = *g bb a g f*. Thus the melody would have us be recollected, meditative; it wishes to give us but an anticipatory taste of the mystery of the Holy Night.

GRADUAL (Ex. 16: 6, 7)

1. *Hodie scietis, quia veniet Dominus,* 2. *et salvabit nos: et mane videbitis* 4. *gloriam ejus* ℣. 1. *Qui regis Israel, intende* 2. *qui deducis velut ovem Joseph.* 3. *qui sedes super Cherubim, appare.* 4. *coram Ephraim, Benjamin, et Manasse.*

1. *This day you shall know that the Lord will come,* 2. *and save us:* 3. *and in the morning you shall see,* 4. *his glory.* ℣. 1. *Give ear, O thou that rulest Israel:* 2. *Thou that leadest Joseph like a sheep;* 3. *thou that sittest upon the Cherubim, shine forth,* 4. *before Ephraim, Benjamin, and Manasses.*

The *corpus* of the Gradual has the same text as the Introit; in its first half, the verse has the same words as the Gradual-verse for the third Sunday of Advent. The melody confines itself to the limits which have become characteristic of Graduals in the second mode, but, like the Gradual for the Midnight Mass, it exhibits some forms of its own. Several passages of both the *corpus* and the verse repeat the same melismas. Compare:

> *Et salvábit nos:*   *et mane vidébitis* =
> *qui sedes*   *super Chérubim, appáre.*

This last group also serves as a setting for *coram Ephraim.* Moreover, *glóriam ejus* = *Bénjamin et Manás-(se)*. The phrasing which so well separates *hódie* and *mane* in the Introit is not so successful here. After *Dóminus* a large pause is marked which, although melodically justifiable, joins *et salvábit* which actually belongs to the first phrase, to the second. The verse is taken from the psalms, the text of the *corpus* from Exodus. But there is a close relationship between the two. In the *corpus* God shows in a special manner how He cared for His people, how, as a good shepherd, He led them into verdant pastures. Then for the last time comes the fervent petition: *inténde* and *appáre*.

The luminous cloud of the Lord's glory rested over the Cherubim of the Ark of the Covenant, and by night it lighted up the path for the tribes of Israel who were wending their way across the desert. The twelve tribes were grouped about the Ark in a square, three to either side, three in front and three in the rear. Now, when the luminous cloud rose, it appeared to the eyes of those who marched behind the Ark, namely, to Ephraim, Benjamin, and Manasses *(Betende Kirche,* p. 286*)*.

We may, if we wish, link the thought of the second half of the verse with the preceding Collect: "Grant that we, who now joyfully receive Thine only-begotten Son as our Redeemer, may also, without fear, behold Him coming as our Judge." The Lord will come again, sitting upon the Cherubim, all the angels forming His train. Then all the tribes of Israel, all mankind, must appear before Him, to hear from His mouth judgement irrevocable. Let us pray to Him today: "Lord, be Thou not to me a Judge, but a Saviour."

ALLELUIA VERSE

1. *Crastina die delebitur iniquitas terrae: 2. et regnabit super nos Salvator mundi.*

1. *Tomorrow shall the iniquity of the earth be abolished: 2. and the Saviour of the world shall reign over us.*

The Saviour is coming as our Redeemer; the Alleluia again stresses this thought. King He will also be, not to impose burdens, but to relieve us of them. The King will likewise be the Lamb of God, to discharge that immense debt which has pressed upon the world ever since Adam's fall. He who will presently be laid in a rough manger will reign from the Cross. That is why the mystery which we are about to celebrate makes us "breathe anew," as the Postcommunion says.

In the most ancient manuscripts this melody is assigned to the Mass for the feast of the Holy Trinity (q.v.). With the same text as on that feast we also hear it sung on the Saturday of Whitsun Week, and with a different text on the feast of the Apostles Philip and James (May 1).

In the first member of the *jubilus, á b g* over *-lúia* becomes *á c b g,* in the second member *b d c b a g* and *á c b á g.* Much like it is the development of the verse. Over *delébitur, g c c* of *Crástina* becomes *g d d;* and at the end of the first phrase the melody again rises to high *d.* The first members of the first and second phrases correspond, and confine themselves to the tetrachord *g–c.* Over *(iníqui)-tas* we also meet the descending motive *c b á g.*

Let us sing this song with the ardor it deserves. If on Good Friday the Jews will cry: "We do not want this man to rule over us!" we shall

today already register a protest against this infidelity by crying: Be
Thou our King!

OFFERTORY (Ps. 23: 7)

1. *Tollite portas, principes, vestras:* 2. *et elevamini, portae aeternales,* 3. *et introibit Rex gloriae.*

1. *Lift up your gates, O ye princes:* 2. *and be ye lifted up, O eternal gates,* 3. *and the King of glory shall enter in.*

After the delicate and fragrant Introit, this song, solemn and majestic in its development, comes as a sharp contrast. It is wholly dominated by the thought of the King of glory; it is filled with deep reverence, but also with the glowing desire to lay open all things to this King, to have everything in readiness for His entrance and to cry to every son of man: Open your heart to the King of glory! For He comes to restore to your soul its lost nobility *(principes)*. He wishes to impress upon you the fact that your soul is eternal and of more worth than all the world. He wishes to grant your soul the inheritance rights to eternal glory. The previous chants emphasized the Person who is coming and what He, the Messias, will accomplish; this Offertory tells us what *we* must do.

A throbbing which ever increases, an onward urge ever growing, runs through the melody. It comes to the fore in the very first phrase with its rising movement. Its low beginning is the only reason why the piece was transposed into the upper fifth. Thus it could be written without the aid of ledger lines. Although the first phrase was satisfied with thirds and seconds, the second phrase at the beginning and at the close is marked by repeated fourths, and with its bold turn over *aeternáles* becomes very impressive. Between these two extremes quiet seconds are inserted. Because of this wise distribution of sudden flights and rests, the climax at *aeternáles* becomes all the more effective. We find a similar, but calmer, development in the third phrase. Peculiar to it is the repeated use of the interval *c a d*: once over *(intro)-íbit* and twice over *(glóri)-ae*. In the somewhat difficult melisma the clivis *d c* might be given slightly more prominence than the bistropha and the other notes. One all but hears a second voice, a voice which, when the text speaks of the King of glory, quietly and fervently adds: "Oh, do raise the gates: open your hearts! The Christchild must not again be turned away, as He was on that wintry night at Bethlehem." The striking close with the fourth *c g a* makes this petition all the more fervent, seems almost like a question, as if there were some fear that His people might this time also neglect to receive Him. Yet He is the King of the entire earth, and all men are His subjects—a truth which is emphasized by the first verse of this Offertory in the ancient manuscripts.

The whole song should resemble a glimpse into eternity, a foretaste of heaven's glory, and a joyous expectation, based on faith, of the dawn of that great day which will shine as no other. *Donec veniat!*

N. Sch. 242, 246, 254, 265.

COMMUNION (Isa. 40: 5)

1. *Revelabitur gloria Domini*: 2. *et videbit omnis caro salutare Dei nostri.*

1. *The glory of the Lord shall be revealed:* 2. *and all flesh shall see the salvation of our God.*

In a few short hours the prophecy of this Communion will be fulfilled. The first antiphon for the first Vespers of Christmas runs thus: "The King of peace is mighty indeed, whose face the whole earth desireth." Soon we shall be privileged to look upon His countenance, to gaze into the blue eyes of the divine Child. At first this chant tells of His glory with quiet reserve, with emphasis on the dominant *f*, as if we had here a plagal mode. To the *d f g* over *glór-(ria)*, *g f g f d* over *(Dó)-mini* comes as answer. The notes *f e f d* over the final syllable of the first word correspond to *f e g f f* over *caro*. But then the melody sings jubilantly of the salvation of our God: *salutáre Dei nostri.* Already we can hear the joyous bells of Christmas; already we hear the same melody and text as in the Communion for the third Mass on Christmas Day.

* * * *

CHRISTMAS DAY
MIDNIGHT MASS
INTROIT (Ps. 2: 7)

1. *Dominus dixit ad me: Filius meus es tu,* 2. *ego hodie genui te.* Ps. *Quare fremuerunt gentes:* * *et populi meditati sunt inania?*

1. *The Lord said to me: Thou art my Son,* 2. *this day have I begotten thee.* Ps. *Why have the gentiles raged:* * *and the people devised vain things?*

With what childlike joy our folksongs speak of the Christchild! They try to please Him, to coax a smile from His rosy lips. They speak to us in a fresh, direct, intimate way. Not so the texts and the plainsong melodies of the Midnight Mass. That Child, lying so poor and helpless and mute in His rude manger, is the one great Word spoken by the heavenly Father before all time, begotten of His own essence. This Child is equal in greatness, holiness, sublimity, and beauty to the Father Himself. *Dóminus dixit ad me*—the Lord spoke to Me who now lie in this manger in the form of man: "Thou art my Son," my Image, whom I embrace with fatherly affection. Today, on this glorious morn of eternity, have I begotten Thee. Today My father's love presents Thee to the world to be its Redeemer and King. That is truly a gaze into eternity, into the essence of the divinity, into the heart of the heavenly Father; a view so sublime and exalted that the soul, overcome with wonderment, bows down in silent adoration. Enraptured it contemplates the mysterious mutual relationship in the life of the divinity, its eternal bestowing and receiving, its eternal being and begetting. And this glorious light of the eternal divine life of joy breaks forth in the dark night of this world, is made manifest in the weak form of an Infant and shines from the mild, gentle eyes of the newborn Child as the aurora which heralds a sun still hidden in a fleecy veil of clouds.

Could such sublime thoughts be sung more worthily, and at the same time more simply, than is done in this Introit? Just as the eternal sonship is necessary, just as it is something perfectly evident to God Himself, so is there likewise an obvious something in this fragrantly tender song that melts away every last vestige of doubt. An effect is thus produced which, in the field of the liturgy, would be quite unattainable by any elaborate tonal effort. *(N. Sch.* 225 f*).*

The antiphon consists of two phrases similar in structure and with the same range of a fifth. They begin with the same motive *(Dóminus = ego)* and close with the same serene rhythm: $d\ e\ d\ c\ |\ c = g\ f\ e\ f\ |\ d$. Both linger on *f*, and thereby make the song more meditative. The cadence over *meus es tu* is frequently found in Introits of the second mode.

The psalm-verse gives us the world's view of this Word of God. There are men who oppose it, fight against it, persecute it. The child in the manger can already see the persecution that awaits Him, from that of Herod to the fateful morning in the court at Jerusalem and up to Golgotha. But the same verse tells us also: *meditáti sunt inánia.* All this raging and fury, all this mad behavior, is futile, like the breaking of a mighty wave that falls back upon itself. He who sits upon the heavenly throne derides them. He has set up His Son as King, and gives Him all the nations of the earth for His inheritance.

At the *Glória in excélsis Deo* we shall, with heartfelt joy at the blessed fact of the Saviour's coming, sing the song which the angels first intoned during the Holy Night on the fields of Bethlehem.

Musica s., 13, 138 ff.; *Gregoriusbote,* 33, 84 ff.; 24, 86 ff.

GRADUAL (Ps. 109: 3, 1)

1. *Tecum principium in die virtutis tuae*: 2. *in splendoribus sanctorum, ex utero* 3. *ante luciferum* 4. *genui te.* V. 1. *Dixit Dominus Domino meo*: 2. *Sede a dextris meis*: 3. *donec ponam inimicos tuos,* 4. *scabellum* 5. *pedum tuorum.*

1. *With thee is the principality in the day of thy strength; in the brightness of the saints, from the womb* 3. *before the day star* 4. *I begot thee.* ℣. 1. *The Lord said to my Lord*: 2. *Sit thou at my right hand,* 3. *until I make thine enemies* 4. *a resting place* 5. *for thy feet.*

All the songs for today participate in the splendor radiating from the Introit of the Midnight Mass. It is not so much the poor manger at Bethlehem, but rather the eternal procession from the Father that is the central point from which all the movements of spirit and heart draw their impulse and life. The Gradual continues the thought of the Introit. From all eternity the Father has begotten the Word, before the day-star was made, before any creature had been called into being. From the very beginning the Word *was*, and the Word was God, and all things that have been made were made by the Word. The Word shines in a sea of infinitely holy light; of this light the day-star is but a tiny spark. "The newborn Child is 'God' from His very birth. From the very beginning He was therefore charged with the fulfilment of His two-fold mission: the destruction of the enemies of God and our salvation. His birthday is the day of His strength and of His victory" (*B.K.*, p. 290).

With the words of this verse the Word of God, now become man, will later give testimony before His enemies of the divine dignity and majesty that is His. These words far transcend the present temporal order. Even today, at the beginning of Jesus' earthly life, they envisage His transfiguration on the day of the Ascension; and the Father will one day force every hostile power to pay homage, to bow down, and adore as the true Son of God the Child who now lies here in the manger.

It is, therefore, the eternal, the sublime, that determines the artistic form of these chants. Hence we ought not to be surprised to note that basically the Gradual employs a quite common, and therefore typical, melody of the second mode (cf. the first Sunday of Lent). The beginning with the solemn fourth *a–e*, which occurs only once in the piece, up to the passage over *virtú-(tis)* is proper to this Gradual. It also has a few passages in common with the melody for the vigil of Christmas, not found in the typical melody; and over *tuos* occurs a cadence of the fifth mode, which, to quote but one example, is sung in the Gradual for the feast of the Assumption over *aurem tuam.*

I, signifies the corpus of the Gradual; II, the verse; a, the passages of the Midnight Mass; b, those of the Mass for the vigil of Christmas:

I a, *in splendóribus sanctórum* | *ex útero* =
   b, *et salvábit nos et mane* | *vidébitis*
II a, *donec ponam inimícos* | *tuos* =
   b. *qui sedes super Chérubim* | *appáre.*

Furthermore, in this Gradual the words *ante lucíferum génui te* and *scabéllum pedum tuórum*, which immediately follow Ia and IIa, have the same melody: considerable reptition therefore results.

ALLELUIA VERSE (Ps. 2: 7)

1. *Dominus dixit ad me: Filius meus es tu,* 2. *ego hodie genui te.*

1. *The Lord hath said to me: Thou art my Son,* 2. *This day have I begotten thee.*

In this verse we meet the same text as in the Introit. We heard the melody for the first time on the first Sunday of Advent (q.v.). With holy joy we sing the florid melisma over the word *hódie* on this blessed night. The subsequent Gospel in its first part contrasts strongly with these solemn words. With striking simplicity it relates how Mary wrapped her Child in swaddling clothes and placed Him in a manger, because there was no place for them at the inn. In the second part, however, the newborn Child is announced to the shepherds as the Saviour, as Christ the Lord; and the angels' *Glória in excélsis Deo* sounds like the echo of the mighty word: "Thou art my Son!"

Springer, *Kunst der Choralbegleitung*, 244 ff.; Wagner, III, 400 ff.; *Musica divina*, 3, 298 ff.

OFFERTORY (Ps. 95: 11, 13)

1. *Laetentur caeli, et exsultet terra* 2. *ante faciem Domini: quoniam venit.*

1. *Let the heavens rejoice, and let the earth be glad.* 2. *before the face of the Lord, because he cometh.*

On this sacred night the Offertory is the only text of the Mass which transmutes directly into joy the solemn grandeur proper to the previous texts and chants. It calls upon the earth to rejoice as the heavens also are rejoicing. What wondrously sweet and overflowing joy marked the visit of the angels! What happiness filled the souls of those two heavenly souls kneeling before the divine Child: Mary in the radiant purity of her unique virgin motherhood, and the quiet, reserved St. Joseph! We also shall participate in this rejoicing. The melody, however, is still dominated by the feelings which filled the previous chants. No buoyant jubilation here, no singing contest with the angels. A word like *exsúltet* surely can be sung in a different fashion than is done here; in many other chants it does receive a prominence commensurate with its meaning. The melody scarcely rises above *f*, which note acts as a kind of dominant in the first phrase. Somewhat more animated is the second phrase; which has a higher melodic line and for its dominant the note *a*, stressed twice over the significant word *Dómini*. Joy comes more to the fore in the two verses which in the ancient manuscripts followed the Offertory proper,[1] both beginning with the words: "Sing ye to the Lord a new canticle" and with the same motive. A fine effect was no doubt achieved in former times when, after each verse, the second half of the Offertory was repeated: *ante fáciem Dómini, quóniam venit*. Now has the Lord revealed Himself (cf. the Communion for the vigil of Christmas). Now we can gaze upon His face; now He is here. The innumerable cries of *Veni*, which for countless centuries were storming the gates of heaven, have now been answered.

The favorite motive, *d g f e*, is introduced in various ways: first with a *salicus*, then with a minor third, and twice with a fourth.

The melody is also used for the feast of the Holy Family, and the greater part of it likewise is fittingly borrowed for the feast of Christ, the King.

COMMUNION (Ps. 109: 3)

In splendoribus sanctorum, ex utero ante luciferum genui te.

In the brightness of the saints, from the womb before the day-star I begot thee.

This Communion belongs to the few pieces that make a prominent use of pentatony (the five-step scale). *F g a* must be regarded as the nucleus. The melody ascends a third above it to *c* and descends a third below it to *d*, each time with avoidance of the semitones. Simplicity is the obvious characteristic of the melody. Only at *lucíferum* does it become somewhat more elaborate. The first and fourth members have corresponding endings; so also the second and third. The descending *g f d* over the final syllable of *útero* and *luciferum* appears in an inverted form over *gé-(nui)* as *d f g*.

Once again we hear expressions of the eternal generation of the Word from the Father. In the Introit and in the Alleluia-verse the Newborn One Himself spoke of it. In the first part of the Gradual and in our present chant the Father is the speaker. This difference between the

---

[1] Wagner, III, 420.

Introit and the Communion is clearly indicated in the annotated manuscripts. In the Introit practically all the neums have the simple and light form; almost everything is tender, fragrant, naive: the divine Child is speaking. In contrast to this, almost all the neums of the Communion are given the broad form. Here we hear the Father, serious and solemn; He is, so to say, conferring upon His Son the dignity of King and Priest. One cannot but admire the delicate artistic sense here displayed in the annotated manuscripts.

Christ accepts our sacrificial gifts, just as He assumed our human nature in order to endow it with His own divine life (cf. the Secret). Thus we are also made to participate in His generation from the Father. To each one of us the Father therefore says: "In the brightness of the saints I begot thee." Instead of "in the brightness of the saints" some translate "in the splendor of holy followers." "We form the brilliant host of His followers, celebrating together with Christ His ultimate day of victory and triumph" *(Betende Kirche,* p. 290 f.).

Revue greg., 9, 227 ff.; *N. Sch., Musica Sacra,* 50, 120.

THE THIRD MASS

INTROIT: Isa. 9: 6)

1. *Puer natus est nobis, et filius datus est nobis: 2. cujus imperium super humerum ejus: 3. et vocabitur nomen ejus, magni consilii Angelus. Ps. Cantate Domino canticum novum: * quia mirabilia fecit.*

1. *A Child is born to us and a Son is given to us: 2. whose government is upon his shoulder: 3. and his name shall be called the Angel of great counsel. Ps. Sing ye to the Lord a new canticle: * for he hath done wonderful things.*

Solemn and sublime were the chants of the Midnight Mass. Now, in the Introit of the third Mass, a new tone is heard. This Introit has not exactly the spirit of the popular *In dulci júbilo,* but approaches it more closely than any of the songs of the Midnight Mass. Indeed, one might almost say that this Introit supplied the inspiration for the song *In dulci júbilo.* After *Puer* with its dulcet fifth comes *d e d;* the second half of the phrase begins in the same manner. There can hardly be any doubt that the parallelism of the text *(Puer—fílius)* influenced the formation of the melody. The difference in the effect of this parallelism compared with that of the first Mass of Christmas with its minor thirds, reminding us of the semidarkness of that night, is well marked. It is well to note, however, that childlike joy, the kind heard in this first phrase, does not always demand new forms of expression, and that the repetition of a favorite motive is one of its chief characteristics. The tristropha brings a relaxation, allowing the following *nobis* to be sung with more color. For us has He been born, this wondrously gracious Child. We bask in His peace, in His benevolence. Rightly, therefore, does this *nobis* receive special emphasis in both parts of the phrase, once with its close on the dominant, the other time on the tonic of the mode. Yet, notwithstanding rhythmic relation in the two instances, the dynamics are different. In the first *nobis* the second *clivis* exercises a decided predominance over the first, while in the second *nobis* the first two notes receive the greater prominence. The same holds true of *natus* compared to the first *nobis*. Thus there results a beautiful melodic interplay, reminiscent, one might almost say, of a cradle song for the Christ Child.

The first phrase sings of the Infant, the second stresses His dominion and divine dignity. Here the Christianized Roman sees realized his old dream of the *imperium*, of the universal kingdom (*B.K.*, p. 292). The melody attains its peak at *impérium*. One best averts the danger of rushing to the highest note at the expense of the others by following the indication of MS. 121 of Einsiedeln, which gives the third note a slightly broader marking. Thus the melodic line can ascend with full solemnity. Care must likewise be taken that the single notes on the first three syllables of this phrase be not sung too short, for they should have the ring of definite and positive avowal. In all this, however, one idea must stand out pre-eminently: this Child exercises His kingly rule peacefully, with unmeasured mildness and love. For this reason it is that the sweet motive which gives such warmth to the first *nobis* again occurs here. Then the melody sinks, slowly and deliberately, like the folds of a king's mantle. Indeed, it almost seems as if a shadow settled upon it. For the royal dignity also reminds us of the burden which already at Christmas rests upon the shoulders of this Child: the burden which will grow and develop until it becomes a heavy cross.

In contrast to this minor third and the semitones we hear a bright major third over *et vocábitur*. It is as though it would like to banish the serious thoughts which insist on entering. It is an effort to introduce the question to which the tristropha and figure over the second *ejus*, like the one over the first *ejus*, give a still more intense form: "What can be the name of this Child?" With a succession of large intervals, a major third, a fifth, and a fourth, we hear the joyful answer: "He is the Angel of great counsel, the One who comes to announce to us the great decision of God, and also to make it effective, as far as in Him lies—our redemption and eternal salvation."

Now the melody comes exultingly: *Cantáte Dómino canticum novum*—"Sing ye to the Lord a new canticle: for He hath done wonderful things." The wonder of wonders, the divine Child in the manger, prompts this rejoicing. Each year He returns to us with renewed love, spins a web of glad magic about our heart, and blesses us with new graces.

Some have thought that the numerous tristrophas in this antiphon were intended to restrain the singer from a too violent show of joy. Be that as it may, these tristrophas should not sound heavy or unwieldy. The piece as a whole ought to be bright and lively. Not without reason are we using the seventh mode (cf. the Introit for the second Sunday of Advent and for the feast of the Ascension), which here never descends below the tonic, but ever strives upward, although the proper dominant of the seventh mode is prominent only in the first phrase. The accented syllables in most instances have a higher pitch than the syllable immediately following, frequently also higher than the preceding syllable.

K.K., 23, 134 ff.; *Choralblatter*, No. 2; *N. Sch.*, 256; *Revue*, 8, 71 ff.; *Analyses*, III, 14 ff.; Wagner, III, 511.

GRADUAL (Ps. 97: 3, 2)

1. *Viderunt omnes fines terrae salutare Dei nostri*: 2. *jubilate Deo omnis terra.* ℣ 1. *Notum fecit Dominus salutare suum*: 2. *ante conspectum gentium revelavit justitiam suam.*

1. *All the ends of the earth have seen the salvation of our God*: 2. *sing joyfully to God all the earth.* ℣ 1. *The Lord hath made known his salvation*: 2. *he hath revealed his justice in the sight of the gentiles.*

As in the Introit, so here again childlike naiveté and lofty grandeur combine to form a liturgical Christmas song, except that here, in accordance with the style of a Gradual-responsory, the sublime predominates in the melodic line as well as in the richness of the melody. The grand beginning with *Vidérunt omnes* already hints at this. Here the customary limits assigned to Graduals of the fifth mode are broken. The Saviour of the world has appeared! Effaced are the national boundaries which separated Jew and Greek and Roman; there comes forth the Catholic Church, the earth-encircling Church, which mediates the salvation of God to all the world, and thus bestows a happiness upon the nations which makes them shout aloud for very joy. Originally this Mass was celebrated at the world-church, St. Peter's. *Vidérunt omnes* has an echo in *omnis* at the end of the *corpus* of the Gradual. Extremely naive is the motive *c b c a* which runs through the *corpus*: *(ter)-rae, (salutá)-re, (no)-stri.* The form over *terra* again recalls the popular *In dulci júbilo.* The frequent occurrence of the tone-sequence *f a c* and its inversion insistently calls to mind our modern F major. But when, as here, the note *b* follows immediately upon *c* ,we are made to realize again that the Lydian fifth mode has a character all its own.

The florid melisma at the beginning of the verse over *Dóminus* is, as we know, a stylistic peculiarity of Graduals. At Christmastide it recalls the words of the Apostle: "But God (who is rich in mercy), for his exceeding charity wherewith he loved us...hath quickened us together in Christ." Into this rich melisma we put our thanks for the profusion of love the Lord has shown us today, that He has revealed His justice to us, has given us the Just One whose coming we have so fervently implored from the clouds above in the *Roráte caeli*. Only the Lord *(Dóminus)* was able to work such a miracle. Three pauses divide this melisma into four parts. The first and second groups are the same, closing with *c d a f*, a motive which in a gracefully shortened form is again heard at the close of *(Dómi)-nus, (conspéc)-tum*, and *(génti)-um*. The third member ends with *c a f*. The beginning of the fourth member, *a f a g f*, immediately ascends to the higher reaches with *a f g a c*, and then the melody rises jubilantly, reminding us of *Dei* in the *corpus*, while the quieter and more devout *salutáre* which follows sounds much like *terrae* there. In an outburst of overflowing joy the melody at *géntium* again stresses the idea that the salvation of the *entire* world has appeared. With *suam* the first two notes are to be sung as a sort of preparation for the subsequent *torculus*; similarly *g a* after the pause should be weaker than the neum which follows; the same holds true of *f g a* before the *pressus*, the summit toward which everything else must tend in an ascending line: all in all a masterful development of incomparable melodic beauty.

Revue, 8, 72; 12, 17; *Greg. Rundschau*, 1, 165 ff.

ALLELUIA VERSE

1. *Dies sanctificatus illuxit nobis:* 2. *venite gentes et adorate Dominum:* 3. *quia hodie descendit lux magna super terram.*

1. *A sanctified day hath shone upon us:* 2. *come ye Gentiles, and adore the Lord:* 3. *for this day a great light hath descended upon the earth.*

This verse continues the thoughts of the Epistle and acts as a transition to the Gospel. The Epistle portrays the greatness and majesty of the Son of God. It exalts Him as the image of the Father, the Creator of the world, who through the power of His word sustains all things, whose throne stands forever, whom the angels adore at the Father's behest. Hence, this Alleluia-verse now cries: *adoráte*—"adore ye the Lord," whereas the preceding Gradual had cried: *jubiláte*!

When we hear the mighty words in the Gospel: "And the Word was made Flesh," we bend our knees before the Babe of Bethlehem. The descent of the melody over *veníte* to low *a*, the prolongation of the dominant *f*—within a passage of florid melismas, a recitation on a single note always produces a solemn effect—truly seem like an eloquent expression of our prayerful adoration.

We have here a typical melody of the archaic form, a favorite for the Christmas season; thus it appears on the feasts of St. Stephen, of St. John, and on Epiphany; likewise on the feasts of St. John the Baptist and SS. Peter and Paul.

Four phrases may be distinguished in the verse. The first and third have practically the same intonation: *Dies = quia hódie*; then follows a recitation on the tonic: *sanctificátus illúxit = descéndit lux*; then the same florid cadence: *nobis = magna*. The second phrase begins with a sort of intonation contrasting with that of the others, then a recitation on the dominant *f*, and a sinple cadence. The fourth phrase is extremely short. It has no intonation of any kind, but a recitation on the dominant like the second phrase (this recitation is longer on the feast of St. John the Evangelist and on Epiphany), and finally a closing cadence. The psalmodic construction of the whole is quite evident.

Both the text and melody probably come from old Byzantium. In some of the ancient manuscripts either a Latin or a Greek text accompanies the melody; in one of the Vatican Library (No. 298, f. 111), both a Latin and a Greek text accompany it.

The great Light, the Light of Light, God of God, true Light of true Light, has come down to us. It transfigures the present day, makes it a holy day indeed. There is nothing blinding, nothing to repel the eye, in this fullness of light; enraptured we contemplate the divine Child, the while we adore Him as the *sol invíctus*, the truly unconquerable Sun.

OFFERTORY (Ps. 88: 12, 15)

1. *Tui sunt caeli, et tua est terra*: 2. *orbem terrarum, et plenitudinem ejus tu fundasti*: 3. *justitia et judicium praeparatio sedis tuae.*

1. *Thine are the heavens, and thine is the earth*: 2. *the world and the fullness thereof thou hast founded*: 3. *justice and judgement are the preparation of thy throne.*

The divine dignity of the Babe of Bethlehem is the first thought, in fact one might say, *the* thought, occupying the mind of the Church today. In opposition to the Arians it was necessary to stress the fact that this Child is equal in essence to the Father, and against the tenets of the Mithraic cults, that on the present day, the day of increasing sunlight, it is not a question of mere symbolism, but of the birth of the divine Sun of Justice in the flesh. The Church, therefore, addresses these words to the newborn Babe: Thine are the heavens, and Thine is the earth. Thou art the Creator and Governor of the world; Thine it is with all its inhabitants. Prominently this *tu* dominates the melodic line, which otherwise never rises above *a*. *Tuae* of the third phrase corresponds to *fundásti*. Nor does the remaining part speak of the poor manger in which the Child is lying. It speaks of His throne, of the exercise of His judicial power, of His zeal for right and justice, of His eternal, immutable judgements. In the same strain run the verses which formely belonged to this Offertory: "Thou art a great God and terrible; Thou wilt slay the dragon of the sea. Mercy and truth shall go before Thy face. Thou strikest down the proud; with the strength of Thine arm Thou wilt cut down Thine enemies. For strong is Thy hand, O Lord, and mighty is Thine arm."

Vigorous words, these. But the melody? Proske, in the preface of his *Musica divina*, makes too sweeping a statement when he says of the church music of the ancients that it avoided all specialized expression. To plain song, at least, a greater freedom of expression must be conceded. But he is right when he characterizes as lyric meditation, or contemplation, that ancient church music which of set purpose avoided any definite emotion. Over this present Offertory, for instance, there hovers a delicate shimmer of light, dreamlike one might almost call it. At *sunt caeli* we find Palestrina (IX, 16, 1) using a sixth *(d–b)*; plain chant, however, is content with simple minor thirds and seconds within the tetrachord *d–g*, and similarly over *ejus* later on; *justítia* likewise confines itself to a tetrachord, *e–a*. Low *f* is the dominant of the entire piece. The first and third phrases have a range of only a fifth; the second, excepting *tu* with its reach of a minor third above the note *a*, has the range of a sixth. All is in an unpretentious style: there seems to be deliberate self-restraint. Large intervals are rare; the few that do occur are quite inert, as in the ascending sequence over *est*, whose nucleus is *f g a g*, an inversion of which is found in *(pleni)-tú-(dinem)*: *e g f g*. At *ejus* the melody effects a retarding tension much like the related melody in the Introit. *Tu* can then sound with full effect. *Justítia* sets in energetically. We may regard the melody over *judícium*, and especially that over *sedis tuae*, as a free variation of *est terra*.

To understand and appreciate this chant, one might imagine the Blessed Mother kneeling before the manger, contemplating her divine Child. Her meditation turns into song, and this tender melody reveals what thoughts are flooding her heart. A tremor of holy ecstasy seizes her: Thou, O Almighty One, art mine, my very own, my Child. And the divine Child (the twenty-seventh verse of the same psalm suggests this thought) addresses the most pure Virgin thus: And thou art my Mother!—Let us kneel at the side of the Mother of God, to pray and sing with her, and in union with her to offer up the gifts of our faith and love and adoration.

(The *"Stabat Mater"* in Liszt's *Christus* closely approaches the spirit of this Offertory.)

COMMUNION (Ps. 97: 3)

Viderunt omnes fines terrae salu-   All the ends of the earth have
tare Dei nostri.   seen the salvation of our God.

We hear this same melody, in a happy adaptation, on the feast of St. Philip Neri (May 26). The jubilant *salutáre* there occurs over the word *exsultavérunt*—my heart and my flesh rejoice. Less happy is the adaptation for the feast of the Holy Family; its adaptation in the Mass of the holy Lance and Nails (on the Friday after the first Sunday of Lent) to the text: "They looked upon Him whom they have pierced, and the foundations of the earth were shaken," is strange, to say the least. No objection can be made to the treatment of the word-accents; but our jubilant *salutáre* is there sung to the very dissimilar *moveréntur*. In all probability the opening word, *Vidérunt*, led to the choice of the melody proper to the Communion *Vidérunt*. These remarks, be it said, are not made merely to find fault. They should help us, rather, to a deeper understanding of the appropriateness and of the beauty of our present Communion song. If we then compare it with the same text used in the first part of today's Gradual, we get an illuminating insight into the stylistic differences of the two chants.

Terrae and *salutáre* mark the high points of the melody. The connection is immediately evident: *salvation* has come to the *world*. The momentous promise so solemnly uttered on the vigil of Christmas that "all flesh shall see the salvation of our God," is now perfectly realized; and from overflowing hearts joyous thanks ascend to God. When we consider, moreover, how great is the number of those who have not yet heard the message of Christmas, who know nothing of the Babe of Bethlehem who came to save them and who would fill the hearts of all with His grace and peace and love; when we consider that we are privileged to look upon Him, that we are even allowed in Holy Communion to taste and see "how sweet He is," then our *salutáre* will have a particularly radiant ring. The notes that come after the lengthened *c* should be sung as two groups of two; the measured rhythm will thus restrain the almost too animated exultation. Rhythmically, *a g e f f* corresponds to *g f a g e* over *(ter)-rae* and *f d f e c* over *De-(i)*.

God is generosity itself; His giving is always on a grand scale. He is the salvation of the entire world. Would that we equalled His magnanimity, and would give our hearts entirely to Him who has become our salvation, our joy, and our delight!

* * * *

ST. STEPHEN, THE FIRST MARTYR

(December 26)

INTROIT (Ps. 118: 23, 86, 23)

1. *Etenim sederunt principes, et adversum me loquebantur: et iniqui persecuti sunt me:* 2. *adjuva me, Domine Deus meus, quia servus tuus exercebatur in tuis justificationibus.* Ps. *Beati immaculati in via:* * *qui ambulant in lege Domini.*

1. *Princes sat and spoke against me: and the wicked persecuted me:* 2. *help me, O Lord my God, for thy servant is exercised in thy justifications.* Ps. *Blessed are the undefiled in the way:* * *that walk in the law of the Lord.*

When we come to Mass on this second Christmas feast we hear, immediately at the Introit, the saint of today describing that which passed in his soul when he stood before the high council. Dispensing with introductory phrases, he speaks to us directly, graphically, impressively. Around him he sees the high priests and scribes *(príncipes)*; from their faces, from their words, he knows that they are his bitterest opponents. He must hear how truth is distorted by the testimony of false *(iníqui)* witnesses; and by this assembly he hears the sentence of death passed against him.

That is the first phrase of this Introit. Its melody consists of three members. The first member, with its series of agitated *porrectus*, each of which sets in on a higher pitch, leads up to the dominant; the second leads back to the tonic: arsis and thesis. The second phrase repeats practically the same formula over *et advér-* and *me loquebán-*. The subsequent double bistropha suggests a mysterious muffled whispering; similarly its recurrence in the Gradual. An agitated up-and-down movement runs through the third member, like the motions of some noble animal at bay: there is indignation at the injustice displayed. It is well to stress the *torculus*, and the syllable following it must also be given its full due. The first note of each neum over *(perse)-cúti* can be sung almost *martellato*.

If in the first phrase the saint looked about himself, he now in the second, looks upward to God. *Deus meus* does not occur in the original psalm-verse, but the composer so merged himself into the feelings of the saint that these words rose spontaneously. The melody becomes urgently pleading. It marks the summit of the entire piece and has the only high *pressus*. Here again the first member lingers on the dominant. Most truthfully can the saint pray: Thou art my God—*Deus meus* .... Thee have I chosen, to Thee have I dedicated myself. In the second and third members the influence of the word-accents in the formation of the melody becomes apparent: *servus tuus exercebátur, tuis*. Though practically the same formula recurs three or four times, this may remind us of the constancy with which the saint withstood all opposition and persevered in the service of his Lord; it may remind us of the fiery zeal with which he offered himself for the great cause. For no one could resist the wisdom and the spirit that spoke in him. With full determination he likewise advances to his death. We have already met the closing formula in the Introit *Gaudéte*; we shall meet it again in the Introit for Epiphany.

The psalm-verse now sings its *Beáti* quietly, almost genially. The purity of heart and fidelity to God here mentioned were the saint's great consolations.

Revue, 4, 65 ff.

GRADUAL (Ps. 118: 23, 86)

1. *Sederunt principes, et adversum me loquebantur*: 2. *et iniqui persecuti sunt me.* ℣. 1. *Adjuva me Domine Deus meus*: 2. *salvum me fac propter misericordiam tuam.*

1. *Princes sat and spoke against me*: 2. *and the wicked persecuted me*: ℣. 1. *Help me, O Lord my God*: 2. *save me for thy mercy's sake.*

The *corpus* of the Gradual has the same text as the first phrase of the Introit, except that the word *Etenim* has been omitted. Similarly, the verse bears some resemblance to the second phrase of the Introit. In both pieces *loquebántur* carries a similar melody; *iníqui* is stressed still more; in both instances *Dómine Deus meus* marks the principal ascent. But there are also specific differences besides those of mode and range. In the Introit the accented syllables helped to form the melody; not a single closing syllable had more than two notes. In the Gradual, on the contrary, it is precisely the final syllables that receive special prominence. Here we also find an interplay of florid melismatic passages with some that are purely syllabic, whereas the entire Introit was developed more regularly and simply: the accented syllable of *persecúti* alone was given three neums. The difference in spirit is even more marked, especially in the verse. At its very beginning the Introit was lively in movement; the solemn beginning of the Gradual, however, seems to lead us to a serious, dignified court-session. At *advérsum me* it gathers momentum, and *iníqui* is still more vigorous: here *f f g a c* becomes *a c d e f*. At *persecúti sunt* the notes, without being hammered out, must be accented well enough to show that the meaning of the word is fully grasped. Thus far the text had a setting almost entirely original; the notation over *me*, however, already acts as a transition to the verse, which employs typical forms only.

The beginning of the verse still reminds us of *et advérsum me* in the *corpus*. Snatches of the melody from the Gradual of the second Christmas Mass follow, and then comes a beautifully articulated melisma, one which on Epiphany we find again over *illumináre* (q.v.). Over *Deus meus* we hear a form which occurs several times, e.g. on the feast of the Assumption *(inclína aurem tuam)*. After the florid melisma a special solemnity attaches to the simple recitation on the low *f* if it is rendered in a sustained (not heavy, or blunt!) manner and in a careful *legato*. Over *tuam* we find the passage *fagf ga a* of *(miseri)-córdiam* a third higher. The closing melisma is quite common; tomorrow we meet it again.

This chant does not in the least sound like the prayer of an outcast, of one who as a victim to fanatical hatred sees a horrible death staring him in the face. Instead, it sounds like the prayer of one whose confidence is boundless, of one who is sure of being heard: an echo, this, of heaven's own songs.

ALLELUIA VERSE (Acts 7: 55)

1. *Video caelos apertos,* 2. *et Jesum stantem* 3. *a dextris virtutis Dei.*

1. *I see the heavens opened,* 2. *and Jesus standing* 3. *at the right hand of the power of God.*

Here a word of the preceding Lesson finds a continuation. Surrounded by enemies raging and furious, Stephen, "full of the Holy Ghost," was privileged to look upon the glory of God. In this perspective he forgot all things of earth. He saw Jesus, to whose cause he had dedicated himself completely, and he saw Him standing, as if He had risen from His throne to help His loyal servant with all His divine power.

We already know the melody from the third Mass of Christmas. Taking into account the divisions noted there it will suffice to add the following particulars:

1. *Vídeo* = 3. *a dextris*
1. *apértos* = 3. *virtútis*
2. *et Jesum stantem,* (4) *Dei.*

OFFERTORY (Acts 6: 5; 7: 59)

1. *Elegerunt Apostoli Stephanum levitam,* 2. *plenum fide et Spiritu Sancto:* 3. *quem lapidaverunt Judaei orantem, et dicentem:* 4. *Domine Jesu, accipe spiritum meum,* 5. *alleluia.*

1. *The Apostles chose Stephen, a levite,* 2. *a man full of faith and of the Holy Ghost:* 3. *whom the Jews stoned, praying and saying:* 4. *Lord Jesus, receive my spirit,* 5. *alleluia.*

Two scenes comprise the Offertory: the first two phrases portray the election of St. Stephen as a deacon; the third and fourth phrases give his prayer while he was being stoned. A solemn quiet hovers about the opening melody. One must guard against singing it too fast, for it should tell in a broad festal manner of the act by which the honor and the order of the diaconate was bestowed upon the saint. He was truly worthy of being chosen,[1] for he was "filled" with faith and with the Holy Ghost. The setting in with the fifth is more than mere chance; so too the further progress of the melody with the descending fourth and the *pressus.* And how austere is then the close over *Spíritu Sancto!* The spirit of the world would certainly be voiced differently.

In the second part one might consider *lapidavérunt,* whose first three *podatus* in the annotated manuscripts are in the broad form, as tone-painting, as depicting the downward flight of the stones. But immediately afterwards we meet the same tone-sequences as we had over *plenum.* To the descending fourth, and also later over *(Dómi)-ne,* a third is added, which makes the melody more virile. The frequent tritones, though most of them are not obvious, contribute to this same end. The second half of the phrase is a quiet preparation for what follows.

What fervor and confidence breathe forth from this prayer! It should be sung with warmth, and above all not too rapidly. After *Dómine* it will be necessary to make a brief pause for breathing. *Ac-(cipe)* and *(al)-le-lúia* remind us of *(Spíri)-tu Sancto* in the second phrase; *spíritum,* of *lapidavérunt* in the third phrase. All the notes after the last minor pause are to be sung *ritardando.*

Dom Jeannin[2] would assign the entire piece to an Ut-mode with a close on the fifth. However that may be, it is quite surprising to find' over *levítam,* a cadence to *c.*

---

1 The word *levitam* is not found in the Acts, but is the free addition of the composer.

2 *Melodies liturgiques syriennes et chaldeennes,* p. 133.

About the same time that we hear the saint praying this *áccipe spíritum meum*, the priest at the altar is saying: *Súscipe, sancte Pater, hanc immaculátam hóstiam*—"Receive, O holy Father...this spotless victim," in preparation for the most holy Sacrifice. Today, on the feast of the first martyr, we must try to appreciate that which is stressed by the Secret on the Thursday after the third Sunday of Lent: "We offer Thee that Sacrifice from which all martyrdom has drawn its source."

COMMUNION (Acts 5: 55, 58, 59)

1. *Video caelos apertos, et Jesum stantem a dextris virtutis Dei*: 2. *Domine Jesu, accipe spiritum meum*, 3. *et ne statuas illis hoc peccatum, quia nesciunt quid faciunt.*

1. *I see the heavens opened and Jesus standing on the right hand of the power of God*; 2. *Lord Jesus, receive my spirit*, 3. *and lay not this sin to their charge.*

The Communion in its first phrase has the same text as the Alleluia-verse; in the second, the same as the fourth phrase of the Offertory. There is a difference, however, in the melodic treatment, much like to that which exists between the Introit and the Gradual, though not in the same degree. The piece has wonderful dramatic power. Here one may nicely see the role played by intervals in plain song. *Video* sets out with quiet seconds; over *apértos* we have a major third. Now the saint's gaze penetrates further into heaven; he sees Jesus. A fourth stands over *et*— and then *Jesum stantem* dominates the entire melodic line. Thus far the arsis. Two energetic *pressus* feature the subsequent thesis. The ardent *Dómine* uses a fifth and an ascent to high *e*. The second part of the phrase is again a thesis. An example of logical development.

The third phrase never extends above *a*; its largest intervals are but minor thirds; toward the end only seconds occur. We are told in the Acts, it is true, that St. Stephen, kneeling, cried with a loud voice: "Lord, lay not this sin to their charge." But the plainsong melody has a different end in view. It seems as if the saint's strength were fast ebbing away; yet before his death he must pronounce this prayer. The melody seems to melt away also. In the Acts the last four words are not to be found. But they proceed from the heart of the saint; they unite his sacrifice and his prayer with that of the Crucified. Christ was nailed to His cross outside the city gates. There also was Stephen stoned. In him the sacrificial power of the Cross achieves its first glorious victory. It is this same power of the Cross that inflamed countless thousands to follow the example of the first martyr.

*　　*　　*　　*

ST. JOHN, APOSTLE AND EVANGELIST

(December 27)

INTROIT (Ecclus. 15: 5)

1. *In medio Ecclesiae aperuit os ejus:* 2. *et implevit eum Dominus spiritu sapientiae, et intellectus:* 3. *stolam gloriae induit eum.* Ps. *Bonum est confiteri Domino:* * *et psallere nomini tuo, Altissime.*

1. *In the midst of the church the Lord opened his mouth:* 2. *and filled him with the spirit of wisdom and understanding:* 3. *he clothed him with a robe of glory.* Ps. *It is good to give praise to the Lord;* * *and to sing to thy name, O Most High.*

The text was taken from today's Lesson, and that in turn from the Book of Wisdom. The Lord has opened the mouth of St. John, has made him to be an Apostle, an Evangelist, a prophet, the writer of the Apocalypse. The Saviour, Wisdom itself, proceeding from the mouth of the Most High, filled the saint with the spirit of wisdom and understanding. For years the saint was privileged to hear the words of life as a favored Apostle; at the Last Supper he drank in wisdom at its source, at the breast of the Saviour, out of His very heart. Standing at the foot of the cross, he received the last words of his Master. How deeply they must have embedded themselves in his heart! He was permitted to take under his care the Mother of Jesus, the Seat of Wisdom; thus he could learn to know even more intimately and thoroughly Him who is the fullness of grace and truth. No one was privileged to taste so deeply of the Lord's sweetness as he, and no one else has written so profoundly of His divinity. The Lord clothed him, moreover, with the robe of glory. How beautiful was this soul in its virginity! So beautiful that it excerised a sort of enchantment over the Lord Himself, for St. John was loved more than any of the other Apostles. How the beauty of this soul grew day by day in the fervor and ardor of its love, and how splendid, in consequence, must its robe of glory have become! To thank God for all this is truly a duty of love.

At the present time this melody is found in the Common of Doctors; it was, however, originally composed for today's feast. The same is true of the Offertory *Justus ut palma*. This Introit is an example of classic repose, and must be sung very sustainedly. The first phrase has two members, each of which begins with a neum resembling a *podatus*; in each instance this is followed by a tristropha and an accented *g*. Everything seems to undulate lightly about *f*, and yet an upward tendency runs through the entire phrase, a tendency which finds a brilliant fulfilment in the second phrase. The *cdfg* here becomes *fgab♭* and *aćc* with the *pressus*, the only one in the entire piece. After this culmination the melody again supports itself, as in the first and third phrases, on *f*. The synonyms *sapiéntiae* and *intéllectus* have similar intonations. Low *c* over the latter word serves as an antithesis to high *c* over *eum* and at the same time as a transition to the third phrase. This phrase also descends to low *c*, but more gracefully and gently, since each of the last two neums sets in with the pitch of the preceding. The second half corresponds to *ejus* at the close of the first phrase. On account ot its range and the emphasis on the tonic *f*, this Introit may serve as a standard example of the (plagal) sixth mode. Of greater moment, however, is the nobility, the enshrined holiness, which breathes from it.

Pal. mus., Vol. 10, and Mocquereau, *Monographies greg.*, I: *L'Introit "In medio"* (Tournai, 1910) discuss the reading and rhythm of this piece.

GRADUAL (John 21: 23, 19)

1. *Exiit sermo inter fratres, quod discipulus ille non moritur. Et non dixit Jesus: Non moritur* ℣. 1. Sed: *Sic eum volo manere,* 2. *donec veniam*: 3. *tu me sequere.*	1. *A saying went abroad among the brethren, that that disciple should not die. And Jesus did not say: He should not die.* ℣. 1. *But: So I will have him to remain,* 2. *till I come*: 5. *follow thou me.*

The text of the Gradual anticipates today's Gospel. Peter had heard the Lord's summons: "Follow me!" But when he saw that John was following the Lord, he said: "Lord, and what shall this man do?" Jesus answered: "So I will have him to remain till I come, what is it to thee? follow thou me." From these words the disciples gathered that John was not to die. But the Lord had only intended to convey the thought that Peter would find death after untold struggles and a bloody martyrdom; John, however, was to remain in quiet labor for the extension of the Church, and, when the Lord would come to receive his soul, would have a serene death, not that of martyrdom.

In the Gradual the words of the Gospel are shortened, and hence not readily understood.

The melody is the same as that of *Ecce sacérdos magnus* and *Christus factus est*. It must be said, however, that the divisions in the *corpus* of this Gradual are better than in that of Maundy Thursday. In the verse one expects another ascent after *donec*, but it is omitted on account of the brevity of the text.

Follow thou me! Filled with love like St. John, we shall interest ourselves in others and care for them; but when God calls, we shall go the way He points out to us, without having any regard for others.

Motet over *manére*: *Revue*, 23, 99 ff.

ALLELUIA VERSE (John 21: 24)

1. *Hic est discipulús ille,* 2. *qui testimonium perhibet de his:* 3. *et scimus quia verum est* (4.) *testimonium ejus.*

1. *This is the disciple* 2. *who giveth testimony of these things:* 3. *and we know that true is* (4.) *his testimony.*

This verse forms the close of today's Gospel. It emphasizes the characteristic mark of an Apostle, expressed by St. Peter before the election of St. Matthias: the Apostles are witnesses of Christ—"Beginning from the baptism of John, until the day wherein He was taken up from us, one of these must be made a witness with us of His resurrection." This testimony all the Apostles confirmed with their life's blood. In a certain sense, St. John also was a martyr (cf. his feast on May 6). This is further justified by the unanimous acclaim of the whole Catholic world, which today shows its special joy in the testimony of St. John. His testimony proceeds from ardent love and depicts for us the most sublime portrait of the Saviour.

This typical Christmas melody is here divided: 1. *Hic est* = 3. *et scimus*; 1. *discípulus ille* = 3. *quia verum est*; 2. *qui testimónium pérhibet de his*, (4). *testimónium ejus.*

OFFERTORY (Ps. 91: 13)

1. *Justus ut palma florebit:* 2. *sicut cedrus, quae in Libano est, multiplicabitur.*

1. *The just shall flourish like the palm tree:* 2. *he shall grow up like the cedar which is in Libanus.*

This Offertory is now found in the Common of Doctors, just as the Introit is. St. John became the teacher of them all. As Evangelist, his symbol is the eagle. The figure of the palm tree signifies much the same thing here: his entire being was turned toward the Sun; his life was lived in heaven, into the deepest mysteries of which he was allowed to peer. In his virginal purity he was immune to all that is earth-bound or burdening. Everything was filled with light and most pure love. In his ardent nearness to God the sweet fruits of which his writings give evidence could attain to perfect maturity. The melody itself suggests the palm with its towering shaft. The second half of *Justus* is repeated over *florébit* and in part over *(Líba)-no*.

In the second phrase, however, the cedar is made to reach higher than the palm. *Sicut* reminds us of *ut pal-(ma)*; *ce-(drus)* with its *abcdca* is a development of the *efgagf* at the beginning of this Offertory; *(Lí)-bano* harks back to *(pal)-ma*: two or three motives are thus manipulated here in a smooth and expert manner. *Multiplicábitur* repeats the fourth which was heard three times at the beginning. The melisma following supports itself on the pressus *áag*, *ǵgf*, and *ffe*. It pictures the spreading branches of the cedar; the development of the melody here is lateral rather than perpendicular.

COMMUNION (John 21: 23)

1. *Exiit sermo inter fratres, quod discipulus ille non moritur:* 2. *et non dixit Jesus: Non moritur:* 3. *sed: sic eum volo manere, donec veniam.*

1. *A saying went abroad among the brethren that that disciple should not die;* 2. *and Jesus did not say: He should not die:* 3. *but: So I will have him remain till I come.*

Here a simple antiphonal melody harks back to the Gospel and the Gradual. Each of the three phrases lifts the accented syllable to *d e*: *ille, dixit, volo.* Furthermore, the last syllable of *Jesus*, as in many other instances where Hebrew words occur, receives the emphasis. *Non móritur* as well as the four preceding notes are the same in both cases. The third phrase begins in the same manner as the second; *manére* is treated with special fondness. *Donec*, if set a fifth lower, would have to be written with *b♭ (dcd cb♭d)*. No doubt the composer wished to avoid this; he therefore wrote the whole piece in a pitch which more closely approaches that in which it is actually to be sung; that is likely the reason for the transposition.

Would that we were like St. John, and might always remain so! Virginal purity adorned his soul. He was filled with a tender and true love of God and the Blessed Virgin. How touchingly he depicts the love of God in his Epistles, and above all in the farewell address at the Last Supper, which he alone records! With most tender solicitude he cared for the Mother of God, whom he was privileged to take under his protection. With an affectionate gesture the Church indicates that Mary today takes him to herself, for the station is at St. Mary Major. Would that we also might be and remain thus until the Lord comes! *Donec véniam*: that is the last word of today's proper chants. The Lord will come again in the next Holy Communion; likewise at the evening of our life. This word should, therefore, be to us, as it was to the early Chris-

tians, a word of admonition, but at the same time a word of consolation
and joyful expectation.

Rass. gr., 7, 9, 417 ff.

*   *   *   *

THE HOLY INNOCENTS

(December 28)

INTROIT (Ps. 8: 3)

1. *Ex ore infantium, Deus, et lactentium perfecisti laudem 2. propter inimicos tuos. Ps. Domine Dominus noster: * quam admirabile est nomen tuum in universa terra!*

1. *Out of the mouth of babes and of sucklings, O God, thou hast perfected praise 2. because of thine enemies. Ps. O Lord, our Lord: * how admirable is thy name in the whole earth.*

A holy awe hovers over the melody. Hence the three descending and
the three ascending fourths in these two short phrases. The first phrase
with its preponderating *g* has a cadence much favored by the second
mode; we heard it recently in the Introit of the Midnight Mass of
Christmas. The second phrase, in which *f* predominates, bears some
affinity to *et lacténtium* of the first phrase.

The Holy Innocents offered God perfect praise; as the Collect of
the feast says, they glorified Him not by words, but by their death. It
is impossible for a creature to show greater glory than this to the Creator. Furthermore, their praise was absolutely pure. Of them today's
Lesson from the Apocalypse speaks as follows: "They are virgins...
and in their mouth there was found no lie; for they are without spot before the throne of God."

Thus should the praise of God resound in the universal Church; it
should be pure and perfect. It ought to be not only an avowal in words,
but rather one which manifests itself in a holy life.

GRADUAL—OFFERTORY (Ps. 123: 7, 8)

Anima nostra, sicut passer, erepta est de laqueo venantium. ℣. 1. Laqueus contritus est, 2. et nos liberati sumus: 3. adjutorium nostrum in nomine Domini, qui fecit caelum et terram.

Our soul hath been delivered as a sparrow out of the snare of the fowlers. ℣. 1. The snare is broken, 2. and we are delivered: 3. our help is in the name of the Lord, who hath made heaven and earth.

Gradual and Offertory have the same text. In the Gradual it is divided into *corpus* and verse; in the Offertory the first three phrases have been drawn into one whole, the last phrase of the Gradual being omitted. Both melodies pulse with rich and radiantly joyful life. The Gradual, it is true, is a composition of various typical melodies, but here they are joined. The melody for the Offertory, on the contrary, shows that it originated from this very text. In the Gradual we find melismatic punctuation on the final syllables of *nostra, venántium, contrítus est, sumus,* while the Offertory broadens only the last syllable of *sumus.*

The Gradual begins solemnly and has a quiet cadence over *nostra.* In the Offertory an ebullient, almost rollicking joy characterizes the first neums. A lightly moving rendition is imperative. Like the lark this song swings aloft exultant and jubilant; we have escaped from the snare of the hunter. *Erépta est* is strongly emphasized in both chants. In the Offertory it is a continuation of the motive over *Anima.* Over *nostra* in the Offertory, first is sung a light bistropha after the *clivis gf,* followed by a *climacus.* With *de láqueo* the Gradual acquires the typical form; the Offertory, however, continues in an exulting strain with the motive of *est,* and yet a third time mounts up to high *b♭.* To a certain extent the last five notes over *láqueo, venántium, nos, sumus* form an antithesis to this overflowing joy, or rather, bring it to a quiet conclusion.

On the third syllable of *láqueus* the Gradual has a florid melisma, such as we find over *et labórem* on the second Sunday of Lent, *Audi fília* on the feast of the Assumption (q.v.), and over *visi sunt* on January 19. According to this it seems always to occur over the third syllable of the first part of the phrase. A form occurs in the Offertory with which we are acquainted from Epiphany (Tharsis); it is repeated over *láqueus* and *liberáti.* The reduplication of the *virga* between the two tristrophas is well substantiated by the manuscripts. Perhaps it wishes to visualize how cleverly the net had been spread, how well everything had been prepared. *Contrítus est* has a triumphant ring; it produces the effect of irony, when the same neums are repeated over *(liberá)-ti.* It seems as if the little birds in their sunny heights, in the ethereal blue, looked down with a smile upon that which human ingenuity had excogitated. The melody continues to exult in a spirit of thanksgiving: We are free! Free for all eternity. Here is inserted a melisma which is not found in the Gradual for the Assumption; it occurs, however, in the Gradual *Ecce sacérdos magnus.* Later we again meet with melodic turns from the Gradual for the Assumption. By a happy coincidence, the verse attains its summit at this spot, a brilliant enhancement compared with the preceding *contrítus est.* The final phrase of the Gradual runs along in a recitative manner, employing *podatus* to emphasize the word-accents. *Dó-*

mini is the only word over which we find a more florid melody; to some extent also the closing syllable of *terram*, which corresponds to the final syllable of the *corpus*. It is to the Creator of heaven and earth that the Holy Innocents are indebted for all their happiness.

In the history of souls, the situation described by the verse is frequently repeated. There is more than one Herod. And there are many innocent children who have happily escaped all the snares of the fowlers and the deceptive devices of the world. And many, very many, have again been freed from them and can not sufficiently thank Christ for the liberty He has granted them.

The feast has a TRACT with a plaintive text; it is composed in the eighth mode. But if it be a Sunday, instead of the Tract the following Alleluia-verse is sung.

ALLELUIA VERSE (Ps. 112: 1)

1. *Laudate pueri Dominum,* 2. *laudate nomen Domini.*

1. *Praise the Lord, ye children,* 2. *praise the name of the Lord.*

The jubilus has the form *a a*^{1} Text and melody have been borrowed from the second Alleluia-verse of the Saturday in Easter Week. We hear the melody over *Allelúia* also on the feast of St. Thomas the Apostle. Similarly, *Laudáte púeri* recurs in the typical melody of the fourth mode, for example, in the Alleluia-verse of the third Sunday of Advent.

With a voice clear as crystal the Holy Innocents fulfill this petition and behest. They cry to us: Ye servants of the Lord, praise the Lord!

COMMUNION (Matt. 2: 18)

1. *Vox in Rama audita est, ploratus et ululatus:* 2. *Rachel plorans filios suos,* 3. *noluit consolari, quia non sunt.*

1. *A voice in Rama was heard, lamentation, and mourning:* 2. *Rachel bewailing her children,* 3. *and would not be comforted because they are not.*

Rachel, an ancestress of the Israelites, wanders about the heights above Bethlehem, bewailing her captured children as if they were dead. That occurred centuries before Herod's ruthless destruction of the innocents; it was a type and a foreboding of the sorrow the mothers of Bethlehem were to experience. But there is one mother's heart which now, even after many centuries, still feels their grief: the Church. Hence, in spite of the Christmas season and the feeling of the Sunday, she sings this pathetic song. The inception on the fifth of the mode, the emphasis on the dominant and the *pressus* over *plorátus* are expressions of gripping sorrow; they almost sound like a shrill outcry.

In the following phrase the minor seconds and the minor thirds produce a gentler ring. The third phrase in its first half supports itself on *c*. The mother's heart is inconsolable, because her children are no more. However true and deep this sorrow may be, it never becomes unruly or distraught. With *dbg* the melody comes to a close; *est* ends on *d*, *(ululá)-tus* on *b*, *suos* on *g*. Through this harmony the grief is tempered.

*   *   *   *

SUNDAY WITHIN THE OCTAVE OF CHRISTMAS

INTROIT (Wisd. 18: 14, 15)

1. *Dum medium silentium tenerent omnia,* 2. *et nox in suo cursu medium iter haberet,* 3. *omnipotens sermo tuus, Domine,* 4. *de caelis a regalibus sedibus venit.* Ps. *Dominus regnavit, decorum indutus est:* * *indutus est Dominus fortitudinem, et praecinxit se.*

1. *While all things were in quiet silence,* 2. *and the night was in the midst of her course,* 3. *thy almighty word, O Lord,* 4. *came from heaven, from thy royal throne.* Ps. *The Lord hath reigned, he is clothed with beauty:* * *the Lord is clothed with strength, and hath girded himself.*

The text speaks of the liberation of Isarel from Egyptian slavery and domination. In the middle of the night came God's almighty word and freed His people. The angel struck Egypt; to the people of God, however, he brought liberty. But today these words have an entirely different import. They tell us of that quiet night in which not only an angel, but in which the Angel of great counsel, the almighty Word of God Himself, deserted His royal throne and descended to us from heaven to be our Saviour. The former was a night of horrors for the Egyptians. This quiet night is a blessed night for us, in which the angels sing new songs, bringing the peace of God to men.

The ascent from the depths fits well to the mysterious text. No little solemnity and majesty is conferred upon the song by means of numerous fourths.

In the first phrase the first three groups show an ascent, but ever again bend downwards: *cd dgf, gag, gbᵇagf, fgac ba*, until finally the tris-

tropha on *c* appears as victor. The first and second phrases exhibit a
textual parallelism, which is not observed by the melody. In its first
half, the second phrase recites on *c*, the third phrase on *a*. At this junc-
ture the recitation becomes still more sustained. With *Dómine* the cadence does not close as *siléntium* in the first phrase with a *clivis*, but
changes to a *podatus*, exactly in the same manner and for the same reason as the word *sitis* in the Introit *Gaudéte* (q.v.). The large pause after
Dómine may surprise some. But in this manner the powerful words can
fully exert their effect upon us: The almighty Word came down from
heaven. Similarly the low inception of *de caelis* seems to cry out to us:
Consider well what this means! We find the same quiet closing cadence
with other Introits of the same mode, for example, in the second Mass
of Christmas.

The Lord is King, even though He is lying in the manger. His robe
of glory is goodness and benevolence, and His strength is love, love even
unto death (Reck).

Very strikingly the psalmodic closing cadence does not set in on
the fifth last syllable, as is the rule, but on the sixth last.

GRADUAL (Ps. 44; 3, 2)

1. *Speciosus forma prae filiis hominum*: 2. *diffusa est gratia in labiis tuis.* ℣. 1 *Eructavit cor meum
verbum bonum*: 2. *dico ego opera
mea Regi.* 3. *lingua mea calamus
scribae velociter scribentis.*

1. *Thou art beautiful above the
sons of men*: 2. *Grace is poured
abroad in thy lips.* ℣. 1. *My heart
hath uttered a good word*: 2. *I
speak my works to the King*: 3.
*my tongue is the pen of a scrivener
that writeth swiftly.*

Now has appeared the most beautiful of the sons of men. Whoever
contemplates Him constantly discovers new attractions and has his
heart captivated. But however swiftly his pen may set down the movements of his heart, still more beautiful and sublime things remain to be
said. None of the soul's faculties can gain an adequate comprehension
of Christ's life and still less how it conforms to His essence: *Nec laudáre
súfficis!* One thing, however remains constantly before the singer's mind:
"I speak my works to the King."

For the first time in the new liturgical year we meet the third mode
in a Gradual-responsory. Of the various types employed, the one chosen
here is found on the Tuesday after the fourth Sunday of Lent, on the
feast of the most Precious Blood (July 1), and on the feast of the Crown
of Thorns (celebrated in some places on the Friday after Ash Wednesday).

The melody toward the end of the *corpus* and the verse is extraordinarily florid. Compare:

> *(diffú)-sa est grátia in lábiis tuis;*
> *(cá)-lamus scribae velóciter scribéntis.*

The *clivis* at the close is to be prolonged. A variety of neums are employed before the final word-accent; thus we have a *torculus* and a *bistropha praepunctis* over *(lábi)-is*, while over *(velóci)-ter* there is a *torculus resupinus*. Then the bistropha follows upon a syllable which is even separated from the preceding neum by a pause. As may be seen by comparing other Graduals of this type, the melisma beginning with *a g a b♭ g f* over *tuis* and *(scri)-béntis* must coincide with the word-accent. As a result, we find the following grouping of endings for this Gradual (I) and for that of the feast of the Precious Blood (II):

I.	*(lábiis)*	*tu-*		*is.*
	velóciter (scri)-	*bén*		*tis.*
II.	*(et)*	*sán-*	*gui-*	*ne.*
	(tres)	*u-*	*num*	*sunt.*

The dactyls are well fitted to the trochees. *Corpus* and verse have in common a sort of *flexa* (1) and a sort of middle cadence (2):

	1.			2.	
I.	*(for)-*	*ma*	I.	*(hómi)-*	*num*
	(cor me)-	*um*		*(bo)-*	*num*
				(Re)-	*gi*
II.	*(ve)-*	*nit*	II.	*(Chri)-*	*stus*
	(cae)-	*lo*		*(San)-*	*ctus*
				(San)-	*guis*

In the *corpus* the first phrase rises to high *e*; *c* dominates the second, surpassed only once by *d*. Similarly we hear high *e* several times in the verse, while its third phrase has the same melody as the second of the *corpus*. The verse foregoes the development which enhances the artistic worth of Graduals of other modes, as well as that of the third.

In more than one passage of the *corpus*, we receive the impression that the piece is composed in the second mode, especially with the words *prae fíliis hómi-(num)*, *lábiis*, *grátia*. We must assign the final cadence of the last word a place among the wandering melismas, which are found in the Graduals of various modes (of the first mode: in the verse of the first Sunday of Advent over *mihi*; of the second mode: in the verse for the Midnight Mass of Christmas over *scabéllum*; of the fifth mode: in the verse for the first Sunday after Pentecost over *(ma)-la*; of the seventh mode: in the corpus of the third Sunday after Pentecost over *te*). *Diffúsa* might well find place in a piece of the second mode; but with *g e*, following upon *f g*, we are again led from the second mode.

The verse begins with an extremely pleasing motive. Over *cor*, the passage *g a b ĉ b c ĉ b* of *(eru)-ctávit* becomes *b c d é d e é d*. The announcement of the sublime word with *verbum bonum* and the signification of this word at *mea Regi* bear the same melody. But that is only accidental. We are struck by the recitation on *a* over *lingua mea cá-(lamus)*.

ALLELUIA VERSE (Ps. 92: 1)

1. *Dominus regnavit, decorem induit*: 2. *induit Dominus fortitudinem, et praecinxit se virtute.*

1. *The Lord hath reigned, he is clothed with beauty*: 2. *The Lord is clothed with strength, and hath girded himself with power.*

That which was only recited in the psalm-verse of the Introit is developed here in an energetic manner. We heard this melody for the first time in the second Mass for Christmas. Over *(alle)-lúia* the *climacus* and *pes* lead to the light *pes subbipunctis*, the apex of the piece; in the second member the *climacus g f e* with the preceding interval of a fifth corresponds to it. Both members have the same closing formula. The verse begins in a most festal manner. Over *decórum* the notes are to be divided into quiet two-note groups; *induit* closes like *(ado)-ráte Dóminum* in the Alleluia of the third Mass for Christmas, and in both cases the following phrase has the same intonation. Through the ascent to *g* and its protraction, *fortitúdinem* receives an admirable preparation. Now it can resound and echo. The close of *virtúte* exhibits the archaic form.

Repeatedly the Church sings of the beauty and the power of Him who has appeared.

OFFERTORY (Ps. 92: 1, 2)

1. *Deus enim firmavit orbem terrae, qui non commovebitur*: 2. *parata sedes tua ex tunc*, 3. *a saeculo tu es.*

1. *God hath established the world, which shall not be moved*: 2. *thy throne, O God, is prepared from of old, thou art from everlasting.*

The power inherent in this song shows itself in the very first interval, a major third. If we substitute a minor third, the significance of the major third at once becomes apparent. Expressive of power are the numerous fourths, and the five tritones, which, ascending or descending run through the whole. It seems to be a song from another world, a hymn of eternity and of the throne of God. If God now stands before

us as the Creator and Preserver of the universe, then His dignity and
His dominion must be acknowledged by all. Today's Gospel, however,
tells us that many will contradict and condemn it. On this Sunday—for
it was already sung in the second Mass for Christmas—it registers a
protest against this attitude of men; it is a solemn avowal of God's
divine prerogatives.

Qui non in the first phrase is influenced by the preceding *orbem*. The
second phrase predominates over the first. In God's own good time heaven
and earth will be destroyed, but His throne will stand unshakeable unto
all eternity. Here the rendition must gain in inner warmth and conviction. Care must be had that *Deus* is not neglected. But above all, following the delicate direction of the annotated manuscripts, both *torculus* of
tunc must be taken broadly. Special solemnity ought also to mark the
ending with *tu es*.

Today the altar is the throne of God. From it also proceeds the
strength which makes our hearts to become worthy thrones of God. And
we shall pledge unflinching fidelity to God's rights.

COMMUNION (Matt. 2: 20)

1. *Tolle puerum et matrem ejus,
et vade in terram Israel:* 2. *de-
functi sunt enim, qui quaerebant
animam pueri.*

1. *Take the child and his mother,
and go into the land of Israel:* 2.
*for they are dead that sought the
life of the child.*

We are struck at first sight by the passages with which both phrases
close: *a c d b a b g ġag g* and *b a c b a b g ġag g.* The beginnings of the
two phrases also show considerable similarity. *Matrem* has a tender and
fervent ring.

Here we perceive how the Child has become a sign which will be
contradicted (cf. the Gospel). Already men have sought His life. But
His persecutors have found their death; the Child with His Mother and
St. Joseph, on the contrary, are allowed to return from exile to their
native land.

Since that time, many persecutors have risen against Him and His
Church. But they have all met their doom. Church History might write
a marvelous continuation of Lactantius' work, entitled *De mortibus per-
secutorum (Concerning the Deaths of the Persecutors)*, composed in the
fourth century. Under the protection of our Lady and of St. Joseph, the
Church's special patron, the Church serenely pursues her way to the
Promised Land.

*   *   *   *

THE CIRCUMCISION OF OUR LORD

(January 1)

INTROIT, GRADUAL, OFFERTORY, and COMMUNION as in the Third Mass for Christmas.

ALLELUIA VERSE (Hebr. 1: 1, 2)

1. *Multifarie olim Deus loquens in prophetis,* 2. *novissime diebus istis* 3. *locutus est nobis in Filio suo.*

1. God who (at sundry times and) in divers manners, spoke in times past by the prophets, 2. last of all in these days 3. hath spoken to us by his Son.

Without a doubt the emphatic words in this passage are those of the second and third phrases. They contain the burden of the joy of Christmastide: in these days the Son of God has come to us and speaks to us; in this manner is fulfilled that for which the bygone centuries yearned and what the prophets foretold. This it is which causes the Apostle to exult and to celebrate the divine splendor of the newborn Babe in the Alleluia-verse. We heard his words previously in the Epistle of the third Mass of Christmas.

The devout and florid melody over *nobis* tells us that we are the fortunate ones, since we are privileged to live in the fullness of time; to us the Son of God addresses His words. The melodic summit, however, is attained over *prophétis*. However great the claim these men may have upon our esteem, placing the emphasis on this word strikes us as somewhat strange.

In quite an unwonted manner a form of expression is here met with which does not confine itself to the individual words, but reproduces a single unified feeling—joy over the fullness of time. Of this joy the entire piece sings.

Allelúia develops in an ascending line (arsis), the first phrase in a descending line (thesis), while the second and third phrases exhibit a combination of the two. The thesis has a short melody of seven, eight, and seven notes respectively. The ascending passage *d f a ċ b a ḋ* over -*lú*- grows out of the preceding *f a ċ g á g*, and continues its effect in *d f ǵ f d ḟ* over *prophétis*, in *ǵ a ḟ e d ḋ*, and in *ċ d ḟ e d ḟ* over *istis*. In the second member we note an instance of a major descending sixth. In the subsequent quiet seconds the tension relaxes. We are well acquainted with the close of the jubilus from the Alleluia for Holy Saturday and that for the first Sunday of Advent.

The first two words of the verse repeat the melody of the first members of *Allelúia* and close on the tonic. All other pauses occur on the dominant, which is somewhat fatiguing. Over *Deus* two-note groups are to be sung; over *nobis*, between the *clivis*, lightly moving bistrophas. The whole is to be rendered with considerable warmth. *In Filio suo* repeats the melody of *Allelúia* with its *jubilus*.

We are struck by the large range of the piece, which is similar in this respect to the Gloria in the ninth Mass, which also belongs to the seventh mode. This melody can be traced to the eleventh century.

*   *   *   *

FEAST OF THE HOLY NAME OF JESUS

(On the Sunday between January 2 and 5, or, if no Sunday occurs between these two dates, on January 2.)

INTROIT (Philipp 2: 10, 11)

1. *In nomine Jesu omne genu flectatur caelestium, terrestrium et infernorum: 2. et omnis lingua confiteatur, quia Dominus Jesus Christus in gloria est Dei Patris. Ps. Domine Dominus noster:* quam admirabile est nomen tuum in universa terra.*

1. *In the name of Jesus let every knee bow of those that are in heaven, on earth, and under the earth: and let every tongue confess that the Lord Jesus Christ is in the glory of God the Father. Ps. O Lord, our Lord:* how wonderful is thy name in the whole earth.*

Today's Introit again is a true overture to the liturgy of the Mass. The very first words provide the leitmotif: *In nómine Jesu*. Except that it substitutes the word *Jesu* for *Dómini*, the first phrase, text and melody, has been borrowed from the Introit of Wednesday in Holy Week. We find a similar melody in the middle and at the close of this phrase, which also brings the first member of the second phrase to a conclusion. In the former edition of these chants, the melody from *caeléstium* to *infernórum* shows a descending line, evidently for the sake of tone-painting. The notation of the ancient manuscripts, however, shows a reciprocal movement and that for internal reasons. It cannot be but that the inhabitants of heaven bend their knee. And upon earth numerous souls will always be found who render this homage from a motive of extreme reverence. But the striking thing is, that those in the nether regions also must bend the knee. Let it be the singer's care to emphasize this fact.

In the second phrase the melodic line is raised, bringing *omnis língua* ("let every tongue confess") brilliantly to the fore. The original is still more effective, since it assigns the reason: "He [Christ] humbled Himself, becoming obedient unto death..." Here, however, the reason forms the second and lower part of the phrase and limps somewhat. The rendition will compensate for this defect. Beginning with *Jesus Christus* (= the third and fourth syllables of *terréstrium*), the two pieces again have the same text and melody.

"The Lord Jesus Christ is in the glory of God the Father." Thus does the Introit wish to stress the sublimity of the name of Jesus. This name is wonderful also upon earth and to be held in honor by all; but many despise and dishonor it. We shall, therefore, repeat the Introit with so much deeper reverence and in the spirit of reparation. What we today so ardently wish and pray for will one day be realized to its fullest extent—when the Lord will appear in the glory of the Father.

Rieg, *Predigten* I, 95 ff.

GRADUAL (Ps. 106: 47)

1. *Salvos fac nos, Domine Deus noster,* 2. *et congrega nos de nationibus:* 3. *ut confiteamur nomini sancto tuo,* 4. *et gloriemur in gloria tua.* ℣. 1. *Tu, Domine, pater noster, et redemptor noster:* 2. *a saeculo nomen tuum.*

1. Save us, O Lord our God, 2. and gather us from among the nations: 3. that we may give thanks to thy holy name, 4. and may glory in thy praise. ℣. 1. Thou, O Lord, art our father and redeemer: 2. thy name is from eternity.

The preceding Epistle closed with the words: "There is no other name under heaven given to men, whereby we must be saved." The Gradual draws out this thought and prays: "Save us, O Lord." The further petition (Isa. 63: 16) proceeds from the heart of the exile; it is expressive of an immense yearning for the homeland and the services of the Temple. There the pious soul would like to praise the name of the Lord and to glory but in one thing, the honor of the Lord.

There is close correspondence between the closing syllables of *(Deus) noster* and *tuo*; both are followed by the same ascent of a fourth. We find the same thing over *Dómine* in the verse (cf. the Gradual for Quinquagesima Sunday). *Tua* and *tuum*, the closing words of the *corpus* and the verse respectively, have extraordinarily florid melodies.

The verse begins and closes like the Gradual for the feast of St. Michael (September 29, q.v.). But from *pater* to *nomen* the melody is borrowed from the verse of Passion Sunday (q.v.). More than usual life and fluency must characterize the singing of this protracted piece. Passages like *nómini tuo* and the tender *Tu, Dómine* allow of great warmth in their rendition.

If the Introit praised the grandeur of the name of Jesus, the burden of this song is: O God, Thou art my Father and my Redeemer. How He is Redeemer and Saviour was demonstrated in the healing of the lame man by the invocation of the name of our Lord Jesus Christ of Nazareth.

ALLELUIA VERSE (Ps. 144: 21)

1. *Laudem Domini loquetur os meum,* 2. *et benedicat omnis caro nomen sanctum ejus.*

1. *My mouth shall speak the praise of the Lord,* 2. *and let all flesh bless his holy name.*

This melody comes from the Sunday within the octave of Corpus Christi (q.v.). *Laudem Dómini,* which exerts an influence on the subsequent *(loqué)-tur os meum,* corresponds to *omnis caro* while *et benedícat* corresponds to *nomen sanctum ejus.*

The Alleluia-verse wishes above all to glorify the *holy* name of Jesus.

OFFERTORY (Ps. 85: 12, 5)

1. *Confitebor tibi, Domine Deus meus, in toto corde meo,* 2. *et glorificabo nomen tuum in aeternum:* 3. *quoniam tu Domine, suavis et mitis es:* 4. *et multae misericordiae omnibus invocantibus te,* 5. *alleluia.*

1. *I will praise thee, O Lord my God, with my whole heart,* 2. *and I will glorify thy name forever:* 3. *for thou, O Lord, art sweet and mild:* 4. *and plenteous in mercy to all that call upon thee,* 5. *alleluia.*

The greater part of this melody has been borrowed from the second Sunday after Epiphany. An easy explanation offers itself for this: formerly the feast of the Holy Name was celebrated on that Sunday. The energetic melody fits very well to the text of the new feast.

Analysis shows that the first phrase is formed out of the first and second phrases and the close of the third phrase of the original composition. Inserted there we find the second *jubiláte* with its incomparably beautiful climax, which, unfortunately, is omitted here. The second phrase of today's Offertory, marking its summit, corresponds to the fourth of the original: *veníte et audíte...* A song of glorification here becomes a resounding festal hymn. *(Ae)-térnum* repeats the melody of *corde* in the first phrase. The third and fourth phrases exhibit peculiarities. Just like the Introit, Gradual, and Alleluia, so the Offertory stresses a special and new quality of the divine Being. While the former emphasized God's sublimity and holiness, the latter places His goodness and mildness and fullness of His mercy in the fore. In this resounding song of praise a tender note insinuates itself—rapture at the Lord's sweetness. *Mitis* in a way is a repetition of *suávis*. *Allelúia*, here treated as an independent phrase, usually brings Offertories of the first mode to a close during Eastertide; but the original, peculiarly, here has the shorter form, generally used at the end of Communions.

COMMUNION (Ps. 85: 9, 10)

1. *Omnes gentes quascumque fecisti, venient, et adorabunt coram te, Domine,* 2. *et glorificabunt nomen tuum:* 3. *quoniam magnus es tu, et faciens mirabilia:* 4. *tu es Deus solus, alleluia.*

1. *All the nations thou hast made shall come and · adore before thee, O Lord,* 2. *and they shall glorify thy name:* 3. *for thou art great and dost wonderful things:* 4. *Thou art God alone, alleluia.*

The melody has been drawn from the sixteenth Sunday after Pentecost. There is, however, a difference in the phrasing of several passages; the close over *Deus solus* is more fluent than in the original, while *magnus es tu* seems to have been composed specially for this text.

All the nations, says the psalm, shall come and adore. How many of them have come today? We at least shall glorify His name after He has entered into us again in Holy Communion. Let us say to Him: Thou alone art God, art my God!

In content and feeling the Communion is related to the Introit. We are to glorify God's name because He is great. Thus two virtues are exemplified in the Mass chants: reverence for the most holy name of Jesus (God Himself chose it), and love and confidence. With what tender love did not the Mother of God speak this name; and millions of men have experienced that Jesus is their Saviour and Redeemer.

*   *   *   *

VIGIL OF EPIPHANY

The chants are the same as those for the Sunday within the octave of Christmas.

*   *   *   *

THE EPIPHANY OF OUR LORD
JESUS CHRIST
(January 6)

The entire liturgy of today's Mass treats of the royal dignity of Him who has appeared and revealed Himself. Indeed, the feast of Christmas already stresses this dignity. But occasionally it also permits us a glimpse of the divine Child in the manger *(Puer natus est nobis)*, and the magic of His charm entrances us. Today everything has the imprint of Christ's kingship and summons the entire world to pay homage to Him.

INTROIT (Mal. 3: 1)

1. *Ecce advenit dominator Dominus*: 2. *et regnum in manu ejus*, 3. *et potestas, et imperium. Ps. Deus, judicium tuum Regi da: *et justitiam tuam Filio Regis.*

1. *Behold the Lord the Ruler is come*: 2. *and kingdom is in his hand*, 3. *and power and dominion. Ps. Give to the King thy judgment. O God:* and to the King's Son thy justice.*

Over this melody must be inscribed the words: majestic, sublime! Like a king's mantle it spreads itself over the text. Beginning with the grand notes of the *Per ómnia saécula*, the introduction to the Preface, it emphasizes the word *advénit* increasingly, over *dóminator* leaps an interval of a fourth, which supports itself on the dominant *f*, lets this dominant resound—it is really the dominant here—and over *Dóminus* rises above it. One seems to see the ruler making his formal entrance, letting his diamonds sparkle. The second phrase again shows an ascending fourth and the clear dominant, which it accentuates still more by means of the *pressus* over *manu* and *ejus*. The repetition of the same motive over these words fits well to the majestic bearing of the whole, and toward the end brings a modulation of exquisite construction on the full tone below the tonic. The third phrase gives plastic form to the word *potéstas* (the descending fourth is to be well brought out); several times it extends above the dominant and closes with a passage corresponding to *Dóminus* in the first phrase.

We may well adduce, as a parallel to the triple division of the Introit, the Christmas hymn: "Lo, how a rose e'er blooming"—no doubt one of the most beautiful. Here also the first and third phrases have corresponding passages, and the middle phrase modulates in the lower fourth.

We ought not to be astonished at the occurrence of the *pressus* on the unaccented syllables in the corresponding passages over *(Dó)-mi-(nus)* and *(impé)-ri-(um)*. Thus the dactylic words are rendered with greater ease and majesty, without jerks or friction; nevertheless they give prominence to the preceding accented syllable by means of the predominating *pes subbipunctis*.

Wagner (III, 286) calls attention to the fact that this entire melody is composed of undulations, each of which attains its melodic summit on the accented syllable of the principal word: *Ecce advénit—dominátor Dóminus—et regnum in manu ejus—et potéstas—et impérium.*

How the centuries watched for the arrival of this King and how ardent were their longings! How often have not the prayers and chants of Advent cried: *Veni Dómine!* What a height did not these yearnings attain in the great O-antiphons immediately preceding the feast of Christmas! Even on the Saturday of Ember Week in Advent this cry was wrung from the heart of the Church: "Come, O Lord, and show Thy face to us, Thou that sittest upon the Cherubim: and we shall be saved"; this *Veni* acts as a prelude to our *Ecce*. Now the sighs have been heard and the longing has been stilled. Now we hear re-echo throughout the land: "Behold the Lord the Ruler is come." But He does not come empty-handed. He bears kingdoms in His hands: the kingdom of truth and of grace and the guarantee for the kingdom of glory. He gives us a share in His power *(potéstas)*. He gives us the power *(potestátem)* to become children of God and therefore co-heirs of His kingdom.

If today kings, princes in the realm of knowledge and research, find no rest until they come to Him, until they prostrate themselves before Him, humble their intelligence and will under His scepter, and with an earnest faith adore Him, the Child, then we see how this Babe reveals Himself as a royal Ruler, how He captures the hearts of men and fills them with happiness.

The psalm-verse emphasizes the judicial power of this King in the form of a wish. Still more does Psalm 71—the royal psalm—show how Christ is the advocate of the poor, how He bestows peace and bread and rich blessings on them, how He reigns over all nations and all times, how all the peoples approach to pay Him homage.

As early as the eleventh century the melody of this Introit has been adapted to the popular Introit *Salve sancta Parens*[1] sung on the feasts

---

[1] *Kirchenmusik*, 11, 33 ff.; *Revue*, 17, 75, 35, 13 ff.; *N. Sch.*, 231; *Benediktinische Monatschrift*, 3, 20 ff.

of the Blessed Virgin. Thus we greet with the same song both the royal
Child and the queen Mother. In this latter melody we possibly prefer
to sing the melodic forms over the accented syllables *Re-(gem)* and
(saecu)-ló-(rum), which occur in today's Introit, over the unaccented
syllables *(Dó)-mi-(nus)* and *(impé)-ri-(um)*. Less happy was the placing
of the *pes* with its fourth, which in today's Introit gives prominence to
the word *potéstas* and its word-accent, on the unaccented syllable of
(saé)-cu-(la).

During the entire octave the same chants are sung; in fact, the entire Proper is the same. But on the octave day itself we hear these words
of St. John the Baptist in the Gospel: *Ecce Agnus Dei*—"Behold the
Lamb of God, behold Him who taketh away the sins of the world."
Then the *Ecce* of the present Introit is vested with a new harmony of
marvelous tenderness. The Ruler comes, not to place burdens upon our
shoulders, but to relieve us of them and to place them upon His own
shoulders, as the Apostle says: "Who His own Self bore our sins in His
body upon the tree."

GRADUAL (Isa. 60: 6, 1)

1. *Omnes de Saba venient,* 2. *au-*
rum at thus deferentes, et laudem
Domino annuntiantes. ℣. 1. *Surge,*
et illuminare Jerusalem: 2. *quia*
gloria Domini super te orta est.

1. *All they from Saba shall come,*
2. *bringing gold and frankincense*
and showing forth praise to the Lord.
℣. 1. *Arise and be enlightened, O*
Jerusalem: 2. *for the glory of the*
Lord is risen upon thee.

Rarely is the connection between the Epistle and Gospel and the
intervening chants so close as on the present feast. The Epistle closes
with the words *Omnes de Saba vénient...*, with which today's Gradual
opens. The words which compose the Gradual-verse, *Surge...*, occurred
at the beginning of the Lesson. Gifts and light, the two leading thoughts,
are melodically spun out. For the Gradual has the same function as the
chorus in the ancient tragedies. The thoughts ought not to be heedlessly
spoken; they should linger in our minds, penetrate into the heart, rouse
it, and incite it to imitation.

Over *(annuntián)-tes* we find repeated the initial motive of *Omnes*,
which recurs in an extended form over *Saba*. The inception on the upper
fourth over *aurum* emphasizes the costliness of the gift. Over *thus de-*
feréntes we hear a resolved major chord, which occurs three times more
in this *corpus*, and enhances the harmony of the song the more, in that
it is regularly woven into the melodic woof with extreme dexterity.

The verse *Surge* immediately sets in on the upper fifth. It resounds the more energetically, since at that time Jerusalem did not comprehend the call and did not heed the admonition. Its people stayed at home and let the Magi go to Bethlehem alone, where the latter discovered the Light of life, the source of their happiness.

In the corpus we sang *c a f*; more forcibly in the verse *d a f*, which recurs again at the end of the florid melisma of *Surge*. *Dómini* closes in a similar manner *(f d c* and *d c a)*. *Illumináre* ("be enlightened") marks the summit of the entire song, not only for the eye, but much more so for the ear. The melody portrays a development and growth like the day, from the first gray streaks of dawn to its noonday splendor. And how regular is this gradation! In the upper third the quietly ascending motive *a f g a c* is repeated as *c a c d f*[1]. This high *f*[1] marks the crowning point. To this large arsis *Jerúsalem* comes as a lingering thesis; *glória Dómini* takes up the musical arsis again and thus points out why Jerusalem can become all light, all bliss. The ascending fourth over *orta est* shines forth in glittering splendor. But with the final neums of *est* comes a pleasant sensation of warm and beneficent light, which streams into the soul and envelopes it.

We hear this same melody on the feast of Christ the King. *(Gregoriusbote*, 42, 148 ff.).*

"All they from Saba shall come." To these *omnes* we also, who with the Magi have been called to the true faith, belong. We were enlightened in holy Baptism, have entirely become light; at that time the glory of the Lord appeared above us while countless others still groveled in the darkness of infidelity. Hence we also bring our gifts—a will of gold and the incense of adoration. Let us likewise offer to the Lord our songs of praise and fervent thanksgiving.

Would that all might become light, that the glory of the Lord might shine over all, and that all might come to Him with gifts and songs!

ALLELUIA VERSE (Matt. 2: 2)

1. *Vidimus stellam ejus* 2. *in Oriente,* 3. *et venimus cum muneribus* (4) *adorare Dominum.*

1. *We have seen his star* 2. *in the East,* 3. *and are come with gifts* (4) *to adore the Lord.*

If the Gradual was a complement and continuation of the Epistle, then the Alleluia-verse acts as a prelude to the Gospel from which it is excerpted. Even though Herod, and all Jerusalem with him, was perturbed at these words of the Magi, only the latter had the courage to speak them and determination enough to execute them, and to rest only when they had actually placed their gifts at the feet of the true King.

The melody was explained in the third Mass of Christmas.

Following the division there given, it will suffice to add these few indications:

1. *Vídimus* = 3. *et vénimus*
1. *stellam ejus* = 3. *cum munéribus*
2. *in Oriénte* (4.) *adoráre Dóminum.*

OFFERTORY (Ps. 71: 10, 11)

1. *Reges Tharsis et insulae munera offerent*: 2. *reges Arabum et Saba dona adducent*: 3. *et adorabunt eum omnes reges terrae*, 4. *omnes gentes servient ei.*

1. *The kings of Tharsis and the isles shall offer gifts*: 2. *the kings of the Arabians and of Saba shall bring presents*: 3. *and all the kings of the earth shall adore him*, 4. *all nations shall serve him.*

In our mind's eye we see an almost interminable procession of those bringing their presents. The Magi from the East have found and still find numerous emulators. These are souls who do not fall short of the "kings" in readiness and joy of sacrifice, in their royal disposition; souls who offer everything they have and are as a sacrifice to Christ, who are a living holocaust, who constitute a perpetual act of adoration. Their sacrifice unites itself with the Eucharistic Sacrifice like the drop of water which the priest mixes with the wine in the chalice at the Offertory. Then comes the Consecration. In Holy Communion Christ Himself becomes their sacrificial food, their wedding banquet. For in these gifts, as the Secret prays, "are offered now no longer gold, frankincense, and myrrh, but He whom those mystic offerings signified is immolated and received: Jesus Christ..."

This Offertory has two parts consisting of two phrases each, which represent a grammatical parallelism. The first part speaks of the sacrificial action which kings of particular countries perform, the second of that of all kings and of all nations. The first refers rather to the external act, while the second refers to its spirit, the act of adoration.

In the first part both phrases have the same range *(f–e)* and a similar ending. *Offerent* develops itself over *addúcent.* In the second part, also, the two phrases have the same range *(f–d)* and a similar ending: the one time on *g*, preceded by *b*, the other time on *f*, preceded by *bb. Múnera ófferent* shows a simliar relationship. The tense *c bb a b b a* finds a pleasant resolution in the subsequent *a gg f g g f.* It must be said that this passage, setting in on the low fifth, with its ascending fourth and the delicate arrangement which follows, is one of the most beautiful of plain songs. It compels the attention of the hearer. The kings come not to show their power, not to conquer countries and to subject peoples, but to submit to the yoke of Christ, to adore Him, and to serve Him. The piece opens with a fanfare; the two tristrophas connected by a virga were already met with (cf. the Offertory for the feast of the Holy Innocents); then astonishment seizes the singer. In the second phrase the swelling of the melody is to be noted: *g a b, g a c, f g a c d, a c d e,* and then the expanding cadence with its solemn seconds. The second group over *Saba* is an extension of the first.

The first part demands a lively tempo; the second will be considerably subdued. The singer is thoroughly imbued with the spirit of reverence and adoration. Into this spirit the three descending fourths (only occurring here) fit admirably. In the fourth phrase, over *omnes* and *gentes* respectively, a *torculus* and a light bistropha are to be sung, yet so that an onward urge runs through the piece to *b♭*, where a relaxation of the tension sets in.

It is striking that this Offertory, as do most of those in the fifth mode, with the exception of that of the fifteenth Sunday after Pentecost, does not extend to high *f*.

The melody is very suitably employed in the votive Mass for the Propagation of the Faith. In the second part of this extended Offertory occur motives from the Offertory of the Sunday within the octave of Epiphany.

COMMUNION (Matt. 2: 2)

1. *Vidimus stellam ejus in Oriente,* 2. *et venimus cum muneribus adorare Dominum.*

1. *We have seen his star in the East,* 2. *and are come with gifts to adore the Lord.*

The first phrase moves joyously. The second breathes the spirit of adoration. Only with *vénimus* do we perceive an echo of the joy of the first phrase. For the closing formula of the first phrase the cadence of the psalm tone of the fourth mode, *b g e,* served as a model. The tritone over *Oriénte*–not so very disturbing since a twofold *b* has preceded it–heightens the peculiar, one might almost say the Oriental, effect of this passage. In three words the unaccented "i" of the second last syllable regularly receives melodic prominence. The fact that the common people accented the Latin language differently from the learned class may be the cause of this; without a doubt plain song was influenced considerably by this so-called "vulgar" Latin.[1]

*   *   *   *

---

1 *Caecilienvereinsorgan,* 49, 124 ff.; *N. Sch.* 237.

FEAST OF THE HOLY FAMILY

(The Sunday within the Octave of Epiphany)

INTROIT (Prov. 23: 24, 25)

1. *Exsultet gaudio pater justi, gaudeat pater tuus et mater tua, 2. et exsultet quae genuit te. Ps. Quam dilecta tabernacula tua, Domine virtutem!* concupiscit et deficit anima mea in atria Domini.*

1. *Let the father of the Just One exult with joy, let thy father and thy mother rejoice, 2. and let her that bore thee be glad. Ps. How lovely are thy tabernacles, O Lord of hosts!* my soul longeth and fainteth for the courts of the Lord.*

Here we address the divine Child. We rejoice in the good fortune which St. Joseph and the Mother of God have been chosen to share, namely, that they can call Him their own, their Child, for whose coming the centuries longed and prayed. It was a purely interior joy, yet so mighty that before it all the world paled into nothingness. Hence this jubilant melody.

This piece is composed of various parts of other Introits. The melody over the first two words we shall hear again in the second phrase of the Introit for the Wednesday in Easter Week over the words *quod vobis pa-(rátum)*, and at the beginning of the Introit on the Friday after Ash Wednesday. *Gaúdeat Pater tuus* sounds like the passage over the words *de láqueo pedes* on the third Sunday in Lent. *Et mater tua*, which limps somewhat, is the same as *patris tui* on the Wednesday in Easter Week. The entire second phrase resembles the third for the thirteenth Sunday after Pentecost. This text, so full of movement and energy, has received a fitting melody.

The small house in Nazareth for many years sheltered *(tabernácula)* the Lord of hosts; there the angels familiarly came and went. The tabernacle, further, is the house of God, in which He dwells with all His strengthening graces. Toward it we ought to turn with yearning, that we may also be about His Father's business, as is related in today's Gospel. Every Christian family, every human heart ought likewise to be a tabernacle of God.

GRADUAL (Ps. 26: 4)

1. *Unam petii a Domino, hanc requiram: 2. ut inhabitem in domo Domini omnibus diebus vitae meae.*

1. *One thing have I asked of the Lord, this will I seek after: 2. that I may dwell in the house of the Lord*

℣. 1. *Beati qui habitant in domo tua, Domine: 2. in saecula saeculorum laudabunt te.*

all the days of my life. ℣. 1. *Blessed are they that dwell in thy house, O Lord: 2. they shall praise thee for ever and ever.*

This Gradual borrows its first phrase and half of the second, text and melody, from the Friday after Ash Wednesday. The last four words are not given there, but we do find the closing cadence of the *corpus.* The melody of the verse, beginning with the third last *neum* over *videam,* is likewise taken from the same Friday. In both phrases, however, the original avoids the somewhat protracted recitation on *c.* The second last syllable extends to high *d.* But this seems to be the rule when a Gradual of the present type closes with a dactylic rhythm (cf. *orta est* in the Gradual for Epiphany).

In truth, Nazareth was the home of the Lord. What was the Temple with all its splendor and glory, what its feasts, compared to the liturgy celebrated in the holy house and the divine praise which ascended thence to heaven? May the Holy Family obtain for us the privilege of living in the house of the Lord all the days of our life, that we may be allowed to join our voices in the unending praise of the Trinity.

ALLELUIA VERSE (Isa. 45, 15)

1. *Vere tu es Rex absconditus,* 2. *Deus Israel Salvator.*

1. *Verily thou art a Hidden King,* 2. *the God of Israel, the Saviour.*

The following Gospel relates how the Saviour remained for three days in the Temple, conversing with the doctors and "asking them questions," pursuing His "Father's business." Then He went down to Nazareth, concealing His divine dignity and power, and was subject to Mary and Joseph. Thus was His life spent in secret, in absolute quiet. As long as He sojourned at Nazareth, the wide world knew nothing of Him, not even Palestine, not even Jerusalem. When later He chose His disciples, they knew nothing or very little of Him. And yet He was King, God, and Redeemer. Even in His quiet and secluded retreat He was at the work of redemption.

This melody is a jewel of plain song. *Allelúia* supplies the melodic material for the first words of the verse. It unites rest and movement. The first member of the *jubilus* gains in strength from its energetic fourths; it has an echo in *(ab)-scónditus.* In its first half the second member of the *jubilus* supports itself on *Allelúia,* in its second half on the first member of the *jubilus.*

OFFERTORY (Luke 2: 22)

1. *Tulerunt Jesum parentes ejus in Jerusalem,* 2. *ut sisterent eum Domino.*

1. *The parents of Jesus carried Him to Jerusalem,* 2. *to present him to the Lord.*

One feels almost sorry that the wonderfully profound *Laeténtur caeli* of the Midnight Mass of Christmas had to sacrifice its music to this purely historical text. But let us inquire more deeply. There is more here than the narration of a simple historical event. The fact that this very melody has been chosen suggests another thought. What joy was felt in heaven over the sacrifice which the Holy Family offered in this presentation of Jesus! It is just this that transfigures the melody: that Jesus, Mary, and Joseph offered this sacrifice to the heavenly Father in complete and joyous resignation to His will. Their sacrificial spirit ought to show us the sentiments with which we should be animated when we attend the Eucharistic Sacrifice.

As far as the word-accents are concerned, the adaptation of the melody is excellent. The perfection of the original with its development over *ante fáciem Dómini* is not attained, it must be freely admitted. *Jerúsalem* predominates over the more significant *sísterent*.

COMMUNION (Luke 2: 51)

1. *Descendit Jesus cum eis, et venit Nazareth,* 2. *et erat subditus illis.*

1. *Jesus went down with them, and came to Nazareth,* 2. *and was subject to them.*

Some may wish to see a kind of tone-painting in the descending line over *descéndit*, and perhaps find the low pitch of *súbditus* extremely suitable for this word. As a matter of fact, however, another of the Christmas melodies has been borrowed here. The brilliant *Vidérunt* of the third Mass for Christmas served as a model. The adaptation is not so good. Because the text was too long in some respects and too short in others, some parts of the melody had to be stretched, others curtailed. Thus *(Náza)-reth* is not an entirely happy copy of *eis*. Then, while in the original the melody over *salutáre* has an exultant ring, it here stands over the insignificant *erat*. Again, the melody fitted to the spondees of the original *(terrae, Dei)* is here distributed over the dactyls *Názareth* and *súbditus*, with evident harm to its fluency.

This text, so full of meaning, demands a fitting rendition. If we would desert our imagined greatness, if we would go to Nazareth and become truly spiritual, then obedience to God and to rightly constituted authority would not appear so difficult, then that peace which enveloped

and filled the house of Nazareth would come also into our hearts, into
our families, and would permeate whole nations.

*   *   *   *

SECOND SUNDAY AFTER EPIPHANY

INTROIT (Ps. 65: 4)

1. *Omnes terra adoret te, Deus, et psallat tibi*: 2. *psalmum dicat nomini tuo, Altissime.* Ps. *Jubilate Deo omnis terra, psalmum dicite nomini ejus: date gloriam laudi ejus.*

1. *Let all the earth adore thee, and sing to thee*: 2. *let it sing a psalm to thy name, O Most High.* Ps. *Shout with joy to God, all the earth,* * *sing ye a psalm to his name: give glory to his praise.*

Gone are the shepherds who knelt before the manger, departed the
Magi who had there adored and offered their gifts. But the spirit of
adoration which animated all of them has remained. It continues to
thrive in the Church. This supplies the theme for the Introits of the
first, second, and third Sundays after Epiphany. Our adoration must
be like mighty granite blocks, over which immense vaults raise themselves, resounding with the joyous songs of praise. We are not only to
prostrate ourselves trembling before the divine majesty; each of these
Introits incites us to sing and to rejoice, for we find these words prominent: *adóret* and *psallat.*

Melodically, also, these thoughts are entwined into one. Each begins with a similar motive. *Psalmum dicat nómini* corresponds to *omnis
terra adóret*, with its ascent to *c* and the descending fourth. The second
phrase is more serene. *Te Deus* finds an echo in *psallat tibi* and even in
tuo. The second last (unaccented) syllable of *(Altís)-sime* carries groups
of neums, in order that a quieter descent may be possible. We find these
groups always on the second last syllable.

Every nation ought to adore God, to sing to His name, and all the
earth should glorify Him. We know how little this admonition is heeded.
This ought to awake in us the resolution to sing this song with so much
more reverence and joy.

GRADUAL (Ps. 106: 20, 21)

1. *Misit Dominus verbum suum,* 2. *et sanavit eos:* 3. *et eripuit eos de interitu eorum.* ℣. 1. *Confiteantur*

1. *The Lord sent his word,* 2. *and healed them:* 3. *and delivered them out of their distress.* ℣. 1. *Let to the*

Domino 2. *misericordiae ejus*: 3. *et mirabilia ejus filiis hominum.*	Lord give glory 2. his mercies: 3. and his wonderful works to the children of men.

The *corpus* of the Gradual has the same melody in its first phrase as on the first Sunday after Epiphany; the same holds true for the beginning of the verse. In the second phrase we find the pleasant melisma known to us from the word *illumináre* of Epiphany. The melody of the third phrase repeats itself in the first half of the verse over *mirabília ejus*. We are struck by the unusual ending of the *corpus*.

It is difficult to explain the frequent repetition of the third-intervals at the beginning of the verse. We met with this construction for the first time on the second Sunday of Advent, but at that time it was enlivened by a variety of neums. The clivis alone produces a slight variation in the melody concealed in the third *ca*, the fourth *cg*, and the ascending fifth *fc*. Wagner *(Stimmen der Zeit*, 58, 136*)* thinks that it wishes to visualize the expansion of the singer's heart, since the liturgical chant recalls to him his own vocation *(confitéri)*. For the early designation of the cantor was *confessor* (cf. the Collects for Good Friday). An admirable effect is afterwards produced by the development over *misericórdiae*. The *pressus*, it is true, constitute the supports of the melody; still one should give close attention also to the notes which precede in every instance. Over *ejus* occurs a partial motive of *eos* in the first part of the Gradual; *(mirabí)-lia* resembles *erípuit eos*. The closing melisma is the same as that in the second Christmas Mass.

Ecce advénit—"Behold, He is come," constitutes the answer to our Advent petition of *Veni Dómine*—"Come, O Lord." Similarly the present *misit* is a fulfillment of our cry: *Mitte Dómine, quem missúrus es*—"Send Him, O Lord, whom Thou art about to send." The Lord has sent His Word, His eternal Word, and the Word was made flesh and dwelt among us; this Word is Jesus, the Saviour; He heals our wounds and saves us from destruction.

How can we thank Him fittingly for this favor? Be comforted: He who has come to us as the mercy of God will Himself direct our song. In today's Sacrifice he again sings to the Father a perfect song of thanksgiving for all the wonderful things He has done to men; He hymns God's wisdom and goodness and power and fidelity, for all these combine in God's mercy.

ALLELUIA VERSE (Ps. 148: 2)

1. *Laudate Deum omnes Angeli ejus*: 2. *laudate eum omnes virtutes ejus.*	1. Praise ye the Lord, all his angels: 2. praise ye him, all his hosts.

The Introit had incited the entire world to adoration and to the praise of God; in the Gradual the eternal Word of God Himself fulfills this service of thanksgiving; in the Alleluia all the choirs of angels join this hymn. Here truly all sing along in the most profound adoration and blissful rapture, and the united hosts never weary of crying: Who is like God? Alleluia!

This melody presents a typical form of the fourth mode; we heard it for the first time on the third Sunday of Advent (q.v.). It does not, however, like all other pieces of this type, ascend to $b\flat$ on the third syllable of the teat. *Virtútes* repeats the preceding formula of *ejus*.

OFFERTORY (Ps. 65: 1, 2, 16)

1. *Jubilate Deo universa terra:* 2. *jubilate Deo universa terra:* 3. *psalmum dicite nomini ejus;* 4. *venite, et audite, et narrabo vobis, omnes qui timetis Deum,* 5. *quanta fecit Dominus animae meae, alleluia.*

1. *Shout with joy to God, all the earth:* 2. *shout with joy to God, all the earth:* 3. *sing ye a psalm to his name:* 4. *come and hear, all ye that fear God, and I will tell you* 5. *what great things he hath done for my soul, alleluia.*

This song of thanksgiving is the most animated, if not of plain song as a whole, then surely of all the Offertories. The pleasant repetition of the text: *Jubiláte...* is paralleled in very few Offertories. Such repetitions are practically unknown in plain song. The first two phrases predominate not only by reason of their length, but above all through the joy that wells up from within: The entire earth is to shout with joy. An effect of tone-painting is produced by the great intervals over *univérsa*. But the singer is more concerned with *jubiláte*. His heart is filled to the point of bursting; he wishes to have his jubilation resound throughout the entire world. He wishes to carry away all things with him and bring them to the throne of God on wings of song. Rapidly the melody falls into the depths; then expanding, ever expanding, it rushes upward. The *pressus* forms—given in the manuscript as trigons—not only divide the movement, but also supply it with new power and energy. However, they should not be emphasized too strongly, lest the delicate melodic line suffer from it. The melody shows a marvelous development and gradation till the outburst with f^1, a twelfth above the lowest note of the piece. We are struck still more by the force of the passage if we compare it with a similar passage, for example that over *corde* in the Gradual *Os justi* from the Mass for a Doctor of the Church. A vigorous tone-sequence relaxes the tension. The only other extended figure we meet with is that over the second *terra*. In place of the $b\flat$ in the first phrase, the second shows an energetic b.

After this unusual development comes comparative rest and relaxation in the third phrase. God's name is pronounced reverently. Its close with the impetuous *pressus* already prepares for the following phrase and has some relation to the third member in the second *Jubiláte*-phrase.

The fourth phrase is an impulsive exhortation to all who fear God. Its three short expressions: "come, hear, I will tell you," not only tend to awaken and attract the attention by the delicate interplay of motives, but they also serve to give us an inkling of powerful movements of the singer's heart. The motive over *omnes* has been borrowed from the third phrase and is introduced like it. Then it gradually dies away, expressing the contents of the message to expectant hearts in its descent to *d*.

In the fifth phrase the singer devoutly ponders all the marvels that God has wrought in him. This inner agitation is still felt toward the end over *ánimae*. The closing *allelúia* really is shorter than that generally found in Offertories, but even the oldest manuscripts have the present form.

This Offertory is also sung on the fourth Sunday after Easter. Indeed, it may have been originally composed for that Sunday. It certainly is striking that not a single Offertory from Advent to Easter, not even those of the great feasts of Christmas and Epiphany, closes with an alleluia except this Offertory *Jubiláte*. What is more, the Sundays after Epiphany received their Mass formularies later than did those after Easter.

Who sings this song? Holy Mother Church. Of her we sang on Epiphany: on that day the Church was wedded to her divine Spouse. This Sunday's Gospel also speaks of a marriage. In the Incarnation Christ assumed a human nature. This the Church knows full well. But she is also conscious of Christ's deed *(quanta)* and sufferings, by reason of which she stands before us pure and immaculate. She knows that in the Eucharist Christ has presented her with a gift than which no more sublime can be found in heaven or on earth, and that in this most exalted Mystery *(tantis mystériis)*, as the Postcommunion so frequently says, He forever remains the source of her life and strength. She sees all the saints with whom Christ has embellished her, all the graces ever bestowed upon man; she looks upon that marvelous bridal array with which He has adorned her. At this she cannot help singing and shouting for joy and happiness.

(Joseph Haas has taken the melody of this Offertory as the theme for a violin sonata with organ accompaniment.)

COMMUNION (John 2: 7, 11)

1. *Dicit Dominus: Implete hydrias aqua et ferte architriclino.* 2. *Cum gustasset architriclinus aquam vinum factum, dicit sponso:* 3. *Servasti vinum bonum usque adhuc.* 4. *Hoc signum fecit Jesus primum coram discipulis suis.*

1. *The Lord saith: Fill the waterpots with water, and carry to the chief steward.* 2. *When the chief steward had tasted the water made wine, he said to the bridegroom:* 3. *Thou hast kept the good wine until now.* 4. *This beginning of miracles did Jesus before his disciples.*

With dramatic brevity the Communion summarizes the Gospel story. Its melody also is a model of realism. Consider first of all the contrast between the first *dicit*, introducing the Saviour's words, and the second *dicit*, introducing those of the chief steward. Already from the intonation we can gather that we have here to do with something unusual. In the tone of extreme astonishment, the singer cries out: "Who can do such a thing?" With the threefold repetition of the same high *torculus* one seems to see the man shaking his head as if unable to comprehend. Naturally, this passage demands a lively rendition. Then there ought to be a considerable pause, after which the second phrase, relating in reverent astonishment the first miracle, is to follow in a solemn manner. It differs from the other phrases by reason of its almost syllabic character. The two parts that compose it are almost alike melodically. In the second part, however, the tritone, no doubt intentionally, comes into prominence, for here *b* is stressed, while in the first part it belongs rhythmically to the preceding accented *c*; besides, the effect of the tritone is almost cancelled by the twofold *g*.

In the first phrase there is nothing striking about the textual treatment of *Dóminus*. It seems that the principle of counting the syllables was applied here, just as it appears in simple psalmody and at the intonation before some cadences, as well as in the solemn Introit-psalmody before the closing cadence of most of the modes. But here we have to do with only three syllables. With this passage compare in the Introit for the Sunday within the octave of Christmas: *siléntium* and *Dómine*; in the Introit for the third Sunday of Advent: *homínibus* and *sollíciti sitis*; furthermore, in the Introit for Epiphany, although the intervals here are different: *Dóminus* and *impérium*. The low inception of *impléte* necessitates the bending over of the last neum. Thus it becomes apparent that plain song can also create vivid contrasts. The expression beginning with *impléte* recites on the tonic, but thrice reaches down energetically to the lower third; while that beginning with *et ferte* supports itself on the dominant *a*. Over the close of the second *architriclínus* we find the same figure repeated as occurs over the first.

Thus in this first public miracle Christ revealed Himself as the Lord and King of creation. An act of the will, a word from His lips, and Nature obeys—the water changes into wine. Today we also have been witnesses of a miracle of change; but of one much more sublime then is here related. This was only a type of and preparation for the Eucharistic transubstantiation. With the former the Saviour began His public Messianic activity. The consecration at the Last Supper is the final stupendous miracle He wrought before His death, but it will continue to the end of days. We have now been privileged to partake of that most excellent wine, the very blood of Jesus Christ, and thus have received a share in the supreme Godhead, as the secret of the fourth Sunday after Easter beautifully puts it. Today He has prepared a marriage banquet for us. Until now, the last, the Messianic era, the Lord has reserved this good rich wine. But its inebriating powers only reveal themselves in us in the measure with which we correspond to our duties *(impléte hýdrias)* and give ourselves over wholly to Christ. This "good wine" is to prepare us for the change of the earthly man into the spiritual, for the eternal, blissful nuptials with the heavenly bridegroom, Christ.

* * * *

THIRD SUNDAY AFTER EPIPHANY

INTROIT (Ps. 96: 7, 8)

1. *Adorate Deum omnes Angeli ejus:* 2. *audivit, et laetata est Sion:* 3. *et exsultaverunt filiae Judae.* Ps. *Dominus regnavit, exsultet terra: *laetentur insulae multae.*

1. *Adore God, all ye his angels:* 2. *Sion heard, and was glad:* 3. *the daughters of Juda rejoiced.* Ps. *The Lord hath reigned, let the earth rejoice: *let many islands be glad.*

Generally the individual phrases of a plainsong chant either exhibit a regular gradation or they are so arranged that the central one marks the summit of the melody. In the present instance, however, the first phrase with its fourths and high pitch—perhaps induced by the thought of the angels in the celestial regions—predominates. In any case, the composer was concerned, above all, to call our attention to the adoring angels at the beginning of the holy Sacrifice. Here they are not so much a model for our own worship of God, as they are the source of our purest joy. For here the Father has adorers according to His own mind, who with their intelligence immerse themselves in God's splendor and tremble before His immensity; adorers, who, with their whole ·will acknowledge their utter dependence upon God. One of their number wished to contest this, to destroy the harmony. But he was cast into hell. Now there is perfect accord, and all the angels offer their homage to God. The Church (Sion) hears it and shouts for joy.

Here again we find expressed the two thoughts *adoráte* and *laetáta est Sion*. Each of the following Sundays after Epiphany repeats the same chants, text and melody.

Audívit shows some similarity to *Judae*: the former has its *pressus* on *a*, the latter on *c*. With *laetáta est Sion* two-note groups are to be sung. In the third phrase *et* is to be treated as an anacrusis, while the following syllable should receive a light secondary accent. After the solemn first phrase, an energetic rendition should mark the remaining two. The text must still be viewed in the light of Epiphany. Christ still stands before us as the "Lord," as the "King." Angels surround and adore Him. In a verse which was formerly sung in connection with this Introit He is addressed thus: "Thou are the most high Lord over all the earth: Thou art exalted exceedingly above all gods." The Church rejoices at His revelation, at the love with which He calls also the heathens into His kingdom (today's Gospel), and at the gifts He dispenses. In the primitive Church the healing of the leper in this Sunday's Gospel signified a type of Baptism; the participation in the heavenly table refers to the Holy Eucharist (*K.L.*).

GRADUAL (Ps. 101: 16, 17)

1. *Timebunt gentes nomen tuum, Domine,* 2. *et omnes reges terra gloriam tuam.* ℣. 1. *Quoniam aedificavit Dominus Sion,* 2. *et videbitur in majestate sua.*

1. *The gentiles shall fear thy name, O Lord,* 2. *and all the kings of the earth, thy glory.* ℣. 1. *For the Lord hath built up Sion,* 2. *and he shall be seen in his majesty.*

In the Gospel which follows upon this chant, the pagan centurion of Capharnaum, filled with reverence at the appearance of the Messias, speaks these words: "Lord, I am not worthy that Thou shouldst enter under my roof." And Jesus marvels at the greatness of this man's faith, which makes the pagan appear like a king over against the Israelites, the "children of the kingdom," as the Gospel calls them. In the marvelous cure of his servant the centurion is privileged to see the glory of the Lord as a reward for his faith.

The entire picture of the feast of Epiphany again rises before our eyes. We behold the heathen and even the kings of the earth streaming to Jerusalem to pay reverent homage to their divine King *(K.L.)*. He builds Sion, His Church, within which all will find place, from the rising of the sun to its setting. And all will be allowed to see and partake of His glory and sit to table with Christ at the Eucharistic marriage banquet. The *corpus* of the Gradual, especially in its lower ranges, proceeds from the heart of the humble centurion. Its first phrase corresponds almost exactly to that of Maundy Thursday. Over *gentes* the annotated manuscripts give almost all the notes a broad form. For the calling of the gentile world to the way of salvation is the greatest event since the Epiphany. Thus the neglect of the lower notes likewise is avoided. Several modes have in common the caesura over *terrae*. We find it again in the verse over *(vidébi)-tur*, as well as in the first part of the Gradual over *tu-(am)*. *Glóriam*, despite its low melodic line, is made effective in the midst of florid neums by its simplicity. Above *tu-(am)* it will most likely be necessary to breathe after the fourth *cg*. This also makes it easier to sing the following eight notes sustainedly.

At the beginning and at the end the verse recites on *f.* Over *Dóminus* let the singer accentuate the *pressus* after the *clivis* and bistropha, yet so that the following deeper notes *a g f* are well heard. Compare it with *Dómino* in the verse for the second Sunday after Epiphany. Over *Sion* the brilliant ascent ought to gain still more in warmth in repetition. *Dóminus* and *Sion* have a similar cadence structure. It has been found that the melisma over *in majestáte sua* forms the close of thirty Graduals.

ALLELUIA VERSE (Ps. 96: 1)

1. *Dominus regnavit, exsultet terra:* 2. *Laetentur insulae multae.*

1. *The Lord hath reigned, let the earth rejoice:* 2. *Let many islands be glad.*

Already in the psalm-verse of the Introit we have heard these words. In this manner the kingdom of the Lord is repeatedly stressed. And King He is, according to St. Augustine *(Tract. 51 in Joannem)*, not to impose burdens upon us, not to collect taxes, not to levy troops, fit them out and let them die in a battle, but to bring peace upon the earth and thus make all peoples happy. Even the most distant are to receive these blessings; rightly, therefore, may they be glad. Here also we hear another thought of Epiphany: the spread of Christianity.

This melody was explained on the first Sunday of Advent.

OFFERTORY (Ps. 117: 16, 17)

For the text with its explanation, see Maundy Thursday.

In the most ancient manuscript the melody is already set to the text *In omnen terram* for the feast of the Apostle Paul (June 30). In our *Graduale* this Offertory is given for the feast of the Apostle Thomas (December 21). It is difficult to discover which is the original composition.

A few minor melodic variants appear as a result of the different accentuation in the two pieces. Today's chant has more dactylic forms: *Dómini, exaltávit me, opera.*

Both texts have great things to tell. In the one the Gospel is carried to the very ends of the earth. Drawn on grand lines, the Catholic Church, embracing all men, stands before us. Here the right hand of the Lord, mighty and wonderful, maintains government. The Lord, as the Gospel we have just heard relates, stretched His hand over the leper, touched him, and said: "I will; be thou made clean," and straightway he was cleansed of his disease. Innumerable times has the right hand of the Lord healed the leprosy of sin, and still He continues to heal it; He lifts us up into the kingdom of grace and of light, awakens us to life, to the true life, so that the soul is forced to shout with joy at the workings of God's right hand and to proclaim the works of the Lord.

COMMUNION (Luke 4: 22)

Mirabantur omnes de his quae procedebant de ore Dei.

They all wondered at these things, which proceeded from the mouth of God.

The real dominant of this piece is that of the eighth mode *(c)*. Only with *de* does the melody gradually change over to the seventh mode. Our general astonishment finds expression in a broad, expansive line. Perhaps the tritone at the end may intimate what it means when God speaks. How marvellous has not His "I will; be thou made clean," shown itself again today! And it can hardly be wondered at that He, the King, declares Himself prepared to accompany the pagan centurion to his sick servant and to heal him... And in the same hour in which He had said: "Go, and as thou hast believed, so be it done to thee," was the servant cured. Besides, how sublime was His teaching! He spoke as one who had power. The common folk treasured His every word. How wonderful was the consolation He poured into their hearts—He who had been anointed to announce the Gospel to the poor and to heal wounded hearts.

Manuscript 339 of St. Gall's and 121 of Einsiedeln give another melody, which belongs to the first mode.

The fourth, fifth, and sixth Sundays after Epiphany have the same chants as the third.

* * * *

SEPTUAGESIMA SUNDAY

INTROIT (Ps. 17: 5, 7)

1. *Circumdederunt me gemitus mortis, dolores inferni circumdederunt me*; 2. *et in tribulatione mea invocavi Dominum,* 3. *et exaudivit de templo sancto suo vocem meam.* Ps. *Diligam te Domine, fortitudo mea:* *Dominus firmamentum meum, et refugium meum, et liberator meus.*

1. *The groans of death surrounded me, the sorrows of hell encompassed me:* 2. *and in my affliction I called upon the Lord,* 3. *and he heard my voice from his holy temple.* Ps. *I will love thee, O Lord, my strength:* *the Lord is my refuge, and my deliverer.*

The first phrase describes spiritual distress; the second, a raising of mind and heart to God. The third phrase already speaks of a favorable hearing, and leads directly to the fervent and thankful, "I love Thee."

Who is speaking these words? The early Christians of Rome on this day marched in solemn procession to the church of St. Lawrence outside the Walls. That was the stational church; there the divine services were held. The opening words of this Mass are, therefore, the words of St. Lawrence, describing his martyrdom on the gridiron, when the flames encompassed him like the torments of hell. In this distress he called upon the Lord, and the Lord heard him, strengthened him, and filled his heart with festal joy (cf. his feast, August 10). Greater than the heat of the fire was the flame of divine love in his heart. St. Lawrence is, moreover, the patron of the catechumens. Those who formerly were accepted on this day, were instructed during Lent, and received Baptism on the Vigil of Easter.

In the large cemetery near S. Lorenzo a sigh, as of death, seems to vibrate in the air. Just so do the first words of this Introit awaken in us that seriousness and penitential spirit which grows steadily from this Sunday till we come to those bitter days when the sighs and groanings of death, veritable sorrows of hell, are to come upon our Lord and Saviour on Calvary and on Golgotha. The Scripture lessons for the coming week deal with the creation of the world, the fall of our first parents, and the fratricide. True groans of death encompassed Adam and Eve when they had to view that first corpse, their own beloved child.

Perhaps there still is in these Sundays (Septuagesima, Sexagesima, and Quinquagesima) a reminder of the final period of the Migration of Nations (the end of the sixth century), when strange hordes brought ruin and tears upon Rome and the surrounding territory. It seems that it was precisely at this time that the pre-Lenten season was incorporated into the liturgical year at Rome (cf. Grisar, *Missale*, 56).

The range of the three phrases is limited. The *d* reaching above the dominant is merely an embellishing note, and is not emphasized. The melody never descends below the tonic. Of the twice-sung *circumdedérunt me*, one is at the beginning of the first phrase, and the other at its end. The second one, with its wide sweep of notes, is not so much tone-painting of *circum* as an indication of the great torment which burdens the soul. The last three notes of this phrase are like the ending found in many Graduals. Here, however, they have not that charming effect so prominent in the Graduals, because they are introduced differently. The second phrase begins almost exactly like the first one. In its second part it becomes quite restless: thrice it leaps up, and thrice it sinks back again, with intervals of a second, a fifth, and a fourth. But this ending does not satisfy; it urges onward. And the expected continuity comes in such a manner that one is reminded of the Psalmist's words that before we call upon God He is already present to us. The third phrase swings up immediately to the dominant in a bright and cheerful manner. *Exaudívit* is admittedly much like *dolóres*, and *sancto suo* resembles *-dedérunt* of the first phrase. Nevertheless, the text demands a different rendition in each case. As in the first phrase, two drops of a fourth occur here also, and then the whole flows calmly on to the conclusion.

Revue, 8, 89 ff.

GRADUAL (Ps. 9: 10, 11; 19, 20)

1. *Adjutor in opportunitatibus in tribulatione*: 2. *sperent in te, qui noverunt te*; 3. *quoniam non derelinquis quaerentes te, Domine.* ℣. 1. *Quoniam non in finem oblivio erit pauperis*: 2. *patientia pauperum non peribit in aeternum*: 3. *exsurge, Domine, non praevaleat homo.*

1. *The helper in due time, in tribulation*: 2. *let them trust in thee, who know thee*: 3. *for thou dost not forsake them that seek thee, O Lord.* ℣. 1. *For the poor man shall not be forgotten to the end*: 2. *the patience of the poor shall not perish for ever* 3. *arise, O Lord, let not man be strengthened.*

In the vicinity of S. Lorenzo, Constantine the Great erected a hospital. Perhaps this Gradual was meant to console the inmates of that institution, to encourage them to trust in God, to beg grace for them to the end that man, the evil in man, the spirit of darkness, might not prevail.

We, as God's own family, should also lovingly remember those who are being visited by physical or spiritual ills, by temptations or by trials.

The verses are taken from Psalm 9, as on the third Sunday of Lent (whose Gradual begins with the last sentence of today's) and on the Saturday of the fourth week in Lent. With this latter our present Gradual has perfect similarity of word and music in *(opportu)-nitátibus* and *in tribulatióne*. The first *non* of the verse is like *(Dó)-mine* in the verse of the other Gradual. Though none of the Graduals in the third mode are easily understood, the one for today presents special difficulties. It lacks a calm and ordered development. The third word goes up to e^1, which is never again reached in the *corpus*. Many fourths occur, but not a single fifth.

Both halves of the first phrase close with the cadence which we meet again in the Introit of the first Sunday in Lent. Endings on *d*, as in the second phrase, are favored by the third mode. The former dominant *b* still occurs, and helps in the formation of the triton, as over *Dómine*.

The beginning of the verse resembles the beginning of the third phrase in the *corpus*. Of more than ordinary difficulty is the execution of the second half of the melisma over *non*. The rich melody at this point is in accord with the general rules for Gradual-verses. In the second phrase the motive is broadened out and repeated over *aetérnum*. The last phrase, with its intense *exsúrge* and its impelling fourths, is most forceful and expressive. The conclusion corresponds to that of the corpus.

TRACT (Ps. 129: 1, 4)

1. *De profundis clamavi ad te, Domine: Domine, exaudi vocem meam. 2. Fiant aures tuae intendentes in orationem servi tui. 3. Si iniquitates observaveris, Domine: Domine, quis sustinebit? 4. Quia apud te propitiatio est, et propter legem tuam sustinui te, Domine.*

1. *From the depths I have cried to thee, O Lord: Lord, hear my voice. 2. Let thine ears be attentive to the prayer of thy servant. 3. If thou shalt observe iniquities, O Lord, Lord, who shall endure it? 4. For with thee is propitiation, and by reason of thy law I have waited for thee, O Lord.*

The Tract leads us from the hospital to the churchyard of S. Lorenzo, and prays *De profúndis* both for and with those who are resting there.
It is a call coming from the depths of a soul which feels itself immeasurably separated from God; it is a cry to the Lord. For the soul of the departed can no longer help itself, and the help of others is also limited
since they also must pray *De profúndis*. This plea therefore voices our
human impotence and our great need of help. The repetition of the
"Lord, Lord" is stylistic peculiarity of all petitions, and indicates the
deep-felt need of divine assistance. Do Thou not observe my iniquities,
O Lord! Mark them not for the Day of Wrath; pronounce not a judgement, signed and sealed, upon my sins. Behold how sin is common to
all mortal flesh, that no one is clean, and no one can redeem himself!
Be Thou my Redeemer! For with Thee is propitiation, and the law which
Thou hast made is the promise of a Redeemer: the sacrifices ordained
by the Law foretell the Lamb that taketh away the sins of the world.
And by Thy own word I know that Thou willest not the death of the
sinner. In this way de we pray with the poor souls.[1]

OFFERTORY (Ps. 91: 2)

1. *Bonum est confiteri Domino,*   1. *It is good to give praise to the*
2. *et psallere nomini tuo, Altissime.*   *Lord,* 2. *and to sing to thy name, O*
                                   Most High.

Mother Church is fond of calling the Mass a sacrifice of praise. If
we sing this text today at the Offertory procession, our sacrifice should
be made glorious through our joyous surrender of self. For this very
reason did St. Lawrence rejoice, that he could be sacrificed for Christ.
This joy in giving must never be wanting, not even now when the
alleluia is silenced.

The parallel between the two sentences is evident enough. *Psállere*
corresponds to *confitéri*, and *Altíssime* to *Dómino*. But in the second
phrase there is an obvious intensifying, for *psállere* means not only "to
praise," but connotes also a playing upon the harp, and *Altíssime* is an
elucidation of the preceding *Dómino*. More clearly than the words does
the music tell us this.

Bonum is a short but charming prelude to the whole selection. *Confitéri* succeeds not only in stressing the accent, but also in bringing the
leading idea of the Offertory well to the fore—evidence again of the
manner in which the musical structure of the chants is guided by the
word-accent and the content of the text. A slight accent should be
given the third *c*. The second phrase is considerably brighter. It no

---

1 M. Faulhaber, *Die Vesperpsalmen der Sonn-und Feiertage*, p. 120 f.

longer rests on the lower *a* and *g*, but on *c*. In fact, it thrice extends above this, with *psállere* even to *e*[1], for both the song and the harp should sing out loud and clear. The *psállere nómini tuo* is taken as one single thought. The melody rises from *g* to *c* each time. In *tuo, c b a b a* of the preceding word seems to be re-echoed, unless one should wish to consider them an amplification of *Dómino* and *(confité)-ri*. The first part of *Altíssime* is bracketed between the ascending and the descending major chord *f a c*. To this the second part must be joined directly, with a slight pause after the first pressus and after *a*. The third part should be sung *crescendo* to the third *pressus*. A sense of abiding joy fills the first phrase, holy enthusiasm is the mark of the second, while the final strains try to bring out the full flavor of the word *Altíssime*.

Analyses, 7, 20 f.

COMMUNION (Ps. 30: 17, 18)

1. *Illumnia faciem tuam super servum*, 2. *et salvum me fac in tua misericordia*: 3. *Domine, non confundar, quoniam invocavi te.*

1. *Make thy face to shine upon thy servant*, 2. *and save me in thy mercy*: 3. *let me not be confounded O Lord, for I have called upon thee.*

By Holy Communion the true Sun arose in our hearts, the Sun of grace, our Redeemer, to transfigure, vivify, and glorify us.

The melody of the first phrase is, so to say, monopolized by the accented syllables, but in such a way that the logical emphasis is well brought out in *fáciem*. In the second phrase the pleading changes to an expression of joyous confidence. God's mercy—how it differs from the pity shown us by men! "Your mercy," so runs the Lord's accusation (Osee 6:5), "is as a morning cloud, and as the dew that goeth away in the morning." But His own mercy is lasting, unstinted, inexhaustible. Our present melody praises this divine mercy in a manner which might almost be called exultant. The third phrase is no longer a plea; it is confiding faith become vocal, calling out, as did Job: "I know that my Redeemer liveth." I shall not be put to shame. *Dómine, non* repeats the melody of *misericórdia*. The second half makes use of the melodies of the first half.

* * * *

SEXAGESIMA SUNDAY

INTROIT (Ps. 43: 23, 26)

1. *Exsurge, quare obdormis, Domine? exsurge, et ne repellas in*

1. *Arise, why sleepest thou, O Lord? arise, and cast us not off to*

finem: 2. *quare faciem tuam avertis, obliviscéris tribulationem nostram? Adhaesit in terra venter noster*: 3. *esxurge, Domine, adjuva nos, et libera nos.* Ps'. *Deus, auribus nostris audivimus*: * *patres nostri annuntiaverunt nobis.*

the end: 2. *why turnest thou thy face away, and forgettest our trouble? Our belly hath cleaved to the earth*: 3. *arise, O Lord, help us and deliver us.* Ps. *O God, we have heard with our ears*: * *our fathers have declared to us.*

The Migration of Nations with its dismal consequences may have been the occasion for these laments. But they are also the prayer of unredeemed mankind, of mankind degenerated, a prey to the lower appetites. These words may well have been the agonized cries of those who watched the waters of the Deluge rising ever higher, for the Breviary this week tells the story of that great flood. Thus may St. Paul have prayed, whose church is the station for today, when his disgust with life well-nigh vanquished him, or when the sting of the flesh caused him such great torture. These words are the cry of the Apostles, almost word for word, when their little boat was so wildly tossed by the waves one stormy night, and the Lord was asleep. So have we also, from sheer necessity perhaps, often prayed for relief from pain or from the shackles of evil desires which threatened to drag us downward. Our Introit is therefore a suppliant prayer from the valley of this death, a plea for resurrection, a preparatory song for Easter, for the day of the Rising *(exsúrge)* of the Lord.

Choral music is often extolled for its calm unimpassioned spirit, for its sedate dignity, for the lucidity which seems to elevate it above all that is earthly and makes it a veritable echo of the songs of heaven. And rightly so. Our present melody is set within the compass of liturgical song, avoids dissonances and startling contrasts, and deprecates unrestrained subjectivism. And yet it shows how deeply and sincerely a chant melody can probe, how intimate the relation is between text and music, and how warm and true its expression.

In the first phrase the first half is ascent (arsis), the second half descent (thesis). Beginning each half is an *exsúrge*, the first one animated, the second impetuous, and both followed by a more quiet recitation on *f*. In the ascent the melody reaches the dominant, and in the descent it goes down to the tonic. The cadence occurring here is much favored by the first and second modes. We may recall having heard it in the Alleluia of the third Christmas Mass *(adoráte Dóminum)*. The next phrase shows by its very first word *(quare)* that it will extend the range of the preceding. A number of fourths occur here, and also the climax of the piece: *obliviscéris*. Though the group of notes for this word is nothing more than a synopsis of the melody over the psalm-verse (*Deus aúribus*), they are most effective here because of their position in the Introit. The composer had in his heart a feeling somewhat akin to that which forced from the Saviour's lips the terrible cry: "My God, why hast Thou forsaken Me?" The almost monotonous *tribulatiónem nostram* reminds us of our daily work, of that deadly sameness which may either numb the soul or be its constant torture. At *adhaésit* the melody tries four times to surge upward, and four times sinks back as if drawn down by a leaden weight. The highest notes of the individual groups form a descending line from dominant to tonic: *a g f e d*.

Now the singer summons all his strength, storming heaven with short yet powerful sentences. How telling is the simple syllabic chant in this instance! The third phrase is melodically like the first; its *ádjuva* is a simpler form of the second *exsúrge*. The second half of the phrase then closes with the anticipated calmness inspired by the subsequent psalm-verse and psalm, which tells of the providence of God in the days of the Egyptian bondage, and of the liberation of Israel's children.

K.K., 24, 13 ff.

GRADUAL (Ps. 82: 10, 14)

1. *Sciant gentes quoniam nomen tibi Deus*: 2. *tu solus Altissimus super omnem terram.* V. 1. *Deus meus, pone illos ut rotam*, 2. *et sicut stipulam* 3. *ante faciem venti.*

1. Let the gentiles know that God is thy name: 2. thou alone art the Most High over all the earth. ℣. 1, O my God, make them like a wheel. 2. and as stubble 3. before the face of the wind.

Rumors of wars and threatened invasions of heathen enemies seem to be referred to in this Gradual. The verse with its request, which strikes us so oddly, begs God to put the enemy to flight with the same despatch that is shown by the autumn wind in heaping together the weeds of the fields and whisking them across the prairie.

By God's grace our enemies are to be robbed of their strength, and we are to be made strong, that we may learn to overcome all things. That is St. Paul's instruction in today's Epistle. We are to preserve this strength throughout our life, and thus show the "gentiles" the enemies of Christ and those who deny Him—that He is truly God. This Easter Christ is to achieve victory in us.

The *corpus* of the Gradual is well planned. There is a well-ordered widening of the range in the phrases *c–a* and *d–b*, as well as in the two following which range from *c–c*. The *nomen tibi* is echoed in *Deus*. Here we find also the words *Deus* and *Altissimus* given a treatment similar

to that found in the Offertory of last Sunday. The cadence in *Altissimus*
is already hinted at in *gentes*. Both the beginning and the end of the first
phrase of the verse are on the dominant, thereby keeping the melody
unusually high in pitch. Closer scrutiny here reveals many similarities
to the ascent to high *f*, so much preferred by Graduals of the fifth mode;
for example, the Gradual for Epiphany *(illumináre)*. Upon this upward
surge follows the middle sentence which again relaxes the tension. The
concluding melisma here employed is found also in many other Graduals
of the first mode; e.g., on the tenth and seventeenth Sundays after Pentecost.   .

TRACT (Ps. 59: 4, 6)

1. *Commovisti, Domine, terram,*
et conturbasti eam. 2. Sana contri-
tiones ejus, quia mota est. 3. Ut
fugiant a facie arcus, ut liberentur
electi tui.

1. *Thou hast moved the earth, O*
Lord, and hast troubled it. 2. Heal
thou the breaches thereof, for it
hath been moved. 3. That thy elect
may flee from before the bow: that
they may be delivered.

Among the foes of whom the Tract makes mention, one naturally
thinks first of exterior enemies, and of the havoc they have caused. In
as far as we have deserved this punishment, it must be acknowledged
as coming from God, and therefore we say, "Thou, O Lord, hast troubled
the earth."

But our souls also have been violently moved. How many in the
course of the past year have begun to tread the downward path despite
the high promise which a careful education and a living faith seemed
to hold out! How often have the burning darts of the evil one wounded
and poisoned the soul! Be Thou, therefore, our Saviour *(sana)*, O Lord,
during this pre-Lenten season and during the coming Lent. Let fly Thy
arrows, Lord, for they will pierce the heart of the enemy. We are Thine
elect, and we, therefore, confidently await Thy special protection and
help.

OFFERTORY (Ps. 16: 5, 6, 7)

1. *Perfice gressus meos in semitis*
tuis, ut non moveantur vestigia mea:
2. inclina aurem tuam, et exaudi
verba mea: 3. mirifica misericordias
tuas, qui salvos facis sperantes in
te, Domine.

1. *Perfect thou my goings in thy*
paths, that my footsteps be not
moved: 2. incline thine ear, and
hear my words: 2. show forth thy
wonderful mercies, thou who savest
them that trust in thee, O Lord.

We do not know if it was after the sad experience of his downfall
that David penned the psalm from which these words are taken. But we

can readily believe that he composed it at that time, if we note the straightforward fervor of this plea. The chant melody likewise seems to have originated in a heart which made the repentant acknowledgement that "it is good for me that Thou hast humbled me, that I might learn Thy commands." Here is humility at prayer, and deep contrition of heart, and the fear that one might belong to those whose hearts are stony ground, who gladly admit the word of God for a time, but give it no firm rooting, with the result that, as today's Gospel says, "in time of temptation they fall away."

Therein we see the earnestness of this melody. But it has a touch of mildness, of spiritual maturity, over it all. There is something appealing in it, much like a song in the quiet of the evening, after a day of storm and stress. Now all is transfigured by the love and the pity of God.

This chant is a song of offering; in the early Church it was likewise a processional song. While it was being sung the faithful advanced to the altar and presented their gifts. These gifts voiced their sacrificial spirit, the spirit without which we cannot follow along the path marked out for us by the Man of Sorrows. In today's Epistle St. Paul shows us clearly along what thorny roads the Lord oftentimes leads His faithful ones. But he also tells us how all-sufficient God's grace is, how it makes us strong in the performance of our daily duties. All these considerations combine to effect a thoughtful and reflective rendition of this chant.

The divisions could hardly be more obvious. Each of the three imperatives, *pérfice, inclína, mirífica,* begins a new phrase. The lingering of the melody at *gressus*—Codex 121 of Einsiedeln has an "x" (= *expectare,* to wait) after each bistropha, and a "hold" over the *clivis*—and the bistropha and tristropha over *moveántur* all seem to breathe confidence. They speak of quiet perseverance in doing the will of God. Thankful joy is discernible in *sémitis,* a joy which perhaps was found only after bitter experience. The formula over *mea* closes the third phrase. *Inclína* swings up with impressive fervor. *Aurem tuam* finds its fuller development in *et exaúdi verba. Mirífica* reminds one of the third phrase in the Introit for Easter Day. In both instances the melody effectively ends the foregoing phrase on *f,* the better to call attention to what follows. The progressive expansion of the melody in this phrase *(f g a)* should be brought out with a *crescendo.* In fact, the whole phrase must steadily grow in fervor until it reaches the confident upward look over *in te* and the tender *Dómine.*

In earlier times this Offertory had four verses. After each verse the words *mirífica misericórdias* were repeated, thus assuring the reception of this consoling truth in the trusting hearts of the faithful.

The Offertory for the feast of St. John Cantius (Oct. 20) has borrowed extensively from this composition.

Revue, 17, 181 ff.

COMMUNION (Ps. 42: 4)

1. *Introibo ad altare Dei*: 2. *ad Deum qui laetificat juventutem meam.*	1. *I will go in to the altar of God* 2. *to God who giveth joy to my youth.*

This is the prayer of the priest at the beginning of Mass, the first of those prayers which are said at the foot of the altar. In this song the faithful make use of the same words, for they also may now approach the altar, there to receive Him who brings joy to their hearts and youthful vigor and energy. Reinvigorated, the soul may then say with the Apostle: "I can do all things in Him who strengtheneth me." Life may bring many trials, and hardships, and disappointments without number; the soul may have experiences much like those of St. Paul; but there ever remains the sweet consolation of saying, "I may go to the altar of God." The altar is the inexhaustible spring of joy and of strength for all.

A festal glow seems to hover over this melody, a joyousness brought out by the rising fourths, the clarion call of the dominant, the graceful intervals *ca cbg, cd da adc*, the broad arcs held together by the word-accents as by a keystone: *Introíbo, ad altáre, Dei*; and all with a pleasing variety. The first and fourth divisions move within the tetrachord *g–c*, the second moves in the fifth *g–d*, and the third small division in the fifth *f–c*.

This happy melody occurs again on the feast of St. Aloysius and in the votive Mass of the Apostles.

Revue, 32, 18, f.

*   *   *   *

QUINQUAGESIMA SUNDAY

"Even more than on the preceding Sundays, there is noticeable throughout today's Mass a restrained joy of Easter, of victory. The light of the Easter sun is breaking through the clouds, revealing the future happenings in the work of our redemption clearly silhouetted against the sky. In the Gospel the Lord announces that He is going up to Jerusalem to suffer, to die, and to rise again. In like manner must we proceed to our own resurrection through suffering and death. Be the journey ever so difficult, we can make it with Christ, we can carry on

by virtue of His strength. When we enter the church today, He becomes
our refuge and our strength, our Leader who will nourish us even now
with the Easter Food, the Food of the strong, in order to bring us through
the desert to the promised land of Eastertide." *(W. K.).*

INTROIT Ps. 30: 3, 4)

1. *Esto mihi in Deum protectorem,
et in locum refugii, ut salvum me
facias:* 2. *quoniam firmamentum
meum, et refugium meum es tu;* 3.
*et proper nomen tuum dux mihi eris,
et enutries me.* Ps. *In te Domine
speravi, non confundar in aeternum:* * *in justitia tua libera me.*

1. *Be thou unto me a God, a protector, and a place of refuge, to save
me:* 2. *for thou art my strength, and
my refuge;* 3. *and for thy name's
sake thou wilt be my leader and wilt
nourish me.* Ps. *In thee, O Lord,
have I hoped, let me never be confounded:* * *deliver me in thy justice.*

The melody of this Introit is divided according to content and text
into three parts, thus affording another instance of the influence which
the text has on the chants themselves.

A happy confidence animates the first part of the song. It is not
impetuous joy, not the exultant joy of a victory-crowned hero. It is
deep-seated happiness, the kind which is born of utter confidence. The
endings to the phrases are delicately done. In every case the final note
is prepared for by the preceding note of the same pitch: *fgf, f, fec, c,
fdec c.* A similar soft effect is produced in most of the accented syllables
by the fact that the note preceding the syllable has the pitch of the
accented one. To this there are but four exceptions—*ut salvum, et propter, tuum,* and *dux*—no doubt because these words are to receive special
prominence. Added to all this we have the warmth of the sixth mode
pervading the whole.

The first phrase is a childlike petition. Beginning with a minor third,
it sinks to *c* and then rises a fourth. Not until this point is reached does
the melody begin to pulse upward above the dominant. The second half
resembles the first: *in Deum* is like *refúgii,* and the second member likewise rises to *a.* The endings, too, are very similar.

In the second phrase the situation is reversed. The first half with its
recitative on the dominant is firm and definite; the descent occurs only
in the second half. A pleasant contrast is thus afforded to the first and
last phrases. Like the first and second, the third phrase also has an
ascending fourth, followed by a bistropha. Here, after an apparent calm
on *g,* the melody rises to a bright *c.* "Thou wilt be my Leader," is the
choir's exultant song. It is the breaking through of joy too long with-
held. Even if I must walk the path of sorrow, I am not alone: Thou art

with me, Thou leadest me, and gladly will I follow. In graceful undulations the melody sinks to the tonic. Thou wilt be not only my Leader;
nay, much more! The emphatic *et* is really arresting, and has the same
effect here in chant as that which Beethoven achieved in the Credo of
his *Missa solemnis* where, after an elaboration of *et*, which heralds great
things to come, he inserts a pause, thereby adding much to the intensity of the passage. In like manner our melody says: Thou wilt even be
my Sustainer. The idea is still more emphasized by the interval of a
fourth, *d–g*, after the repeated *c–f* interval. Thou art indeed the Good
Shepherd. I shall henceforth place my entire trust in Thee; never shall I
then be led astray.

Psalm 30, from which this Introit takes its text, was the prayer of
David in his greatest need. Now David is the type of Christ. And when
He was hanging on the cross, Christ prayed one of the verses of this
psalm aloud: "Into Thy hands I commend My spirit." We shall, therefore, also pray this Introit with great fervor, and thus come closer to
the very heart of Christ. The melody colors the words even at this early
date with the light of the Easter dawn.

Analyses, VII, 8 ff.

GRADUAL (Ps. 76: 15, 16)

1. *Tu es Deus, qui facis mirabilia solus:* 2. *notam fecisti in gentibus virtutem tuam.* ℣. 1. *Liberasti in brachio tuo* 2. *populum tuum*, 3. *filios Israel et Joseph.*

1. *Thou art the God that alone dost wonders:* 2. *thou hast made thy power known among the nations.* ℣. 1. *With thy arm thou hast redeemed* 2. *thy people*, 3. *the children of Israel and of Joseph.*

We heard many sublime things foretold about the Messias, especially during the Christmas cycle. Now He Himself speaks of His
suffering: He is to undergo deep disgrace—and death. But we do not
wish to err like the disciples at Emmaus, who said: "We hoped that it
was He that should have redeemed Israel." Hence the solemn profession in the Gradual: "Thou art God," and, "Thou alone dost wonders."
How heathen Egypt *(géntibus)* and Pharaoh rued the day they had to
acknowledge Thy power! How mighty the arm with which Thou didst
redeem Thy people! But all that was mere prototype of the wonders
which Thy redemptive work will effect, of the freedom which Thou wilt
give us, and by means of which Thou wilt make us Thy chosen people.
It is Thy love which will accomplish all.

The Pasch of the Old Testament was but a shadowy likeness of the
Christian Pasch with its Easter victory and its Easter joy.

If the Graduals were not admittedly made up of typical formulas, one might easily claim that in this Gradual the text is responsible for the melodic structure: Thou art *(c–g)* God *(d–b)*, that dost *(e–c)* wonders *(g–d)* alone *(d–c)*. A rising quint and numerous *pressus* give the second phrase even more force. This melody is in all probability peculiar to the present text. Its final cadence resembles that over *(so)-lus,* and the phrases following begin in both instances with a fourth, in accordance with the rules for symmetry. The final cadence of the third phrase is quite common. We hear it again at the end of the *corpus* in the Gradual for the third Sunday in Lent. The first phrase of the verse concludes in the same manner as the body of the Gradual on Passion Sunday. The florid melisma at the end also occurs in the aforementioned Gradual, although there it is found in the first phrase. Wagner (III, 381) considers it a variant of the melisma over *non* of the verse on Septuagesima Sunday. The very last tones of the verse agree with *(pópu)-lum* of the preceding phrase.

The rendition should be very animated.

TRACT (Ps. 99: 1, 2)

1. *Jubilate Domino omnis terra: servite Domino in laetitia.* 2. *Intrate in conspectu ejus, in exsultatione.* 3. *Scitote quod Dominus ipse est Deus.* 4. *Ipse fecit nos, et non ipsi nos: nos autem populus ejus et oves pascuae ejus.*

1. *Sing joyfully to God, all the earth: serve ye the Lord with gladness.* 2. *Come in before his presence with exceeding great joy:* 3. *Know ye that the Lord he is God.* 4. *He made us, and not we ourselves: but we are his people, and the sheep of his pasture.*

This song, in the middle of the pre-Lenten season, is like a breath of Easter morning; one might almost think it too jubilant. But Holy Mother Church knows why she asks us to sing in this strain today: even now we are to rejoice over the graces given us through the Redemption; even now we are to thank the Good Shepherd that we are sheep of His pasture. Here again, as in the Gradual, we acknowledge that He is God. Only divine love could have prompted the forfeiting of life for the sake of the sheep; neither we nor any power on earth could have made us children of God: *Ipse fecit nos.*

OFFERTORY (Ps. 118: 12, 13)

1. *Benedictus es Domine, doce me justificationes tuas:* 2. *benedictus es Domine, doce me justificationes tuas:*

1. *Blessed art thou, O Lord, teach me thy justifications:* 2. *blessed art thou, O Lord, teach me thy justifica-*

3. *in labiis meis pronuntiavi* 4.   tions: 3. *with my lips I have pro-*
omnia judicia oris tui.   nounced 4. *all the judgments of thy*
    mouth.

The blind man healed by the Saviour followed Him and glorified God. "And all the people, when they saw it, gave praise to God." We now add our own song to the chorus of praise coming from the one healed and from the people; we sing a *Benedíctus* to the Son of David, whose help the blind man so earnestly besought. To this song of praise we subjoin the plea, "Teach me!" Our understanding must increase, our heart must expand if our song is to ring out whole-heartedly. But we may also ask for the humility which justified the publican *(descéndit justificátus)*. Teach me to have faith, O Lord, and confidence, the two virtues necessary for the granting of Thy great gifts: "As thou hast believed, so be it done to thee"; or, to use the words of today's Gospel, "Thy faith hath made thee whole." Teach me also that I must suffer as Thou didst suffer *(opportébat pati Christum)*. Teach me to love, as Thou didst love. Out of love Thou goest to Thy death, to repay the debt of honor to the Father and to merit life for us. Teach me as Thou didst teach St. Peter, in whose church we are assembled today. At first he, too, failed to understand Thy prediction of suffering and death; but later, by his martyrdom, he gave proof of the great love he had for Thee. Teach me love, the love which will make me ascend Calvary and persevere under the cross. Teach me that love of my fellows which is forgetful of self and "endureth all things" (Epistle); for love, Thou didst tell us, is Thy chief commandment.

As in the Offertory for the second Sunday after Epiphany, the chant here repeats the first sentence, using also the same melody. Not until the second *tuas* is there any further addition to it. Over this same *tuas* the climax of the whole piece is found. Such repetitions might be taken alternately by a soloist and the choir, or by a smaller and a larger group in the choir.

The third phrase is markedly quieter, at first proceeding in seconds only. After the breathing mark there is first repeated the motive of phrases one and two over *(justificati)-ónes*, which is therefore sung three times, and then the motive which occurs over the second *tuas*. The fourth phrase stresses the words *ómnia* and *oris* with fourths that only with difficulty they awaken in us any sympathetic response. The highest notes of the successive groups over *(o)-ris tui* form the descending line *c b♭ a g f e*.

May our lips speak the same words which fell from the lips of the Lord? Is our heart unspotted? Formerly another verse, which was like-wise sung a second time with a more ornate melody, belonged to this

Offertory: "Let no iniquity have dominion over me;" and in the secret for today we beg God to "cleanse us from our sins, and sanctify the bodies and minds of Thy servants for the celebration of this sacrifice." We choir members shall accordingly try to banish all that is inharmonious from our souls, that our song may ring out clearly and joyfully, as did the blind man's in today's Gospel.

COMMUNION (Ps. 77: 29, 30)

1. *Manducaverunt, et saturati sunt nimis,* 2. *et desiderium eorum attulit eis Dominus:* 3. *non sunt fraudati a desiderio suo.*

1. *They did eat, and were filled exceedingly,* 2. *and the Lord gave them their desire:* 3. *they were not defrauded of that which they craved.*

According to content, the first phrase is superior to the second; the melody, however, makes the second more prominent. Its final cadence very closely resembles the close of the first division in the responsories of Matins which are assigned to the second mode. Its first half has *g* as its recitative, its second half, *f*. The beginning of the third phrase makes emphatic use of the dominant, followed by the motive which closes the first phrase; the opening notes of the first are employed in the second half.

The same melody, but shortened somewhat to accommodate a shorter text, is found on the feast of St. John Capistran (March 28).

Only that divine Food which was offered to us in this Holy Communion can adequately fill the yearning of our heart, in as far as that is possible here below. At this holy Banquet we acquire that feeling of full satisfaction, of perfect composure, which helps us turn a deaf ear to the deceitful promises of the world. The conviction becomes ever more clear: God alone suffices. May our longing increase with every reception of Holy Communion, together with a corresponding deepening and intensifying of the joy in our hearts! With the strength afforded by this Food we shall then advance confidently into the promised land of Easter peace and Easter happiness.

* * * *

ASH WEDNESDAY

A. BLESSING OF THE ASHES

ANTIPHON *Exaudi* (Ps. 68: 17)

1. *Exaudi nos Domine, quoniam benigna est misericordia tua:* 2. *secundum multitudinem miserati-*

1. *Hear us, O Lord, for thy mercy is kind:* 2. *look upon us, O Lord, according to the multitude of thy*

onum tuarum respice nos, Domine.
Ps. Salvum me fac Deus: quoniam
*intraverunt aquae * usque ad ani-*
mam meam.

tender mercies. Ps. Save me, O God,
*for the waters have come in * even*
unto my soul.

It is a serious time, this season upon which we are now entering.
But in this very first antiphon the Church aims at giving us a consoling
thought, one which is to sink deeply into our consciousness. The high
range of the notes and the resounding tristrophas give animated voice
to the words expressing God's mildness and mercy. Be our guilt ever so
great, depressing, or shameful, though the floodwaters of sin penetrate
our very soul, the benignity of God and His mercy are greater still. The
miseratiónum tu-(arum) occurs also on the second Sunday of Lent with
the same notation. *Nos Dómine* is an amplification of *-árum.*

Of the chants which may be sung during the distribution of the
ashes, we shall here discuss only the last two.

ANTIPHON *Juxta vestibulum*
(Joel 2: 17; Esther 13: 17)

1. *Juxta vestibulum et altare plo-*
rabunt sacerdotes et levitae min-
istri Domini, et dicent: 2. *Parce,*
Domine, parce populo tuo: 3. *et ne*
dissipes ora clamantium ad te,
Domine.

1. *Between the porch and the altar*
the priests, the Lord's ministers,
shall weep, and shall say: 2. *Spare,*
O Lord, spare thy people; 3. *and*
shut not the mouths of them that
sing to thee, O Lord.

Plorábunt—"They shall weep"—is the word which characterizes
the spirit of this chant. The first half of the first phrase rests on *f*, and
goes beyond it only to lay stress on the word-accent. The *e–f* preceding
plorábunt, demanded by the rules, serves to combine these two parts of
the melody. Special emphasis is then put on the dominant *a* in the following group of notes, as well as in the second and third phrases, with
the result that the melody is heavy, depressed. A leaden weight seems to
burden the singer. *Parce Dómine* is an urgent entreaty. We are still Thy
people, despite the fact that we have sinned. Shut not the mouths that
praise Thee, and close not Thy heart against our pleading. Have mercy,
O Lord!

RESPONSORY *Emendemus* (Esther 13; Joel 2)

1. *Emendemus in melius, quae*
ignoranter peccavimus: 2. *ne subito*
praeoccupati die mortis, quaera-

1. *Let us amend and do better*
those things in which we have
sinned through ignorance: 2. *less*

mus spatium paenitentiae, et invenire non possimus. * 3. *Attende Domine, et miserere: quia peccavimus tibi. Adjuva nos, Deus salutaris noster: 2. et propter honorem nominis tui, Domine, libera nos.* * *Attende Domine... Gloria Patri*
...

suddenly prevented by the day of death, we seek time for penance, and be not able to find it. * 3. Attend, O Lord, and have mercy: for we have sinned against thee. ℣. 1. Help us, O God, our Saviour: 2. and for the honor of thy name, O Lord, deliver us. * Attend, O Lord ... Glory be to the Father...

Responsories occurring in the Divine Office and in blessings have the general arrangment A B A. But generally only a part of A is repeated. There are even more typical melodies here than in the Gradual-responsories. The verse with its *Glória Patri* is such a typical melody, and consequently no account is taken of the meaning of the text. The first half of the verse has the recitation on the dominant together with a five-syllable middle cadence. The second half recites on the tonic. Without exception, the final cadence begins at the fifth last syllable: *Dó-*

$\overset{5\ \ 432\ \ 1}{}$ $\overset{5\ 4\ 3\ \ 2\ \ 1}{}$

mine líbera nos and *Spíritui sancto.*

The *corpus* of the Responsory has many typical turns: *peccávimus* = *non possímus* and also the second *-vimus tibi*; and *spátium paeniténtiae* = *Atténde Dómine et miseré-(re)*. The melody greatly resembles the Responsory *Obtulérunt* of Feb. 2. But the second phrase of our present chant has a character peculiar to itself; with its heaped-up fourths it well represents the excited state of the singer's soul. He is moved by the words with which the priest placed the ashes on his sinful head: "Remember, man, that thou art dust, and unto dust thou shalt return." Here, as well as on Palm Sunday and on the feast of the Purification, the Responsory rounds out the first ceremony of the day, and leads over to the Solemn Mass which follows it.

THE MASS

INTROIT (Wisd. 11: 24, 25, 27)

1. *Misereris omnium, Domine, et nihil odisti eorum quae fecisti, 2. dissimulans peccata hominum propter paenitentiam, 3. et parcens illis: 4. quia tu es Dominus Deus noster. Ps. Miserere mei Deus,*

1. Thou hast mercy upon all, O Lord, and hatest none of the things which thou hast made, 2. and overlookest the sins of men for the sake of repentance, 3. and sparing them: 4. for thou art the Lord our God. Ps.

*miserere mei: * quoniam in te confidit anima mea.*　　　　*Have mercy on me, O God, have mercy on me: * for my soul trusteth in thee.*

After the Church has earnestly prayed, both at the blessing of the ashes and in her chants during their distribution, that God show His mercy to her children, she here voices the conviction that her prayers have been heard: "Thou hast mercy upon all, O Lord." His divine heart is full of pity for the poor, even for the most forsaken. His love for His creature is lasting, even when this creature turns its back upon its Creator. Progressing in full-step intervals, the melody has the ring of conviction, of confident hope. The opening motive is heard again in *ómnium Dómine* and *nihil*. The note *a* predominates in the first half of the phrase, the note *f* in the second.

In the second phrase, *propter paeniténtiam* emerges rough and rugged, like a mountain ridge which must first be scaled and crossed before one can reach the beautiful valley of peace which lies beyond. God "overlooks" our sins that we may do penance, that we may have time for introspection, for sorrow and atonement. The Responsory *Emendémus* has already told us that God's patience in this matter is not a license to sin. But if we turn to Him with true contrition He will also turn to us, will become *Deus noster*, "our God." The more sincere our penance and our conversion, the closer will He be to us. The composer cleverly gives the words *Deus noster*, at the end of the Introit, the same melody that *paeniténtiam* has, except that it is a fifth lower. The logical connection is, therefore, indicated by the melodic correspondence. In its deeper setting the melody has, moreover, none of that ruggedness or severity which we noted before. Our God is the God of peace. Contrariwise, the effect of *paeniténtiam* is all the more severe because of the appealing melody over *hóminum* which precedes it. We have already met this formula in the Introit *Gaudéte* and elsewhere.

The third phrase, despite its brevity, is treated as an independent sentence. It follows the closing cadence over *paeniténtiam* and precedes the new sentence opening over *quia*; the annotated manuscripts, therefore, call for a broad rendition of the *climacus* over *parcens*. Consolation and repose pervade this short phrase, but the rising third at its end prepares us for more vigorous lines, and thus serves as a solemn introduction to the fourth phrase. Here the melody becomes rich in neums; it breathes a prayer of thanks for the good fortune of those who have been raised from the slough of sin to the fatherly heart of God. The proportions are worthy of notice. *Tu* is divided by the *mora vocis*, eight notes to the first part and eight to the second. *Dóminus* and *De-(us)* likewise have eight, and -*us* and *noster* seven and eight notes respectively. The psalm-verse prays in this strain: Since Thou, O Lord, hast pity on all, and lovest everything that Thou hast made, show mercy also to me. In Thy immeasurable mercy do I place all my hope.

Musica s., 45, 25 ff.

GRADUAL (Ps. 56: 2, 4)

1. *Miserere mei Deus,* 2. *miserere mei:* 3. *quoniam in te confidit anima mea.* Ỿ. 1. *Misit de caelo, et liberavit me:* 2. *dedit in opprobrium conculcantes me.*

1. *Have mercy on me, O God,* 2. *have mercy on me:* 3. *for my soul trusteth in thee.* Ỿ. 1. *He hath sent from heaven, and delivered me;* 2. *he hath made them a reproach that trod upon me.*

Corpus and verse have perfect similarity of ending: *(me)-a* = *me*. In the *corpus* both the first and the second sentences descend to low *c*. The second *miserére mei* is more forceful than the first, but this is probably due not so much to the text itself as to the rules for melodic development. The third phrase and the greater part of the second phrase of the verse are sung in the same manner on the tenth Sunday after Pentecost. In the first phrase of the verse the prominence given to the high *c* is the outstanding feature. Its first half closes with the same formula as that over the word *David* in the Gradual *Sacerdótes* of the second Mass for a Confessor-Bishop.

The words of the *corpus* are the same as those we heard in the Introit. They would impress on us the fact that we can never have too much confidence in God's merciful love. The singer thankfully acknowledges the guidance of almighty God and his liberation from the enemy.

TRACT (Ps. 102: 10)

1. *Domine, non secundum peccata nostra,* † *quae fecimus nos:* (—) *neque secundum iniquitates nostras* (—) *retribuas nobis.* 2. (Ps. 78: 8, 9). *Domine, ne memineris iniquitatum nostrarum:* † *cito anticipent nos* (—) *misericordiae tuae, quia pauperes facti sumus nimis.* 3 (Hic geniflectitur.). *Adjuva nos Deus salutaris noster:* (—) *et*

1. *O Lord, repay us not according to the sins* † *we have committed,* (—) *nor according to our iniquities* (—). 2. (Ps. 78; 8, 9). *O Lord, remember not our former iniquities:* † *let thy mercies speedily prevent us* (—), *for we are become exceeding poor.* 3. (Here all kneel down.) *Help us, O God, our Saviour:* (—) *and for the glory of thy name, O Lord, de-*

propter gloriam nominis tui, Do-mine, libera nos: † *et propitius esto peccatis nostris, propter nomen tuum.*

liver us: † *and forgive us our sins for thy name's sake.*

This tract is not found in the oldest manuscripts. It would seem that it received its present form no earlier than the twelfth century. The similar middle cadences are indicated above by the mark †, and the caesura (—). In the first verse the phrasing of the text and the melodic phrasing are not quite parallel. The second and third verses have much in common. In the third verse, the introductory notes and the prolonged clinging to *a* reveal the underlying emotion of the soul; it is a suppliant call, heartfelt and urgent. It presents one of the more dramatic moments of the liturgy, the kneeling of all the faithful to the accompaniment of this chant. We cry to the Lord: Thy Being and the glory of Thy Name demand that Thou enter the lists for us and grant us Thy lasting help.

OFFERTORY (Ps. 29: 2,3)

1. *Exaltabo te Domine, quoniam suscepisti me,* 2. *nec delectasti inimicos meos super me:* 3. *Domine clamavi ad te, et sanasti me.*

1. *I will extol thee, O Lord, for thou hast upheld me:* 2. *and hast not made mine enemies to rejoice over me:* 3. *O Lord, I have cried to thee, and thou hast healed me.*

How can this text belong here, at this solemn opening of Lent? On Easter Day we should readily understand it as the victorious song of the Risen One, as a second stanza to the Easter Introit with its *tecum sum*, as a song of victory, or as the glorified Saviour's song of exultation after all the wounds that had been inflicted upon Him. But today it seems out of place. We must not forget, however, that the Lenten season which we are now ushering in is but the great preparation for Easter. Moreover, the melody itself does not course upward in extraordinarily bright and jubilant tones, but adapts itself, more than does the text itself, to the prevailing spirit of the day.

This was the day on which public sinners were thrust out of the church to do public penance. Not till Maundy Thursday were they again permitted to participate in the divine service. This must have reminded the faithful in a most vivid manner of what they themselves owed to the grace of God, to that divine help which ever led them on, which protected them against the allurements of the enemy and the contagion of sin. The same grace makes them participants today in the blessings flowing from the Eucharistic Sacrifice.

Perhaps this song can be taken as coming from the heart of St. Sabina, in whose church the station was held on this day. Then it would be the thanksgiving of the saint for God's help during her martyrdom, and therefore also an encouragement toward a renewal of the spirit of sacrifice in us.

Our sincere thankfulness for the grace of regeneration should be reflected in *suscepísti me*. This passage, which sounds much like a resolved major chord, must not be rendered hastily. Though we might feel that this chant is of the fifth mode, the whole piece nevertheless contains turns so characteristic of the second mode that to assign it to the fifth mode with an augmented third *(a)* over the tonic *(f)*, is hardly defensible. There is, morevoer, a frequent recurrence of the chief repercussion of the second mode and the immediate following of the tonic by the dominant, which latter is usually broadened out or continued in the following note-group *(here a—ccc)*. A skillful rendition of this chant will obviate the monotony which would otherwise result in such passages. One should, therefore, avoid giving any prominence to the *c* in the conclusion over *sanásti*; that note should be comparatively subdued. The second phrase widens the ascending range, and favors intervals of fourths. Rather unexpected is the array of neums over the unimportant word *super*, just as it was over the last syllable of *quóniam*. If the melody here reaches its climax, we must no doubt attribute it to tone-painting, for that seems to be the purpose of the groups over *super* ("above, higher"). Compare the Gradual for the third Advent Sunday, for instance. The close of this second phrase with *a g* has the effect of a modulation, the kind favored by the second mode. *Dómine* in the third phrase should not be sung heavily; it should rather indicate a childlike confidence in God. *Clamávi ad te* repeats the melody of *inimícos meos*. *Sanásti me* calls for an impulsive *crescendo*.

The transposition of this piece by a fifth is, no doubt, due to the fact that *suscepísti me* would, in its normal position, have been written $b\flat\ d\ f\ d\ b\flat\ b\flat\ c\ b\flat\ b\flat$, a notation which would appear strange so low on the staff.

COMMUNION (Ps. 1: 2, 3)

1. *Qui meditabitur in lege Domini die ac nocte,* 2. *dabit fructum suum in tempore suo.*

1. *He who shall meditate upon the law of the Lord day and night,* 2. *shall bring forth his fruit in due season.*

The two phrases have similar endings. But the first speaks radiantly of God's law, and emphasizes the dominant, whereas the second rises but once to high *c*. The law of God, His holy word! How willingly we should open our hearts to it and receive it as the precious seed it is! How carefully we should cultivate it in loving meditation, and with hearty good will make it our rule of life! From the quiet of our inmost soul—the calm, deep melody reminds us of this quiet—it will develop outwardly in our practical life and bring forth fruits in due season, fruits which will endure forever, even when eternity begins and time is no more.

But our song is also a song for Holy Communion. The new covenant is sealed by the institution of the Holy Eucharist, and the Saviour's first commandment is simply: "Do this for a commemoration of Me." Our meditation on the law of God must also include this command concerning the Blessed Eucharist and all that is bound up therewith. Day and night we must ponder this great truth and make it the treasure to which our heart will, according to today's Gospel, ever remain attached. Then will the life-giving sap and the life-giving strength of Christ, the true Vine, flow into us and bring forth rich fruit.

The text is taken from Psalm 1. From now until the Friday preceding Palm Sunday the Communion text on week days is taken from the psalms, from Psalm 1 to 26. On five days, however, the texts are taken from the current Gospels, and the accompanying melodies are almost entirely syllabic. Thursdays are likewise exceptions, because originally the Thursdays in Lent had no Mass of their own.

*   *   *   *

FIRST SUNDAY IN LENT

In the temptation of Christ narrated in today's Gospel, the tempter quotes verses of Psalm 90. Now he must hear these verses, applied in their proper sense, of course, many a time during the Lenten season. A fine irony is revealed thereby. Today, in fact, the songs are taken exclusively from the ninetieth psalm. But there is another reason for the profuse employment of this pslam today: it is the song which best expresses confidence in God. Now that the great days of penance and mortification are at hand, and we give ourselves entirely to God, we are, according to the teaching of the current liturgy, justified in relying on the special protection of the Most High. He will guard His own against all the enemies of the soul, against sin and concupiscence and the evil spirit. (R. Tippmann, *Die Messen der Fastenzeit*, p. 27.)

INTROIT (Ps. 90: 15, 16)

1. *Invocabit me, et ego exaudiam eum: 2. eripiam eum, et glorificabo eum: 3. longitudine dierum adimple-*

1. *He shall call upon me, and I will hear him: 2. I will deliver him, and glorify him: 3. I will fill him*

bo eum. Ps. Qui habitat in adjuto-
*rio Altissimi, * in protectione Dei*
caeli commorabitur.

with length of days. Ps. He that
dwelleth in the aid of the Most
*High, * shall abide under the pro-*
tection of the God of heaven.

We have now entered the serious season of Lent, the season of penance. Much is expected of us during this time. But the prospect should not dismay us; sadness or weariness are entirely out of place. For we are not to carry on the fight alone. Now more than ever the Lord will be our help. We may call upon Him, and He promises to hear us (first phrase). He will remove all obstacles, all ground for complaint; He will "deliver us;" He will even—Oh, the wonder of it!—glorify us (second phrase). And that which He now promises us is, moreover, to be our lasting possession, is to fill the yearning of our hearts for all eternity (third phrase).

The words of the Introit found their fulfillment in the Saviour Himself. His long and fervent prayer was answered by reason of the piety with which He prayed. He was freed from all pain and from all His enemies; He was glorified, and both the fullness of days and the fullness of joy overflowed into His sacred humanity. That is the wonderful panorama which Mother Church unfolds for us on this very first Sunday in Lent.

We must also pray this Introit as if it were coming from the hearts of the catechumens. The station today is at St. John Lateran, the mother-church of all Christendom, dedicated to St. John the Baptist. There, on the night preceding Easter, the catechumens will find the dearest wish of their heart granted; there the Sacrament of Baptism will remove from them the power of their enemies and free them from the vicious world and from the darkness of sin. There they will be received into the Communion of Saints, obtaining thereby a claim to the glory of heaven.

These thoughts are of themselves sufficient to prevent us from giving a somber interpretation to the present Introit. The fact that it belongs here, to the first Lenten Sunday, will not hinder us from singing it as a joyous, sunny song, transfigured by the goodness of God.

The first phrase twice touches the note *f*, but only in passing; in the main it restricts itself to the tetrachord *g–c*. The word-accents are well defined and usually occur on the dominant *c*. The second phrase is built around the magnificent *glorificábo*, which truly sings of glory. Its closing word is like the first *eum*, but a bit more restricted. *Gló-(ria)* is like *e-(go)* of the first phrase, and *erípiam* resembles *invocábit*. The third phrase begins on the dominant, and assigns to *diérum* and *eum* the same notation that *eum* of the second phrase has. *Adimplébo* is the counterpart of *glorificábo:* the former has *e* as its lowest note, the latter has *e* as its highest. All the depths of the soul, be they ever so profound, will find their perfect satisfaction in the glory of God. Although this phrase is much like the preceding one, the emphasis given to *d* in the first half and the descent to *e* in the second half succeed in individualizing it. Parallel sentence structure, clear delineation and presentation of what is important, pleasing contrasts and cadences: those are the features of this chant.

The same melody is used on Trinity Sunday and on the feast of St. Joseph Cupertino.

In the psalm-verse the final cadence, by way of exception, begins not on the fifth last, but on the sixth last syllable.

Caecilia, 29, 18 f.; *Gregoriusbote,* 25, 10 ff.

GRADUAL (Ps. 90: 11, 12)

1. *Angelis suis* 2. *mandavit de te,* 3. *ut custodiant te* 4. *in omnibus viis tuis.* ℣. 1. *In manibus porta-bunt te,* 2. *ne unquam offendas* 3. *ad lapidem* 4. *pedem tuum.*

1. To his angels 2. hath he given charge over thee, 3. to keep thee 4. in all thy ways. ℣. 1. In their hands they shall bear thee up, 2. lest at any time thou dash 3-4. thy foot against a stone.

According to the words of the Epistle, a servant of God must prove himself "in much patience, in tribulation, in necessities, in distresses, in stripes, in prisons, in labors, in watchings, in fastings." The Apostle is describing his own life. But in the introduction he notes this word of the Lord: "In an acceptable time have I heard thee, and in the day of salvation have I helped Thee." The verses of this Gradual point to a special kind of divine help and protection; they are the very verses quoted by the devil in today's Gospel. But in the Gradual the Church tells us this· he who does not willfully place himself in danger, who is not more wise than it behooveth to be wise, but humbly places his confidence in God, for such a one these words will ever remain true. They are our consolation in all the trials and temptations we may have to undergo.

God Himself has put us in the care of the angels, of His own angels. In the prayers of the Breviary this verse resounds throughout the whole of Lent.

The melody is a typical one, and is employed for a great variety of texts. Here we shall discuss only those texts which occur on Sundays and feast days and in the Requiem Mass. In *Paléographie musicale* (Vol. II) are published two hundred and nineteen manuscripts, dating from the ninth to the seventeenth century, in all of which this melody is faithfully adhered to, with but negligible variations, for the text *Justus ut palma.*

The structure of the melody is psalmodic in character. Both the *corpus* and the verse have four phrases, each of which has some sort of intonation *(initium),* then a recitation on the dominant either alone or elaborated, finally a prominent cadence with or without a *jubilus.* It must be admitted, however, that there is a lack of that pleasing alternation of simple psalmody with its ascending middle cadence and descending final cadence.[1] The *corpus* has the dominant *c*, the verse in its first half the dominant *d*. This has given rise to the custom of assigning the melody to the seventh mode. Others again assign it to the fifth mode, with a close on the upper third (cf. the Gradual for the first Sunday after Pentecost, *Musica s.,* 45, 105 f).

In the following scheme the letter a) designates the Gradual from the Mass of a Confessor not a Bishop, b) that from the Mass of the Dead, c) that from the Mass of St. Matthias, d) that from the Mass of the first Sunday in Lent, e) that from the Mass of the twenty-first Sunday after Pentecost, f) that from the Mass of St. Joachim (q.v.), g) the corresponding parts of the Gradual for Easter, h) the same from the Gradual for the Midnight Mass for Christmas.

CORPUS

Initium.		Dominant, simple or ornate.			Cadence, with or without jubilus.		
		First Phrase					
1		**2**			**3**	**4**	**5**
a) Ju-		stus ut palma flo-			ré-		bit.
b) Ré-		quiem ae-			tér-		nam
c) Ni-		mis hono-			rá-	ti	sunt
d) An-		gelis			su-		is
e) Dó-		mine re-			fú-	gi-	um
f) Dispérsit					de-		dit
		Second Phrase					
1	**2**	**3**	**4**	**5**	**6**	**(7)**	**8**
a) sicut	ce-	drus		Lí	ba-		ni
b)	do-	na	e-	is	Dó-	mi-	ne
c) a-	mí-	ci	tu-	i	De-		us
d) man-	dá-	vit		de	te		
e)	fa-	ctus	es		no-		bis
f) pau-	pé-	ribus		ju-	stí-	ti-	a . . .

---

[1] *Pal. Mus.,* III, 36 ff.; *N. Sch.,* 203.; *Wagner,* III, 370 ff.

Third Phrase

	1	2	3	(4)	5
a)	mul-	tipli-	cá-	bi-	tur
b)	et	lux per-	pé-	tu-	a
c)	ni-	mis confor-	tá-	tus	est
d)	ut	custódi-	ant		te
e)	a	generati-	ó-		ne
f)					
g)	ex-	sul-	té-		mus
h)	ante	lu-	cí-	fe-	rum

Fourth Phrase

	1	2	3	4	5	6	7	(8)	9
a)	in	do-				mo	Dó-	mi-	ni.
b)		lú-	ce-			at	e-		is.
c)	prin-	ci-	pá-		tus	e-	ó-		rum
d)	in	óm-	ni-	bus	vi-	is	tu-		is.
e)		et				pro-	gé-	ni-	e.
f)		saé-						cu-	li.
g)						in	e-		a.
h)	gé-		nu-			i	te.		

VERSE

Initium.			Dominant.		Cadence.		

First Phase

	1	2	3	4....	5	6	(7)	8
a)	Ad	an-	nun-	tián-	dum	ma-		ne
b)	In	me-	mó-	ria	ae-	tér-		na
c)	Di-	nu-	me-	rá-	bo	e		os
d)	In	má-	ni-	bus	por-	tá-	bunt	te
e)	Priús-				quam	mon-		tes
f)	Potens				in	ter-		ra
g)	Confité-			mini				
h)	Di-	xit	Dó-	minus Dómi-	no	me-		o

Second Phrase

	1	2	3	4	5́	6
a)		mi-	sericórdi-	am	tu-	am,
b)		e-		rit	ju-	stus:
c)	et	su-	per	a-	ré-	nam
d)	ne	un-	quam	of-	fén-	das
e)		fíe-	rent, aut formaré-tur		ter-	ra
f)		e-	rit　se-	men	e-	jus:
g)						
h)	sede	a	dex-	tris	me-	is

Third Phrase

	1	2	3	4́	(5)	6
a)	et	veritá-	tem	tu-		am
b)	ab	auditió-	ne	ma-		la
c)		[Text too short]				
d)		[Text too short]				
e)	et	orbis:	a	saé-	cu-	lo
f)	ge-	nerátio	re-	ctó-		rum
gh)						

Fourth Phrase

	1	2	3	4	5	6	7́	8
a)	per						no-	ctem.
b)	non					ti-	mé-	bit.
c)	multi-			pli-	ca-		bún-	tur.
d)	ad		lápi-	dem	pe-	dem	tu-	um.
e)	et	in	saécu-	lum	tu	es	De-	us.
f)	be-			ne-	di-		cé-	tur.
g)		miseri-		córdi-		a	e-	jus.
h)		pe-		dum		tu-	ó-	rum.

The melody was transposed, since ordinarily the gamut *d c e♯ d c* would have resulted over *mandávit*. The motive *é f d a é a g* in the third phrase of the *corpus* is varied somewhat in the first phrase of the verse: *é d c b é a g* and *é f d b é a g*, and entirely at the end *é d é b á b c (a)*. In the verse the principal accents receive a gentle preparation through a *pes*: *por-tábunt, of-féndas*... Corresponding passages were indicated by slurs.

TRACT (Ps. 90)

The entire ninetieth psalm with the exception of verses eight to ten now follows. Each verse has an almost identical mediant †; if this sign appears twice in a verse, the mediant occurs twice also. Several verses have a caesura, indicated by (—).

1. *Qui habitat in adjutorio Altissimi, † in protectione Dei caeli commorabitur.* 2. *Dicet Domino: Susceptor meus es, † et refugium meum, Deus meus (—): sperabo in eum.* 3. *Quoniam ipse liberavit me de laqueo venantium, † et a verbo aspero.* 4. *Scapulis suis obumbrabit tibi, † et sub pennis ejus sperabis.* 5. *Scuto circumdabit te veritas ejus: † non timebis (—) a timore nocturno.* 6. *A sagitta volante per diem, † a negotio perambulante in tenebris, † a ruina et daemonio meridiano.* 7. *Cadent a latere tuo mille, † et decem millia a dextris tuis: † tibi autem (—) non appropinquabit.* 8. *Quoniam Angelis suis mandavit de te, † ut custodiant te (—) in omnibus viis tuis.* 9. *In manibus portabunt te, ne unquam offendas † ad lapidem pedem tuum.* 10. *Super aspidem et basiliscum ambulabis, † et conculcabis (—) leonem et draconem.* 11. *Quoniam in me speravit liberabo eum: † protegam eum, (—) qoniam cognovit nomen meum.* 12. *Invocabit me, et ego exaudiam eum: † cum ipso (—) sum in tribulatione.* 13. *Eripiam eum, et glorificabo eum: † longitudine dierum adimplebo eum, † et ostendam illi salutare meum.*

1. *He that dwelleth in the aid of the Most High, † shall abide in the protection of the God of heaven.* 2. *He shall say to the Lord: Thou art my protector, † and my refuge, my God (—): in him will I trust.* 3. *He hath delivered me from the snare of the hunters, † and from the sharp word.* 4. *He will overshadow thee with his shoulders, † and under his wings thou shalt trust.* 5. *His truth shall compass thee with a shield: † thou shalt not be afraid (—) of the terror of the night.* 6. *Of the arrow that flieth in the day, † of the business that walketh in the dark † of ruin, or of the noonday devil.* 7. *A thousand shall fall at thy side, † and ten thousand at thy right hand: † but to thee (—) it shall not approach.* 8. *For he hath given his angels charge over thee, † to keep thee (—) in all thy ways.* 9. *In their hands they shall bear thee up, lest thou dash † thy foot against a stone.* [The phrasing here is not happy.] 10. *Thou shalt walk upon the asp and the basilisk, † and thou shalt trample under foot (—) the lion and the dragon.* [This verse has a proper middle and closing cadence.] 11. *Because he hath hoped in me, I will deliver him: † I will protect him, (—) because he hath known my name.* 12. *He shall call upon me, and I will hear him: †*

with him (—) am I in tribulation.
13. I will deliver him, and I will
glorify him: † I will fill him with
length of days, † and I will show
him my salvation.

OFFERTORY—COMMUNION (Ps. 90: 4, 5)

1. *Scapulis suis obumbrabit tibi*
Dominus, 2. *et sub pennis ejus*
sperabis: 3. *scuto circumdabit te*
veritas ejus.

1. *The Lord will overshadow thee*
with his shoulders, 2. *and under*
his wings thou shalt trust: 3. *his*
truth shall compass thee with a
shield.

With the exception of the word *Dóminus,* which is wanting in the Communion, the two pieces have the same text. Both also exhibit three well-marked phrases. This is best shown in the Communion, which closes each phrase with the same cadence, has an ascending line in the first half of each phrase and a descending line in the second half. Three parts are also distinguished in the Offertory. The first and third phrases correspond; by way of contrast the second moves upwards. Here the motive over *obumbrábit* returns at the beginning of the second phrase. We find it also at the beginning of the Communion. The powerful motive over *tibi* appears in a varied form with *véritas ejus* and *(circúm) -dabit.*

In the Communion *(obum)-brábit* finds an echo in *(circúm)-dabit* and *véritas.* The responsories in the fourth mode at Matins generally close the third phrase with the melody *sperábis.*

The Offertory has a vigorous, rousing ring. In the Communion there is an admixture of tenderness, of tranquility. But it also manifests clear joy with the jubilant *et sub pennis,* just as the Offertory attains a degree of gentleness through this, that every second neum over *circúmdabit* sets in on the same pitch with which the preceding one closed.

Scápulis and *sub pennis* are generally regarded as meaning the same thing and translated as such. In the clear triple division of the pieces, in the difference of the first phrase from the third, one may perhaps leave *Scápulis* its usual meaning of "shoulders," and refer the phrase to the strength of divine protection. If, in accordance with the words of Holy Scripture, the Lord supports the entire universe upon His three fingers, what confidence ought it not to inspire when He reaches us His hand, when He protects us with His shoulders and fights for us! The second phrase makes us feel how securely we are lodged under His wings. In the Communion especially the soul exults that it is privileged to rest

on the bosom of God. In the third phrase we are told: You are protected
on all sides *(circum)*. If God's truth, and His entire truth, encompasses
you, then there is no vulnerable spot left in you; you need fear nothing,
for God's protection will remain true to you.

*   *   *   *

SECOND SUNDAY IN LENT

In olden times the divine services of the night of Saturday in Ember
Week were prolonged until Sunday morning. For this reason there was
no solemn Mass on the present day. Its formulary was composed only
later (fifth century). With the exception of the Tract, all the chants
have been borrowed from the preceding Wednesday.

INTROIT (Ps. 24: 6, 3, 22)

1. *Reminiscere miserationum tuarum, Domine,* 2. *et misericordiae tuae, quae a saeculo sunt:* 3. *ne unquam dominentur nobis inimici nostri:* 4. *libera nos Deus Israel ex omnibus angustiis nostris.* Ps. *Ad te, Domine, levavi animam meam:* * *Deus meus in te confido, non erubescam.*

1. *Remember, O Lord, thy bowels of compassion,* 2. *and thy mercies that are from the beginning of the world;* 3. *lest at any time our enemies rule over us:* 4. *deliver us, O God of Israel, from all our tribulations.* Ps. *To thee, O Lord, have I lifted up my soul:* * *in thee, O my God, I put my trust, let me not be ashamed.*

This song is an expression of deep humility. What would happen to
us if God were not merciful, if His mercy were not eternal! How entirely
dependent upon it we are! Hence we dare to remind Him of His mercies.
He never forgets them; for they are a part of His essence. For this reason
also, the Introit speaks of *Thy* commiseration, of *Thy* mercy.

The parallelism between the first two phrases of the text is repro-
duced in the melody. Both phrases vigorously accent the note *f*; both
have the same range *(d–a)* and similar endings; finally, *misericórdiae* is
only a repetition of *miseratiónum.* In both instances the *torculus* enlivens
the serene melodic line.

Now begins a new part. The melody also throws off some of its reserve. In its range of a sixth, the intervals grow larger. The first part
confined itself to thirds only; here we meet with five intervals of a fourth.
Next to *f*, *g* is the dominating note. A certain restlessness makes itself
felt. The pious soul looks about herself; she sees herself surrounded by
enemies, wily and formidable, numerous and inexorable. Whoever does

not acknowledge the Lord *(Dómine,* in the first part*)* becomes their slave, is dominated by the world, evil passions, and the devil. We pray: Do not allow our enemies to rule over us. But we must also add: Let them never again gain power over us. The more painfully we have been made to feel the heaviness of their yoke, the more fervent and heartfelt will be this prayer and this song. We divine what the composer wished to say with the gamut *dg ǵf* over *inimíci* and *gfág g* over *nostri.* Here a *crescendo* comes spontaneously.

Then a third time we pray with the ascending fourth: *líbera nos:* Thou art the God of Israel; Thou hast selected this nation as Thine own people. Thou art our God also, and hast elected, bought, and redeemed also us. Deliver us, then, from all our distresses. Be Thou at our side especially then, O Lord, when that greatest of all trials will come, when we are about to enter through the narrow *(angústiis)* portals of death[1].

The feeling proclaimed in the very first notes is effectively retained throughout, but in the second part it becomes more lively.

The psalm-melody recites on *a,* which up till now had only been touched transiently, and then rises above it, full of confidence in God.

Caecilia, 29, 19 f.

GRADUAL (Ps. 24: 17, 18)

1. *Tribulationes cordis mei dilatatae sunt:* 2. *de necessitatibus meis eripe me, Domine.* ℣. 1. *Vide humilitatem meam,* 2. *et laborem meum:* 3. *et dimitte omnia peccata mea.*

1. *The troubles of my heart are multiplied:* 2. *deliver me from my necessities, O Lord.* ℣. 1. *See my abjection,* 2. *and my labor:* 3. *and forgive all my sins.*

The text expresses entirely the spirit of the Introit. Indeed, it has become still more earnest with the reading of the Lesson. There the Apostle had cried: "This is the will of God, your sanctification." We are all aware how difficult is this life's task, how the heart, desirous of love, has to struggle, how arduous the conflicts of life really are. And we frequently feel exhausted and miserable, because we have often added our personal failings to the burden of life. At the sight of all these miseries, we address to the Lord this threefold petition: Deliver us, see our abjection, forgive us our sins.

And the melody? It sounds entirely different. It throws a festal garment over the agitated text. Certain of the fulfillment of its prayer, it sends rays of beneficent light over a sorrowful countenance and into a wounded heart—as a reflection of eternal light.

---

1 In the votive Mass for the grace of a happy death, this melody forms the second phrase.

The friendly F-major chord—at least so it strikes us—is often heard, both in an ascending and in a descending line. Several times occurs the descending fourth *c–g*. The close of the *corpus* corresponds with *meis.* The verse repeats its first motive and prolongs it. The melodic development of its second and third phrases will be explained on the feast of the Assumption. *Meis* in the *corpus* and *meum* in the verse tend to produce the same effect as a modern modulation to A minor. Similarly, we should like to speak of *ómnia* as a modulation to C major.

TRACT (Ps. 105: 1, 4)

The closing cadences of all the verses, with the exception of the last, are alike. From verse to verse the range of the melody is extended.

1. *Confitemini Domino, quoniam bonus:* † *quoniam in saeculum* (—) *misericordia ejus.* 2. *Quis loquetur potentias Domini:* † *auditas faciet* (—) *omnes laudes ejus?* 3. *Beati qui custodiunt judicium,* † *et faciant justitiam* (—) *in omni tempore.* 4. *Memento nostri, Domine, in beneplacito populi tui:* † *visita nos in salutari tuo.*

1. *Give glory to the Lord, for he is good:* † *and forever* (—) *endureth his mercy.* 2. *Who shall declare the powers of the Lord:* † *who shall set forth* (—) *all his praises?* 3. *Blessed are they that keep judgement,* † *and do justice* (—) *at all times,* 4. *Remember us, O Lord, in the favor of thy people:* † *visit us with thy salvation.*

The Gospel, which contains the episode of the Transfiguration, comes as an answer to the final petition of the Tract. And at the consecration and in Communion the salvation of God descends upon us.

OFFERTORY (Ps. 118: 47, 48)

1. *Meditabor in mandatis tuis, quae dilexi valde:* 2. *et levabo manus meas ad mandata tua, quae dilexi.*

1. *I will meditate on thy commandments, which I have loved exceedingly:* 2. *and I will lift up my hands to thy commandments, which I have loved.*

Diléxi with its lightly moving torculus dominates the melodic line and colors the entire piece. Now we hear a song of love, which by love alone can be fully grasped. For he only can love commandments to whom the command is an expression of the will of the beloved, who makes it his care to fulfill all the desires of the beloved, for whom—as it was with the Saviour—it is a joy to do at all times that which is most pleasing to the Father. Such is the conviction here expressed. Another thought may be added: the commandments lead us higher, away from the mean things of this earth, up to the Tabor of union with God. Thus the commandments establish the peace of the heart—indeed, even the temporal welfare of nations. We shall, then, meditate on Thy commandments and stretch forth our hands to fulfill them with all fidelity.

The piece begins like the pealing of bells. In some places the church bells have the tones of these first four or six notes. The motive over *in mandátis* runs through the whole. It occurs over *et levábo, manus meas,* and *ad mandáta*. The three-note groups in the second half of the first phrase tend to enhance the elevated feeling of the piece.

The second phrase is divided in the same manner as the first. Here also the second half sets in on the dominant. Before it, however, the melody makes a pronounced modulation to the second under the tonic, a figure appearing quite frequently in the second mode. The second *diléxi* has no addition in the text, like the first. But it seems that the extended melody says more here than the simple *valde*. It sings of the rest and the happiness of the soul which willingly bears the sweet yoke of the Lord. The second group repeats the motive over *(me)-as*. Now follow two groups corresponding to one another. Everything must be light and tender and fragrant.

The Gospel closed with the words: "This is my beloved Son...hear ye Him." The Offertory is the song of those fortunates who hear the word of God and do it. Still closer is the connection between the Gospel and the Offertory of the preceding Wednesday. There the Gospel reads thus: "Whosoever shall do the will of My Father that is in heaven, he is My brother, and sister, and mother."

COMMUNION (Ps. 5: 2, 4)

1. *Intellige clamorem meum: intende voci orationis meae, Rex meus et Deus meus:* 2. *quoniam ad te orabo, Domine.*

1. *Understand my cry: hearken to the voice of my prayer, O my King and my God:* 2. *for to thee will I pray, O Lord.*

After the Mass I must again descend from the Tabor of union with God to the affairs of workaday life, from the brilliant heights, where it was so good to be, to the darkness of this world with its dangers, its scandals, its temptations, and its sufferings. Stay Thou with me, O Lord, for the night cometh. With its broad *podatus*, its lingering on the dominant, and the stressing of *b*, this song prays almost with violent outbursts. How different is this beginning, compared to the simple *Reminíscere* of today's Introit! *Inténde*, parallel to *Intélligs*, is simpler; for this reason *voci oratiónis* receives so much more prominence.

We pray to the King. On Tabor He manifested His royal dignity. His countenance shone like the sun, His garments became white as snow, and the Covenant of the Old Law paid homage to Him. But this transfigured King is now *my* King, my God in Holy Communion. From *Deus meus* on, the melody with its two- and three-note groups becomes more serene.

In the second phrase composure gives place to confidence. *Orábo* is an evident lifting of the soul to God. With tender sequences and a rhythm corresponding to that of the first phrase the whole comes to a close.

*   *   *   *

THIRD SUNDAY OF LENT

INTROIT (Ps. 24: 15, 16)

1. *Oculi mei semper ad Dominum, quia ipse evellet de laqueo pedes meos*: 2. *respice in me, et miserere mei,* 3. *quia unicus et pauper sum ego.* Ps. *Ad te Domine levavi animam meam:* * *Deus meus in te confido, non erubescam.*

1. *My eyes are towards the Lord, for He shall pluck my feet out of the snare*: 2. *look thou upon me, and have mercy on me,* 3. *for I am alone and poor.* Ps. *To thee, O Lord, have I lifted up my soul:* * *in thee, O my God, I put my trust, let me not be ashamed.*

In the Rome of the early Christian centuries the solemn services on the third Sunday of Lent were held in the Church of St. Lawrence. There the Christians gathered and, especially on Sundays, thanked God for the grace of Baptism and the sonship of God, which they attained through it. Thither also came the catechumens, those who sought Baptism. At the church of the deacon St. Lawrence, their patron, they were examined today, and on seven other days of Lent, about the doctrine they had studied, and inquiry was made into their manner of life. For this reason, also, the present Sunday was called the Sunday of scrutinies, of examinations. Prayers were said over the catechumens and the first exorcism performed in order to destroy the power of the devil in their souls.

Hence the composer of this Introit was concerned in a special manner to give prominent expression to one word, the word which predominates over the rest of the antiphon: *evéllet*—He liberates me, plucks my foot from the snare, frees me. Whatever of consolation and joy (a joy like that of Easter) this word contained, was to penetrate into the heart of the catechumens; at the same time it was to arouse a vehement longing for happiness, for the freedom of the children of God. *Evéllet* takes the part of a leitmotif, receiving a wonderful development especially in today's Gospel. However great Satan's power may be, a superior power will take the field against him. Christ will conquer him, will cast him out from the souls of men and despoil him of the weapons in which he had placed his trust. Thus prays the Introit: *Oculi mei*— my eyes are ever fixed upon the Lord. Text and melody exhibit a pleasing, symmetric construction.

In the first part we look up to God; in the second we beg Him graciously to look down upon us. Each part, in its second phrase, adduces a reason. "My eyes are towards the Lord," *quia*... "for He shall pluck my feet out of the snare;" in the second part: "look Thou upon me," *quóniam*... "for I am alone and poor." In the first phrase, the melody, corresponding to its text, tends upward: *Oculi mei*...and especially *evéllet*. In the second phrase we must regard it as more than mere coincidence that there are four descending fourths over the petition: Look Thou upon me.

Oculi, setting in with an interval of a fifth, reminds us of the first word of the Introit for the third Mass of Christmas, *Puer*. The melody over *me* is also known to us from the same Introit. There it occurs over the word *nobis*. Similarly the close: *sum ego*, sounds like that of the Christmas Introit over *Angelus*. Then, like *impérium* in the Christmas melody, *evéllet* ascends to high *f*. In the present Introit, however, the development is more ornate, it is drawn on a grander scale, and the accents with the frequent *pressus* forms are more energetic.

With unflinching eye the singer gazes upward to God. This is shown not only by the protraction of the dominant, but especially by the annotated manuscript reaching back as far as the tenth century. Over *semper* they demand a broad rendition of all the notes—a valuable psychological indication. We meet the cadence of *Dóminum* again at the end of the second part over *únicus*, and in a somewhat extended form over *(miserére) mei*. The unsatisfactory cadence at the close of the first part would lead us to expect a continuation.

The second part, *réspice*—"look upon me"—is melodically more tender, more fervent, more suppliant, but its range is less extended. *Réspice* still has a range of a sixth *(g–e)*; the subsequent members of the phrase, however, confine themselves to a fifth *(f–c)*. The harsh tritone over *pauper* agrees well with the subdued feeling.

In the psalm-verse a light secondary accent on the third syllable further increases the rest and the rhythmic clearness. Thus, after the introductory formula over *Ad*, quiet two-note groups follow. In the second half of the verse the significant little word *te* "(in *Thee* ...I put

my trust") must not be neglected; still the flow of the whole must not
be interrupted by it.

If, in the first place, the Church prayed in the stead of those who
are preparing for Baptism, she has to pray for many today who after
Baptism have again become the prey of the devil, who have again strayed
into his snares, from which they cannot or will not liberate themselves.
From our own experience we know that he does not very readily resign
his domination over a man; that, like a spider, he spins his webs, employing our evil propensities and the seductions of the world to ensnare us.
We are well aware of the difficulty of the struggle and the extent of our
weakness. This calls for much and fervent prayer; we must fix our eyes
on the Lord *(Oculi mei semper ad Dóminum)*, we must implore Him to
look down upon us in his mercy.

GRADUAL (Ps. 9: 20, 4

1. *Exsurge Domine, non prae-*
valeat homo: 2. *judicentur gentes in*
conspectu tuo. ℣. 1. *In convertendo*
inimicum meum retrorsum, 2. *in-*
firmabuntur, et peribunt a facie tua.

1. *Arise, O Lord, let not man pre-*
vail: 2. *let the gentiles be judged in*
thy sight. ℣. 1. *When mine enemies*
shall be turned back, 2. *they shall*
be weakened and perish before thy
face.

In every instance, the final syllable of each part has a very florid
melody, two of which are the same: *tuo* and *tua*. Extended rhythms,
therefore, bring both these parts to a close. Perhaps the similarity of
the thought expressed by the text must be assigned for the correspondence: *in conspéctu tuo* and *a fácie tua*=in Thy sight. Smaller rhythms
close the first half of each phrase in the first part. *Dómine* and *gentes*
correspond. After this descent, the second part opens each phrase a
fourth higher. (Cf. the rule for the adaptation of phrases.)

The prayer for divine assistance in the fight becomes still more
urgent here than in the Introit. Man, the evil in man, and the evil one,
must not carry away the victory. We sang the first five words at the close
of the Gradual for Septuagesima Sunday, but with another melody.
Homo alone in both cases preserves some similarity. In plain song it
makes a world of difference in the melodic development whether there
is question of the beginning of a piece or of a phrase working toward a
close. In the first instance the passage shows great agitation, while we
begin the second quietly. This song is the continuation of the verses
from Psalm 9, which itself finds a continuation on the Saturday after
the fourth Sunday in Lent. In mode, style, and text, these three pieces
form one whole, pointing perhaps still to that time when, according to

the testimony of St. Augustine (fifth century), an entire psalm was sung after the Lesson. In any case, this practice did not extend much beyond the eighth century, for some of the manuscripts of the period, as those of Rheinau and Monza, already show the Gradual as consisting only of the *corpus* and the verse.

After beginning with the typical forms, the melody develops itself in an independent manner. For *homo* the annotated manuscript of the tenth and eleventh centuries demand a broad rendition of all the notes, save the first *c*. This gives the melody a serious, almost violent, ring. In the Epistle St. Paul had said: "You were heretofore darkness, but now light in the Lord." This melody impresses the sentiment strongly upon us: Do not again become darkness; do not again subject yourself to the yoke of the prince of darkness! *Non praeváleat homo*! Between the passages *judicéntur* and *in conspéctu*, melodically alike, a rhythm to *Dómine* interposes itself over *gentes*.

The verse is a song of thanksgiving for divine help already granted, and thus anticipates the fulfillment of the preceding petition.

As compared with the *corpus*, the melody of the verse shows an amplification. Several times it extends to high *e*. Over *retrórsum* the florid melisma has a victorious ring. A second and third time the motive over *fácie* is repeated. Before the third repetition, however, we find ascending groups in pleasing contrast. Whenever plain song repeats a motive, it generally introduces it differently with the third repetition, or gives it a different ending.

In the Gospel of this Sunday Christ shows Himself as the valiant Conqueror, who defends His house, His property, the human soul, against the attacks of the enemy.

TRACT (Ps. 121: 1, 3)

1. *Ad te leravi oculos meos, qui habitas in caelis.* 2. *Ecce sicut oculi serrorum in manibus dominorum suorum:* 3. *et sicut oculi ancillae in manibus dominae suae:* 4. *ita oculi nostri ad Dominum Deum nostrum,* * *donec misereatur nostri.* 5. *Miserere nobis, Domine, miserere nobis.*

1. *To thee have I lifted up mine eyes who dwellest in heaven.* 2. *Behold, as the eyes of servants are on the hands of their masters:* 3. *and as the eyes of the handmaid are on the hands of her mistress:* 4. *so are our eyes unto the Lord our God,* * *until He has mercy on us.* 5. *Have mercy on us, O Lord, have mercy on us.*

From the Introit to the Tract our sentiments of prayer become more and more fervent. *Oculi mei*—"My eyes are ever on the Lord:" thus begins the Introit. The Tract continues to pray earnestly. In the two-fold *miserére* at the end, its sighs attain their summit. The Gospel assures us that this prayer was not in vain. In the healing of the possessed dumb man God's affection and power manifest themselves to us in a marvelous manner.

One might be tempted to regard the ascending line over *ad te levávi* as word-painting, referring it to the raising of the eyes to God. Since, however, the Tract *Qui séminant* of the Mass *Intret* for several martyrs employs the same tone-sequence with another text, it will be well to be careful and conservative with one's explanations. In general Tracts seldom touch the domain of expressive music.

The second and third verses have the same melody, though a somewhat simpler form. It never extends beyond *c*. These two verses may be sung somewhat more softly, to be followed by the fourth and fifth verse in a more lively style. This Tract reveals no regular construction. Only the fourth verse has the middle cadence, generally employed in each verse, with its interval of a fourth, its *pressus*, and close on *f*; hence a full tone below the finale of the mode. *Oculos* and *óculi* in the first and fourth verses, on the contrary, speaking of the eyes of the servants and of the handmaid, have a descending line. In the second verse, and in the third, which sounds almost like it, the second last member closes on *f*, the last on *g*. Both notes exert an influence on the preceding neums; *f* demands *b♭*, while *g* calls for *b*. The typical Alleluia-melody of the eighth mode, that, for example, of the first Sunday of Advent, exhibits a similar structure at the end. The last verse harks back to the second and third verses, makes its petition tender and suppliant by stressing its *b♭*, and then renders it impressive by means of the threefold *clivis* and the accentuation of the fourth, the whole resembling a hurling motion. Codex 339 of St. Gall's gives these three clives in juxtaposition, while otherwise it carefully separates the individual neums which do not belong so closely together. Codex 121 of Einsiedeln places the letter "c" *(celeriter,* rapidly*)* over the first two clives. Every musician will know how to appreciate these indications.

OFFERTORY (Ps. 18: 9, 12)

1. *Justitiae Domini rectae, laetificantes corda,* 2. *et dulciora super mel et favum:* 3. *nam et servus tuus custodiet ea.*

1. *The justices of the Lord are right, rejoicing hearts,* 2. *and sweeter than honey and the honeycomb:* 3. *for thy servant will keep them.*

Even on the second Sunday of Lent the Church had lovingly sung of the Lord's commandments. But the sound of the Offertory of the third Sunday of Lent is still more sweet in the hearts of the faithful and in our hearts. It sings along serenely, not taking any audience into consideration; it rejoices in the revealed truth and is an expression of the soul's good fortune in being able to walk with simplicity and love in the ways of God. It is the song of a soul firmly grounded, of a soul that has tasted the sweetness of the Lord. It is like the morning prayer of a child, fresh as the dew, whose eyes reflect its innocence, and who has as yet no inkling of the world's wickedness and does not realize how bitter commerce with it may become.

The motive over *Dómine* runs through the entire piece. We hear it over *rectae*, and even before, over *justítiae*, then in *corda*, and beautifully expanded over *dulcióra*. The second phrase modulates to *c*, which is a fourth lower than the tonic. While the first and second phrases contented themselves with seconds and thirds, the third phrase also has fourths. Everything up to the last notes very evidently belongs to the sixth mode. Suddenly we meet with a surprising melodic turn. Now the passage *agfg gf* becomes *agf gfe e*. Occasionally the masters of polyphony also close with an unexpected key, as is shown by some of Schubert's songs. In itself there is nothing peculiar about the ending on *e*. In this, or in a somewhat expanded form, it frequently occurs in pieces of the fourth mode, for example, in the Gloria of the fourth Mass. In that selection, however, sixteen preceding phrases end on *e*. But here final *e* for the first time comes at the very end. That is the striking feature. After the bright, open melody of the sixth mode it comes as a question, a slight doubt. Is what you say true? Will you remain faithful? Will you be of the number of those whom the Lord in today's Gospel calls blessed because they hear the word of God and keep it? In the Gospel of the present Sunday the Blessed Virgin is set before you as a model. She deserves the encomium, for she was privileged to bear in her womb the Saviour, the Word of God, but still more because no one else heard and observed God's word as she did. Will you keep your promise? In today's Mass formulary the Missal has a decided and clear *custódit*: Thy servant *keepeth* Thy commandments. In the earlier editions of the *Liber Gradualis* (1883 and 1895), published under the supervision of Dom Pothier, the Offertory patently closed with the sixth mode: *agf agf f*, as did also the Medicean edition. The older reading, however, demands *custódiet*: He *will keep* them, is determined to keep them. And the old melody, closing on the half tone, is far removed from victorious certainty. It sounds like a fervent petition: Lord, give me the strength for it through Thy holy Sacrifice.

In the psalm and in the text of the Missal before the words *et judícia tua* we find the strange neuter form *dulcióra*: Thy judgements are sweeter than honey.

COMMUNION (Ps. 83: 4, 5)

1. *Passer invenit sibi domum, et turtur nidum, ubi reponat pullos suos: 2. altaria tua Domine virtutum, Rex meus, et Deus meus: 3. beati qui habitant in domo tua, in saeculum saeculi laudabant te.*

1. *The sparrow hath found herself a house, and the turtle a nest, where she may lay her young ones: 2. thine altars, O Lord of hosts, my King, and my God: 3. blessed are they that dwell in thy house, they shall praise thee for ever and ever.*

The Communion offers modal peculiarities. First it closes on *a*, showing that it is transposed. But now the question might arise whether it is a transposition of a fifth or a fourth—actually it is a transposition of a fifth. Over the closing note is a full step and a minor third. A fourth lower, this would result in *e f♯ g e e*, impossible to plainsong notation. A fifth lower, however, it becomes *d e f d d*—the closing formula of the first mode. The reason for the transposition lies with *pullos*. A fifth lower it would demand an *e♭: f e♭ g f f g d d*. The ancient plainsong notation however, found it impossible to write *e♭*, but could quite easily transpose a fifth higher to *b♭*.

Futhermore, the third and first modes are fused here. The intonation of *passer* and the melody over *virtútum* point to the third mode. The closing cadence of the third mode, *ccc a c b a*, corresponds to *c b a* over *(vir)-tútum*. From *Deus meus* on the piece moves in the first mode. *Rex meus* contracts its interval over *(De)-us meus*. Here follows a modulation to the full tone below the tonic, much affected by the first mode.

The antiphonal chants for the third Sunday of Lent exhibit various forms of modulation. The Introit in the seventh mode modulated to the full tone below the finale after the *f* over *miserére mei*; we find the same in the Tract of the eighth mode after the *f* over *nostrum*. The Communion of the first mode also modulates to the full tone below the finale over *Deus meus*, and the Offertory, really in the sixth mode, modulates to the fourth below the finale over *favum*. Each time the modulation agrees with a break in the text, therefore in the thought.

In the three phrases of this piece there is mention of a threefold kingdom. The first speaks of the realm of Nature, of the birds and the nests in which they harbor their young. We are struck by the numerous *podatus* forms, which may, in the composer's mind, indicate the fluttering of birds. That which is expressed pictorially in the first phrase, in the second becomes a reality, even though mysteriously, in the realm of mystery, in the kingdom of grace. From the altar and its Mystery flow the strength by which the Lord of hosts—the melody stresses this word —becomes our King, our God. There the soul has found her earthly home; there she is harbored safely and securely; thence she draws a marvelous fecundity. Such was the yearning of the catechumens: to be privileged to draw nigh to the altar. And the penitents, who had to remain outside the church during Lent, how will they envy the good fortune of those who come out with the Saviour in their heart! The third phrase refers to the kingdom of glory, to the house of God, where we shall sing praises for a blessed eternity. How luminous the melody here is! There we shall sing Alleluia in unending Paschal joy. There we shall forever sing our joyous thanksgiving for the boon God has bestowed upon us; for now *evéllet* of the Introit has become full reality. There we shall sing an everlasting *Redemisti nos*—Thou hast redeemed us with Thy blood; our soul has escaped like a bird from the snares of the fowler: the snare is torn and we are freed. For this happiness the Mysteries of the altar are to prepare us. Holy Communion gives us the strength requisite to attain eternal glory. Our praying and singing in the house of God is a preparation for that more sublime song of eternity. May God's merciful love one day bring us all together in that celestial choir!

*   *   *   *

FOURTH SUNDAY OF LENT

Even more than on the second Sunday of Advent (q.v.), the station "at the church of the Holy Cross in Jerusalem," in which the solemn services were conducted at Rome, has determined the selection of the liturgical texts of today's Mass. All the chants contain allusions to Sion or Jerusalem. Only the Offertory in its present form is an exception.

INTROIT (Is. 66: 10, 11)

1. *Laetare Jerusalem: et conventum facite omnes qui diligitis eam:* 2. *gaudete cum laetitia, qui in tristitia fuistis:* 3. *ut exsultetis, et satiemini ab uberibus consolationis vestrae.* Ps. *Laetatus sum in his quae dicta sunt mihi:* * *in domum Domini ibimus.*

1. *Rejoice, O Jerusalem, and come together all you that love her:* 2. *rejoice with joy, you that have been in sorrow:* 3. *that you may exult, and be filled from the breasts of your consolation.* Ps. *I rejoiced at the things that were said to me:* * *We shall go into the house of the Lord.*

The liturgy of this Sunday's Mass is the spring of the Easter liturgy, the anticipation of Easter joy. The same melodies which close the ardently longed-for Alleluia on Holy Saturday *(g c a b a a g)*, today, like true overtures, begin the Mass *(f bb g a ǵ f)*. The joy of motherhood, which the Church will experience at the baptism of so many new children, gives this song its bright and festal character. She anticipates their happiness in the possession of true freedom, and in the fulfillment of their desires through Christ. It is as if the Lenten season and penitential sorrow had already disappeared; as if the unrest brought about by doubts concerning the faith, and disquietude *(tristítia)*, as also the sorrows occasioned by the necessities of this present life, had long been overcome; it appears as if that blessed time in which God will dry away all tears had already dawned—when we shall be permitted to enter the Father's house and drink of the cup of solace.

The joys here portrayed are of various intensities. At *gaudéte* this joy is rather subdued, at *laetáre* it tends toward fuller expression, and at *exsultétis* it attains a glorious climax. But even here the melody observes a restraint peculiar to liturgical hymns. It contends itself with the range of a seventh.

Laetáre has *bb* for its highest note; this will dominate the third member of the first sentence. *Jerúsalem* has as its highest note *c*, upon which the second member of the sentence supports itself. The *clivis* on the last syllable of *Laetáre* is to be extended somewhat. The *convéntum fácite* is almost like the ringing of bells. It may also be interpreted as the far-reaching sound of the herald's proclamation. We meet it again on the first Sunday after Pentecost in *et pauper sum ego*. The first sentence closes with quiet sequences.

The second sentence introduces a new summons to joy. The final cadence of the solemn tone of the lesson, *é g á f*, is beautifully continued over *cum laetítia*. Between the similar forms over *(tristí)-tia* and *(fu)-istis*, which are characterized by the melancholic effect of the repeated *bb*, there is placed on the first syllable of this word an energetic *b*.

The third sentence returns to the solemn tone of the first sentence and even amplifies it. The vivid *exsultétis* closes with the dominant, while a tristropha prepares for the brilliantly executed *satiémini*: "you shall be filled," you shall drink to satiety from the streams of eternal bliss. The word closes with a kind of modulation in A minor *(a b a)*, which renders the second part of the sentence with its recurring *bb* all the more effective. The broad intervals, fourths and fifths, also indicate the fullness of consolation; but this is achieved most effectively by the rich final cadence which rhymes with the first sentence. This, as well as the melody over *convéntum fácite*, might readily be written to five-eighths time. The final syllable of *ubéribus* is rendered softly. The execution should bring out the sweetness of divine consolation.

Where so much joy and happiness await us we cannot but join with all our heart in the sentiment of the verse of the psalm: *Laetátus sum*. That is the answer to the *Laetáre* of the antiphon.

N. Sch., 77; K.K., 24, 29 ff.; Analyses, I, 12 ff.; Rass. gr., 9, 5 ff.; Caecilia, 29, 20 f.

GRADUAL (Ps. 121: 1, 7)

1. *Laetatus sum in his quae dicta sunt mihi.* 2. *In domum Domini ibimus.* ℣. 1. *Fiat pax in virtute tua:* 2. *Et abundantia in turribus tuis.*

1. I rejoiced at the things that were said to me: 2. We shall go into the house of the Lord. ℣. 1. Let peace be in thy strength: 2. And abundance in thy towers.

The *corpus* has the same text as the psalm-verse of the Introit. The melodic style, however, is very different. The psalm-verse of the Introit carries only one note over each syllable of the text, and accordingly remains purely syllabic. The Gradual, however, practically throughout carries groups of notes over each syllable of the text. The Introit verse is composed according to a fixed formula, which remains the same in all Introit psalm-verses of the fifth mode, regardless of the content and sentiment of the text. Graduals as a rule, make use of a variety of formulas and are, therefore, essentially embellishing music. Today, however, the number of typical formulas is almost negligible, and consequently we may consider it an original composition.

But also here psalmodic construction is evident:

Intonation	Middle Cadence (dominant)	Final Cadence (tonic)
Laetátus	*mihi*	*íbimus,*
Fiat	*pax*	*tua:*
	abundántia	*tuis.*

The first sentence of the *corpus* is an arsis conceived on a grand scale. The middle cadence contains a pleasant undulation. The second sentence is a thesis and a return to the tonic. This made possible a bright development of the verse. Actually, it contains a petition: *Fiat*—"may it come to pass." What we hear, however, is not a petition and supplication, but a portrayal of interior and exterior joy, and a cheerful thanksgiving for these gifts. As to melody, two sentences are to be distinguished: *Fiat pax* brings the same rich middle cadence as *sunt mihi* above, with the exception that the word *pax*, so full of meaning, is brought into prominence more plastically and brilliantly. At *tua* the melody returns again to the fundamental of the mode. The second sentence is built up in a similar way. The middle cadence, however, contains a significant extension here. The larger intervals and the tarrying on the high seventh above the fundamental seem to try to give expression to the abundant fullness of blessing.

The desire of the singer is the attainment of peace and prosperity; for peace without prosperity is quiet misery, and prosperity without peace is unenjoyable happiness, as St. Chrysostom says. In the mouth of the Israelites, returning from exile, this psalm was a jubilant greeting to Sion. Peace has again entered the hearts of many during these holy weeks before Easter. They have gone into the house of the Lord, and God with His grace has again entered into their hearts. They have been filled with divine consolation in the reception of Holy Communion.

The Gradual is a preparation for the Gospel of this Sunday, which recounts the miraculous multiplication of the loaves, is a preparation for the institution of the Holy Eucharist and its never-failing peace. We hear it again in the votive Mass for peace.

TRACT (Ps. 124: 1, 2)

1. *Qui confidunt in Domino sicut mons Sion: † non commovebitur in aeternum, † qui habitat in Jerusalem. 2. Montes in circuitu ejus: † et Dominus in circuitu populi sui, † ex hoc nunc et usque in saeculum.*

1. *They that trust in the Lord shall be as Mount Sion: † he shall not be moved for ever † that dwelleth in Jerusalem. 2. Mountains are round about it: † so the Lord is round about His people, † from henceforth now and forever.*

The intervals of fourths over *montes* endeavor to picture for us the jagged mountains. Over *sui* we meet an easily recognizable form of what Ernst Kurth, in his *Grundlagen des linearen Kontrapunktes* (pp. 26 ff.), calls "*Schleuderbewegung.*" We receive the impression that there is a gathering and concentration of forces in preparation for the leap of the interval. Codex 339 of St. Gall's here uses only light neums to be sung straight on, evidently requiring a fluent and impelling rendition, reminiscent of the preparatory twirls of a sling.

OFFERTORY (Ps. 134: 3, 6)

1. *Laudate Dominum quia benignus est: 2. psallite nomini ejus quoniam suavis est: 3. omnia quaecumque voluit, fecit in caelo et in terra.*

1. *Praise ye the Lord, for he is good: 2. sing ye to his Name, for he is sweet: 3. whatsoever he pleased, he hath done in heaven and on earth.*

The introductory word *Laudáte* is significant from a twofold consideration: on account of its rich melody and its extended range. Both these elements, however, are lacking as the melody progresses. It never passes beyond the range of a fifth. It would seem that it was not so much the thought of singing and playing for God that occupied the mind of the author, but rather this thought: "God is good." In a similar manner does he emphasize, with almost the same melodic turn, the thought: "sweet is His name" after the motive over *psállite* in the Introit of the first Christmas Mass. It is this thought that gives the chant its sweet and restful character. It governs also the third sentence, which treats of the omnipotence of God. A modulation to the full step below the tonic closes the second sentence. Then *ómnia* rises up solemply, and we expect a development, but the repetitions over *vóluit, fecit,* and over *caelo et in terra,* which are enlivened only by fourths, preserve the quiet character. No boisterous song which might arouse the listeners should be allowed here. It is a quiet song, a joyful prayer of thanksgiving for the goodness of God manifested in the miracle of the multiplication of the loaves (Gospel) and in the miracle of the Eucharist which is continually being performed.

The Offertory is the only chant of today's Mass that does not contain an allusion to Jerusalem. Formerly, however, it contained more verses, the last of which runs thus: "Ye that fear the Lord, praise the Lord. Praised be the Lord of Sion, who dwelleth in Jerusalem." It was this concluding word that carried an unusually rich melody.

COMMUNION (Ps. 21: 3, 4)

1. *Jerusalem, quae aedificatur ut civitas, cujus participatio ejus in idipsum*: 2. *illuc enim ascenderunt tribus, tribus Domini, ad confitendum nomini tuo, Domine.*

1. *Jerusalem which is built as a city, which is compact together*: 2. *for thither did the tribes go up, the tribes of the Lord, to praise thy name, O Lord.*

The word *Jerúsalem* is treated with evident affection. Hence, whenever any certain tone is prolonged and the melody lingers about it, it conveys the picture of a well-grounded city, or at least suggests such an image. The brilliantly aspiring melody which follows, however, stresses the point that more important than these external advantages are the spiritual benefits which this city of peace imparts to its inhabitants. The climax of the entire piece comes at the words *illic enim ascendérunt tribus* with a melody full of sweet harmony, and an excellent expansion of the motives of *ejus in idípsum*. In the Rome of the Middle Ages, as Grisar *(Das Missale,* p. 46*)* says, "even the ascent to today's station church 'in Jerusalem' was a reality, since it went from the Lateran down into a valley, then higher up again. Even today, despite the filling in of the lower parts of this valley, this is still discernible from the course of the old city walls which are found at that place." The purpose of the rising melody, however, is not only to portray. It rings out like the echo of the joyful songs that the Israelites, dressed for the solemn occasion, sang on their pilgrimage to Jerusalem; or like an anticipation of the songs that came from the hearts of the catechumens, when, on the night before Easter, vested in their white robes—the symbol of purity of heart—they were permitted to go up to the altar from the baptistry in order to take part in the sacrificial banquet *(participátio)*.

In the Epistle of this Sunday St. Paul speaks about the heavenly Jerusalem. Thither, to our true home, we all direct our pilgrimage. There we shall find brothers and sisters who know themselves intimately united with us. And all of us have communion with them (that is how we may translate the words: *cujus participátio)*. The bread of life is our viaticum. Therefore bravely on toward the eternal Easter, to never-ending joy, to the never-ceasing praise of God. When next the solemn services shall be held at the "Holy Cross in Jerusalem," Good Friday, with its deeply impressive honoring of the holy cross and its lovable dwelling on the wounds and the love of Christ, will have come. At that time, too, the Church will emphasize the fact that through the cross alone has joy come over the whole world. The joys that run through the present Sunday also flow from the cross of Christ, as does all peace and happiness.

*   *   *   *

PASSION SUNDAY

INTROIT (Ps. 42: 1, 2)

1. *Judica me, Deus, et discerne causam meam de gente non sancta*: 2. *ab homine iniquo et doloso eripe me: quia tu es Deus meus, et fortitudo mea.* Ps. *Emitte lucem tua et veritatem tuam:* * *ipsa me deduxerunt, et adduxerunt in montem sanctum tuum, et in tabernacula tua.*

1. *Judge me, O God, and distinguish my cause from the nation that is not holy*: 2. *from the unjust and deceitful man deliver me: for thou art my God and my strength.* Ps. *Send forth thy light and thy truth:* * *they have conducted me, and brought me unto thy holy hill, and unto thy tabernacles.*

The forty-second psalm, from which these words are taken, forms a part of the preliminary prayers of the Mass, on account of its verse: "I will go unto the altar of God, to God who giveth joy to my youth." But even before it was used for this purpose it was sung on the present Sunday. We are reminded of this old custom when today, and on the following days until Holy Saturday exclusive, this psalm is not said at the foot of the altar lest it be said twice—by the priest and choir.

If we permit the melody to work on us, or even if we merely glance at the notation, one phrase immediately draws our attention. It is *éripe me*—"deliver me!" It is the cry of a heavily oppressed heart. How effective must it have been formerly, when after each verse of the psalm, the antiphon and with it this cry of affliction was heard. Along with it, the second thought of this Introit was stressed, the thought of trust: "For Thou art my God and my strength." But the entire melodic development works up to a climax with *éripe me*.

Who is it that prays thus? Since today is Passion Sunday, our first thought is that it is Christ Himself. Today's Epistle tells of Him that He offered Himself as a spotless victim to the Father by the Holy Ghost. No doubt, the words or thoughts of this Introit belonged to that Introit, that introductory prayer, with which our dear Lord and Saviour began His Passion on Mount Olivet. He sees Himself betrayed by Judas, "the unjust and deceitful man;" he sees Himself before a tribunal, verily before a "nation that is not holy." How must His inner Self have cried to the Father: *Júdica me*—"Judge me, O God, and distinguish my cause:" *éripe me*—"deliver me!" Apparently this appeal is not heard, nor the prayer: *émitte lucem tuam*—"Send forth Thy light," for darkness covered the face of the earth when the Jews crucified the Lord. He prays: "Send forth . . . Thy truth;" but will have to cry: "My God, My God, why hast Thou forsaken Me?" And yet God was His God and His strength. The Easter sun will come to dispel the darkness of Calvary. And Golgotha, in spite of its tragedy, was a holy mount and the anteroom to the sublime tabernacle of glory. And the first song of the risen Christ is a song of praise to the Father for His fidelity: "I arose, and am still with Thee."

As Christ prays so the Church prays, for she is one with Him. Thus also does the individual Christian soul pray. Only too frequently we perceive ourselves to be an unholy nation, an unjust and deceitful man that would delude us, deceive us, and turn us away from truth and fidelity. The more we enter into ourselves by a searching self-examination, the more fervently shall we cry to our God and our strength: *éripe me*—"deliver me!"

But we also know that in the mystery of the holy Mass God's light shines before our eyes and His fidelity reveals itself. Here we are upon His holy mountain, in His tabernacle; we approach closely to Him. He enters into our soul with His light and His truth.

The first and third phrases have the same ending, while the second has a similar close a fifth higher over *(éri)-pe me*. Thus the whole is varied and rounded out. There is some resemblance between the first half of the first two phrases and the second half of the third phrase. The seconds and the minor third in the first phrase begin apathetically. But already *causam meam* betrays inner agitation. The sorrow, thus far concealed with difficulty, comes to the surface in the second phrase with gathering force. "From the unjust and deceitful man deliver me!" With *a, bb, b, c,* the melody works up to *d.* This results quite naturally in a forceful *crescendo.* In the annotated manuscript of the tenth and eleventh centuries the third phrase is introduced with great delicacy of feeling with broad notes, over which is placed "t" *(tenére,* to hold*).* Thus impressiveness is added to the subsequent assertion: "for Thou art my God and my strength." Similarly, on the final syllable of *fortitúdo,* "Thou art my strength," the same manuscripts have almost all the neums marked broadly.

GRADUAL (Ps. 142: 9, 10)

1. *Eripe me, Domine, de inimicis meis:* 2. *doce me facere voluntatem tuam.* ℣. 1. *Liberator meus, Domine, de gentibus iracundis:* 2. *ab insurgentibus in me exaltabis me:* 3. *a viro iniquo eripies me.*

1. *Deliver me from mine enemies, O Lord:* 2. *teach me to do thy will.* ℣. 1. *Thou art my deliverer, O Lord, from the angry nations:* 2. *thou wilt lift me up above them that rise up against me:* 3. *from the unjust man thou wilt deliver me.*

The Gradual continues the principal petitions of the Introit. Both cry out: *éripe me;* both speak of the unjust man *(hómine iníquo, viro iníquo).* Whereas the Introit had prayed: "Send forth Thy light," the Gradual implores the Lord thus: "Teach me to do Thy will." Both are filled with an unshakable confidence. *Deus meus, et fortitúdo mea* of the Introit corresponds to *liberátor meus* in the Gradual. In the *corpus* we find more supplication: *éripe me,* while the verse is more expressive of confidence: "Thou wilt lift up; Thou wilt deliver me." Melodically, also, the verse represents an increase, as is the case in most Graduals.

The melody belongs to the third mode, which is employed in nine different Graduals in the period from Septuagesima Sunday to the Tuesday in Holy Week, while during the entire remaining part of the liturgical year it occurs only nine times in all. It is composed of varying formulas, which are adapted in various groupings over different texts. We have, therefore, to do here with a typical melody, and hence are not so much concerned with interpretation of the text as with its embellishment. Upon closer inspection, however, several peculiarities may be noted, among them the plaintive closing motive *b a g a f f e,* which occurs over *fácere, iracúndis, in me, iníquo,* and *(erípies) me.* Above all, however, the passage over a *viro iníquo* produces a striking effect. The beginning bears some resemblance to that of the third Sunday of Lent. *Meis* and *tuam* with their florid cadences divide the *corpus* into two distinct phrases. The latter gave a corresponding ending to the *corpus* and verse on the third Sunday of Lent. The verse has three phrases. In many passages the old dominant of the third mode *(b)* is still plainly discernible. At the beginning of the verse, *c b c d a* must be regarded as an arsis; that which follows as thesis. The third member begins here with a contraction of the second member and then repeats the thesis like motive of the first member.

(Cf. the Gradual for Quinquagesima Sunday.)

TRACT (Ps. 128: 1, 4)

1. *Saepe expugnaverunt me a juventute mea.* 2. *Dicat nunc Israel:* † *saepe expugnaverunt me* (—) *a juventute mea.* 3. *Etenim non potuerunt mihi:* † *supra dorsum meum* (—) *fabricaverunt peccatores.* 4. *Prolongaverunt iniquitatem sibi:* † *Dominus justus concidet* (—) *cervices peccatorum.*

1. *Often have they fought against me from my youth.* 2. *Let Israel now say:* † *Often have they fought against me* (—) *from my youth.* 3. *But they could not prevail over me:* † *upon my back* (—) *the wicked have wrought.* 4. *They have lengthened their iniquities:* † *the Lord, who is just, will cut* (—) *the necks of the sinners.*

In every instance the beginning of the verses is different. Special attention should be paid to that of the first and second verses. To look upon the florid melody over *saepe* as mere word-painting, representing frequency, would indeed betray a too superficial understanding: for if one remarks how the annotated manuscript, for example Codex 121 of Einsiedeln, give a broad form to almost every note, how each of the descending thirds is marked with an episeme and besides this also with "t" *(tenére,* to hold*)*, the thought suggests itself that the singer was casting a glance backward over all the struggles that had broken in upon him and was reliving all the hard and bitter things they had brought to him, and in this mood had sung this heavy melody. Similarly, the second verse with its threefold "x" *(exspectáre,* to wait*)* after three groups of notes, with a broad construction over the last four notes, which moreover are marked with "t", seems to reveal a similar feeling. After these serious beginnings we soon meet frequent joyous passages, proper to Tract-melodies of the eighth mode. The fundamental thought of the entire piece is: *non potuérunt mihi,* which we should like to see given melodic prominence rather than the second *mea.* The second last member closes on *f,* the last on *g.* Both notes influence the preceding neums: *f* demands *b♭,* while *g* calls for *b: cc ag a b♭ g f, a ca bg g aa g.* The typical Alleluia-melody of the eighth mode, sung, for example, on the first Sunday of Advent, has a similar closing formula. Toward the end, the first and third verses have an identical melody; the closing neums of the second verse also are alike. By the middle cadence with its modulation to *f,* the second verse is divided at *Israel,* the third at *mihi,* the fourth at *sibi.* With *dorsum meum* the word-accent is prepared by two neums, exactly as with *concídet,* and before the *expugnavérunt me.* Then the syllable after the accent dies away quietly. In the last verse we find a florid melisma over the accented syllable of *Prolongavérunt,* which also occurs over the second syllable of *étenim* at the beginning of the third verse. As happens frequently, plain song resolves the word *étenim* into its two constituent parts, *et†enim.*

The song marks the opening of the mighty struggle upon which Christ is now entering. From His youth, from His very childhood, He was harassed, so that He had to be saved by flight from His country. In the Gospel of Passion Sunday we hear again how His enemies intended to stone Him; indeed, they already had the stones in their hands. What means did they not employ to render Him and His work odious? How have not the wicked wrought upon His back at the scourging? How did they not lengthen their iniquities in that long night and on that terrible Good Friday? But they did not conquer Him. In spite of their machinations, Easter Day dawned. As He had been, so has His Church been worried from her youth, from the days of the first Pentecost, when the Apostles were scourged, to our own time. The Christians have been persecuted and slaughtered, churches and cloisters have fallen a prey to vandalism. The researches of so-called scholars and the intrigues of diplomats and statesmen have exerted all their powers against her. But *non potuérunt,* they were not able to overcome her. Christ has given His promise and will fulfill it to the end of days: and all the fury of hell shall not avail against her.

OFFERTORY (Ps. 118: 17, 107)

1. *Confitebor tibi, Domine, in toto corde meo:* 2. *retribue servo tuo: vivam, et custodiam sermones tuos:* 3. *vivifica me secundum verbum tuum, Domine.*

1. *I will confess to thee, O Lord with my whole heart:* 2. *render to thy servant: I shall live and keep thy words:* 3. *enliven me according to thy word, O Lord.*

This bright, joyous text of the antiphon—and verse which was attached to it in the most ancient manuscript—may surprise us on Passion Sunday. It does, indeed present petitions: "enliven me; incline my heart in Thy testimonies;" but the other thoughts predominate: "Thy judgements are delightful" *(jucúnda)*, and, with a florid melody, "I have loved Thy law." Thus this Offertory continues the thoughts of the second and third Sundays of Lent. We may point out that, from Passion Sunday on, the Missal does not stress the sufferings of Christ so much as does the Breviary in its hymns and antiphons. We never find somber tones exclusively in the Church's mourning. When she thinks of her beloved dead, she does not act like those who have no hope; she sees eternal light rising before them, and asks that this eternal light be theirs. And the most heartfelt sympathy with the sufferings of the Crucified One does not hinder her from singing of Christ's resurrection on Good Friday, and from singing of His cross: "For by the wood the whole world is filled with joy."

The Offertory bears some relation to the Gospel of the Sunday. Christ is accused by the Jews of having a demon; His enemies condemn Him as a blasphemer and therefore wish to stone Him. We, on the contrary, sing: "I will confess to Thee ... with my whole heart." In the Gospel Christ speaks: "Abraham your father rejoiced that he might see My day: he saw it [in spirit], and was glad." Abraham's longing and joy has been realized. The day of Christ has come. We see Him and experience His presence at every holy Mass. Hence the grateful words: "I will confess to Thee, O Lord, with my whole heart" (first phrase). The Saviour continues: "Amen, amen I say to you, if any man keep My word, he shall not see death for ever." This gives us an understanding of the solemn protestation of the Offertory: "I shall live and keep Thy words" (second phrase). But humbly and confidently we add: "Enliven me according to Thy word, O Lord" (third phrase).

The melody has a bright and joyous ring. It is characterized by symmetry and harmony. The first and third phrases have the same longer closing formula over *meo* and *Dómine*, while the second has it a minor third higher over *tuos*. These corresponding cadences give to the whole the qualities of song construction. In each case they already set in a fourth before the finale: over *(cor)-de* and *(tu)-um* with *g ff e (d)*, over *(sermó)-nes* with *b♭ a g (f)*. A trained ear will recognize a resolved F-major chord over *in to-(to)*, *-o vi-(vam)*, *et custó-(diam)*, *vivífica*, *verbum*. In other instances too this piece shows a predilection for small formulas: *tibi* and *toto* with a descending fourth, as also *Dómine, vivam, custó-(diam)*. The formula *g a f d f* over *(to)-to* likewise deserves mention;

it is repeated over *(retríbu)-e* and in a shortened form over *verbum* as *f g f d f.*

If we compare the three phrases of the piece, it can scarcely be asserted that any single one of them is more significant than the others or reveals a greater tension of soul. In this fact, from a purely artistic point of view, lies the defect of our present Offertory. The fact that the second and third phrases in each case set in with the closing note of the preceding phrase causes some monotony. The initial motive of the piece is found frequently; for example, in the Introits *Roráte* and *Gaudeámus,* and in the Offertory *Jubiláte.* In the second phrase the question arises whether or not a larger pause ought to be made after *servo tuo.* Generally we translate: "Render to Thy servant that I may live." This interpretation is corroborated by the manuscript of St. Gall's (339) and of Einsiedeln (121), which do not place an episeme over the last two notes of *tuo,* as is almost always done in similar passages. They intend, therefore, that *vivam* be added immediately. The melody as such, however, seems to demand a pause. Melodically, *vivam et custódiam* surely belong together. The passage over *sermónes tuos* frequently recurs in pieces of the fifth and sixth modes (cf. the Introit *Réquiem).* In the third phrase the cadence *secúndum* is somewhat disturbing, because it separates the preposition too much from its substantive, unless the rendition be a fluent one. So much the more pleasant is *vivífica* ("enliven me") and *verbum.* The latter is a happy continuation of *toto,* while *(retríbu)-e* may be looked upon as a contraction of that word. Compare also the melodic movement over *(in) me* in the verse of today's Gradul with *verbum.*

N. Sch., 232, 239 f.

COMMUNION (I Cor. 11: 24, 25)

1. *Hoc corpus, quod pro vobis tradetur: hic calix novi testamenti est in meo sanguine, dicit Dominus:* 2. *hoc facite, quotiescumque sumitis, in meam commemorationem.*

1. *This is my body which shall be delivered for you: this is the chalice of the new testament in my blood, saith the Lord:* 2. *this do as often as you receive it, in commemoration of me.*

Christ is Highpriest. He offered Himself to the Father as a spotless victim as He does today in the Mystery of holy Mass, and sings to Him a perfect song. With His own blood He accomplished the salvation of mankind on the wood of the cross, so that whence death came, thence also life might rise again (Preface of the Cross). He has won eternal redemption and eternal life, which He bestows upon all those who group themselves around Him in faith, who hear His word and keep it.

Some of the melody's peculiarities, no doubt, arise from its affinity to the Ambrosian Liturgy of Milan, where it is still sung today (*Rass. gr.*, 7, 506 ff.). But it has become much more effective in its Gregorian dress.

This song takes us into the midst of the scene of the Last Supper, at its most solemn moment. The words we hear are the most powerful heard since the creation of the world; words embodying in themselves wonder upon wonder, effecting the profoundest Mystery of the Holy Eucharist. Hence we may well expect that the plainsong melody has great things to tell. But it has still another characteristic. The frequent succession of three full tones, *f g a b* (tritone), ascending over *vobis tradétur* and over *calix novi*, and descending over *meo sánguine* and *meam commemoratiónem*, imparts to the song harsh, painful features. They seem to remind us of the Saviour's words on the eve of His passion, to re-create, as it were, the feelings which at that time filled His heart. Not only did He have a premonition of them, but He foresaw them most clearly, and felt beforehand all the tortures with which His body would be afflicted and with which His blood, establishing the New Covenant, would be shed. This pain is present throughout the piece. With great difficulty *vobis tradétur* seems to ascend, as if it had to pause for rest and recuperate strength after each full tone. The annotated manuscript here have three neums with broad markings. By reason of the similar closing formulas over *tradétur*, *Dóminus*, and *commemoratiónem*, one might distinguish three phrases. The first phrase supports itself on *g* and only once extends to *b*. By its emphasis on *b*, the second phrase wishes to state the fact that a new covenant has been called into being. In this phrase we hear a single *c*. A new division begins with *hoc fácite*. Emphatically the melody ascends to *c* and lets it resound. Manuscript 121 of Einsiedeln has here not only an episeme for the first neum, but also "t" *(tenére,* prolong, draw out this note*)*. Here the melody appropriately grows in warmth and solemnity, especially over *quotiescúmque* with its protracted high *e*. Over *meam* the same form returns a fourth lower. The Lord has given the command which called our liturgy into being, the command which incites to participation in the sacrificial Banquet, which builds our altars, and the churches and cathedrals that house them. It seems as if the light of transfiguration were sweeping over the countenance of the Saviour, joyful at the immeasurable blessing that the Holy Eucharist will produce, blissfully contemplating all the love it will wake in grateful hearts. The harsh ending tells us that Communion is the fruit of Christ's sacrificial death.

Musica s., 52, 3 ff.

*   *   *   *

PALM SUNDAY

A. THE BLESSING OF THE PALMS AND THE PROCESSION

The chants and prayers are arranged as at holy Mass. In place of the Introit we have the following antiphon

ANTIPHON (Matt. 21: 9)

1. *Hosanna filio David: benedictus qui venit in nomine Domini.*
2. *Rex Israel: Hosanna in excelsis.*

1. *Hosanna to the Son of David: blessed is he that cometh in the name of the Lord.* 2. *O King of Israel: Hosanna in the highest.*

Here the very first word again supplies the leading thought of the celebration, the fundamental idea. The blessing of the palms and the procession anticipate the resurrection. The large interval of a fifth at the beginning and toward the close of the antiphon tend to rouse and enhance the festal joy. Philologically the word *Hosánna* means "save now, save," and implores a blessing upon the Son of David entering Jerusalem. But perhaps at that time already, as at present, it was an expression of jubilation. Therefore, *Hosánna in excélsis* does not mean that God is to send down His help from on high. Rather it is an exhortation to the inhabitants of the celestial regions to join in the rejoicing of the exultant multitude on earth. In the Son of David all of God's prophecies have been fulfilled. In Him we meet the divine, we meet God Himself.

This cry has been perpetuated throughout the centuries, and no Mass is now celebrated in which the King of glory is not greeted in this manner. With what affection did our most famous composers treat the *Benedíctus* with its *Hosánna*.

This melody bears some resemblance to an archaic Greek composition dating from the second century before Christ.

Moehler, Geschichte der alten und mittelalterlischen Musik, I, 18 (Sammlung Goeschen) and *Musica s.* 44, 193 ff.

THE RESPONSORIES

Between the Lesson, describing the oasis with its seventy palms, and the Gospel, which narrates the triumphal entry of Jesus, two responsories are inserted, either of which may be sung. In the present instance both of them strike us as strange. One of them leads us to the meeting of the Sanhedrin, which determined upon the death of Jesus. Its melody reveals a powerful, even passionate dramatic force. The rendition is not easy.

THE SECOND RESPONSORY (Matt. 26: 39, 41)

A. 1. *In monte Oliveti oravit ad Patrem*: 2. *Pater, si fieri potest transeat a me calix iste*. 3. * *Spiritus quidem promptus est, caro autem infirma*: 4. *fiat voluntas tua.* B. ℣. *I. Vigilate et orate, II. ut non intretis in tentationem. A. 3.* * *Spiritus....*

A. 1. *On Mount Olivet he prayed to his Father*: 2. *Father, if it be posible, let this chalice pass from me* 3. * *The spirit indeed is willing. but the flesh is weak*: 4. *thy will be done. B. ℣. I. Watch and pray, II. that ye enter not into temptation. A. 3.* * *The spirit....*

The procession began from Mount Olivet. This responsory speeds ahead of the incidents in the order of their occurrence and transports us to the scene of Christ's agony on the same Mount of Olives, thus setting up a rather somber background to this joyful celebration.

The melody has the form A B A, like the responsory *Emendémus* on Ash Wednesday. In A the first half of the first phrase ascends to the dominant; in the form of a sequence the second half comes to the tonic. The second and third phrases begin on the dominant. The third closes with a modulation to the full tone below the tonic. *Iste* sets the formula over *(Oli)-véti* a full tone lower.

B, the verse, has an entirely typical melody. Both of its two phrases have an introductory formula; then in I the wonted recitation on *c* follows which is very brief here on account of the brevity of the text, together with a frequent five-syllable middle adence; in II recitation on *g*, and always a five-syllable closing cadence, here from *tentationem* on.

Wagner, III, 197 and 343; Johner, *Der greg. Choral*, 96 and 102.

At the distribution of the blessed palms the antiphons *Púeri Hebraeórum* are sung.

Pueri Hebraeorum, portantes ramos olivarum, obviaverunt Domino, clamantes, et dicentes: Hosanna in excelsis.

The Hebrew children carrying olive branches, met our Lord, crying out, and saying: Hosanna in the highest.

Pueri Hebraeorum vestimenta prosternebant in via, et clamabant dicentes: Hosanna filio David: benedictus qui venit in nomine Domini.

The Hebrew children spread their garments in the way, and cried out saying: Hosanna to the Son of David: blessed is he that cometh in the name of the Lord.

These energetic songs well deserved to become the common property of the faithful. They are similar in construction, yet present a

ag f ga a

pleasing variety. The first antiphon sings *o-li-va-rum*, while the second

a g f fg g

in the corresponding place sings *-nebant in vi-a*. Especially in the second antiphon does the influence of the word-accents on the melody make itself felt. These songs were very popular formerly.

THE PROCESSION OF THE PALMS

Through their blessing the palm boughs were elevated to the dignity of sacramentals, capable of mediating grace for us. The blessing, however, has still another purpose; it is the psychological preparation for the elevated feeling manifested in the palm procession. It explains to us the symbolism of this procession and asks for the graces which are to prepare us for this solemn act. Then only can real joy and true enthusiasm quicken us. The palms anticipate triumphs over the prince of this world: thus the Church, in poetic strain. They announce beforehand that our Saviour will fight with the prince of death for the life of the world and that by His death He will conquer. And the olive branches tell us that in the Son of God the fullness of mercy has been manifested to the world.

Of the charming antiphons which the Church offers us we shall adduce the following only:

1. *Ante sex dies solemnis Paschae, quando venit Dominus in civitatem Jerusalem, occurrerunt ei pueri: 2. et in manibus portabant ramos palmarum, et clamabant voce magna dicentes: 3. Hosanna in excelsis: 4. benedictus qui venisti in multitudine misericordiae: 5. Hosanna in excelsis.*

1. *Six days before the solemnity of the Passover, when our Lord was coming into the city of Jerusalem, the children met him* [solemn inception, emphasis on seconds, but then a great development, a clear major chord over *quando ve-(nit), Jerúsalem, occurrérunt*]. 2. *and carried palm branches in their hands, and cried with a loud voice, saying* [deep middle phrase, forming a kind of

contrast and making the subsequent Hosanna so much the more effective]. 3. *Hosanna in the highest* [magnificent swellings, both in the first and in the second group of *Hosánna*]. 4. *blessed art thou who hast come in the multitude of thy mercy* [harking back to the melody of the second phrase and telling emphasis on *multitúdine*]. 5. *Hosanna in the highest* [jubilant and spirited repetition of the melody.]

1. *Occurrunt turbae cum floribus et palmis Redemptori obviam:* 2. *et victori triumphanti digna dant obsequia:* 3. *Filium Dei ore gentes praedicant: et in laudem Christi voces tonant per nubila: Hosanna!*

1. *The multitude go out to meet the Redeemer with flowers and palms:* 2. *and to a triumphant conquerer* [how effective is the interval of a fourth and the recitation on the dominant!] *they pay homage:* 3. *nations proclaim the Son of God: and their voices rend the skies in the praise of Christ: Hosanna!*

Cum Angelis et pueris fideles inveniamur, triumphatori mortis clamantes: Hosanna in excelsis.

Let us join with the angels and children singing to the conqueror of death: Hosanna in the highest.

What a mighty impression these melodies must have produceu when sung by an immense concourse, rejoicing in their faith! And in the early centuries Palm Sunday was a solemn popular feast. Thus attests the pilgrim Etheria (c. 385), and so it was throughout the entire Middle Ages. Its procession enjoyed the same favor and popularity as was attained ín later centuries by the Corpus Christi procession.

RETURN OF THE PROCESSION

When the procession returns into the church, it finds the doors locked. Suddenly from the interior of the church a joyous song to the victorious King Christ resounds, the renowned *Glória laus*[1], composed by Bishop Theodulf of Orleans (✝821).

---

1 *C.-O.*, 46, 45 ff.; *Revue*, 3, 115 ff.; *Civilta catt.*, 57, II. 3 ff. and 159 ff.

A. *Gloria, laus, et honor, tibi sit Rex Christe Redemptor:* B. *Cui puerile decus prompsit Hosanna pium.*

A. *All glory, praise, and honor be, O Christ, Redeemer King, to thee,*
B. *Whom children hailed with joyous song, Hosanna in sweet melody.*

The first halves of the two verses have some resemblance.

The singers outside the church repeat this distich. Then the singers inside intone:

1. *Israel es tu Rex, Davidis et inclyta proles: Nomine qui in Domini, Rex benedicte, venis.*

1. *Thou David's Son of royal fame, Who in the God of Israel's name Art come our praise and love to claim.*

Here the verses have the same spirited melody.

After each of the following verses the singers outside the church add the *Glória laus.* Thus there results an energetic alternate song.

2. *Coetus in excelsis te laudat caelicus omnis, Et mortalis homo, et cuncta creata simul.*

2. *The angels host laud thee on high, All creatures too in earth and sky And mortal man takes up the cry.*

3. *Plebs Hebraea tibi cum palmis obvia venit: Cum prece, voto, hymnis, adsumus ecce tibi.*

3. *The Hebrews came with branches fair, And we with hymns and suppliant prayer Would in thy gracious triumph share.*

4. *Hi tibi passuro solvebant munia laudis: Nos tibi regnanti pangimus ecce melos.*

4. *Thee on thy way to death they praise, To thee exsultant psalms we raise, Who reignest unto endless days.*

5. *Hi placuere tibi, placeat devotio nostra: Rex bone, Rex clemens, cui bona cuncta placent.*

5. *To thee this day, O gracious King, Whom their devotion pleased, we sing, Do thou accept the praise we bring.*

As the procession re-enters the church, the following is sung:

RESPONSORY Ingrediente Domino

A. 1. *Ingrediente Domino in sanctam civitatem,* 2. *Hebraeorum pueri, resurrectionem vitae pronuntiantes,* 3. * *Cum ramis palmarum Hosanna clamabant in excelsis. B. Ẏ. I. Cumque audisset populus, quod Jesus veniret Jerosolymam, II. exierunt obviam ei. A.* 3. * *Cum ramis ...*

A. 1. *As our Lord entered the holy city,* 2. *the Hebrew children declaring the resurrection of life,* 3. * *With palm branches, cried out: Hosanna in the highest. B. Ẏ. I. When the people heard that Jeuss was to come to Jerusalem, II. they went out to meet him. A.* 3. * *With palm branches ...*

The construction here is the same as in the responsory *Emendémus* on Ash Wednesday. The third phrase corresponds to the first: *civitátem* = *clamábant in excélsis,* with a slight simplification in the middle. In the second and third phrases the joy of the multitude waving palms strives to go beyond the limits of the typical form. Here again the third phrase modulates to the full tone below the tonic; the closing cadence also has five syllables: *óbviam ei.*

B. THE MASS

INTROIT (Ps. 21: 20, 22)

1. *Domine, ne longe facias auxilium tuum a me,* 2. *ad defensionem meam aspice:* 3. *libera me de ore leonis, et a cornibus unicornuorum humilitatem meam. Ps. Deus, Deus meus, respice in me,* * *quare me dereliquisti? longe a salute mea verba delictorum meorum.*

1. *O Lord, remove not thy help to a distance from me,* 2. *look towards my defence:* 3. *deliver me from the lion's mouth, and my lowness from the horns of the unicorns. Ps. O God, my God, look upon me,* * *why hast thou forsaken me? far from my salvation are the words of my sins.*

The jubilant Hosanna is no longer heard. The multitudes have dispersed and the Saviour is alone. Even now He experiences what that lonely hour of vigil on the Mount of Olives will hold for Him. Even now the feeling, which on the cross will cause Him to cry out: "O God, My God, why has Thou forsaken Me?" has overtaken Him. In most abject distress, in the face of a sea of sorrows which unmercifully overwhelms Him, He cries in this Introit: "O Lord, remove not Thy help to a distance from Me!" This Introit like others wells up melodically from the depths (cf. the luminous Introit for the second Mass of Christmas). Our Introit receives its somber character more especially from the double descent of a fifth over *Dómine ne longe*, thus protracting the initial *Dómine*. A light accent should be placed on the second, not the third, note of *Dó-(mine)*. *Tuum* exhibits special tenderness: Thou, O Lord, art the only One that can yet help me.

In the second phrase *áspice* sounds like the cry of one harassed to death. Look Thou upon me with the eyes of Thy mercy and of Thine omnipotence! The Introit for Pentecost has a similar passage. There, however, *sciéntiam vocis* is only a majestic echo of *orbem terrárum*. *Aspice* marks the only high point of today's Introit. At Pentecost the *d*, which had already been sung twice, lessens the effect of the interval of a fourth; in the present piece, however, the interval of a fourth comes abruptly. The *torculus* over *meam* tends to retard and to weaken, making the outcry *áspice* so much the more impressive.

The third phrase no longer exhibits great agitation. It has a range of only a fifth. Its special means of expression is the repeated emphasis on the dominant *c*, and, following the lead of *áspice*, it stresses the second imperative, *líbera me*. How fervent is the petition of the one who is praying: I am Thy Son, Thy well-beloved Son. The repeated *a* over *de ore le-(ónis)* and the repeated *g* over *unicornuó-(rum)* share some of the impressiveness of the high *c*. In the Offertory of the Requiem Mass, *de ore leónis* with its interval of a fourth and *pressus* is more effective. Here it merely repeats the formula of *a me*, which occurs also over *(cór)-nibus* and in an abbreviated form over *auxílium*. In this phrase the accent is placed on *líbera me*. The whole molds itself into a favorite cadence of the eighth mode. The ascending *f a c*, so frequently employed in the eighth mode, is here avoided throughout. Generally it is used to adorn bright and joyous texts and is found only once in connection with a supplicating text in the Introit for the sixteenth Sunday after Pentecost over *tota*. In a somewhat veiled and descending form we meet it here over *tuum a me*.

Quiet resignation characterizes the end of the song. Nevertheless the prayer wells up once more almost vehemently: "O God, my God, why hast Thou forsaken Me?" The repetition of the first word already betrays the interior agitation. Forsaken Me! Now one disciple is about to betray and sell Me, another to deny Me, then all the rest flee! Even God Himself seems to forsake Me!

Why has the Lord taken all this sorrow upon Himself? On account of our sins!

N. Sch., 267 ff.

GRADUAL (Ps. 72: 24, 1–3)

1. *Tenuisti manum dexteram meam*: 2. *in voluntate tua deduxisti me*: 3. *et cum gloria assumpsisti me.* ℣. 1. *Quam bonus Israel Deus rectis corde!* 2. *mei autem pene moti sunt pedes,* 3. *pene effusi sunt gressus mei*: 4. *quia zelavi in peccatoribus,* 5. *pacem peccatorum videns.*

1. *Thou hast held me by the right hand*: 2. *and by thy will thou hast conducted me*: 3. *and with glory thou hast assumed me.* ℣. 1. *How good is God to Israel, to them that are of right heart!* 2. *but my feet were almost moved,* 3. *my steps had well nigh slipped*: 4. *because I had a zeal on occasion of sinners,* 5. *seeing the peace of sinners.*

The sacred Passion dominates the liturgy of today's Mass. But if we listen a bit sharply we hear other notes also; if we scrutinize a bit closely, we discern lights springing up here and there in the night of sorrows, foreshadowing a great morning—the dawn of Easter. The Epistle speaks of the voluntary sacrificial death of Christ, but at the same time of the glory He has thus won for Himself. Similarly in the Gradual the gaze of Christ passes to the Paschal solemnity, to His Ascension, when the Father will unite Him to Himself in glory. Looking back upon His earthly life, He thanks the Father for His protection. This, even in His bitterest sufferings, remains the chief sentiment of His heart: "How good is God!" True, He also thinks of His sufferings; He sees beforehand that His feet will no longer bear Him, that laden with His cross, He will stumble and falter, and all this because zeal against sin and zeal for His Father's glory consumes Him. But the joy of the coming glory transcends all sorrow. This thought was stressed still more in earlier times when the initial words were repeated. Even in the subsequent Tract, filled as it is with tragedy, at least the concluding verses speak of the blessing of the Passion for redeemed mankind.

In its three phrases the *corpus* presents three thoughts. The final syllables of each phrase bear a florid melisma. The second phrase ascends upward; to balance this, the third phrase makes the same cadence after *glória* as the first phrase. Melodically, a new fourth phrase begins with *assumpsísti*, having the same motive which opened the second phrase. Pauses in the text and in the melody do not entirely agree. A frequent reversion of the melody from *f* over *d* to *c* characterizes the first phrase. It is the expression of a quiet resignation.

According to content and sentiment, the first phrase of the verse still belongs to the *corpus*. Although we seem to be singing in the first mode, nevertheless the interval of a fourth over *corde*, the inception on the dominant *a*, and the last five or six notes over *videns* lead us back to the fourth mode. The melody of *rectis corde* is repeated over *moti sunt pedes*; *gressus mei* repeats the formula of *(dedu)-xisti me* in the *corpus*. Other slight repetitions are also found. The verse, moreover, ascends higher than the first part, which never goes above *b♭*.

TRACT (Ps. 21: 2–9, 18, 19, 22, 24, 32)

The present Tract seems to be the account of an eyewitness, rather than a prophetic hymn composed a thousand years before the accomplishment of these events.

Here again the mediant is indicated by the sign †; the caesura, by (—).

1. *Deus, Deus meus, respice in me,* † *quare me dereliquisti?* 2. *Longe a salute mea* † *verba* (—) *delictorum meorum.* 3. *Deus meus clamabo per diem, nec exaudies:* † *in nocte, et non* (—) *ad insipientiam mihi.* 4. *Tu autem in sancto habitas,* † *laus Israel.* 5. *In te speraverunt patres nostri:* † *speraverunt* (—) *et liberasti eos.* 6. *Ad te clamaverunt, et salvi facti sunt:* † *in te speraverunt* (—) *et non sunt confusi.* 7. *Ego autem sum vermis, et non homo:* † *opprobrium hominum* (—) *et abjectio plebis.* 8. *Omnes qui videbant me, aspernabantur me:* † *locuti sunt labiis et moverunt caput.* 9. *Speravit in Domino, eripiat eum:* † *salvum faciat eum* (—) *quoniam vult eum.* 10. *Ipso vero consideraverunt et conspexerunt me:* † *diviserunt sibi* (—) *vestimenta mea, et super vestem meam miserunt sortem.* 11. *Libera me de ore leonis:* † *et a cornibus unicornuorum* (—) *humilitatem meam.* 12. *Qui timetis Dominum, laudate eum:* † *universum semen Jacob* (—) *magnificate eum.* 13. *Annuntiabitur Domino generatio ventura:* † *et annuntia-*

1. *O God, my God, look upon me,* † *why hast thou forsaken me?* 2. *Far from my salvation* † *are the words* (—) *of my sins.* 3. *O my God, I shall cry by day, and thou wilt not hear:* † *and by night, and it shall not be imputed* (—) *as folly in me.* 4. *But thou dwellest in the holy place,* † *the praise of Israel.* 5. *In thee have our fathers hoped:* † *they have hoped:* (—) *and thou hast delivered them.* 6. *They cried to thee, and were saved:* † *they trusted in thee* (—) *and were not confounded.* 7. *But I am a worm and no man:* † *the reproach of men* (—) *and the outcast of the people.* 8. *All they that saw me have laughed me to scorn:* † *they have spoken with the lips, and wagged the head.* 9. *He hath hoped in the Lord, let him deliver him:* † *let him save him* (—) *seeing he delighteth in him.* 10. *But they looked and stared at me:* † *they parted* (—) *my garments among them, and upon my vesture they cast lots.* 11. *Deliver me from the lion's mouth:* † *and from the horns of the unicorn* (—) *my lowness.* 12. *Ye that fear the Lord, praise Him:* † *all ye, the seed*

bunt caeli justitiam ejus. 14. *Populo qui nascetur quem fecit Dominus.*

of Jacob (—) glorify him. 13. *There shall be declared to the Lord a generation to come:* † *and the heavens shall show forth his justice.* 14. *To a people that shall be born, which the Lord hath made.*

For the Passion the choir sings a simple melody, with middle and closing cadence. High *f* is the dominant, prepared for by the low *d* on the first syllable of the phrase. The Chronicler closes his melody in every instance with *é g á f*, so that almost regularly the choir begins with a sixth *(d)*.

OFFERTORY (Ps. 68: 21, 22)

A. 1. *Improperium exspectavit cor meum, et miseriam: B.* 2. *et sustinui qui simul contristaretur, et non fuit:* 3. *consolantem me quaesivi, et non inveni: C.* 4. *et dederunt in escam meam fel,* 5. *et in siti mea potaverunt me aceto.*

A. 1. *My heart hath expected reproach and misery: B.* 2. *and I looked for one that would grieve together with me, and there was none:* 3. *I sought for one to comfort me and I found none: C.* 4. *And they gave me gall for my food,* 5. *and in my thirst they gave me vinegar to drink.*

The whole is divided into three parts, each of which sets in with low *f*. In part B the theme is announced. It speaks of profound reproach —the melody here and here alone descending to low *c*—and of misery, reaching its climax over *misériam*. These are the two extremes of the phrase. But He who complains thus is resigned to all things; this is evidenced by the slow and measured ascending seconds, the subsequent fourths, and the tarrying on high *c*.

Part B is concerned with the psychic sufferings of Jesus. His heart beat only for others, consumed itself for others. If anyone, then surely the suffering Saviour was justified in expecting that all those whom He had healed, whom He had assisted, whom He had given true peace of heart would accompany Him on His way of sorrows. He looks about Him. Where are they? *Non fuit.* Not one is at hand. Four times the tenderly complaining motive *b d c ée b b* pleads for sympathy. But in vain. Over *contristarétur* the annotated manuscripts have practically only simple neums, which demand a fluent rendition. There is here no question of labored expressions of misery, but rather of subdued, tearful reproaches. This brings *non fuit* with all its broad neums into sharper relief. No doubt the parallelism of the text necessitated similar introductions for *et sustínui* and *consolántem*. The second *et non* sets in a note lower and then ascends to a bewildering high *e*. The strikingly swift descent with *invéni* only heightens the artistic effect of this passage. That which is not denied the poorest wretch, that bit of heartfelt sympathy which accompanies even the most hardened criminal to his death —this was denied to the Saviour; not a single, mild, loving word, not a glance of pity alleviated His sufferings. And then as if the tortured breast could no longer contain all this woe, there escapes from His lips the cry of this harsh, painful *et non invéni*. Perhaps such combinations of notes made a different impression upon the ancients than they do upon us.

Part C gives us an inkling of the tortures which the Saviour, who was harassed by fever, expressed in His cry: "I thirst." All ages, however, have seen a deeper import in this cry than the mere expression of bodily pain. He received vinegar and gall, His tormentors made sport of His sufferings, they ridiculed Him and laughed at Him, and thus elevated His sufferings to the plane of the infinite. Expressive of these sentiments, the melody once more rises to high *e* and then, as if burdened with sorrow, descends with harsh tritones.

The quiet phrase *et dedérunt ... fel* interposed between these two high points shows artistic finesse. It has the smallest range of any of the phrases (only a fifth). We find no protractions or accents with a *pressus*, no fourths, but predominantly seconds and the simple repetition of the formula which had already been employed over *misériam*. The relaxation here from the high tension of the preceding part affords the singer an opportunity to gather new strength for that which is to follow. Codex 339 of St. Gall's gives the first seven notes over the word *fel* a broad form, thus in a way indicating to us the amount of bitterness latent in this word. The annotated manuscripts give prominence to the fact that the thrice-prolonged and accented *c* over the doleful, subsiding *acéto* should not work to the detriment of the lower *a*; and thus in spite of the stirring, even violent feelings, the beauty of the melodic line is preserved intact.[1]

In the most ancient manuscript the Saviour voices His reproaches in three other verses of Psalm 68, but He also knows that the time of grace and the fullness of God's bounty has now come.

In the holy sacrifice of the Mass the Saviour appears, as it were, suffering and dying among us. But He ought no longer look in vain for consolation and sympathy. Let us present ourselves to Him under the symbols of bread and wine, which the priest now lifts up to God.

---

[1] *N. Sch.*, 270 ff.

COMMUNION (Matt. 26: 42)

Pater, si non potest hic calix transire, nisi bibam illum: fiat voluntas tua.

Father, if this chalice may not pass away, but I must drink it, thy will be done.

How suitably this text has been chosen for a Communion song! The chalice which Jesus accepts here has become for us the chalice of salvation. The blood which we drink flows from the wounds of the Crucified. In today's Mass liturgy we hear for the first time the childlike word, "Father," which sets in with a tender bistropha on the dominant. The passage *dc bdc b* over *bibam illum* corresponds to *ag fag g* over *(po)-test hic calix.* In the minor thirds and the half tone, it is true, we still perceive something of the painful. But *b* here partakes of the nature of a leading note and with melodically logical necessity leads to the *c* over *fiat*, to that heroic word: "Thy will be done!"

It is characteristic of all these chants that the Saviour Himself speaks to us. He opens His heart to us and lets us gaze into the depths of woe and shame. He manifests to us His yearning for consolation and sympathy. How close He has come to us in these texts and still more in these heartfelt melodies; so close that we almost feel His breath, that we almost perceive the palpitations of His heart. We have need of such a Saviour, for He is our consolation. Under the influence of His love and grace we also shall find the strength to pray: Father, Thy will be done!

*   *   *   *

MAUNDY THURSDAY

In early Christian ages the faithful were wont to congregate toward evening for the Eucharistic celebration,[1] in order thus to become intimately united to the Saviour in the Cenacle. The Secret used to form the introduction to the celebration. The Mass of the Catechumens is of later composition. The Introit is taken from the Tuesday in Holy Week.

INTROIT (Gal. 6: 14)

1. *Nos autem gloriari oportet in cruce Domini nostri Jesu Christi:* 2. *in quo est salus, vita, et resurrectio nostra:* 3. *per quem salvati, et liberati sumus.* Ps. *Deus misereatur nostri, et benedicat nobis:* * *illu-*

1. *But it behooves us to glory in the cross of our Lord Jesus Christ:* 2. *in whom is our salvation, life, and resurrection;* 3. *by whom we are saved and delivered.* Ps. *May God have mercy on us and bless us:* *

---

[1] *C. O.*, 51, 41 ff.

<table>
<tr><td>minet vultum suum super nos, et misereatur nostri.</td><td>may he cause the light of his countenance to shine upon us, and may he have mercy upon us.</td></tr>
</table>

The Introits of Tuesday, Wednesday, and Thursday of Holy Week speak of the holy cross, but stress also the glorification of the Crucified. Before the Saviour descends to the depths of His Passion and its affronts, before the flood of sorrows bursts upon Him, He stands before us in all His splendor.

The text of this Introit might well be an inspiration for a paean of triumph and of victory, arousing enthusiasm and advancing in lively rhythm. But such is not the case. It would seem as if the composer, before he wrote his song, had meditated with tender sympathy on the sacred Passion and had come to realize that for many all this would be in vain. With tears of compassion in his eyes he began to sing with this tender melody, made almost sorrowful through the thrice-repeated half-time interval, the *Nos autem*.

A similar feeling is awakened if we answer the question: Who, then, are the others? as implied in the opening words: "But it behooves *us*." The Apostle has already said that the cross is foolishness to the heathen and a scandal to the Jew, but how is it regarded at the present time? The blasphemies of the moderns must fill us with indignation and sorrow and with a deep sympathy for our wounded Love, we shall strive to fathom the melody of *Nos autem*. If we then ask ourselves what our relation to the Crucified is, how we regard in practice the cross God has laid upon us, then we shall sing, not with arrogance, but humbly and modestly: *Nos autem*.

The major third over *opórtet* is not without purpose. Here it seems as if the holy cross were being slowly elevated before us; with *nostri* it stands before us in all its glory; the cross of *our* Lord. As the melody gradually increases, so also must the *crescendo* grow, till it attains its greatest ardor with *nostri*. Especial care must be taken that this high *c* be not sung unprepared, not raw and cold and angular, as were the timbers of the cross on Golgotha.

The second phrase develops and confirms the theme announced in the first phrase. The human blood which reddens the trunk of the cross has become for many the drink of "salvation," supplying new life and courage and strength to overcome sorrow and woe and death. From it emanates eternal, blessed, glorified life. In the melody the second half of the first phrase is repeated.

Textually the closing phrase forms a parallel to the second phrase. Here, as above over *autem* and often in plainsong, the tristropha serves to set the following word in greater relief: *salváti*—"we are saved." *Liberáti* repeats the motive of *resurréctio*, to which *(glo)-riári* and *autem* are also related. With evident love the composer tarries on *sumus*, just as he gave *nostri* and *nostra* above melodic prominence.

The psalm-verse with its somewhat harsh *b* following upon the exclusive use of *b♭* in the antiphon is a cry for mercy, for enlightenment and blessing, so that the mysteries of the cross, its sufferings and its love may be revealed to us.

At the end of days the cross will appear in the clouds of heaven. To those who courageously took up their cross and followed the Crucified, to those who, sacrificing their all furthered the interests of the Crucified, this cross will be a boon. Then, indeed, will the cross and the Crucified in the fullest sense be their salvation, their life, their resurrection; then will the petition of the psalm-verse become a jubilant song of thanksgiving. Thou hast had mercy upon us. Now Thy glorious countenance shines upon us and, overcome with joy, we gaze into the depths of Thy redeeming love.

Musica s., 45, 49 ff.

Today the *Glória in excélsis Deo* is solemnly intoned by the organ and sung to the accompaniment of the church bells. Today is the birthday of the Eucharistic Christ.

GRADUAL (Philipp. 2: 8–9)

1. *Christus factus est pro nobis obediens usque ad mortem*, 2. *mortem autem crucis. ℣. 1. Propter quod et Deus exaltavit illum*, 2. *et dedit illi nomen, quod est super omne nomen.*

1. *Christ became obedient for us unto death*, 2. *even the death of the cross. ℣. 1. Wherefore God also hath exalted him*, 2. *and given him a name which is above every name.*

The *corpus* of the Gradual moves predominantly in a lower pitch about the fundamental note *f* and descends below it to *d* and *c*, thus giving *a* also a certain importance. All this would point to the plagal form of the F (sixth) mode.

The verse has an entirely different character. It strives upward to the dominant of the fifth mode, sounds it, and even goes a fifth above it. This fits excellently to the text. In the *corpus* there is mention of the lowliness of Christ, in the verse of His glorification.

Whether or not this be an original composition is difficult to say. The fact that Codex 339 of St. Gall's has only the initial notes of the florid melismas over *illum* and *nomen*, thus presupposing the existence of the piece, bears no weight. The corresponding passages in the Gradual for the feast of St. Sylvester, *Ecce sacérdos magnus*, are likewise indicated only by their first notes. The fact, however, must not be overlooked that the melody over *nobis* works like a cadence, hence that it demands, or at least will bear, a greater pause. This is not the case in the present Gradual. Taken by themselves, the first five words do not express an independent thought. It is different with the Gradual *Ecce sacérdos magnus*, which, with the exception of a single passage in the verse, has exactly the same melody as today's Gradual. The same holds true of the Gradual *Exiit sermo* sung on the feast of St. John the Evangelist (q.v.). Hence, it seems more likely that one of these two Graduals is the original. *Et dedit illi nomen* is also heard in the Gradual for the second Sunday in Lent and for the Assumption. The close of the verse occurs in no fewer than thirty Graduals.[1]

In spite of all this, however, we shall consider today's text and melody as one whole and render them thus. The *corpus* expresses grateful love for all that Christ in His abasement did for us. *Nobis* helps to produce this effect. The annotated manuscripts give practically every note here the broad form. The interpretation of *Caecilia* (29, 49 ff.) seems somewhat forced when it regards *obédiens* as an agitated melodic movement and sees in it the natural repugnance which the youthful heart of Christ felt in the face of death and of the terrible death struggle He was to undergo. This interpretation would furthermore intimate that the resolved major chord over *usque* is restful, insofar as it reconciles Christ to the terrible duty imposed upon Him by obedience. The descending fourth of *crucis* may serve to visualize for us how the Saviour with the cry: "Father, into Thy hands I commend My spirit," bowed His head and died.

If the *corpus* narrated the things Christ did for us, then the verse narrates what the Father did for Christ: *exaltávit illum*—He hath exalted Him. The melody here sounds like the ringing of Easter bells, vieing with the joys of heaven. The recitation on *c* over *exaltávit* and afterwards on *d* over *dedit illi* gives a more plastic form to the subsequent neums. As if in holy protest, we anticipate the glorification of the Saviour's name which will be blasphemed so terribly in the succeeding days, the nscription of which we shall find on the cross over the head of the Victim. Here the melody modulates to *c* like the middle cadence in psalmody. The psalmodic structure, moreover, betrays itself by the intonation at the beginning of the verse and by a sort of *flexa* on *a*, the last note of *illum*. At the low inception with *quod est* we reverently bow before the holy name of Jesus.

---

[1] Wagner, III, 384.

OFFERTORY (Ps. 117: 16, 17)

1. *Dextera Domini fecit virtutem,*
2. *dextera Domini exaltavit me:* 3.
non moriar, sed vivam, et narrabo
opera Domini.

1. *The right hand of the Lord*
hath wrought strength, 2. *the right*
hand of the Lord hath exalted me:
3. *I shall not die, but live and shall*
declare the works of the Lord.

The selection closes on *a*, showing that it has been transposed. In this manner it comes closer to its natural pitch, and consequently its low passages can be written without the aid of ledger lines.

The three clearly discernible phrases have each as their principal development the ascent to high *d* in their second half. A still closer relation exists between the first and third phrases, insofar as they have their ending on the dominant and employ the same range. Similarly, the melody over *(Déxte)-ra Dó-(mini)* is heard in an abbreviated form over *vivam*. But *virtútem*, with its prolonged and accented *d* and the descending fourth, produces in consonance with its text a more powerful effect than *ópera*. The second phrase closes a major second below the fundamental—a modulation much favored by the second mode. The inception and continuance on the dominant indicate this thought: I shall not leave hold of this hand. Over *exaltávit* the three notes after the bistropha *c a d* are to be united into one figure, after which the *pressus* is to be stressed. A lively rendition should characterize the third phrase. Here annotated manuscripts almost throughout have simple neum forms and twice mark the melody with "c"*(celeriter,* rapidly*).* The word *Dómini*, recurring thrice, shows us how freely plainsong treats the three syllables of the word. To the first syllable it assigns notes as follows: two, four, and one; to the second: five, one, and one; to the third: two, one, and nine respectively.

Who is it that prays in this manner? In the first instance our thoughts turn to Christ. It is the eve of His death. He casts a glance in retrospect upon His Messianic activity and upon all the miracles His divinity wrought. He looks ahead to that which still awaits him. Well does He know that the right hand of the Lord will exalt Him, as, indeed, the Gradual jubilantly announced in its verse. He does not die, but in death obtains eternal life for Himself and for all the world. And in His resurrection and glorification, with His Church, He is an eternal, personal hymn of praise of the great deeds of God. Thus, invested with power and grandeur, certain of victory, He steps across the threshold of death.

But we may also consider this Offertory in the light of the Eucharist. Psalm 117, from which it has been taken, belongs to the number of those

which were wont to be sung at the Passover, hence which Christ also
sang at the Last Supper in the Cenacle. The Eucharist is a miracle, an
honor and a glory to the Church, and a fountain of the richest life. Here
is fulfilled the word of the Lord: "He that eateth My flesh ... hath everlasting life." Hence the Church and with her the Christian soul sings:
Non móriar—"I shall not die, but live." I shall attain to a life of eternal
blessedness, and I shall laud the works of God and forever give Him
thanks for the great things He has wrought in me. But the soul is already
inspired to announce the works of the Lord. For in celebrating the liturgy we recount His works and benefits and give thanks in a manner
which is worthy and just and unceasing.

Finally, this song may also be placed in the mouths of the penitents
who today are again received into the church. The most ancient manuscripts assign it to the third Sunday *post Theophaniam (=Epiphaniam,*
q.v.) in connection with the Gospel in which the Lord in such a loving
manner stretches forth His hand and heals the man stricken with leprosy.
With evident delight the melody lingers over the word *Déxtera.* Imagine
the sentiments of thanksgiving and profound joy with which the penitents and their mother, the Church, prayed these words at the moment
of reconciliation! Consequently the text permits of various interpreta-
tions. In this manner we see how the liturgy can be made ever to bear
new fruit. Renewed observation and contemplation of its peculiarities,
its texts, and its melodies always reveals new relations, thus producing
new and profound joy.

COMMUNION (John 13: 12, 13, 15)

1. *Dominus Jesus, postquam coenavit cum discipulis suis, lavit pedes eorum, et ait illis:* 2. *Scitis quid fecerim vobis, ego Dominus et Magister?* 3. *Exemplum dedi vobis, ut et vos ita faciatis.*

1. *The Lord Jesus, after he had supped with his disciples, washed their feet, and saith to them:* 2. *Do you know what I, your Lord and Master, have done for you?* 3. *I have given you an example, that so you do also.*

In ancient times slaves washed the feet of their lords, and no special
significance was attached to the action. It is entirely different when the
"Lord Jesus," the "Lord and Master," performs this service—He of
whom the Gospel of the present day speaks with such majesty: He
knew "that the Father had given Him all things into His hands, and
that He came from God, and goeth to God." For this reason the Communion begins on the dominant of the mode; and the return to this

dominant and the use of the same motive over *ego Dóminus et Mágister* surely does not occur by chance.

A contrast to this melodic curve opening downward is formed by the curve opening upward, met with for the first time over *cum discipulis suis* and recurring frequently, indeed, almost too frequently. The melody would narrate the events of the Communion in a restful tone, but lays very special stress on one word. The chant had been practically syllabic; over *Scitis*, however, it grows into a melisma and ascends majestically. Codex 339 of St. Gall's prolongs the first four notes. Such a melody is calculated to stamp itself on our hearts, there to re-echo and ever again remind us of the example given us by the "Lord Jesus," so that we may imitate it and become like Him.

If we approach the table of the Lord filled with such sentiments of of humility and subjection, then surely the Lord will grant us the grace to realize more fully that which He has done for us.

During the procession with the Blessed Sacrament the hymn *Pange lingua* is sung.

We meet the first three words again tomorrow in the hymn for the adoration of the Cross. St. Thomas used the latter as a model for his Corpus Christi hymn, whose two final stanzas *Tantum ergo* and *Genitóri* are heard at every solemn benediction with the Blessed Sacrament. The melody[1] with its three phrases cannot compare, it is true, with the virile character of the hymn to the Cross; still, it also is filled with a strong, quiet joy. In the second and still more in the third phrase this joy is subdued through reverence for the great mystery. This is shown in the descent of a fifth, the graded diminution of the range, and the avoidance of large intervals in the third phrase. Each phrase has its arsis and thesis. In the first and third phrases the arsis exerts its influence even in the second half of the phrase. Concealed in the second and third phrases is the closing cadence of the fourth mode: *a b g e*.

* * * *

GOOD FRIDAY

When at the beginning of the service[2] the priest and his assistants approach the altar they are not accompanied by song; nor does a single candle burn upon the altar. Clad in black vestments they cast themselves at the foot of the altar and, with their faces to the ground, pray in

---

[1] Wagner, III, 478, f.
[2] *C. O.*, 51, 57 ff.

silence. When sorrow overpowers us, then words fail us. And today the most terrible scene will be enacted, for Christ dies upon the cross between two criminals. With this announcement the pious soul trembles, for she remembers the words of the first Tract: The crucifixion is the work of divine justice, but at the same time it is our work. We are not innocent of the blood of this Just One. On the cross, moreover, is accomplished the separation of the spirits. The cross is the great dividing point *(in medio)* of the world's history. The great and final parting will take place when the Crucified will come again as the Holy One "from the shady and thickly covered mountain," when His glory will fill the heavens, and the whole world will resound with His praise.

FIRST TRACT (Heb. 3: 2, 3)

1. *Domine, audivi auditum tuum, † et timui: † consideravi opera tua, et expavi.* 2. *In medio duorum animalium innotesceris: dum appropinquaverint anni, cognosceris: † dum advenerit tempus, ostenderis.* 3. *In eo, dum conturbata fuerit anima mea: † in ira, misericordiae (—) memor eris.* 4. *Deus a Libano veniet, † et Sanctus de monte umbroso et condenso.* 5. *Operuit caelos majestas ejus: † et laudis ejus plena est terra.*

1. *O Lord, I have heard thy hearing, † and was afraid: † I considered thy works, and trembled.* 2. *In the midst of two animals thou shalt be made known: when the years shall draw nigh, thou shalt be known: † when the time shall come, thou shalt be shown.* 3. *In the time when my soul shall be troubled: † in anger of mercy (—) thou shalt be mindful.* 4. *God shall come from Libanus, † and the Holy One from the shady and thickly-covered mountain.* 5. *His majesty hath covered the heavens: † and the earth is full of his praise.*

The sign (†) indicates the mediant, while (—) indicates the caesura. In the first verse the mediant occurs twice. The ascending fourth *d–g* with the prolonged *f* joined to it, which is heard several times, seems to be a peculiarity of this Tract. The melisma which closes the third verse, is only found again at the very end of the piece. In the fifth verse we hear a melody over the first two words which is also sung in the Alleluia-verse of Christmastide, for example, in the third Mass for Christmas over the third phrase.

SECOND TRACT (Ps. 139: 2-10, 14)

1. *Eripe me, Domine, ab homine malo: † a viro iniquo (—) libera*

1. *Deliver me, O Lord, from the evil man: † from the unjust man (—)*

me. 2. Qui cogitaverunt malitia in corde :† tota die (—) constituebant praelia. 3. Acuerunt linguas sicut serpentes: † venenum aspidum (—) sub labiis eorum. 4. Custodi me, Domine, de manu peccatoris: † et ab hominibus iniquis (—) libera me. 5. Qui cogitaverunt supplantare gressus meos: † Absconderunt superbi (—) laqueum mihi. 6. Et funes extenderunt in laqueum pedibus meis: † juxta iter scandalum (—) posuerunt mihi. 7. Dixi Domino: Deus meus es tu: † exaudi Domine (—) vocem orationis meae. 8. Domine, Domine virtus salutis meae: † obumbra caput meum (—) in die belli. 9. Ne tradas me a desiderio meo peccatori: † cogitaverunt adversum me: ne derelinquas me (—), ne umquam exaltentur. 10. Caput circuitus eorum: † labor labiorum ipsorum (—) operiet eos. 11. Verumtamen justi confitebuntur nomini tuo: † et habitabunt recti cum vultu tuo.

rescue me. 2. Who have devised wickedness in their heart: † all the day long (—) they designed battles. 3. They have sharpened their tongues like a serpent: † the venom of asps (—) is under their lips. 4. Keep me, O Lord, from the hand of the sinner: † and from unjust ones (—) deliver me. 5. Who have proposed to supplant my steps: † the proud have hid (—) a net for me. 6. And they have stretched out cords for a snare for my feet: † by the wayside they have laid for me (—) a stumbling block. 7. I said to the Lord: Thou art my God: † O Lord (—), the voice of my supplication. 8. O Lord, Lord, the strength of my salvation: † overshadow my head (—) in the day of battle. 9. Give me not up, from my desire to the wicked: † they have plotted against me: do not forsake me (—), lest at any time they should triumph. 10. The head of them compassing me about: † the labor of their lips (—) shall overwhelm them. 11. But the just shall give glory to thy name: † and the upright shall dwell with thy countenance.

This Tract describes, above all, the psychic tortures which Christ, the true Paschal Lamb, underwent when He sacrificed Himself. The Lesson immediately preceding spoke of the Paschal lamb. At the very hour in which the blasts of the trumpet from the Temple indicated the time for the slaughter of the Paschal lamb of the Jews, the true Paschal Lamb was expiring upon the cross. The heart which had so ardently loved is betrayed, condemned, and repudiated. The people which Christ called His own has "the venom of asps under its lips." Raising His thoughts to God the Father He prays: I said to the Lord: "Thou art My God," soon to be followed by the cry: "Why hast Thou forsaken Me?" But He also perceives the blessing that will flow from His sufferings. He sees, as the closing verse says, hosts of human beings who have been redeemed through His tortures.

The Lessons and the Tracts serve only as a preparation for the Passion, the climax of the first act in today's drama. The second act brings the great prayers of intercession. In these mention is made of the *Confessóres*, who are named between the ostiaries and the virgins. Some are of the opinion that those who sing in church are meant here, since *confitéri*—the praise of God, is their office.

The unveiling and adoration of the cross make up the third act.

THE UNVEILING AND ADORATION OF THE CROSS

Thrice in an ascending scale the *Ecce lignum crucis* is intoned by the priest and continued by his assistants. Then all kneel and, filled with deepest reverence, sing: "Come, let us adore!"

During the adoration of the cross the choir sings the *Improperia*, those subdued, imploring lamentations of an unappreciated and despised love. No artist has painted the scene of the crucifixion so graphically as do these simple words and notes. They are the last words of the dying Messias-King to His people; not the words of condemnation or of judgment, but words calculated to soften stony hearts. They are spoken by the tender voice of the Author of grace, a voice offering pardon, asking only for one thing—understanding and love.[1]

Popule meus, quid feci tibi? aut in quo contristavi te? responde mihi. ℣. Quia eduxi te de terra Aegypti: parasti crucem Salvatori tuo.

O my people, what have I done to thee? or in what have I afflicted thee: answere me. ℣. Because I led thee out of the land of Egypt, thou hast prepared a cross for thy Saviour.

The import of these words—the questions, the petitions, the complaints, the bitter sorrow, and the remnant of hope for the nation's conversion—has been voiced in a truly marvelous manner by the melody. With restrained grief it rises from a heart wounded in its holiest sentiments, swelling perceptibly over *aut in quo*, then prolonging itself softly, as if Christ's gaze were fixed questioningly upon His people, penetrating their souls with all seriousness. The Saviour then progressively describes the love with which He guided His people, how He fed them with manna, planted them as a most beautiful vineyard. And ever again we hear the lamentation: *Popule meus*.

---

[1] *C. O.*, 51, 60 ff.

These complaints of the dying Saviour apply to us also. What shall we answer Him? In our helplessness the Church directs us to reply with an act of homage to the "holy God," to the "strong God," to the "immortal God," coupled with cries for mercy. Originally, no doubt, *Agios o theós* was addressed to the Holy Trinity; today, however, it is applied to Christ Crucified. On the cross He became as sin, and immolates Himself between two thieves for the sins of the world; we, nevertheless, laud Him as the "Holy God." On the cross He is an object of misery, weak forsaken by all, yet we praise Him as the "strong One." On the cross His discolored countenance already bears the marks of the agony of death, still we celebrate Him as the "immortal One," and with full voice appeal to Him: "Have mercy upon us."

This last invocation attains a powerful climax with *g a b♭* and *a b c* up to the prolonged and accented *c* over *eléison*. This illustrates beautifully how the high point of a melody is carefully prepared and then suddenly broken off. Besides *c*, the notes *b* and *a* in this phrase are prolonged, just as in the preceding appeals *f* and *a* received special accents. In all probability this melody with the text found its origin in the Orient.

The lamentations of the Saviour will not be silenced, but become more tender, more heartfelt, more sad. His strength seems to be diminishing gradually. Let us analyze only a few verses.

1. *Ego propter te flagellavi Aegyptum cum primogenitis suis: et tu me flagellatum tradidisti.* 3. *Ego ante te aperui mare: et tu aperuisti lancea latus meum.* 5. *Ego te pavi manna per desertum: et tu me cecidisti alapis et flagellis.* 9. *Ego te exaltavi magna virtute: et tu me suspendisti in patibulo crucis.*

1. *For thy sake I scourged Egypt with its firstborn: and thou didst scourge me and deliver me up.* 3. *I opened the sea before thee: and thou with a spear hast opened my side.* 5. *I fed thee with manna in the desert: and thou hast beaten me with buffets and scourges.* 9. *I have exalted thee with great strength: and thou hast hanged me on the gibbet of the cross.*

Between the individul verses the choir sings *Popule meus*.

The melody could scarcely be more simple. It moves within the range of a fifth and recites in both parts of the phrase on the third. Only the beginning and the close of each half bring some variety. It is a kind of psalmody having intonation, a *flexa* with more lengthy verses *(Aegýpto)*, middle cadence with two accents and a preparation; then a second intonation and closing cadence with two accents and a preparation. But in the final verse over the dactylic word before the last accent an *e* is placed upon the unaccented syllable. How powerfully this melody moves along, despite the like-sounding motives of *Ego* and *et tu*; or is it perhaps precisely because of this similarity in face of the powerful textual contrast, that the Saviour would say: Since I was so prodigal with My love for thee, I might have expected some love in return, but thou...!

Suddenly a new feeling and sentiment is brought to the fore. Thus far the liturgy gave prominence to thoughts of sorrow, complaint, and heartfelt sympathy. But now, even on Good Friday, joy makes itself felt in the antiphon *Crucem tuam* and the hymn *Pange lingua*. The resurrection-motive which was heard in the first Lesson for today is again utilized, and over the first four words we hear the melody of the *Te Deum*: *eg ga a ag abca*. It avoids *b♭*, which imparted such a tender character to the Introit of Maundy Thursday, and replaces it with *b*, which breathes the joy of victory.

Crucem tuam adoramus, Domine: et sanctam resurrectionem tuam laudamus et glorificamus: ecce enim propter lignum venit gaudium in universo mundo. Ps. *Deus misereatur nostri, et benedicat nobis:* * *illuminet vultum suum super nos, et misereatur nostri.*	*We adore thy cross, O Lord: and we praise and glorify thy holy resurrection: for by the wood of the cross the whole world is filled with joy.* Ps. *May God have mercy on us, and bless us:* * *may he cause the light of his countenance to shine upon us: and may he have mercy on us.*

The festal and elevated feeling of the antiphon continues to resound in the hymn *Pange lingua*.[1] It extols the cross as noble and rich in blessing, and the death of Christ as a voluntary sacrifice of the Lamb of God. Of particular beauty are the following stanzas:

Crux fidelis, inter omnes Arbor una nobilis: Nulla silva talem profert, Fronde, flore, germine: * *Dulce lignum, dulces clavos, Dulce pondus sustinet.*	*Faithful Cross! Above all other, One and only noble Tree! None in foliage, none in blossom, None in fruit thy peers may be; Sweetest Wood and sweetest Iron! Sweetest Weight is hung on thee.*
Flecte ramos, arbor alta, Tensa laxa viscera, Et rigor lentescat ille, Quem dedit nativitas: Ut superni membra Regis Miti tendas stipite.	*Bend thy boughs, O Tree of glory! Thy relaxing sinews bend; For a while the ancient rigor, That thy birth bestowed, suspend; And the King of heavenly beauty On thy bosom gently tend!*

---

[1] *Revue*, 10, 51 ff.

The melody with its majestic lines and large intervals rises to pathetic jubilation—a striking contrast to the tender and gentle complaints of the *Impropéria*. The first verse is the arsis, the second thesis, and the third merely a melodic repetition of the second. Thus we find it has the less artistic form *abb*, rare in plainsong. The second and third verses with their ending *d f ed d* correspond to the close of the first verse with *g c ba a*. *Inter omnes* is also related with *a c cb ag* and *(fron)-de, flore* with *da ag ed*.

A peculiarity of this hymn is its responsorial form. What was originally the fourth last stanza appears as a refrain and is repeated in whole or only with its third verse after each stanza; evidently this arrangement is Syriac in form.[1] In the ancient manuscripts of plainsong this hymn, as well as the following *Vexilla Regis*, bears the name of its composer, Venantius Fortunatus (†c. 600)—one of the few instances of an author's mention.

The liturgy now continues with the Mass of the Presanctified. A procession is formed in silence, and without song or audible prayer it proceeds to the chapel or to the sepulchre in which the Blessed Sacrament is preserved. Here, indeed, the sight of the altar adorned with lights and flowers, fills us with the sentiments of Maundy Thursday. On the return to the high altar the hymn *Vexilla Regis* is sung.

Is the descending line of the first verse to imitate the fluttering of the King's banners? The third verse shows an ascending movement. The fourth verse in its beginnings is like the first, but closes like the second half of the second verse. This hymn does not attain the warmth of the *Pange lingua*, but its structure is of more artistic value.

May Christ Crucified be our light and our strength in life, and our hope in death! Let us pray that at that moment the petition of today's first Tract may be fulfilled in us: "In the time when my soul shall be troubled ... be mindful of mercy."

*   *   *   *

HOLY SATURDAY

After the blessing of the fire and the incense at the entrance of the church, the procession proceeds to the main altar. The deacon, following the cross, carries a three-branched candlestick decorated with flowers. He lights one arm of this candle and sings: *Lumen Christi*—"The light of Christ." All those participating in the procession kneel and

---

1 *Jahrbuch' uer Liturgiewissenschaft*, II, 8?.

answer: *Deo grátias*. This is repeated, as the second and third arms are lit, always in a higher pitch and with increased joy.

Who will count all those who have earnestly sought after God and after truth! How often in their stress of soul have they implored on bended knee the light from above. And when of a sudden it flared up in their soul, when they recognized Christ, the Risen One, and recognized in His resurrection the most convincing proof of His divinity and the divinity of His Church, a sincere *Deo grátias* welled up from their hearts; and the more brightly the light of Christ shone into their hearts, the more they felt themselves enriched in the possession of the truth, and ever again they cried: *Deo grátias*.

We also join in this cry and, united in festal procession, place ourselves among the followers of this light. It has become for us the light of life, leading us on to eternal, unending life.

In the magnificent *Exúltet* which follows, the deacon announces the joy of Easter, chanting the "triumph of so great a King" and the blessedness of redemption.

After the fourth, the eighth, and the eleventh prophecy a Tract is sung in the brilliant eighth mode. On Good Friday the Tracts were composed in the more serious second mode.

On the way to the baptismal chapel the Tract *Sicut cervus* is sung.

TRACT Sicut Cervus (Ps. 41: 2–4)

1. *Sicut cervus desiderat ad fontes aquarum:* † *ita desiderat anima mea ad te, Deus.* (—) 2. *Sitivit anima mea ad Deum vivum:* † *quando veniam, et apparebo ante faciem Dei mei?* 3. *Fuerunt mihi lacrimae meae panes die et nocte,* † *dum dicitur mihi per singulos dies: Ubi est Deus tuus?*

1. *As the har panteth after the fountains of water:* † *so my soul panteth after thee, O God.* (—) 2. *My soul hath thirsted for the living God:* † *when shall I come and appear before the face of God?* 3. *My tears have been my bread day and night,* † *while they said to me every day: Where is thy God?*

The yearning of the catechumens for the new life, for the life in God, receives striking expression here. After the many days of anxious doubt, after bewailing their estrangement from God, they were now to appear before His face, were to become His children and receive this personal God into their heart.

After the blessing of the baptismal fount it was customary in the early Church to administer solemn Baptism. We might here gratefully recall our own Baptism and all the great things it brought us, the interior beauty it conferred upon our soul, and the rare good fortune it bestowed upon us in making us children of God. To recall the day of Baptism was always a source of greatest pleasure to the saints, and Dante's one great wish was that he be crowned poet laureate in the same place where the saving waters of Baptism had made him a child of God.

From the baptismal chapel the procession returns to the main altar; during this time the Litany of the Saints is chanted.

THE LITANY OF THE SAINTS

These invocations afford us a glimpse of the Church triumphant. They show us the power of baptismal grace when the serious, purposeful, persistent striving of man co-operates with it. All these saints became in their lifetime ideals of moral perfection. Like ourselves, they had to struggle against such enemies of the soul as the Litany enumerates, against sin and the assaults of the devil. With Christ's grace, however, they conquered all. And yet, exalted though they be in the possession of high degrees of virtue and blessed in their heavenly home, they are nevertheless close to us. Together with them we form one holy Church. Consequently when we cry: "Pray for us," our petition is not in vain. Rather the refrain is taken up by our sainted brethren, who have a great affection toward us, who long for our presence, and whose prayers and merits are made available to us as a help toward the realization of the day when we may be joined to them before the throne of God.

The range of the melody of the first invocations confines itself to the tetrachord *g–c*; from *Pater de caelis Deus* on, to the tetrachord *a–d*. From *Propítius esto* on, the melody has the range *f–d*; from *Peccatóres* on, the range *g–e*. Thus the various divisions show a growth in range of the melody and a steady upward tendency from *c* to *d* and *e*.

After the last *Te rogámus* a longer pause is made, so that the *Agnus Dei* with its *b♭*, so striking in this connection, come not too abruptly. This is the *Agnus Dei* of Mass XVIII.

If we consider the Kyrie an introduction, a threefold division becomes apparent, of which the middle part with its downward movement forms in a certain sense a contrast to the first and third parts.

To the accompaniment of the Easter *Kyrie* the priest, clad in joyous white vestments, approaches the altar and presently intones the *Glória in excélsis Deo*. True, we heard it only on Maundy Thursday, but seemingly weeks have passed since then. Mighty things have been accomplished in the meantime, and gripping scenes have been enacted in the shadow of the cross! But now all that has passed; the joyous ringing of bells announces to all the world the victory and joy of Easter, the new life in Christ for all mankind and especially for the neophytes.

The prescribed time of silence is over and the organ again booms forth to join in the jubilation. Great joy and solemnity accompany the salutation *Agnus Dei* in the Gloria today, for Christ has shown Himself to be the true Lamb; He has sacrificed Himself for us.

ALLELUIA

How shall we adequately render this word of praise? We should like to announce it to the whole world with cries of vehement exultation. And our chant? The melody sets in with the minor third, known to us from the Preface. Later editions of plain song that begin with a fourth are in error. After the first few notes we might surely expect a greater interval; but the melody again sinks back and repeats the same formula. This is followed not by a quiet *clivis*, but an onward-urging *pes*; finally there is an interval of a fourth.

Wagner[1] has called attention to the fact that the melody over *Alle-*agrees with that of the *Per ómnia saécula saeculórum*, and that the *jubilus* on *a* bears some resemblance to the *Dignum et justum*.

All this would depict for us the Church just awaking from a deep sleep, and not yet realizing that after so many days of enforced silence she is again allowed to sing *Allelúia*. The *Allelúia* is repeated three times, each time in a higher pitch, making it necessary to begin in a subdued, low pitch.[2] But steadily the joy grows, steadily the jubilation increases. And once the climax has been reached, the melody continues impressively on high *c* with *Confitémini* (Ps. 117, 1).

1. *Confitemini Domino, quoniam bonus: 2. quoniam in saeculum misericordia ejus.*

1. *Praise ye the Lord, because He is good: 2. because his mercy endureth for ever.*

The first half of either verse has the same close, in which there seems to re-echo a motive of the preceding Tract. The whole ends with the final motive of *Allelúia*. The text is explained in the verse of the Gradual for Easter Sunday.

TRACT (Ps. 116: 1–2)

1. *Laudate Dominum omnes gentes:* † *et collaudate eum omnes populi.* 2. *Quoniam confirmata est super nos misericordia ejus:* † *et veritas Domini manet in aeternum.*

1. *Praise the Lord all ye Gentiles:* † *and praise him all ye people.* 2. *Because his mercy is confirmed upon us:* † *and the truth of the Lord remaineth for ever.*

---

[1] III, 397.

[2] Another interpretation would hear in this threefold repetition the blast of trumpets.

We heard this song on the Ember Saturday of Lent. How devout and joyful it sounded today when at the solemn administration of Baptism individuals of all nations experienced the plentitude of divine mercy, when they formed an alliance with the God who is eternally faithful.

After the priest has received Holy Communion, renewed jubilation sweeps through the house of God. *Allelúia* resounds again in a melody which in its simplicity, its brevity, and its harmony has all the characteristics of a true folksong.

In the *Magníficat* that follows, the Blessed Virgin assumes the role of chanter and praises the Lord who has wrought such great marvels upon us, who has thrust the mighty from their seats and exalted the lowly, who has filled the hungry with good things and in His mercy has adopted us as His own children. The full effect of this pleasing, powerful, and gripping song can only be realized by actual participation in the services on Holy Saturday morning.

ANTIPHON Vespere Autem

Vespere autem sabbati, quae lucescit in prima sabbati, venit Maria Magdalene, et altera Maria, videre sepulcrum, alleluia.

In the evening of the Sabbath: which dawns in the first day of the week, came Mary Magdalen, and the other Mary, to the sepulchre: alleluia.

With *lucéscit* joy overruns the almost typical limits of the melody.

For the dismissal of the community, the deacon does not employ the usual formula; his heart is too full. He must continue with a twofold *allelúia* the Easter jubilation which he intoned in the *Exsúltet*. Go, he tells us, and bring gladness into a world languishing for want of joy; carry into it a spirit of goodness and purity, and revivify it with consolation and strength.

Our answer is a spirited *Deo grátias, allelúia, allelúia*. For we realize what we are taking away with us, and how rich we have become through Christ and His liturgy. We know that the Church, her divine claims substantiated by the miracle of the Resurrection, has resisted all the attacks of violence and pretended learning and come forth victorious. We believe in the power of truth, in the might of grace; and filled with the spirit of the primitive Church, filled with the courage and strength of the martyrs, we cry: *Deo grátias, allelúia, allelúia*.

*   *   *   *

EASTER SUNDAY

INTROIT (Ps. 138: 18, 5–6)

1. *Resurrexi, et adhuc tecum sum, alleluia:* 2. *posuisti super me manum tuam, alleluia;* 3. *mirabilis facta est scientia tua, alleluia, alleluia.* Ps. *Domine probasti me et cognovisti me:* * *tu cognovisti sessionem meam et resurrectionem meam.*

1. *I arose, and am still with thee, alleluia:* 2. *thou hast laid thy hand upon me, alleluia:* 3. *thy knowledge is become wonderful, alleluia, alleluia.* Ps. *Lord, thou hast proved me, and known me:* * *thou hast known my sitting down, and my rising up.*

The opening word of today's Introit *(Resurréxi)* brings us directly to the mystery that is being celebrated. Christ Himself, gloriously risen, speaks this word to His heavenly Father. He has fulfilled the duty with which His Father had charged Him, and now He directs His first thought, His first prayer, to the Father. This took place during that "truly blessed night which alone deserved to know the time and hour when Christ rose again from the dead," as the Church sang yesterday in the *Exsúltet.* Then the Risen One lifted His eyes and heart to the Father and prayed: *Resurréxi et adhuc tecum sum.* It is all inner fervor, this melody, breathing intense love, like a song coming from the quiet, unalterable depths of eternity itself. Exclusively personal, it has no thought of its listeners; no impetuous cries of triumph disturb it. But it is not gloomy or dismal; it is a smile of purest joy. It clothes the text with lights and colors to which we should otherwise have remained entirely oblivious, and thus it opens up new avenues to the understanding of the Paschal Mystery.

1. "I arose, and am still with Thee"; that is, I am again with Thee. From the bosom of the Father, the second Person of the Blessed Trinity descended to us, assumed a nature capable of suffering, and thus to a certain extent forsook the glory which knew naught of pain or sorrow. He was, so to speak, cut off from the glory of the Father. And how keenly He felt this separation on the cross! But now He is again "in the glory of God the Father." He contemplates His glory, the boundless, golden, eternal glory which henceforth is proper to His human nature also. And He looks into the vastness of future time, which is blessed because all mankind is to share in His resurrection. The font of salvation is now opened to all, and its saving waters will bring us to glory, so that we may be united to Jesus our Head, and may be with the Father as He Himself is with the Father. Alleluia!

The real dominant of the melody and of the *Resurréxi* is *f*, which pervades the entire piece as a tristropha; it must be sung very lightly; it is, so to say, a quivering from very joy. *Adhuc tecum sum* has *g* for its dominant. Five notes precede the word *tecum* and five follow it. The entire first phrase confines itself to the tetrachord *d–g*. Its *allelúia* is also sung as proceeding from the heart of the risen Christ. But it may serve in all three phrases as our own cry—a jubilant, expressive Amen to the words of the Redeemer (*Analyses*, III, 10).

2. "Thou hast laid thy hand upon me." Even when He was in the grave the hand of the Father rested protectingly over His Son. Then it permitted Him to shatter the fetters of death and to arise to a new life. Perhaps one may also apply these words to the hand of God demanding justice which weighed so terribly upon the Saviour that it forced from Him the words: "Only against Me He hath turned, and turned again His hand all the day" (Lamen. 3: 3). But today Christ substitutes the glad Alleluia: Alleluia for His sufferings, for His death, and for the fruits of His redemption.

The calm melody with its strong accent on *f* may serve as a picture of the quietly sheltering hand of God. *Super* and *manum* remind us of the first *alle-(lúia)*. Toward the end, the second *allelúia* must grow in warmth and thus prepare for the third phrase. The rising melody has the same end in view. This second phrase has three members, like the first, but a greater range: *d–a*.

Now the third phrase may begin with all solemnity. It has four members, a tone-range of *c–a*, and a fourth which introduces a sort of modulation to low *c*. Amazement seems ever to grow in the heart of the Risen One. If we abstract from the first note, then the first *allelúia* is but a slightly shortened form of *et adhuc tecum sum*, and the second *allelúia* a repetition of the *allelúia* which follows that phrase.

The gaze of the risen Christ turns back to the days of eternity when divine mercy conceived the plan *(sciéntia)* of redemption. God was to become man, the Impassible One was to suffer, the Eternal to be destroyed, but from this death a new and fruitful life was to emerge; mankind, a nonentity before the majesty of God, was destined to obtain in the divine person of Jesus eternal reconciliation, unending glorification. Human power and malice were indeed to triumph for a short time, but then God's wisdom, omnipotence, and goodness were to assert themselves so much the more gloriously. All these apparent contradictions found a wonderful solution *(mirábilis)* in the resurrection of Christ. It is through this that our faith and our hope have received their foundation and corroboration.

In the psalm-verse, the God-man once again speaks of the trial which the Father had imposed upon Him. But He, the second Adam, stood the test. He is today the Blessed One who has proved Himself, who is adorned with the crown of life (Jas. 1: 12). Out of His abasement, out of His repose in the tomb *(séssio)*, the glory of the resurrection blossomed forth.

Whereas the Phrygian cadences *e g f f e* of the Introit proper have a tender ring, the somewhat severe psalmody expresses the virile joy of victory. Thereupon we tenderly and devoutly repeat the entire Introit. Thus this chant will impart to our soul genuine Easter joy, restrained, broad and deep, and we shall thank Mother Church that with this song, so uninviting at first sight, she leads us into the riches of the Easter liturgy.

   K. K., 23, 29 ff.; *Analyses*, III, ff.; *Choralblaetter*, Nr. 3.

GRADUAL (Ps. 117: 24, 1)

1. *Haec dies quam fecit Dominus*: 2. *exsultemus* 3. *et laetemur in ea*: ℣. 1. *Confitemini Domino* 2. *quoniam bonus*: 3. *quoniam in saeculum misericordia ejus.*

1. *This is the day which the Lord hath made*: 2. *let us be glad* 3. *and rejoice therein.* ℣. 1. *Give praise to the Lord*, 2. *for He is good*: 3. *for His mercy endureth forever.*

In the Introit the risen Lord spoke to His Father. Here all Christendom breaks forth in loud rejoicing and praises the Father because He has had commiseration upon His Son and because the season is now past in which it seemed that the Father would pity Him no more. To that terrible Friday, the handiwork of men, succeeded the day which the Lord hath made. God's heart has again inclined toward His Son, and now His mercy endures forever. All this is told us by the marks of the passion on the glorified body of Christ. The blissful life of the divinity has become a permanent acquisition of the sacred humanity. Christ died once; He dies no more.

How powerfully this song must have impressed the neophytes! In the early morning hours of Easter Sunday the churches gleamed with the dazzling white of their baptismal robes, which were perhaps even more beautiful than the silvery sheen of the Angels at the tomb. For the first time the neophytes experienced the happiness of being children of God; now their hearts overflowed with joy and thanksgiving that the Lord had delivered them from the hand of the enemy (Gradual for the coming Tuesday). And the assembled faithful rejoiced to know that the neophytes, for whose enlightenment and conversion they had stormed heaven for many long years, were now in the possession of baptismal innocence and of the true faith. This thought alone was enough to make well up from their innermost hearts the song: "Give praise to the Lord, for He is good and His mercy endureth forever."

It was on Easter evening, moreover, that the Lord not only wished peace to His disciples, but left to the entire world an unfailing source of peace in the Sacrament of Penance, which He instituted on this very day. This is the day, therefore, on which He bestowed upon His Church that great treasure of solace and consolation, which since that time has rejoiced the hearts of millions. Indeed, "the Lord is good and His mercy endureth forever."

The melody has much in common with the typical melody which was explained on the first Sunday of Lent (q.v.). But it also possesses noteworthy peculiarities. The first motive opens the chant in an almost dreamy manner; the following *Dóminus*, however, rises up in radiant tones. *Laetémur in ea* is more gracefully developed than in the former melody: *c cdc a, dc ded c, ec efdb c*. *Quóniam bonus* soars brilliantly above all else. The thought of God's goodness permits the singer to forget the limits to which the melody is otherwise confined. Although there is so much enthusiasm displayed, there is nevertheless a careful plan. The melody reaches its peak in *Quóniam*, and never thereafter does it rise to *f*, which has hitherto dominated the tonal line. The repeated *e c a*, which we feel to be a minor chord, and the broadening of the low *g* create a tension which finds a brilliant resolution in the G-major triad with its prolonged high *g*. The *clivis* which follows serves as transition to the tender *bonus*, which is to be rendered with great fervor.

Musica s., 45, 74 ff. and 105 f.

ALLELUIA VERSE (I Cor. 5: 7)

Pascha nostrum immolatus est Christus.   Christ our Pasch is immolated.

This most striking thought of today's Epistle has called into being one of the most beautiful creations of choral chant. Here the triumphal shout of Easter is best realized. It is melodic thanksgiving and jubilation and revelry. For now, in very deed, the great work of our redemption is an accomplished fact.

Over the *Allelúia* and in the first four notes of the first phrase of the *jubilus*, the melody shows an ascent, which in turn is answered by a descent in three groups of delightful turns. The first and second member of the *jubilus* have an identical ending; the third member in its second half reminds one of the close of the Alleluia on Holy Saturday.

The beginning should almost be *piano*, but should steadily gain in fervor and warmth. *Pascha nostrum*: how much grateful love *nostrum* shows! *Immolátus* must be an exultant shout. The rich melisma has the form *a a¹ b c*. Let *a¹* be a resounding amplification of *a* after which, however, the next nine notes are to recede somewhat in volume; *b* in turn should come a little to the fore, while great eagerness should be evident in *c*. Strange to say, *a* and *a¹*, with a different introduction, however, and at a lower pitch, are to be found over *univérsi* in the last verse of the Tract on the Ember Wednesday in Lent.

Revue, 31, 33 f.

SEQUENCE

The joyfulness of the *Allelúia* continues *(Sequentia)* to resound in the Sequence, which owes its origin to Wipo (✝c. 1048), an ecclesiastic at the courts of Conrad II and Henry III. The Alleluia-verse supplies the theme for the I strophe: *Sing the Paschal Victim's praise!* With a powerful motive, the following two strophes then set in. IIa. *A Lamb the sheep did save; and Christ back to the Father, sinless, sinners gave.* IIb. *Death and Life clashed in mysterious strife; Life's Captain, dead, now lives and reigns instead.*

The four succeeding strophes are a dialogue between the choir and Mary Magdalen. With the motive beginning an octave lower than that of IIa *(acd)*, the melody now becomes somewhat more calm. IIIa 1. *O Mary, say, what sawest thou by the way?* 2. *The tomb of the living Christ; and the glory of Him risen.* IIIb 1. *I heard the angelic word: I bowed to see the bands, the shroud.* 2. *Christ my hope is risen, and He is gone before you into Galilee!*

Again the jubilant motive of IIa resounds. It springs from exultant, unshakable conviction. IV. *Christ from the dead is truly risen! Victorious King, to us kind pity show. Amen. Alleluia.* As far as *victor Rex* the melody is full of power, upn which a confident *miserére* with a softer coloring follows. A hearty *Amen, Allelúia* brings this marvelous song to a close.

OFFERTORY (Ps. 75: 9, 10)

1. *Terra tremuit et quievit,* 2. *dum resurgeret in judicio Deus,* 3. *alleluia.*

1. *The earth trembled and was still,* 2. *when God arose in judgment,* 3. *alleluia.*

We cannot sing this melody too solemnly or too majestically. Although employing the fourth mode, like the Introit, in spirit it differs radically, being full of force and irresistible power. One is tempted to cry out: Though you plant both feet solidly upon the earth, there is no escaping; you must experience how at some period this solid earth and all things mundane will be shaken and destroyed. And all the world's clamor, its pomposity and boasting, its presumption to independence and autonomy, its singing and exultation will one day become mute when God comes in judgment. The magnificent Easter triumph which the *Victor Rex* gained over His enemies, over death and over all the powers of this world, guarantees also His final victory. The quaking of the earth on Easter morn is only a prelude to the mighty cataclysm which will come to pass at the end of time.

The first phrase ascends gradually. After *trémuit* it rests on the dominant of the mode, depicting perhaps, the fear of all creation. With *et* the melody reaches a height seldom attained by the fourth mode and strains the attention: even the boastful world will at some time come to feel exceedingly small and dejected. The final neums of this phrase were also used to conclude the first phrase of the Offertory of the Midnight Mass at Christmas. The second phrase bears some resemblance to the first. It also begins and ends with *d*, closes its first half with *a*, and twice reaches high *c*. Here the melody gains in amplitude and becomes more expressive of victory, especially at *judício* with its quint, the *pressus*, and the harsh *gbaga*. *Allelúia* in its first member is related to that on the feast of the Ascension, although the latter is in the first mode. Now the melody no longer reaches to *c*—the *b* which preceded it even becomes *b♭*—the whole becomes more tender, more personal. He who is one day to appear as our Judge, today again becomes our Redeemer in the Holy Sacrifice.

COMMUNION (I. Cor. 5: 7, 8)

1. *Pascha nostrum immolatus est Christus, alleluia:* 2. *itaque epulemur in azymis sinceritatis et veritatis,* 3. *alleluia, alleluia, alleluia.*

1. *Christ our Pasch is immolated, alleluia:* 2. *therefore let us feast with the unleavened bread of sincerity and truth,* 3. *alleluia, alleluia, alleluia.*

The first phrase has the same text as the *allelúia* after the Gradual. There it overflows with joy, like a rushing paean of triumph which is to inundate all the earth; here it is in an intimate Communion song, in which the exultation is more reserved. There an authentic mode is employed (7); here a plagal (6). In the former melody everything strives toward the dominant and above it, while here it centers about the final note, almost too much so; the lowest note is a fourth below and the highest a fourth above the finale, as if it had been measured with a rule *(f–c, f–b)*. But despite this modest means of expression the melody throbs with the consciousness of fresh life.

It may seem strange that *itaque* carries so rich a melody, and stranger still that the neums should fall to the syllable *-ta-*. This is due to the influence of early colloquial Latin, which put the accent on the syllable immediately preceding the enclitic *-que*. It is quite logical that the word should have such a rich melody, for it wishes to stress this thought with special emphasis: Since Christ has offered Himself as your Pasch, *therefore* we are able to celebrate the Paschal feast and unite ourselves with Him in Holy Communion. We are, moreover, to celebrate it in sincerity and truth. For after the Paschal lamb had been slaughtered in the Temple, the Jews were no longer permitted to have any leaven in their houses. In like manner, the old leaven of sin may no longer have any place in the Christian's heart, now that Christ has offered Himself for us. Consideration of the sacrificial death of Christ and of the ardent love that prompted it ought to enkindle us and induce us to lead a pure and holy life.

Christus is a graceful response to *(Pas)-cha no-(strum)*. The two-note group in the first *allelúia*, in the last five notes of *(i)-taque* and *(equ)-lémur*, and the first four notes of *á-(zymis)* and *veri-(tátis)* produce a pleasing effect. The spirited ascent in the third phrase, which reaches its summit in the third *allelúia*, is likewise highly effective.

Musica s., 52, 49 ff.

*   *   *   *

EASTER MONDAY
INTROIT (Ex. 13: 5, 9)

1. *Introduxit vos Dominus in terram fluentem lac et mel, alleluia:* 2. *et ut lex Domini semper sit in ore vestro, alleluia, alleluia.* Ps. *Confitemini Domino, et invocate nomen ejus:* * *annuntiate inter gentes opera ejus.*

1. *The Lord hath brought you into a land flowing with milk and honey, alleluia:* 2. *and that the law of the Lord may be ever in your mouth, alleluia, alleluia.* Ps. *Give glory to the Lord, and call upon his name:* * *declare his deeds among the gentiles.*

Here the neophytes, who wore their white robes at all the divine services of Paschal Week, are addressed. Baptism has led them into the land flowing with milk and honey, into the Promised Land of holy Church with its life-giving and invigorating sources of grace, with its sweet consolation. Hence it was that at Baptism they actually were given milk and honey to taste. Perhaps the journey they have just completed was made under a blistering sun and through the burning sand of the desert. But today their hearts are overjoyed at the loving guidance with which God has led their souls.

In its first part, the melody shows special favor to *vos* and *fluéntem lac et mel*. We are acquainted with the ascent over *fluéntem* from *egrediéntem* of the *Vidi aquam*. It occurs again immediately in the second phrase over *ut lex Dó-(mini)*. Similarly, the close of the first phrase is found in an abbreviated form over the two last *allelúia.* *Semper* shows special vigor.

After God has led you with such love, He may surely expect His will to be sacred to you, His law at all times to be in your mouths and in your hearts and to be accomplished in your lives. Grateful love demands this. But your eternal salvation is likewise assured thereby. It is just this faithful observance of His law that will lead you through all the dangers and allurements of the world, and bring you safely home to the eternal Easter, into the true Promised Land.

We may regard these words as coming from the mouth of St. Peter, whose basilica is the station for today. By way of admonition he also raises his voice: Let the life of Christ fill your hearts. "Then it seems as if a tear flowed down the cheek of Peter" (*K. L.*).

GRADUAL (Ps. 117: 24, 2)

Haec dies ... [as yesterday]. ℣. 1. *Dicat nunc Israel, quoniam bonus*: 2. *quoniam in saeculum misericordia ejus.*

This is the day ... [as yesterday]. ℣. 1. *Let Israel now say that He is good*: 2. *that His mercy endureth forever.*

Haec dies resounds throughout Easter Week until Saturday, when it appears in the form of the *Allelúia.* Today we may again sing the jubilant *quóniam bonus* in all its wonderful Easter glory.

ALLELIUA VERSE (Matt. 28: 2)

1. *Angelus Domini descendit de caelo*: 2. *et accedens revolvit lapidem, et sedebat super eum.*

1. *An angel of the Lord descended from heaven*: 2. *and, coming, rolled back the stone, and sat upon it.*

The first member of the *jubilus* with its downward rolling movement is a sharp contrast to the upward tendency of the two members which flank it. It occurs again, but slightly changed, over *de caelo*. The second member of the *jubilus* recurs over *revólvit lápidem. Accédens* is modeled upon *allelúia.* This piece is assigned to the eighth mode, and actually closes on *g*. But if we compare it with the Alleluia now sung on the feast of the Assumption, then it does not seem improbable that we here have the C mode with a close on the fifth above.

The angel at the tomb occupies the mind of the Church considerably. We have met him already in the Gospel for Holy Saturday, and throughout the week he appears in the antiphons for Vespers and Lauds. Today we see him also in the Alleluia-verse and in the Offertory.

OFFERTORY (Matt. 28: 2, 5, 6)

1. *Angelus Domini descendit de caelo, et dixit mulieribus*: 2. *Quem quaeritis, surrexit, sicut dixit, alleluia.*

1. *An angel of the Lord descended from heaven, and said to the women*: 2. *He whom you seek is risen as he said, alleluia.*

At an early date this melody was set to the text *Posuísti* for the feast of St. Gorgonius (Sept. 9), was used also for the feast of St. Matthew, and finally was introduced into the Mass *Laetábitur* common to martyrs. It is also sung on the feast of the Assumption to the text *Assúmpta est.* He who can abstract from the historical side and look at these Offertories from a purely melodic point of view accordng to the relation of word and sound and according to their phrasing, will without much hesitation place *Posuísti* first, *Assúmpta* second, and *Angelus* third. In the Offertory *Posuísti* the words *corónam* and *pretióso*—"Thou hast set on his head a crown of precious stones"—receive a most effective treatment. With *vitam pétiit* a new thought begins melodically, to which *tribuísti ei, allelúia* is admirably proportioned. In like manner, the climaxes of *Assúmpta est* occur on the words *gaudent* and *collaudántes*, while *ángeli* and *benedícunt*, respectively, after the great development bring pleasant relaxation and rest. *Benedícunt*, it is true, produces this effect too dependently. The motive which in the two other Offertories is given to *sicut dixit* and to *tribuísti ei*, respectively, drops away entirely. But the first phrase of the Offertory for the feast of the Assumption rounds out beautifully. It will well repay one's efforts to compare the Offertories with one another:

1. a) *Angelus Dómini descéndit*
   b) *Posuísti Dómine in cápite ejus*
   c) *Assúmpta est María in caelum*

2. a) *de caelo et dixit muliéribus*:
   b) *corónam de lápide pretióso*:
   c) *gaudent Angeli collaudántes*

3. a) *quem quaéritis, surréxit sicut dixit, allelúia.*
   b) *vitam pétiit a te, tribuísti ei, allelúia.*
   c) *benedícunt Dóminum, allelúia.*

In this Offertory, one becomes painfully aware of the omission of the ormer verses. Its present form does not entirely satisfy. Happily today's Gradual gives some indication of the melody of at least one of these verses.

The melody of the third verse has been adapted to the Offertory *Beáta es virgo*, which is now given in the Votive Masses of the Blessed Virgin from Easter till Pentecost. *Pérmanes* does not allow of such an adaptation; i t is the same as *allelúia* in the Offertory for Easter Monday. *Surréxit* of today's Offertory and *Creatórem* of the former have identical melodies.

In today's Offertory we are tempted to invert the two principal parts, to sing the narrative part first in a subdued manner and then to swing up to the higher regions (which now occur over *caelo* and *muliéribus*) with the words of the angel concerning the resurrection. But even in its present arrangement the melody appeals, because it has a certain elegance of movement, fluent melodic line, and charming motivation. How fine, for instance, is the line *d c a ǵfa a* over *Dómini*, the descent and ascent over *descéndit* and at its close the resemblance to the motive over *(An)-ge-(luś)*, the contraction of this motive with the first part of *descéndit* by the notes *f ǵag*, the notes *a g a c c* over *Dó-(mini)*, which is answered by *b g a c c* over *(muli)-é-(ribus)*! The two well-proportioned groups over *(sur)-réx-it* expand rhythmically over the second syllable of *allelúia*; the *allelúia* itself with its tense *(g) b*, whose solution *(g) cc* comes only after four notes, produces a delightful effect. We might almost speak of an intentional retarding of the leading note. *Dixit* with its energetic *pressus* likewise challenges attention. What was promised at that time has now become full reality. The Lord is truly risen. These words, together with the glorious *allelúia*, constituted the refrain to the verses. It is somewhat tiresome to meet the frequent close on the tonic; only three times is there a variation.

The pious women who gave evidence of such noble courage and tender love in coming to the tomb of the Saviour, well deserve that their names be mentioned with honor in the liturgy. This happens more than once in this solemn Paschal Week. Indeed, the Oriental Church has a special feast on the second Sunday after Easter, called the feast "of women bearing myrrh." May they teach us how to become true searchers after God, how to place all our powers in the service of Jesus and His cause, His Church, and how to approach the altar with the true sacrificial spirit! At the Eucharistic Banquet the Risen One will then appear also to us in the splendor of His glory.

COMMUNION (Luke 24: 34)

Surrexit Dominus, et apparuit Petro, alleluia.

The Lord hath risen, and hath appeared to Peter, alleluia.

Today's Gospel tells us: "The Lord hath appeared to Simon"; the Communion, however, uses the name Peter, which is more familiar to the people. St. Peter's church was the scene of today's solemn service. How great is the forgiving love of the Saviour as shown by this appearance! He is almost compelled to demonstrate this love to St. Peter even on the feast of Easter. To us also the Risen One has appeared today in Holy Communion.

Appáruit seems like an inversion of the final motive over *(Dómi)nus.* In an *allelúia* unusually long for a Communion, grateful joy finds expression for the love shown us in the redemption. To *d c a b é* corresponds *á b a g é.* It was only to avoid the key *b♭* that the melody was transposed a fifth higher.

*   *   *   *

LOW SUNDAY

INTROIT (I Pet. 2, 2)

1. *Quasi modo geniti infantes alleluia*: 2. *rationabiles, sine dolo lac concupicsite, alleluia, alleluia, alleluia.* Ps. *Exsultate Deo adjutori nostro:* * *jubilate Deo Jacob.*

1. *As newborn babes, alleluia:* 2. *thoughtful, and without guile, desire ye the milk, alleluia, alleluia, alleluia.* Ps. *Rejoice unto God our helper:* * *Sing aloud to the God of Jacob.*

The newborn child, in accordance with its instinct of self-preservation, desires the milk of its mother. For this it needs no admonition. Thus should we also, in order to preserve the supernatural life, have a spontaneous longing for the nourishment of our souls, for truth, and for the Holy Eucharist. That is the wish of holy Mother Church. In ancient times she impressed this strongly upon the neophytes, who had put off their white baptismal robes yesterday. At present she sings it for first communicants. And with true maternal solicitude she sings it for us all. She cries out to us: Preserve the spirit of the children of God, remain simple, humble, and submissive to Him. Remain *rationábiles*, children of the spirit; do not become children of the flesh. Remain *sine dolo*; preserve the truth without falsity, and love without envy. And come to me and nourish yourselves upon the stores which Christ has confided to me. Then deep joy will fill your hearts; God will be your Helper and you will rejoice and exult in His sight.

The song is extremely simple, almost naive. After it has risen to the tonic of the sixth mode *(f)*, it clings to it as if in fear. It moves about this note, several times descends lower, but always strives toward it again. This is especially shown with *infántes, al-(lelúia)*. The plagal form of the F mode could scarcely be evidenced more clearly. Melodically, *rationábiles*, with its harmonious line, is the highest point of the song. Its constituent notes are but a syllabic part of the psalm-verse of the Introit: *adjutóri nostro*. The Introit for the vigil of Christmas resembles this melody to some extent. After *sine dolo* there is a sort of break. It is for this reason that in the translation it has not been connected with the subsequent *lac*, as some do who translate thus: "Desire after the unadulterated milk"; it must be considered a separate phrase. *Concupíscite* is a pleasing variant of *(do)-lo*. Of the three *allelúia* the second forms a contrast to the two others, which are identical with the exception of one single note. After the preceding *d*, the first sets in on *c*, while the third sets in on *d* after the preceding *c*; thus the beginnings are pleasantly varied.

In the psalm-verse, since the second half of the text is very short, the melody cannot unfold itself entirely.

FIRST ALLELUIA VERSE (Matt. 28: 7)

1. *In die resurrectionis meae, dicit Dominus,* 2. *praecedam vos in Galilaeam.*

1. *On the day of my resurrection, saith the Lord,* 2. *I will go before you into Galilee.*

Manuscript 121 of Einsiedeln assigns this Alleluia to Thursday in Easter Week. The *jubilus* has the form *a a¹ b*. It seems that the composer was much concerned about the words *In die*, but wanted to give still more prominence to *praecédam vos* which soars a fifth above the surrounding melody. This seems rather strange to us, and makes us doubt whether the composition at hand is entirely original.

There is a free adaptation of text here. The words which are placed in the mouth of the risen Christ were spoken by the angel on Easter morning to the women at the tomb: "And going quickly, tell ye His disciples that He is risen: and behold He will go before you into Galilee; there you shall see Him." The singular melody is perhaps influenced by the fact that we have to do here with an extraordinary solemn appearance of the Risen One, at which, according to the testimony of St. Paul, more than five hundred disciples were present.

SECOND ALLELUIA VERSE (John 20: 26)

1. *Post dies octo, januis clausis*
2. *stetit Jesus in medio discipulorum*
suorum, 3. *et dixit: Pax vobis.*

1. *And after eight days, the doors being shut,* 2. *Jesus stood in the midst of his disciples,* 3. *and said: Peace be to you.*

Manuscript 339 of St. Gall's and 121 of Einsiedeln know nothing of this melody.

The motive which sets in over -*lúia* appears again in the third member of the *jubilus*; in the second member it sinks pleasingly a third lower; the second parts are identical in the first and second members, but in the third there is a slight difference.

The first two phrases of the verse are clearly psalmodic in structure:

Intonation	Middle Cadence	Closing Cadence
Post dies	*octo*	*jánuis clausis*
Stetit Jesus	*in médio*	*discipulórum suórum*

The third phrase repeats *Allelúia* with its *jubilus*.

This Alleluia serves nicely as an introduction to the following Gospel. During the eight days after Jesus' appearance in the Cenacle on the evening of Easter Sunday the disciples, no doubt, asked about Him and yearned for His presence. For him who seeks, whose heart is filled with longing, a period of eight days seems a painfully long time. Suddenly Jesus stands in their midst. He comes with that blessed greeting: "Peace be with you!" He comes again with His cheering goodness, which seems to have become even more warm and profound since the resurrection. In today's Eucharistic celebration this appearance of Jesus will be renewed. The Saviour wishes to come to us, to address also to us His joyful *Pax vobis*, to give us His peace, yes, even to give Himself.

The explanation of the OFFERTORY is given on Easter Monday.

COMMUNION (John 20, 27)

1. *Mitte manum tuam, et cognosce loca clavorum, alleluia:* 2. *et noli esse incredulus, sed fidelis, alleluia, alleluia.*

1. *Put in thy hand, and know the place of the nails, alleluia:* 2. *and be not incredulous but believing, alleluia, alleluia.*

This Communion song reflects in a pleasing manner the goodness of the Saviour, His winsome, touching love for us. Here He speaks as to an invalid whom one wishes to spare all exertion. The melody prefers simple seconds and avoids all larger intervals. What a contrast to the impetuosity of a Thomas with his pretentious demands! The Good Shepherd very carefully frees the erring lamb from the thorns in which it is entangled. The piece must be sung very devoutly and tenderly. And yet, with all its simplicity, it has its contrasts. Inserted among the Saviour's words we find a comparatively florid and bright *allelúia*, with which the melody also reaches its peak. At the end are two *allelúia*, which likewise extend to high *b♭*. There is also an interval of a fourth between *fidélis* and *allelúia*. These *allelúia* are the jubilant thanks of the Church for the Saviour's goodness.

Also to us the Risen One directs these words: "Put in thy hand." In early times the Christians were wont to receive the Holy Eucharist in their hands. Our faith enables us also to touch His sacred wounds and united with Him we cry out in sincere thanksgiving: "My Lord and my God, alleluia!"

*   *   *   *

SECOND SUNDAY AFTER EASTER

INTROIT (Ps. 32: 5, 6)

1. *Misericordia Domini plena est terra, alleluia:* 2. *verbo Dei caeli firmati sunt, alleluia, alleluia. Ps. Exsultate justi in Domino:* * *rectos decet collaudatio.*

1. *The earth is full of the mercy of the Lord, alleluia:* 2. *by the word of the Lord the heavens were established, alleluia, alleluia. Ps. Rejoice in the Lord, ye just:* * *praise becometh the upright.*

Tender and mellow tones (thrice the half-tone interval recurs) which sing of God's mercy mark the beginning of this piece. For today is the Sunday of the "Good Shepherd." Everything breathes of His goodness His love, His understanding pity. He knows His own. He acknowledges every indication of good will; He recognizes our weakness and knows how to have compassion on us. All the earth must in very deed praise His merciful love, for He has given His life for everyone. Than this there is no greater love, as He Himself has declared. The melody develops very gradually. The notes *d–f* at the beginning become *e–f–g* over *Dó-(mini)* and *f–a* on the third syllable of *allelúia*, yet so that the first phrase rests on *f*.

A more energetic spirit is evidenced in the fourths of the second phrase and the accent on *g*. We are speaking here of God's almighty *fiat* This one word sufficed to stabilize the heavens. But to unlock for us the heaven of divine mercy, the Word of God went to a most cruel death.

At this thought a heartfelt *allelúia*—the apex of the melody—must ascend from our hearts. We summon all the just to join in our song. The only other time we hear this bright, jubilant melody is at the end of the Introit of the Rogation Mass and in the more recent Introit for the feast of St. Paul of the Cross (April 28). As usual in the fourth mode, the psalm-verse has *a* as its dominant. Thus we have the gradation: the first phrase *f*; the second *g*; the psalm-verse *a*.

FIRST ALLELUIA VERSE (Luke 24: 35)

1. *Cognoverunt discipuli Dɔmi-num Jesum* 2. *in fractione panis.*

1. *The disciples knew the Lord Jesus* 2. *in the breaking of the bread.*

SECOND ALLELUIA VERSE (John 10: 14)

1. *Ego sum pastor bonus:* 2. *et cognosco oves meas,* 3. *et cognoscunt me meae.*

1. *I am the Good Shepherd:* 2. *and I know my sheep,* 3. *and mine know me.*

These two Alleluia-verses pave the way for the Gospel. There the Lord will say: "I know Mine and Mine know Me, as the Father knoweth Me, and I know the Father." Both Alleluia speak of recognition of the Lord. The former leads us back to Emmaus and permits us to experience in ourselves the happiness of the disciples. Their hearts were burning within them when that mysterious traveling Companion spoke to them. But now they recognize the Lord Jesus in the breaking of the bread. Originally this melody was sung to the text *Dómine Deus, salútis meae,* which is employed at present on the twelfth Sunday after Pentecost. Its explanation will likewise be found there.

Similarly, the melody of the second Alleluia is not original. In the ancient manuscripts as well as in the present Gradual it is assigned to the feast of the holy Martyrs Marius, Martha, Audifax, and Abachum (January 19). The *jubilus* of *Allelúia* exhibits the form ab, cb, d. The verse repeats the melody of *Allelúia* and its *jubilus* over *cognósco oves meas* and over *et cognóscunt me meae.* Since the original is not drawn out, the similarity of sound between the words prompted this repetition. The effect is not an entirely happy one, because we hear the same melody four times. Two small variations, however, should be mentioned. The beginning of the second and third phrases is lighter than that of *Allelúia.* In the same manner, *meas* avoids the *pressus* at the close of the *jubilus,* for as yet there is here no question of a complete ending. The inception with the dominant over *Ego sum* is remarkably effective, even though we here have a text that has been substituted.

Christ knows His own as He knows the Father. These words ought to be for us an infinitely great consolation. The Saviour's knowledge of the Father includes of itself His immeasurable and unending love for Him.

OFFERTORY (Ps. 62: 2, 5)

1. *Deus, Deus meus, ad te de luce vigilo*: 2. *et in nomine tuo levabo manus meas, alleluia.*

1. *O God, my God, to thee do I watch at break of day*: 2. *and in Thy name I will lift up my hands, alleluia.*

Christ is the shepherd and bishop of our souls; today's Epistle applies these terms to Him. He keeps a faithful watch over His sheep, never resting, never slumbering. Hence it is but fitting that my first waking thought be directed to Him, that my heart turn to Him at the first streak of dawn *(de luce)*. And this the more, since on this morning He again desires to be mine entirely, and wishes me to partake of His divine life in the Eucharistic Banquet. Just as at the Offertory the priest lifts up his hands together with the sacrificial gifts of bread and wine, so shall I also lift up my hands and offer myself as an oblation, singing my Alleluia in the joy of the Holy Ghost and confiding in the omnipotence of His grace *(in nomine tuo)*. In early times these sentiments were expressed by these verses: "I come before Thee, to see Thy power and Thy glory. Thou hast been my Helper. And I will rejoice under the covert of Thy wings." In the Offertory the divine Redeemer prays to His heavenly Father and protests His continual readiness to be sacrificed. Here and now He becomes the Lamb which is offered for us on the altar.

In the quiet first phrase, *luce* is the only word which rises to somewhat greater prominence. Is this perhaps to remind us of the sudden flashing of the light? The tone-sequences over the second syllable are heard at various times: in the *Vidi aquam*, where there is mention of flowing water with *aqua ista*; in the Offertory *Invéni David*, when it speaks of flowing oil with the words *óleo sancto*. Proper to almost all pieces of the second mode is the close of the first phrase on *c*. Only here the seconds, without any *pressus*, have not that strong modulatory power shown, for example, in the Introit *Mihi autem* for Apostles. In its first half, the second phrase is somewhat more lively, setting in immediately on the dominant and taking on a more ornate melody with *in nomine tuo*, upon which is placed a fourth as an antithesis to that occurring in the first phrase. The second part returns to the simple, almost naively pastoral style of the first phrase, which feeling is strengthened by the minor third *d–f*, the usual combination of dominant and tonic in pieces of the second mode.

COMMUNION (John 10: 14)

1. *Ego sum pastor bonus, alleluia*: 2. *et cognosco oves meas, et cognoscunt me meae, alleluia, alleluia.*

1. *I am the good shepherd, alleluia*: 2. *and I know my sheep, and mine know me, alleluia, alleluia.*

We have been allowed to participate in the breaking of the Bread. In Holy Communion Christ appeared as the true light in our hearts and has made us happy. Each Holy Communion is a pledge that the Good Shepherd will not rest until He has successfully led us to the springs of eternal life. He alone is the Good Shepherd. Hence *Ego* occupies a very emphatic position at the beginning of the piece. We shall remain united to Him, and if other voices entice us and seek to influence our judgment, then we shall turn to Him alone and listen only to His voice. We know Him and bend our knees before His presence. He, the "Only-Begotten of the Father, full of grace and truth," dwells in our hearts as the Word of God became flesh.

The Communion has the same text as the second Alleluia-verse, but a different development. The two phrases *et cognósco* and *et cognóscunt*, it is true, begin with the same motive. But in place of the parallelism in the Alleluia, the melody in the present case over *et cognósco oves meas* shows a lively upward swing with the range of a sixth. It portrays the great love of the Good Shepherd for His sheep. But *et cognóscunt* has only seconds and its range is but a third: compared to His knowledge of us, our knowledge of Him will always be fragmentary. Tenderness breathes from the half-tone intervals at the beginning, and yet there is also firmness shown in the double note (as found in our present version). Cf. Wagner (II, 147) concerning the notation of this passage in the old manuscripts. In the notation of Montpellier which is given there, the hook does not belong to the neums, but to the letters *ef*. Remarkably simple is the *allelúia* which is inserted between the words of the Saviour, and also the two *allelúia* which are attached at the end, since this cry usually is sung with great spirit (cf. the *allelúia* in today's Introit). Here they strive to be nothing more than the simple melody of a shepherd in the fields.

Revue, 20, 133 ff.

* * * *

THIRD SUNDAY AFTER EASTER
INTROIT (Ps. 65: 1, 2)

1. *Jubilate Deo omnis terra, alleluia*: 2. *psalmum dicite nomini ejus,*

1. *Shout with joy to God, all the earth, alleluia*; 2. *sing ye a psalm*

alleluia: 3. date gloriam laudi ejus,   *to his name, alleluia: 3. give glory*
4. *alleluia, alleluia, alleluia.* Ps.   *to his praise,* **4.** *alleluia, alleluia,*
Dicite Deo, quam terribilia sunt opera   *alleluia.* Ps. *Say unto God: How*
tua, Domine! * *in multitudine vir-*   *terrible are thy works, O Lord!* *
tutis tuae mentientur tibi inimici   *in the multitude of thy strength*
tui.   *thine enemies shall lie to thee.*

A twofold division is made by the melody. The first part is subdivided by the imperatives, *Jubiláte, dícite,* and *date.* Each of these words
in its own way strives upward to *c,* and each has its last syllable on *f,*
the lowest note of this first part. The first and third phrases close on the
tonic; the close of the second on *a* is a pleasing variation, the first part
of whose *allelúia* repeats the motive of *psalmum.* This *allelúia* may also
be found in Introits of the third mode, for example, that of Wednesday
in Whitsun Week. We may consider the motive over *dícite* as a model
for the extension over *nómini ejus* and *glóriam laudi ejus.*

The threefold *allelúia* constituting the second part is in effect another imperative: "Praise ye the Lord!" But the melodic line differs
from the imperatives above. First it descends to *d,* then to *c,* and finally
soars upward with impelling force to *c.*

Although the melody has a rather limited range (the first part confines itself to a fifth), still there is something impressive about it. With
its numerous fourths it endeavors to work itself into the hearts of the
people and to propel them into that atmosphere of joy with which it is
itself filled. How vigorously *omnis terra* is stressed! All countries are to
join in this jubilation. That should, at any rate, be the effect on ourselves
as a result of meditating on the wonderful works of God, on the realization of His plan of salvation, the redemption through Christ's death
upon the cross, our predestination to eternal glory. The very thought is
enough to make the entire earth prostrate itself in humble obeisance before God's face with its heart filled with joy. This will one day come to
pass; at the great final resurrection all the earth will pay reverence to its
King, its Lord, its God. Then those, too, who now boastfully pose as
enemies of Christ and His kingdom, will of sheer necessity throw themselves on their knees in adoration, and the entire celestial host will sing
to Him its eternal Alleluia.

FIRST ALLELUIA VERSE (Ps. 110: 9)

Redemptionem misit Dominus   *The Lord hath sent redemption to*
populo suo.   *his people.*

At St. Gall's, in the tenth century, this melody was sung on the
Thursday of Whitsun Week. Codex 121 of Einsiedeln lists it among the

Alleluia at the end of the manuscripts. We became acquainted with it and its *jubilus* in the Christmas season. While the verse has a different close there, in today's melody the ending runs harmoniously into the *jubilus* of *Allelúia*. Only the Lord can send redemption to His people; rightly, therefore, are the words *Redemptiónem* and *Dóminus* and their accented syllables brought into prominence.

SECOND ALLELUIA VERSE (Luke 24: 46)

1. *Oportebat pati Christum, et re-surgere a mortuis,* 2. *et ita intrare in gloriam suam.*

1. *It behooved Christ to suffer these things,* 2. *and so to enter into his glory.*

Codex 339 of St. Gall's does not mention this melody; Codex 121 of Einsiedeln, however, assigns it to the Wednesday of Easter Week. With its rise to the tonic *(e)*, its repetition of the major chord *c–e–g*, and the use of similar motives, it reminds one of the Alleluia *Amávit eum* in the Mass for Doctors of the Church. Considered in this light, this Alleluia, as well as the *Amávit eum*, might be assigned to the C mode, with its close on the third.

The *jubilus* has the form *a a b b c*; part *a* has a pleasant interchange of *porrectus* and *torculus*, while quiet seconds follow the energetic ascending fifth in part *b*. *Oportébat* reminds us of *Allelúia*, *intráre* of the motive *a*, *mórtuis* shows the infleunce of *b*, and *in glóriam* repeats *et ira*. Some have tried to show that the first half of the Alleluia-*jubilus* with its low pitch refers to the suffering *(pati)* and that the second (higher) half expresses the joy of Easter. As far as musical comprehension of the text is concerned, we had best consider the rendition from the standpoint of declamation. We should rather stress *Oportébat*, and still more *pati*, and place special emphasis on the words *ita* and *glóriam*. This is the way the melody develops.

Christ was under no absolute obligation to suffer, but all His suffering was included in God's plan of redemption, and hence "the servant of God" (as Isaias calls the Messias) was impelled to fulfill this duty; it became, so to say, a necessity *(Oportébat)*. Now His work is done. Similarly, the glory of the resurrection had to follow upon His suffering and death, and it is on this glory that the Alleluia congratulates the Lord.

OFFERTORY (Ps. 145: 2)

1. *Lauda, anima mea, Dominum:*
2. *laudabo Dominum in vita mea:*
3. *psallam Deo meo, quamdiu ero, alleluia.*

1. *Praise the Lord, O my soul,*
2. *in my life I will praise the Lord:*
3. *I will sing to my God as long as I shall be, alleluia.*

In the first phrase the singer rouses himself to the praise of God
with a fervor which is in no wise obtrusive or spectacular, but which
for that very reason makes a more profound impression on a receptive
spirit. The second and third phrases immediately draw the practical
conclusions: *laudábo, psallam.* This is the singer's occupation not merely
for the moment, but for all the time of his life; it is his vocation. As long
as blood courses in his veins, as long as his heart beats within his breast,
this sacred obligation should urge him on. For God's mercy attends him
all the days of his life. The verses which formerly accompanied these
verses ran as follows: "I will sing to the Lord as long as I live. Who
keepeth truth forever; who executeth judgment for them that suffer
wrong; who giveth food to the hungry. I will sing to the Lord as long as
I live, alleluia. The Lord lifteth up them that are cast down; the Lord
looseth them that are fettered; the Lord keepeth the fatherless and the
stranger and the widow. The ways of sinners he will destroy. The Lord
shall reign forever; thy God, O Sion, unto generation and generation. I
will sing to the Lord as long as I live, alleluia."

Only the Lord can effect all this. Hence the word *Dóminum* towers
prominently above all else. The ascending endings of the first *Dóminum*
and of *mea* are necessitated by the lower beginning of the following phrase.
Perhaps the same reason applies for *meo.* Rhythmically these similar
endings effect a great calmness, to which the identical or at least very
similar intonations of *Lauda, psallam,* and *allelúia* contribute. Perhaps
two neums on the unaccented syllable *(quám)-di-(u)* are accounted for
by the fact that colloquial Latin preferred to retain the accent on the
stem syllable. The final *allelúia* is common to all the Offertories of the
fourth mode during the Paschal season. Perhaps it received its form
from the present Offertory, since its first part resembles *psallam* and its
close *mea.*

COMMUNION (John 16: 16)

1. *Modicum et non videbitis me,
alleluia*: 2. *iterum modicum, et
videbitis me,* 3. *quia vado ad Patrem, alleluia, alleluia.*

1. *A little while, and now you shall
not see me, alleluia:* 2. *and again a
little while, and you shall see me*: 3.
*because I go to the Father, alleluia,
alleluia.*

Here the Saviour says to His Apostles: Only a short time remains
until the separation. It will begin in a few hours and will be completed
on the evening of Good Friday. But it will last only a short time, for
they will see Him again on Easter Day. In the first phrase the melody
reflects the sorrow of parting by its stress on the tonic and by its descent

a fourth below it. In *íterum módicum,* which sets in on the lofty tenor and emphasizes it, as well as in the ascending melodic line over *vidébitis me,* we see expressed the joy of reunion. Between the two sentences, as is only natural, an *allelúia,* redolent of the spirit of Easter, is interpolated, and receives further melodic amplification in the twofold *allelúia* at the end of the melody.

When we participate in the Eucharistic Banquet, we cannot see the Saviour; His divinity and His humanity are veiled. But we can contemplate Him with the eyes of faith. And the purer our heart is, the deeper does this gaze penetrate. This sight and possession and enjoyment, it is true, is short-lived *(módicum),* and here below it will never be perfect; it will ever be a *módicum.* But Christ is going to the Father, and we may therefore sing a joyous *allelúia.* He goes to prepare a place for us, that we may see Him face to face throughout a blessed eternity. But, according to the words of St. Augustine[1], He is also preparing us for this dwelling. Occasionally we become painfully aware that this work of preparation is going on. But it is to last only for a little while *(módicum)* after which we shall also be allowed to chant the eternal alleluia.

*   *   *   *

FOURTH SUNDAY AFTER EASTER

The lively expression of joy and thanksgiving for divine assistance which we find in the Masses for the fourth and fifth Sundays after Easter are, no doubt, influenced, as H. Grisar remarks *(Das Missale im Lichte roemischer Stadtgeschichte,* p. 85), by the general rejoicing which followed the overthrow of barbarian hordes through divine intervention. Perhaps there is reference to the raising of the siege of Rome under Wittiges (A.D. 538).

INTROIT (Ps. 97: 1–2)

1. *Cantate Domino canticum novum, alleluia:* 2. *quia mirabilia fecit Dominus, alleluia:* 3. *ante conspectum gentium revelavit justitiam suam, alleluia, alleluia.* Ps. *Salvavit sibi dextera ejus:* * *et brachium sanctum ejus.*

1. *Sing ye to the Lord a new canticle, alleluia:* 2. *for the Lord hath revealed his justice, alleluia:* 3. *in the sight of the gentiles, alleluia alleluia.* Ps. *His right hand hath wrought for him salvation:* * *and his arm is holy.*

A rising line marks the development of the melody. The first part of the first phrase has a range of a fourth, the second of a fifth; the sec-

---
[1] *Tractatus 68 in Joann.*

ond and third phrases have a range of a sixth. The motive of *Cantáte Dómino* recurs over *fecit Dóminus* and the following *allelúia*. It is not, however, proper to this Introit. We heard it over *sine dolo* in the Introit for Low Sunday. Closer examination, in fact, shows that these two Introits are similar in more than one way. They have the same mode and the same range; the close of the first phrase and almost the entire second phrase, moreover, show great similarity. Compare:

(novum) allelúia: quia mirabília fecit Dóminus, allelúia, and *(infántes) allelúia: rationábiles, sine dolo.*

The small variant here observable shows the refined sense the ancients had for forming endings. The formula over *sine dolo* has its final *torculus* a third below the tonic, thus facilitating immediate continuance of the melody over *lac*. The *allelúia* after *Dóminus*, however, brings the entire second phrase to a close; for this reason the final *torculus*, suggestive of pleasant rest, is placed a fourth below the tonic. This at the same time provides a pleasant contrast to the endings of the first and third phrases.

The third phrase begins with a sort of inversion of the preceding motive, vigorously stresses *revelávit*, and accords still greater prominence to *justítiam suam*. According to melodic sense, the second last *allelúia* finds its fulfillment in the resolved major chord of the subdominant. The last *allelúia* is almost the same as the one which ends the first phrase.

From the obvious similarity of this chant with the Introit *Quasi modo*, and from its restricted range, we can readily infer that it is not intended as a powerful song of victory, but rather a heartfelt song of thanksgiving for the wonder of wonders which the *Father* has wrought in the resurrection of His Son. He made known His justice to all the nations. He has accepted the expiatory sacrifice of His Son, and has glorified and transfigured Him because of it; He has manifested His beloved Son as the Just One, through whom alone the world can attain to salvation and justification.

The resurrection must also be ascribed to Christ Himself. For He indeed has the power to lay down His life and the power to take it up again. On the cross His right hand was cruelly pierced by a nail and His sacred arm was most painfully wrenched out of place. But by His own strength He overcame everything: sin, suffering, and death.

Since today's Gospel and Communion treat of the coming of the Holy Ghost, we may likewise attribute the marvelous deeds to His activity, to the glory which, according to Christ's own assertion, He bestowed upon Him, and the wonders which He has not ceased to work in the Church from the first Pentecost until the present time.

Would that we might sing to the Father and to the Son and to the Holy Ghost a new canticle, with renewed love, renewed joy, renewed gratefulness, and in the same spirit as the Risen Christ sang the new canticle of His glorified humanity to the Father on Easter morning. The deeper we penetrate into God's marvels, the more spontaneously, the more lively, the more joyously will this song well from our hearts.

FIRST ALLELUIA VERSE (Ps. 117: 16)

1. *Dextera Dei fecit virtutem*: 2. *dextera Domini exaltavit me.*

1. *The right hand of the Lord hath wrought strength*: 2. *the right hand of the Lord hath exalted me.*

These words are known to us from the Offertory for Maundy Thursday. At that time they were spoken in anticipation; but now, after the feast of Easter, they are a glorious reality; each Sunday after Easter celebrates the victory of the Mighty One, who in the power of His own arm triumphed over death and sin. On the feast of the Invention of the Cross the same text is employed in the Offertory. First the Saviour had to be lifted up, nailed to the cross, and only then did He enter into His glory.

The beginning of *Allelúia* and the endings over *Dei, (vir)-tútem* and *Dómini* exhibit characteristics of the first mode. To the descending line over the first *déxtera* the ascending line over the second comes as an answer. In the *jubilus* the formula *gabaga* resembles *abćaga* over *me.*

SECOND ALLELUIA VERSE (Rom. 6: 9)

1. *Christus resurgens ex mortuis, jam non moritur*: 2. *mors illi ultra non dominabitur.*

1. *Christ rising again from the dead, dieth now no more*: 2. *death shall no more have dominion over him.*

Psalm 117 continues the text of the first Alleluia-verse with the words: "I shall not die, but live." In the second Alleluia-verse the words of St. Paul repeat the same thought, correlating it directly with the general theme of the Easter season. The melody lingers on this one fundamental joyous thought, that death is now become an impossibility for Christ. The bitter flood of trial and suffering which overwhelmed Him can nevermore disturb His body or His soul. Now is He "the Prince of Life," as the Easter Sequence refers to Him, and no power can ever diminish the plenitude of His bliss.

This thought is expressed by means of parallel phrases, a device often met with in the psalms. The first phrase uses the principal motives of *Allelúia* with its *jubilus, ab, ac, d: Christus = Alle-(lúia), resúrgens =* the expansion of *(Alle)-lúia, ex mórtuis = jam non móritur = ac* and *d.* The divisions of this first verse are evident: the arsis to *mórtuis*, here a logical pause on the dominant of the mode; beginning with *jam*, the thesis, and a pause on the tonic. A correspondence exists between the closing formulas of *(re)-súrgens* and *mórtuis*. *Mors* in the second phrase is not a recalling of the death agony, but a cry of triumphant joy. Boldly it soars up on a seventh, stresses the high note, then adds an animated *torculus*. The repetition sets in with a lively interval of a sixth, an uncommon occurrence in plain song. Then it moves to a victorious completion in *climacus* groups which, incidentally, should not be sung rapidly. *Non dominábitur* repeats *Allelúia* with its *jubilus*, thus giving the jubilant melody over *mors* undisputed first rank.

The modal peculiarity of the piece lies in this, that it is assigned to the first mode, but throughout avoids the note *b*, and that *mors* resembles the *jubilus* of the Alleluia *Amávit eum* from the Mass for Doctors of the Church, assigned to the fourth mode (cf. also the second Alleluia-verse for the third Sunday after Easter).

On the feast of Christ the King we meet the same melody.

OFFERTORY

The explanation was given on the second Sunday after Epiphany (q.v.). There is hardly any doubt that originally it was composed for this Sunday. On the former Sunday it invited the entire world to admire the love which God showed to men in the incarnation of His Son. But today we exult in thanksgiving for Christ's resurrection and the glory which it makes accessible also to us. What great things *(quanta)* are contained in the words of the Apostle! "But God, who is rich in mercy, for his exceeding charity wherewith he loved us, even when we were dead in sins, hath quickened us together in Christ ... and hath made us sit together in the heavenly places" (Ephes. 2: 4 ff.).

COMMUNION (John 16: 8)

1. *Dum venerit Paraclitus Spiritus veritatis,* 2. *ille arguet mundum de peccato, et de justitia, et de judicio, alleluia, alleluia.*

1. *When the Paraclete shall come, the Spirit of truth,* 2. *he shall convince the world of sin and of justice and of judgment, alleluia, alleluia.*

Here, for the first time in the Mass-chants after Easter, there is mention of the Holy Ghost, the Spirit of truth, of His coming and of His activity. As the Gospel more fully explains, He comes to convince the world of its sin, the greatest sin, its rejection of the Son of God, its resistance to the truth taught by the Apostles and the Church and announced to all the world. He comes also to show it justice, namely, the justice of the cause of Jesus. He whom the world condemned as a blasphemer and a seducer is risen and ascended into heaven; hence He alone is holy, He alone is just. The Holy Ghost also prepares for judgment. At the death of Jesus He already dealt a mortal blow to the prince of this world; but at the final judgment He will fully glorify the Son of God. Against the proofs adduced *(árguet)* by the Spirit of truth, no pretentious learning and no power on earth can prevail. Truth will infallibly conquer. Hence *árguet* rightly marks the summit of the melody. For this reason, also, a twofold brilliant *allelúia* is added to this serious text, and for the same reason *ille* is vigorously stressed. The concluding formula *b–a–g* with the weighty full-step intervals in *peccáto, justítia,* and *judício,* cannot be entirely unpremeditated. The melody over *Spíritus veritátis* is a citation from the beginning of the Communion *Ego sum pastor bonus* for the second Sunday after Easter, or vice versa. Both Communions are also employed as responsories at Matins.[1]

The antiphon for the Magnificat on Tuesday after the fourth Sunday after Easter has the same text and also some melodic resemblance.

Our song must be sincere homage to the Spirit of truth, and at the same time a defiant challenge to all the vain pretences of a world which tries to ignore God. Today's Holy Communion will strengthen this resolve. As often as we communicate, we announce the death of the Lord until He will come as the Holy One, the Judge of all the world.

*   *   *   *

FIFTH SUNDAY AFTER EASTER

(Cf. the remarks at the beginning of the fourth Sunday)

INTROIT (Is. 48: 20)

1. *Vocem jucunditatis annuntiate, et audiatur, alleluia:* 2. *nuntiate usque ad extremum terrae:* 3. *liberavit Dominus populum suum, alleluia, alleluia.* Ps. *Jubilate Deo omnis terra:* * *psalmum dicite nomini ejus, date gloriam laudi ejus.*

1. *Declare the voice of joy and let it be heard, alleluia:* 2. *declare it even to the ends of the earth:* 3. *the Lord hath delivered his people, alleluia, alleluia.* Ps. *Shout with joy to God, all the earth:* * *sing ye a psalm to his name, give glory to his praise.*

One might imagine that the Easter joy would gradually diminish in the successive Introits for the Sundays after Easter, for the more we

---

[1] *Revue,* 20, 137.

recede from this feast, the closer we approach the day of the ascension and the departure of the Lord from this earth. But it does not. Other rules come into play here. The melodies for the Introits of the first, second, and fourth Sundays are devout, rather than jubilant. Into these the brilliant third Sunday is inserted. Now, rising above all these, comes the Introit of the fifth Sunday: a clarion call of real Easter joy which would resound to the uttermost ends of the earth, as if conscious of the fact that never was there a more consoling message brought to cheer mankind.

In its first half, the first phrase has an energetic ascent for its arsis, followed by a similarly proportioned thesis. How delicate the melodic line here is, avoiding everything rough or severe! By preference the new neum sets in on the last note of the preceding one *(dge–eg–ga–acb*, and the descending *ca–ag–gag)*. After a brief arsis the second half brings a drawn-out thesis with the tetrachord *d–g*. Strength is thus gained for a renewed, powerful ascent. The second phrase begins with the same motive as the first, but increases greatly in force with the fourth over *usque*. The effect is heightened still more by the two identical clives. And now comes a loud cry of joy with the *torculus*. It is not only tone-painting, but the manifestation of long-pent-up, surging joy in the heart of the singer. The third phrase brings the message itself. One might expect a still greater enhancement of the melody here. But a further development upward is hardly possible, for the third mode, the one selected for this piece, very rarely reaches above the high *e* used over *extrémum*. And a repetition of that note might sound weak. Moreover, how is a royal message announced? First a fanfare and the rolling of drums, and then the solemn and quiet proclamation of the message. The greater and the more unexpected its contents are, the warmer and more mysterious will be its ring. That is the case here. The message announces our freedom from ignoble bondage, and the cessation of that misery of soul which once seemed so hopelessly abject because no man could help. It announces our citizenship in a kingdom whose Ruler is the God of infinite love. What is more, it promises a life of eternal bliss in this kingdom. Hence we shall sing these words not so much with rousing joy as rather with deep emotion and heartfelt thanksgiving. But with the twofold *allelúia* joy breaks forth anew. Over *suum* it has already reverted to the motive of the first phrase over *audiátur*; this it varies pleasantly toward the end and culminates in the florid neums over the final *allelúia*.

This melody was adopted for the Introit of the feast of the Immaculate Conception; and also, though less happily, for the feast of St. Anthony Mary Zaccaria (July 5).

Analyses, I, 31 ff.

FIRST ALLELUIA VERSE

1. *Surrexit Christus, et illuxit nobis,* 2. *quos redemit sanguine suo.*

1. *Christ is risen, and hath shone upon us,* 2. *whom he redeemed with his blood.*

In the eternal liturgy of heaven the saints never tire of singing: "Thou, O Lord, hast redeemed us to God, in Thy blood, out of every tribe, and tongue, and people, and nation, and hast made us to our God a kingdom" (Apoc. 5: 9, 10). Little wonder that the Church on earth again and again intones this hymn. Today we hear it in the Introit and in this Alleluia. As a city set on a hill cannot remain hid, so this *redémit* attracts the attention by its notation and still more by its rendition. It sets in a fifth higher than the preceding *nobis*; the following *sánguine* begins a fifth lower. Not infrequently plainsong employs this method of plastic expression (cf. the word *aetérni* in the Communion *Beáta víscera* —the Son of the *eternal* Father whom Mary bore in her womb). Similarly here the emphasis is: We have been *redeemed* through the blood of Christ. Joyful remembrance of this fact urges us to express our thanks again and again. Here it is done in a simple yet affectionate manner by the two *pressus* over *sánguine*. The conjoined formula repeats the ending of *(illú)-xit nobis*. We might delineate the second phrase thus: high-low; and the first: low-high. The first half of the first phrase enlivens its simple melodic line with three *pressus*: *feddc, efggf, edffe*; the second half strikes out more boldly. We might, however, expect more light over *illúxit*. Four times *allelúia* with its *jubilus* varies the tone-sequence *g f e d*, and introduces it in three different ways.

By Christ's resurrection our redemption was perfected and sealed, and if Christ now appears in His splendor, this is a consoling assurance that we also, as the Apostle told us in the Epistle for Holy Saturday, shall appear with Him in glory.

SECOND ALLELUIA VERSE (John 15: 28)

1. *Exivi a Patre, et veni in mundum:* 2. *iterum relinquo mundum,* 3. *et vado ad Patrem.*

1. *I came forth from the Father, and came into the world:* 2. *again I leave the world,* 3. *and go to the Father.*

Seldom does an *allelúia* begin immediately on the dominant of the mode, as this one does. The melody soars to heights which but few singers can reach. It should, therefore, be taken a minor or a major third lower.

Allelúia with its jubilus has the following divisions:

a   b   a   c   a¹

Al - le - lú - ia | ... | ... | ...

The verse confines itself almost completely to motives a and b:
Exivi a=a¹, *et veni*=a¹, *iterum*=b, *(relin)-quo*=a¹, *mundum*=a¹, *et
vado*=a, *ad Patrem*=b. Or one might say, more simply, that with the
exception of the last four notes, it repeats *Allelúia* with its *jubilus*. The
last thought thus receives an extremely florid melody. The composer
had no intention of giving melodic symmetry to the symmetry of the
text. In *veni in mundum* he avoided any such effect as the masters of
polyphonic music aimed at in the *descéndit de caelis* of the Credo. Nor
did he have any intention of working out a contrast between the two
thoughts, a contrast which would express Christ's departure from this
world and His return to the Father in a more brilliant, more jubilant
manner. One and the same spirit pervades the entire piece. In the frequently repeated minor third *d–f* of the festal melody there lies hidden
a feeling akin to quiet grief, to the pain of separation. The Son of God
left the Father and for a short time bade farewell to the glory that was
His; He came into this world to humiliate Himself and to die. Heaviness
fills the disciples' hearts because the Master leaves them to go to the
Father and will not return until later to take them to Himself.

The text is taken from the Gospel which follows; hence this Alleluia
is a transition and introduction to the Gospel.

If one were to sing the passage *vado ad Patrem*, even though it resembles many another passage, with more fervor and warmth, as if rejoicing from one's heart with the Saviour that He is now about to go
back to His Father, no one could take it amiss.

We, in imitation of Christ, have gone forth from the Father and
have been sent into this world in order to fulfill a mission, a mission
which we must never lose sight of, no matter how persistently the allurements of the world cry for our attention. This resolve must ever remain firm in our minds: "I must go to the Father; I must seek God in
everything." Then we shall surely find Him, and death itself will not be
able to affright us. With childlike confidence we shall say: "I go to the
Father."

OFFERTORY (Ps. 65: 8, 9, 20)

1. *Benedicite gentes Dominum
Deum nostrum et obaudite vocem
laudis ejus:* 2. *qui posuit animam
meam ad vitam, et non dedit com-
moveri pedes meos:* 3. *benedictus*

1. *O bless the Lord our God, ye
gentiles, and make the voice of his
praise to be heard:* 2. *who hath set
my soul to live, and hath not suffered
my feet to be moved:* 3. *blessed be*

Dominus, qui non amovit depreca-   the Lord, who hath not turned away
tionem meam, et misericordiam   my prayer, and his mercy from me
suam a me, 4. *alleluia.*   4. alleluia.

The present Sunday is the last before the feast of the Ascension. Christ looks back upon His earthly life and His passion. How often His enemies sought His life! Day and night, as He Himself says. On the Mount of Olives His soul was sorrowful nigh unto death. Burdened with the cross, He totters toward Calvary. With a mighty cry He calls to His Father. But His appeal seems to fall on deaf ears; there is no pity for His distress. Now, however, He has been heard; He lives again, and it is a life of glory immeasurable. The Father's grace is poured over His most sacred humanity as a stream of the "oil of gladness." Now He can waver no more. No matter how His enemies rage, He will ever remain the central figure of all history.

We shall, therefore, sing this song in the spirit of Christ, as a continuation of that canticle which He intoned in the Introit for Easter Sunday. The two songs are closely related; both express a joy which, though outwardly subdued, fills the soul to its very depths. Considering the melody in this light, we can better understand the absence of melodic development, the modest range (only a sixth, if we abstract from the descent to the lower third at the beginning over *amóvit*) despite the length of the piece, and the repetition of large melodic groups: *(no)-strum et obaudíte ro-(cem) = (a)-móvit deprecatiónem me-(am), laudis ejus = pedes meos, et non dedit = commovéri, benedíctus = qui non a-(móvit).*

The first phrase, with its almost depressing beginning, is a far cry from the joyous exultation of the Introit; and yet the two basically express the same thought. In the second phrase, however, we have a fresh and animated motive, which may be considered an amplification of *Dóminum* in the first. There it runs *c e g f f*; here, especially in the more simple form over *ánimam, d f a g f*. In a slightly varied form it appears over *suam* in the third phase.

The chief repercussion of the second mode *(d–f)* is employed frequently, almost too frequently, *f* generally appearing as a bistropha or a tristropha. Special care must be given these notes, lest they sound clumsy; the whole selection, in fact, should be sung fluently. We may also make the song our very own, thanking God for the new life which Easter has brought to us, for the new life of grace which in His mercy He has perhaps repeatedly conferred upon us when we strayed from the right path. He has graciously heard our prayer for mercy and made our joy complete. Now we are about to offer the holy Sacrifice, the noblest and most efficacious prayer, in the name of Jesus. That is what promotes the growth in us of the new life which Christ brought us; that is what gives us perseverance till the day of our glorification. How rich we are in Christ. May we never cease praising Him.

COMMUNION (Ps. 95: 2)

1. *Cantate Domino, alleluia*: 2. *cantate Domino, et benedicite nomen ejus*: 3. *bene nuntiate de die in diem salutare ejus, alleluia, alleluia.*

1. *Sing ye to the Lord, alleluia*: 2. *sing ye to the Lord, and bless his name*: 3. *show forth his salvation from day to day, alleluia, alleluia.*

Today, it would seem, the Church is continually exhorting us to sing, to exult, to offer thanks. This Communion harks back to the happy melody of the Introit. The *crescendo* which one naturally expects in the repetition of the cry *Cantáte* is effected with a graceful broadening of volume and range. We shall meet *Dómino* again in the Communion for the feast of the Ascension, *nomen* in the same chant at the close of the second *allelúia* and again at the end of the *annuntiáte. Bene nuntiáte,* which begins a fifth higher than the close of the preceding phrase and carries a florid melody, fared very well at the hands of the composer. In annotated manuscripts each *clivis* is marked broadly. *Diem* reminds us of *nuntiáte.* At *salutáre* we see why the piece is transposed; normally, that is, a fifth lower, we should have *eb.* With its tritone the melody here seems to enter a kind of twilight; but this vanishes immediately, dispelled by the bright *allelúia,* a fifth higher. The *allelúia* are not such as are usually found in Communions, but rather in Introits. Everything palpitates and sparkles with life.

Now that the Saviour is in our heart, our song should be most spontaneous. When the aged Simeon was privileged to look upon "the salvation of God," a joyous, youthful song surged to his lips. But we were not merely allowed to see the Lord, but also to receive Him into our hearts. May our song ascend to the heavens to glorify His holy name. Continually He fulfills the promise made in today's Gospel: "Amen, amen, I say to you, if you ask the Father anything in My name, He will give it you." How radiantly happy and confident this assurance should make us!

* * * *

ROGATION DAYS

For the *Exúrge,* see February 2. Compare what was said on Holy Saturday concerning the Litany of the Saints.

INTROIT (Ps. 17: 7)

1. *Exaudivit de templo sancto suo vocem meam, alleluia*: 2. *et clamor meus in conspectu ejus, introivit in aures ejus, alleluia, alleluia.* Ps. *Diligam te, Domine, virtus mea*: * *Dominus firmamentum meum, et refugium meum, et liberator meus.*

1. *He heard my voice from his holy temple, alleluia*: 2. *and my cry before him came into his ears, alleluia, alleluia.* Ps. *I will love thee, O Lord, my strength*: * *the Lord is my firmament, and my refuge, and my deliverer.*

As on the feast of the Epiphany and of the Purification, so also to-day we have at the beginning of the Introit the use of the significant past tense: *Exaudívit.* In the Litany which preceded we often placed the petition: *Te rogámus, audi nos.* We have been heard, and now subjoin the Introit as a song of thanksgiving. Its first phrase is so sincere and simple that it brings to mind one who has only recently been relieved of some great sorrow or pressing anxiety, and finds need to orientate himself to his new and improved conditions. Only in the second phrase does the melodic line become more comprehensive and sing of triumphant joy. Poor though I be, my cry has nevertheless reached His ears and heart, alleluia. The melody over *vocem* is repeated over *aures.* The *alleluia* at the end of the first and the second sentences rhyme; *meam* concludes in a similar manner. The parallelism of the text is intensified by the melody of the second phrase.

The two final *allelúia* also conclude the Introit of the second Sunday after Easter. Otherwise the Introits of the fourth mode have a different ending in Paschal time.

The first verse of the psalm from which the Antiphon has been taken usually constitutes the psalm-verse of the Introit. Today's choice could not have been more happy. God has approached us with such an insurmountable love that we can but meet Him with the heartfelt words: "I will love Thee, O Lord, my strength." Thou hast become "my firmament, and my refuge, and my deliverer."

ALLELUIA VERSE (Ps. 117: 1)

1. *Confitemini Domino, quoniam bonus*: 2. *quoniam in saeculum misericordia ejus.*

1. *Give praise to the Lord, for he is good*; 2. *for his mercy endureth forever.*

The text of the Alleluia is the same as that of Holy Saturday, as is also the melody over the first two parts and, with the exception of the final vocalize, over the last two words. Even the Tract-form cadence, which on Holy Saturday concludes both half phrases, is here found over *quóniam.* In other respects this verse with its preceding *allelúia* has a melody of its own, as well as the atmosphere of gratitude and serenity which is proper to Introits.

OFFERTORY (Ps. 108: 30, 31)

1. *Confitebor Domino nimis in ore meo: et in medio multorum laudabo eum, qui astitit a dextris pauperis, 2. ut salvam faceret a persequentibus animam meam, 3. alleluia.*

I will give thanks to the Lord exceedingly with my mouth, and in the midst of many I will praise him, because he hath stood at the right hand of the poor. 2. to save my soul from persecutors, 3. alleluia.

Those who sing in church do so in the name of the Catholic people. The singer praises God *in médio multórum*—"in the midst of many." Today he sings in the name of all those who have taken part in the procession, who with him have invoked the saints and have directed to Almighty God the petitions: *Líbera nos Dómine* and *Te rogámus, audi nos.* He represents all those Catholics, spread over the entire world, whose prayers have at one time or other been answered, and who, with the help of God's saving grace, have been protected against persecution, violence, and adulation, against cunning and seduction. The saints in heaven also join our song, for it was likewise through God's grace that they were liberated from sin and misery and were admitted to eternal bliss. The one perfect form of thanksgiving, however, is that which Christ offers to the Father in the holy Sacrifice of the Mass.

The melody over the first three words recalls the beginning of the Introit *Roráte caeli* of the fourth Sunday of Advent. Between the two conspicuous words *Confitébor* and *nimis* there is inserted a simple recitation on *a*, to which the recitation on *g* over *et in médio multó-* corresponds. The melody following this latter repeats the same figures *c ga fa ag gc* as are noted over *nimis in ore meo.* The idea of divine praise, which permeates the first part of the Offertory, is brought to a climax by the special prominence given the word *eum.*

The second part of the text, which gives the reason why the singer feels the urge to praise God, begins with *qui ástitit.* In the Vatican Gradual this second part is not preceded by a major pause; as a matter of fact, the cadence over *eum* is not a final cadence. A major pause, moreover, would interrupt the flowing movement and disturb the inherent inner joy. Intervals of a fourth become numerous, making effective especially *déxteram* and the broad, sonorous *salvam.* The melody over *persequéntibus* is found in the Introit of Ash Wednesday, pitched once as today and once a fifth lower; it recurs in the lower pitch over the final *allelúia* of today's Communion. A new expression of joy comes to the fore with *ánimam*, and concludes with a quiet cadence over *meam*. Heart-felt gratitude, however, expresses itself once more in the florid and rhymed harmonies of the *allelúia*. This same melody also concludes the Offertory of the eighth Sunday after Pentecost.

COMMUNION (Luke 11: 9, 10)

1. *Petite, et accipietis: quaerite, et invenietis: pulsate et aperietur vobis:* 2. *omnis enim, qui petit accipit: et qui quaerit, invenit:* 3. *et pulsanti aperietur, alleluia.*

1. *Ask, and you shall receive; seek, and you shall find; knock, and it shall be opened to you:* 2. *for everyone that asketh receiveth; and he that seeketh findeth;* 3. *and to him that knocketh it shall be opened, alleluia.*

This melody might well be considered a model of musical tension with a concomitant relaxation. The very words: "Ask, seek, knock," expressed as they are in a higher tone of voice, depict this feeling of tense-ness. The result of heeding these commands: "You shall receive, you shall find, it shall be opened unto you," will naturally be expressed in a more quiet and lower tone of voice. This indicates in general the out-lines of the melodic development in the first and second phrases. The close of the second *aperiétur* with *d ff* makes the promise which is given all the more prominent and trustworthy. A fitting preparation is also thus afforded the *allelúia*.

The first and second phrases show many similarities. Both divisions of the second phrase, which are practically identical as to melody, are an extended form of *Pétite* and *ínvenit*, while *pulsánti* is an abbreviation of *pulsáte*.

These words of the Saviour, taken from today's Gospel, should find application not only within the house of God, but in our everyday life as well. They are fulfilled in a wonderful way time and again at Holy Mass. We asked the Father for bread and in turn received heavenly Manna in Holy Communion. We sought out the Saviour and found Him; we knocked and He opened for us all the treasures of His goodness and love. Outside the house of God we should also ask for heaven's grace and blessing; there also, if we seek we shall find Him, and if we knock it shall be opened to us. The more intimately we remain united with our Eucharistic Saviour, the more abundantly will He give us all that is conducive to our eternal salvation.

*   *   *   *

THE ASCENSION OF OUR LORD

INTROIT (Acts 1: 11)

1. *Viri Galilaei, quid admiramini aspicientes in caelum? alleluia:* 2. *quemadmodum vidistis eum ascendentem in caelum, ita veniet,* 3. *alleluia, alleluia, alleluia.* Ps. *Omnes gentes plaudite manibus:* * *jubilate Deo in voce exsultationis.*

1. *Ye men of Galilee, why wonder you, looking up to heaven? alleluia:* 2. *he shall so come as you have seen him going up into heaven.* 3. *alleluia, alleluia, alleluia.* Ps. *O clap your hands, all ye nations:* * *shout unto God with the voice of joy.*

When we met the Saviour at Christmas, we greeted Him with the seventh mode. The motive *dc éd dd* over the accented syllable of *Galiláei* reminds us also of *nobis* in the Introit for the third Christmas Mass. Now the seventh mode leads the Lord back to the Father, who today will speak that long-promised word: "Now sit Thou at My right hand." On Bethlehem's fields once the angels sang; today we again hear angels. They seem to have a special preference for the seventh mode in plainsong. Their words are addressed to the Apostles, who find it impossible to turn their eyes away from heaven, whither their dearest Lord and Master has ascended. And here the angels do not say, as the Acts of the Apostles report: "Why *stand* you looking up to heaven?" but: *Quid admirámini aspiciéntes*—"Why *wonder* you, looking up to heaven?" This word also supplies the key to the understanding of this Introit. The Apostles may not stand still and rest. Now is the time of labor, of strife, of suffering. Now they must fulfill the commission with which the Lord charged them. Now they must sow the seed in tears, in sweat, and in sorrow. Not till later will the time come for repose, for blissful contemplation of God. Perhaps the angel wished to stress another thought: "It is difficult for you to realize that your dearest Lord has departed from you. You cannot but wonder, and it is wonder that tends to make you sad. But be comforted! He will come again; you will see Him; and never again lose sight of Him. Just as true and real as His ascension is today, will His return be with power and majesty." This consoling thought, finds expression in the jubilant cries of *allelúia*. And St. Luke tells us (24: 52) that the disciples returned to Jerusalem "with great joy."

This rejoicing seems to increase still more in the psalm-verse: "Oh, clap your hands with joy, all ye nations." When the Holy Father enters St. Peter's (today's station, by the way, is at St. Peter's), the enthusiasm and the applause of the people is surprisingly vehement and inspiring. But how trifling even that will appear, when compared to the greeting which will be shouted out by all the peoples of all the centuries when Christ will again appear at the end of the world!

Today we also exult and rejoice, because the work which the Father gave His Son to do is now perfected. His glorification is ours also. He has, in the words of today's *Communicantes*, set at the right hand of the Father's glory the substance of our frail human nature which He had taken to Himself, and He says to the Father: "Father, I will that where I am, they also may be whom Thou hast given me."

The melody calls for an easy and joyous rendition. Codex 121 of Einsiedeln gives evidence of a fine esthetic sense by employing light neum constructions everywhere except over *allelúia*, and in five places notes a "c" *(=celeriter)* and once "st" *(=statim)* over this chant.

The neums over *Galilaéi* reminds us of the intonation of the solemn melody for the psalm-verse. One might also assert that there is a correlation between the first of the three last *allelúia* and the middle cadence of the psalm-melody *(plaúdite mánibus)*, although there is an obvious difference between the *pes* with accented *d* and the *clivis* with accented *f*. Moreover, in the *allelúia* this *f* is sung a second time, which individualizes it still more. It marks the summit of the entire piece. In the rendition, this *climacus*, and all the *allelúia* in fact, demand a most hearty rendition. Our joy should be voiced wholeheartedly. The rhythmic motive over *admirámini, dedc c* (4 plus 1), runs through the entire piece, recurring over *aspici-(éntes), vidístis e-(um), (ascendén)- tem in cae*—and over the second *caelum*. After the accented syllable of *aspiciéntes* the melody sinks a fifth. This makes the following line, expressing the heavenward gaze of the disciples, more effective.

In the second phrase, the melody moves lightly about *c*. Nevertheless *quemádmodum* and *ita véniet* are brought well to the fore. Special gravity and majesty are produced by the pause on *c*. The quiet second *allelúia* forms a contrast to the enthusiastic first *allelúia*, while the third strikes a mean between the other two.

Revue, 21, 107 ff.; *Analyses*, III, 28 ff.; *Der Chorbote*, 2, 26 ff.

FIRST ALLELUIA VERSE (Ps. 46: 6)

1. *Ascendit Deus in jubilatione,*
2. *et Dominus in voce tubae.*

1. God is ascended with jubilee, 2. and the Lord with the sound of a trumpet.

For the melody, see the third Sunday of Advent. Like the verse for the Introit, this text is taken from Psalm 46, which is eminently suited to the Ascension. It was originally sung after a victory gained by the Israelites, and was meant to tell how the God of the Covenant, enthroned upon the ark, was borne to Mount Sion amid the acclaim of His people and the sound of trumpets. At that time the Lord was invisible. Today He ascends to heaven before the eyes of His disciples: *vidéntibus illis*, according to the words of the fifth antiphon at Vespers. Alleluia-verse and Offertory give prominence to the significant word *Ascéndit*. As a parallelism to them we may mention the Alleluia-verse and the Offertory of the feast of the Assumption, where *Assúmpta est* ("she was taken up") stands first. He, our Lord and Saviour, ascended on high by His own power, accompanied by much rejoicing. This joy is above all in His own soul, which, only a few short weeks ago, was sorrowful unto death upon this very Mount of Olives. Joyous shouts of angels likewise surround Him; some angels are escorting Him and others are awaiting Him in heaven. Then there is also the ineffable joy of the saints whom He is leading to their reward.

Perhaps its seems strange that the word *Dóminus* appears as an independent melodic phrase. On the third Sunday of Advent the heartfelt *et veni* and on Pentecost *et creabúntur*, both complete thoughts, occupy this place. But here, too, the word *Dóminus* is to be especially stressed. For Christ has shown Himself the Lord over life and death, over nature, grace, and glory; He is the living Ark of the Covenant, which bears in its heart the law of redemptive love and the manna of eternal life, and is now entirely immersed in the radiant light of glory.

SECOND ALLELUIA VERSE (Ps. 67: 18, 19)

1. *Dominus in Sina in sancto, ascendens in altum,* 2. *captivam duxit captivitatem.*

1. *The Lord is in Sinai, in the holy place, ascending on high,* 2. *he hath led captivity captive.*

This song also presupposes a victory over the foes of God's people; several of the enemy are being led along in the triumphal procession as captives. In this victory the Lord has revealed Himself in His majesty as on Mount Sinai, when He gave Moses the Decalogue. Still more gloriously and majestically Christ today mounts above all that is earthly and makes His entry into the heavenly court. By a happy coincidence, the most significant neum of this piece stands above the word *ascéndens*. St. Paul comments on this psalm-verse: "Now that He ascended, what is it, but because He also descended first into the lower parts of the earth? He that descended is the same also that ascended above all the heavens, that He might fill all things" (Ephes. 4: 7–10). Now He leads captives captive. Sin, death, and hell, which formerly made man their captive, have become His booty. But also those who had previously been confined to limbo as in captivity today enjoy the privilege of entering into blissful captivity with Christ. "And the Mount of Olives, the place of ascension to heaven, expands over the entire earth; each hour the joyous multitude of the freed, newly captured children of God, now gloriously going to their home, grows larger. Those liberated from purgatory and limbo were the first to chant this Alleluia of the Ascension. The Apostles and the disciples, who saw the glory of this ascending Master, have joined them to augment the choir, and at their side millions are singing before the throne of God, the palm of victory in their hands. A yearning to join this choir and sing this wondrous Alleluia pervades the heart of every Christian" (*Caecilia*, 29, 65 ff.).

OFFERTORY (Ps. 46: 6)

This Offertory has the same text as the first Alleluia; its melody, however, is original. By quiet seconds it solemnly ascends upward. One seems to see the radiant form of the Lord rising from the earth and majestically soaring up to heaven. Rightly does this spot mark the climax of the piece. This line must be sung very sustainedly. A great *crescendo* must develop, which is to swell to *forte* over *jubilatióne*. In the second half of the first phrase the feeling changes slightly. The Lord ascends in jubilation. What broad lines the melody here assumes; how it rings and echoes with its *pressus* with the stress on high *c*! And still, how solemn the closing cadence is! In the verse which was formerly joined to this, the enthusiasm is even greater. We there find the following passage:

	aGG	ccc	Gccc	Gccc	aFG	GaG	GaG
in voce		ex-	sul-	ta-	ti-	ó-	nis.

The second phrase begins with the same motive as *in*. The sequence *acgg* rounds out to the pleasant *agcaa*, which calls for full and satisfying tones. *Allelúia* is the usual closing word in Offertories during the Easter season. Compare the *allelúia* of Easter Sunday, whose solemn pathos re-echoes in our present melody.

With the sound of trumpets the Lord ascended. With the sound of trumpets He will come again, and mightily will they then call out *(Tuba mirum spargens sonum.)* Today, however, at least in spirit, we go with joyful heart to the altar of sacrifice to participate in that great procession which accompanies the Saviour on His ascent into heaven.

In the ancient manuscripts this Offertory is assigned to the Sunday within the octave of the Ascension. In place of it was sung the Offertory *Viri Galilaéi*, having the same text as the Introit. Its melody resembles that of the Offertory *Stetit Angelus* for the feast of St. Michael (September 29). *Ascéndit* has the same richly descriptive melody as *ascendéntem* in the Offertory formerly sung on this feast.

COMMUNION (Ps. 67: 33, 34)

Psallite Domino, qui ascendit super caelos caelorum ad Orientem, alleluia.

Sing ye to the Lord, who mounteth above the heaven of heavens to the east, alleluia.

The texts of the first Alleluia and the Offertory are taken from Psalm 46; those of the second Alleluia and the Communion from Psalm 67. From the standpoint of mode, however, the Offertory and the Communion belong togèther. Again we meet a prominent rising line over *ascéndit super*. But it is more effectual here, preceded and followed as it is by two short, low-pitched phrases. Plainsong, it seems, likes to assign high notes to *super*. *Caelos* and *caelórum* are similarly treated.

We believe that Christ has ascended to heaven, has gone up toward the rising sun. Similarly do we, when we go to the altar, to the sacrificial banquet, go toward the rising sun; for the church should have its high altar facing eastward. Then we sing psalms to the Lord, our hearts filled with sincere thanksgiving.

*   *   *   *

SUNDAY WITHIN THE OCTAVE OF THE ASCENSION

INTROIT (Ps. 26: 7, 9)

1. *Exaudi, Domine, vocem meam, qua clamavi ad te, alleluia:* 1. *tibi dixit cor meum, quaesivi vultum tuum, vultum tuum Domine requiram:* 3. *ne avertas faciem tuam a me, alleluia, alleluia.* Ps. *Dominus illuminatio mea, * et salus mea: quem timebo?*

1. *Hear, O Lord, my voice with which I have cried to thee, alleluia:* 2. *my heart hath said to thee: I have sought thy face, thy face, O Lord, I will seek:* 3. *turn not away thy face from me, alleluia, alleluia.* Ps. *The Lord is my light, * and my salvation: whom shall I fear?*

In the present instance the melody of the psalm-verse in a way eclipses that of the antiphon. Although it preserves its recitative and syllabic character and has no such groups of neums as the antiphon, nevertheless, on account of its high pitch, its stressing of the dominant *a*, its ascent to high *g* in both halves of the verse, it possesses a brightness and freshness which is lacking in the antiphon. Instead, the antiphon breaths a lyric tenderness. Perhaps it is a longing for the Spouse of the Church, for Him whose countenance is no more visible since Ascension Day. And when the Church looks about her on earth, what does she see?

A thousand dangers surging up against her! Now she can only implore heaven that the Lord turn not away His eyes, His grace, His high favor from her. How different is the present text from those of the fourth and fifth Sundays after Easter! And the change in the spirit of the melody is even more striking. In accordance with the Master's instructions, the disciples, together with Mary, the mother of Jesus, are assembled in the Cenacle, fervently praying for the Consoler, the Holy Spirit, who is to strengthen them so that they may bear witness to Christ. Heartfelt prayer: that is the basic idea of the antiphon.

The psalm-verse has a bright and hearty ring, as if Pentecost had already arrived and all fear for the sufferings of the apostolate had vanished: "The Lord is my light and my salvation. Who, then, can make me afraid?" It sounds like the answer to the suppliant *Exaúdi*. In the mystery of the Holy Eucharist, which is truly an anticipation of the Parousia, the final coming of the Lord, all the longing of the Church is satisfied. Even now His eternal light illuminates the pathway of life, our round of daily work; and we are invested with His strength.

The antiphon begins with a motive proper to the third mode. Compare, for instance, the beginning of the Introit for the fifth Sunday after Easter. In its normal position, that is, a fifth lower, we should have here *dd e♭ c f*. It is on account of this *e♭* that the piece was transposed. The motive over *clamávi ad te*, which always descends before an accented syllable and thus gives prominence to the latter, is heard again in the second phrase over *quaesívi* and in the third over *avértas*. The petition is thereby made all the more urgent. Worthy of note also is the gradation of introductory intervals: *g c* at the beginning of the first phrase, *a d* at the beginning of the second, *a ef* from *me* to *allelúia*.

In earlier times the station was at the church called *Sancta María ad Mártyres*, the former Pantheon. It was there that the picture of the Lord's face, called *Verónica nostra* by Dante, was preserved in a coffer secured with thirteen keys. Later this casket was transferred to St. Peter's. How significant and appropriate it was to sing this Introit, in which there is such frequent mention of the Lord's face, before this picture![1]

FIRST ALLELUIA VERSE (Ps. 46: 9)

1. *Regnavit Dominus super gentes*: 2. *Deus sedet super sedem sanctam suam.*

1. *The Lord hath reigned over all the nations*: 2. *God sitteth on his holy throne.*

---

[1] Schuster, *The Sacramentary*, II, 379.

The *jubilus* presents a graceful interplay of motive with the *climacus + pes* and the *climacus + clivis*. Its middle part is the most prominent. Setting in a fifth higher than the ending of the preceding word, as *super omnes* does, the word *Deus* receives still greater prominence by its ascending melody, which again goes over into a *climacus + clivis*. Perhaps there is attempted tone-painting here, as in other pieces containing this word (cf. the Communion for the Ascension and the Gradual for the third Sunday of Advent). The two ascending *clives* over *Re-* receive an augment over *-gnávit*. This melody does not say much concerning God's kingly rule over all nations; *Deus* must therefore be made so much the more impressive. The entire piece is to be sung with a quiet and measured movement.

As King over all the world, Christ is enthroned at the right of the Father. We rejoice in His glorification. God's beauty now transfigures His most sacred humanity.

SECOND ALLELUIA VERSE (John 14: 18)

1. *Non vos relinquam orphanos:*
2. *vado, et venio ad vos,* 3. *et gaudebit cor vestrum.*

1. *I will not leave you orphans:*
2. *I go and I come to you,* 3. *and your heart shall rejoice.*

After the somewhat cold first Alleluia, we here have a song full of consolation, soothing the pain of separation and banishing the feeling of loneliness and isolation, a song of glad returning. "Through the Holy Ghost the Lord will come into our inmost heart, will be one with us, will be much closer to us than He was formerly to the Apostles when He dwelt among them in the flesh. Our heart will feel His nearness and will rejoice." (*W. K.*)

Here we have one of the most devout melodies cast in the first mode; no doubt, it purposely avoids a greater range in order to penetrate the more readily into our heart.

Allelúia consists of two groups which are almost identical: a lower one within the tetrachord *c–f* over the first two syllables of *Alle-* and a higher one with the tetrachord *f–b♭* over the two final syllables *-lúia*. The two groups complement each other and form a symmetrically constructed whole.

The *jubilus*[1] has the form *a a a*[1] *b*. Designedly the fifth *d–a* marks the peak of the theme of the *jubilus*; in an energetic line it combines all that precedes. Its first note begins Alleluia; the second closes it; moreover, these two notes predominate in both groups. The theme of the *jubilus*[1] is taken from the figure over *-lúia*, the higher group. This expresses

---

[1] Wagner (III, 412) gives a fine explanation of the divisions.

most fully its character of an overflowing of joy inspired by God. The descending *climacus* is repeated. It seems a third *climacus* would like to join, but suddenly the melody bends backward. The general rule, that the selfsame formula should not be employed more than twice in the same way, is here adhered to not only in the smaller detail, but is also observed on a larger scale in the form $a\ a\ a^1\ b$ of the entire *jubilus*. At first a^1 is little more than a repetition of a, but the *pressus* after the first four notes causes the melody to veer over to the thesis, which reaches completion in the two smaller mutually corresponding groups that follow. The high points of the successive figures form the stepwise descending line $b\flat\ a\ g\ f$, an effective form of cadence structure. A similar arrangement is found in the Alleluia for the twenty-third Sunday after Pentecost.

In the verse, *Non relinquam* resembles *allelúia*; in *vado* the melody rises to an accented $b\flat$, thus becoming strikingly tender and gentle. The descending group over *vénio* reminds us of *Alle-*. The verse melisma on the accented syllable of *gaudébit* presents a succession of descending two-note figures *(clives)* in its first part; in the second part it has ascending *podatus* until it comes to a close on a.

The OFFERTORY was explained on the feast of the Ascension.

COMMUNION (John 17: 12, 13, 15)

1. *Pater, cum essem cum eis, ego servabam eos, alleluia*: 2. *nunc autem ad te venio*: 3. *non rogo ut tollas eos de mundo, sed ut serves eos a malo, alleluia, alleluia.*

1. *Father, while I was with them, I kept them whom thou gavest me, alleluia*: 2. *but now I come to thee*; 3. *I pray not that thou shouldst take them out of the world, but that thou shouldst keep them from evil, alleluia, alleluia.*

Let us first consider this piece from a musical viewpoint only. The final *alléluia* is the same as the one which occurs at the end of the first phrase. *Ut serves eos a malo*, together with the penultimate *allelúia*, is practically nothing more than a shortened repetition of *ut tollas eos de mundo*. And this entire third phrase bears considerable resemblance to the second half of the first. Hence two large phrases can be distinguished melodically, each of which has two parts. In the first, *Pater, cum essem cum eis* and *nunc autem ad te vénio*, the melody tends vigorously upward to a height rarely attained by the fourth mode. The second phrase glides downward on an easy decline, enlivened only by the word-accents. *Ad te vénio* with its accented c marks the summit of the piece. Hence, we may not compare it with *eis* of the first phrase, since in the latter word the note *a*, rather than *c*, bears the accent. *Vénio*, setting in a third above the tonic, stands out very prominently, and is excellently suited to its text: "Now I come to Thee." It is a veritable reaching up of the Saviour's arms to His heavenly Father, a taking wing and leaving this realm of space and time, a song which wells up from the heart after a difficult mission happily fulfilled. Truly can He say to the Father: "I have finished the work which Thou gavest Me to do."

It seems strange, therefore, that *cum essem cum eis* should receive a similar melody. Why the great expansion over these words? Did the composer perhaps first sing *ad te vénio* and then try to create a parallel in the first half of the first phrase?

A special tenderness, as if coming from the very heart of Jesus Himself, is revealed in the second half of each phrase. With what motherly care He shielded His disciples from everything that might have harmed them when His enemies sought to exploit their ignorance and inexperience! When He was immersed in a world of suffering on the Mount of Olives, how concerned He was that nothing happen to His disciples! Those who were entrusted to Him He again confides to the hands of the Father and implores Him to keep them out of harm's way. The two *allelúia* at the end continue these heartfelt desires of Jesus.

In the Cenacle, after the first Eucharistic Banquet, Jesus had prayed thus. In Holy Communion we are again "given" to Him. Now within us He prays to the Father, as He taught us to pray in the final petition of the Lord's Prayer: that we, laboring in the world and for the good of the world, may remain untainted by its spirit; that we may be in the world like a ray of the sun which, though it furnishes light and warmth, nevertheless remains free of the sin that is committed in its light.

Rass. gr., 7, col. 420.

* * * *

WHITSUNDAY

INTROIT (Wisd. 1: 7)

1. *Spiritus Domini replevit orbem terrarum, alleluia:* 2. *et hoc quod continet omnia, scientiam habet vocis, alleluia, alleluia, alleluia. Ps. Exsurgat Deus, et dissipentur inimici ejus:* * *et fugiant, qui oderunt eum, a facie ejus.*

1. *The Spirit of the Lord hath filled the whole earth, alleluia:* 2. *and that which containeth all things hath knowledge of the voice, alleluia, alleluia. Ps. Let God arise, and let his enemies be scattered:* * *and let them that hate him, flee from before his face.*

The very first word tells us that today's feast is dedicated to the Holy Ghost and His marvelous workings. In the same manner the first word at Christmas *(Puer)* directed our attention to the divine Child, and the first word of the Introit for Easter *(Resurréxi)* indicated the song which the Risen One sings to His Father. What a tender and devout ring that melody had! Today, however, our song tells of a power which sweeps everything before it, of a force which nothing can withstand. There is a feeling of mystery about its low-pitched beginning. But then the melody expands with tempestuous speed, expands until it fills the entire earth. But it is no devastating hurricane, breaking the nations as a reed and making poor humanity cry out in despair. It rather resembles a storm of spring, imparting new strength to an aging world, from which new creations rise: the marvel of the Catholic Church, the phenomenon of holiness on the sinful earth, the prodigy which bears God in its heart as the sweet guest of the soul. Hence, in spite of all its impetuosity and power, this song is extremely pleasant to our musical sense. Upon the broken D-minor tritone over *Spíritus* follows the brilliant F-major tritone over *replévit*, over the penultimate *allelúia*, and in a descending line over *-rum, alle-(lúia)*. A profusion of light pours out from the C-major chord, descending from the upper e^1, and gleams again, though in a milder form to correspond with the more serene text, over *habet vocis* as e^1ca.

"The Spirit of the Lord hath filled the whole world." In the beginning He moved over the waters, put life into inert matter, disposed and ordered it, and thus perfected creation. On the day of the Incarnation He descended upon the most pure Virgin and consummated the miraculous creation of Christ's humanity. On Pentecost He perfects the new creation of the Church founded in Christ's blood and by His love and His power makes her exceedingly fruitful. He fills the entire world not only in its length and breadth, but also in its depth, with the riches of His grace and His most intimate union. He is the Spirit of the "Lord," of the Father and the Son, God of very God.

For a discussion of the text of this Introit, cf. Wagner, II, 66. Compare also the first phrase with the second antiphon of today's Vespers. With *replévit* a broadly expanding *crescendo* should set in. One must exult with the universal Church. It is not mere word-painting, such as one finds, for instance, in C. M. Weber's *Oberon* in the passage *"rund um die ganze Welt"* ("round about the world") in the aria *"Ozean, du Ungeheuer."* In this chant we have rather a glimpse into eternity, and an enraptured wonderment at the greatness, the wisdom, and the power of Him who fills the whole earth.

Et hoc in the second phrase is a slavish translation of the Greek, in which language *Pneuma* (Spirit) is a neuter noun. We should naturally expect *et hic* here, taking the masculine *Spíritus* into consideration. After *et hoc* a very short pause for breathing is to be recommended. Then *quod cóntinet ómnia* is to be sung straight on; and even after the last word the pause should be very slight. In this manner the gradation *g a c¹(ómnia), bc¹ d¹(sciénti-), a d¹ (-am habet)* is brought out more clearly. The cadence after *vocis* requires a resolution and receives it in the following *allelúia*. For this reason the three *allelúia* may not be considered as an independent third phrase, although their length might tempt one to do so; they must be taken as a necessary conclusion and coda-like extension of the second phrase. There is some resemblance between the two phrases. Taking the principal notes into consideration, one might sketch them thus:

First phrase:	*dfaf fac d¹e¹c gc af fag;*
Second phrase:	*fgc d¹e¹c a af fag.*

With the exception of one note, the final *allelúia* is the same as the one at the end of the first phrase. With its limited range and fourfold stressing of *a* it harmonizes with the *allelúia* after *vocis* and is the expression of quiet joy, while the penultimate *allelúia* with its bright ring and the accentuation of the tenor *c* harks back to the jubilant festal spirit of the entire antiphon.

Since the Holy Ghost sustains and rules all things, nothing can be hidden from Him. He hears everything, all verbal and all silent longing, and every sigh for glorification which goes through creation as a whole and through each individual soul. He hears our singing and praying, too, all of it, and accepts it graciously.

Perhaps there was still another thought in the mind of the composer today. The Holy Ghost is the Spirit of knowledge; He has the most perfect possible knowledge of Himself. But He has also the power and the means to manifest His being. As God once revealed Himself on Sinai amid thunder and lightning, so He makes Himself known today in the fiery tongues, in the roar of the mighty wind, in the impressive sermon of the prince of the Apostles, and in the miracle of tongues wrought upon the Apostles.

Psalm 67, of which only the intonation here appears, portrays the history of Israel from the time of its liberation from Egypt to the establishment of God's kingdom on Sion, as a triumphal procession which God Himself leads through the desert to the consternation of His enemies and for the glory of His people (*W. K.*). Today the psalm is for us a confiding look into the future. The Church realizes that she has many enemies who hate her and who do all in their power to destroy her. Thus it was already on the very first Pentecost, and thus it will remain throughout the centuries. But the Church knows no fear: God fights for her. When He arises and shows His flaming countenance, all the enemies are instantly dispersed. The final victory is to the Church. Hence she sings: *Glória Patri et Fílio et Spirítui Sancto.*

Whoever lives himself into this song seems to feel that the Spirit of the Lord filled also the heart of the composer and bestowed upon him this power of song. May the Holy Ghost likewise fill our hearts, that our chant may penetrate into the hearts of the faithful like Pentecostal grace!

Revue, 7, 172 ff.; 23, 135 ff.; *Analyses*, IV, 21 ff.; *Mus. divina*, 1, 9 ff.; *Choralblaetter*, No. 5.; *Tribune de Saint-Germain*, 11, 203 ff.

FIRST ALLELUIA VERSE (Ps. 103: 30)

1. *Emitte Spiritum tuum*, 2. *et creabuntur*: 3. *et renovabis faciem terrae.*

1. *Send forth thy Spirit*, 2. *and they shall be created*; 3. *and thou shalt renew the face of the earth.*

Today there is a clear connection between the Alleluia and the preceding Lesson, a relationship which is not so obvious on some other days, and often is lacking entirely. In a vivid, captivating manner the marvel of Pentecost was held before our eyes. How wondrous were its effects. The Spirit had descended upon the Apostles, who a short time before were much like the lifeless clay of Adam's body before God had breathed a soul into it. Now they have become a new creation; they are filled with life, wisdom, courage, and energy; are determined to carry the richness of life which they received to the ends of the world and renew the entire earth. Oh, may He come again, this Holy Ghost, and again effect a new creation! That is the suppliant cry of the present Alleluia-song.

How vitally necessary the Holy Ghost is to us! And how many men there are who know nothing of Him, who no longer know the meaning of spirit and grace and purity and the supernatural life. They have lost all religious sense. The material world alone captivates them. Would that the Spirit who in the beginning swept over the waters, might once again sweep over this matter and vivify it! How fervently this petition rises from the heart of the Church! And yet we clothe it in the jubilant cry of *Allelúia*, because we know that we have a right to this Spirit in virtue of the fact that we have been redeemed.

SECOND ALLELUIA VERSE

1. *Veni Sancte Spiritus, reple tuorum corda fidelium*: 2. *et tui amoris in eis ignem accende.*

1. *Come, Holy Spirit, fill the hearts of thy faithful*: 2. *and kindle in them the fire of thy love.*

This melody must be numbered among the most impressive and most beautiful in the entire Graduale. "Here all kneel"—that is the simple rubric. And when at high Mass the bishop with his assistants kneel down at the throne, when all those in choir bend the knee, then this one wish is uppermost: Would that I might sing this chant with that deep fervor with which it was first conceived and then sung throughout the centuries, with that depth and ardor with which the Blessed Virgin called upon the Holy Ghost during the novena preceding Pentecost Day! Like the dew from heaven its tones should sink into the hearts of the faithful.

It seems almost presumptuous to analyze this melody; one fears to dissect so fragrant a flower. There is a threefold accent in the *allelúia* with its *jubilus*: the second time with an interval of a fourth, the third time with an interval of a fifth. Twice the ending is formed with *c d*, once with *e d*. The *allelúia* furnishes the theme, the verse the variations. *Veni* resembles *allelúia*. That which follows, as far as *fidélium*, derives its melodic material from the second member. *Et tui amóris* utilizes the motives of the third phrase. It is impossible to sing this passage too tenderly; and yet one ought to introduce a *crescendo* in the repetition. For the longing after the pure, deep, faithful, enrapturing love of the Holy Ghost is ever increasing. After the development has reached its climax, the quiet thetic forms *éfedéd* should diminish in volume. With the *pressus*, which occur several times in the piece, blunt increase in volume must be avoided. It must be prayerful throughout: humble, reverent, yet confiding withal.

The Sequence is composed of five double strophes[1], each of which is made up of three spondaic verses. According to the latest investigations, its authorship must be assigned to Stephen Langton, chancellor of the University of Paris (✝ 1228).

In its first verse the first strophe uses the melodic material of the second *allelúia*, *c d e f e d c d*; it is, therefore, its melodic continuation, just as in content it is a further development of the Alleluia's fervent supplication. Thus we have here a *Sequéntia* (continuation) in the full sense of that word. From the depth of our indigence the motive rises, is heard a fourth higher in the second verse, and with a change of interval

---

[1] Wagner, I, 274.

in the third verse, thus presenting the form $a\ a^1\ a^2$. The interval of a sixth between the second and third verses is quite rare in plainsong. Surprising, too, is the rise of the final syllable of the word at the end of the verse. The same thing occurs in some of the following pairs of strophes. The first pair of strophes sings of the Holy Ghost as the source of light and of the soul's riches:

1a. *Come, O Holy Spirit, come;*   1b. *Come, thou father of the poor,*
And from thy celestial home   *Come, thou source of all our store,*
Shed a ray of light divine.   *Come, within our bosoms shine.*

The second pair of strophes sets in on the dominant and with joyful confidence rises an octave above the tonic. They praise the Holy Ghost as the source of consolation in trials and sufferings. Here the rendition ought to be somewhat more forceful:

2a. *Thou of all consolers best,*   2b. *In our labor rest most sweet,*
Thou, the soul's most welcome guest,   *Grateful coolness in the heat,*
Sweet refreshment here below.   *Solace in the midst of woe.*

The third pair of strophes sets in on the octave, a proceeding unknown to the classic period of plainsong composition and hardly to be found before the eleventh century. How stirring is this plea for the saving light! The passage *d d c b c d c* at the beginning was taken over, it seems, from *(in la)-bóre réquies*. In the third verse, *b♭ a g f* corresponds to *d c b a* of the first:

3a. *O most blessed light divine,*   3b. *Where thou art not, man hath*
Shine within these hearts of thine,   *nought,*
And our inmost beings fill.   *Nothing good in deed or thought,*
     Nothing free from taint of ill.

Thus far the Sequence was almost continually rising and expanding. In the subsequent pair of strophes the melody describes a curve and becomes appreciably more tender. Graceful harmony marks the lines of the first and second verses: *bab cbag = feƒ gfed*.

The third verse is almost the same as the opening motive in the Sequence for Corpus Christi *(Lauda Sion)*. This is the only pair of strophes which close on the tenor. Care must be taken that the first note of each verse be not prolonged, otherwise a trivial three-eighths time will result:

4a. *Heal our wounds; our strength*   4b. *Bend the stubborn heart and will*
     renew;   *Melt the frozen, warm the chill;*
On our dryness pour thy dew;   *Guide the steps that go astray.*
Wash the stains of guilt away.

After this decrease in range and volume, the former liveliness and impressiveness returns in the final pair of strophes: in fact, it is even increased. Fiery and turbulent as the flashing of the tongues of fire in the "mighty wind" is the ring of the first and last members; they can well bear to be sung forte. They have descending fifths at the beginning, and endings which correspond to one another *(acba=dfed)*. The middle verse is more quiet. The final strophe again sets in on the octave. Just as the very first strophe insistently prays *Veni* four times, so the last pair four times has *da*: Give, O Holy Spirit!

5a. *Thou on those who evermore*
Thee confess and thee adore
In thy sevenfold gifts descend.

5b. *Give them virtue's sure reward,*
Give them thy salvation, Lord;
Give them joys that never end.
Amen. Alleluia.

The composer of this song was a veritable harp of God, on which the Holy Ghost Himself played. Its tones will continue as long as mankind looks up in heartfelt prayer to the "Father of the poor."

Whoever realizes the neediness of his own heart, whoever can sympathize with all that moves the heart of his fellow man, whoever reflects while he peruses the text and the melodic development, upon the work of the Holy Ghost in souls and in the Church, will of his own accord arrive at the rendition which is most suitable for this magnificent song.

OFFERTORY (Ps. 67: 29, 30)

1. *Confirma hoc Deus, quod operatus es in nobis:* 2. *a templo tuo, quod est in Jerusalem,* 3. *tibi offerent reges munera, alleluia.*

1. *Confirm this, O God, which thou hast wrought in us:* 2. *from thy temple, which is in Jerusalem* 3. *kings shall offer presents to thee, alleluia.*

On Christmas (first and third Masses), on Easter, and on Pentecost the Offertory belongs to the fourth mode. But how varied is the feeling! At Christmas it is a meditative, blissful, intimate song, not intended for the big outside world; at Easter, a melody full of power and weight, a pean of victory; and now, on Pentecost Day, a fervent yet joyously moving prayer, calling upon the Holy Ghost much like today's second Alleluia. Solemnly the melody increases over the first words. *Hoc* presages great things. The strange beginning of *Deus* only tends to make the petition the more intensive: God alone can supply our needs. To the ending with the *pressus* at the close of the first half of the verse corresponds that of the first phrase over *nobis*. With the tristropha, the only one in the piece, the melody reaches its peak. Most thankfully we acknowledge the great things which God has worked in us. And we beg that these *magnália Dei* may not be taken from us, that the Spirit of grace may establish and "confirm" us against all attack from within and from without, that the life of grace may more and more penetrate our entire being, may spiritualize and transfigure it, so that, like the sacrificial gifts which are now placed upon the altar, Christ may through the working of the Holy Ghost be glorified in us by our putting on His spirit of sacrifice. With what deep emotion we ought to chant this song! Over *operátus es* the *torculus gag*, must predominate. Then we must take care that *in nobis* be not harsh and blunt; it should rather be sung with special warmth.

In its first half the second phrase also closes with a *pressus* as the first did, continues with *f*, and also reaches high *c*, though only once. *Tuo* and *est* correspond. The melody makes the phrase more independent than it actually is. Here we are, no doubt, to think of the new Jerusalem which the Spirit of God has bestowed upon us, or of the Cenacle with its marvels, or of the wonderful sanctifying activity of the Catholic Church.

If the Spirit can again be active in our souls, can establish and "confirm" them, what, then, will His effect be? Simply this, that we shall function properly as participants in the kingly priesthood, and shall offer our gifts, not in a sorrowful or forced manner, but magnanimously, in the joy of the Holy Ghost. *Tibi* and *reges* have a similar ring. *Offerent* is rightly assigned a prominent position. The three *torculus* over *múnera* are arranged in climactic order. *Allelúia* repeats the melody of *hoc Deus* in the first phrase.

The first phrase adverts to the things which God has done for us, while the second reminds us of the dignity and burden of our kingly priesthood.

Revue, 3, 3 ff.

COMMUNION (Acts 2: 2, 4)

1. *Factus est repente de caelo sonus advenientis spiritus vehementis, ubi erant sedentes, alleluia: et repleti sunt omnes Spiritu Sancto, loquentes magnalia Dei, alleluia, alleluia.*

1. *There came suddenly a sound from heaven as of a mighty wind coming, where they were all sitting, alleluia: 2. and they were all filled with the Holy Ghost, speaking the wonderful works of God, alleluia, alleluia.*

In most Masses the *Ite missa est* harks back to the melody of the Kyrie. In a similar way this Communion reminds us of the festive enthusiasm of the Introit. With striking clearness it portrays in the first phrase the sudden coming of the Holy Ghost. One seems actually to hear the mighty wind in the recurring fifths and the ascent to f^1 with its interval of a fourth. That is word-painting which, although it violently urges us along, is nevertheless enjoyable. In spite of all His might and power, the Spirit who comes is the Spirit of order, of life, and of love.

The structure of the Communion is strikingly plain, and its affiliation to psalmody unmistakable. The two phrases have in their first half an energetic and lively ascent with the tenor d, and in their second half a more quiet, meditative spirit with the proper tenor c and a descent to the tonic. This division extends even to the two final *alleluia:* the first shows an animated upward movement, the second closes quietly.

The first phrase speaks of the coming of the Paraclete, the second of His activity. One becomes aware of the freshness and liveliness with which *Factus est* sets in, if one transposes the *pes* from the final syllable to the accented syllable and notes the contrast. With *Puer* in the Christmas Introit such a procedure is very suitable to praise the dear Christ-child, but here a more energetic rhythm is called for. As for the rest, the word-accents play the leading role in the formation of the melody. The second phrase is less sparkling, less striking than the first. Nevertheless, with its bright, joyous ascent over *Spiritu Sancto*, with the accentuation of *magnália*, with its florid melody and the tritone b–f, impelling us to admiration of the marvel here recounted, it has a beauty all its own. Filled with the divine life, with the Holy Ghost, the Apostles are impelled to praise and glorify the great things God has done, just as Mary, who is sitting in their midst, filled with the Holy Ghost, sang her *Magníficat* and glorified God, who had done "great things" *(magna)* to her.

"In a certain way, the miracle of Pentecost becomes visible in Holy Communion. The Holy Ghost, it is true, does not come in the form of fiery tongues, but in the form of bread He enters into our hearts; for Christ is filled with the Holy Ghost. And although the species disintegrate, the Paraclete wishes to remain with us, to take hold of us spiritually, and fill us with holy enthusiasm" *(W. K.)*

* * * *

MONDAY IN WHITSUN WEEK

In content the INTROIT is closely related to that of Easter Monday. Today, too, the neophytes are to shout with joy over the "honey-sweet" mystery of the Holy Eucharist. For the explanation of the melody, see the feast of Corpus Christi.

FIRST ALLELUIA VERSE (Acts 2: 4)

1. *Loquebantur variis linguis*   1. *The apostles spoke in divers*
Apostoli 2. *magnalia Dei.*   *tongues* 2. *the wonderful works of*
                                           God.

Again and again the Church marvels, this week, at the astounding
miracles of tongues. Repeatedly she reminds us of God's almighty rule
in the history of mankind in general and of each individual soul in particular.

The *allelúia* has two parts, the first of which confines itself to the
tetrachord *c–f*, while the second reaches up to high *c*. We met a similar
melody on the Sunday after the Ascension. The first member of the *jubilus* shows a fine manipulation of the motive: *f g a b♭ a g* and *e f g á g f*;
the second member also has two related tone-sequences. *Loquebántur* is
a further development of *alle-* while *-lúia* and the greater part of the
jubilus are repeated as far as *linguis*. Before this word a short pause is
indicated, while in the corresponding passage in the *jubilus* we have a
half pause, which is well justified by the *pressus* with the modulation to
c. Here, however, the related words *váriis linguis* are to be joined together as closely as possible. *Apóstoli* may also be regarded as the continuation of *-lúia*, but here the threefold *c* far outweighs the *f* which begins the group. For this reason we do not sing *b♭* here, but a strongly
accented *b*. It is interesting to note the display of power resulting from
the *f* with its subsequent *b♭*, and the *c* with its subsequent *b*.

OFFERTORY (Ps. 17: 14, 16)

1. *Intonuit de caelo Dominus,* 2.   1. *The Lord thundered from*
et Altissimus dedit vocem suam: 3.   *heaven,* 2. *and the Most High gave*
et apparuerunt fontes aquarum,   *his voice*: 3. *and the fountains of*
alleluia.   *waters appeared, alleluia.*

The Offertory is borrowed from Tuesday in Easter Week. Throughout the octaves of Easter and of Pentecost we hear the rushing fountains of water, reminding us that we were reborn out of water and the
Holy Ghost. Hence it is that the melody reaches its highest point in the
third phrase of our present chant. A grateful and joyous spirit pervades
the entire piece.

The close of *allelúia* corresponds with *Dóminus* in the first phrase.
This and the second phrase have the same range, but a different melodic
development. In its second half the second phrase closely follows the
tone-sequences of the first mode. A light secondary accent on the last
note of *vo-(cem)* will help to clarify the rhythm. The preceding notes

may be considered as a simplification of the motive $b\flat\ g\ \hat{f}\ e\ d\ f\ f$ over *caelo*; the first two neums over this word are heard again over *(apparu) -é-(runt)*.

On Pentecost the Lord let His voice be heard in a special manner: suddenly from heaven *(de caelo)* came the noise of a mighty wind. But it was not like the reverberation of thunder, for it marked the coming of the Holy Ghost, of Love itself.

COMMUNION (John 14: 26)

Spiritus Sanctus docebit vos, alleluia: quaecumque dixero vobis, alleluia, alleluia.

The Holy Ghost shall teach you, alleluia, whatsoever I have said to you, alleluia, alleluia.

The words of the Saviour may be regarded as a solemn solo, and the cries of *allelúia* as the grateful, joyous answer of the community.

The intrusion of the first *allelúia* is somewhat disturbing to the clear psalmodic construction of this antiphon, which has an obvious intonation, middle cadence on the tenor, and a final cadence. The accented syllable consistently occupies a higher position than the following syllable. Thus the melody follows the natural declamation of the words.

Christ, who has just come into our hearts in Holy Communion, addresses us as He once did His disciples: Let yourselves be instructed by the Holy Ghost. He will lead you to all truth, and the truth will make you free and happy. Alleluia.

To announce the "great things of God" *(magnália Dei)* in the liturgy ought to be for us a sacred and sweet duty, to which we should dedicate ourselves heart and soul.

*   *   *   *

TRINITY SUNDAY
(The first Sunday after Pentecost)

It was not until 1334 that this feast was extended to the universal Church. As early as the eighth century, however, the Mass formulary had been composed for a votive high Mass in honor of the Holy Trinity. In the earliest manuscripts we can therefore find the chants for this feast. But in great part they are only accommodations of melodies from other texts. The Introit has its melody from the first Sunday of Lent, the Gradual and the Offertory from the feast of SS. Peter and Paul, and the Communion is a free adaptation of the Communion *Feci judícium* from the second Mass for a Virgin Martyr.

In and by Himself God is infinitely happy. A sea of delight issues from the Father to the Son, and from both of these it overflows upon the Holy Ghost, and again flows back from Him. And yet it seems that something in the essence of the infinite God seeks for some further complement. Nothing is wanting to His perfect happiness, but He would share His love with others and pour blessings, grace, and happiness upon them from His own overflowing Heart. Every act of God toward His creatures is therefore an act of charity. Still more resplendent, however, does God's mercy appear when He offers reconciliation and forgiveness to sinful man after he has trodden God's holiness underfoot, when He renovates the temple of the soul which man in his folly has wasted and destroyed, and adorns it with His gifts of grace. We can never sufficiently thank God for this great love. What a price He paid for our redemption! Today, then, we hear this phrase repeated in the Introit, Offertory, and Communion: "He hath shown His mercy to us." The entire Mass formulary becomes one great "Glory be to the Father…" as a conclusion to the work of redemption begun at Christmas and brought to completion at Pentecost. Each of today's chants begins with an exhortation to praise God; Introit: *Benedicta*; Gradual, Alleluia-verse, and Offertory: *Benedictus;* Communion: *Benedicimus*. Few Mass formularies exhibit such unified structure.

INTROIT (Tob. 12: 6)

1. *Benedicta sit sancta Trinitas, atque indivisa Unitas*: 2. *confitebimur ei, quia fecit nobiscum misericordiam suam.* Ps. *Domine Dominus noster: * quam admirabile est nomen tuum in universa terra!*

1. *Blessed be the Holy Trinity and undivided Unity:* 2. *we will give glory to him, because he hath shown his mercy to us.* Ps. *O Lord, our Lord: * how wonderful is thy name in the whole earth.*

The melody was explained on the first Sunday of Lent. Its adaptation here is not an entirely happy one. Particularly unfortunate is the fact that the ascending melody over the accented syllable of *glorificábo eum* is here fitted to the unaccented syllable *(confité)-bi-(mur ei)*. It seems that the seven syllables of this text were parcelled out to the seven groups of notes which are carried by the seven syllables of the original with no reference to the word-accent. Furthermore the second half of the first phrase begins with the motive which in the original brings the first phrase to a close. Nevertheless, the entire feeling of the original is admirably suited to that of our present Introit: it is a joyously moving song of thanksgiving.

Gregoriusblatt, 28, 106 ff.; *Gregoriusbote,* 25. 10 f.; Revue, 7, 124 ff.

GRADUAL (Dan. 3: 55, 56)

1. *Benedictus es, Domine, qui intueris abyssos,* 2. *et sedes super Cherubim.* ℣. 1. *Benedictus es Domine, in firmamento caeli,* 2. *et laudabilis in saecula.*

1. *Blessed art thou, O Lord, who beholdest the depths,* 2. *and sittest upon the Cherubim.* ℣. 1. *Blessed art thou, O Lord, in the firmament of heaven,* 2. *and worthy of praise forever.*

There are times, many times in fact, when we stand face to face with inscrutable mystery. The most eminent naturalists, for instance, have made statements such as this: "It is something we do not know and never expect to know." Mysteries there are also in the human heart; yes, even in the depths of our own heart. But for the world's Creator there is no mystery: all things are evident to Him. In the Epistle we have just heard the words: "Of Him, and by Him, and in Him, are all things." He need inquire of no one. He knows what is in man. He is the Searcher of the hearts and the reins, and before Him the darkness is as the noonday brightness (Ps. 138: 11). Even the most noble creatures in the spiritual creation, the Cherubim, stand infinitely lower than He and are privileged to be His footstool. God reigns above all; who can praise Him worthily? Yet behind the ramparts of heaven a marvelous song resounds unceasingly. It is the praise and glory which each person of the Most Holy Trinity offers the others. They alone perfectly realize how praiseworthy God is. This song re-echoes unto all eternity, and the angels and saints of heaven join in with this never-ending *Glória Patri* . . . .

The melody has been borrowed from the feast of SS. Peter and Paul. Instead of *in firmaménto caeli* the ancient manuscripts read *in throno regni tui*: Blessed art Thou on the throne of Thy empire.

ALLELUIA VERSE (Dan. 3: 52)

1. *Benedictus es, Domine Deus patrum nostrorum,* 2. *et laudabilis in saecula.*

1. *Blessed art thou, O Lord God of our fathers,* 2. *and worthy of parise forever.*

The Gradual is the only song today which does not treat explicitly of God's mercy, but of His infinite splendor. In the Alleluia-verse this same thought is emphasized. The merciful love of God is, however, implicitly contained in the reference to the patriarchs and prophets of the Old Law, which was but a prelude to the fullness of grace of the New Covenant. Even in the most ancient manuscript the melody, which was explained on the vigil of Christmas, is assigned to this Mass.

OFFERTORY (Tob. 12: 6)

1. *Benedictus sit Deus Pater, unigenitusque* (2.) *Dei Filius,* 2. *Sanctus quoque* (3.) *Spiritus*: 3. *quia fecit nobiscum misericordiam suam.*

1. *Blessed be the Father, and the only-begotten* (2.) *Son of God* 2. *and also* (3.)*the Holy Spirit*: 3. *because he hath shown his mercy towards us.*

The figures in parentheses indicate the fine divisions in the original melody for the feast of SS. Peter and Paul, and show that our present Offertory has little regard for the proper phrasing. It is gratifying to note, however, that the words *Benedíctus, Pater, unigénitus, Spíritus,* and *nobíscum* are brought clearly into the foreground. Similarly, the melodic development over *Sanctus quoque* may well serve to increase our reverence for the Holy Ghost and the entire mystery of the triune God.

Let us give thanks! But let us do so mindful of the fact, mentioned in the today's Secret, that our thanksgiving can be acceptable only if God's grace is working to make of us an eternal sacrifice to Himself!

COMMUNION (Tob. 12: 6)

1. *Benedicimus Deum caeli,* 2. *et coram omnibus viventibus confitebimur ei*: 3. *quia fecit nobiscum misericordiam suam.*

1. *We bless the God of heaven,* 2. *and before all living we will praise him*: 3. *because he has shown his mercy to us.*

The first phrase is very faithful to its original (see p. 229); not so the second. The melody over *qua fecit,* which here opens the third phrase, forms the close of the second phrase in the original. Here again the phrasing is not entirely happy. Small heterogeneous pieces compose the last part: *nobíscum* is like *scuto* in the Communion for the first Sunday of Lent; the close is found in a number of chants, for example in the Introit for the tenth Sunday after Pentecost over *in aetérnum.*

We still are numbered among the living who can praise and thank God. In each holy Mass the triune God makes holy our sacrificial gifts and converts them into the sacrifice of Christ, and in the sacrificial Banquet the Father and the Holy Ghost, together with the Son, join themselves to us, and thus prove that their life and mercy are truly infinite.

*   *   *   *

CORPUS CHRISTI

With the words *Exsultáte—jubiláte* of the Introit-verse is announced the theme of today's feast, of the Mass, and of the procession which follows. The psalm from which these words have been taken was once sung at the feast of Tabernacles, which was celebrated in the open, in tents constructed of boughs in memory of the tent-life of Israel in the desert. Hence it also refers to the dwelling of God with us in the desert of this world, and to today's festive procession in the open over a path decorated with boughs (*W. K.*). Today Mother Church's heart overflows with joy—with joy that extends beyond the confines of the church building. All Nature is to exult with her. And, conversely, Nature, with her trees now wearing their most beautiful green, with her wreaths and garlands, is allowed to make a solemn entry into the church. For this is also her festal day. From her the Saviour has selected the two species, bread and wine, under the appearance of which He gives Himself to us.

In 1264, under Pope Urban IV, this feast was extended to the universal Church; its liturgy was composed by St. Thomas Aquinas (✛ 1274). The melodies have been borrowed from earlier Sundays or feasts; the following Introit, for instance, has received both text and melody from the Monday in Whitsun Week.

INTROIT (Ps. 80: 17)

1. *Cibavit eos ex adipe frumenti alleluia:* 2. *et de petra, melle saturavit eos,* 3. *alleluia, alleluia, alleluia.* Ps. *Exsultate Deo adjutori nostro:* * *jubilate Deo Jacob.*

1. *He fed them with the fat of wheat, alleluia:* 2. *and filled them with honey out of the rock,* 3. *alleluia, alleluia, alleluia.* Ps. *Rejoice to God our helper:* * *sing aloud to the God of Jacob.*

Profound awe and reverence for the true Manna marks the beginning of this piece; yet it sounds like the joyous ringing of bells. This Manna is the nourishment of our souls! That is the thought of the first phrase, which never extends beyond the tenor, but twice descends to low *a*. The accented syllable of *ádipe* carries only a single note, while the following unaccented syllable has a tristropha. We meet this construction rather frequently. Compare, for example, the Introit for the fourth Sunday after Pentecost *(Illuminátio)*, the Offertory for the fifteenth Sunday after Pentecost *(Dóminum)*, the Offertory for the sixteenth Sunday after Pentecost *(Dómine)*, the Communion for the seventeenth Sunday after Pentecost *(Dómino)*.

The second phrase augments the initial motive of the first phrase: *acdf* becomes *cdfg* over *melle*; and, as further development, *dgffga*. Rightly does *saturávit* mark the summit of the piece. Before the melody reaches it, however, there is a retarding motive (cf. *dolo* on Low Sunday), downward bent, making the development of *saturávit* all the more brilliant. This second phrase speaks of the sweet consolation which the Holy Eucharist brings to us; of the spiritual satiety which strengthens us against all the allurements of the world. The three *allelúia* may be regarded as an independent phrase. Here the ascending fourth over *saturávit* is answered by a descending fourth. The second *allelúia* closes on *c*, like *eos* above; on account of its *e* it can very effectively modulate to a full tone below the tonic. This song must proceed from a heart in which joy reigns supreme.

N. Sch., 295 ff.

GRADUAL (Ps. 144: 15, 16)

1. *Oculi omnium in te sperant, Domine*: 2. *et tu das illis escam in tempore opportuno.* ℣. 1. *Aperis tu manum tuam*: 2. *et imples omne animal benedictione.*

1. *The eyes of all hope in thee, O Lord*: 2. *and thou givest them meat in due season.* ℣. 1. *Thou openest thy hand*: 2. *and fillest every living creature with thy blessing.*

God is the Creator and the Preserver of the natural world. But He is still more concerned about preserving and promoting the life of the soul. If we look at Him today, if by our steady gaze we become one, so to speak, with the altar and the Blessed Sacrament, then He will not let us wait in vain, but will bestow upon us streams of blessing and of vital power.

In the manuscript the melody with this text is assigned to the twentieth Sunday after Pentecost. The *corpus* of the Gradual and the verse have the same florid closing cadence: *opportúno—benedictióne*. The first phrase of the *corpus* unfolds until it reaches the tenor and closes with a cadence known to us from the fourth Sunday of Lent: *mihi*. Over *(il)-lis* the final groups of neums appear a third lower. It is surprising to see that the unaccented syllable of *Aperis* carries such a florid melisma. P. Wagner (II, 66) thinks that the melody was originally composed for a Greek text and only later transferred to a Latin one; this opinion, however, is contested by *C.O.* (49, 126). A similar line of *pressus*, but with a finer grouping, is met with in various Tracts, for example the second verse of the first Tract on Good Friday over *médio*, and in several Graduals, that of the second Sunday after Epiphany over *(misericórdi)-ae* in the verse. *Manum* resembles the first half of *(Dómi)-ne*, while *imples* reminds us of *(témpo)-re*. The entire piece calls for a lively rendition.

According to *K.L.* the Gradual and the Alleluia-verse have the following mutual relations: the Gradual is taken from the Old Testament, treats of Nature, and tells of God the Provider, who hears His creatures

saying their grace before meat. The Alleluia-verse is taken from the
New Testament, is a prelude to the Gospel, and treats of grace and of
the Food of the soul.

ALLELUIA VERSE (John 6: 56, 57)

1. *Caro mea vere est cibus, et
sanguis meus vere est potus*: 2. *qui
manducat meam carnem, et bibit
meum sanguinem, in me manet et
ego in eo.*

1. *My flesh is meat indeed, and
my blood is drink indeed*: 2. *he that
eateth my flesh and drinketh my
blood, abideth in me, and I in him.*

With what earnestness the disciples on the way to Emmaus besought the Lord to remain with them, for the night was approaching!
Here our Saviour not only gives us the assurance that He will remain
with us, but that He will remain *in* us when we are united with Him in
Holy Communion. Thus the indefectible Light itself, the Light which
can never be dimmed, is within us! Our souls will be the house where
Truth dwells, where falsehood can never intrude. We shall be filled with
the life and strength from which all the saints, whom we rightly admire, have drawn. Hence He truly is what our hungering and thirsting
soul needs in life and still more in death. Our present song expresses
thanks for these many graces.

Allelúia with its *jubilus* has the form *abc*; no inner relationship
exists between it and the melody of the verse. Several times during the
year we meet this melody: first, on Corpus Christi; second, on the feast
of the Transfiguration; third, on the feast of St. Lawrence; fourth, on
the feast of St. Michael (second Alleluia); and fifth, on the feast of the
Holy Rosary. In the most ancient manuscripts it is found with the text
Laetábitur justus: "The just shall rejoice in the Lord, and shall hope in
Him: and all the upright in heart shall be praised." The melody is entirely begotten of the text, an energetic song of exultation, which leaves
this earth far below it and soars up to the ethereal blue—describing the
joy and the delight of the singer. The original, unfortunately, is no
longer sung. In it the beauty and clarity of the structure, which is psalmodic in character, is better revealed. Two phrases begin with an intonation and then have a florid middle cadence. In the first phrase there
follows not a mere recitation on the tenor, but a very ornate melisma
with a repetition; finally comes the closing cadence. The melody of
allelúia with its *jubilus* is joined to the last words of the verse to form
the third phrase. In the first part of the original an independent thought
is expressed: "The just shall rejoice in the Lord," thus fully justifying
the pause on the dominant after the middle cadence. But *b* towers above

the two *a* parts. A brief survey will show the relation between the original composition and the adaptations mentioned and numbered above.

FIRST PART

Intonation		Middle Cadence
Laetábitur	*justus*	*in Dómino*
1. *Caro mea*	*vere est cibus*	*et sanguis meus*
2. *Candor est*	*lucis*	*aetérnae*
3. *Levíta*	*Lauréntius*	*bonum opus*
4. *Concússum*	*est mare*	*et contrémuit*
5. *Solémnitas*	*gloriósae*	*Vírginis*

Florid Melisma	Closing Cadence
Et sperá-	*-bit in eo*
1. *vere est potus, qui mandúcat*	*meam carnem*
2. *et spéculum sine má-*	*-cu-la*
3. *operá-*	*-tus est*
4. *térra*	[without closing cadence]
5. *Maríae ex sémine*	*Abrahae.*

SECOND PART

Intonation	Middle Cadence	Closing Cadence
et lauda-	*-búntur*	*omnes*
1. *et bibit*	*meum*	*sánguinem*
2. *et*	*imágo*	*bonitátis*
3. *qui per signum*	*crucis*	*caecos*
4. [irregular]	*ubi Archángelus*	*Míchael descendé-*
5. *ortae*	*de tribu*	*Juda*

THIRD PART

recti corde
1. *in me manet et ego in eo.*
2. *illíus.*
3. *illuminávit.*
4. *-bat de caelo.*
5. *clara ex stirpe David.*

The structure is clearest in the verse *Laetábitur*. Of the others, verse 2, that is, that of the feast of the Transfiguration, bears the closest resemblance. The third also is good. In 1, a new thought begins with the melisma that is repeated, thus handicapping the effectiveness of the melody; for its upward surge, about which there can be no doubt in this type of Alleluia, is thereby weakened. The third part, whose melody is formed somewhat differently, does not give the feeling of a finished organic whole in which all parts are attuned to one another.

SEQUENCE

The Sequence owes its origin to St. Thomas Aquinas. In superb language it enunciates the dogma of the Holy Eucharist. Its accompanying melody was composed by Adam of St. Victor (✠ c. 1192). In its original form it was a hymn to the cross, for which the Alleluia *Dulce lignum* (May 3) supplies the initial motive *(egagcbag)*. In the double strophe *Dogma datur* and *quod non capis* this motive returns a fourth higher *(egagcbag = dcdcfedc)*. All the strophes close on the tonic and most of them with the formula *ag fg g*. Occasionally this is preceded by *a b* or *c b*. Less often we have *c ag fg g* or *ga fg g*. The individual verses close on the dominant or on *c*. Toward the end the closings on the dominant increase; the final double strophe has it thrice.

At Beuron this chant is sung in six minutes. This observation is not made with any intention of prescribing a set tempo, but merely to show that even this Sequence takes a comparatively short time to sing.

1a.   Praise, O Sion, praise thy Saviour, * Shepherd, Prince, with glad behavior, * Praise in hymn and canticle: 1b. Sing His glory without measure, * For the merit of your Treasure * Never shall your praises fill.

2a.   Wondrous theme of mortal singing, * Living Bread and Bread life-bringing, * Sing we on this joyful day: 2b. At the Lord's own table given * To the twelve as Bread from Heaven, * Doubting not we firmly say.

3a¹.   Sing His praise with voice sonorous; * Every heart shall hear the chorus * Swell in melody sublime: 3a². For this day the Shepherd gave us * Flesh and Blood to feed and save us, * Lasting to the end of time.

3b¹.   At the new King's sacred table, * The new Law's new Pasch is able * To succeed the ancient Rite: 3b². Old to new its place hath given, * Truth has far the shadows driven, * Darkness flees before the Light.

4a.   And as He hath done and planned it, * "Do this," hear His love command it, * "For a memory of me." 4b. Learned, Lord, in Thy own science, * Bread and wine, in sweet compliance, * As a host we offer Thee.

5a.   Thus in faith the Christian heareth: * That Christ's Flesh as bread appeareth, * And as wine His Precious Blood: 5b. Though we feel it not nor see it, * Living Faith that doth decree it * All defect of sense makes good.

6a.   Lo! beneath the species dual * (Signs not things), is hid a jewel * Far beyond creation's reach! 6b. Though His Flesh as food a- bideth, * And His Blood as drink—He hideth * Undivided under each.

7a.   Whoso eateth It can never * Break the Body, rend or sever; * Christ entire our hearts doth fill: 7b. Thousands eat the Bread of Heav- en, * Yet as much to one is given: * Christ, though eaten, bideth still.

8a.   Good and bad, they come to greet Him: * Unto life the former eat Him, * And the latter unto death; 8b. These find death and those find heaven; * See, from the same life-seed given, * How the harvest differeth!

9a.   When at last the Bread is broken, * Doubt not what the Lord hath spoken: * In each part the same love-token, * The same Christ, our hearts adore: 9b. For no power the Thing divideth— * 'Tis the sym- bols He provideth, * While the Saviour still abideth * Undiminished as before.

10a.   Hail, angelic Bread of Heaven, * Now the pilgrim's hoping leaven, * Yea, the Bread to children given * That to dogs must not be thrown: 10b. In the figures contemplated, * 'Twas with Isaac immo- lated, * By the Lamb 'twas antedated, * In the Manna it was known.

11a.   O Good Shepherd, still confessing * Love, in spite of our trans- gressing,— * Here Thy blessed Food possessing, * Make us share Thine every blessing * In the land of life and love: 11b. Thou, whose power hath all completed * And Thy Flesh as Food hath meted, * Make us, at Thy table seated, * By Thy Saints, as friends be greeted, * In Thy paradise above.[1]

OFFERTORY (Lev. 21: 6)

1. *Sacerdotes Domini incensum et panes offerunt Deo: 2. et ideo sancti erunt Deo suo, 3. et non pol- luent nomen ejus, alleluia.*

1. *The priests of the Lord offer incense and loaves to God: 2. and therefore they shall be holy to their God, 3. and shall not defile his name, alleluia.*

---

[1] Transl. by Msgr. Henry, in Britt's *Hymns of the Breviary and Missal.* (Benziger Bro- thers 1922.)

Through Holy Orders priests—and they alone—have received the power to offer the Sacrifice of the New Covenant. Consequently their lives must be holy. But they act as the mediators of *our* Sacrifice, and for this reason we, too, must be holy. Let bread and incense be the symbols of our labor, our prayer, and our sacrificial spirit. If we rise superior to selfishness, to worldly pleasure, to the world's way of thinking and acting, and go up to the altar of sacrifice with hearts vibrant with pure love of God, like incense, which seeks only what is above and is consumed for God, then are we a kingly priesthood, a holy nation.

The melody has been borrowed from Whitsunday (see p. 225), fits fairly well to the text whose content is related to it, and has received a rather good adaptation.

COMMUNION (I Cor. 11: 26, 27)

1. *Quotiescumque manducabitis panem hunc, et calicem bibetis, mortem Domini annuntiabitis, donec veniat:* 2. *itaque quicumque manducaverit panem, vel biberit calicem Domini indigne, reus erit corporis et sanguinis Domini, alleluia.*

1. *As often as you shall eat of this bread and drink the chalice, you shall show forth the death of the Lord, until he come:* 2. *therefore whosoever shall eat this bread or drink the chalice of the Lord unworthily, shall be guilty of the body and blood of the Lord, alleluia.*

The Offertory took its melody from Whitsunday. It was natural, then, to borrow the Communion melody from the same Mass. But there is a great difference in content and spirit between the two. Here the rendition should be inspired by the intensely serious text.

Taking only the text into consideration, this Communion is a direct continuation of the Communion for Passion Sunday (p. 148). Every Eucharistic celebration, every Holy Communion announces the death of the Lord. Bread and wine are consecrated separately. By virtue of the words of consecration, under the species of bread the Body of the Lord is represented, as it were, bloodless and lifeless, just as the Blood of the Lord is, so to say, separate in the chalice. But our faith tells us that under both species Christ is totally present. Christ is present: how pure, then, must be our heart! What a frightful sacrilege does he commit who communicates unworthily! For him the bread of life and the chalice of salvation open the door to destruction, to damnation.

After the impressive *Dómini* we may not disregard the significant *indígne*. After *córporis* or after *erit* a very slight pause is recommended. The words *donec véniat* receive an independent melodic phrase. Therein is voiced the guarantee that the Holy Eucharist, the holy Sacrifice, and

Holy Communion, with their infinite blessings will be preserved in the Church and will continue until the end of time, until the Lord will come for the final judgment. Then shall we see Him as He is, face to face, and with ineffable bliss we shall be allowed to immerse ourselves in His glory.

The *allelúia* at the end, which sounds rather strange after the words of the text, is demanded, first of all, by the analogy with the Introit and the Offertory. Secondly, it softens the seriousness of the words and gently leads back to the fundamental idea of the entire feast, the *mentis jubilátio*, to the grateful exultation of the heart, which again is given full play in the procession.

Musica Sacra, 52, 85 f.

*   *   *   *

SUNDAY WITHIN THE OCTAVE OF CORPUS CHRISTI

INTROIT (Ps. 17: 19, 20)

1. *Factus est Dominus protector meus, et eduxit me in latitudinem:* 2. *salvum me fecit, quoniam voluit me.* Ps. *Diligam te Domine fortitudo mea:* * *Dominus firmamentum meum, et refugium meum, et liberator meus.*

1. *The Lord hath become my protector: and hath brought me forth into a large place:* 2. *he saved me, because he was well pleased with me.* Ps. *I will love thee, O Lord, my strength:* * *the Lord is my stronghold, and my refuge, and my deliverer.*

When the evening of his life was approaching, David looked back upon all that the long years had brought him. There had been much suffering; many had been inimical to him; bitter woe, the torture and affliction of turbulent passions, had saddened his heart. But by far outweighing all this was the help which God had bestowed upon him, the protection which had come upon him from on high. Hence he cries out with a grateful heart: "The Lord has become my Protector! I will love Thee, O Lord, Thou my strength!"

The saints in heaven voice the same sentiments: "The Lord hath become my Protector, and hath brought me forth into a large place." Their happiness now is boundless. They are forever freed from all that is small and mean and imperfect, from all that formerly oppressed them, from all that was defective. Now they enjoy perfect liberty. They have been saved, and forever sing a canticle of grateful love.

We who still tarry upon earth surely have every reason to thank God for having become our Protector, for having led us into the open, into the perfect liberty of the children of God, and for having become our Redeemer from a motive of pure love. Our thanks ought to be especially sincere when we think of the Eucharistic Saviour and of the protection which His grace affords us against all the enemies of our soul, against whatever oppresses it, weakens it or obscures its vision. How entirely is He who was made flesh become our protector in the Holy Eucharist! What love will He not show us in this Sacrament until the very end! When we consider this, then surely the words *Díligam te* must well up from our inmost hearts. I shall attempt to repay Thy infinite love with my own poor love. Thou art my strength against all the violence of my unchecked nature, Thou art my refuge and my rescue, to whom I may have recourse in my every need.

In the first phrase joy continually tends toward development, until the motive over *edúxit me* attains its full measure with the words *in latitúdinem*. It is the song of one who suddenly finds himself free and in broad daylight after a long imprisonment in a narrow, dark, and dank dungeon. It ought not cause surprise that this same melody occurs in the Introit *Státuit*. Here also it transfigures that loftiest of all themes: the dignity of the priesthood. The ascent at *protéctor meus* bears some relation to the *Dóminus prope* of the Introit *Gaudéte* (Third Sunday in Advent): it is also somewhat reminiscent of the beginning of the Introit on the feast of St. Stephen.

The construction is apparent at first sight. Of the two phrases which compose the piece, the first has its half cadence and its full cadence on the dominant (*a*), the second at times on the tonic of the mode (*d*). The first phrase exhibits an arsis laid on a grand plan, while the second is a clear thesis. Whereas *f* is banned from the first half of the first phrase, the note *b♭* occurs four times; the second half is influenced by high *c*, and *b* occurs thrice. At *edúxit* the two *podatus* are to be interpreted broadly. The first phrase has a descending fourth (*d–a*) over *edúxit*; the second phrase two descending fourths (*g–d*). The motive over *me fecit* is heard again over *vóluit* with a quiet closing formula which releases the tension of the fourths.

GRADUAL (Ps. 119: 1, 2)

1. *Ad Dominum, cum tribularer, clamavi,* 2. *et exaudivit me.* ℣ 1. *Domine, libera animam meam a labiis iniquis,* 2. *et a lingua dolosa.*

1. *In my trouble I cried to the Lord,* 2. *and he heard me.* ℣ 1. *O Lord, deliver my soul from wicked lips,* 2. *and a deceitful tongue.*

This Gradual continues the thoughts of the Introit and is a joyfully animated song of thanksgiving for favors granted. A retrospective glance at the help which the singer has received from God's bounty gives him courage confidently to present his new petitions in the verse. Wicked lips afflict him also, speaking what is unjust *(lábiis iníquis)*, accusing him without cause, and calumniating him. And even if the Epistle for the Sunday says: "Wonder not if the world hate you," this hate, nevertheless, presses heavily upon the soul. Others come with honeyed words, but they are false *(língua dolósa)*; they wish to deceive and seduce. Lord, save me from this peril!

The ordinary construction of Graduals, which assigns a plagal mode to the corpus and the corresponding authentic mode to the verse, is followed here in the first words *Ad Dóminum;* but then the melody immediately changes over to the authentic form and emphasizes it almost more than the verse. The verse thrice closes on the tonic; the *corpus* never. The melody over *dum tribulárer* has for its schema the middle cadence of the simple psalm-tone of the fifth mode *f a c–d c;* that over *exaudívit,* the close of the solemn tone of the lessons, *é g á f,* which receives still greater amplification in the verse over *língua.* In the verse care must be taken that the bistropha and the two tristrophas be interwoven into the whole in an elastic yet subdued manner. The seconds over *líbera ánimam* should have a soothing effect. We hear the same sequence of tones over *meam* that appeared in the close of the *corpus* of the Gradual. *Lábiis* and the central group of notes over *dolósa* are related. The melismas over *iníquis* have been taken over from those over *clamávi* in the first part. In the ancient manuscripts this Gradual is assigned to the Friday after the second Sunday in Lent.

ALLELUIA VERSE (Ps. 7: 2)

1. *Domine Deus meus, in te speravi; 2. salvum me fac ex omnibus persequentibus me, 3. et libera me.*

1. *O Lord my God, in thee have I put my trust; 2. save me from all them that persecute me, 3. and deliver me.*

The Alleluia with its *jubilus* has the form a b b[1]. *Allelúia* is the arsis; the *jubilus* is the thesis. Twice the descent is retarded and held together by a *pressus.* In the verse three great curves swing upward as arses, to which a triple descending thesis corresponds.

Arsis	Thesis
1. *in te sperávi*	1. *salvum me fac*
2. *ex ómnibus*	2. *persequéntibus me*
3. *et líbera (me)*	3. *me*

The closing neum of each arsis, *a b c a a*, returns in the closing neum of the thesis a fifth lower as *d eĵd d*. The close of the third strophe *(me)* is in a richer strain, thus swelling the melody of the thesis considerably. It resembles to some extent the *jubilus* of *allelúia*. With this melodic arrangement that of the text naturally does not agree, as is readily apparent from its punctuation. A little difficulty is experienced in the beginning of the verse *Dómine Deus meus*. It possesses the character of a thesis, although no arsis actually precedes it. One might say that it is a free repetition of the thesis of the *jubilus*.

Dómine Deus suggests quiet repose in the fatherly arms of God; *in te sperávi*, a most firm trust in Him who is the Author of earthly changes, who directs and governs them all. However great the difficulties that arise, this trust in God remains unshaken. *Omnibus* and *líbera* may perhaps suggest the tribulations of the Psalmist who, pursued by his enemies, places all his confidence in God alone. The rich melismas on the last word, with their downward movement, speak of rest. This impression is strengthened when *allelúia* with its *jubilus* is repeated.

OFFERTORY (Ps. 6: 5)

1. *Domine convertere, et eripe animam meam*: 2. *salvum me fac propter misericordiam tuam.*

1. *Turn to me, O Lord, and deliver my soul*: 2. *O save me for thy mercy's sake.*

Marked by a special style and a childlike naivete of tone, this Offertory stands alone among all the Offertories. Only the Offertory *Dómine in auxílium* of the sixteenth Sunday after Pentecost is related to it, for it follows the same mode, the sixth, and confines itself almost to the same range. Soon, however, it shows a tendency to form melismas, while here syllabic chant predominates with a trustful adherence to the tonic *f*. The stressed syllable tends to form a *pes*; twice indeed it becomes a *torculus*. The second phrase bears the same features as the first, although the melody is somewhat more ornate. The closing neums of the third last and the second last syllable are freqnuetly emphasized in the sixth mode. It would almost appear as if the melody wished to tone down the strong expression *éripe me* ("loose me from"). *Salvum me foc* has an entirely different coloring from the petition in the Alleluia-verse. The theme of the whole might be put thus in the words of Morikes: "O Lord, into thy hands let all things be placed—the beginning and the end."

But when we consider the Gospel, how it was selfishness which kept the invited guests from the "great banquet," then we shall pray earnestly: O Lord, free me from blindness and delusion, from all dangers that threaten my soul, and let me taste what Thou hast prepared for me in Thy banquet.

The two additional verses which are given in the old manuscripts for the Monday after Passion Sunday are similarly suggestive of rest. Only the word *Dómine* of the first verse is somewhat more ornate. In the second part of the second verse the melody assumes the brighter coloring of the fifth tone and even becomes melismatic over the second last word, *ossa*. The confident *salvum me fac propter misericórdiam tuam* brings the whole to a close.

COMMUNION (Ps. 12: 6)

1. *Cantabo Domino, qui bona tribuit mihi*: 2. *et psallam nomini Domini altissimi.*

1. *I will sing to the Lord, who giveth me good things*: 2. *and will make melody to the name of the Lord most high.*

As is apparent from the closing note *a*, this piece was transposed a fifth higher, since the final interval is a full step. Ordinarily the ending would run thus: *d e d*. If the beginning of the piece is transposed a fifth lower, then we have *b c̆ e♭ c e♭*. According to the old notation, this *e♭* could only be written a fifth higher, namely as *b♭*. Besides acting as the passing note, the *e♭* also plays the role of tenor. On the Wednesday of Ember Week in Lent the Offertory, which is composed in the fourth mode, begins almost exactly like the melody over *Cantábo Dómino*. Why was not the Communion composed in a similarly easy style? Evidently because it had in view what was to follow. For from *qui bona* on, the second tone, to which the entire piece is assigned, makes itself heard. In the Introit for the fourth Sunday after Pentecost, which certainly belongs to the second mode, the passage *qui bona tríbuit mihi* recurs over the words: *et salus mea, quem timébo*. The combination of the fourth and second mode—here effected by *c* (ordinarily *f*)—signifies an ascent over against the tenor *e♭* which preceded it. And only after the singer has lived himself into the new mode does the *b=e* occur twice, although each time as passing note, so that compared to the preceding *b♭=e♭*, it is not at all disturbing.

In the second part of the Communion, the melody shows a rise seldom found in a plagal mode. The name of the Most High must be glorified. He, although infinitely superior to all that is mundane, has deigned in His love to look upon man. Yet more, He has associated himself most intimately with man; He has become one with him in Holy Communion. He could not bestow a greater good *(bona tríbuit)* than Himself—all His holiness, all His merits, graces, and gifts above measure.

Were we able fully to comprehend this immense boon, how our hearts would exult! In this manner we must conceive the joy expressed in the melody. If the formula for this Sunday's Mass were not much older than that for the feast of Corpus Christi, we should be tempted to say that it is an echo of the jubilation with which we paid our homage to the Eucharistic Lord as He moved through the streets several days ago. And if we are depressed because we are unable to thank God as is His due, then we possess the sweet consolation that the Saviour in our breasts is our canticle of praise—that He offers adequte praise to the Father for us. Manuscript 121 of Einsiedeln endeavors to bring closer to us the full meaning of *Altissimi*, by giving the four *torculus* and the two deepest notes—the second mode is wont to indulge in these plunges—a broad marking.

* * * *

FEAST OF THE MOST SACRED HEART OF JESUS
(Friday after the Octave of Corpus Christi)

In the seventeenth century, St. Margaret Mary Alacoque, of the Order of the Visitation, strove earnestly to obtain the recognition and institution of the present feast. Only in 1856 did Pius IX prescribe its celebration for the universal Church. Pius XI gave it an octave and raised it to the same rank as the feasts of Christmas and Ascension. It was assigned a new Mass formula and Office by a decree of January 29, 1929. The present Mass formula has various points in common with the Mass *Miserébitur* hitherto prescribed for the universal Church and the Mass *Egredímini* permitted to some localities. The thought which pervades today's feast is indicated by the Preface. In that beautiful composition the pierced Heart of our Lord is glorified as the sanctuary of divine liberality, from which flow streams *(torréntes)* of mercy and grace.

INTROIT (Ps. 32: 11, 19)

1. *Cogitationes cordis eius in generatione et generationem; 2. ut eruat a morte animas eorum et alat eos in fame. Ps. Exsultate justi in Domino, * rectos decet collaudatio.*

1. *The thoughts of his heart to all generations; 2. to deliver their souls from death and feed them in famine. Ps. Rejoice in the Lord, O ye just, * praise becometh the upright.*

The words of the Introit point to the significance of the Sacred Heart of Jesus in the history not only of the world but of the individual soul. That it might deliver humanity from eternal death, the Heart of Jesus itself went into death. In order to appease the hunger of souls and bring salvation to the world, this Heart offered its very flesh and blood, yes, its own Self together with its overflowing truth and love. And this offering was not an isolated event of the remote past only, but continues from generation to generation—*in generatióne et generatiónem*. To be an inspiration at all times and daily to bring divine consolation is the constant yearning, desire, and will of the Sacred Heart. How manifold have been its experiences with the souls of men and how varied the reactions to its all-embracing love! There have always been and will always be souls that requite love for love by making a complete oblation of self. But there are also the great number of those who close their souls to the influences of divine love, who are irresponsive to the many gifts of grace, and who show themselves faithless even to the point of hatred. In spite of all this, the Heart of Jesus has not become embittered; although wounded, it continues to pour forth the riches of its merciful love. It is ever faithful, prepared to give help *in generatióne et generatiónem*. As the Mother of God sings of the mercies of the Lord that continue from generation to generation, so the Preface of today reminds us that the fire of love in the Sacred Heart continues to burn without interruption.

The words *et generatiónem* should not be sung too hastily. As the melody develops, our grateful love should likewise develop. This will be effected the better, the more we realize how much the merciful love of God means to us throughout our life. And just as this love embraces all creation, we would desire all creation to rejoice and sing the praises of the Sacred Heart. The fact that numberless holy souls in heaven and on earth join in our song of jubilation is a matter of encouragement and comfort to us. As members of this great family of God we employ the words of Psalm 32 to express our sense of gratitude to divine Providence that it has created all things, that it directs and knows all things, and that it is ever present to help us in attaining our eternal salvation. The initial verses of this same psalm describe the joy of the just, the concluding verses the rejoicing of our own soul, for "in His holy name we have trusted."

Like the text, which is composed of different verses of the same psalm, the melody is a combination of various parts of several Introits. The melody over *Cogitatiónes Cordis eius in generatió-(ne)* shows some similarity to that over *Dómine refúgium factus es nobis a generatió-(ne)* at the beginning of the Introit for Tuesday after the first Sunday of Lent. The fact that both excerpts end with the same word may have brought about this association. The following *et generatiónem* repeats in abbreviated form the melody over *convéntum fácite* in the Introit *Laetáre* of the fourth Sunday of Lent.

The entire second phrase *et eruat* is the same as the third phrase of the Introit *Laetáre*. In the original melody, *exsultétis* depicts a feeling of jubilation, the accented syllable of *satiémini* is effectively emphasized, while the wide intervals of a fourth and fifth, together with the agreeable melody which stresses the word accent of *consolatiónis*, give us a premonition and experience of the fullness of divine consolation. On account of its abbreviated text, today's new Introit had also to contract the original melody.

GRADUAL (Ps. 24: 8, 9)

1. *Dulcis et rectus Dominus*, 2. *propter hoc legem dabit delinquentibus in via.* ℣. 1. *Diriget mansuetos in judicio*, 2. *docebit mites vias suas.*

1. *The Lord is sweet and righteous*: 2. *therefore he will give a law to sinners in the way.* ℣. 1. *He will guide the mild in judgment*: 2. *he will teach the meek his ways.*

The Epistle depicts St. Paul on bended knee praying for us to the Father of our Lord Jesus Christ that our inner man might be strengthened and that Christ might dwell in our heart, and that, rooted and founded in His love, we should comprehend the glory of our vocation and the charity of Christ which surpasses all understanding. This divine charity forms the theme of the present Gradual, the words of which afford us great comfort. God is good to His creatures and faithful: He is all-high, all-powerful, all-sublime, and awe-inspiring (Wolter, *Psallite sapienter*, I, 330). The psalm excerpt which forms today's Gradual continues with the words: "All the ways of the Lord are mercy and truth." Indeed, the Lord is merciful and faithful even to those who err in the way—or as others would translate: who fail against the law. And without doubt, to this class we must also ascribe ourselves, the more so if we carefully and truthfully scrutinize the actions of our own life. Notwithstanding the complaint of our Saviour in the Reproaches of Good Friday: "Thou art become to Me exceeding bitter," He remains *dulcis*, sweet and gracious. Notwithstanding His complaint: "All have turned from righteous ways," He remains faithful, and wills not the death of the sinner. Out of the fullness of His love He gives us the Law, imparts to us enlightenment and grace, affords us the means whereby we can be absolved from the guilt of sin that we might again realize peace in our souls, and gives us the strength to order our life in accord with His divine will. If we but allow Him to lead and guide us, then surely will His charity also permeate our being. His words will teach us how to become meek and humble, and will instill into us a desire to share with others His peace and contentment. On our part, let us promise this good and faithful God henceforth to remain true to His ways, those straight paths that lead to eternal life.

The melody over *et rectus Dóminus* might be derived from the Gradual *Concupívit rex* of the Mass *Vultum tuum* (the second for a Virgin not a Martyr). The florid neums over *et* are found over the significant *rex* in the latter Mass. It is more probable, however, that today's melody is to be sought in the Gradual of the twenty-second Sunday after Pentecost (q.v.). At any rate, the beginning over *Dulcis (ecce)* and the entire melody from *delinquéntibus* to the end is taken from that Gradual.

A note of importance seems to permeate the entire melody. *Dulcis* is sung somewhat slowly and subdued. The thoughts suggested at the beginning of the text are well accommodated to the range of a fifth over *Dóminus*. The neums over *mansuétos* are also employed over *(inquirént)-tes* on All Saints. The coda of *judício* is identified as a wandering melisma. The rich vocalization over *suas* occurs frequently as a termination of Graduals in the first mode.

ALLELUIA (Matt. 11: 29)

1. *Tollite jugum meum super vos* 2. *et discite a me, quia mitis sum et humilis corde: et invenietis requiem animabus vestris.*	1. *Take my yoke upon you* 2. *and learn of me, because I am meek and humble of heart: and you shall find rest to your souls.*

That burdened souls might find their rest in Him is the great desire of our divine Saviour. To this end He pleads with us that we take His yoke upon ourselves and follow His example. Consider the yoke which He bore! Fully conscious of His divine dignity and majesty He humbled Himself and descended to the lowest depths of humiliation and abjection; He became an object of bitterest scorn, underwent most cruel and painful tortures, and climaxed His life by death upon the cross. But He bore this yoke willingly, He embraced His cross lovingly and kissed it tenderly. And now He pleads with us to bear our yoke submissively, to lose our own will in His divine will, to subject our desires to His divine dispensation, in fine, to accept our state of life with its concomitant hardships as something which is to the advantage of our souls, as the yoke appointed for us to bear. Then we shall find rest to our souls.

The Gradual melody is the only one of today's Mass which is not modeled on some other melody. The sincerity and warmth which characterize its first part make it immediately appealing. Alleluia with its *jubilus* has the form $a + b + c$ (c^1). The *pressus* on *aa, gg* and *ee* enliven the movement. *Tóllite jugum me-(um)* is similar to *-lelúia* with its *jubilus*. The motive over *Tóllite* recurs in a slightly modified form over *ju-(gum)* and *quia*. The melody over *(me)-um super vos* and *(qui)-a mitis sum* shows an effective rhyme which, with its tender melody reminiscent of the *Improperia* of Good Friday, fits the text well. Although the melody at the conclusion is effective harmoniously, it all but isolates the *húmilis corde* which follows and with which it is logically connected. In view of this, the pause after *mitis sum* should be made very short. The richly developed melody over *et* and its inception of a sixth after the first pause recurs, with the exception of the first three notes, over *ré-(quiem)*. The same might be referred to that over *mors* in the Alleluia of the fourth Sunday after Easter. The melodic distinction given the word *réquiem* is well merited. Its somewhat austere character indicates that this rest can be attained only at the price of constant vigilance.

The Tract for votive Masses after Septuagesima employs recognized typical forms. Lengthy vocalizes are avoided except at the very end. The descent of a fourth at the beginning of the third phrase happens rarely at this place in Tracts. The text as such mirrors the underlying thought of the feast: the goodness and love of the Sacred Heart.

The Alleluia for Paschal time is the same as that for All Saints (q.v.).

OFFERTORY (Ps. 68: 20)

1. *Improperium exspectavit Cor meum et miseriam,* 2. *et sustinui qui simul mecum contristaretur et non fuit;* 3. *consolantem me quaesivi et non inveni.*

1. *My heart hath expected reproach and misery,* 2. *and I looked for one that would grieve with me but there was none:* 3. *and for one that would comfort me, and I found none.*

The Gospel led us to Golgotha and pictured to us our dead Saviour "whom they have pierced," whose side they opened with a spear. Unconcerned about strict chronology, the Offertory permits us to listen to a last word which the dying Christ directs to mankind. Text and melody repeat the first three phrases of the Offertory of Palm Sunday (q.v.) and give us an insight into that which the Heart of Jesus endured.

Even today Christ awaits—but in vain—many who come not. They have neither time nor heart for Him; neither is there a grateful remembrance of that love for which He underwent a most cruel death. Let us, therefore, share His grief with Him the more intimately. By a worthy rendition of this touching song we shall move the faithful assembled in the house of God to correspond more fully to the expectations of the Sacred Heart.

OFFERTORY for Votive Masses during Paschal Time
(Ps. 37: 7, 9)

1. *Holocaustum et pro peccato non postulasti; tunc dixi: Ecce venio.* 2. *In capite libri scriptum est de me ut facerem voluntatem tuam:* 3. *Deus meus, volui et legem tuam in medio cordis mei,* 4. *alleluia.*

1. *Burnt offering and sin offering thou didst not require: then I said, Behold I come.* 2. *In the head of the book it is written of me that I should do thy will:* 3. *O my God, I have desired it and thy law in the midst of my heart,* 4. *alleluia.*

The melody is taken from the Offertory for the Dedication of a Church (q.v.). With a slight variation in its concluding text, this same melody was sung in the Sacred Heart Mass *Egredímini* and from there passed over to the text of the present Mass. In the original there are three phrases differing from one another in text and sentiment. The first phrase portrays a simple heart *(in simplicitáte cordis)* joyfully bringing sacrifice. Today's Offertory emphasizes the words *pro peccáto.* The second phrase of the original further stresses the "great joy," the enthusiastic spirit of sacrifice, which unites the people with its king, David. Today, by happy chance, the gradation of melody takes place over the words *voluntátem tuam.* The third phrase of the original brings a fervent prayer: "Preserve this will of their heart." The closing syllable of *voluntátem* (today: *médio)* once more vibrates with the joy of the first two phrases. *Dómine Deus* (today: *cordis mei)* reverts to the charming simplicity of the first phrase.

In reality there is one main thought which permeates the entire Offertory of the new feast. Mankind throughout the centuries has expended great care and energy in its sacrificial services. Yet after calm reflection it must admit that all its offerings and sacrifices do not suffice, and can neither efface nor compensate for the soul's guilt. But then a voice from heaven resounds: Behold, I come and achieve an offering of limitless efficacy, which entirely satisfies the demands of God, a sacrifice which is all adoration, all atonement, all praise of God. Thy command, O my God, is my will and the desire of my Sacred Heart. And these glad tidings of the Heart of Jesus we realize again and again in the sacrifice of the Mass. As an Offertory song these words then have a special import and make a direct appeal to us. When Christ says: "I come," let us answer: "I will go with Thee." When He says *vólui*—"I have desired" —let us answer: "I also desire; may Thy law be deeply inscribed in my heart and pervade my life, my very being. Enkindle in my heart the fire of Thy love for sacrifice."

COMMUNION (John 19: 34)

1. *Unus militum lancea latus eius aperuit, et continuo exivit sanguis et aqua.*

1. *One of the soldiers with a spear opened his side, and immediately there came out blood and water.*

Like the Offertory, the Communion emphasizes the thought of Christ's sufferings. The soldier who opened the side of Christ certainly had no premonition of the blessings his action presaged. The Heart of Jesus is opened and will remain open forevermore, "a rest for the pious and a refuge of salvation for the penitent" (Preface). The water and blood which flowed from His side are symbols of the graces bestowed in Baptism and in the Holy Eucharist.

The melody resembles that of the feast of St. Boniface (June 5). The adaptation of the text on that feast is more happy and more fluent. The melody over *mílitum láncea la-* corresponds to that over *sánguis et a-(qua)*.

COMMUNION for Votive Masses during Paschal Time (John 7: 37)

1. *Si quis sitit, veniat ad me et bibat, alleluia, alleluia.*

1. *If any man thirst, let him come to me and drink, alleluia, alleluia.*

There are many voices to entice the one who is seeking happiness, but these voices, as a rule, lead only to disillusionment and bitter disappointment. One alone has the right to call us who at the same time has the power to satisfy our desires, and that one is our divine Saviour, whose Sacred Heart embodies within itself the plenitude of all happiness. He gives us a foretaste of this happiness in Holy Communion, which in turn prepares us for an eternal happiness where in unending joy and gratefulness we shall sing: Alleluia, alleluia.

The strikingly simple and concise melody models itself on the Communion of Low Sunday, as comparison of the following will show: *quis sitis* and *Mitte...tuam*, *véniat ad me* and *et (cla)-mavérunt, et bibit all. all.* and *sed fidélis all. all.* The word *me* is emphasized to good advantage and has the effect of a leitmotif. It recalls to mind the goodness and love with which the Sacred Heart received the doubting Thomas, who was permitted to lay his hand in the side of the Saviour and feel the pulsing of His Sacred Heart. Filled with faith and happiness let us exclaim with him: "My Lord and my God!" Would that we might sing the praises of the Sacred Heart with that feeling, yes, if possible with that perfection, with which the Saviour sang the praises of God while on earth.

*   *   *   *

THIRD SUNDAY AFTER PENTECOST
INTROIT (Ps. 24: 16, 18)

1. *Respice in me, et miserere mei, Domine*: 2. *quoniam unicus et pauper sum ego*: 3. *Vide humilitatem meam, et laborem meum*, 4. *et dimitte omnia peccata mea, Deus meus.* Ps. *Ad te Domine levavi animam meam:* * *Deus meus, in te confido, non erubescam.*

1. *Look thou upon me and have mercy on me, O Lord*: 2. *for I am alone and poor.* 3. *See my abjection and my labor.* 4. *and forgive me all my sins, O my God.* Ps. *To thee, O Lord, have I lifted up my soul:* * *in thee, my God, I put my trust; let me not be put to shame.*

"At that time the publicans and sinners drew near unto Jesus to hear Him"—thus the Sunday's Gospel. And they heard from Him that word for which their souls were famishing: the call of the Good Shepherd, who opened His compassionate and forgiving heart even to them; who would not rest till He had found the lost sheep and pressed it to His bosom. Where such love is shown, confiding prayer again becomes easy. Not by chance has the sixth mode been selected for the sweet melody of today's Introit, which runs entirely in this vein. The text, it is true, speaks of loneliness and distress of heart, of misery and suffering, and requests forgiveness of all sins. But over all this the melody spreads a warm, invigorating light, issuing from the very heart of the Good Shepherd. Assurance of being heard pervades all, in accordance with the psalmverse: "In Thee I trust, let me not be put to shame."

In the first half of the first phrase occur the petitions *Réspice* and the ascending *miserére*, both words supporting themselves on the tone *f*. Besides placing special stress upon the petitions by the fifth above the tonic, the second half of the phrase gives their reason: "I am alone and poor." *Unicus* repeats the motive of *Réspice* a fifth higher, and the striking *pauper sum ego* stands in the same relation to it as the more modest *miserére* to *Réspice*. Its execution must do full justice to the melodic ascent. It is very expressive of thanks. The concluding notes remind us of the first announcement of Easter in the Introit *Laetáre* at the words *et convéntum fácite*, and of *salutári tuo*, with which we laud God's blessedness on the first Sunday after Pentecost. As a smile among tears, so is this melody to the text. At first the second phrase adheres to *c* with some pertinacity, which is to be expressed by a *crescendo*, especially since the fourths *c–g* and *g–c* impel toward it. But the downward movement, at first only alluded to, is carried into effect by *aaa (vide humi-)*, *ggg (-litátem)*, *ff (meam)* as far as *fddc*, as a contrast to the upward tendency of the first phrase. *Et labórem*, by its emphasis on the tonic, re-establishes the equilibrium. The third phrase has not only the same range as the second, but also some melodic resemblance: witness the descent to *c*, which is answered by a melodic reversal over *peccáta*. Quiet now steals over the heart of the singer. Thirds are the greatest intervals in the melody. From the Requiem Mass we are already acquainted with the seconds that occur in the closing formula, which also are sung in the above-mentioned Introit *Laetáre* with the words *dilígitis eam*.

GRADUAL (Ps. 54: 23, 17, 19)

1. *Jacta cogitatum tuum in Domino: et ipse te enutriet.* ℣ 1. *Dum clamarem ad Dominum,* 2. *exaudivit vocem meam ab his, qui appropinquant mihi.*

1. *Cast thy care upon the Lord, and he will sustain thee.* ℣ 1. *Whilst I cried to the Lord,* 2. *he heard my voice from them that draw near unto me.*

In the Epistle we heard St. Peter: "Cast all your care upon Him [the Lord], for He hath care of you" (1 Pet. 5: 7). Almost the same words are employed in the *corpus* of the Gradual. Leading us away from the affairs of our workaday existence, the melody rapidly brings us to Him "who shall sustain us." According to the indications of the manuscripts, we are to interpret the four notes over *Dó-(mino)* broadly, thus showing our unshakable trust in God. This first part, ending on the dominant, bears all the markings of an arsis. From *et ipse* on, the thesis begins with the employment of the conventional formulas. The first part is terse—a bold, confident shaft *(jacta)*—while the second sings with great freedom and evident joy of the divine Sustainer. In the verse, *Dum clamárem* and *exaudívit* receive the same melodic treatment. The Saviour's words come to mind here: "As thou hast believed, so be it done to thee." From the Graduals for Laetare Sunday and for the feast of St. Cecilia we are acquainted with the formula over *Dóminum*. We should prefer to hear it over *exaudívit* ("He has heard me"). Twice more the closing formula of *clamárem* recurs over *exaudívit* and *his*, which seems to mar the construction somewhat. The ornate groups of neums over *mihi* beautifully enlarge upon the close of the *corpus* which we heard over *enútriet*.

With but few changes, the melody of this Gradual has been borrowed from that for the feast of St. John Damascene (March 27).

ALLELUIA VERSE (Ps. 7: 12)

1. *Deus judex justus, fortis et patiens:* 2. *numquid irascitur per singulos dies?*

1. *God is a just judge, strong and patient:* 2. *is he angry every day?*

To judge from the pauses indicated, *allelúia* with its *jubilus* has five parts. A rising motive is repeated thrice almost in the same style, but each time takes a different development and a different thesis. The half pause between the third and fourth members produces a disturbing effect, hampering the musical development of a melody which beyond doubt belongs to the finest to be found in the Graduale. Care must be taken not to rush too precipitately to the higher notes. Not without reason does Codex 121 of Einsiedeln assign a broad construction to the rising notes. Nevertheless, the rendition must not drag; the exultation which pervades this chant must be clearly indicated. The two first members of *allelúia* are characterized by the ascending fourth and fifth and the descending fourth and by a strong emphasis on *g*, the tonic of the mode. In the second part of the *jubilus c* predominates. A similar relation exists between the two parts of the following verse. In the first part the two first members of *allelúia* are twice repeated over *Deus judex justus* and *fortis et*. In the latter case, the descending fourth is replaced by a full note. But after the rising fifth, the development is different each time, and the climax is reached over *pátiens*. The fact that this word, speaking of God's longanimity, receives prominence, tempers to some extent the text of an Alleluia-verse which is unusually serious, and introduces us to the consoling Gospel in which the Good Shepherd, full of tenderness and long-suffering, pursues the erring lamb and does not rest until He has placed it upon His loving shoulders. If then the verse, continuing in two corresponding parts, voices the question "Is he angry everyday?" we must recall the beginning of the Epistle of the Sunday: "Be you humbled, therefore, under the mighty hand of God; that He may exalt you in the time of visitation." But the whole again ends with *allelúia*.

While plainsong in general is very adept in joining individual phrases and parts of phrases, we here find, less happily all the beginnings of the melody on the tonic.

OFFERTORY (Ps. 9, 11-12, 13)

1. *Sperent in te omnes, qui noverunt nomen tuum, Domine*: 2. *quoniam non derelinquis quaerentes te*: 3. *psallite Domino qui habitat in Sion*: 4. *quoniam non est oblitus orationem pauperum.*

1. *Let them trust in thee who know thy name, O Lord*: 2. *for thou hast not forsaken them that seek thee*: 3. *sing ye to the Lord, who dwelleth in Sion*: 4. *for he hath not forgotten the cry of the poor.*

A fifth marks the range for the first three phrases: the first going from *g–d*, the second and third from *f–c*. Hence, the song produces no great tension. One is almost tempted to say that the lamb on the shoulders of the Good Shepherd is singing its song of thanksgiving in a reserved and unostentatious manner, and is urging us to trust in God. It has understood what today's parable wishes to teach; it has come to know the Saviour in His most winsome, most appealing character. The triple repetition of the cheerful motive with which the piece began—over *nomen, quaeréntes,* and *psállite*—fits very well to the modest style of the whole, although it is each time developed in a different manner. Both neums over *tuum* are marked broadly in manuscript 121 of Einsiedeln and thus help to call particular attention to the word. Truly, he who has come to the full knowledge of Christ can do nothing else than place his entire trust in Him; for "God does not forsake those who trust in Him." This conviction is shown especially by the restful seconds which bring the second phrase to a close. Yea, He pursues His sheep even though they do not seek Him, for He wishes to bring them peace and happiness. The calm recurring seconds over *hábitat in Sion* breathe the same spirit of peaceful indwelling in God. Still the final *f* of this passage is a surprise, one to make us meditate, suggesting perhaps the thought: Do you fully realize what this means: God dwells in Sion, dwells in you, dwells in His Church, and is prepared to offer Himself again for you in the holy Sacrifice of the Mass? The closing phrase has a character all its own. Possessing a range of an octave, it effects a certain elaboration of the motive: over *quóniam non, ed ga bab;* over *oblítus, fe fg aga;* over *oratiónem, cdf eg aa,* and with this word seems to try to picture how our prayer rises from the depth of misery directly to God. *Páuperum* presents the same melody, though a fifth lower, with which the first phrase over *Dómine* closed.

COMMUNION (Luke 15: 10)

Dico vobis: gaudium est Angelis Dei super uno peccatore paenitentiam agente.

I say to you: There is joy before the angels of God upon one sinner doing penance.

Significantly this piece begins immediately on the dominant of the mode. For Jesus is speaking, and He speaks a new word, a word full of consolation. Who would think that when a sinner does penance there is an increase in the joy of the angels in heaven, and that this joy is renewed as often as a human heart is brought to look into itself and is converted *(super uno)*!

The first part is developed about the note *c*; the second, about *a*.

Codex 121 of Einsiedeln has a broad virga and "t" over *est,* whereby a *ritardando* is indicated, with evident good effect.

At St. Gall's, at Einsiedeln, and in some other places this Sunday's Communion was sung on the twenty-second Sunday after Pentecost, today's being replaced by *Ego clamávi*. This Communion, however, fits well to the Gospel of the Sunday, and at the same time acts as an admonition to those faithful to whom the liturgy of the Mass has not yet brought reconciliation with God and true interior peace.

If the text is clearly enunciated, it will be seen how well the simple melody brings the word *gáudium* into prominence.

There is joy in heaven, and peace in the heart of him who has again found his way back to God. The Father of the prodigal son crowns His kindness by preparing the most sumptuous banquet for him in Holy Communion.

*   *   *   *

FOURTH SUNDAY AFTER PENTECOST

INTROIT (Ps. 26: 1, 2)

1. *Dominus illuminatio mea et salus mea, quem timebo?* 2. *Dominus defensor vitae meae, a quo trepidabo?* 3. *qui tribulant me inimici mei, ipsi infirmati sunt, et ceciderunt.* Ps. *Si consistant adversum me castra:* * *non timebit cor meum.*

1. *The Lord is my light and my salvation: whom shall I fear?* 2. *The Lord is the protector of my life: of whom shall I be afraid?* 3. *My enemies that trouble me have themselves been weakened and have fallen.* Ps. *If armies in camp should stand together against me,* * *my heart shall not fear.*

Few selections in the entire Graduale have a melody so easily understood, so lucid in structure, and of such regular development as this Introit. From the introduction to the Preface we are familiar with the opening motive, which recurs throughout the entire piece. It begins the second phrase a fourth higher, and comes to a climax in the third, being heard also over *a quo*. Thus all three phrases are closely knit together. No lengthy pause must be made between them; they must follow one another in a lively, almost impetuous sequence, as an expression of most complete confidence in victory. Perhaps the early Christians sang this song in the dim, wan atmosphere of the catacombs. But the hearts of those who sang were full of light: for Christ had enlightened them. And even if their brothers and sisters above were led to martyrdom and thrown before the beasts, inwardly they possessed the courage and strength of lions: the victorious Lion of the tribe of Juda had imparted His fearlessness to them. Self-possessed and unafraid they entered the lists against the entire world, contemning death. For they were invested with the firm conviction that all these attacks would be repelled by the Church and that all their enemies, though they now appeared as mighty hosts strongly encamped *(castra)*, would finally collapse utterly.

The manner in which the interrogative pronouns *quem* and *a quo* are melodically treated has given rise to special theoretical explanations on the handling of interrogatives in chant compositions *(Gregoriusblatt* 1920, 33 ff.; *N. Sch.* 248). It remains to be seen if this procedure is justified. Let it be noted, however, that the entire passage *et salus mea, quem timébo* with its descending close agrees with *qui bona tríbuit mihi* in the Communion for the second Sunday after Pentecost, in which there is not the slightest idea of interrogation. Similar instances, for example the Offertory *Invéni David servum meum*, could be quoted. On the other hand, the interrogation in *trepidábo* produces a very marked effect. It sounds like a challenge. And though foes may summon *(tríbulant)* all their forces, naught shall come of it. How telling is the comparison between the stormy *tríbulant* and the simple *infirmáti sunt* with its delicate irony! All the mighty fortresses which are built to hinder the advance of the Church tumble down like houses of cards. One is reminded of the verse, "The arrows of children are their wounds" (Ps. 63: 8). *Cecidérunt* closely resembles the closing word *timébo* of the first phrase. Over *illuminátio* and *infirmáti* the principal as well as the preceding secondary accent is short, whereas the following syllable always has more than one note. In the first nocturne of this Sunday's Office the story of David and Goliath is related. There stood the giant, a terror to the entire Jewish host *(si consístant advérsum me castra)*. David alone showed no fear. The Lord was his light and his salvation! And how miserably did that colossus come to grief *(infirmáti sunt)*! A stone from David's sling sufficed to lay him low.

GRADUAL (Ps. 78: 9, 10)

1. *Propitius esto, Domine, peccatis nostris*: 2. *nequando dicant gentes*: 3. *Ubi est Deus eorum?* ℣ 1. *Adjuva nos, Deus salutaris noster* 2. *et propter honorem nominis tui, Domine, libera nos.*

1. Forgive us our sins, O Lord, 2. lest the gentiles should at any time say: 3. Where is their God? ℣ 1. Help us, O God our Saviour: 2. and for the honor of thy name, O Lord, deliver us.

The fourth, fifth, and sixth Sundays after Pentecost have the three Graduals in the same succession as they occur in the liturgy of the Ember Saturdays of Lent and of September. At St. Gall's and other places these seem to have been sung also at a second Mass on the Ember

Saturday in Whitsunweek. They belong to the fifth mode. The structure of the text is brought out plastically by the melody. A quieter, simpler style distinguishes the *corpus* of the Gradual from the more extended and ornate melismas of the verse. Compare the close of the first phrase of the verse *(noster)* in the Gradual for the fourth Sunday. The verses of all three Graduals have the same closing melisma; in fact, from *cca ba* they are identical and only minor variations occur before that. This melisma forms the final phrase in about thirty Graduals. Abstracting from this, however, one must admire the richness of form, the variety, and the harmony of these verses. As we know, the ornate melismas after the first words of the verse are a part of its peculiar style. Here a wonderful opportunity is offered the singer to put forth the best that is in him. Perhaps here as in many other places, it should be made clear that the *praise* of God occupies the first place, and that the *petitions (*in the present selection *exáudi* and *líbera)* ought to be subordinated to this primary purpose. Rendered in this spirit they will, humanly speaking, produce the greatest impression on the heart of God. Melodically, the thoughts *salutáris noster* (God is our Saviour), *Deus virtútum* (God of hosts), and *Dómine refúgium* (the Lord is our refuge) stand forth in the most brilliant light.

All three Graduals have the first word accented on the second syllable. It is clearly shown here that the accent tends to raise the tone. The first syllable is a minor third lower in every case. And the bistropha or the *pes quassus* over the accented syllable would seem to indicate that the accent, besides prolonging the tone, also strengthens it.

This Gradual *(Propítius esto)* is also sung on the Thursday after the second Sunday in Lent. Its theme is as follows: Because of our sins we deserved punishment and castigation. But should this misfortune fall upon us who are Thy people, O Lord, then the Gentiles would say that our God is too weak and powerless to shield us. Thus, O Lord, it is in reality a question of Thy honor. In order to preserve and increase this, do Thou save us, O Lord!

Dómine forms the answer to *esto.* We meet a textual turn in the Offertory for the fourth Sunday after Pentecost similar to that here employed with *ne quando dicant gentes.* Naturally, we should expect a tenser conclusion here. The question *ubi est Deus eórum?* seems to have been worked into the rising movements of *ubi* and *eórum.* It is almost impossible to decide whether the composer intended this as such, or whether an established formula was employed. Then one might still ask why such a suitable formula was selected. *Adjuva nos* harks back to the beginning of the verse in the Gradual for St. Stephen. Toward the end of that verse one finds the same recitation on the tonic, which is here replaced by the extended recitation on the dominant note at the beginning of the verse. Special care must be taken that these passages be not hurried. Correctly woven into the rhythmic whole, they produce a marvelous effect. But there is nothing restful about the inner melismas over *honórem*. Here the singer must let himself be captivated by the urge of the melody, which only begins to subside gradually after the *torculus*, in which high *f*¹ occurs, is reached. Many will not be able to sing these florid groups in one breath; they may make a short pause after the fifth note over *(ho)-nó-(rem)*.

GRADUAL for the fifth Sunday after Pentecost
(Ps. 83: 10, 9)

1. *Protector noster aspice Deus*: 2. *et respice super servos tuos.* ℣ 1. *Domine Deus virtutum*, 2. *exaudi preces servorum tuorum.*

1. *Behold, O God our protector*: 2. *and look on thy servants.* V 1. *O Lord God of hosts*, 2. *give ear to the prayers of thy servants.*

This same Gradual is sung on the Monday after the first Sunday in Lent. Between *noster* and *áspice* an interval of a sixth occurs—a somewhat rare occurrence in chant. This song is a longing prayer for a gracious glance from the eye of God. The *corpus* as well as the verse have the same closing melisma. One may find the entire passage *exáudi preces servórum tuórum*, text and melody, repeated in the Gradual for the feast of the Dedication of a Church. According to Codex 121 of Einsiedeln, all eight notes over *preces* are to be sung broadly.

GRADUAL for the sixth Sunday after Pentecost
(Ps. 89: 13, 1)

1. *Convertere, Domine, aliquantulum*, 2. *et deprecare super servos tuos.* ℣ 1. *Domine, refugium factus es nobis*, 2. *a generatione et progenie.*

1. *Return, O Lord, a little*; 2. *and be entreated in favor of thy servants.* ℣ 1. *Lord, thou hast been our refuge*, 2. *from generation to generation.*

Only the syllable *-vér-* comes into prominence in the Gradual *Convértere Dómine*; in other respects it resembles the beginning of the Gradual for the fourth Sunday after Pentecost in the two opening words. The text prays very modestly: "Lord, turn to us, only a little." Nevertheless, the heart of the singer beats somewhat faster, and he sings these words with marked impressiveness. *Super servos tuos* has been taken from the preceding Gradual. On the feast of SS. Peter and Paul, Trinity

Sunday, Immaculate Conception, and on certain other days, the entire verse is sung. The burden of today's prayer is this: May God, who throughout the centuries has seen all human beings in their trials and their pain, in their struggles and their suffering, and who has throughout assisted them with His grace—how many in heaven could tell of His powerful help!—be merciful also to us, His servants!

ALLELUIA VERSE (Ps. 9: 5, 10)

1. *Deus, qui sedes super thronum et judicas aequitatem*: 2. *esto refugium pauperum in tribulatione.*

1. *O God, who sittest upon the throne and judgest justice*: 2. *be thou the refuge of the poor in tribulation.*

Few alleluiatic verses are so well developed as this one. It belongs to the very essence of such verses to distribute the ornate melismatic groups over several words. The rich melody over *thronum* seems to fit the text extremely well, and portrays fittingly the grandeur of the throne of the Almighty. But borrowing of a Gradual melody is very apparent here: viz., from a verse on the Sunday within the Octave of Epiphany over *pacem*, and from the verse in the Mass *Salus autem*, of the Commune Sanctorum, over the word *corde*. The most ancient manuscripts do not give this Alleluia for the Sunday's Mass, and it cannot be traced back farther than the eleventh century. One point, however, deserves attention. The verse ends on the petition: *esto refúgium* ("be Thou the refuge of the poor in tribulation"). But here there is no cry for deliverance: it is exclusively a glorification of God's might. This is the prayer of petition in its noblest form, in accordance with the Psalmist's behest: "Cast thy care upon the Lord and He will sustain thee."

The motive after the first pause in the *jubilus* of *allelúia* repeats itself a step lower after the second pause. A second time we have the formula *b c a g*, with a conclusion much resembling a coda. *Allelúia* is therefore composed in the form a b b¹. The verse begins with the first motive of *allelúia*.

The text can be linked up with the preceding Epistle. In the passage read, the Apostle speaks of the deep longing that runs through all creation, the yearning for the liberty and the glory of the children of God. This same longing and sighing pervades the Alleluia-verse with its petition.

OFFERTORY (Ps. 12: 4, 5)

1. *Illumina oculos meos, ne unquam Obdormiam in morte*: 2. *ne-*

1. *Enlighten my eyes, that I may never sleep in death*: 2. *lest at any*

quando dicat inimicus meus: prae-   time my enemy say: I have pre-
valui adversus eum.   vailed against him.

Two voices are discernible in this Offertory. One proceeds from a soul in the most dire need, abandoned and persecuted. Its prayer is as fervent and as urgent as can be. In the oldest manuscripts this Offertory is assigned to the Saturday before the third Sunday in Lent, and still is sung on that day. The Gospel story of the Prodigal Son immediately precedes it. Hence the prayer seems to proceed from the soul of the Prodigal. Surely moments and hours were not lacking when in his soul almost all the light was extinguished, when the frightful darkness of the night, of despondency even, seemed to overpower him, when the mocking laugh of his enemies already rang in his ears: *Praeválui*—"Now I have Thee in my power. All attempt to escape is futile." But far greater than the strength of the enemy was the omnipotence of divine love and of divine mercy. We may also think of those who are walking along the edge of a precipice and who, when the light fails, are dashed down the abyss, beyond all hope of salvation; of those who, caught in a complexity of temptations, do not even realize their situation. For them also the Offertory prays: *Illúmina.* A note of melancholy is apparent in the melody. The singer is conscious of his condition and it makes his prayer ever more intense. Over *me-(os)* we have *g bb a bb g f*, proceeding from *f a g á f d* over *Illú-(mina)*; *ne-(quándo)* is then added as a development. Now the melody recedes as if exhausted. But with *morte* it receives new strength. Their very importance causes the three *c*'s to be heard. Hence the rhythmic markings of the manuscripts emphasize the fact that the four succeeding low tones be given a broad rendition. This makes the passage very effective. After the *f* over *me-(os)* breath may be taken, and a new start made with the second *f*.

The second phrase corresponds almost exactly to the first, with the twofold division and subdivision of each member into two parts, and has practically the same length. Because of its position at the beginning of the second phrase, the second *nequándo* is given a different melodic treatment. The repetition of the same motive over *dicat* and *inimícus*, with the heavy accent upon the high *c*, is evidence of the keen feeling in the heart of the singer. As often as the following phrase begins with *d*, a concluding *f* as over *me-(us)*, is the general rule.

But now, in the stirring *praeválui*, a second voice is heard. It comes as a call from hell, as a precipitate dash upon the victim, a horrible entwining in the tentacles of some frightful monster, a descent into the eternal night of death. Here *á g c̹ c c̹ g e* over *morte* in the first phrase occurs a fifth lower with the notes *d̹ e c f́ f́ff d e c*. A cold shiver seizes us. Here drama and realism are portrayed as one would scarcely expect to find them in plainsong. The passage might have a paralyzing effect upon us, did we not know that in the holy Sacrifice God's power will be made evident, mightily overcoming every enemy of our soul, and bringing us every needed grace. Of this divine strength we become partakers in Holy Communion. In the ancient manuscripts this Offertory has the following conclusion: "Look upon me and hear me. I will praise the Lord, who has bestowed His graces *(bona)* upon me." *Praeválui* seems in a certain sense an allusion to yesterday's Magnificat antiphon: *Praeváluit David in Philistaéum.* David conquered the Philistine with a sling and a pebble from the brook. But it also mentions the source of this heroic strength when it adds: *in nómine Dómine*—"in the name of the Lord."

The similarity of ending over *morte* and *eum* is still more accentuated in the old manuscripts, since *morte* as well as *eum* has a *virga* and a *climacus* (not a *pes subbipunctis* in the one case). Over *eum* in the motive of *meus, (e g f e f f f)* expands into *g a g d f f f.*

A better effect will be obtained if the piece is sung a tone higher.

COMMUNION (Ps. 17: 3)

1. *Dominus firmamentum meum, et refugium meum, et liberator meus:* 2. *Deus meus adjutor meus.*

1. *The Lord is my firmament, and my refuge and my deliverer:* 2. *my God is my helper.*

In content, in feeling, and in mode this Communion is much like the Introit. We now go out into everyday life with its demands upon our energies—but God is our strength. Soon we are again threatened by dangers and death-dealing arrows—but God is our refuge. If we meet opposition interiorly—God is our helper. Just now He has again become my God *(Deus meus)* in Holy Communion. Hence I have every reason to be consoled. "May the Sacrament we have received......be our sure defense" (Postcommunion).

Quickening and strengthening confidence pervades this melody. This is already indicated by beginning on the dominant of the mode; also by the accumulation of the *pressus* of which there are no fewer than seven in this short chant. One is immediately struck by the similar endings over *firmaméntum meum* and *adjútor meus.* But the opening *f é f d́ f c* over *Dóminus,* repeated a third higher over *Deus* as *a ǵ a f́ e d,* has a very definite appeal. To this must be added the sober descent and confident ascent over *refúgium meum* and the victorious, well-prepared accent over *liberátor.* It is a song of joyful and unshakable confidence in God. In this manner the Apostles might have sung after the miraculous catch of fishes related in today's Gospel. Fired with this confidence, they went forth into the wide world to become fishers of men. At the behest of God they cast out their nets, and never was their work done in vain. Their trust in God was without any *if* or *but*; it was solid as granite and bright as the rays of the sun (Oberhammer, III, 106).

* * * *

FIFTH SUNDAY AFTER PENTECOST

INTROIT (Ps. 26: 7, 9)

1. *Exaudi, Domine, vocem meam, qua clamavi ad te*: 2. *adjutor meus esto, ne derelinquas me, neque despicias me, Deus salutaris meus.* ℣. *Dominus illuminatio mea et salus mea*: * *quem timebo?*

1. *Hear, O Lord, my voice with which I have cried to thee*: 2. *be thou my helper, forsake me not, nor do thou despise me, O God, my Saviour.* ℣. *The Lord is my light, and my salvation,* * *whom shall I fear?*

The first half of the first phrase moves in the lower range in simple seconds. Are they the expression of reverence before the majesty of God? Or of that quiet confidence which places all things in the hands of God? Has the singer, perhaps, quieted down only after much difficulty, so that now, during his singing of the Introit, the consciousness of his burden breaks upon him afresh? In the second half of the first phrase a certain agitation makes itself felt, not so much in the descending as in the ascending thirds. The annotated manuscripts, moreover, indicate a broad rendition of all the neums over *qua clamávi*, as an expression of grievous affliction. Still the singer rouses himself to confidence in the almost brilliant *adjútor meus esto* with its swelling melody. No such marked pause, however, may be made after *derelínquas me* as after *esto*. Both petitions—"forsake me not, do not despise me"—must follow rapidly one upon another. The similar passages *qua clamávi: ǵa ǰd ḋc e, despícias: ǵa ǰd ég e* and *salutáris meus: ǵa ǰg ég f*, however simple they may be, still contribute their share toward making the whole more unified. *Deus* is the direct antithesis to *esto*. The closing formtion *ad te* bends the otherwise expected *clivis* (compare the close of the antiphon with *meus*) to a *podatus*, an almost universal rule in chants of the fourth mode when the following phrase begins with low *d*, or still lower. P. Wagner (III, 338) thinks indeed that in the treatment of the responsories of the Office, the ascending fourth (or fifth) after *d* is the determining factor. The present case, as well as the passages *non credis, quia,* and *est, allelúia,* in the Communion *Tanto témpore* (May 1), perhaps permit of a broader interpretation of the above rule. In any case, Wagner is correct when he observes (*ibid.* 339): "The highly developed sense of the early singers for an effective and natural concatenation of melodic members reveals itself to the observer again and again" (cf. above p. 6).

The somewhat oppressive mood of the antiphon is lightened in the psalm-verse with its high dominant and cheerful *b*. By this contrast the otherwise typical melody adds a hearty "Yea" and "Amen" to the text: "The Lord is my light and my salvation."

How often has not that call for assistance, *Exáudi*, winged its way to heaven! And each time it had its own ring, and each heart gave it its own coloring, and every sorrow gave it its own accent of confidence —from the radiant hopefulness of a child's prayer to the poignant cry of some stricken heart tempted to despair. Choral chant has some knowledge of this also. It would be worth our while to compare, for instance, the treatment of *exáudi* in the Introits of the Tuesday after the fourth Sunday in Lent and of the Sunday after Ascension, in the Gradual for the feast of the Dedication of a Church, and in the Offertory of the Monday after the third Sunday in Lent.

For the Gradual see p. 259.

ALLELUIA VERSE (Ps. 20: 2)

1. *Domine, in virtute tua laetabitur rex*; 2. *et super salutare tuum exsultabit vehementer.*

1. *In thy strength, O Lord, the king shall joy*; 2. *and in thy salvation he shall rejoice exceedingly.*

The upward tendency of *Allelúia* is cut short by the lively downward movement in the first member of the *jubilus*, only to appear so much the more firmly and powerfully afterwards. It is not difficult to distinguish the two motives, which gracefully complement each other: the first tends upward, while the second is characterized by its vigorous accent.

a) $\acute{f}$ g f $b\flat$ a g b) $b\flat$ g f $\overbrace{aa}$ f

   f g f $b\flat$ g f f d c $\overbrace{ff}$ c

   d f e g f d c c d $\overbrace{cc}$ a

   f a g c c c a g a $\overbrace{gg}$ f

In the verse, *Dómine* borrows its melody from *Allelúia*, and *virtúte* from the third member of the *jubilus*. Here the verse reaches its zenith; it mentions the source of all life, of all purposeful activity, the fountain inexhaustible. In the first phrase the singer is filled with jubilation. But that which follows is quite unexpected. What does the ornate melody over the insignificant *et* mean? One is tempted to assume that we here have a borrowed melody, one which originally belonged to some other text. In contrast, how fitting is the use of this melody on the feast of the Most Pure Heart of the Blessed Virgin Mary (in some places this feast is celebrated on the third Sunday after Pentecost) with the words: *Magníficat ánima mea Dóminum!* This is the first phrase; in the second we meet the rich melody in question over the words *et exsultávit.* If we now sing these rich melismas with the word *et,* we treat them as a *jubilus* of *allelúia* and sing them in the spirit of *exsultábit* which occurs only later on. In any case, the presentation must be very flexible. We must consider this phrase as the expression of unbounded joy, which does not confine itself to individual words. After the *climacus c b♭ a g,* high *c* is to be sung straight on both times without any lengthening. In this manner, *exsultábit veheménter* gives expression to the melody of *allelúia* and the *jubilus* with genuine rejoicing.

OFFERTORY (Ps. 15: 7, 8)

1. *Benedicam Dominum, qui tri-buit mihi intellectum:* 2. *provide-bam Deum in conspectu meo sem-per:* 3. *quoniam a dextris est mihi, ne commovear.*

1. *I will bless the Lord, who hath given me understanding:* 2. *I set God always in my sight:* 3. *for he is at my right hand, that I be not moved.*

This melody offers an opportunity to observe how plainsong can give new and refreshing variations to the same motive. Beginning with *f,* it works its way up to *c,* now in steps of seconds, now in major and minor thirds, and then descends again to the lower tones. Compare *qui mihi—intelléctum—providébam Deum—in conspéctu meo—quóniam—a dextris.* One might readily consider these passages a simplification of the solemn motive with which the piece began—*é d d a b á g a é c c a.* Let there be no pause after *benedícam,* but add *Dóminum* immediately with a good *crescendo.* In general, the whole chant demands a lively presentation. It is a song of thanksgiving for divine illumination, for insight into God's economy, into the mysterious workings of grace in the individual soul and in the entire Church. It is the joyful song of the pilgrim who sings of his resting place in God; also a song of victory over the enemies of the soul. For since God is with us and in us, how can there be any faltering? Hence we hear nothing of fear or pusillanimity, of sadness or weariness. Our God-given insight into the riddle of life helps us in every emergency; it makes us joyful, courageous, and confident of salvation. In this spirit the melody must be sung. Nevertheless, certain portions should be given broader interpretation in accordance with the rhythmic indications in the manuscripts; *(intel)-léctum, meo*, and *semper* are to be treated in this manner. Strange to say, the *clivis* is marked with "c" *(celeriter*—rapidly*)*, where a slower rendition might be expected. *Mihi* again descends to low *c*, thus giving the third phrase the same range as the first. It is characteristic of the authentic modes that the tonic of the mode, which was used twice in the beginning of the piece and avoided after that, here makes its reappearance. The melisma over *commóvear* gains in perspective when we compare the group *ǵ f g f̌ f d* of the first member with the group *ǵ f g f̌ f e* in the second, the former being a preparation for the latter. A *crescendo* is to mark *ǵ f á g f*. The following group, with its sober seconds, then leads over to the conclusion.

Some singers may find it necessary to pause for breath after *conspéctu meo*, as well as after *dextris est*.

COMMUNION (Ps. 26: 4)

1. *Unam petii a Domino, hanc requiram*: 2. *ut inhabitem in domo Domini omnibus diebus vitae meae.*

1. *One thing I have asked of the Lord, this will I seek after*; 2. *that I may dwell in the house of the Lord all the days of my life.*

If we wish to sing this text according to its sense, we shall emphasize the very first word *Unam*, and still more *hanc*. Later, when we come to speak of the goal whither all our longing tends, special stress should be laid upon *inhábitem* and *domo Dómini*. The melody develops exactly according to these ideas. It seems only natural that the piece should begin on the dominant. At *hanc* the suppliant soul with all its ardor cries out: "O Lord, grant me but this one thing!" Then peace envelopes it, reflected by seconds progressing in the style of a sequence according to the common formula. The next phrase, beginning a fourth higher, introduces a new arsis based on the dominant. The thesis takes its inception with *ómnibus*; *vitae meae* forms a grateful response to *requíram*. The melody over *Dómino* is repeated note for note in the Introit for the third Sunday in Lent over the word *Dóminum*. Similarly, the adjacent half-phrase in both songs has the same movement; in our present selection, however, the highest note receives particular emphasis.

Even if we are obliged to leave the church after the Sacrifice today, we nevertheless remain in union with our Lord and with the Church. For the Master of the house has united Himself to us in Holy Communion. And just this one desire is His, that He may dwell in our hearts by His grace and remain there all the days of our lives, until He may offer us a lodging in His heavenly mansion where we shall no longer lack anything, where our every longing will be perfectly satisfied in the contemplation and possession of Himself.

*   *   *   *

SIXTH SUNDAY AFTER PENTECOST

INTROIT (Ps. 27: 8, 9)

1. *Dominus, fortitudo plebis suae, et protector salutarium Christi sui est:* 2. *salvum fac populum tuum, Domine, et benedic hereditati tuae, et rege eos usque in saeculum.* Ps. *Ad te Domine, clamabo, Deus meus, ne sileas a me:* * *ne quando taceas a me, et assimilabor descendentibus in lacum.*

1. *The Lord is the strength of his people, and the protector of the salvation of his Anointed:* 2. *save, O Lord, thy people, and bless thine inheritance, and rule them forever* Ps. *Unto thee will I cry, O Lord:* * *my God, be not thou silent to me, lest if thou be silent to me, I become like them that go down into the pit.*

Today's Introit begins in the same manner as that for the fourth Sunday after Pentecost, and is also cast in the same mode. The *usque in sáeculum* and the preceding *(fortitú)-do plebis suae* resemble *cecidérunt* in the former. The present Introit, however, differs greatly in development and in sentiment. The range of the former is from low *a* to high *b♭*; here it is only from *a* to *g*, beyond which it never goes. In the former there is but slight difference between the individual phrases, and one experiences something almost oppressive—as if the psalm-verse, which speaks of those who descend into the pit, supplied the leading thoughts for the singer. Still, the fourths over *(fortitúdo) plebis* and especially over *(pro)-téctor*, as well as the vigorous accents of *suae* and *rege* following the frequent stress of the dominant and the return to the tonic, produce an enlivening effect. They energetically express the thought: We are Thine inheritance, O Lord, and Thou shalt be our King!

Two musical phrases are distinguishable, each beginning with low *a* and again returning to it after having reached their peak with *g*. Here, even more than elsewhere, we must be guided by the text, which is most thought-provoking. In the first part David praises the Lord as the "strength of His people" and gratefully recalls the armor of divine grace which has been bestowed upon him, the Lord's anointed. It is also a prayer of thanksgiving. The second part is a prayer of petition. But the king's petition is not for himself; it is for his people, or, more correctly, for the people of God. He says to Him: It is Thy people, Thy

inheritance, which Thou hast acquired for Thyself. Thus he adduces
for it the most forcible recommendation possible. These words of the
second part have been incorporated in the *Te Deum*, except that *in
saéculum* is replaced by *in aetérnum*.

This Introit exhorts us who are assembled for divine service not
to think only of ourselves and our own personal needs, but rather of the
entire people of God, of that corporate whole to which we are privileged
to belong. The solemn annointings at Baptism and Confirmation impress upon us that we are the elect of God, the inheritance which He so
dearly purchased at the cost of His own blood. With these sentiments
we should sing *salvum fac, bénedic,* and *rege.*

The petition made in the psalm receives wonderful fulfillment in
the Gospel. It is impossible for the Saviour to remain mute; He cannot
look upon the sufferings of His people in silence. Hence He speaks the
consoling word: "I have compassion on the multitude." He does not wish
His people to resemble those shepherdless ones who go to destruction.
He is ever providing the necessary nourishment, lest they faint on the
way. The blessing which He pronounces over the seven loaves and the
few fishes really refers to His people. He leads them to rich pastures, so
rich that even after the four thousand are sated, an abundance still remains. All that was there enacted materially is only a symbol of His
wondrously compassionate work in the Holy Eucharist.

This Introit is to be sung at least a fourth higher and in a lively
tempo.

For the GRADUAL see p. 259.

ALLELUIA VERSE (Ps. 30: 2, 3)

1. *In te, Domine, speravi, non
confundar in aeternum:* 2. *in tua
justitia libera me, et eripe me:* 3.
inclina ad me aurem tuam, 4. *ac-
celera, ut eripias me.*

＊ 1. *In thee, O Lord, have I hoped,
let me never be confounded:* 2. *deliver me in thy justice, and release
me;* 3. *bow down thine ear to me,*
4. *make haste to deliver me.*

The beginning of this verse forms the conclusion of the *Te Deum*;
the second part of the Introit of the Sunday made a similar allusion. It
is not necessary to add that the *Te Deum* was not the source of these
texts, but that they were taken from the twenty-seventh and thirtieth
psalms. Melodically, the words *in te Dómine sperávi* and *inclína ad me
aurem tuam* are the same; similarly *non confúndar* and *éripe me,* as well
as *accéle-(ra)* and *erípi-(as).* At *aetérnum* there is an evident caesura,
fully justified by the text, for a new part begins with *in tua.* Then follow petitions based on the invincible confidence in God which was ex-

pressed in the first part. Hence the pause after *éripe me* must not be too prolonged; the melody does not come to a final close here any more than at *confúndar*, which has the same melody and which is followed merely by a short pause. The same is true with the large pause after *tuam*, which corresponds to the half pause after *sperávi* above. Both parts have the range of a sixth. By way of exception, the verse bears no assonant relation to *allelúia* or its *jubilus*. At *confúndar* and the corresponding *éripe*, the six notes before the quilisma are to be sung broadly according to Codex 339 of St. Gall's; this adds weight to the words. In *allelúia* also, the first three notes over -*le*- and -*lú*- are to be sung broadly. Thus a modest ascent is achieved —*ascensiones pudicae*, as the anclients put it. Of special beauty is the simple yet harmonious recitation over *libera me*; centrally placed, it produces the effect of a mellow solo in the midst of a powerful male chorus. This also tends to make the petition so much the more striking.

For the OFFERTORY see Sexagesima Sunday, p. 104.

Today we might combine this prayer with the Epistle of the Sunday. The Apostle tells us that Christ was awakened from the dead through the glory of the Father; he exhorts us for this reason to walk in newness of life and to look upon ourselves as men who, having died to sin, now lead a life unto God. We are indeed conscious of human frailty, but we know also the desire of the Christian soul to live in newness of life and for God alone. Hence the soul prays in deep humility, but at the same time with full confidence in the might of divine grace: "Make perfect my steps in Thy paths." The Offertory is a processional: we carry our "gifts" to the altar; this procession is the symbol of the course of our lives.

In the holy sacrifice of the Mass the Lord continually repeats the marvel of His benevolence and renews the sacrifice of the cross. He bestows graces upon us, that through our concelebration of the Mass, we may effectually die to sin and grow together with Christ both in the likeness of His death and also in the likeness of His resurrection, as today's Epistle has it.

COMMUNION (Ps. 26: 6)

1. *Circuibo, et immolabo in tabernaculo ejus hostiam jubilationis:* 2. *cantabo, et psalmum dicam Domino.*

1. *I will go round, and offer up in his tabernacle a sacrifice of jubilation*: 2. *I will sing, and recite a psalm to the Lord.*

The beginning is filled with awe, and reminds one of a reverential bow. But then the singer is impelled to pour forth his jubilation vigorously and enthusiastically. The holy Sacrifice with all the honor it gives the Holy Trinity, with all the blessings it brings to souls, especially in the sacrificial Banquet, has become a sacrifice of jubilation. Filled with these sentiments, the pious soul prepares to return again to the life that awaits its outside. There also it will not forget to sing and play before the Lord and to remain a cheerful giver.

The melody rises in a well-graduated ascent, its highest points forming the ascending line *c d e f g a*. How clearly *hóstiam jubilatiónis*, with its recitative on high *g* and the graceful conclusion, rings out! The second phrase returns more to the spirit of the introductory *Circuíbo*. But in *dicam* the song reasserts the tone of jubilation. Both phrases close with the same formula. The reason for the transposition to *c* is found in the beginning of this chant. Usually we should have *f c eb*. We are here dealing with a formula which begins many pieces, especially antiphons of the eighth mode. Thus the Magnificat antiphon for the first Vespers of Christmas, set a whole step lower, begins as follows:

$$f \; c \qquad\qquad eb \; f \; g \; f \qquad\qquad f \; g \; f \; f$$
$$Cum \qquad\qquad ortus \qquad\qquad fuerit$$

The same holds true of the beginning of the Introit for the first Sunday of Advent.

*   *   *   *

SEVENTH SUNDAY AFTER PENTECOST

In comparison with the preceding Sundays, a change of feeling now becomes apparent in the antiphonal chants. The former were serious, entreating, imploring confidence. Now they have a tone of joyous exultation.

INTROIT (Ps. 46: 2)

1. *Omnes gentes, plaudite manibus*: 2. *jubilate Deo in voce jubilationis.* Ps. *Quoniam Dominus excelsus, terribilis:* * *Rex magnus super omnem terram.*

1. *O clap your hands, all ye nations*: 2. *shout unto God with the voice of joy.* Ps. *For the Lord is most high, he is terrible:* * *he is a great King over all the earth.*

The exhortation to be glad, to shout aloud for sheer joy, could hardly be expressed better than in these words of the Introit. It is the triumphal shout of Easter. The melody, however, is not correspondingly impetuous, and can scarcely be regarded as a substantial enhancement of the text. The sixth mode, the one used here, is mild and limpid in character. Besides, in its plagal form, it usually has very narrow limits in the higher range, and here is especially unpretentious. Only once does it go beyond the dominant *a* in the brilliant *jubiláte* which, with its *a é b c a*, can be regarded as a development of *f a g a f* over *Omnes* and *(exsultati)-ó-(nis)*. Otherwise it rests upon the tonic *f*, and several times descends below it. Only well-known formulas come into play. *Omnes* resembles *Stetit Angelus* in the Offertory of September 29, while *pláudite mánibus* employs the common formula of the Alleluia-verse of Christmastide: for example, that of the third Christmas Mass over *adoráte Dóminum* or that of the Introit of the preceding Sunday over *plebis suae*. Just as an actual clapping of hands, in accordance with the summons of the Introit, is entirely out of question in the Roman liturgy, so also is the indicated joyfulness quite restrained and subdued.

Perhaps the psalm-verse, which speaks of the "terrible" God, removed some of the rich coloring of the antiphon. Although this text must be considered a most serious one, and although it may be true that reverence and joy constitute the extremes of all true church music, still it must be noted here that all the other verses of the psalm in question glorify the Lord with great jubilation as the victorious God who procured our salvation.

Each Sunday recalls to mind the marvelous victory which Christ achieved on Easter morning, that victory which He also intends should be ours. That is the reason why the most high God makes such intimate contact with us in the Eucharistic mysteries; that accounts for the fact that almighty God treats with our souls so respectfully: that He may fully realize the marvels of His resurrection and glorification in us.

Manuscripts 339 of St. Gall's and 121 of Einsiedeln omit this psalm-verse and substitute the fourth verse, *Subjécit*—"He hath made the peoples subject to us."

GRADUAL (Ps. 33: 12, 6)

1. *Venite, filii, audite me:* 2. *timorem Domini docebo vos.* ℣. 1. *Accedite ad eum et illuminamini:* 2. *et facies vestrae non confundentur.*

1. *Come, children, hearken to me:* 2. *I will teach you the fear of the Lord.* ℣. 1. *Come ye to him and be enlightened;* 2. *and your faces shall not be confounded.*

Only when the soul is permeated with the fear of God will the exhortation of the Apostle in today's Epistle: "Now yield your members to serve justice, unto sanctification" (Rom. 6: 21), and that of the Lord in the Gospel, to do the will of the Father who is in heaven and to bring forth good fruits, be carried into effect. This lesson is brought home forcibly in the *corpus* of the Gradual. The first phrase shows an upward

tendency, while the second is, in the main, a descent of thirds: *b c a f—
g a f—e f d—e c*, and exhibits a very common coda. The verse calls attention to our good fortune in being permitted to approach so closely to our God in the *mysterium* of the Mass, to be enlightened by Him, to be radiant with His own blessedness. This melody is explained on June 29. Let us only note here how spiritedly the important words *eum* and *illuminámini* sing out their full joy in the topmost notes of the melody.

ALLELUIA VERSE (Ps. 46: 2)

1. *Omnes gentes plaudite mani-bus*: 2. *jubilate Deo in voce exulta-tionis.*

1. *O clap your hands all ye nations*: 2. *shout unto God with the voice of joy.*

It seems as if this ornate melody were a recompense for the restraint of the Introit which has the same text as above. *Allelúia* rises in thirds: *d–f, f–a, a–c.* In the *jubilus*, the second member resembles the first, except that the beginning and the end differ somewhat. The verse is composed of two parts. In the first *b♭* dominates, while the second is marked by a sharply contrasted *b.* But the difference is still more sharply defined. *Omnes* already introduces the third mode, which changes only with *mánibus*, from whence a sort of modulation leads back to the first mode. The second part, on the contrary, stresses the Doric *b.* After the pause, *b♭ c g g f* over *gen-(tes)* is raised to *c d b♭ b♭ g.* We may divide the melismas over *plaúdite* into three groups, of which the second is a repetition of the first. Why is the quilisma with *a* missing in the first group? Perhaps because the third *g–b♭* has a brighter effect than the simple seconds, and hence is better suited to the first summons, *plaúdite.* The melody tends upward, but only to sink back again. After the second *f aca*, it emphasizes *c* and then soars above it. These notes must come prominently to the fore. A clear understanding of the melodic gradation is evidenced in manuscript 121 of Einsiedeln by the broad *torculus* and the *pressus* in this passage. This is the summit that was to be attained: it must therefore be brought out strongly. We hear the entire strain repeated in the *jubilus* of the Alleluia *Amávit eum Dóminus* in the Mass for Doctors of the Church. There also the melody, after a twofold repetition, soars above its highest note. The Alleluia, however, is assigned to the fourth mode. As for the strange manipulation of the text, which assigns rich melismas to the unaccented syllable *(pláu)-di-(te)*, it must be remarked that the popular Latin, no doubt, exerted its influence by stressing the unaccented "i" in the second last syllable; other examples of this may be found in the words *spíritum, vídimus,* and *munéribus.*

We are introduced into another world by the second phrase with its stressed tritone, marked with a lengthened *virga* and a *pressus* with "t" *(tenére,* to hold*)* in manuscript 121 of Einsiedeln. Keen mountain air seems to surround us; these impetuous seconds are surcharged with energy. It is like the exultation of men who are returning from the bitter strife and perils of war. Only when the melody again enters upon the *jubilus* does the tender *b♭* reappear. Into this verse put all your joy at having been redeemed. (*K. L.*)

OFFERTORY (Dan. 3: 40)

1. *Sicut in holocaustis arietum et taurorum, et sicut in millibus agnorum pinguium:* 2. *sic fiat sacrificium nostrum in conspectu tuo hodie, ut placeat tibi,* 3. *quia non est confusio confidentibus in te, Domine.*

1. *As in holocausts of rams and bullocks, and as in thousands of fat lambs;* 2. *so let our sacrifice be made in thy sight this day, that it may please thee:* 3. *for there is no confusion to them that trust in thee, O Lord.*

It is surprisingly rare to find Offertory and Secret mutually complementary in thought. Today, however, the relation between the two is unmistakable. Hence we shall immediately subjoin the Secret: "O God, who hast ratified the divers victims of the Law by one perfect sacrifice: receive the oblation of thy devoted servants, and hallow it with a blessing like to that wherewith thou didst hallow the gifts of Abel; so that what each has offered in honor of thy majesty may avail for the salvation of all." Both Offertory and Secret speak of the numerous sacrifices that were offered in the Old Dispensation. But it was precisely this variety in the kinds of sacrifice that showed the insufficiency of all of them. It was only the unique Eucharistic Sacrifice that finally brought perfection and infinite value. Sacrifice is offered to the glory of the divine majesty; hence the Offertory prays that God may find it acceptable. It should, however, also redound to our salvation, and for this reason the Offertory continues: "There is no confusion to them that trust in Thee." Naturally, our motives in offering the oblation must be pure. It does not suffice to cry "Lord, Lord" (cf. the Gospel); we must immolate our will to the will of God, and formulate this resolve in ourselves: "May all things be done that God wills and in the manner in which He wills them" (*Katholische Kirchenzeitung,* Salzburg, 1927, p. 265).

This Offertory is an excerpt from the prayer which Azarias and the three youths recited in the fiery furnace. The entire prayer, as well as the subjoined canticle *Benedícite,* which is said in Lauds for Sunday, does not occur in the original Hebrew text. St. Jerome incorporated it

into the Vulgate from Theodotion's Greek translation. The young men
in the furnace are no longer able to offer sacrifice in order to obtain God's
mercy. Hence they tender Him their contrite and humble spirit. Their
inner disposition is to compensate for the sacrificial gifts. May their
sacrifice today be in the sight of God as if they came with rams and
bullocks, with thousands of fat lambs, that He may find pleasure in it.
(*Theologie und Glaube*, 19, 409 ff.)

The melody is pleasingly restful, preferring intervals of seconds.
In the passages *Sicut in holocáusto aríetum* and *(si)-cut in míllibus agnó-
rum pínguium* there are seconds only; they also predominate in the last
phrase. Considering the length of the piece, the range is quite limited.
Some resemblance to this Offertory, both in melody and text, is seen in
that of the eighteenth Sunday after Pentecost, but the latter has a more
extended range. Both avoid high *f*, which is wont to occur rather frequently in the fifth mode, especially in Graduals. It is heard in only one
Offertory—in that of the fifteenth Sunday after Pentecost in the expressive passage: "With expectation have I waited for the Lord." This
Sunday's Offertory is more subdued. It almost appears as if the words
which immediately precede our present text occupied the mind of the
composer: "In a contrite and humbe spirit may we be accepted"—words
which find their full significance in the Offertory prayers of the Mass.
They also help us here in evoking the proper disposition for singing this
piece.

To the first *Sicut* with *f g a b♭ a,* the second with *a c d e d* corresponds. Similarly, the cadence at the end of *pinguium* is repeated over
sacrifícium nostrum. The only large interval occurs in this second phrase,
over *in con-(spéctu).* The text reminds us of that passage in the Canon
of the Mass which the priest, bowing profoundly, recites after the consecration: "We most humbly beseech Thee, almighty God, command
these things to be carried up by the hands of Thy holy Angel to Thine
altar on high, in the sight of Thy divine majesty *(in conspéctu divínae
majestátis tuae).*" This petition is effectively answered. The Eucharistic
Sacrifice ascends straight to heaven, and God finds pleasure in it. For
it is the Sacrifice of His well-beloved Son. God graciously accepted the
oblation of the three youths in the fiery furnace. But what of our sacrifice? *Sic fiat sacrifícium nostrum*—"May our sacrifice be offered up in
Thy sight......that it may be pleasing to Thee." We mean not only the
sacrifice which we offer up as singers at divine service; but the sacrifice
of our lives as well. We must be permeated with the spirit of Christ.
How earnestly therefore, we should voice this petition! Once it has been
granted, we can have no more reason to be afraid, for the Lord provides
for us. We hear the same motive repeated over *pláceat tibi, non est con-*

fúsio, confidéntibus in te, and somewhat simplified over *Dómine,* the first
and last time with a slight variati on. Its ascending line symbolizes the
confident lifting of our eyes to God. The smooth descent *c a ǵ a f* seems
to indicate a trustful placing of ourselves in the fatherly arms of God.

With the similar closing neums over *(Dómi)-ne* with their repetition,
compare the twofold *f a c a* in the Alleluia-verse over *pláudite* and the
passage over *(sanctificávi) te* in the Gradual for the feast of St. John the
Baptist. Everything breathes of rest and blissful happiness.

COMMUNION (Ps. 30: 3)

1. *Inclina aurem tuam,* 2. *ac-*   1. *Bow down thine ear,* 2. *make*
celera, ut eripias me.   *haste to deliver me.*

Special impressiveness is added to this simple prayer by the fivefold repetition of one single motive, although with a little variation each
time. The passage *ǵ a ǵ f ǵ a a* over *tuam* becomes *ǵ a ǵ f é f f* over *(accé)-
lera, ǵ a ǵ f g* over *éru-(as),* over *(éru)-as* first simply *ǵ a ǵ f,* and then
ǵ a ǵ f e. "Bow down Thine ear!" For now Thou art so near to me in
Holy Communion. Better than myself dost Thou know all my difficulties and perplexities, all the dark recesses of my spirit, all that remains
since the time when I was yet "a servant of sin" (Epistle). Thou know-
est all the perils that threaten me from false prophets and their wiles,
all that hampers me in fulfilling the will of Thy Father faithfully and per-
severingly (Gospel). I know that without Thy grace I can do nothing;
hence I cry now, as in the prayer *Deus in adjutórium* which begins the
canonical hours: *accélera*—make haste to deliver me from all evil and
confirm me in all good.

✴   ✳   ✴   ✳

EIGHTH SUNDAY AFTER PENTECOST
INTROIT

See February 2 for the explanation. Proceeding from a jubilant
heart, this Introit is a song of thanksgiving for God's merciful love, for
all the graces which have become our portion in the midst of His Temple,
in the Church which He founded. Who can comprehend the greatness
of His gifts; who can number them, from that first great grace of divine
adoption in Baptism, to that of the present day, when the Eucharistic
Saviour again imlores mercy upon us and makes us more intimate partakers of the sonship of God! Never shall we be able to praise and glorify
this great God as He deserves.

Revue gr., 9, 136 ff.

GRADUAL (Ps. 30: 3)

1. *Esto mihi in Deum protec-*
torem, et in locum refugii, 2. *ut*
salvum me facias. Ẏ. 1. *Deus, in*
te speravi, Domine, 2. *non con-*
fundar in aeternum.

1. *Be thou unto me a God, a pro-*
tector, and a place of refuge, 2. *to*
save me. Ẏ. 1. *In thee, O God, have*
I hoped, O Lord, 2. *let me never be*
confounded.

The *corpus* of the Gradual shows the influence of melismatic punctuation in the grouping of the neums at the end of *(protectó)-rem,* in
(refúgi)-i with its similar conclusion, and in the close of *(fáci)-as.* The
melodic development is gradual but constant. While the first half has a
range of a ninth, the second phrase has a range of a tenth. A refreshing
effect is produced by the very unusual turns over *refúgi-(i)* and *salvum*
me. The authentic form is strongly emphasized in the verse; it never descends lower than the tonic and vigorously stresses the dominant *c.* Although, melodically speaking, *Dómine* opens the second phrase of the
psalm-verse, it is actually drawn to the first phrase by the incomplete
cadence.

We are not allowed to live according to the flesh. That is the admonition of the Epistle. Consequently, we stand in need of the protecting grace of God and a place of refuge in His holy Church in all our
difficulties, be they interior or exterior. We are to place all our trust in
God, that firm trust which emanates from the spirit of sonship of which
the Epistle speaks.

ALLELUIA VERSE (Ps. 47: 2)

1. *Magnus Dominus, et lauda-*
bilis valde, 2. *in civitate Dei nostri*
in monte sancto ejus.

1. *Great is the Lord, and exceed-*
ingly to be praised; 2. *in the city of*
our God, in his holy mountain.

These selfsame words have been heard in the psalm-verse of the
Introit. Here, however, *nimis* is replaced by *valde,* and the word *nostri*
is entirely omitted. Several translations of the Scriptures prior to St.
Jerome give this *valde.* In the Introit the contemplation of God's essence
raised the singer to brilliant heights *(secúndum nomen tuum).* In the
same manner the melody here seems to attempt to soar to the regions
where God dwells *(magnus Dóminus).* It is seldom that the seventh mode
essays such flights. We should expect a close on the tonic with *valde.* Instead of this, however, the motive which opened the verse, and which
has already been heard over *Allelúia,* is repeated. In the second phrase
of the verse we have a repetition of the *jubilus* of *Allelúia.* Since no con-

clusion follows as yet, *Dei* has a quite simple melody. Strikingly simple is also the syllabic chant over *in monte sancto ejus*.

Allelúia with its *jubilus* has the form *a b b c c*[1]; the *climacus resupinus* forms the nucleus of the entire group. Care must be taken that the third member be more than a mere echo of the second, although the conclusion *cd cdd* is to be sung more quietly both times, somewhat in echo fashion. In place of the minor third of *c*, the member *c*[1] has a fifth, which brings the whole to a vigorous close. The *b* members predominate over the *c* members. Some resemblance to this Alleluia is found in that of the fourth Sunday after Pentecost. The most ancient manuscripts do not contain this melody.

OFFERTORY (Ps. 17: 28, 32)

1. *Populum humilem salvum facies, Domine,* 2. *et oculos superborum humiliabis:* 3. *quoniam quis Deus praeter te, Domine?*

1. *Thou wilt save the humble people, O Lord,* 2. *and wilt bring down the eyes of the proud;* 3. *for who is God, but thou, O Lord?*

The rite of oblation at Mass, with its washing of the hands, is well calculated to arouse and deepen true humility in us. Only "in the spirit of humility and with a contrite heart" is it possible for us and our sacrifice to find acceptance with the Lord. Humility alone leads to prudence, to the prudence which, according to today's Gospel, is characteristic of the children of light. Thus endowed, however, we may confidently hope for deliverance.

From the very beginning of the first phrase the melody grows with each succeeding word, until it soars to jubilant heights with *salvum fácies*. Thus we sang in the Introit *Laetáre* at the words *convéntum fácite* (cf. p. 137) as well as in the Introit *In virtúte tua* at the word *laetábitur*, in both of which joy is the predominant note. Here, too, we are filled with hope while awaiting salvation from the Lord. A similar cadence with a fifth over *Dómine* occurs twice in the Offertory *Gloriabúntur* of June 26, which is sung several times in the course of the year.

Superbórum in the second phrase accords somewhat with *húmilem* of the first. As *salvum fácies* is brought into prominence there, so *humiliábis* is stressed here. A feeling of victory, confidently overcoming all obstacles, pervades the melody. This impression is strengthened by the rhythmic four-note groups.

The third phrase, imitating the first two, begins on *f*. The half tone over *Deus* tends to accentuate the question, "Who is God?" *Prae-*

ter te, which follows, makes the phrase sound like the battle cry immortalized in the name of St. Michael. "Thou alone art the Lord:" that is the meaning of the passage over *Dómine.* The motive over the first eight notes expands in the following group and again contracts in the two neums immediately preceding *-mine.* We find the same concluding cadence in the Mass for Rogation Days. In this phrase, the somewhat harsh ending of the first *Dómine* of the Offertory is tempered by the intercalated *a.* Just as the Lord is terrible in His dealings with the proud, so is He gracious and affable to the humble of heart.

Húmilem may, however, also be understood of an entire people that is lowly. Thus the Offertory points out the antithesis between the Epistle and the Gospel: the spiritual man versus the earthly man; the children of light versus the children of this world. (*K. L.*) What is more elevating than the divine grace which is infused in those who participate in the sacrificial Mystery!

COMMUNION (Ps. 33: 9)

1. *Gustate et videte, quoniam suavis est Dominus:* 2. *beatus vir, qui sperat in eo.*

1. Taste and see that the Lord is sweet: 2. blessed is the man that hopeth in him.

This antiphon is composed of only two phrases. Both have a marked rise in their first parts, with a pause on *a.* Their second parts are identical: *sperat in eo* corresponds with *(su)-ávis est Dominus.* Still each little phrase has its peculiarities. The first is a lively exhortation; hence the rise to high *c* and the tarrying there with a double tristropha, a neum rarely used in the Communion. The exhortation is to resound and to penetrate into all hearts. The second phrase is a simple assertion and never rises above *a.*

This is the oldest Communion song to be found with its psalm in all the liturgies, oriental as well as occidental. How heartfelt it must have sounded, coming from the lips of those who were returning from the altar with the sweetest and most savory of foods in their hearts! What longing it must have awakened in the souls of the faithful who were still on the way to receive Holy Communion!

Whoever loves the Eucharistic Saviour will not only gladly and frequently carry this exhortation into effect, but will also, as far as he is able, make others partakers of this same great joy.

The Greek equivalent for sweet is *chrestos*; hence the play on words: Taste and see that it is Christ (Chrestos) the Lord. (*K. L.*)

*   *   *   *

NINTH SUNDAY AFTER PENTECOST

INTROIT (Ps. 53: 6-7)

1. *Ecce Deus adjuvat me, et Do-minus susceptor est animae meae:* 2. *averte mala inimicis meis,* 3. *in veritate tua disperde illos, protec-tor meus, Domine.* Ps. *Deus, in nomine tuo salvum me fac:* * *et in virtute tua libera me.*

1. *Behold, God is my helper, and the Lord is the protector of my soul* 2. *turn back the evils upon mine enemies,* 3. *and cut them off in thy truth, O Lord my protector.* Ps. *Save me, O God, by thy name,* * *and de-liver me in thy strength.*

Man's weakness is great, and many a sad experience confirms the fact that the admonition in today's Epistle, "He that thinketh himself to stand, let him take heed lest he fall," is not sufficiently taken to heart. Clever and tireless enemies seek out the weaknesses of man in order to destroy the life of his soul. Nevertheless, we must not grow despondent, for *Ecce Deus ádjuvat me*—"God is my helper;" such is the clear and as-suring theme of the Introit. *Ecce*, with its start on the dominant (*N. Sch.*, 51) of the mode, wishes to say: "Do not consider only the enemies of your soul, but look especially, or better, look exclusively to God. He will be your Helper." Therefore it is not without reason that the *c* over *Deus* is doubled and that *Dóminus* in the second part of the first phrase is made emphatic by a fourth. If the Lord God is for us, who can op-pose us? The manuscripts indicate with special markings that the notes over *Deus ádjuvat me* should be given a broad interpretation. Hence they rightly demand a solemn rendering of this passage to express our deeply-rooted confidence. From the second phrase on *(avérte)*, a certain restlessness and apprehension becomes evident. Perhaps it is holy anger, calling for vengeance. Some relationship exists between the passages over *mala* and *illos*. But the manuscripts wish above all to emphasize the *pressus* over *illos*. Hence the bistropha with its succeeding *clivis* are here marked with "c" (*celeriter*, rapidly); or "st" (*statim*, immediately) is interpolated between the bistropha and the *clivis*, while in the corre-sponding passage over *mala* "t" *(tenere*, to prolong)* and an episema are placed over the *clivis*. The called-for acceleration of the neums which precede the *pressus* makes the latter stand forth prominently. Only with *protéctor meus*, which may be considered a prolongation of *est ánimae meae*, does the confidential feeling of the beginning return to the text and still more to the melody, which closes with well-known and pleas-ing seconds.

More than once the effect of the melody is heightened by what we may call the "resolved" F-major scale.

Here the question is very pertinent: Is a Christian allowed to pray thus: *avérte mala*—"turn back the evils upon mine enemies"? If these words proceeded from personal hate, then indeed they would be unchristian, and such a prayer would never find acceptance in the sight of God. Even David refrained from laying hands upon Saul when the latter was powerless before him. But since God desires the salvation of our souls, the enemies of our souls are also the enemies of God, and for that reason are we allowed to beseech God to render His and our enemies harmless, and to let their efforts toward the destruction of souls and the kingdom of God come to naught. Has not God promised His help to those who approach Him with confidence? Hence we call upon His fidelity *(veritáte)*, on His goodness and love, and leave it entirely to His wisdom how He will supply us with help against our foes. If, however, there is question of the interior enemies of salvation, such as self-deceit, concupiscence, lust, and so forth, then these words lose their questionable character, and we are allowed to use them in serious and earnest prayer. When we have to deal with exterior dangers, such as ignorance and seduction, then we give *avérte mala* its proper meaning by adding *et in veritáte tua dispérde illos*: subdue Thy foes *through* Thy truth, gain them over *to* Thy truth, destroy ignorance, save the wayward! (Reck, II, 150.)

GRADUAL (Ps. 8: 2)

1. *Domine Dominus noster,* 2. *quam admirabile est nomen tuum in universa terra!* ℣. *Quoniam elevata est magnificentia tua super caelos.*

1. *O Lord, our Lord,* 2. *how admirable is thy name in the whole earth!* ℣. *For thy magnificence is elevated above the heavens.*

One can hardly claim that this melody exhibits any melodic turns which do not occur also in other similar selections; nevertheless, melody and text are happily matched. Deep reverence marks the beginning of the piece. With *quam admirábile* joy is added to amazement. Reverence seems to predominate with *nomen tuum*, while *in univérsa terra* again has a lighter coloring. Thus there is a delightful interplay of reverence and joy. In the Gradual for the feast of the Dedication of a Church we sing the same melody over *inaestimábile* as we do here over *admirábile*. *Est* disturbs the even flow somewhat. We find that the melody over *(univér)-sa* also closes the *corpus* of the Gradual in the third Christmas Mass. In both cases the same idea is enunciated. The verse begins with an evident ascent, which one might wish to see extended in *magnificéntia* to high *f*, as in other Graduals, but the short text does not allow it here. The composer was more intent on giving a satisfactory conclusion. With *(eleváta) est*—most likely the composer did not intend tone-painting—the *torculus* is to be taken broadly in every instance. A unified impression is given the whole by the repetition of the form *á g ǵ c c* over *admirábile, in univérsa, eleváta,* and *magnificén-(tia)*.

ALLELUIA VERSE (Ps. 58, 2)

1. *Eripe me de inimicis meis, Deus meus*: 2. *et ab insurgentibus in me libera me.*

1. *Deliver me from mine enemies, O my God*: 2. *and defend me from them that rise up againt me.*

There was mention of the enemies of the soul in the Introit. Here we meet them again, and they induce the singer to beseech God fervently for deliverance and salvation. The same text is set to music in the Offertory for Wednesday after Passion Sunday. An ornate melisma occurs over *insurgéntibus* in both instances. That of the Alleluia-verse, however, cannot compare with the dramatic effect produced by the Offertory. In the latter we see clearly how the foes go forth in battle array, how their number ever grows, how things come to such a pass that God alone is able to help. The word receives a quieter construction in the Alleluia-verse. Its first two members are identical. The coda-like close with its seconds in both parts strives to still all excitement. In spite of this, however, unrest is again felt to some extent in the third member with its fourth and the descent to low *a*. In the annotated manuscripts the neums over *Eripe* and *Deus meus* in the first phrase are given the broad form. Sorrow oppresses the singer. His prayer flows from a heavy heart; at least that is what the rhythmic marks indicate. But the *Revue Grégorienne* (9, 112) remarks: "At the thought of God, the soul forgets its incipient fear. It is so conscious of the divine presence that when it sings *Deus meus* it no longer thinks of the enemies it spoke of just before. It lets itself be rapt into pure contemplation." In all this praying and beseeching it must not be forgotten that the petition is framed by *Allelúia*. In the melodic turn over *inimicis meis* we are reminded of the effective passage *de ore leónis* in the Offertory of the Mass for the Dead —effective because it enhances the earnestness of the phrase. Until the repetition of the *jubilus* is reached with *libera*, all pauses close on the tonic. Though this is somewhat inartistic, it fits quite well into the quiet mood of the entire phrase. The Alleluia has the form *a b b¹*.

The melody is of very ancient provenance. As early as the eleventh century it was fitted to the words *Ave María* in the Advent votive Mass of the Blessed Virgin.

Today's OFFERTORY was explained on the third Sunday of Lent. On the present Sunday, however, after the threatened destruction of the city of Jerusalem in the Gospel, we shall sing it in a somewhat more subdued fashion and more fervently ask for the grace of fidelity.

COMMUNION (John 6: 57)

1. *Qui manducat carnem meam, et bibit sanguinem meum, in me manet,* 2. *et ego in eo, dicit Dominus.*

1. *He that eateth my flesh, and drinketh my blood, abideth in me* 2. *and I in him, saith the Lord.*

Today's Epistle was "written for our correction," that the same fate may not befall us which was visited in a horrible manner upon the many Israelites who fell victims to the temptations of idolatry, of fornication, of murmuring against God. A like effect is produced by the Sunday's Gospel, in which Jerusalem is made to hear the announcement of its annihilation because it did not recognize the things that were unto its peace. For this reason we ought to pray with special fervor before Holy Communion: "Make me always cleave to thy commandments, and never suffer me to be separated from thee." But hark! In Holy Communion Christ will be to you a word of solace, a word that will take from you all fear, and will make you feel perfectly safe: "He that eateth My flesh, and drinketh My blood, abideth in Me." Be not afraid; His love, His grace, His help will always be at hand. The melody begins with an almost supernal simplicity. In the second half-phrase the first half-phrase is given a more elaborate form. The endings of the parts of the phrase *(meam* and *meum)* are characterized by corresponding formulas. No doubt this is the technical reason why the more important words *carnem* and *sánguinem* do not stand out so prominently. Now follows the expressive *in me manet* with a descending fourth, which must be given special warmth. It is answered by a rising fourth in *ego in eo.* Thus both thoughts are placed in strong relief: Thou in me and I in Thee. The prolonged *b♭* at the beginning of *dicit,* which has been avoided thus far, wishes to impress upon us the "Thus saith the Lord." His word is of unfailing efficacy and harbors in itself the fullness of consolation.

This song is sung also on the Thursday after the second Sunday of Lent. In olden times it was used on the fifteenth Sunday after Pentecost, and in place of it was sung *Primum quáerite,* which is now employed on the fourteenth Sunday.

*   *   *   *

TENTH SUNDAY AFTER PENTECOST

INTROIT (Ps. 54: 17, 18, 20, 23)

1. *Cum clamarem ad Dominum, exaudivit vocem meam, ab his qui appropinquant mihi*: 2. *et humiliavit eos qui est ante saecula, et manet in aeternum*: 3. *jacta cogitatum tuum in Domino, et ipse te enutriet.* Ps. *Exaudi, Deus, orationem meam, et ne despexeris deprecationem meam*: * *intende mihi, et exaudi me.*

1. *When I cried to the Lord, he heard my voice, against them that draw near to me*; 2. *and he who is before all ages, and remains for ever, humbled them*: 3. *cast thy care upon the Lord and he shall sustain thee.* Ps. *Hear, O God, my prayer, and despise not my supplication*: * *be attentive to me and hear me.*

Each of the three phrases closes with the same melodic formula. Besides, the first and second phrase also have the preceding neums in common over *(appropin)-quant mihi* and *aetérnum*. In general, a close relation exists between these two phrases, even exteriorly, since both are made up of three members, while the third phrase has only two; and their interior relation is still more intimate. The first phrase speaks of the fruits of prayer; the second of the manner in which prayer is heard. Hence, these two preliminary statements may serve as two premises, from which the third follows as a conclusion; therefore "cast thy care upon the Lord!"

The first phrase with its upward striving expresses both an earnest petition and the tension of soul which accompanies it. Then comes a thankful, brilliant *exaudívit*: I have been heard. The second phrase several times extends beyond the highest note of the first. In the small phrase *qui est ante sáecula* we twice hear the fourth *g–c*, and once the fourth *a–d*. We get some inkling of the eternity of God, which is without beginning, from the large intervals. Some purely syllabic passages occur in the third phrase. Its melodic line is the symbol and expression of a certain effort, a conquering of the difficulties which present themselves to wavering, doubting, short-sighted human beings who ought to live entirely by faith and throw all their care upon the Lord. If this is done —how quiet and sure is the tone of the seconds over *et ipse te!*—then He will nourish and sustain us with paternal affection and will royally reward all our hopes and expectations. Even today we shall see the fulfillment of these words in the sacrificial Banquet.

We may sing the words of the psalm-verse in the spirit of the publican of whom the Gospel makes mention. He does not confide in himself; he does not look upon himself as just. He realizes, moreover, that God would have enough reason to despise his prayer. But it is just this humble consciousness of his own sinfulness that guarantees the granting of his petition. He went to his house justified.

This Introit is also sung on the Thursday after Ash Wednesday.

GRADUAL (Ps. 16: 8, 2)

1. *Custodi me, Domine, ut pupillam oculi*: 2. *sub umbra alarum tuarum protege me.* ℣. 1. *De vultu tuo judicium meum prodeat*: 2. *oculi tui videant aequitates.*

1. *Keep me, O Lord, as the apple of thine eye*: 2. *protect me under the shadow of thy wings.* ℣. 1. *Let my judgment come forth from thy countenance*: 2. *let thine eyes behold the things that are equitable.*

In the liturgical evening prayer called Compline we each day hear the words used in the corpus of the Gradual. Whoever can pray thus knows that he is dear to the heart of God. How careful we are that not even a speck of dust enters our eye! We may expect the same and even greater anxiety and love on the part of God toward our soul, for its welfare and salvation. The present melody proceeds from such a disposition. A pleasing repose hovers over its beginning. One seems to hear melodies of the low plagal mode with the dominant *f*. The same holds true of the quiet sequences of seconds over *óculi*. But through it all a flash of light, which proceeds from *pupíllam*, is discernible.

In the second phrase we gaze at a new picture—a picture of wings, of mighty pinions, under which we seek protection. Here the melody is broadly delineated, becoming the outburst of a heart that knows what a hidden life in God means and that prays for this boon with full confidence.

A new mood appears in the verse; it is a resolute prayer, such as can come only from a heart that rests securely in God and is conscious of no grave offense. Are we sinful men allowed to address God thus, the Omniscient who never judges from appearances, to whom the innermost secrets of the heart are open? Strictly speaking, Christ alone with His most pure and immaculate heart can pray in this manner. But Christ makes our concerns His own and makes supplication for us to the Father. With a courageous upward swing the melody at the very beginning ascends to the dominant *a* and beyond it, with a strong accent on high *c*. The *corpus* had a similar treatment, but here it is more lavishly employed, so that the verse serves as an enhancement of the *corpus*, although both have the same range. The first phrase is well divided and has a cadence over *pródeat* corresponding admirably to the text. It must be admitted that the well-marked cadence on the tonic over *tui* is not so happy. The text here allows no marked pause. After the first pause over *tui* a sort of sequence of thirds begins, which was still more emphasized in earlier times, since after the pause not a doubled *c* of the same pitch was sung, but a lower note, most likely *b c*, as the graphic representation of the neums seems to demand. Thus the original sequence of notes would be *b c a g, a b♭ g f, g a f d*. The conclusion of *aequitátem* also occurs on the seventeenth Sunday after Pentecost, on Friday of the Ember Week in Lent, on Sexagesima Sunday, and in the Gradual *Sacerdótes*.

ALLELUIA VERSE (Ps. 64: 2)

1. *Te decet hymnus, Deus, in Sion*: 2. *et tibi reddetur votum in Jerusalem.*

1. *A hymn, O God, becometh thee in Sion*: 2. *and a vow shall be paid to thee in Jerusalem.*

We are well acquainted with these words from the psalm-verse of the Introit *Requiem*; here in the Alleluia-verse, however, they must receive a more brilliant and livelier interpretation than in the funeral Mass. But even there no gloomy rendition should disfigure them. Here we have a song of praise, a grateful paying of vows, witnesses of just so many favors granted. The choice of the lively seventh mode and what has the effect of a bright major chord in *allelúia* is most happy. A correspondence exists between the endings of the second and third members of the *jubilus*. *Te decet hymnus* is chanted with emphasis on the accented syllables. From the standpoint of melody, we have two phrases, of which the first extends as far as *votum*, building on the psalm-melody of the seventh mode to the middle cadence inclusive. This appears again, more richly developed, over *Sion* and is repeated over *votum*. The incisions over *Deus* and *reddétur* resemble a *flexa*. Over *Jerúsalem* the closing melisma is particularly ornate. Here not only the *jubilus* of *allelúia* is repeated, but we find numerous neums interpolated before it, which usually prolong the upper note of the fourths *c–f* into a tristropha or a *pressus*. It is not easy for the singer to live himself into these melismas. They are foreign to our feelings and cannot readily be developed and for this reason they demand a limpid, fluent presentation. Perhaps this ornate melody already foreshadows the idea which was formulated in the later Middle Ages by Bishop Sicard of Cremona (✠ 1215) in his work entitled *Mitrale* (Migne, *P. L.*, 213, 394): "Almost in every instance when the word 'Jerusalem' occurs in a song, long neums are attached to it, in order to give a picture of the exultation of the heavenly Jerusalem."

In the most ancient manuscripts this Alleluia has yet a second verse, whose melody was used with the Alleluia on the feast of St. Alexius (July 17), but without the extraordinarily ornate closing melisma. In its second half the *jubilus* of the verse resembles that of the fourteenth Sunday after Pentecost.

For the OFFERTORY see the first Sunday of Advent.

The publican did not even dare to lift his eyes to heaven. But he had elevated his heart to God *(ánimam meam levávi)*, and God deigned to look upon the sinner. On account of his sins, the publican felt himself forever estranged from God, but in His loving-kindness God was near to him. His prayer was inspired with great confidence, and he was not confounded. He went to his house justified, his heart filled with divine grace and peace. Whoever prays as this publican did will not be put to shame.

"In the holy Sacrifice the parable of the Gospel renews itself. You entered the church as a humble publican; in the Kyrie and the Gradual you struck your breast: that was your pilgrimage to Sion (Alleluia-verse); now gracious words of pardon fall from the mouth of the Lord" (*K.L.*).

COMMUNION (Ps. 50: 21)

1. *Acceptabis sacrificium justi-tiae,* 2. *oblationes et holocausta, super altare tuum, Domine.*

1. *Thou wilt accept the sacrifice of justice,* 2. *oblations and holo-causts, upon thine altar, O Lord.*

Soon the priest will pronounce these words in the *Placeat*: "May the homage of my bounden duty be pleasing to Thee, O Holy Trinity; and grant that the sacrifice which I, though unworthy, have offered in the sight of Thy majesty, may be acceptable *(acceptábile)* to Thee." Such must be the prayer of the sacrificing priest. But the sacrifice which Christ has just offered finds gracious acceptance in heaven, as the Church well knows. Hence the determined and joyful beginning of the melody. It is the sacrifice of justice, the fitting sacrifice, which Jesus Christ "the Just" has offered; the sacrifice which has again reconciled the offended justice of God. It is in truth a burnt offering in which the love of Christ to the Father consumed itself; a holocaust, since Christ Himself was unable to give more. To this sublime sacrifice, which was now offered on the altar (how pensive the melody becomes here!), are added our sacrificial gifts *(oblatiónes)*: all the renunciations, all the sufferings courageously borne, the persevering performance of our duty we have placed on the paten and in the chalice. Taken up into Christ's oblation, as the drop of water into the wine at the Offertory, and united with Christ's sacrifice, these gifts find acceptance before the Lord.

The cadence over *justítiae* is typical in responsories of the fourth mode. No doubt its close on *e–f* and not *f–e* (as in *Dómine*) is employed to effect an easier and more flexible union of the first and second phrases. This cadence has also appeared over *Acceptábis* in a shortened form. Here the concluding *e–f* is found for the same reason as above. The member which immediately follows begins with *d* and an interval of a fourth, just as the second period is always introduced in the responsories of the fourth mode. In this Communion, therefore, as in many others, the structure of the responsories is imitated. The second phrase is more quiet, with a strong accent on *f*. Only with the expressive *altáre* is any prolongation noticeable. We sing this same song on the Thursday after Ash Wednesday.

The presentation should be lively and joyful.

"In the sacrificial banquet the publican receives a pledge of his justification. *Ite, missa est*—he goes to his house justified" (*K. L.*).

* * * *

ELEVENTH SUNDAY AFTER PENTECOST

INTROIT (Ps. 67: 6, 7, 36)

1. *Deus in loco sancto suo:* 2. *Deus qui inhabitare facit unanimes in domo:* 3. *ipse dabit virtutem, et fortitudinem plebi suae.* Ps. *Exsurgat Deus, et dissipentur inimici ejus:* * *et fugiant, qui oderunt eum, a facie ejus.*

1. *God in his holy place:* 2. *God who maketh men of one mind to dwell in his house:* 3. *he shall give power and strength to his people.* Ps. *Let God arise, and let his enemies be scattered:* * *and let them that hate him flee from before his face.*

The text of the antiphon is divided into three phrases, which division the melody faithfully observes. An upward tendency is apparent in the first and third phrase, while the contrary is true of the second; the latter is melodically more significant. Hence we have here the form A B A. The need for contrast is based on purely musical grounds, since the text offers no reason for it.

Three thoughts are presented: (1) God abides in His holy places: in heaven, in the Church, in the heart of him who has the life of grace. We owe Him reverence and adoration. (2) God wishes to unite all those who enter His house into one family, into one heart. This phrase breathes of love. (3) If the mystery of strength already abides in this unity, then God provides special power *(Exsúrgat)* for the struggle against His foes, who are at the same time ours.

First phrase: Like the Introit of the ninth Sunday after Pentecost, this one also begins immediately on the dominant,[1] with a descending line to the tonic. A vigorous emphasis marks the word *Deus*. Care must be taken that the doubled notes be not too prolonged. The rest of the phrase is solemn and reverential. Each of the disyllabic words has the accented syllable lengthened, so that the whole sounds like a succession of solemn spondees—*Deus, loco, sancto suo*. The final *clivis* over *(lo)-co* corresponds to that over *(sanc)-to*. They must not be made too short.

Second phrase: Here, as in the preceding phrase, the word *Deus* is marked by its accent and melodic independence; and just as the former properly begins only with *in loco*, so does the latter with *inhabitáre*. After *Deus* a short pause or prolongation is not at all out of place. This second *Deus* is more tender and quiet than the first, a fitting introduction to this phrase, which no longer speaks of the majesty of God, but of His goodness. Both word-accents in each of the two members, *inhabitáre* and *unánimes*, have a correspondingly important musical accent. The second *porrectus* must be sung more lightly than the first; then must follow a steady *crescendo* to the musical climax, which speaks of the workings of divine mercy with the word *facit*. Let only a slight prolongation be made on the *clivis* of *(fa)-cit*. A still better effect is obtained if the two members—*facit* and *unánimes*—are joined without a pause. In case of need, breath might be taken, imperceptibly, before *facit*. If a full pause is given after *domo* and only a half pause after *suo*, this must not cause confusion. We are not dealing here with mathematical values. The cadence on *domo* permits of no long pause; it urges forward to completion.

Melodically speaking, the third phrase has two members, of which the second comprises the words *plebi suae*. The first bears some resemblance to the first phrase of the antiphon and has, moreover, the same spirit of solemn affirmation. Happy trustfulness is suggested by the accented dominant and the fourth. A sharp, clear pronunciation of the consonant "t" before the "v" will contribute much to bring out the symmetry between *dabit* and *virtútem*. This part moves in the four-note range *a–d*, emphasizing the *c*, while the following *et fortitúdinem*, employing a similar range *(f–b♭)*, stresses *a* and for the first time strikes *b♭*. The cadence closes a part of a phrase, but not the entire piece, and

---

1 *N. Sch.,* 52.

therefore no considerable pause is allowed after it. In its upward movement, *plebi suae* reminds us of *qui inhabitáre* in the first phrase. The principal accent on *ple-(bi)* occurs with its highest neum, *b♭c*. A broad construction should be given to the cadence-like *torculus* over *su-(ae)*.

Revue, 24, 170 ff.; *Analyses*, 5, I, 3 ff.

GRADUAL (Ps. 27: 7, 1)

1. *In Deo speravit cor meum, et adjutus sum: et refloruit caro mea,* 2. *et ex voluntate mea confitebor illi.* ℣. 1. *Ad te, Domine, clamavi:* 2. *Deus meus, ne sileas: ne discedas a me.*

1. *In God hath my heart confided, and I have been helped: and my flesh hath flourished again,* 2. *and with my will I will give praise to him.* ℣. 1. *Unto thee have I cried, O Lord:* 2. *O my God, be not thou silent: depart not from me.*

A marvelous effect is produced here in the steady development of the melody and the comparatively rapid close after the climax has been reached. The first phrase is quiet, confined to a fifth; it is only the low *c* at the very end that brings an expansion with a modulation in the plagal form of which the F mode is so fond. It is like a quiet retrospect on the working of God. But now thanksgiving and jubilation come to the fore: "With my will I will give praise to Him." This phrase begins a sixth higher—a rare occurrence in plainsong—and extends far above *a*, the peak of the first phrase. And yet the thanksgiving here expressed is not so joyous and ringing as that of many other pieces. The note *b♭*, which dominates the phrase, has a tendency to hold back the exultation, and the close over *illi* is more like an indecisive faltering than a song of joy.

After an introductory formula, the verse has the same ornate melismas as are heard on Maundy Thursday and on other days. The first part of the Gradual modulates to low *c*; by way of contrast the verse goes up to high *c*. Thus far there is no difficulty in following the melodic development. But the following petitions, *ne síleas*, and *ne discédas* (the latter has a common closing formula) have no intrinsic relation with one another or with that which precedes. *Ne síleas*, moreover, loses much of its effectiveness simply because the preceding melody is already developed in so splendid a manner.

Who is to sing this song? If it is true that every Sunday is a miniature Easter, then it is true especially of this Sunday. The Epistle which precedes our present Gradual again impresses upon us the fact that Christ died for our sins, that He arose from the dead on the third day according to the Scriptures, that He appeared to Peter, to the eleven, and to more than five hundred brethren. We may, therefore, place this song in the mouth of the Risen One. Its first phrase resembles the spirit of the Easter Introit. "My flesh hath flourished again." How radiant is Christ in His springtime beauty and splendor, after His body has undergone the most horrible sufferings! How sweet is this song of thanksgiving when it comes from the heart of Jesus! In the verse, the risen Christ seems to look back on His sufferings and His abandonment, when the Father seemed to turn a deaf ear to His *Deus meus* and to be immeasurably distant. But in ancient times the present Gradual did not close with these petitions. To round out the piece the *corpus* of the Gradual was repeated in the spirit of reconciliation, thus making it more like a song of thanksgiving.

With these same words St. Paul might have given thanks that by the grace of God he is what he is, and that this grace has not remained inoperative in him—thoughts which close today's Epistle. We all have good reason to give thanks from the bottom of our hearts, because we have been saved by the same good tidings. In like manner does the deaf-and-dumb man of today's Gospel thank the Lord, for He did not remain silent, but pronounced His almighty *Ephpheta*—"Be thou opened!"

ALLELUIA VERSE (Ps. 80: 2, 3)

1. *Exsultate Deo adjutori nostro*   1. *Rejoice to God our helper,* 2.
2. *jubilate Deo Jacob:* 3. *sumite*   *Sing aloud to the God of Jacob:* 3.
psalmum jucundum cum cithara.   *take a joyful psalm with the harp.*

Allelúia has the form a b c. Similarly, a begins the first and third phrases of the verse. In each case, however, the treatment of the word-accent is different, with corresponding differences in the dynamics. *Exsultáte* and *súmite* are admittedly nothing more than introductions to the words which follow them. The imperative which begins the second phrase also rises a fourth above the opening note. Principal and secondary accents are treated in the same way as in *exsultáte (=jubiláte)*. In the b-member, *e d e f d* and *b a b c d c* correspond. The passage over *Deo* is heard again over *nostro* and *(Ja)-cob*, while *(adjutó)-ri* occurs in an extended form over *psalmum* and *jucúndum*. Were it left to us we should most likely in all three cases have distributed the neums as with *psalmum*, instead of placing a single note on the accented syllable and an ornate melisma over the closing syllable. In the votive Mass of the Most Pure Heart of Mary during Paschal time, the melody is sung in the same fashion; the alleluia for the twenty-third Sunday after Pentecost also bears a slight resemblance to it.

If we sang the Gradual in the spirit of Easter as coming from the heart of the risen Lord, then this Alleluia ought to be the expression of our joy at having received the help of God's grace in holy Baptism. In that Sacrament He freed us from sin, made us to speak and understand spiritually, and in the Holy Eucharist He makes us sharers in His divine life. When we hear the words of this verse and of the whole psalm, the strains of the Introit *Cibávit eos* for Monday in Whitsun week and for Corpus Christi seem to resound again in our hearts, for they sing of the Saviour's Eucharistic love for us, and urge us to teach the whole world how to share in our joy.

OFFERTORY

This Offertory was explained on Ash Wednesday. We continue to offer thanks for the grace of Baptism. The "Ephpheta" of today's Gospel, together with the ceremonies that attended it, has been incorporated into the rite of Baptism, and has produced its effect in us in the most sublime sense. "Be thou opened!" the priest cried, and our ear opened itself to the word of God, our tongue loosed itself for the praise of God, and our eye looked upon the marvels of grace which God had worked in our soul. We were made children of God and heirs of heaven, partakers of Christ unto life eternal. If a prayer of thanksgiving forced itself to the lips of him who had been deaf and dumb, then surely we must pray and sing: I will extol Thee, O Lord, for Thou hast protected me; Thou hast received me into Thy Church, hast broken the power of my mortal enemy and hast begun to heal the wounds of original sin. Mayest Thou remain with me, that my enemies may no longer rejoice over me.

COMMUNION (Prov. 3: 9, 10)

1. *Honora Domino de tua substantia,* 2. *et de primitiis frugum tuarum:* 3. *et implebuntur horrea tua saturitate,* 4. *et vino torcularia redundabunt.*

1. *Honor the Lord with thy substance,* 2. *and with the first of all thy fruits:* 3. *and thy barns shall be filled with abundance,* 4. *and thy presses shall run over with wine.*

These four phrases are like so many strophes of an intimate and appealing song, one over which the good odor of the earth, the fragrance of gardens and of fresh wine seems to hover. According to the text there are two pairs of phrases: the first two mention what we are to do; the other two speak of the generosity with which God will repay us. While the third phrase expresses astonishment over God's bountiful goodness, the second soars upward in the spirit of self-sacrifice. The first and fourth phrases have the same range, both descend to *c* and have the same extended finale.

The first phrase has the same beginning as today's Gradual. Over *tua* and *substántia* the first *f* ought to be prolonged. You are not to offer any kind of gift, but the noblest, the best, the first fruits. This gradation of thought is paralleled by that of the melody in the second phrase, while the warm-toned cadence over *primítiis*, which also exerts some influence on that which follows, speaks with the tender, cordial voice of love. The ending of *tuárum* corresponds with that of the first and fourth phrases. In the third phrase the melody becomes even more luminous than in the second. We are struck by the sudden beginning of *hórrea* with an interval of a fourth, as if it were a cry of wonder at the immensity of God's goodness! *Vino* in the fourth phrase closes on a *pes* and the following word begins a fifth lower, a frequent occurrence in pieces of the first and eighth mode (cf. the Introit *Gaudéte*, p. 27, and the Introit *Dum médium siléntium*, p. 69.). The *Revue Gregorienne* calls this musical turn a "smiling interrogation mark." *Torculária*, reminding us of *impleántur*, brings the joyous answer. Here again the secondary as well as the principal accent receive very curt treatment.

Clearness and joy characterize the melody, rather than solemnity. Holy Communion is the life-giving bread, the never-failing wine which gives strength to the soul.

Would that we choir directors ever derived new energy from the celebration of the sacred Mysteries, in order to glorify the Lord with all our strength *(substántia)* and to offer Him the noblest and the best!

Revue, 24, 174 ff.; *Analyses*, 5, 7 ff.

* * * *

TWELFTH SUNDAY AFTER PENTECOST

INTROIT (Ps. 69: 2, 3)

1. *Deus, in adjutorium meum intende*: 2. *Domine, ad adjuvandum me festina*: 3. *confundantur et revereantur inimici mei, qui quaerunt animam meam.* Ps. *Avertantur retrorsum, et erubescant*: * *qui cogitant mihi mala.*

1. *Incline unto mine aid, O God*: 2. *O Lord, make haste to help me*: 3. *let mine enemies be confounded and ashamed, who seek my soul.* Ps. *Let them be turned backward, and blush for shame,* * *who devise evils against me.*

All the canonical hours of the daily Office open with the first two phrases of the Introit and are generally sung in a rather simple style.

In the present instance the melody climbs to unusual heights, which is already indicated by the use of the C clef on the second line. The first two phrases are impelled onward by great anxiety of soul; they voice the most abject misery. We can imagine how the man in today's Gospel cried for assistance after the robbers had beaten him almost to death. He had seen the priest approach and confidently looked forward to being rescued. But the priest passed by, indifferent. Similarly had he seen the Levite coming toward him, but he also kept aloof. How he must have cried then to God for help: *Inténde,* imploring Him to send relief at once, for he was bleeding to death: *festína!*

By means of the *pressus* over *Deus* and the strengthening of the note over *(adju)-tó-(rium),* special emphasis is placed on the first phrase, while the whole step below the *c* gives it unusual force. We shall better understand the melody if we picture it written a fourth lower: its essential notes then would be *ǵ c á g á f ǵ a c d c* and *á f á g g* at the end. These are tone-sequences with which the eighth mode has made us well acquainted. The second phrase, which ought to be compared with the rich Offertory on the Thursday after the fourth Sunday in Lent, could be transposed in the same manner. We should then have an *f♯* over *mei.*

To judge merely from the melodic structures, the third phrase is the most calm. But in the development of the motive of *confundántur* over *revereántur,* and in the prominent syllabic chant, a tension is evident which is readily felt by the singer, a tension which calls for release in the second half of the phrase and especially stresses the important words *ánimam meam.* A host of evil spirits go about the world, seeking the ruin of souls (cf. the prayers after Mass). Evil men assist them in their task. Many hardly realize the dangers by which they are surrounded, or with what terrifying speed they are rushing to perdition. For them the Church prays with motherly solicitude and cries to heaven: *Deus in adjutórium!* May the strength of the enemies be broken and their influence come to naught!

In the Epistle we hear the Apostle admonishing us: "Not that we are sufficient to think anything of ourselves, as of ourselves; but our sufficiency is from God." And the Collect remarks that it is only by virtue of God's grace that His faithful serve Him loyally and worthily. All this urges us to pray the more fervently: *Deus in adjutórium meum inténde!*

GRADUAL (Ps. 33: 2, 3)

1. *Benedicam Dominum in omni tempore:* 2. *semper laus ejus in ore meo.* ℣. 1. *In Domino laudabitur*	1. *I will bless the Lord at all times:* 2. *his praise shall be ever in my mouth.* ℣. *In the Lord shall my*

anima mea: 2. *audiant mansueti, et* *soul be praised*: 2. *let the meek hear,*
laetentur.   *and rejoice.*

This melody is marked with irregularities. It has not that lucid construction so evident in Graduals of the fifth and sixth modes, which places the principal melodic ascent in the verse. Here the ascent is found in the *corpus*, which several times goes up to *f* and even to *g*, whereas the verse reaches *f* only once. Surprising, too, is the closing of the *corpus* on *c a b a*, the usual ending of the transposed Doric mode. Not only is the ending Doric; the entire extended phrase *in ore meo* with the preceding ten notes is sung in the Gradual of the tenth Sunday after Pentecost, which belongs to the first mode, over the words *prótege me*. This is no doubt one of the longest accommodations in a strange mode. Not quite so extended is the appropriating of the second group of notes over *mansuéti*, which is taken from the third mode. Here one may also compare the second and third groups over the word *meus* in the Gradual for Passion Sunday. The close of *mea* and *mansuéti* recurs in the Gradual *Justus ut palma*, which is ascribed to the second mode, over the word *multiplicábitur* and before *per noctem*. The melody over *laudábitur ánima mea* bears a great resemblance to that over *laudábimur tota die* on the twenty-third Sunday after Pentecost, which latter is, however, set a fourth higher. In both cases there is question of the seventh mode.

The importance of the melismatic punctuation again comes prominently to the fore. Compare *(Dómi)-num, (témpo)-re, (e)-jus, (me)-o*; in the verse, *(Dómi)-no, (me)-a, (mansué)-ti, (laetén)-tur.* Over *Dómino* the verse has the same melody as the first part of the Gradual over *Dóminum*.

Mode, style, and text of this Gradual find their continuation in the Gradual *Clamavérunt* of the Mass *Salus autem*. Both are taken from the thirty-third psalm. Compare the remarks on the Gradual for Septuagesima Sunday.

The Graduals *Dómine, praevenísti* on March 19 and *Benedícta* on July 2 are assigned to the fourth mode, no doubt because the first part of the Gradual, which is to be repeated, closes on *e*. The verse belongs undoubtedly to the first mode. One would expect to find the determining factor after the close of the corpus. Since, however, in ancient times the first part of the Gradual was not repeated after the verse, but the verse *Clamavérunt*—clearly belonging to the seventh mode, as is also indicated in our Graduale—followed, the entire piece was assigned to the seventh mode with good show of reason.

The Psalmist stresses the point that we are to praise God at all times. For in Himself God already is *laudábilis nimis*. He can never be praised sufficiently. If we then consider His love for us and His beneficence, the obligation of thanking Him must weigh heavily upon our souls and ever inspire us with new love. What immense riches we possess in Christ! Of this today's Epistle reminds us when it shows that the New Dispensation is far superior to and more glorious than the old, and that God's grace has called us and qualified us for this New Law. But especially in the house of God ought our singing and praising so to resound, that it "may arouse joy in the hearts of the faithful." St. Benedict in his Rule (Chapter 47) stipulates that only he should be allowed to sing or read in choir who can fulfill this task to the edification of those present. He should do it with humility, dignity, holy fear, and in obedience. In the same manner we ought to perform our sacred service for the honor of God and the joy and edification of the faithful.

ALLELUIA VERSE (Ps. 87: 2)

1. *Dómine Deus salútis meae:* 2. *in die clamavi et nocte coram te.*

1. *O Lord the God of my salvation:* 2. *I have cried in the day, and in the night before thee.*

Allelúia has the form a b c c¹. The frequent *pressus* are introduced in various ways. Over *(Al)-le-(lúia)* a group of four notes precedes the *pressus*; the same is true of the close of the *jubilus: é f e d ée—ĝ a g a ǵǵ.* In the b-member, groups of three notes precede: *é b a co—ĝ a b aa*; in c and c¹, groups of two notes: *ĝ a cc—b g aa.* The effectiveness of the melodic line will be increased if the *pressus* be not accented too strongly; in fact, the preceding notes should be stressed a little more. The address to God composes the first phrase of the verse. Here there is melodic tenseness, ascending until it closes on the old dominant of the third mode. "Thou art the God of my salvation." This grateful avowal is the best recommendation for the petition which follows. The *pressus* helps to make the plea more impressive. The extreme limits of this descending curve give the melodic line *c b a g f e,* which is, however, enlivened by thirds. *Dómine Deus* must be sung solemnly. The annotated manuscripts here have broad markings almost exclusively.

In connection with the Gospel which follows, this song sounds like a cry for the redemption of a world sick unto death.

On the feast of the Precious Blood and of St. Benedict Joseph Labre (April 16) the same melody is sung.

We here have poignant sorrow transfigured by the Paschal Alleluia. Our thoughts revert to Mother Church, sorrowfully awaiting the day of her resurrection. Perhaps your own soul will have to sing a similar Alleluia chant. (*K. L.*)

OFFERTORY (Ex. 32: 11, 13, 14)

1. *Precatus est Moyses in conspectu Domini Dei sui, et dixit:* 2. *precatus est Moyses in conspectu Domini Dei sui, et dixit:* II. 3. *Quare, Domine, irasceris in populo tuo?* 4. *Parce irae animae tuae:* 5. *memento Abraham, Isaac et Jacob, quibus jurasti dare terram fluentem lac et mel. III.* 6. *Et placatus est Dominus de malignitate, quam dixit facere populo suo.*

1. *Moses prayed in the sight of the Lord his God, and said:* 2. *Moses prayed in the sight of the Lord his God and said:* II. 3. *Why, O Lord, is thine indignation enkindled against thy people?* 4. *Let the anger of thy mind cease:* 5. *remember Abraham, Isaac, and Jacob, to whom thou didst swear to give a land flowing with milk and honey. III.* 6. *And the Lord was appeased from doing the evil, which he had spoken of doing against his people.*

Here everything—the content, the construction, the expression—is on a grand scale. One can almost see the palpitations of the singer's breast, as it rises and sinks under the excessive emotions that rush in upon his soul. Everything is at stake: the salvation of an entire people. God has threatened it with destruction because it adored the golden calf. He had promised Moses, however, that He would make him the father of a new and better people. Hence Moses threw everything into the balance to save his people, the very nation which had so frequently embittered his life. That was spirit of the spirit of God! Here was shown a mercy akin to that of the Good Samaritan of the Gospel.

The three divisions of the piece are indicated in the above translation: I. Introduction; II. Supplication of Moses; III. Response.

I. We can divine the meaning of this prayer at the very outset. The beginning of *In con-(spéctu)*, with its low fifth, lets the prayer ascend from the very depths of the soul. The form over *Dei sui* with its tritone occurs in a varied shape over *(i)-rascéris, in pópulo*, and *tuae*, besides coming in the repetition. Over the first *dixit* we meet the closing neums frequently used in the eighth mode. Compare the passage over *surréxit* in the Offertory for Easter Monday. We find the same first phrase repeated in the Ambrosian Antiphonary *(Paléographie musicale*, VII, 197*)*. The words *Precátus* and *Moyses* are slightly amplified by the addition of a *clivis*; the close of *dixit*, on the contrary, has been considerably shortened.

II. Violent agitation is expressed by the cumulation of fourths, bistrophas, tristrophas, *pressus*, and tritones. Ever more vehement becomes the beating of the singer's heart. As if to storm the gates of heaven itself, he now cries: *Meménto!* Lord, Thou hast pledged Thy word. Thou *canst* not destroy us. The fourth over *Quáre* becomes a fifth, then a sixth, and the agitation grows apace, until some relaxation is afforded with the descending fifth over *(Ja)-cob*. Nevertheless, the tension is still evident in *terram*. In the presentation, a short pause must be made after *lac*. The heaping of neums over the twice-sung *et* strikes us rather oddly.

III. The third part begins with the tone of assurance. We regard this passage as a resolved major chord. *Malignitá-(te)* is placed between two motives of like sound. The rich melody over *pópulo* with the development *ć a ć b g, á c a ć a f* assures us that Israel is again God's people. Quiet seconds form the close. The avoidance of tritones is no doubt intended.

Moses is but a weak type of Christ and His redemptive work. Christ not only prayed for us: He gave Himself completely for us. He can, therefore, not only point to the promises of God; He can show His wounds and the blood which was shed "unto the remission of sins," as the priest prays at the consecration. He is the "High Priest who came to effect a reconciliation in the time of God's wrath." Hence He also expects of us that we assist at the holy Sacrifice in the spirit of reconciliation and with a love which is not self-centered, but is prepared to immolate itself for others.

COMMUNION (Ps. 103: 13, 14, 15)

1. *De fructu operum tuorum, Domine, satiabitur terra*: 2. *ut educas panem de terra, et vinum laetificet cor hominis*; 3. *ut exhilaret faciem in oleo*, 4. *et panis cor hominis confirmet.*

1. *The earth shall be filled with the fruit of thy works, O Lord*: 2. *that thou mayest bring bread out of the earth, and that wine may cheer the heart of man*: 3. *that he may make the face cheerful with oil*: 4 *and that bread may strengthen man's heart.*

As last Sunday, so today again we have a harvest song, a song of thanksgiving for the blessings of grain, wine, and oil which God has bestowed upon man. His paternal goodness not only supplies the necessaries of life; it aims also at bringing joy to our heart: twice this thought is expressed here. It is precisely in these passages that the melodic climaxes occur. Joy wants to pour itself out, communicate itself, and inflame the hearts of others. It receives special emphasis not only through its high position, but also through the *pressus*, the only one used in this Communion, in contrast to that of last Sunday. Besides this contrast, in spite of the fact that it employs the same sixth mode, this Communion has a quieter melody, a more limited range, and smaller intervals, for even fourths are excluded. All is more unassuming here; but at the same time more intimate and cordial. The entire first phrase confines itself to seconds, and the chant is almost purely syllabic. The second phrase has *f* for its recitative, with emphasis of the accented syllables. It is the word-accent, in fact, which usually determines the melodic development: *f ǵ a f* over *edúcas, f g b♭ a b♭ a* over *vinum, á c a͡a g a* over *laetíficet.* The third phrase retains the joyous spirit of the second and, in spite of its brevity, has individual charm in the consonant passages *č a b♭ ǵ a g f̂ g ǵ f* over *(ex)-hílaret* and *f̂ d é f ďed č d ďc* over *in óleo.* With *et panis* we should like to see a new phrase begin on account of the text and the melodic arrangement. Here we have the rare case of a phrase ending wit a half tone *(e f).* Although the *e* before the final note accords with our ideas of harmony, still the ancients considered a close with a half tone an imperfection.

The Eucharistic allusion of these verses becomes most evident when they are used in a Communion song. For how many has the Eucharist stilled the longings of the heart, satisfied the craving for heavenly food! For how many has it been the source cf joy and inspiration. The fruit of Thy works O Lord, the Eucharistic Sacrifice, has satisfied the longings of our soul. There we see Christ as the Good Samaritan. Wine and oil He pours into our wounds, and a love that knows no limits. When we read at the end "that bread may strengthen man's heart," then let us pray: O my Saviour, now I must again go forth into life with its struggles, its trials, its many temptations. Take Thou my troubled heart into Thy hand and impart to it strength, constancy, and fidelity.

* * * *

THIRTEENTH SUNDAY AFTER PENTECOST

INTROIT (Ps. 73: 20, 19, 23)

1. *Respice, Domine, in testamentum tuum, et animas pauperum tuorum ne derelinquas in finem:* 2. *exsurge Domine, et judica causam tuam:* 3. *et ne oblivscaris voces quaerentium te.* Ps. *Ut quid Deus reppulisti in finem:* * *iratus est furor tuus super oves pascuae tuae?*

1. *Have regard unto thy covenant and forsake not to the end the souls of thy poor:* 2. *arise, O Lord, and judge thy cause, and forget not the voices of them that seek thee.* Ps. *Why, O God, hast thou cast us off unto the end:* * *why is thy wrath kindled against the sheep of thy pasture?*

Violent emotions stir the heart of the singer today. Apprehension that God may turn away forever His face from His wayward people seizes it; fear that He may break the covenant, mankind's only hope, because so many have become unfaithful to it. Hence this violent, almost passionate, clamoring, especially in the second part over *exsúrge Dómine*. "Perhaps it was the dire distress, caused by the migration of Nations, that forced this lamentation from the Church; we might now substitute as her reason the sinfulness of so many of her children" (*K. L.*). The singer knows, however, that he can pray in the name of the whole Church: we are *Thy* people, Thy poor, the lambs of Thy pasture, this matter is Thy concern. And that consoles him for God will not abandon His Church to any hostile power, and no malice or evil scheming can ever prevail against her.

Today's Gospel tells the story of the lepers' cleansing. With what loud voices did they not cry: "Jesus, Master, have mercy on us!" But even more urgent than this will be the plea of him who has experienced what is the leprosy of the soul, what a shameful thing sin is, how it impoverishes man utterly, and what a terrible thing it is to desert one's Creator and to break the covenant so solemnly ratified. Our present song is born out of this bitter realization. But there is confidence in it also: The divine Shepherd of souls does not forget us, He does not forsake us, for behold, in the holy Sacrifice He comes down upon the altar and gives Himself as food to His poor sheep!

The melody will gain in lucidity if we consider the pause after *causam tuam* the same as that after *testaméntum tuum*. Thus are formed two parts; the first half dramatically enlivened by the imperatives *Réspice*, *exsúrge*, and *júdica*; while the second half with *ne derelínquas*, *ne obliviscáris*, and the emphasis on the dominant *c*, is considerably more quiet. Toward the end the chant again becomes more insistent by reason of the *pressus* over *derelínquas* and *quaeréntium*.

The first half of the phrase forcefully presents the three most important words; the second half avoids all larger intervals. It is the suppliant petition of the "poor." The final cadence is borrowed from the fourth mode. After the turbulent *exsúrge Dómine*, *et júdica* sets in on the dominant, just as *in testaméntum* after *Dómine* above; *tuam* is an abridgment of *tuum*; *ne obliviscáris* harks back to *et júdica*; *voces* closes on *c*, like *tuorum* above.

GRADUAL (Ps. 73: 20, 19, 22)

1. *Respice, Domine, in testamentum tuum:* 2. *et animas pau-*

1. *Have regard, O Lord, to thy covenant, and forsake not to the*

perum tuorum 3. *ne obliviscaris in finem.* ℣. 1. *Exsurge Domine,* 2. *et judica causam tuam*: 3. *memor esto opprobrii servorum tuorum.*

end the souls of thy poor, ℣. 1. *Arise, O Lord,* 2. *and judge thy cause*: 3. *remember the reproach of thy servants.*

With the exception of the last phrase, the Introit and Gradual have the same wording. But how different is the mood the latter expresses! Here *Réspice* and the entire first phrase have a quieter tone, although the second phrase is more lively than *et ánimas paúperum* in the Introit. In the Gradual the prayer of the "poor" becomes more perceptible by means of the *b♭* after the *b*, which immediately precedes, through the stressing of the minor third, but especially by the urgent fourths and the emphasis on *b♭* and *c*. Then the melody presents a regular cadence, quite uncalled for by the text. The pause should be very short. Songs adorned with many neums, such as Graduals and Alleluias, naturally have more divisions than other pieces. Thus what was one phrase in the Introit is here divided into three melodic phrases. The third phrase begins like *in testaméntum* above, but imparts a special fervor to the petition. There are but few fifth-mode Graduals which are so animated in their first part as this one.

The verse, however, is typical throughout. The final neums of *Dómine* come to a climax with increasing power. Few singers will be able to chant the whole on one breath. In case of necessity, breath might be taken after *d e d͡d b. Causam* in the second phrase repeats the final neums of *Dómine* and those over *et jú-(dica)*; *tuam* presents the same motive thrice, and then adds a cadence. *Oppróbrii* reiterates the cadence of *(tuó)-rum* from the first part of the Gradual. We Thy servants have become a laughing stock, an object of contempt to Thy enemies. Forget us not, desert us not; judge Thou *Thy* cause! This is not sung in the vigorous style of the Introit, however, but with a typical Gradual-melody which is predominantly joyful in character.

ALLELUIA VERSE (Ps. 89: 1)

1. *Domine, refugium factus es nobis*: 2. *a generatione et progenie.*

1. *Lord, thou hast been our refuge*: 2. *from generation to generation.*

This Alleluia comes like a song of thanksgiving for the granting of the petitions mentioned in the Gradual. Would that we might hear the prayers of all the nations of the Christian centuries thanking God that He has provided a place of refuge in His Church, a shelter against the darts and arrows of the evil one, an asylum of rest after the sorrows and hardships of life, a haven where the soul, hungering for truth and grace, may find sustenance! If we could hear all these songs of thanksgiving, from those which were sung in the catacombs to those we now hear in all the churches of Christendom, how our hearts would be aflame with gratitude for all that God means to us in His Church.

Allelúia has four members, each of which ascends to high *e*. That is also the upper limit of the first phrase. The second phrase, however, soars above it to *f*. In the first and third members of *Allelúia* a slight pause occurs on the note *b*. We meet the second neum of the second member again over *es* and *no-(bis)*. *Dómine* rises in majestic seconds. In *refúgium* a concatenation of motives is apparent: *d̄ e d̄ b* and *ĉ d ĉ a* are joined to one another by *ĉ d ĉ b*. The cadence over *refugium*, which recurs in a shortened form at the end of *(generati)-óne*, seems almost too final for a word in the middle of a sentence. The ornate neums over *(generati)-óne* sound as if they were borrowed from the words *Juxta est Dóminus* of the Gradual *Clamavérunt*. The melodic line, here crowned by a *torculus*, is more graceful than that of the Gradual with its *pressus*. *Et* harks back to *a*.

OFFERTORY (Ps. 30: 15, 16)

1. *In te speravi, Domine*; 2. *dixi: Tu es Deus meus*, 3. *in manibus tuis tempora mea.*

1. *In thee, O Lord, have I hoped*: 2. *I said: Thou art my God*, 3. *my times are in thy hands.*

In content and melody this Offertory strongly resembles that of the first Sunday of Advent. Like the latter it ascends from the depths, from the acknowledgment of human indigence and helplessness. In both pieces *Dómine* receives similar treatment. The close over *témpora mea* can also be regarded as a variant of that over *ánimam* in the other Offertory. But the singer will soon discover the difference between the two. In the first place, today's Offertory is more serene. Similar or identical tone-sequences are found in the ending of *sperávi*, over *(Dó)-mi-(ne)*, over *Deus* and *meus*. Our present melody avoids large intervals—the greatest is a third—as well as modulation to *c*, so much favored by the second mode. This melody is also brighter in character. The development with *dixi* and *in mánibus* may not be very apparent, but still one readily senses the freedom that underlies it. It is the song of carefree confidence. In spite of its length, the melody of the first Sunday of Advent never reaches high *a*, as today's does.

There is great similarity in the compass of the three phrases. In the first phrase the first note, lengthened by a quilisma, is extremely effective, especially in this text. In the second phrase the *podatus* after the tristropha should receive a good accent; the same over *Tu*. The climax over *Deus meus* is obvious enough. This is really the sense of the melody: O God, Thou art my God. After *meus* a short pause is allowable. Everything strains toward further development with *in mánibus*. It seems but natural that *f g á g a f (mánibus)* should follow *d e f̂ e d̂ (Deus)* and *d e f ĝ f e (meus)*. A slight secondary accent may be placed on the fifth note over *má-(nibus)*. Quiet yet effective two-note groups thus make up this half of the phrase.

Included in the gifts which we bring to the altar is the oblation of ourselves to God; we confide entirely in Him, and place in His hands both life and death, both time and eternity. There we shall be safe (*W.K.*). At a nuptial Mass the spouses similarly place their entire lives in God's hands, for this Offertory is also sung in the Mass *Pro Sponso et Sponsa*. And even if we are conscious of the leprosy of sin with which we are afflicted, we know for certain that to our suppliant cry, "Jesus, Master, have mercy on us," He will reply with His almighty word: "Arise, go thy way: for thy faith hath made thee whole."

Special beauty attaches to the verses which formerly were sung in connection with this Offertory: (1) "Make Thy face to shine upon Thy servant; save me in Thy mercy. Let me not be confounded, O Lord, for I have called upon Thee." (2) "O how great is the multitude of Thy sweetness, O Lord? Which Thou hast hidden for them that fear Thee? Which Thou hast wrought for them that hope in Thee, in the sight of the sons of men." And each verse closed with the joyfully confiding refrain: *In mánibus tuis témpora mea.*

COMMUNION (Wisd. 16: 20)

1. *Panem de caelo dedisti nobis, Domine, habentem omne delectamentum,* 2. *et omnem saporem suavitatis.*

1. *Thou hast given us, O Lord, bread from heaven, having in it all that is delicious,* 2. *and the sweetness of every taste.*

It is the Lord who has given us the Holy Eucharist. That is the first thought suggested by the melody, which progresses almost stepwise, emphasizing *f–f, g–g, a–a, c–c,* until the word *Dómine* surmounts it all. Pronounce the words of this phrase distinctly and see how well the chant follows the natural development of the text. The Bread of heaven hast Thou given us, O Lord! Only Thou wast able to give it. Thy wisdom alone could conceive such a gift; Thy love alone could bestow it upon us. In very truth, "Thy sustenance showeth forth Thy sweetness to Thy children," as the subsequent verse of the Book of Wisdom puts it.

The second thought is: This Bread is full of *sweetness*. The text alone rings with the joy of it, but the melody strives to make it still more prominent. *Omne* in the second half of the first phrase is sung on the dominant. (According to a stylistic requirement which is generally observed in florid songs such as Graduals, a new melodic phrase is here formed for the same thought.) Its first half is characterized by the predominating *d*; the second is introduced by a surprising fifth and closes with the cadence customary with the fifth and sixth modes.

We have again been made partakers of this precious food from heaven. That is the Lord's answer to our supplication and lamentation in the Introit. He does not forget or forsake us. He comes into our hearts, bringing His peace, which contains all sweetness in itself. Would that we might thank Him as we ought! This heavenly food is to prepare us for heaven, for a heavenly life even on this earth. Its sweetness will detach us from all earthly joy.

*   *   *   *

FOURTEENTH SUNDAY AFTER PENTECOST

INTROIT (Ps. 83: 10, 11)

1. *Protector noster aspice, Deus, et respice in faciem Christi tui:* 2. *quia melior est dies una in atriis tuis super millia.* Ps. *Quam dilecta tabernacula tua, Domine virtutum!* * *concupiscit, et deficit anima mea in atria Domini.*

1. *Behold, O God, our protector, and look on the face of thy Christ:* 2. *for better is one day in thy courts above thousands.* Ps. *How lovely are thy tabernacles, O Lord of hosts!* * *my soul longeth and fainteth for the courts of the Lord.*

The first phrase has a middle cadence on the finale and a final cadence on the dominant after an emphatic *b*. It is dominated by the petitions *áspice* and *réspice*. *Aspice* is not an outcry, as it is in the Introit for Palm Sunday; nevertheless the fourth and the accented *c* make it quite insistent. Without God the weakness of man is indeed wont to fall, as today's Collect tells us. It is extremely difficult constantly to comply with the admonitions of today's Epistle and to crucify our flesh with its vices and concupiscences. Assistance from above is absolutely necessary if we would folllow the dictates of the *spirit* always and in all things. Hence this *áspice* and *réspice*. But *Christi tui* receives still greater stress. When we have congregated in the house of God *(átriis tuis)*, we may pray to Him: We are Thy anointed, Thy Christ; we belong to the mystic body of Christ, having become conformable to the image of Christ through sanctifying grace. Hence we may expect Thy special protection. The love which Thou bearest to Thy Son Christ overflows upon Thy chidren, the Christians, Thy anointed ones.

In singing this piece care must be had that the low *d* over *(Pro)-té-(ctor)* be not slighted. It is the beginning of a *crescendo* which must increase till it reaches *c*. Perhaps this *d e f g a* served as a model for the *f g a c d c* over *(fáci)-em Christi*; it is heard again over *super míl-(lia)*.

The beginning of the second phrase on *b♭* tends to make the closing melisma of the preceding *tui* mellow and tender (cf. *N. Sch.*, 249). For here we are speaking of the consolation that our soul so eagerly receives in church, in the house of God. Here we ever become more conformable to the image of Christ; here our soul finds its true home in the heart of God. Were it to taste all the joy of the world for a thousand days or a thousand years, it would still be homesick and would long for its true happiness—union with God. The *b♭* over *quia* and over the similar *mélior* is influenced by the following *f*, just as later *c* over *una* calls for *b*. *Una* is emphasized, but *míllia* has the richest melisma of the entire composition. But however grateful we may feel for the treasures of grace which are available in God's holy place, still a yearning fills our hearts for that great day which shall know no evening, for the contemplation of Christ *(in fáciem Christi)*.

GRADUAL (Ps. 117: 8, 9)

1. *Bonum est confidere in Domino, quam confidere in homine.* ℣ 1. *Bonum est sperare in Domino, 2. quam sperare in principibus.*

1. *It is good to confide in the Lord, rather than to have confidence in man.* ℣. 1. *It is good to trust in the Lord, 2. rather than to trust in princes.*

An antithesis exists between God and the world; that was the theme of the Introit. In the Epistle flesh and spirit, in the Gospel God and Mammon are placed in opposition. The Gradual loudly proclaims the same thought. And were worldlings endowed with all power and wealth, they would yet remain mere men, mortal men, incapable of bestowing upon us lasting happiness. David, the composer of Psalm 117, knew this from his own experience as well as from the history of his nation. God alone is the source of true happiness of heart: His fidelity is never wanting; His riches are boundless; His love is eternal.

Hardly a single musical turn is found in the *corpus* which does not occur also in other Graduals of the fifth mode. Thus the beginning of the first phrase bears great resemblance to that of the fourth and sixth Sundays after Pentecost. The first phrase of the verse is also much like

the second phrase of the Gradual for the second Sunday in Lent (q.v.).
Its second phrase echoes the second phrase on the fourth Sunday after
Pentecost. The melodic development is not influenced by the meaning
of the individual words; it is purely harmonic, or, better perhaps, it
portrays but one sentiment: that of joyous confidence in God.

ALLELUIA VERSE (Ps. 94: 1)

1. *Venite, exsultemus Domino*:
2. *jubilemus Deo salutari nostro.*

1. *Come, let us praise the Lord
with joy*: 2. *let us joyfully sing to
God our Saviour.*

Allelúia has the form a b c; in the same manner the verse opens
with a and closes on c. Melodically, two sentences can be distinguished,
each with an intonation *(Venite, salutári)*, middle cadence *(Dómino,
nostro)*, and final cadence *(Deo*, and the closing neums over *nostro)*. The
melody has therefore different divisions than the text. Over *exsultémus*
we meet the accented *f* for the first time, preceded and followed by a
minor third, which is again sung over *Deo* and several times over *nostro*.
On the tenth Sunday after Pentecost the second half of this extremely
ornate melisma also occurs at the close of the Alleluia-verse. There,
however, the crowning notes are only *f g f̂ d*, while here they are *ĝ a f̂ d*.
Formerly this Alleluia had yet another verse (Wagner, III, 402 f.).

In the early Christian centuries this song was sung during the procession which led the newly baptized to the baptismal font each day
during Easter Week. For was it not the fountain of supernatural life and
bliss? Was it not there that the Lord had shown Himself as the Saviour?
This salvation and happiness flowed from Christ's death and resurrection. The verse is indeed an appropriate song for Sunday. In connection
with the Mass formulary of today, it reveals the choice made between
God and the world: *"Venite, exsultemus Domino!"* (Cf. *Kirche und
Kanzel*, 1927, 289 f.)

OFFERTORY (Ps. 33: 8, 9)

1. *Immittet Angelus Domini in
circuitu timentium eum,* 2. *et
eripiet eos*: 3. *gustate et videte, quoniam suavis est Dominus.*

1. *The angel of the Lord shall en-
camp round about them that fear
him,* 2. *and shall deliver them*: 3. *O
taste and see that the Lord is sweet.*

The three phrases composing this song have a very modest range:
the first and third confine themselves to a sixth; the second to a fifth.
There is here no dramatic scene, no vehement cry for help; it is rather
a song of consolation and confidence. Even though the world surges

about us, enticing or threatening, we have nothing to fear, for God is our Helper. We must take care not to make any considerable pause between the first two phrases, which compose the first part of the Offertory. In content and spirit the second part resembles the Introit. There we sang: "Better is one day in thy courts above thousands"; now we reaffirm the same thought with: "O taste and see that the Lord is sweet."

We are reminded of the *Vidi aquam*, which we sing at the sprinkling of the holy water during the Easter season, in the introductory formula over *Immíttet*, which occurs also at the beginning of the Communion *Hoc corpus* of Passion Sunday. The passages over *Angelus* and *(ti)-ménti-(um)* are almost identical. Each syllable of the word *Dómini* begins with the same motive, which is, however, continued in a different manner on the final syllable. *(E)-rípiet* and *est* have a similar melody. Following the analogy of like passages, the Benedictines of Solesmes indicate the rhythmic division *éd bc áa f* over *(cir)-cúitu, (vi)-dé-(te)*, and *Dó-(minus)*. In the final *allelúia* of the Offertory for the Rogation Mass, the same formula is employed. According to the monks of Solesmes the grouping of the neums has a melodic, rather than a musical, signification. From *gustáte* on, the second part is more lively, as well as richer melodically. As a result of their fourths, *d–a, c–g*, the imperative forms *gustáte* and *vidéte* effect a similar impression.

Holy angels form a protecting wall about us. But Christ Himself is the Angel of the Lord, the Angel of the great counsel, as He is called in the Introit for the third Mass of Christmas. He comes in the mystery of the Mass, descending upon the assembled congregation. He comes with all His love, all His power, and frees us from all that may harm soul or body. But it is not only His presence that is to delight us: the angels of the Lord invite us: *gustáte et vidéte*. In Holy Communion He becomes our very food. These are the words which form the oldest and most cherished Communion-song of the early Church (cf. the Communion for the eighth Sunday after Pentecost).

COMMUNION (Matt. 6: 33)

1. *Primum quaerite regnum Dei,*
2. *et omnia adjicientur vobis, dicit Dominus.*

1. *Seek first the kingdom of God,*
2. *and all things shall be added unto you, saith the Lord.*

The Communion wishes to impress firmly upon our minds the final thought of today's Gospel. In our whole mode of life, in our inner soul as well as in our external dealings with others, the kingdom of God, of Christ the King, is to be formed and realized. That alone is the guarantee of true peace and welfare and happiness. Then all things else will be added. Thus saith the Lord.

The melody is not so much a fervent exhortation as an expression of trust in the fulfillment of these words, or even of hearty thanks for all that divine Providence has in store for us. *Regnum Dei* is made impressive by means of a chord resembling a tritone. For everything depends upon this, that God, God exclusively, be acknowledged and obeyed as the true King.

We may sing the last two words somewhat softly, thus placing the preceding more prominently in relief.

Plainsong delights in using the turn *g b a g* which occurs over *Dei*. The school of Palestrina, however, avoids it on account of the leap made from the accented first note of the group of four.

There is some resemblance to this melody in the Communion for the feast of St. Andrew the Apostle.

*   *   *   *

FIFTEENTH SUNDAY AFTER PENTECOST

INTROIT (Ps. 85: 1, 2, 3)

1. *Inclina, Domine, aurem tuam ad me, et exaudi me*: 2. *salvum fac servum tuum, Deus meus, sperantem in te*: 3. *miserere mihi, Domine, quoniam at te clamavi tota die.* Ps. *Laetifica animam servi tui*: * *quia ad te, Domine, animam meam levavi.*

1. *Bow down thine ear, O Lord, to me, and hear me*: 2. *save thy servant, O my God, that trusteth in thee*: 3. *have mercy on me, O Lord, for I have cried to thee all the day.* Ps. *Give joy to the soul of thy servant*: * *for to thee, O Lord, have I lifted up my soul.*

Deus meus, sperántem in te forms the melodic nucleus of this Introit. Confidence in God is its theme. From this the many petitions, the many imperatives, receive their character: Thou art my God; in Thee I trust. Calmly, and with a wealth of assurance, the seconds ascend to high *c*. At the end of each word, however, a slight bending back of the melody occurs: *g–f, b–a, c–a*; in this manner the thesis that follows is prepared for and introduced. It is quite impossible to sing this passage too fervently or too ardently. Confidence is sustained by reverence, and here we pray: *Deus meus.* In the first and third phrases, as well as in the psalm-verse, *Dómine* must be well delineated.

The first phrase supports itself on *a*, the second on *g*, the third on *f*. The first half of the first phrase is made forceful by *a*; while the second half surprises us by its descent into the lower range. We have met the same intonation in various other chants. After the accent with the *pressus*, the remaining notes over *Dómine* are modest and tender in character.

In the second phrase the three notes over *salvum* are to be stressed. The concatenation of the thirds *a–f*, *g–e*, *f–d* characterizes the third phrase, as do also the low notes in its second half. It almost sounds like a *De profúndis*, a call from the depths of human helplessness. *Clamávi* is a suppliant cry and resounds throughout the day. Over *miserére*, as frequently happens, principal and secondary accent have only one note, while each of the following syllables has three.

Whoever examines his conscience according to the admonitions of today's Epistle will feel himself impelled to pray as this chant does. For we find it extremely difficult to persevere, to do good untiringly, to take care that we be not tempted. It is hard for us to bear the burdens of others; each of us finds his own burden—the responsibility for all his acts of commission and omission—heavy enough. Surely we have every reason to cry to God: "Bow down Thine ear, hear me, heal me, save me, have mercy on me!" But we ought also to pray with confidence. There should be no gloomy coloring to our song, not even in the third phrase. In the verse the Psalmist himself dares to pray: "Give joy to the soul of Thy servant."

Let us consider the final words of the psalm-verse: "To Thee, O Lord, have I lifted up my soul." Is it true? Is my prayer and song an elevation of my being, of my whole personality, to God? Is it truly a *Glória Patri*?

Revue, 9, 111 f.

GRADUAL (Ps. 91: 2, 3)

1. *Bonum est confitere Domino* 2. *et psallere nomino tuo, Altissime.* ℣. 1. *Ad annuntiandum mane,* 2. *misericordiam tuam,* 3. *et veritatem tuam per noctem.*

1. *It is good to give praise to the Lord:* 2. *and to sing to thy name, O most High.* ℣. 1. *To show forth in the morning* 2. *thy mercy,* 3. *and in the night thy truth.*

Both parts of the Gradual have the same prolonged close: *Altíssime* =*per noctem*, except that the unaccented syllable -*si*- in the first word has a *clivis* of its own. The beginning of the *corpus* and the ascent over *confitéri* with the cheerful major scale have a pleasant ring. From then on, however, the melody moves within the tetrachord *a–d*, and several times repeats *d c b c*. Here a fluent presentation and a proper emphasizing of the significant accents will avert the danger of monotony.

In the verse we meet the melody with which we are acquainted from the verse for Maundy Thursday; it is marked by the vigorous final cadence over *mane*. Any considerable pause after *mane* is incompatible with the text.

The beginning of this verse alone is proper; the rest, as far as *misericórdiam* inclusive, is sung on the fourth Sunday after Pentecost. Compare also the verse for Maundy Thursday. *Mane* has an energetic final cadence, which in other pieces agrees with the divisions of the text. No lengthy pause is allowable here—one of the few instances in which the divisions of melody and text do not coincide. *Tuam* is known to us from the passage over *Dóminus* in the Gradual for Easter Sunday and from *tuam* in the Gradual for the feast of the Assumption. *Et veritátem tuam* has been taken over from the Gradual *Justus ut palma*, both text and melody; an appropriation, consequently, from the second mode. In both Graduals the verses have the same wording, but up to this point the melody differs. *Per noctem* again veers back, rather abruptly, it must be admitted, to the fifth mode.

In the psalms the mercy and fidelity of God are frequently combined. Today's Gospel mentions an extraordinary instance of His mercy. "When the Lord had seen, being moved with mercy toward her [the widow], He said to her: 'Weep not'." God does not exercise His mercy at particular moments; it accompanies us, as Psalm 22 says, all the days of our life. In Psalm 32 we read: "All his works are done with faithfulness." God's fidelity, however firm and unshakable it may be, has nothing about it that is either difficult or irksome. It is the fidelity of a merciful God. For this great favor we can never thank Him sufficiently. The hour of dawn drives home this truth most forcibly. For at that time particularly is God's mercy made manifest in the liturgical Sacrifice with especial splendor. Throughout the entire day, and even during the night *(per noctem)*, this song ought never to cease. Even when the night of bitter woe breaks in upon us we should hold fast to the mercy and fidelity of God, and thereby sublimate and transfigure all our sorrows. This Gradual is like the prelude to the praise given by the assembled throng in today's Gospel: "There came a fear upon all of them, and they glorified God, saying: A great prophet is risen up among us, and God hath visited His people."

ALLELUIA VERSE (Ps. 94: 3)

1. *Quoniam Deus magnus dominus,* 2. *et Rex magnus super omnem terram.*

1. *For the Lord is a great God,* 2. *and a great king over all the earth.*

Quóniam—"for"—introduces the reasons for the glad Alleluia call. Because God is so great, so sublime, we are impelled to glorify His greatness in new ways. There is nothing we are more in need of than an ever-expanding, ever-widening and deepening concept of the Deity. This is what we intend to impress upon the minds of the faithful by this song. Over the word *magnus*, in both instances, the melody seems to hover lovingly. In the Alleluia for the eighth Sunday after Pentecost we also laud God's immensity. On that day the melody wishes rather to extol His sublimity; today, however, the fullness and extent of His power. He is Lord and King over the entire world. His power reaches even where that of all men, be they the mightiest earthly rulers, is weak and ineffectual. Death itself is not exempt. When He says *Surge*—"arise," Death must give up his victims. Now God uses His regal power in order to render us happy; hence the joyful tone.

This Alleluia was formerly sung in the Easter procession. It has the structure a b c (=a¹) d (=b¹) and the archaic form, which does not round off the close of the verse with the melody developed by the *jubilus*.

The psalmodic construction of the seventh mode is still evident in the verse. The two phrases composing it have like introductions: *Quóniam Deus* and *et Rex*; a similar middle cadence, which in the first phrase is on the fifth above the tonic *(magnus)*, and in the second phrase, as in many other Alleluias of the seventh mode (e.g., that of the fourth Sunday after Pentecost), upon the third above the tonic *(rex magnus)*; finally, very similar closing cadences, *Dóminus* and *omnem. Terram* has a melody by itself, which in its beginning harks back to *magnus* of the first phrase, and in its cadences agrees with the close of the Alleluia-verse on the feast of the Dedication of a Church. In its beginning, *omnem* employs a melodic turn which is proper to the Alleluias of the second mode (see, for example, that of the third Mass of Christmas).

OFFERTORY (Ps. 39: 2, 3, 4)

1. *Expectans expectavi Dominum, et respexit me:* 2. *et exaudivit deprecationem meam,* 3. *et immisit in os meum canticum novum,* 4. *hymnum Deo nostro.*

1. *With expectation I have waited for the Lord, and he had regard to me:* 2. *and he heard my prayer,* 3. *and put a new canticle into my mouth,* 4. *a song to our God.*

In the Gospel we heard the narrative of the miracle wrought at the city gate of Naim. We do not know if the youth's mother had a lively faith in the omnipotence of Jesus, and if she was, perhaps, expecting Him to come to her aid. But of this we are certain: the Lord looked upon her lovingly, and tenderly said: "Weep not!" And we know that she sang a new song to Him, such as had never before come from her heart, when she could again look into her son's animated eyes and when the Lord placed the warm hand of her child into her own. It was a song of praise to God.

St. Augustine comments upon this Gospel: "That her son was called again to life was the joy of the widowed mother; that the souls of men are every day called to life is the joy of our Mother the Church." Frequently Mother Church has to wait a long time, has to pray much, before the mercy of God reawakens the souls of her children to life. But daily she must also thank Him for such marks of kindness. Today's Offertory is a song of thanksgiving coming from the very depths of her maternal heart. God Himself has placed it upon her lips. Furthermore, in the Holy Eucharist He has given her the most perfect song of praise and thanksgiving that can ascend to heaven.

The melody over the first three words vividly pictures the raising of the eyes to God, the begging for His grace; it is almost too noticeable, in fact. For the theme of today's Offertory is not expectation and longing, but rather thanksgiving: He has looked upon me, He has heard me, He has placed a new canticle into my mouth.

The first phrase has a range of a seventh and two endings on *c*. *Respéxit me* has a triumphant ring. *Dóminum* receives the same treatment, for example, as *ádipe* in the Introit for Corpus Christi. The second phrase confines itself to a range of a fifth and never extends beyond *d*. It has its endings on *a* and repeats the same thought as the second part of the first phrase. The third phrase, with a range of a sixth *(g–e)*, begins with the same sparkling motive as *respéxit* in the first phrase and closes still more brilliantly than the former with a modulation to *c*. Its joy overflows into the fourth phrase. In this passage the tonic of the mode appears for the very first time. Over *Deo g a* and *d c b g* are to be sung broadly and solemnly. The whole chant must be delivered in a lively fashion.

COMMUNION (John 6: 52)

1. *Panis, quem ego dedero, caro*   1. *The bread that I will give is*
mea est 2. pro saeculi vita.   *my flesh 2. for the life of the world.*

Vita—"life!" That is the last word of today's proper chants. Christ is our life. He showed Himself to be the Ruler of life by reawakening the youth of Naim. He is our life in the Holy Eucharist, the living and life-giving Bread. Only through Him can the world attain to life and only by His power can its life be increased and developed.

Holy joy welled up from the heart of the Saviour when He spoke the prophetic words we sing here. This joy is reflected by the brilliant and exultant melody. It attains its summit and greatest expansion precisely over the word *vita*. The thought, "life of the world," forms an independent musical phrase, being, however, strongly influenced by the melody over *mea est* in the first phrase. Here we have a descending fourth, followed by a *pes* and a *clivis*, while in the former instance there was a descending fifth with a descending *pes* and *climacus*. These sequences of tones and the surprising beginning over *Panis* are well calculated to rouse in our souls reverent astonishment at the marvels spoken of. For this reason, too, the word *ego* is especially emphasized by the melody.

The two phrases differ in this, that the first supports itself in the first half on *a* and reaches low *d* four times in its second half, while the second phrase in its first half stresses *g* and four times strikes high *c*.

Some time—thus we hope and pray—the Risen One will also cry to us: "I say to thee, arise," and will lead us into the life of eternal blessedness. For this is His solemn promise: "He that eateth my flesh, and drinketh my blood....... I will raise him up in the last day."

*   *   *   *

SIXTEENTH SUNDAY AFTER PENTECOST
INTROIT (Ps. 85: 3, 5)

1. *Miserere mihi Domine, quoniam ad te clamavi tota die*: 2. *quia tu Domine suavis ac mitis es, et copiosus in misericordia omnibus invocantibus te.* Ps. *Inclina Domine aurem tuam et exaudi me*: * *quoniam inops et pauper sum ego.*

1. *Have mercy on me, O Lord, for I have cried to thee all the day:* 2. *for thou, O Lord, art sweet and mild, and plenteous in mercy to all that call upon thee.* Ps. *Bow down thine ear to me, O Lord, and hear me:* * *for I am needy and poor.*

This Introit begins like the Introit *Laetábitur justus*, now in the Common of a Martyr not a Bishop, which in the old manuscripts opens the Mass for the feast of St. Vincent. There it is a cry of joy; here a prayer for mercy. How can the two be reconciled? Perhaps we may explain today's melody in the same manner as we did that for the third Sunday after Pentecost. The acknowledgment that God is good and mild and overflowing with mercy, and the mood produced by it is all contained in the first phrase. There is no misery portrayed in the melody, no inner strife. Assurance fills the singer's heart: my Redeemer lives and His heart is open to my incessant *(tota die)* prayer. How touching and how tender is the melody of the second phrase! With its minor thirds and semitones it seems to proceed from the heart of Jesus Himself. If major thirds and whole steps be substituted in their place, it will soon become apparent what the composer's intention in this passage was. We seem to hear the Saviour Himself singing: *mitis sum*—I Myself am goodness and mildness. And this goodness, this mildness, this mercy is infinitely boundless in width and depth; it is inexhaustible. To impress this upon the hearts of the faithful so well that it will never be forgotten, in any condition or state of life, not even when oppressed by sin, that is the aim of today's Introit. Someone has said of this melody that the cry for mercy continually grows more unrestrained. (*Betende Kirche*, p. 366). The melody, however, does not place any special stress upon this point. It wants to console, to encourage, to instill confidence. What a deep impression *copiósus* must have made when, in former times, it was repeated after every verse!

On the Friday after Passion Sunday, the melody for the Introit begins like today's. At its very beginning, however, instead of an interval of a fourth it has a third; but that chant, it must be noted, belongs to the fifth mode. The spirit of the Introit *Miserére* is predominantly joyful. In the first half of the second phrase the presentation must obviously be more tender and cordial. According to the annotated manuscripts, *(su)-ávis ac mitis* is to be prolonged slightly. *Copiósus* must be sung with all possible brilliancy. One readily notes some resemblance to *benígna est misericórdia* in the first antiphon for the blessing of the ashes on Ash Wednesday, which is filled with the same spirit; also the similarity between *(Dó)-mine* and *(misericór)-dia*. The composer seemed almost too careful in his plan of giving the second syllable of a dactyllic word more than one note. The melody thus avoids all ungraceful angles.

Whoever sings and prays in the spirit of this melody can never feel entirely poor or miserable. For in the holy Sacrifice of the Mass the fountains of eternal mercy are unceasingly operative.

GRADUAL

The explanation of the Gradual will be found under the third Sunday after Epiphany. In the Epistle St. Paul depicts the richness of the glory of Christ, which He bestows upon us "abundantly," so that we are filled "unto all the fullness of God." In return for such goodness we can only reverently thank God and with the Apostle "bend the knee to the Father of our Lord Jesus Christ." In the new Sion, which is His Church, we behold His glory and experience His gracious dealings with us.

The Apostle speaks to us as a prisoner, as a symbol of the suffering Church in her earthly exile. Around her the darkness grows ever deeper, but in the same degree she gains in grace and glory. Affliction should purge the members of the Body, should cause their love and faith to increase, and thus lead them into the depths of Christ and into His glory. In this manner the Lord "builds" His new Sion, His glorified Church, of well-known stones; there He will dwell as Victor and King.(Bomm, *Volksmessbuch*).

ALLELUIA VERSE (Ps. 97: 1)

1. *Cantate Domino canticum novum*: 2. *quia mirabilia fecit Dominus.*

1. *Sing ye to the Lord a new canticle*: 2. *for the Lord hath done wonderful things.*

The reverent surprise with which the Gradual began, continually mounts in the course of the piece and finally develops into a song of joy. It continues in the Alleluia in a bright tone and with gentle persuasiveness, striving to captivate hearts, urging them on to joy in the Lord. Were we to strive to contemplate the wonderful things of God, the marvels of His grace, of His mysteries, the prodigies of the Eucharistic Sacrifice; were we to make an earnest effort to penetrate into this world, then this song would give new stimulus and energy every time we should assist at Mass. Then our whole soul would sing out this melody as a small recompense to God for the gift of His only-begotten Son.

Over *Cantáte* the melody swells as far as the *pressus* on *c*; then it relaxes somewhat, only to prepare for a greater climax with *Dómino*. Our song is intended for the Lord, and for Him alone. The third significant word of this verse, *mirabília*, is made prominent like the first two, but it may be sung with still greater warmth. The tempo must, of course, be quite lively.

So far as the melody is concerned, this Sunday's Alleluia is much like that of the twenty-second Sunday after Pentecost. Both have the same twofold division, clearly indicated by the melody. It is difficult to determine which is the original composition. The probability seems to favor the twenty-second Sunday after Pentecost, for in the most ancient manuscripts the Alleluia *Cantáte Dómino* is not mentioned, while in manuscript 121 of Einsiedeln the text is given, but without any neums, although a place was reserved for their insertion. Three small variants seem to be mere printing mistakes:

Sixteenth Sunday	Twenty-second Sunday
(Dómi)-no gf	*Dóminum ge*
(Dó)-mi-(nus) fgaga	*(eó)-rum faga*

Over the second last word:

bistropha   tristropha
                                         preceded by low *d*.

The preceding note was added, perhaps, because plainsong does not generally begin a new phrase with a tristropha, or because the longer text brought a change with it. Final *gf* sounds decidedly more pleasant and provides for a better sequence. For this reason we have after *Dómino* a pause cutting the two middle lines, while that after *Dóminum* cuts only the topmost line.

Revue, 21, 97 ff.

OFFERTORY (Ps. 39: 14, 15)

1. *Domine, in auxilium meum respice:* 2. *confundantur et revereantur, qui quaerunt animam meam, ut auferant eam:* 3. *Domine, in auxilium meum respice.*

1. *Look down, O Lord, to help me:* 2. *let them be confounded and ashamed that seek after my soul to take it away:* 3. *look down, O Lord, to help me.*

Both text and melody of the first part are presented twice. The twenty-third Sunday after Pentecost offers the only similar case. It reminds us of the early practice of repeating a part (usually the last) of the antiphon after every verse that was joined to the Offertory. It should be noted how beautifully this repetition is introduced by the tense, forward-urging cadence over *eam*. The melody has a narrow range, is tender and fervent. Its simplicity is surpassed only by that of the Offertory of the second Sunday after Pentecost. Numerous *pressus*, however, make it fairly eloquent. The text would allow of a quite different melodic treatment, and has in fact found such also in plainsong. Compare the turbulent Communion *Erubéscant et revereántur* on the Tuesday of Holy Week, or the indignant Communion *Confundántur supérbi* from the Mass *Loquébar* in the Common of a Virgin and Martyr. But all such excitement is foreign to the Offertory for this Sunday.

Who prays thus? Surely it is the soul that knows how its adversary the devil goes about, seeking *(quaerens)* whom he may devour; the soul that sees itself surrounded by foes whom it cannot overcome by its own strength. It looks to the Lord, to Him who loves it and can give it all things, and begs for a loving glance and assistance. When we think of the words addressed by our Saviour to Saul the persecutor: "Why persecutest thou me?" and infer from this that He regards Himself one with the Church in all that threatens and harasses it, then we may place these words upon the lips of the Saviour Himself, who is now to offer Himself again upon the altar. Then we may be certain that Christ prays thus to the Father for us; and so we sink readily into the quiet atmosphere of the melody. We enter into its spirit even more when the repetition *Dómine in auxílium meum réspice* is sung tenderly and devoutly. Now we understand why all three phrases are given about equal importance: a strongly contrasting phrase in the middle would be somewhat disturbing. The same motive occurs over *qui quaerunt* and *ut áuferant*. The word-accent is especially emphasized by the fourth and the prolonged note. Over *in auxílium*, however, no fourth occurs. Perhaps this is due to the fact that in this instance two syllables precede the word-accent, while in both other cases a single syllable precedes.

The two verses which the ancient manuscripts add to this Offertory on the Friday after the second Sunday in Lent had an unusually ornate melody on their last word. So much the more impressive must have been the simple *Dómine*, which is likewise repeated in the manuscripts.

COMMUNION (Ps. 70: 16, 17, 18)

1. *Domine, memorabor justitiae tuae solius:* 2. *Deus, docuisti me a juventute mea,* 3. *et usque in senectam et senium, Deus, ne derelinquas me.*

1. *O Lord, I will be mindful of thy justice alone:* 2. *thou hast taught me, O God, from my youth,* 3. *and unto old age and grey hairs, O God, forsake me not.*

Let us first of all consider the middle phrase: *Deus, docuísti me a juventúte mea*. It takes its inception a fourth higher than the preceding note, adheres to the dominant high *c*, has a group of two and of three notes over *me-(a)* and the preceding syllable, and a pleasing harmony. It is a soul's grateful expression for the loving care that God has taken of it from its youth to the present day, even until today's Communion, for this is a Communion song. Whoever considers all this sees the debt of gratitude become infinitely great. But he finds his consolation in Him who has come in Holy Communion, whose thanksgiving is infinite in value.

The first and last phrases are not so cheerful; in fact, one must say that they are almost heavy, depressing. This results from the frequent descent of the melody to low *d*, the accentuation of the tonic *g*, and the repetition of the same formula: *Memorábor=senéctam, justítiae=sénium,* and the same motive a fourth higher over *solíus=(de)-re-(línquas).* The thought of God's justice may become extremely oppressive, as well as the prospect of lonely old age here referred to. And the repetition of *senéctam* and *sénium* compels us to think of all the unwelcome concomitants of old age. When loneliness creeps into my heart, when those desert me on whose love I had reckoned, or if they shall have left this life before me, when in the evening of my life the awful meaning of Thy justice, O God, flashes up in my mind, when the very thought of Thy loving kindness since the days of my childhood only tends to increase my responsibility, and when the night approaches, then, O God, be Thou at my side, desert me not. However great the similarity of the first and third phrases may be, still the latter shows an evident development, an increase of feeling, an intensely prayerful attitude. *Usque* must be sung slowly and impressively; so also *Deus* with the *pressus*, which corresponds to the single note in the first phrase over *tuae*; then the expansion of *fga* over *so-(lius)*, corresponding to the twofold *f a c* over *ne de-(relinquas)*. Hence this third phrase must have a more tender ring than the first. Even though the thought of God's justice is appalling, still it is not entirely devoid of consolation. It would be a mistake to consider this melody an outgrowth of anguish or despondency. In His justice God places no greater burden on any man's shoulders than he is able to bear. Men often judge harshly, because frequently they overlook the circumstances which lessen the grievousness of the offense. God knows all things; He, and He alone, knows the true motives behind every act. His justice, moreover, is always tempered with mercy.

"This Communion portrays an entire life's history: the Saviour of thy childhood, thy youth, thy manhood, thy old age" (*K. L.*).

* * * *

SEVENTEENTH SUNDAY AFTER PENTECOST

INTROIT (Ps. 118: 137, 124)

1. *Justus es, Domine, et rectum judicium tuum*: 2. *fac cum servo tuo secundum misericordiam tuam.* Ps. *Beati immaculati in via*: * *qui ambulant in lege Domini.*

1. *Just thou art, O Lord, and thy judgment is right*; 2. *deal with thy servant according to thy mercy.* Ps. *Blessed are the undefiled in the way*: * *that walk in the law of the Lord.*

We begin today's Introit with an act of faith; "Thou art just, O Lord, and all that Thou commandest and orderest is just." With this declaration all questioning, all scrutiny, all doubt is silenced. And the ultimate decision which God will announce on Judgment Day is likewise just. The closer we come to the end of the liturgical year, the more frequently does the Church hold this thought of the great judgment before our eyes. Shall we be able to endure it, this manifestation of God's justice? If we consider this, then we shall think it a kindness on God's part that we are now allowed to appeal to His mercy: now we understand why the melody of the second phrase is so stirring, almost turbulent: we seem to stretch out to grasp the merciful hand of God. His justice alone can return to us the purity which we perhaps lost on the difficult and dangerous journey through life. It is His merciful love alone that can give us the requisite strength henceforth to remain true to His commandments, especially to that principal one mentioned in today's Gospel—love of God and of neighbor.

The rapid ascent of the melody to high *e* is quite common in Introits of the first mode; for example, *Salus autem* and *Sapiéntiam* from the Mass for several Martyrs, and especially the Introit *Suscépimus Deus*, which is sung on the eighth Sunday after Pentecost and on February 2. There we find a similar beginning with a fifth and the same melody over the words *(mi)-sericórdiam tuam* as we have here over *judícium tuum*. In the former piece, however, the development is drawn on larger lines and is easier of comprehension, while in today's Introit *tuo* leads over to the conclusion somewhat too suddenly. The pause after *tuo* is justified only by the necessity for taking breath. The melodic continuity—compare *e c a c* with the subsequent *c a f g f*—is thereby broken. Far better would be the effect if the whole could be sung without any interruption. In a large choir, the individuals might breathe at different places. *Tuo* is also the only word with melodic shifting, since the accented syllable is lower than the following syllable. The ending of the second phrase expands the closing motive of the first phrase a fifth lower.

Revue gr., 11, 123 ff.

GRADUAL (Ps. 32: 12, 6)

1. *Beata gens, cujus est Dominus Deus eorum*: 2. *populus, quem elegit Dominus* 3. *in hereditatem sibi.* ℣. 1. *Verbo Domini caeli firmati sunt*: 2. *et spiritu oris ejus* 3. *omnis virtus eorum.*

1. *Blessed is the nation whose God is the Lord*: 2. *the people whom he hath chosen for his inheritance.* ℣. 1. *By the word of the Lord the heavens were established,* 2. *and by the spirit of his mouth* 3. *all their power.*

If the sevenfold unity of which the Epistle has just spoken binds us all together; if we walk worthy of the vocation to which we are called; if we support one another with all meekness, humility, patience, and charity; if we are careful to keep the unity of the spirit in the bond of peace, then are we a blessed nation, then God is our God—we are His inheritance and He, the Eternal, will one day be our inheritance and reward exceeding great.

The first phrase of the verse corresponds to the second in the Introit for the second Sunday after Easter (cf. p. 191). God's almighty word has called into existence the heavens with their innumerable stars and thus created a world of light and order and harmony. If we bring our wills into perfect accord with that of God, then we call into being in our interior and around us a cosmos of marvelous light, order, and harmony.

In the *corpus* each of the three phrases ascends to *c*. Emphasis is added in the third phrase by the *b*. The love of God which led Him to predestine us to glory is apparently alluded to here. Over *sibi fg fd fa* is interposed between two identical members. The first four notes are again used to bring the piece to a close. At the beginning of the verse, a preliminary *f* prolongs its effect in the subsequent *bb*; then the accented *c* calls for *b*. The cadence over *Dómini* is found in pieces of various modes. Here, as above with *Dóminus*, the *pressus* before the final note effectively enhances the close. The words *caeli firmáti sunt* are brought well to the fore. *Ejus* has a cadence like *Dóminus* above. Mention was made of the same closing melody in the Gradual for the tenth Sunday after Pentecost.

ALLELUIA VERSE (Ps. 101: 2)

1. *Domine, exaudi orationem meam,* 2. *et clamor meus ad te veniat.*

1. *O Lord, hear my prayer,* 2. *and let my cry come unto thee.*

The Alleluia has the form a b b¹. The first part of b is repeated on a reduced scale in b¹, while the second part is expanded. Both phrases open on *a*, as well as the repetition with *ad te*. *Exáudi* bears the middle cadence in the first phrase; *meus* in the second. *Meam* and *(véni)-at* carry the final cadences. The psalmodic construction is unmistakable. Special vehemence issues from the cry *exáudi*. On the twenty-third Sunday after Pentecost we meet it in exactly the same form.

When we hear the words of the Gospel: "Thou shalt love the Lord thy God with thy whole heart," then there is need to pray for love; and when we hear the passage concerning Christ's divinity, then there is great need to pray for faith.

OFFERTORY (Dan. 9: 17, 18, 19)

1. *Oravi Deum meum ego Daniel dicens;* 2. *Exaudi, Domine, preces servi tui:* 3. *illumina faciem tuam super sanctuarium tuum:* 4. *et pro-*

1. *I, Daniel, prayed to my God, saying:* 2. *Hear, O Lord, the prayers of thy servant:* 3. *let thy face shine upon thy sanctuary:* 4.

pitius intende populum istum, su-   *and favorably look down upon this*
per quem invocatum est nomen   *people upon whom thy name is in-*
tuum, Deus.   *voked, O God.*

In the first phrase the one who prays mentions his name—a rare occurrence. The introduction is quiet, never going beyond the tenor of the mode *(a)*. Daniel prays to his Lord and God in the oppression and the hardships of the Babylonian captivity. His beloved people, once the elect of God, is pining away in a strange land, beaten and scattered. Hence that emphatic cry of the melody: *Exáudi*—"Hear, O Lord, the prayers of thy servant!" After the large interval of a fourth follow quiet seconds, thus making *Exáudi* all the more impressive. *Preces* accords with *Deum* in the first and *pópulum* in the fourth phrase. At the end, *tui* is turned upward *(e f)* because the following phrase begins with *dg*. In the second phrase, only *exáudi* receives prominence; the third phrase initiates a greater development. For was not this the prophet's most bitter grievance, that the sanctuary in Jerusalem had become a heap of ruins? Oh, let Thy glorious countenance once more regard this spot, the the place which Thou Thyself hast chosen! The melodic turn *c ǵa ef ǵa* over *super sanctuá-(rium)* is frequently employed in Graduals belonging to the third mode. *Tuam*, like *tuum* in the fourth phrase, is accentuated. The first part of the fourth phrase, however, is made still more impressive. The passage *ḋg ág g* at the beginning of the third phrase becomes *ǵc ḋc c* here. "Favorably look down upon this people," that is, the chosen people. It is Thy people, bearing Thy name. The tone-sequence *fg cd* combines *istum* and *super*, according to the rules which effect contrast in uniting phrases or parts of phrases in the first and eighth modes. *Deus* repeats its first member. An ornate closing melisma, such as the one here, is practically a stylistic necessity in Offertories.

For these modern times Daniel's Offertory prayer is also most opportune. We confidently hope to emerge from the present collapse of spiritual faith and Christian morals with the help of God's grace; we long for the religious renascence into the realm of the "King of Love," for that rebirth which must be effected, however much the foolish and malicious world may oppose it. Mankind must find the true answer to the two momentous questions which have been its greatest concern throughout history, the two points brought up in today's Gospel: the question of the greatest commandment and that of the person of Christ. (Oberhammer).

In the Eucharistic Sacrifice, Christ, the Son of the Living God, does look favorably upon us. There He manifests His infinite love to the Father and to us.

COMMUNION (Ps. 75: 12, 13)

1. *Vovete, et reddite Domino Deo vestro, omnes qui in circuitu ejus affertis munera*: 2. *terribili, et ei qui aufert spiritum principum*: 3. *terribili apud reges terrae.*

1. *Vow ye, and pay to the Lord your God, all you that round about him bring presents*: 2. *to him that is terrible, even to him who taketh away the spirit of princes*: 3. *to the terrible with all the kings of the earth.*

Few Communions have such a serious text as this one. Generally they speak words of consolation and of the goodness of God, or present our humble yet confident petitions. Here, however, God is twice called "the Terrible," before whom all the kings of the earth tremble. He appears here, as in the Introit, as the judge of the earth (to whom today's Gospel also makes reference) when the Lord says to His Lord—the Father to His Son—that He will subdue all His enemies and make them His footstool. He will crush all the obstinacy of earthly potentates, will take their courage from them—or, as others translate it, will rob them of their breath—all their pride and self-esteem will be as nothing in the sight of His glory and majesty.

The first *terribili* sets in on the dominant, and with its major third is the most significant word of the entire melody, just as the phrase which it opens surpasses the other two. In the first phrase, the increase of the melody over the first three words seems to parallel the thought: you must not only make vows: rather you must keep and fulfill them. Over *Dóminus* the word-accent has only a single note, while the following unaccented syllable supports a tristropha, a common occurrence. Over *in circúitu ejus* the melody describes a semicircle as if imitating the sense of the words. The second *terríbili* likewise begins on the dominant and then reverently bows before the majesty of God.

The fear of the Lord, of Him who will one day judge the whole world, must also underlie our activity in church music. In our worship we can never be too reverent. For, while we live, we can receive into our hearts Christ, our Saviour, our Redeemer and Consoler, whose greatness we adore, whose arrival for judgment we await.

*   *   *   *

EIGHTEENTH SUNDAY AFTER PENTECOST

Up to the seventeenth Sunday after Pentecost inclusive, the Introits were taken from the psalms. Beginning with the present Sunday, the text will be taken from other books of Holy Writ, with the exception of the Introit for the twenty-second Sunday. Upon closer examination, all the texts sung today, the Alleluia-verse excepted, appear as parts of an ancient formulary for the Dedication of a Church:[1] with the Introit and the psalm-verse *Laetátus sum...* we enter the house of the Lord; the Gradual with the words of the same psalm and the Offertory treat of the altar and the sacrifice; the Communion urges us to bring our sacrificial gifts and to offer our worship in God's house. Just when this formulary was transferred to the present Sunday is not known. In very early times this Sunday followed immediately upon the autumnal Ember Days; since the services of Ember Saturday were prolonged throughout the night till morning, the day did not have a Mass proper to it.

INTROIT (Ecclus. 36: 18)

1. *Da pacem, Domine, sustinentibus te,* 2. *ut prophetae tui fideles inveniantur:* 3. *exaudi preces servi tui, et plebis tuae Israel.* Ps. *Laetatus sum in his quae dicta sunt mihi;* * *in domum Domini ibimus.*

1. *Give peace, O Lord, to them that patiently wait for thee,* 2. *that thy prophets may be found faithful:* 3. *hear the prayers of thy servant, and of thy people Israel.* Ps. *I rejoiced at the things that were said to me:* * *we shall go into the house of the Lord.*

To be a Christian, as Cardinal Newman remarks, is to keep on the lookout for Christ. Again holy Mother Church invites us to maintain this watchfulness. In fact, she considers it one of her most important and sublime duties. She is especially alive to this obligation during Advent and toward the end of the liturgical year. We belong to those who await the Lord *(sustinéntibus te)*, who prepare for His coming and are predisposed by the action of divine grace. It is for this reason that we today pray for peace and all that comes in its train. As the palsied man in this Sunday's Gospel longed to be cured, and only attained full recovery and true peace after the Lord said to him: "Thy sins are forgiven thee," so in the Introit we cry *Da pacem* and toward the end of Mass, *Dona nobis pacem.* Streams of peace will the Lord cause to flow into the hearts of men—so the prophets sang. Lord, show that they are *Thy* prophets *(tui)*, the men whom Thou hast sent, and therefore fulfil what Thou hast promised by them.

---

[1] In the fifth century the dedication of a church in honor of St. Michael was celebrated at Rome on September 30 (later the twenty-ninth) and the Sunday occurring about this time was called the first *post natale basilicae s. Angeli* or simply *post sancti Angeli* (G. Morin Les veritables origines du chant greg.).

Lend an ear to the prayers of Thy servant. By the mouths of the prophets, the Messias had had Himself pictured as the servant of God. Therefore the Father was well pleased in Him. He still prays in the same way for us today and again becomes our Mediator in holy Mass, and this assures the acceptance of our prayers. Not in vain do we await Him: He will come. He who is our peace enters our heart in Holy Communion, bringing us peace and the pledge of life eternal. Hence the joy we experience when we are told that we may enter into the Lord's house. What riches it lavishes upon us every day!

The first phrase is reminiscent of the Introit *Roráte caeli*, with which it is also closely allied in spirit. Identical with it is the first phrase of the well-known Introit *Státuit*. The continual use of *b♭* in the first and second phrases tends to make the melody tender and devout, while the frequent repetition of the same motive or of a similar one makes it impressive. This motive is composed of the notes *á b♭ g á g* over *(Dó)-mine*, which remains the same in its first part, but changes slightly in its second over *susti-(néntibus)*, *tui*, *preces*, *tuae*. It produces its greatest effect over *tuae*, because it sets in here with a major third, while in the other cases only a whole step precedes. The petition: "We are Thy people," gains in intensity thereby.

GRADUAL

For the explanation of this chant see the fourth Sunday of Lent. Today we thank God with the Apostle for the grace which is given us in Christ Jesus, for in Him we have become rich in all things. But our thoughts and our longings also extend beyond to the house of God in heaven, to His peace and blessedness. "The incense which curls upward at the Gospel and my uplifted hands are both symbols of my yearning for heaven" (*K. L.*). We may also be confident that God will make us steadfast to the end, that we may be "unto the end without crime, in the day of the coming of our Lord Jesus Christ."

ALLELUIA VERSE (Ps. 101: 16)

1. *Timebunt gentes nomen tuum, Domine*: 2. *et omnes reges terrae gloriam tuam.*

1. *The gentiles shall fear Thy name, O Lord*: 2. *and all the kings of the earth Thy glory.*

Allelúia has the form a b b c c¹. The b shows an upward tendency, c goes downward, while c¹ is a union of arsis and thesis. Part a opens the verse; b, c and c¹ are heard again over *nomen tuum*, and with slight variation over *terrae*. Thus *Allelúia* supplies the theme for the verse.

The first phrase of the verse has a range of a seventh. One rarely sees a descent like that to *b* over *Dómine*. The second phrase has the wide range of a tenth, and is dominated by the word *reges*. The singer wishes to say that not only all the nations will pay homage to the Lord, but also the kings: all the kings of the earth will worship God. What is their paltry glory, even if they be veritable sun gods, compared to that which Christ will reveal at His final coming? Before Him all things will crumble into dust. There will be no dallying about the ceremonial of reception. Only one thing will remain to be done: to bend the knee and adore, to tremble in reverence before Him who alone is the Lord, the King of glory.

With a feeling of certainty that could scarce be greater, the melody proclaims this truth: *Timébunt*, "they shall fear." This faith is most deeply engraved in the consciousness of the Church. She looks forward with confidence to the coming of her King: already today she greets Him with the cry of Alleluia.

OFFERTORY (Ex. 24, 4 - 5)

1. *Sanctificavit Moyses altare Domino*, 2. *offerens super illud holocausta*, 3. *et immolans victimas*: 4. *fecit sacrificium vespertinum in odorem suavitatis Domino Deo*, 5. *in conspectu filiorum Israel*.	1. *Moses consecrated an altar to the Lord*, 2. *offering upon it holocausts*, 3. *and sacrificing victims*: 4. *he made an evening sacrifice to the Lord God for a savor of sweetness*, 5. *in the sight of the children of Israel*.

According to the context, the participles *ófferens* and *ímmolans* are closely akin. A great caesura, however, is introduced into the melody by the cadence over *(holo)-cáusta*, and further on prominence is given to *et ímmolans* which is hard for us to grasp. Similarly, in relation to the other phrases, the third receives undue amplification. Here we cannot apply as a measure of perfection the carefully planned and artistic development which we so admire, for instance, in Graduals of the fifth mode. In spite of this, however, the melody has beauties of its own.

The first word is simply narrative, confines itself to a tetrachord *(f–b)*. What we now feel to be a bright major chord, we hear over *altáre* and *odórem* and in a descending line over *(con)-spé-(ctu)*. The soothing close of *(Dó)-mino* echoes somewhat over *(ví)-ctimas, (vesper)-tínum*, and *Deo*. To the descending fourths at the beginning and end of the second phrase, the strongly accented ascending fourth over *(ho)-lo-(cáusta)* comes as an answer. Over *illud* two bistrophas are to be sung after the *clivis*, followed by an accented *torculus*. The third phrase is introduced like *Móyses* above. *(Suavi)-tátis* resembles *(holo)-cáusta*; *Dó-(mino)* repeats the first four notes of the last-mentioned word. The fourth phrase abounds with groups of neums and in its lower part brings a delightful new movement. It is extremely rare in plainsong that a melody closes on the leading note *f̂ g é f ĝg f.*

Is this descent of the melody to signify the deep impression which the sacrifice of Moses made upon the Israelites? God had given His law upon Mount Sinai. The sacrifice was now to ratify the covenant which God had made with His people. The New Testament has been sealed in like manner by bloody sacrifice, by an evening *(vespertínum)* oblation, for it was about the ninth hour when Jesus bowed His head on the Cross and gave up the ghost. This sacrifice is renewed at Mass. What a high consecration *(sanctificávit)* attaches to the altars of our churches! How sublime the Sacrifice that is offered upon them! With what pleasure does not our heavenly Father regard it! Then is fulfilled what the priest asks for at the offering of the chalice—it ascends with the savor of sweetness. And we are allowed to be witnesses *(in conspéctu)* of this mystery. What is more, we ourselves are drawn into the mystery. We become, as today's Secret says, partakers of the one supreme Godhead.

COMMUNION (Ps. 95: 8, 9)

1. *Tollite hostias, et introite in atria ejus*: 2. *adorate Dominum in aula sancta ejus.*

1. *Bring up sacrifices, and come into his courts*: 2. *adore ye the Lord in his holy court.*

The first phrase speaks of an action; the second of the spirit with which that action is to be performed. *Tóllite* sets in on a high pitch: let there be no hesitation, no indifference in the offering of the sacrifice or in the sacrificial procession! The two imperatives *Tóllite* and *introíte* have the same note progression, *d c b,* and consequently they are also closely related melodically. *Hóstias* towers above both these words. The third member of the phrase is quieter, never extending beyond *c* and the modest interval of a minor third.

The solemnly descending line in the second phrase expresses the idea of adoration—a profound bow, a prostration before the majesty of God. In the annotated manuscripts each of the clives over the words *(ado)-ráte Dóminum* is marked with a hold, thus enhancing the impression of reverence. But the solemn spirit is made less formidable by the fact that each new *clivis* opens on the same note with which the preceding closed.

In the church our humble gifts of bread and wine are converted into the Lord Himself; under the sacred species we adore Him who offers

Himself for us and gives Himself to us in Holy Communion. *In aula* is related to *ejus* of the first phrase. It closes on *b♭* like the second *ejus*, while *sancta* closes on *c*. Instead of the quiet, solemn two-note groups of the preceding member, we here have three-note groups. The suspended close on *b♭* may serve to remind us that we are still awaiting the eternal courts of God, the eternal liturgy of heaven. With one exception, the accented syllable is always higher than the following syllable.

K. L. translates and explains *Tóllite hóstias* thus: "Take unto yourselves the hosts!"

*   *   *   *

NINETEENTH SUNDAY AFTER PENTECOST
INTROIT

1. *Salus populi ego sum, dicit Dominus*: 2. *de quacumque tribulatione clamaverint ad me, exaudiam eos*: 3. *et ero illorum Dominus in perpetuum.* Ps. *Attendite populæ meus, legem meam*: * *inclinate aurem vestram in verba oris mei.*

1. *I am the salvation of the people, saith the Lord*: 2. *in whatever tribulation they shall cry to me, I will hear them*: 3. *and I will be their Lord forever.* Ps. *Attend, O my people, to my law*: * *incline your ears to the words of my mouth.*

The Introits after Pentecost thank God for graces bestowed and rejoice in His splendor and greatness. At the same time they are often prayers of petition and supplication; in fact, all those from the second Sunday on are of this kind. Today, on the nineteenth Sunday, as also on the twenty-third Sunday, God answers all these cries; He responds to the petition of Psalm 34: "Say to my soul, 'I am thy salvation'. " Today He says: "I am the salvation of the people," and on the twenty-third Sunday: "I think thoughts of peace." On both Sundays God Himself speaks—both times with the same introductory formula: *dicit Dóminus*. The Introit for the twenty-third Sunday is more intimate, for not only is the Lord Himself speaking, but He is speaking directly to us, is addressing us. Today's chant, however, is more general in tone.

Calmness and goodness are suggested by the seconds and the minor thirds in the first phrase: I am the salvation of the people, the savior in tribulation, the protector in dangers, the only true happiness of the people. In the Holy Eucharist God is "our salvation, our life, and our resurrection." He not only heals all the wounds of the soul; He implants in it the germ of immortality, of an eternal life in glory. The introduction shows some resemblance to the beginning of the Introit for the fourteenth Sunday after Pentecost. Similarly, *ad me* and *eos* in today's melody are related to *una* in the former; *in perpé-(tuum)* reminds us of *super míl-(lia)* in the same piece. *Dóminus* finds a corresponding motive over *(per)-pétuum* at the end of the melody. At the end of the first phrase, however, the *clivis* is converted to a *pes*, because the subsequent phrase begins on low *d*. The distribution of the neums over *Dóminus* here and in the third phrase, as well as over *perpétuum*, results from the fact that plainsong is not fond of dactylic endings, but prefers spondees. (*N. Sch.* 233 f).

The second phrase with its interval of a fourth and its harsh *a b* is not intended to portray distress, but rather to emphasize, clearly and definitely, that when the need is greatest God's assistance is nearest. *Clamáverint ad me* and *exáudiam eos* have almost the same melody: to the measure of our faith and confidence God's generosity will correspond. There is a slight but noteworthy difference, however. Over *(ex)-áu-(diam)* we might have sung *g ga g* as over *(cla)-má-(verint)*; the equal accentuation on the two words would have suggested this. Since, however, a different construction was preferred, and the melody descends to *e*, the only one of this phrase, and has a quilisma after *f*, it is evidently intended to emphasize the words: "I will hear them."

In its first half the third phrase harks back to the quiet style of the first. But there follows immediately a portrayal of God's eternal fidelity, of His indefatigable desire to help. Hence the fourth and the accent on high *c*. We may consider the closing neums over *(Dómi)-nus* as a variation of those over *(e)-go sum, ad me* and *eos*.

Since God declares Himself ready to assist us everywhere and at all times, we should also willingly accept the admonition: "Attend, O My people, to My law!" His law assures us of temporal and eternal happiness. And if He, the Lord, is so prepared to help us, then we ought to be proud to acknowledge His sovereignty always and in all things.

GRADUAL (Ps. 140: 2)

1. *Dirigatur oratio mea sicut incensum in conspectu tuo, Domine.* ℣ 1. *Elevatio manuum mearum 2. sacrificium vespertinum.*

1. Let my prayer be directed as incense in thy sight, O Lord. ℣ 1. The lifting up of my hands 2. as an evening sacrifice.

David is far from the sanctuary, sunk in poverty and distress. He yearns to offer a sacrifice to the Lord. But there is nothing at hand. Hence he lifts up his hands, his prayer, his whole soul, to God.

We may look upon today's Eucharistic celebration as the solemn evening sacrifice at the close of the liturgical year. Just as formerly the Christians prayed with outstretched arms and extended hands, and as

the priest still lifts up the sacrificial gifts, so do we now raise our hearts
to God. This new oblation of ourselves, this new love for Him, should
in this infinite Sacrifice ascend in His sight as clouds of aromatic incense. (*W. K.*).

In imitation of incense, this energetic song strives higher, ever
higher; it is tone-painting on grand lines. Upon *Dirigátur* with *ǵd d d*
follows *orátio mea* with *ǵc b d d̂ e f*, then *sicut incénsum* with *cd ég g*;
then in the verse *Elevátio* with *c d̂ g f̂ g a*; similarly *mánum*. As an antithesis to this we meet a rhythmic motive, generally in the lower part
of the range, first at the close of *(Dirigá)-tur* as *c d aa g*, in like manner
in the expanded *(tu)-o*, in the verse over *Elevátio f d cc a*, again in the
same word *f g ee d*, and finally over *meárum* with its diminished chord
d f dd b and the *b* which here serves as a leading tone, and which receives
its natural resolution in the *c* immediately following. The same relations
obtain at the conclusion, with *(vespertí)-num*.

The *corpus* of the Gradual has five members; the last, however, is
little more than a coda. At the end of the second and third phrases we
find a forward-urging *clivis*. The fourth member corresponds to the
first in its tendency to move in the lower part of the range.

In the verse we have an evident enhancement of the melody. One
might well think of Moses, who, praying on the mount with outstretched
arms, procured victory for the Israelites. He was not allowed to drop
his arms; similarly this present melody, although it sinks from time to
time, always strives upward again with energetic accents, till *meárum*
brings a relaxation of the tension. In the last phrase this upward tendency again becomes apparent twice. It is principally this which dif-
ferentiates it from the almost identical close of the Gradual on Laetare
Sunday. The entire melody of the verse has been adopted for that of
the feast of the Sacred Heart.

ALLELUIA VERSE (Ps. 104: 1)

1. *Confitemini Domino, et invocate nomen ejus*: 2. *annuntiate
inter gentes opera ejus.*

1. *Give glory to the Lord, and call
upon his name*; 2. *declare his deeds
among the gentiles.*

Most Alleluias reach their full development only in the verse. On
the third Sunday after Pentecost and on the present Sunday, however,
it takes place in the *jubilus*. And it is just today that the verse might
well have lent itself to a solemn denouement. Who can sufficiently
praise God's deeds of kindness! Formerly this song was sung in the
Easter procession. How often in the course of centuries has God shown

Himself the salvation of His people! Who could number the times He
did so, or thank Him sufficiently? How this song should resound throughout the entire earth, so that even the heathens *(gentes)* might hear it.
But there are also various degrees in thanksgiving and praise, with corresponding variance in form. Gratitude cannot always be jubilant, as
the *Confitémini* on Holy Saturday is, for instance, or the Gradual for
Easter Sunday. In the present instance the exultation confines itself to
the range of a seventh and several times repeats the tonic and the dominant, *a* and *c* respectively—if we are really dealing here with the
second mode. Perhaps it is fundamentally the key of F, with the conclusion taking a chord in terce position. If in place of the do clef we were
to substitute the fa clef on the same line, then the note *b♭* would occur
over *et (invocáte)* and over the closely allied *ó-(pera)*. To avoid having
the notation set too low, the piece was transposed a fifth higher.

The rendition should be cheerful and lively. In its first part the
Alleluia resembles that for the feast of the Dedication of a Church
(Adorábo). *Dómino* repeats the melody of *Allelúia*. There is very little
difference between the two phrases; both close the first part on *g*. *Annuntiáte* is well drawn out. The clives which occur at the close hark back
to a similar figure over *(oblivi)-scáris* in the Gradual for the thirteenth
Sunday after Pentecost. Throughout this chant the word-accents are
given due prominence. This melody has been accomodated to the verse
for the feast of St. John Capistran in Paschal time.

OFFERTORY (Ps. 137: 7)

1. *Si ambulavero in medio tri-bulationis,* 2. *vivificabis me, Domine:* 3. *et super iram inimicorum meorum extendes manum tuam,* 4. *et salvum me fecit dextera tua.*

1. *If I shall walk in the midst of tribulation,* 2. *Thou wilt quicken me, O Lord:* 3. *and Thou wilt stretch forth Thy hand against the wrath of mine enemies,* 4. *and thy right hand shall save me.*

If in the Introit the Lord said: "I am the salvation of the people:
in their every distress will I hear them," then the Offertory says Amen
to this assertion. And so it is: whatever be my distress and tribulation
in a world full of sensuality and allurements, at a time when many have
lost the true life of the soul, sanctifying grace, or have not even a concept of it, being entirely destitute of the "wedding garment"—among
so many who are estranged from Thee, Thou wilt yet save me, wilt
preserve the life of my soul, and in the end grant me life eternal. The
evening mood which pervades today's liturgy teaches us how we may
use this Offertory as the evening-prayer of life. At the last hour we shall

experience the most dire distress; then the rage *(ira)* of our foes will be increased, for they are well aware that all depends on these final moments. But we place all our trust in the holy Viaticum. That will be our defense against the evil one and will lead us safely to eternal bliss. And when the priest extends his hand over us in Extreme Unction, then God's hand rests protectingly upon us *(exténdes manum tuam)*, so that we may happily attain our eternal salvation.

Logically the first and second phrase belong together; they should therefore not be separated by too great a pause. Beginning and end of the two phrases are alike. In these two phrases, as well as in the later ones, we meet numerous fourths. These give life and buoyancy to the piece. To this must be added the strengthening of *(vivifi)-cá-(bis)*, which gives added impressiveness to our Amen. The third phrase has a beginning similar to the first, descending like it to low *d*. We are acquainted with the melody over *exténdes* from the Offertory of Easter Monday: *Surréxit*. In the spirit of Easter, confident of victory, the singer bursts out into a joyous strain over *manum tuam*. He knows what it means to have God's almighty hand resting upon him. *Tuam* calls for a continuation. The simple recitative *et salvum me* which follows, set as it is in the midst of a florid melody, has an especial solemn character and must not be sung too rapidly. Over *tua* the melody is to be divided into two bistrophas and a *clivis*, followed by an energetic *pressus*.

The same melody has been accommodated to a shorter text for the feast of St. Philip Neri.

COMMUNION (Ps. 118: 4, 5)

1. *Tu mandasti mandata tua custodiri nimis*: 2. *utinam dirigantur viae meae, ad custodiendas justificationes tuas.*

1. *Thou hast commanded thy commandments to be kept most diligently*: 2. *Oh, that my ways be directed to keep thy justifications.*

This song sets in on the dominant of the mode, thus emphasizing the first words: Thou hast given Thy commandments. Thou indeed hast a right to do this, for Thou art the Lord. But Thy commandments are the source of our joy and happiness. Would that we might ever realize this and ever walk faithfully along the way Thou hast marked out for us! Solemnity, even majesty, marks the beginning of the first phrase, and the quint with *cu-(stodíri)* emphasizes the same feeling. According to the annotated manuscripts the notes over *(ni)-mis* are to be given a broad rendition.

By the frequent repetition of *b♭* the second phrase is made tender, almost oppressively so, for the singer knows that he has not always directed his steps according to God's ordinances. It pains him to realize, that, like the men in today's Gospel, he has given more care to his fields and his business than to the invitation to the King's banquet. Bitterly he repents the fact that he has several times lost the wedding garment. Hence, filled with contrition and the consciousness of his own weakness, he asks for God's grace. In the spirit of the following Postcommunion he prays that the salutary effects of the Holy Eucharist may serve to free him from his evil inclinations, may renew him in Christ and make him imitate Christ, so that he may always cling to God's commandments. The second half of the third phrase has seconds exclusively. *Justificati-(ónes)* faithfully repeats the melody of *(cus)-todién-(das)*. All in all, it is a simple, humble prayer.

*   *   *   *

TWENTIETH SUNDAY AFTER PENTECOST

In the Epistle for today the Apostle gives us the guiding principles for all our work with ecclesiastical music: "Be ye filled with the Holy Spirit, speaking to yourselves in psalms and hymns, and spiritual canticles, singing and making melody in your hearts to the Lord: giving thanks always for all things, in the name of our Lord Jesus Christ, to God and the Father" (Eph. 5: 18–20).

INTROIT (Dan. 3: 31, 29, 35)

1. *Omnia quae fecisti nobis, Domine, in vero judicio fecisti,* 2. *quia peccavimus tibi, et mandatis tuis non obedivimus:* 3. *sed da gloriam nomini tuo,* 4. *et fac nobiscum secundum multitudinem misericordiae tuae.* Ps. *Beati immaculati in via:* * *qui ambulant in lege Domini.*

1. *All that thou hast done to us, O Lord, thou hast done in true judgment:* 2. *because we have sinned against thee and we have not obeyed thy commandments;* 3. *but give glory to thy name,* 4. *and deal with us according to the multitude of thy mercy.* Ps. *Blessed are the undefiled in the way:* * *who walk in the law of the Lord.*

It is rare that the preliminary prayers and the Introit accord, for in origin and development they are quite distinct from one another. On this Sunday, however, the agreement could scarcely be more manifest. At the foot of the altar the priest, bowing profoundly, prays: "I have sinned," while the choir sings: "We have sinned against Thee and have not obeyed Thy commandments." Thus prayed Azarias in the fiery furnace at Babylon, acknowledging his guilt together with that of his people. He solemnly confesses also that God is absolutely *just (in vero judício)* in punishing His sinful people with exile and all the hardships accompanying it. How much lamenting and murmuring would be stilled if we would contritely acknowledge our guilt and, like Daniel and the thief on the cross, humbly confess: We indeed suffer justly, for we receive the due reward for our deeds!

Large intervals and strong emphasis on the dominant characterize the peculiar style of the first phrase. It is as though the singer felt the mighty hand of the Lord. To a great extent this phrase sounds like the second in the Introit for the tenth Sunday after Pentecost.

The second phrase is more subdued. Only twice, in fact, does it reach the tenor: "We have sinned against thee and we have not obeyed thy commandments." In contrast to the *c* of the first phrase, *a*, a third below the dominant, here predominates.

The third phrase and the beginning of the fourth, on the contrary, exhibit great solemnity in the slowly ascending seconds, in the stress on the dominant, in the repetition of the same, and the similar melodic lines over *da glóriam* and *nómini*: "Give glory to Thy name." But how can any new splendor be added to the name of God? How can it gain in dignity? In this, simply, that God pities and forgives, that He pours upon us the full measure of His mercy. Hence it is that the Introit prays so solemnly, so fervently, so earnestly, especially with the words *et fac*. Similar sentiments are expressed in the preliminary prayers: "Show unto us, O Lord, Thy mercy, and grant us Thy salvation." In order to lessen the monotony of the neums over *secúndum multitúdinem* within the tetrachord *e–a*, it is well to stress the neums appearing over the word-accents. *Misericórdiae* is much more effective: a longing expectation of God's mercy. If the first part of the Introit spoke of a just God, the second part turns to a *merciful* God. Before the beginning of the fourth phrase the melody descends to low *d*. Thus is created a contrast, which makes the following phrase so much the more effective. (cf. p. 4).

Then the psalm-verse sings of the happiness attendant upon a spotless mode of life. To a certain extent such a life is a foretaste of the life to come, and this thought confers a special consecration and a solemn ring to our song of praise *(Da glóriam nómini tuo)*.

The syllables which carry the accent are higher in almost every instance than those immediately following; often also higher than the syllable which precedes the accented one.

GRADUAL

This melody was explained on the feast of Corpus Christi. Perhaps it is a remnant of a prayer at the *agapae* or love feasts, at which the early Christians were wont to assemble at the close of the liturgical celebration. It sighs after the future heavenly country and its present guarantee, the holy Eucharist. (*K. L.*).

ALLELUIA VERSE (Ps. 107: 2)

1. *Paratum cor meum, Deus, paratum cor meum*: 2. *cantabo et psallam tibi gloria mea.*

1. *My heart is ready, O Lord, my heart is ready*: 2. *I will sing, and will give praise to thee, my glory.*

Here we have an echo of the Epistle: "singing and making melody in your hearts to the Lord." The melody was explained on the fourth Sunday of Advent. With the present text the second *parátum*, in its repetition, receives a fine melodic augmentation. Sad to say, the number of those whose hearts are really so prepared is small. Even among those who have been called to sing in the house of God the heart often lags far behind the voice.

This thought ought to spur us on to praise God with our *whole* heart. With good reason we sing twice: "My heart is ready!" We do not sufficiently realize the fact that God is our glory, that He, the infinitely sublime God, lowers Himself to our level, lifts us out of the dust, and makes us partakers of His divine life. This is so great an honor that no one in the whole wide world could bestow the like upon us, a nobility no one but God could confer. Thus He becomes our glory, our pride; and the very thought should urge us to sing of Him and to praise His goodness with all our heart.

OFFERTORY (Ps. 136: 1)

1. *Super flumina Babylonis, 2. illic sedimus et flevimus, 3. dum recordaremur tui, Sion.*

1. *Upon the rivers of Babylon, 2. there we sat and wept, 3. when we remembered thee, O Sion.*

Babylon and Sion—what a contrast! There heathenism with all its abominations; here the site of the holy temple of God in all its glory, with its many songs and festivities. There exile, a strange country, poverty and want; here home with its loved ones. In that far country homesickness was always gnawing at one's heart: how could one play or sing the songs of the Lord?

But what is Babylon compared to the great Babylon of the Apocalypse, and what is Sion compared to the heavenly City. The earthly Babel with its coarseness, its filth, its passions, its seductions—and the heavenly Sion with its luminous beauty and purity, its peace, and its eternal Alleluia! He who is filled with a lively faith and has a deep understanding of all that Babel signifies, is seized with insatiable longing for the heavenly Sion. And especially now in late autumn, when the fading leaves fall from the trees, and when so much in nature is dying off, there wells up in the heart of the true child of God an intense yearning for the home beyond, where all is different, where there is eternal spring, eternal life, eternal love.

It is of this homesickness that our piece is singing. How beautifully have the two thoughts *flúmina Babylónis* and *Sion* at the beginning and at the end of the song been drawn out! And then this recurrent rise and fall of the melody, stretching out, as it were, toward eternal life, only to sink back again! Each of the three phrases reaches high *c*, but only in passing; it occurs only once in the middle phrase. The average pitch is *a*. No violence, no impassioned or explosive grief is expressed; only a very subdued wailing and weeping. Care must be taken that the tempo be not too slow. *Babylónis* sounds a bit like restrained rage. Over *illic* both neums must be prolonged. As if pressed down by pain, the motive over *sédimus* and *flévimus* sinks ever lower—*á b c a, ǵ a b♭a, f̂ g a g*. The closing cadence of *flévimus* continues that of *flúmina*. Over *recordarémur* (surely the appropriate spot!) the only high *pressus* occurs, testifying to the unemotional character of the piece in general. One might wish that *tui* were more pregnant with meaning. In its very simplicity, however, with the repetition of the same motive, this song succeeds in telling us much. It was in *Sion*, above all places, that the singer wished to pour forth his grief and his yearning. He repeats the neums of *dum recordarémur* and, proceeding in almost dreamlike fashion, his voice dies away as if it were stifled in tears. We who are now singing are still in a strange land, but we are allowed these songs of home, these echoes of the heavenly songs, for they are to us a source of consolation. We know that through Christ we have become citizens of heaven and that He will come again into our hearts as a new pledge of future glory. In a few moments He will appear before our eyes in the mystery of the Mass; and in the sacrificial banquet we are united with Him and with all heaven.

Babel sings and plays and shouts and dances, entirely oblivious of the heavenly Sion. But we want to belong to those who, homesick yet optimistic, are ever striving to reach the fatherland beyond.

COMMUNION (Ps. 118: 49, 50)

1. *Memento verbi tui servo tuo, Domine, in quo mihi spem dedisti;* 2. *haec me consolata est in humilitate mea.*

1. *Be thou mindful of thy word to thy servant, O Lord, in which thou hast given me hope:* 2. *this hath comforted me in my humiliation.*

In the Offertory there was a breath of *Meménto mori*. Here we dare to ask God to remember us, but we do it humbly and reservedly, in the manner in which the repentant thief on the cross spoke his *meménto*. It is a consolation for us to be allowed to pray thus. The three similar endings: *Dómine, dedísti, mea* reflect quiet and confidence. The turning of the *clivis* over *Domini* into a *pes* is necessitated by the low *d* which opens the following melody. Large ascending intervals would be disturbing; hence the melody avoids them. *Servo* with its descending fourth gives a pleasing development: second *a–g*, third *a–f*, fourth *g–d*. The accentuation of the dominant is the only evidence that the heart of the singer is really beating somewhat more rapidly. With its *b* and its *pressus*, the second phrase has about it something new, something reassuring, which soars above the entire preceding melodic line. It restricts itself to intervals of seconds. The half-step progressions toward the end agree admirably with the text. It is a humble prayer, one which encourages us to rely entirely on the grace of God.

To the official at Capharnaum the Saviour spoke the consoling words: "Go thy way, thy son liveth." And he fulfilled His promise. This ought to enkindle confidence in our hearts; a firm hope in Him must revive and strengthen our weary soul. God keeps His word! May the Word of God, the Word Incarnate, which has entered our hearts in Holy Communion, grant us grace and strength to observe His word and keep also the word which we have pledged to Him.

This piece well demonstrates how plainsong prefers to treat the principal word-accent lightly and briefly; thus *verbi tui servo* and *mihi*; this rule extends even to the secondary accent over *consoláta* (Mocquereau, *Nombre* II, 221).

For the rhythm of the first phrase cf. *N. Sch.* ,34.

*   *   *   *

TWENTY-FIRST SUNDAY AFTER PENTECOST

INTROIT (Esther 13: 9, 10, 11)

1. *In voluntate tua, Domine, universa sunt posita,* 2. *et non est qui possit resistere voluntati tuae:* 3. *tu enim fecisti omnia, caelum et terram, et universa quae caeli ambitu continentur:* 4. *Dominus univer-*

1. *All things are in thy will, O Lord,* 2. *and there is none to resist thy will:* 3. *for thou hast made all things, heaven and earth, and all things that are under the cope of heaven:* 4. *thou art the Lord of all.*

sorum tu es. Ps. Beati immaculati in   Ps. *Blessed are the undefiled in the*
via: * *qui ambulant in lege Domini.*   *way*: * *who walk in the law of the*
    Lord.

A fleeting glance at the melody shows that it attains to no great
heights. The piece moves below the dominant of the fourth mode, below
a, almost throughout. Not until the verse does the dominant play an
important role. But this, in turn, necessitates a lower pitch for the antiphon. An unmistakable gravity pervades the whole. A glance at nature
out in the open, no doubt, will awaken the same feeling. Late autumn
brings great changes: a multitude of beings vibrant with life must perish;
violent gusts of wind sweep the withered leaves from the trees; many a
flower has been vanquished by the frost and droops its head as if tired
of life. Everywhere the picture of change, of death. One alone remains
immutable, immortal, eternal: the God of peace. All things are in His
hand; by His will are they directed and governed.

Thoughts such as these help to give us some inkling of the meaning of the melody. This chant wished to sing of nothing but repose, reminding us of the sea which, although it can rage and foam and toss
today is calm and placid, hardly disturbed by a ripple.

The first phrase really has *f* for its dominant, like the Introits for
the second Sunday of Lent, for Easter, and for the second Sunday after
Easter. The first phrase confines itself to a third. Very slowly the melody
begins to increase. The range of the first phrase is *c–g*, of the second
d–a, of the third and fourth *c–a*; there is, therefore, some development
in the melody. The accented syllables with few exceptions carry a *pes*
or an expansion of the *pes*. But there are various degrees of accentuation
according as the first note of the *pes* is of the same pitch as the preceding
one *(voluntáti* in the second phrase*)*, a second lower *(voluntáte tua* in th
first phrase*)*, a second higher *(*the first *univérsa)*, or a third higher *(*the
second *univérsa)*. Here, as in *possit*, the *pes* encompasses a third. *Non*
is still more strongly accented. No one can long resist the divine will
Many indeed now shout out their "I will not serve"; they wish to dis
regard the admonition of the Apostle in today's Lesson: "Take unto
you the armor of God, that you may be able to resist *(resístere)* in th
evil day, and to stand in all things perfect." Against many such St
Stephen's complaint might well be directed: "You always resist the Hol
Ghost." But when the Lord will come at the last day for the universal
judgment, then this *non* will receive an absolute value; no longer will
anyone dare to offer any resistance. Such thoughts are suggested by the
liturgical year which is now rapidly coming to its close.

The ascending fourth *d–g* over *non* is balanced by the descending
a–e over *possit*. Variation in the melody is secured by this *e*; any othe

interval would tire. The second phrase begins on the low *d* and is joined with the preceding by means of the ascending *e f*.

The third phrase gives the reason why God can demand perfect obedience. Everything that the heavens and the earth contain owes its existence to His almighty will alone. *Omnia* and *ámbit* have a similar ring; *caelum et terra* and *univérsa* are practically identical, for they express related thoughts. In the rendition these passages must follow rapidly one upon another with a strong, though not exaggerated, emphasis on the word-accent. The formula at the end of *continéntur* always stands over the final syllable of a word (compare *ómnibus* in the Introit for the second Sunday in Lent; and *Israel, mihi, sibi* in the Tract for Passion Sunday, where the formula is still more developed).

Special solemnity should characterize the final phrase with its reverent close: *Dóminus universórum tu es*. Care must be taken that the tempo be not too slow. Strangely enough, the *climacus* repeats the same notes, *g f e*, while similar passages, for example, the ending of the Introit for the second Sunday of Lent, have the much more pleasing formula *á g f ǵ f e e*.

In the psalm-verse the good fortune of those is praised who dispose their entire lives according to the holy will of God. Thus was rewarded the fidelity of Mardochai, whose prayer is used as the antiphon of to-day's Introit. God averted from him and from his people the evil which Aman contemplated, and made them to see days of gladness.

GRADUAL (Ps. 89: 1. 2)

1. *Domine, refugium factus es nobis,* 2. *a generatione et progenie.* ℣. 1. *Priusquam montes* 2. *fierent, aut formaretur terra et orbis;* 3. *a saeculo,* 4. *et in saeculum tu es Deus.*

1. *Lord, thou hast been our refuge,* 2. *from generation to generation.* ℣. 1. *Before the mountains* 2. *were made or the earth and the world was formed;* 3. *from eternity* 4. *and to eternity thou art God.*

Perhpas someone is tempted to see tone-painting in the florid melody over *montes*—the rising mountains, the depressed valleys, and finally the highest peaks. In Graduals, however, one must be extremely careful about making pronouncements of this kind, and more especially here, for our present chant is entirely typical; a melody frequently used and here adopted note for note. It was explained on the first Sunday of Lent.

The Gradual-verse belongs to that small number of pieces in which the phrasing is not entirely satisfactory, since the divisions of the text and the melody do not correspond. The words *Priúsquam montes fierent* belong together, but the melody makes an extended cadence over *montes* and begins a new melodic part with *fíerent*. Farther down one feels instinctively that, after the large cadence over *terra*, *et orbis* limps along without much meaning. As a matter of fact, all Graduals of this type begin a new division with the bistropha which is here placed over *et*. In *Paléographie musicale* (II, 43) the following musical division is indicated: *Priúsquam montes | fíerent aut formarétur terra et orbis*; it places the large cadence, which the Vatican Gradual sets over *terra*, on the word *orbis*. Codices 339 of St. Gall's and 121 of Einsiedeln have the same phrasing as the Vatican Gradual.

One easily notes the relation between the Gradual and the preceding Epistle. In the latter St. Paul writes to the Ephesians concerning our struggle against the deceits of the devil, who comes armed with fiery darts. Where shall we find a shelter to protect ourselves? The Gradual presents uncounted multitudes to our gaze: generations upon generations come before God's throne as if to offer thanks, and they make this profession: "Thou, O Lord, hast become our shelter, our place of refuge. Under Thy protection we were shielded against all the enemies' thrusts. For who could have harmed us, seeing that Thou wast for us? Thou art the eternal God, who wast before the hills were made, and unto all ages is Thy might."

ALLELUIA VERSE (Ps. 113: 1)

1. *In exitu Israel de Aegypto*, 2. *domus Jacob de populo barbaro.*

1. *When Israel went out of Egypt*, 2. *the house of Jacob from a barbarous people.*

As has already been mentioned in the introduction, no inner relationship exists between the Graduals and the Alleluia-verses. On the present Sunday, however, one may be established. The Gradual treats of God's benign dealings with *all* peoples, while the Alleluia speaks of His loving care for *one* nation. That Israel was allowed to depart from Egypt, from the nation under whose dominion it had to suffer terribly; that the opposition of a Pharaoh (cf. the Introit) was broken; and, to supplement the thought from the second verse of the psalm, that it could enter the Promised Land—all this was the ordinance of God. Formerly this song was sung in the procession of thanksgiving which each day in Easter Week led the neophytes to the baptismal font. There they had been freed from the Egypt of unbelief and darkness and from the slavery of the prince of this world, and had been led into the Promised Land of the Church, whose means of grace offer infinitely more than the land flowing with milk and honey. But the procession itself also has a symbolic meaning. It represents the departure from this world of ours and the entrance into the heavenly Jerusalem. For this reason Psalm 113, the first verse of which is here employed, is sung in some localities at funerals. This eschatological conception fits extremely well to the thoughts which permeate the close of the liturgical year.

Psalm 113, from which this verse is taken, was among those said at the eating of the Paschal lamb, which Christ Himself therefore sang with His Apostles at the Last Supper before His *éxitus*, before His departure from this earth.

Cardinal Schuster (*The Sacramentary*, III, 180) comments strikingly on the words *de pópulo bárbaro*: "As far as purely exterior culture is concerned, the Egyptians were far in advance of the Jews. And yet the subjects of the Pharaohs are called a barbarous people by the Scriptures. For material and artistic progress is not the only criterion of true culture, but rather spiritual life and spiritual development. From this standpoint the Israelites far surpassed the most famous nations of antiquity and thereby proved that their faith was supernatural."

The melody over the word *allelúia* sounds as if it might have been borrowed from the fourth mode. As a matter of fact, the Alleluia *Amávit eum* from the Mass for a Doctor has almost an identical tone-sequence.

Twice more in the *jubilus* we meet the *pressus dd c*; it confers a strong accent. In every instance, however, it is introduced differently, thus avoiding monotony. The *jubilus* has two parts, the first of which has three subdivisions: the fourth in subdivision b is rounded out by means of connecting notes in b[1]; in c the motive thus produced appears a second higher. We shall have to consider the repetition of *d ff* an augmentation rather than an echo.

Neither *allelúia* nor its verse is conspicuous for any particular ardor. But a lively tempo is to be recommended, for we are singing a song of thanksgiving. Very striking is the development over *ex Aegýpto* with a fifth on the insignificant *ex* and then the descending fourth. We are to consider, it seems, what the words "out of Egypt" really signify. The chord of resolution over *pópulo* has a joyous ring.

OFFERTORY (Job 1)

1. *Vir erat in terra nomine Job,* 2. *simplex et rectus, ac timens Deum*: 3. *quem Satan petiit, ut tentaret*: 4. *et data est ei potestas a Domino in facultate et in carne ejus*: 5. *perdiditque omnem substantiam ipsius, et filios*: 6. *car-*

1. *There was a man in the land whose name was Job,* 2. *simple and upright, and fearing God*: 3. *whom Satan sought that he might tempt*: 4 *and power was given him from the Lord over his possessions and his flesh*: 5. *and he destroyed all*

nem quoque ejus gravi ulcere vul-   *his substance and his children: 6.*
neravit.   *and wounded his flesh also with a*
     grievous ulcer.

With its purposely restricted range, this piece expresses heartfelt sympathy for the patient Job. This compsasion must be all the more noble, since here are portrayed the sufferings of a man who was "simple and upright, and fearing God," who really had not deserved his misfortunes personally, and who stands before us exhibiting an imcomparable greatness of soul. When we regard this melody we can understand why the ancients called the second mode elegiac and used it extensively in the antiphons of the Office of the Dead.

The Vatican Gradual divides this piece into six phrases, of which the first, third, and fifth begin with almost the same motive. The similar passages over *simplex* and *rectus* serve to emphasize the same thought. This similarity holds good of *facultáte* and *et in carne* further on. In the Introit we were able to point out a like procedure. With *quem Satan* the melody takes on a new and tenser turn, even though the formula over *tentáret,* which recurs over *fílios,* over *vulnerávit,* and in an expanded form over *Dómino,* again relaxes the tension somewhat. So much more effective is the fourth phrase, *et data,* in whose first half high *d* plays the role of dominant. The twofold division in *facultáte* and *et in carne* is more fully developed in the fifth and sixth phrases. A deep melancholy is manifested in the final phrase with its prominent accents, its repetition of the same motive $\overset{\frown}{cc}$ *b a g a,* which was heard over *ut* in the third phrase.

The piece has been transposed by a fifth, most probably only for practical reasons, in order to render ledger lines unnecessary.

At the present time we have just this one verse. In the Antiphonary of St. Gregory several more verses follow, in which the dramatic element becomes almost passionate. This is apparent even exteriorly from the frequent textual repetitions, which are otherwise quite rare in plainsong. The last verse, a vehement cry for the joy which every human heart demands, nine times repeats the words *ut vídeam bona* (cf. Wagner, I, 110, and especially III, 430 f.).

Job is a figure of Christ, and his sufferings are a type of Christ's sufferings. For this reason the Book of Job was read during Holy Week. Even on his couch of suffering Job protests his innocence, but his friends do not believe him and assert that his sins are the cause of this awful visitation of God's justice, which afflicted him so much that he had to cry out in his distress. In the same manner Christ, who is Holiness itself, suffers for our sins, which He took upon Himself in merciful love. He too is jeered at in His agony. If with this Offertory we enter the inner circle of the sacrificial action in which Christ renews the sacrifice of the cross upon the altar, then we may not entirely forget the sufferings which the delicate and tender body of Christ and the soul of "the most beautiful of the children of men" had to undergo upon the cross. We shall again draw new strength and courage from holy Mass in order to bear all our sufferings and trials with perfect resignation to God's will.

COMMUNION (Ps. 118: 81, 84, 86)

1. *In salutari tuo anima mea, et in verbum tuum speravi*: 2. *quando facies de persequentibus me judicium?* 3. *iniqui persecuti sunt me, adjuva me, Domine Deus meus.*

1. *My soul is in thy salvation and in thy word have I hoped*: 2. *when wilt thou execute judgment on them that persecute me?* 3. *the wicked have perscuted me: help me, O Lord my God.*

The phrase has a quiet melody. It is not so expressive of longing and yearning as of childlike confidence which places all things in the hands of God. One would hardly suspect, from the mood of this phrase, that a storm, such as the second and third phrases speak of, can still disturb the soul. The inception on the dominant *a* over *quando* and the tarrying on this note are like an urgent knocking at the door of mercy. How often has this *quando*, "when"—"when, O Lord, will our deliverance come?"—risen in fervent pleading to heaven! We have here an instance in which an extremely common form, the recitation on a single note, becomes the means of powerful expression, for all the other words of this text touch the dominant only transiently, while over *quando* it receives particular stress. Thus the second phrase and the still more climactic third phrase sound like the cry of a hunted soul which finds shelter only with its Lord and God.

In the third phrase, first half, we find the formula of psalmody proper to the Introit-verses of the first mode. And it is precisely here that the piece reaches its climax.

It seems that the similar closes of the phrases over *sperávi, judícium*, and *meus* are to breathe calm into the turbulent soul. The quilisma over *(judí)-ci-(um)* is very striking.

We are making this a Communion song; for now the "salvation of God" is come to us, and we may place all our trust in the incarnate Word of God now dwelling within us. No matter how long the time of probation and trial, how numerous or unjust our aggressors may be, the Lord will come on His great day to judge them all.

*   *   *   *

TWENTY-SECOND SUNDAY AFTER PENTECOST

INTROIT (Ps. 129: 3, 4)

1. *Si iniquitates observaveris Domine, Domine quis sustinebit?* 2. *quia apud te propitiatio est, Deus Israel.* Ps. *De profundis clamavi ad te Domine:* * *Domine exaudi vocem meam.*

1. *If thou shalt observe iniquities, O Lord, Lord, who shall endure it?* 2. *for with thee is propitiation, O God of Israel.* Ps. *From the depths I have cried to thee, O Lord:* * *Lord, hear my voice.*

How difficult we find it to forgive and forget! What efforts it costs us to condone a wrong, and to bear no malice when a request for forgiveness is made! What if God were to treat us in this manner! What if He would immediately mete out punishment after every sin? Who would be able to stand it? God indeed looks upon *(observáveris)* our sins and weighs them in the balance of His holiness and justice, but His mercy prevents His justice from punishing sin on the instant and also from punishing a repented sin in the manner it deserves. Thus also this Introit, like that of last Sunday, shows us God's absolute greatness, but here it is pictured in the pleasing light of comprehending love that is both merciful and forgiving.

The divisions of the melody are evident enough. To the soaring ascent of the first phrase, a second, filled with rest and relaxation, answers. All three members of the first phrase close on the half tone *b c*. *Dómine* here carries the same melody as in the Introit for the twentieth Sunday after Pentecost, with this difference that there it closes with *c b*, instead of with *b c* as in the present melody. There the second phrase begins with a higher note; here on a lower. The very same reason holds for the close of *sustinébit*. Here again the following phrase sets in a third lower. It might also be pointed out that we have to do with a question, and that the tension contained in a question naturally evolves itself in an ascending melodic movement. If we could have had our own way about it, we should perhaps have given more prominence to the significant *quis* than is done here. If the first half of the phrase has *c* for its dominant, then the second receives special force from its dominant *d*. Care must be taken that the recitation be not too precipitous on this *d*; in fact, a moderate *martellato* might be recommended. It seems as if a trembling before God's holiness pervades the melody.

The second phrase, however, brings rest. It never extends beyond *c* and has only minor thirds and seconds in the beginning. Over the accented syllable of *propitiátio* the melody becomes an expression of fervent thanks; it comes to full bloom in the more florid melismas over the word *Deus*. Only with God can we find such judgment and forgiveness. The final groups of neums are frequently seen at the close of the Introits of the third mode (cf. the Introit for the fifth Sunday after Easter and that for the tenth after Pentecost). The last two groups of neums represent a rhythmically united and inseparable whole; they always occur over the two final syllables. That explains the peculiar treatment accorded *Israel*. All in all, this Introit well agrees with the spirit of All Souls' Day and is very fitting at the end of the liturgical year.

With the same confidence with which we sing the Introit we are also to sing the psalm-verse. And though I should be sunk in the abyss of utter need and utter helplessness, still shall I cry to Thee, O God, and Thou wilt not despise my humble supplication.

The Introit also teaches us to look with humble confidence to that great day, mentioned twice in today's Epistle, when Christ Jesus will reappear on earth.

GRADUAL (Ps. 132: 1, 2)

1. *Ecce quam bonum, et quam jucundum habitare fratres in unum!* ℣. 1. *Sicut unguentum in capite,* 2. *quod descendit in barbam,* 3. *barbam Aaron.*

1. *Behold how good and how pleasant it is for brethren to dwell together in unity.* ℣. 1. *It is like the precious ointment of the head,* 2. *that ran down the beard,* 3. *the beard of Aaron.*

The Epistle shows with what "tender love" the Apostle regarded the community at Philippi, what heartfelt wishes for this community inspired him—an ideal picture of shepherd and flock. Would that it were so everywhere! Would that all who congregate in the churches on Sundays were bound together spiritually in an enduring bond! This is the happy condition which the Gradual tries to portray.

Ecce at the beginning of the piece is full of meaning; the melody has something important to tell us. *Habitáre* with its quint is just as pregnant. In this phrase, *a* is a sort of tonic supporting the ascending melody. *Unum* receives prominence from its *pressus*; the two subsequent notes, *a g*, are to be sung broadly according to the annotated manuscripts. The closing melisma with the rhythm *é f d f̂ a ǵ a g e f̂ g* is an abbreviation of the ornate formula which ends the first part of the Gradual on the seventeenth Sunday after Pentecost. This first part has also been adopted as the Gradual for the vigil of the feast of the Immaculate Conception.

Florid melismas and a rising melodic line characterize the verse. On All Saints' Day we meet the neums which occur here over *(unguént)-*

tum over *(iniquirén)-tes.* The coda of *(cápi)-te* belongs to the wandering melismas and occurs in almost all modes in the form of a cadence. The ornate melody over *(Aa)-ron* frequently closes Graduals (compare *Timéte* for All Saints' Day and *Dómine praevenísti* for the feast St. of Joseph and in the Common of Abbots). A typical Alleluia melody of the third mode, illustrated on the twentieth Sunday after Pentecost, has the same ending.

The melody of the verse is in no way tone-painting; it is almost too imposing for the text which it accompanies; it disregards the typical in the text; it practically disregards Aaron himself, the one on whom the balsam flowed from beard to garment on the day of his consecration. It aims primarily at portraying the blessings of the Communion of Saints, the unity of the Church, the streams of grace and holiness and glory which flow from the mystic Head, Christ, in loving generosity and with unutterable sweetness upon all His members.

In the ancient manuscript this melody is assigned to the feast of the martyrs John and Paul (June 26); it was also sung—according to Codex 121 of Einsiedeln—in a votive high Mass *De Caritáte*: for Charity.

ALLELUIA VERSE (Ps. 113: 11)

1. *Qui timent Dominum, sperent in eo*: 2. *adjutor et protector eorum est.*

1. *They that fear the Lord, let them hope in him*: 2. *he is their helper and protector.*

Compare the melody of the Alleluia-verse for the sixteenth Sunday after Pentecost with that of today. Without doubt we should have given melodic preponderance to the second phrase of our present text. The melody does not sound like an exhortation, but speaks rather of a comforting sense of security under the protecting hand of God.

St. Paul opened the Epistle with the words: "We are confident in the Lord Jesus, that He who hath begun a good work in you will perfect it unto the day of Christ Jesus." The verse generalizes this same thought. If the fear of God brings forth the same fruits as it did with the Philippians; if it leads to this, that "charity may more and more abound in knowledge and in all understanding"; if one is "sincere and without offense unto the day of Christ," filled with the fear of the Lord—then this fear serves "unto the glory and praise of God," then there is good reason for the confidence which regards God as the indefatigable Helper and universal Protector unto the day of the coming of Christ.

OFFERTORY (Esther 14: 12, 13)

1. *Recordare mei, Domine, omni potentatui dominans*: 2. *da ser-*

1. *Remember me, O Lord, thou who rulest above all power*: 2. *and*

monem rectum in os meum, ut pla-
ceant verba mea 3. in conspectu
principis.

give a well-ordered speech in my
mouth, that my words may be
pleasing 3. in the sight of the
prince.

Everything, her own welfare as well as that of her people, depended on the audience which Esther was to have with the king; of this she was well aware. For this reason she turned in fervent prayer to Him who exercises dominion over all rulers, who knows also how to direct the heart of kings according to His own will. The melody emphasizes the words *Recordáre* and still more *Dómine.* Then it lingers on *g* with stately solemnity, here again stressing God's immensity and majesty. This first phrase, as well as the first half of the second, which repeats motives taken from the second part of the first phrase, moves quite sedately. Now, however, the unrest in Esther's heart can no longer be concealed. "O Lord, I rely entirely upon Thee and upon Thy wisdom. Place the right words on my lips that I may find favor." These words are brought out with a vivacity that is almost dramatic. *(Plá)-ceant* repeats the motive of *me-(um)*, but this renders the petition all the more impressive. The melodic finale is composed of two words. Over *conspéctu*, however, the melody is drawn out indefinitely. Such drawing out comes as a surprise at the end of an Offertory which has this florid closing melisma as its most prominent feature, and especially since there seems to be practically no development of the melody at hand. The melisma has the following grouping: a b a c d(= ½b). Here there is need for clear division, correct accent, and dynamic shading. In group a, a *torculus* with an apostropha is to be sung, then a *torculus* and a tristropha. As far as possible, *f* ought to recede in favor of the other notes. In groups b and d, however, when the note *f* occurs with the *pressus*, it is to be stressed. In c, the note *g* may receive an accent. In d, the growth of the intervals —third, fourth, fifth—demands an increase in volume. Perhaps we may consider this somewhat strange passage as a repeated impulse to self-encouragement, for the interview at the palace, and a diminution of energy, for purposeful reflection, until in the final member with its *pressus* and growing intervals, the *clivis ǵ f* and the *podatus f g* (both of which are to be well accented) definitely bring back the feeling of full determination.

Now Esther is the Church. She acts as our mediatrix. With her and in her Christ, who lives forever, prays, in order to intercede for us in the holy Sacrifice of the Mass. He knows which word finds favor in the Father's sight; for He Himself is the Word of the Father, that most beloved Son in whom the Father is well pleased.

We singers of the Church's chants, however, shall cry out: Give me to sing worthily, O Lord! The words which we pronounce are such as can please Thee, for they are mostly Thy words, words which Thou hast spoken or inspired. But also our melodies must ring true if they are to please Thee. And they will have the correct ring if we but conform our lives to that which we say with our lips.

COMMUNION (Ps. 16: 6)

1. *Ego clamavi, quoniam exaudisti me Deus: 2. inclina aurem tuam, et exaudi verba mea.*

1. *I have cried, for thou, O God, hast heard me; 2. Oh, incline thine ear, unto me and graciously hear my words.*

In the first phrase the singer gratefully acknowledges that as often as he called upon God he found relief. The descending melody over *clamávi* sounds like the confession of one's own helplessness and insufficiency. So much the more surely and convincingly does it soar up over *quóniam*, using the motive of *ego: f̂ g, ǵ a, g á b, b̂b c, á d d,* with a slight bending back of the melodic curve. The melody should therefore be rendered accordingly. Now follows the almost turbulent petition, in which the melody soars a third above the dominant of the eighth mode: "Oh, incline also today Thine ear to me and graciously hear my prayer. Behold, I now bear Thy beloved Son in my heart. I pray in His name, in union with Him, and He intercedes for me. Do Thou hear Him!" On *exaudísti* there is an ascending fourth, *a–d*, and over *exáudi* a descending fourth, *d–a*.

If a song is supposed to be natural, direct, alive, true, and warm, then this song meets all the requirements. It is, therefore, hard to understand why this expressive melody was appropriated for the text used on the feast of the Holy Shroud (celebrated in some places on the Friday after the second Sunday of Lent): "Joseph buying fine linen, and taking him down, wrapped him up in the fine linen."

* * * *

TWENTY-THIRD SUNDAY AFTER PENTECOST

INTROIT (Jer. 29: 11, 12, 14)

1. *Dicit Dominus: Ego cogito cogitationes pacis, et non afflictionis:*

1. *The Lord saith: I think thoughts of peace, and not of affliction: 2.*

2. *invocabitis me, et ego exaudiam vos:* 3. *et reducam captivitatem vestram de cunctis locis.* Ps. *Benedixisti Domine terram tuam:* * *avertisti captivitatem Jacob.*

You shall call upon me, and I will hear you: 3. *and I will bring back your captivity from all places.* Ps. *Lord, thou hast blessed thy land:* * *thou hast turned away the captivity of Jacob.*

The words of today's Introit are an excerpt from the letter which the Prophet Jeremias wrote at God's behest to the captive Jews at Babylon. They must have been a soothing balm for those tired and wounded hearts. God had experienced untold infidelities and offenses at the hands of His chosen people, and yet He thinks thoughts of peace and not of affliction. He still promises to hear their prayers, still promises to bring them back from their captivity into the Promised Land.

We are not yet in the Promised Land. The deathlike picture of all nature in this bleak November vividly brings the fact home to us. We know it also from the affliction of heart which frequently weighs more heavily upon us than captivity: we are exiles, living in that state of flux called time. Suddenly a word strikes our ear, enters our heart; a word not spoken by man, for men are powerless: it is the Lord, and He speaks of *peace.* He pronounced this word when He sent His beloved Son upon earth; He published it by the mouth of an angel on Christmas night. And how often Christ the Saviour uttered His *Pax vobis!* He is still uttering it today, and suiting the action to the word.

Majesty marks the opening of the melody; the theme is blessed peace. Over *cogitatió-(nes)* the motive of the beginning is repeated, followed by the bright major chord; then its tones sink again, sweetly, blissfully, like rays of sunshine into our heart. God thinks thoughts of peace. Would that we, too, might always think them! But how often we fail to recognize what serves unto our peace, and thus force the Lord to discipline us *(afflictiónis)*, until, made homesick once more by our desolation of soul or by some external affliction, we transfer our affection and longing to Him who alone can be our peace, our happiness. The cadence over *afflictiónis* is the same as that which is repeated twice in the Introit *Réquiem.* It places before him who is conversant with plainsong the thought of those still awaiting the full peace of the Lord in purgatory. All the melodic pauses and incisions in this first phrase fall on the note *f.* The melody loses somewhat in variety thereby, but it preserves the quiet feeling which is proper to this phrase. This phrase, moreover, towers far above the other two: its text is longer, its range is more extended, its neums are more ornate. The usual thing in chant, however, is to have the phrases more nearly in climactic order.

The second phrase is restricted to a fifth. A contrast is formed by the *b* in the first phrase and *b♭* in the second. There is a certain unrest in *invocábitis* ("you shall call upon me") which soon is eased by the dominant-like fivefold *b♭* which seems to say: Be comforted, the Lord will grant your prayer; you have, it is true, often forgotten Him, have despised and deserted Him, but He thinks only of your peace.

In the third phrase, with its range of an octave, the tonic *f* plays a prominent part. Perhaps this is to indicate the oppression of captivity, just as is done with the same word in the Offertory for the third Sunday of Advent by lingering on the dominant. In the second half of the phrase, however, *de cunctis* rises with such firm assurance that neither men nor circumstances can weaken it. Even to those who have gone farthest astray, the road to their fatherland, to reconciliation, to peace, will not be closed. Indeed, the Lord Himself proffers His guiding and protecting hand *(redúcam)*; He Himself wishes to lead them home (cf. Reck, II 378). Happy he who grasps this hand!

First the Lord says: "I will hear; I will bring back." With the abandon of faith the congregation immediately responds with words which assume that the promise is already fulfilled: "Lord, Thou hast blessed the land: Thou hast turned away the captivity of Jacob." The church into which we are now filing is already heaven for the community; the processional entrance itself becomes in a certain sense an anticipation of the procession of the just, when, after the Last Day, they will follow Christ into full glory. The house of God, into which we enter now for the celebration of the sacred Mysteries, is heaven upon earth. We are coming closer to the Parousia: though it is still sacramentally veiled, it is already pre-realized in the Eucharist *(Jahrbuch fuer Liturgiewissenschaft,* IV, 148 f.).

This is the Lord's promise: "I will hear; I will bring back." And in the regions of bliss—for it is November, the month of All Saints—thousands of the blessed make joyous melody, because He has led them to eternal peace, to freedom, and to the glory of the children of God.

GRADUAL (Ps. 43: 8, 9)

1. *Liberasti nos, Domine, ex affligentibus nos:* 2. *et eos qui nos oderunt, confudisti.* ℣. 1. *In Deo laudabimur tota die,* 2. *et nomini tuo confitebimur in saecula.*

1. *Thou hast delivered us, O Lord, from them that afflict us:* 2. *and hast put them to shame that hate us.* ℣. 1. *In God we will glory all the day,* 2. *and in thy name we will give praise for ever.*

In the Epistle we heard the words: "But our conversation is in heaven; from whence also we look for the Saviour, our Lord Jesus Christ, who will reform the body of our lowness, made like to the body of His glory." With unhesitating faith, as if this were already effected, Holy Church sings in the Gradual a spirited song of freedom and thanksgiving. All those who opposed and hated her have fallen. Even our bodies, which were the source of untold miseries, may now, in recompense for renunication and suffering and mortification, expectantly look forward to the transfiguration of Christ. If we read in the same Epistle of the enemies of Christ, that their glory is in their shame, then God is the pride and glory of His children; Him will they praise for all eternity.

The two phrases of the *corpus* of the Gradual place the activity of God at the beginning and at the close: *Liberásti—confudísti*. Those who afflict and hate are in the center. In both phrases the psalmodic construction of the melody with intonation, recitation on *c*, a sort of middle cadence with its close on the dominant *d* or the mediant *b* respectively, and final cadence on the tonic, is still recognizable. The formula over the first *nos* recurs in the verse over *(tu)-o*, while the neums over *confú-(disti)* remind us of those over *(Dómi)-ne*. The ending over *(confu)-dísti* employs a motive frequently heard in Graduals of the fifth mode. Compare the passage *terra* in the Gradual for the third Mass for Christmas. Here the motive sets in on *g*, but has instead of the half tone *c b* (in the fifth mode) the full tone *d c*.

The verse has the same florid melisma over *Deo* as the Gradual-verse for the third Sunday of Advent (q.v.). Rightly does *laudábimur tota die* mark the climax of the piece. The second part of the verse is comparatively simple and quiet, the chant being almost syllabic. The motive over *confitébimur* is repeated over *in saecula*. We find the same closing melisma on the Sunday within the octave of Epiphany.

ALLELUIA VERSE (Ps. 129: 1, 2)

1. *De profundis clamavi ad te, Domine: Domine exaudi vocem meam.*

1. *From the depths I have cried to thee, O Lord, Lord, hear my voice.*

The words *Allelúia* and *De profúndis* and *Dómine* of the verse have the intonation of the ornate Introit-psalmody as their model. Consequently there is hardly any justification for speaking of tone-painting with the words *De profúndis* in spite of the upward movement. Its form a b b b^1 c c^1 resembles that of the Alleluia for the Sunday after Christ's ascension. In b^1, however, the *pressus* does not occur on *e*, but on *c*. The melody of the verse has two independent members, of which each has an intonation, a sort of middle cadence, and a closing cadence. *Exáudi* is an enhanced form of the supplicating *clamávi*. It was sung in the same spirit on the seventeenth Sunday after Pentecost; the Alleluia-verse for the eleventh Sunday likewise bears considerable resemblance to our present one.

If we say that today's Gradual is sung by the choir of the blessed, by the Church triumphant, then the Alleluia with its verse is sung by the Church militant and the Church suffering. We have not yet reached the goal of perfect liberty. Many things handicap us. And a great many children of the Church have drawn far away from God. But no abyss is so deep that God's merciful love cannot reach down to its very bottom. God will stretch forth His helping hand to everyone who proves that he has at least some good will. For He heals those who have been afflicted for many years, as the Gospel says; even the dead He brings back to life.

There is nothing oppressive about the melody; in fact, there is a certain throb and swing in it. As to the text, we must think not so much of the Office of the Dead as rather of one of the songs which the Jews sang on their pilgrimage to Jerusalem. And for our dear departed we have but one wish: that they may complete their pilgrimage to the heavenly Jerusalem as soon as possible.

OFFERTORY (Ps. 129: 1, 2)

1. *De profundis clamavi ad te, Domine*: 2. *Domine exaudi oratio-nem meam*: 3. *de profundis clamavi ad te, Domine.*

1. *From the depths I have cried out to thee, O Lord*: 2. *Lord, hear my prayer*: 3. *from the depths I have cried to thee, O Lord.*

The Offertory has almost the same text as the Alleluia-verse; here, however, we have the word *oratiónem* instead of *vocem*. A much more earnest tone pervades the melody. Out of the depths the melodic line comes forth, almost as in the Offertory for the first Sunday of Advent. As in the former melody, so here, too, it strives upward. But repeatedly it sinks back to the tonic, on which all the pauses are made, and even below it. There is something almost painful in *te* with its *b*, which is generally avoided in Offertories of the second mode. In the ancient annotated manuscripts each note over *clamávi*, with the exception of the quilisma, carries a broad marking. It is a cry coming from a heart burdened with grief. In the second phrase the melody twice begins with the dominant and rises above it. As in the Alleluia so here, too, the climax occurs on the word *exáudi*. In both pieces *clamávi* has a similar melody. *(Ex)-áudi* repeats the form of *Dómine*; the florid *meam* is characteristic of Offertories. To the ascending motive over *De profundis* the descending *f d c a* at the end of *meam* comes as an answer; it then bends upward to *c c d* to prepare for the low beginning of the third phrase, which is an exact repetition of the first. Formerly the two following verses of Psalm 129 *(Fiant aures tuae* and *Si iniquitátes)* were also sung with this Offertory; between each pair were interpolated the words *De profúndis clamávi at te, Domine,* which also brought the whole to a close. These verses only tended to increase the earnestness of the composition.

With the Gospel as a background (the healing of the woman troubled with an issue of blood and the awakening of the daughter of Jairus) our cry ascends to the Lord. In a life filled with sickness, disease, lamentation for the dead, our yearning for perfect redemption and absolute freedom from all species of misery is most intense. This longing comes to the fore in spite of all the self-denial and willing submission we may have. It will accompany our every good deed. I am still wandering in the depths; my life is spent in a desert where tears and sorrows are my lot. But some day I shall be quiet and happy, and like the healed woman and the child of Capharnaum brought back to life, I shall thank the Saviour, and I shall live on with all the others who have arisen.

COMMUNION (Mark 11: 24)

1. *Amen dico vobis: quidquid orantes petitis, credite quia accipietis, et fiet vobis.*

1. *Amen I say to you: Whatsoever you ask when you pray, believe that you shall receive, and it shall be done to you.*

In the two half-phrases which constitute this song, the first part in both instances extends above the range of the second part. Each inception, if we disregard the introductory formula, is on the dominant: *quidquid, crédite, et*; this gives the piece an added feeling of assurance. The endings show a descending line: *vobis=a, pétitis=g, accipiétis=f vobis=ed.* It is to be noted that the accented syllables are always higher than the succeeding syllables, and generally carry several notes. *Amen* is a striking exception. The form *d a b♭,* over its second syllable, is in all other cases on the accented syllable, for example, *Suscépimus, Gaudeámus, Praecéptor.* The same might easily have been done here. Perhaps the Greek pronunciation of *Amen,* which accents the second syllable, influenced the present arrangement. But more important than this detail is the bold continuation the melody makes with its leap of a fourth.

August majesty marks the beginning of this chant. Here He speaks who rules over all things, who has in His hand life and death, time and eternity, who needs but will and things are made, who can grant all that is asked of Him. Here is the answer He makes to our petitions in the Alleluia-verse and in the Offertory. Here He renews the promise given in the Introit: "You shall call upon me, and I will hear you." But we must pray, pray with confidence, with full certainty of being heard. Now at the end of the liturgical year, when the Apostle admonishes us in the Epistle to "stand fast in the Lord," a great need makes itself felt: the prayer for perseverance, the prayer for life eternal, the prayer that our names also may be inscribed in the Book of Life (Epistle). He has again heard the petition of the Lord's Prayer: "Give us this day our daily bread." We have received Him *(accipiétis)*, the Bread of Life. He has come into our hearts in Holy Communion. That is our guarantee that sometime we may also enter upon eternal life.

*   *   *   *

Special Feasts Of Our Lord And The Saints

(Proprium de Sanctis)

ST. ANDREW, APOSTLE

(Nov. 30)

INTROIT (Ps. 138: 17)

. 1. *Mihi autem nimis honorati sunt amici tui, Deus*: 2. *nimis confortatus est principatus eorum.* Ps. *Domine, probasti me, et cognovisti me*: * *tu cognovisti sessionem meam, et resurrectionem meam.*

1. *To me thy friends, O God, are made exceedingly honorable*: 2. *their principality is exceedingly strengthened.* Ps. *Lord, thou hast proved me and known me*: * *thou hast known my sitting down, and my rising up.*

At the Last Supper Christ said to His Apostles: "I will not now call you servants: for the servant knoweth not what his Lord doth. But I have called you friends: because all things whatsoever I have heard of My Father, I have made known to you" (John 15: 15). He initiated them into those profound mysteries of His divinity, otherwise impervious to the mind of man. He imparted to them powers that not only pierced but elevated into the very heavens. Never was there a truer friend and never has friend given so generously as Christ gave to His Apostles.

Christ's Bride, the Church, shares the sentiments and emotions of her divine Founder. And hence she exclaims on the feasts of the holy Apostles: "To me Thy friends, O God, are made exceedingly honorable." With splendor she honors the Apostles in her divine services, although the feasts of the Apostles are no longer days of obligation. Numberless churches have been dedicated to their memory! Together with the Queen of the Apostles, their name is daily invoked during the sacrifice of the Mass!

Solemn and ever-increasing awe pervades the melody until it reaches its proper climax on the accented syllable of *honoráti*. It is a truly festal melody requiring a worthy, joyful rendition. The feeling of awe is even more vividly expressed in the preceding *nimis* with its descending interval of a fourth, which recurs again at the words *(tu)-i*, *De-(us)*, and introduces the modulation to *c*.

The second phrase is characterized by a strong accentuation of the tenor *f*, which is here the true dominant. The power which God has given his Apostles and through them to the Church will endure to the end of days, and no other power either on earth or in hell will prevail against it. With an interval of a fourth the second *nimis* begins immediately on the dominant, while *confortátus* repeats the motive of *hono-(ráti)*. Twice the melody ascends to *a*, where it is particularly effective over *eórum*. The triple repetition of *c d f g* over the words *Mihi autem ni-(mis)*, *(a)-míci tui*, and *(prin)-cipátus* is so skillfully interwoven with the whole that it is scarcely noticeable.

In the psalm-verse the Apostle himself prays to the Lord. It was a source of wonderful consolation to him to know that amid all his toils and labors the eye of his beloved Master followed him and saw all that he had done and suffered for Him. In a martyr's death the Apostle has stood the test *(probásti me)* victoriously.

This Introit is sung also on the feasts of the Apostles SS. Thomas, Matthias, Barnabas, within the Octave of SS. Peter and Paul, James the Elder, Bartholomew, Luke, Simon, and Jude.

The melody was made use of extensively in the Introits for the feasts of St. Ignatius the Martyr, of the Stigmata of St. Francis of Assisi, and of the Holy Innocents. Compare also the Gradual for the feast of St. Matthias.

For an explanation of the Gradual *Constítues* see the feast of SS. Peter and Paul.

ALLELUIA VERSE

1. *Dilexit Andream Dominus* 2. *in odorem suavitatis.*

1. *The Lord loved Andrew* 2. *in the odor of sweetness.*

In the oldest manuscripts we find this melody given for the present-day Alleluia *Justus ut palma* in the Common of Abbots. It is difficult to determine which of the texts inspired the melody. We might conceive the florid melisma over the word *odórem* as tone-painting of the word *cedrus* in the Alleluia *Justus ut palma*, imitative of the giant growth and the wide spread of the branches of this tree. The melody for today's Gradual is the same as that on the feast of the Purification and on the Friday and Saturday of the Pentecostal Ember Days.

The melody of *Allelúia* tends to reach a climax. This climax, which is repeated by the melody, is indicated by the *climacus* at the beginning of the *jubilus*. The varied progression of the second *climacus*, first *f g* and then *c d*, is charming indeed. The *pressus* is characteristic of the second and third members of the *jubilus*. The figure *d f e d c* in the second member becomes *g a f e d* in the third member, which latter, besides being strengthened, is provided with an upbeat in the fourth member.

The verse sets in with grand solemnity on the dominant *a*. *Diléxit*— Andrew was beloved of the Lord—is expressive of something great and happy. The melodic turn over *(André)-am Dó-* was noted previously in the last member of the *jubilus*. The extended melisma over *odórem* is of pellucid construction. A suggested grouping might combine the second *clivis* with an unextended *climacus* where a division point is then observed, thus: *ć e ǵ a b♭ g á e f e d* | *f e ǵ e f e c* | *é d f d*. Several of the old manuscripts declare in favor of this method of phrasing. The joining of *climacus* and *clivis* rounds off the melody in a pleasing manner. Careful examination, however, shows that all annotated manuscripts declare in favor of the phrasing given in the Vatican Gradual. The first note of every second *clivis* is lengthened. Thus, before resting on the tonic *d* of this descending curve, the voice imparts a special relief to the clives *a–e*, *g–e* and *f–d*, thereby adding particular charm to the melody. *Odó- (rem)* is sung with a *crescendo* which diminishes as we approach the final *f–d*. The repetition is sung in the same manner. The two accordant groups which follow are subjoined in a fervent and delicate manner so as to make the effect of the whole that of sweet-scented balsam. These and other considerations might induce us to consider *Diléxit Andréam* an original composition.

Revue gr., 8, 135 ff.; 9, 58 ff.

OFFERTORY (Ps. 138: 17)

1. *Mihi autem nimis honorati sunt amici tui Deus*: 2. *nimis confortatus est principatus eorum.*

1. *To me thy friends, O God, are made exceedingly favorable*: 2. *their principality is exceedingly strengthened.*

Holy Mother Church finds it difficult to realize fully the dignity and power which Christ bestowed upon His Apostles. For this reason the same text that we have in the Introit is repeated here. The melodic development is also very much the same, although the Offertory, as becomes its meditative character, is more impressive. As in the Introit, the first phrase up to *nimis* shows a gradual development. The melody then descends, giving the following *honoráti*, which is inclosed within the limits of an interval of a fourth, an opportunity to develop more fully.

The second half of the first phrase in both Introit and Offertory is serene and thetic in character. A solemn reverential awe pervades the *nimis* of the second phrase, which reaches its climax over *confortátus est* and *eórum*.

The powerful motive over *autem nimis* with its resolved major chord *f a c*, its tristropha *ccc* and the extended intervals of a fourth *c–g–c* are heard again over *(confor)-tátus est*, and with a slight variation over *(princi)-pátus eórum*. The three first syllables of *confortátus* and *principátus* employ the same melodic figure; likewise the closing figures of the first *(ni)-mis* and *(eó)-rum*, *(De)-us* and *est*.

COMMUNION (Matt. 4: 19, 20)

1. *Venite post me: faciam vos fieri piscatores hominum: 2. at illi continuo, relictis retibus et navi, secuti sunt Dominum.*

1. *Come ye after me: I will make you to be fishers of men: 2. And they immediately, leaving their nets, and their boat, followed the Lord.*

In the first sentence the Lord summons Peter and his brother Andrew, while the second sentence relates how both of them immediately heeded His call. The Lord calls them from the midst of their life occupation—they were at the moment letting down their nets into the sea— to an entirely new vocation, one which as yet lay veiled before them. This new calling demanded of them numerous sacrifices and labors and bitter disappointments—innumerably more than their previous vocation— and finally determined their death on the cross. Hearing the word of Christ and obeying it was for them, however, but the work of a moment. The melody beginning on the dominant emphasizes this thought, and its continuance on the dominant realizes for us the enduring sacrifice they are bringing. It is not difficult to conceive that they were very fond of their fishing nets and intimately attached to their little ship! Although the word *navi* does not occur in the Gospel, we are grateful for its insertion here so that, realizing the greatness of their sacrifice, we may appreciate it the more fully. The first phrase is the more quiet, although there is a certain solemnity in the twofold descent of the interval *g–d* and the ascending *g–c*: here the Lord, the King of the Apostles, is speaking.

This expressive melody is as a fresh breeze from the sea. Together with the Communion of the Vigil *Dicit Andréas*, it forms one of the gems of the Graduale.

* * * *

FEAST OF THE IMMACULATE CONCEPTION OF THE BLESSED VIRGIN MARY

(December 8)

INTROIT (Isa. 61: 10)

1. *Gaudens gaudebo in Domino, et exsultabit anima mea in Deo meo:* 2. *quia induit me vestimento salutis: et indumento justitiae circumdedit me,* 3. *quasi sponsam ornatam monilibus suis.* Ps. *Exaltabo te, Domine, quoniam suscepisti me:* * *nec delectasti inimicos meos super me.*

1. *I will greatly rejoice in the Lord, and my soul shall be joyful in my God:* 2. *for he hath clothed me with the garments of salvation: and with the robes of justice he hath covered me,* 3. *as a bride adorned with her jewels.* Ps. *I will extol thee, O Lord, for thou hast upheld me:* * *and hast not made my enemies to rejoice over me.*

The Immaculate Virgin herself, radiant in the light of grace, soaring guiltless over a world laden with sin, the very spouse of God adorned with all-wonderful jewels, introduces today's festal Mass. She knows, however, the source of her beauty and is aware of her singular dignity. She knows that great things have been done unto her. Sin, which up to that time had infected every human being born into this world, was held in abeyance from the time of her conception; while the earth was covered with darkness, the Almighty clothed her in light. Hence in the Introit she chants her gratitude to God, a *Magnificat*, as it were, in its original setting. Today she sings: *Gaudens gaudébo in Dómino*; later on: *Magníficat ánima mea Dóminum.* Today we hear: *Et exsultábit ánima mea in Deo meo*, while the mountains of Judea re-echo the words: *Et exsulátvit spíritus meus in Deo salutári meo.* Today it is *Quia induit me*; later on: *Quia fecit mihi.*

How shall this melody be rendered? Without doubt it should have a ring of sincerity and graciousness emanating most tenderly from the depths of the soul; it should be characterized by solemnity yet be joyful, coming withal from a being all light, all grace, elevated to the proximity of God.

The melody, however, was not originally intended for this text. Excepting the neums of the last few words, it is taken from the Introit of the fifth Sunday after Easter. There it is a song of victory, of liberty, of thanksgiving, which we fittingly place today on the lips of the Blessed Virgin. For this reason also text and melody are of the same mold.

The first sentence begins softly and tenderly on the half step *e–f* and the minor third, whence the intervals are extended to the dominant *c*. *Dómine* is full of joyful movement, designating as it does the source from which all this happiness emanates. Summarizing it all in a word, we might exclaim: Joy in the Lord! The second half of the first phrase reflects the parallelism of the text *(gaudébo—exsultábit)* in the melody, which becomes more fervent over the words *Deo meo*. Here the soul fuses, as it were, with its God. And well may Mary sing in this singular strain, for the angel will shortly say unto her: "The Lord is with thee!"

Like the various members of the first phrase, so the second phrase and the first half of the third phrase form parallel verses. The initial motive is similar to that at the beginning of the Introit. In a word, with the argument which it introduces, a more definite sounding double *f* replaces the corresponding tender *e f*. The interval of the fourth *a–d* leading over to the dominant creates a bold transition. In the first phrase this transition is soon abandoned, while here it is made the continual support of a new movement, which has a tense preparation over *vestiméntis*, reaches its climax on the *torculus c e d*, and then closes with undiminished power. These phrases are an outcry of ecstatic jubilation over the salvation that has come to the Blessed Virgin. She is indeed the first and most beautiful fruit of salvation; Christ has clothed her with the mantle of justice. In the first phrase the closing cadences over *Dómino* and *meo* were on *e*, over *salútis* and *me* they are on *g*.

The melody of *quasi sponsam* offers a new thought. The Blessed Virgin is represented as "a bride adorned with her jewels." These words are sung on the descending melody with such charming humility as only the *ancílla Dómini*, the handmaid of the Lord could sing them. And notwithstanding the miracles of grace which had been wrought upon her, she ever remained the humble handmaid of the Lord. Unceasing gratitude, however, urges her on, and once more she receives the great graces of which she has been made the recipient, once more she gives vent to her feelings of amazement, joy, and gratitude.

In the psalm-verse the Blessed Virgin addresses her God directly: "I will extol Thee, O Lord, for Thou hast not made my enemies to rejoice over me." Reference is here made to the hereditary foe of the human race, the devil, who in hellish glee mars newly created souls with the stain of sin. Today, however, his song of triumph is silenced, for, with his head crushed, he lies powerless under the foot of the Virgin. The repetition of the Introit fittingly projects the image of the Mother of God into the background of this picture and completes it in every detail.

GRADUAL (Jud. 13: 23)

1. *Benedicta es tu, Virgo Maria, a Domino Deo excelso,* 2. *prae omnibus mulieribus super terram.* ℣. 1. *Tu gloria Jerusalem,* 2. *tu laetitia Israel,* 3. *tu honorificentia populi nostri.*

1. *Blessed art thou, O Virgin Mary, by the Lord the most high God,* 2. *above all women upon the earth.* ℣. 1. *Thou art the glory of Jerusalem,* 2. *thou art the joy of Israel,* 3. *thou art the honor of our people.*

The text of the Gradual is intimately connected with the high honor paid to Judith after her victory over Holofernes. In like manner Mary is presented to us in the role of victor over sin. She is the solitary boast of our tainted nature, the blessed among women. Hence, millions salute her today in terms of highest reverence and glowing love: Thou art our pride, our joy, our crown of honor.

In the Introit Mary was the person speaking; in the Gradual she is the person spoken to.

The present melody was composed for the text *Constítues* of the feast of SS. Peter and Paul. The adaptation could not have been more happy. The text of the day imparts to the melody fresh energy, a fullness of joy and enthusiasm. How full of reverence the words *Benedicta es tu*, how ardent and lovely the *María*! The extended development due to the word-painting over *omnem terram* in the original fits perfectly to the word *excélso*. *Glória Jerúsalem* revels in astonishment, admiration, and delight.

ALLELUIA VERSE (Cant. 4: 7)

1. *Tota pulchra es, Maria:* 2. *et macula originalis non est in te.*

1. *Thou art all fair, O Mary:* 2. *and there is in thee no stain of original sin.*

In relation to the preceding Gradual, it is rather difficult to assign a definite position and sentiment to the present chant and to characterize it properly. It must be sung neither heavily nor slowly, but rather with a spirit of naive joy and admiration. The melody is not original to this text, but was sung in the 12th century on the feasts of the Assumption and St. Agnes.

If we combine *allelúia* and *jubilus* into one in accordance with the pauses, there will be four members. *Allelúia* is amplified in the second member and repeated at the end of the third and fourth members as a soft refrain. The -*lúia* is characterized by a contrary ascending movement, being somewhat extended at the beginning of the third member and correspondingly abbreviated at the beginning of the fourth member. The *pressus* serve to enliven the melody. A comparison might be drawn between the ascending melody previous to the refrain and the last Kyrie of Masses 9 and 10.

The first phrase of the verse is beautifully rounded off. *Tota* prepares for the spiritual warmth given *pulchra*, while *María* ends the phrase like to the glow of a mild sunset. How beautiful is Mary, immaculately conceived! Indeed, she has been the inspiration of a Murillo and numberless others, and yet the essence of her beauty defies the skill of every artist.

The first and only express mention of original sin in today's feast is made in the second phrase. The groups *ag acb g* over *ori-* correspond to *gcb cde a* over *mácula*. Most singers will be obliged to breathe at this place. What follows presents some further difficulties as to comprehension and rendition. The *torculus* and *climacus* must be considered as organic, linking elements. The sentence is to be taken as a whole. The emphasis on *mácula* must not be wrongly interpreted, for we might emphatically exclaim: Original sin—is not in thee!

Revue, 6, 160; 26, 277 ff.; *Analyses*, 8, 25 ff.

OFFERTORY (Luke 1: 28)

1. *Ave Maria, gratia plena*: 2. *Dominus tecum*: 3. *benedicta tu in mulieribus. Alleluia.*

1. *Hail Mary, full of grace*: 2. *the Lord is with thee*: 3. *blessed art thou among women. Alleluia.*

We have here the rare instance where a new melody has been composed for the Mass text of a later feast. The melody was written by the Benedictine Dom Fonteinne and adapted by his confrere Dom Pothier. Fervor, delicacy, and sublimity combine to effect an harmonious whole.

Ave begins soft and tender, reverently continuing the salutation of the Angel which concludes the Gospel of today's feast. With what joy might God Himself today have saluted Mary who, like an early morning dawn, shedding light in the wake of a receding darkness, prefigures the dissolution of the dark night of sin at the approach of the Sun of salvation. We, too, greet thee, mild and gracious Lady, in thy immaculate conception and in thy life of motherly solicitude to become an eternal dispenser of grace and mercy. As in the Gradual, Alleluia, and Communion, the word *María* is here treated with evident love.

Grátia begins in a somewhat dreamy mood, but waxes increasingly powerful, as though the singer had joyfully glimpsed in Mary's soul the broad, shoreless expanse of her many graces. Part of the melody is reminiscent of *María* in the Gradual. The modulation to *c* is likewise peculiar to chants of the fifth mode.

The second phrase is more serene, never going beyond *c*. It contains a mysterious allusion to the dignity of that divine motherhood which conveniently demanded the immaculate conception of the Blessed Virgin.

The third phrase, on the other hand, sets in with brilliance immediately. Thou art the promised one, the blessed, the chosen among all the daughters of Eve. Be thou praised, alleluia! The melody over this last word is similar to that over *María* of the first phrase. The descent to low *d* is peculiar to the eighth mode. The piece might be more effective if low *d* did not occur in each of the three phrases.

Comparison of today's *Ave María* with that of the fourth Sunday in Advent will be very instructive. The final phrase of that composition is lacking here. The fact that *muliéribus* there is not final, as it is in the present case, would make the use of its melody for today impossible. This may also have occasioned the new composition for this feast.

COMMUNION

1. *Gloriosa dicta sunt de te, Maria:* 2. *quia fecit tibi magna qui potens est.*

1. *Glorious things are told of thee, O Mary:* 2. *for he who is mighty hath done great things unto thee.*

The melody was originally composed for the text *Dico autem vobis* of the Mass *Sapiéntiam* for the Common of many Martyrs. In the early ages it was the melody for the Communion of the feast of St. Hippolytus, who is commemorated two days before the feast of the Assumption of the Blessed Virgin. It may possibly have been borrowed from the former for the Communion *Optimam partem* of the Assumption, and thence transferred to today's feast. Here there is a more faithful adherence to the original than on the Assumption, where the text of the second phrase is somewhat abbreviated. The festive, serene character of the melody seems to have been inspired by the text. The motive *g a b č g g* over the third syllable of *Gloriósa* undergoes a slight change over *magna* and enlarges over *qui potens est*. The descent to low *d* over *tibi*, a fourth below the tonic, which is characteristic of the eighth mode, forms the antithesis to the interval *g–c*. This formula is well known from the psalmody of the first mode with final cadence D ad lib. Annotated manuscripts have *leniter*—gliding downward gently—written at this point. On the feast of the Immaculate Conception the Communion closes with an accent on the third last syllable, necessitating a slight change in the melody. On the feast of the Assumption and in the original melody the close is more energetic and effective.

Scripture, the Church in her liturgy, and her saints speak in glowing terms of the Blessed Virgin. And yet it is impossible to narrate and portray all the great things that God has wrought in and through Mary from the day of her conception and how she has proved herself to be the Mother of mercy. The closing phrase of the Communion reminds us once more that it was only the omnipotence of God which made it possible for Mary to enter this world pure and without the stain of original sin on her soul.

Having received our Lord in Holy Communion we should with grateful hearts repeat the words of the Magnificat: "The Lord hath done great things unto me." Surely, it is a wonderful condescension that God almighty deigns to come into our souls.

*   *   *   *

ST. THOMAS, APOSTLE
(December 21)

When this feast is of the second class only, it is not celebrated on a Sunday of Advent.

For the Introit refer to the feast of St. Andrew, and for the Gradual to that of St. Matthias. The Alleluia is proper. Its opening melody occurs on the feast of the Holy Innocents. The Offertory is sung on the feast of St. James (July 25). The Communion is the same as that on Low Sunday, *Allelúia* being omitted.

*   *   *   *

PURIFICATION OF THE BLESSED VIRGIN
OR CANDLEMAS
(February 2)

The first chant of today after the blessing of the candles extols Christ as the light of the gentiles. The procession as also the liturgy of the Mass, would glorify Him as the King of light. True, He makes his entrance into the Temple as a babe in arms, clinging and looking to His mother. Similarly our own thoughts and sentiments revert to that same blessed Mother. It is not without reason that the Church has chosen the title "Purification of the Blessed Virgin Mary" for today's feast.

LUMEN (Luke 2: 32)

Lumen ad revelationem gentium, et gloriam plebis tuae Israel.

A light to the revelation of the gentiles, and the glory of thy people Israel.

Both parts of this vigorous antiphon are well balanced. In the second half *f a* serves merely as an introduction for the accent on *glóriam* = *Lumen.* The first half closes with *á g á g f*, the second half with *á a b a g.*

A kind of rondo form results from the repetition of this antiphon after each of the verses of the *Nunc dimíttis* (Luke 2: 29–31), which has ever been heard in the Church since the day the aged Simeon sang it in the joy of the Holy Ghost.

1. *Nunc dimittis servum tuum, Domine * secundum verbum tuum in pace.*

2. *Quia viderunt oculi mei * salutare tuum;*

3. *Quod parasti * ante faciem omnium populorum:*

4. *Gloria Patri. . . .*

1. *Now thou dost dismiss thy servant, O Lord * according to thy word in peace.*

2. *Because my eyes have seen * thy salvation.*

3. *Which thou hast prepared * before the face of all peoples:*

4. *Glory be to the Father. . . .*

(The customary intonation must be omitted at the beginning of the third verse on account of the brevity of the text.)

It is somewhat surprising that the final cadence G, that is, *ć b c á g* is employed, since in the Antiphonale the cadence *ć a c d́ c* is used for this antiphon (the fourth in Lauds for February 2) and as often as the antiphon begins on *c.*

The present feast is a connecting link between Epiphany and Easter. Today Christ, the Light, enters the Temple, where at some future time He will solemnly proclaim: I am the Light of the world. Mankind, however, prefers darkness to the light and is bent upon extinguishing it in its heart. Christ became a sign unto many, but was contradicted; at the crucifixion the Light of the world was overshadowed by darkness. On Holy Saturday, however, the triumphant cry *Lumen Christi*, followed by a grateful *Deo grátias*, is heard.

EXSURGE DOMINE (Ps. 43: 26)

Exsurge, Domine, adjuva nos: et libera nos propter nomen tuum. Ps. Deus, auribus nostris audivimus: * patres nostri annuntiaverunt nobis.

Arise, O Lord, help us, and deliver us, for thy name's sake. Ps. We have heard, O God, with our ears: * our fathers have declared to us.

The first notes of this antiphon are well known to us from the *Per ómnia saécula*. Similar melodic treatment are accorded *ádjuva nos* and the definitive *líbera nos*: the *e* following the former acts as an impellent for the latter. The present *Exsúrge* is devoid of the stormy excitement and the feeling of abandonment by God depicted in the Introit of Sexagesima. True, today's chant is impressive—the repetition of the same formula emphasizes this—but it is simpler, more ardent, more confident. It is also sung on Rogation Days immediately before the procession.

Of the various antiphons sung during the procession, we take note of the following one only.

ADORNA

In the first two phrases the second half repeats the melody of the first half.

1. *Adorna thalamum tuum, Sion et suscipe Regem Christum*: 2. *amplectere Mariam, quae est caelestis porta*: 3. *ipsa enim portat Regem gloriae novi luminis*: *subsistit Virgo, adducens manibus Filium ante luciferum genitum*: 4. *quem accipiens Simeon in ulnas suas praedicavit populis Dominum eum esse vitae et mortis, et salvatorem mundi.*

O Daughter of Sion, adorn thy bridal chamber, and welcome Christ the King: 2. *greet Mary with loving embrace, for she, who is the very gate of heaven*, 3. *bringeth to thee the glorious King of the new light. Though in her arms she bears a Son begotten before the day star, yet ever she remaineth a pure virgin.* 4. *Hers was the Child whom Simeon, taking up into his arms, declared unto all peoples to be the Lord of life and death, the Saviour of the world.*

Sion, in the first verse, refers to the Church. In the second verse the singer is inspired by the thought of the "King of the new light," and thenceforward the melody becomes brighter.

Special emphasis is given the word *eum*, for *He* is the Lord. The whole produces the effect of a royal hymn, a festive echo of Christmastide, which delighted in singing of Christ the King. The identical form of the motive over *Sion* recurs four times; that over *glóriae* three times; that of *novi lúminis* over *(ad)-dúcens mánibus*, and again with a slight change over *Dóminum eum esse.*

According to Wagner (I, 51, and 207) these chants are of Greek origin. *Rass. gr.*, is of a different opinion (8, 193, and 438 ff.; 9, 51 ff.).

RESPONSUM (Luke 2: 26, 27, 28, 29)

1. *Responsum accepit Simeon a Spiritu Sancto, non visurum se mortem, nisi videret Christum Domini: 2. et cum inducerent puerum in templum, accepit eum in ulnas suas, 3. et benedixit Deum, et dixit: 4. Nunc dimittis servum tuum, Domine, in pace.*

Simeon received an answer from the Holy Ghost, that he should not see death before he had seen the Christ of the Lord; 2. and when they brought the Child into the temple, he took him into his arms, 3. and blessed God, and said: 4. Now dost thou dismiss thy servant, O Lord, in peace.

In comparison with the foregoing, the present chant is much more quiet and reserved. It reflects the reverent, serene happiness of the aged Simeon. The motive over the word *Simeon* with its *pressus*, swelled as it were with ardent desire, recurs over *Sancto* and *templum*. A second motive appears over *Dómini* and *dixit*, which is somewhat more developed over *Dómine* and artistically so over *pace*. In the same manner the aged Simeon feels himself rich with the fullness of divine peace. A third motive introduces the second and third phrases, and partly also the fourth phrase.

On re-entering the church, the following Responsory is sung.

OBTULERUNT

*A. Obtulerunt pro eo Domino par turturum, aut duos pullos columbarum: * Sicut scriptum est in lege Domini.*

*A. They offered for Him to the Lord a pair of turtledoves, or two young pigeons: * As it is written in the law of the Lord.*

B. I. Postquam impleti sunt dies purgationis Mariae, secundum legem Moysi,

B. I. After the days of the purification of Mary, according to the law of Moses, were fulfilled,

II. tulerunt Jesum in Jerusalem, ut sisterent eum Domino.

II. they carried Jesus to Jerusalem, to present Him to the Lord.

*A. * Sicut scriptum est. . .Gloria Patri. . . .*

*A. * As it is written. . .Glory be to the Father. . . .*

The division of syllables *eum Dómino* and *(Spi)-rítui Sancto* is readily recognized. The construction is identical with that of the Responsories *Emendémus* on Ash Wednesday and *Ingrediénte* on Palm Sunday. The melody is closely related to that of the former. Compare also the Response *In monte Olivéti* of Palm Sunday.

Let us attend the holy Sacrifice with the same disposition that Mary had when offering her Child in the Temple.

INTROIT (Ps. 47: 10, 11)

1. *Suscepimus, Deus, misericordiam tuam in medio templi tui*: 2. *secundum nomen tuum Deus, ita et laus tua in fines terrae*: 3. *justitia plena est dextera tua*. Ps. *Magnus Dominus, et laudabilis nimis*: * *in civitate Dei nostri, in monte sancto ejus*.

1. *We have received thy mercy, O God, in the midst of thy temple*: 2. *according to thy name, O God, so also is thy praise unto the ends of the earth*; 3. *thy right hand is full of justice*. Ps. *Great is the Lord and exceedingly to be praised*: * *in the city of our God, in his Holy Mountain*.

With these words the priest might have greeted the first entrance of our Lord in the arms of His Mother into the Temple; with the sound of the trumpets the Levites might have saluted Him, and with jubilation the entire populace might have bade Him welcome. But, alas! the priests know no songs to honor Him, the trumpets of the Levites are silenced and the people have no word of welcome to offer. Simeon alone sings his immortal *Nunc dimittis*, and the prophetess Anna rejoices with him—then silence again in the Temple.

In this majestic melody, the Church offers that which Sion denied its King. She values the fact that He came with a heart full of tender mercy and that she is privileged now to receive Him for whom the centuries had prayed: "Show us, O Lord, Thy mercy." In the Postcommunion of the first Sunday of Advent she still prayed: "May we receive... Thy mercy," and continued this petition throughout the week. Today her prayer is heard, and with a grateful heart she cries: *Suscépimus*—we have received. In like manner, to the Advent petition *Veni*—Come, she could joyfully respond on Epiphany: *Ecce advénit*—Behold He is come.

Let the very confines of the earth resound with His praises. And even though the infant hand be small, it embodies within itself the fullness of that righteousness from which we also have received, and by which we are made children of God. For this reason, despite His humble appearance, the Church greets Him with the words of the psalm-verse: "Great is the Lord, and exceedingly to be praised."

At first glance our attention is attracted by the extended intervals at the beginning of the second phrase. It would seem as though the singer wished to clarify our notion of the majestic essence of God. The entire middle phrase overtops the first and third phrases rather prominently. The cadence over *fines terrae*, which forms the close of the first phrase as well, imparts to both a well-rounded finish.

In the first phrase *a* is the predominant note, *c* being sounded only in passing. The second phrase is dominated by *c*, the third by *f*. Briefly, we might say that the first phrase is characterized by *f–a*, the second by *a–c*, the third by *d–f*. An apparently insignificant but important note forms the transition to the third phrase. Despite an indicated major pause here, the note effecting the transition makes for a short rest only. Codex 121 of Einsiedeln inserts at this place "st" (*statim*, at once) which in modern music corresponds to an *attaca subito*. The third phrase should be rendered in broad, full tones, every word being given due prominence.

Today's Introit forms the favorite chant of many singers. *K. K.,* 23, 3 ff.; *Revue gr.,* 9, 136 ff.

GRADUAL (Ps. 47: 10, 11, 9)

1. *Suscepimus, Deus, misericordiam tuam in medio templi tui*: 2. *secundum nomen tuum, Deus, ita et laus tua in fines terrae.* ℣. 1. *Sicut audivimus,* 2. *ita et vidimus,* 2. *in civitate Dei nostri, in monte sancto ejus.*

1. *We have received thy mercy, O God, in the midst of thy temple*: 2. *according to thy name, O God, so also is thy praise unto the ends of the earth.* ℣. 1. *As we have heard,* 2. *so we have seen, in the city of our God, and in his holy mountain.*

This *corpus* repeats the text of the first two phrases of the Introit and bears some melodic similarity to it: *(tu)-am tem-(pli), secúndum no-(men)*. In general, this part is characterized by solemn serenity. The melody of the verse is practically the same as that of Maundy Thursday. The florid melisma over *illum* of the latter is unhappily wanting here.

The prophecy of Malachias (Lesson of the feast) has been realized, and "we have received Thy mercy, O God." In His holy temple we behold Him, the Angel of the covenant, the Angel of the great counsel (Introit of the third Mass of Christmas). And this is the house of God, in which we render Him homage and offer Him our worship of adoration.

ALLELUIA VERSE

1. *Senex puerum portabat*: 2. *Puer autem senem regebat.*

1. *The old man carried the Child*: 2. *but the Child governed the old man.*

The melody was explained on the feast of St. Andrew.

Like Simeon we also should be governed by the divine Child; He alone should be our Lord and our King. Our soul in consequence will be endowed with a maturity attained comparatively seldom even by advanced age; it will radiate inner purity, sound judgment, and steadfastness. We can then apply to it the words of St. Ambrose speaking of St. Agnes: "a brilliance of mind unrestrained." In all humility let us pray as did Cardinal Newman even before his conversion: "I loved to choose and see my path; but now, lead Thou me on."

The TRACT which is sung while the blessed candles are being distributed has the same text and the same divisions as the *Nunc dimittis*. The Antiphon *Lumen* is added as a fourth verse.

OFFERTORY (Ps. 44: 3)

1. *Diffusa est gratia in labiis tuis* 2. *propterea benedixit te Deus in aeternum*, 3. *et in saeculum saeculi.*

1. *Grace is poured abroad in thy lips*: 2. *therefore hath God blessed thee forever*, 3. *and for ages of ages.*

At the beginning of the Christmas season we referred these words to the charm and beauty of the divine Child (see Gradual of the Sunday after Christmas). Today, at the close of the Christmas season, these same words glorify the Mother of the divine Infant. It has ever been the wish of the artist to portray the exterior charm of the blessed Mother, but never has the ideal conception of her been successfully materialized. To comprehend fully the beauty of her soul one would needs require eyes of faith and a soul as pure and rich in graces as Mary's. The Archangel Gabriel at first sight of her exclaims: *Ave, grátia plena*—"Hail, full of grace." This angelic salutation is developed and paraphrased in the first phrase of the Offertory. The term *plena* corresponds to *diffúsa*. Would that we might sing this melody with the reverence and glowing love of the Archangel! Following the low-pitched and rather reserved introduction, *grátia* continues in a bright, ascending melody. The *climacus* here and over *lábi-(is)* later must be sung *crescendo*. *Tuis* modulates into a full step below the tonic. The second phrase, which is a development of the Archangel Gabriel's *benedícta tu*, terminates in the same manner. Following the ascending intervals of a fourth in the first phrase we have here descending intervals of a fourth. The melody

c d cc g a is re-echoed in the following *g b aa g g a. Deus* should be given
the expression it demands. The word *aetérnum* is accorded particular
splendor. The preceding torculi *c d c* reach their climax in *d e c*. The
final cadence should be sung broadly.

In the third and final phrase the singer, dwelling emphatically on
high *c*, would conclude his pean by describing for us eternity, endless
in extent. As in the second phrase, the neums here should be given pre-
cedence over the bistropha and tristropha. This finale is well rounded
off, having a conclusion similar to that of the first two phrases. The
Lessons of some feasts of the Blessed Virgin ascribe to her the words:
"I shall not cease in all eternity." And truly, she will be blessed for all
eternity and will ever be the dispenser, the mediatrix of blessings. She
will never cease to console, to succor, and to heal.

The present feast invests the person of the Mother of God with a
peculiar charm. She appears as if transfigured by sorrow. She realizes
what the offering of her Son in the temple presages, for she hears there
the ominous words: "And thy own soul a sword shall pierce." And additional beauty and charm is imparted to her soul by the royal response:
Fiat—Be it done. As the Mother of Sorrows she becomes the fountainhead of blessing and consolation for mankind.

In the oldest manuscripts this melody is noted on the feast of St.
Agnes (January 21). The tempo should be bright, the rendition light
and airy.

COMMUNION (Luke 2: 26)

Responsum accepit Simeon a Spi-   Simeon received an answer from
ritu Sancto, non visurum se mor-   the Holy Ghost, that he should not
tem, nisi videret Christum Domini.   see death, until he had seen the
                                          Christ of the Lord.

The melody is narrative in character. Its musical line is defined by
the word-accents.

As in response to his ardent expectation and prayer, Simeon received a special inspiration of the Holy Ghost, and what thus far he had
beheld merely in spirit became for him today a blessed reality. He was
privileged before his death to look upon the "Christ of the Lord," to
take Him into his arms, to press Him to his bosom. In Holy Communion
we too may look upon Christ and receive Him into our hearts. My Blessed
Saviour, be Thou my light and consolation in the hour of death and re-

ceive me into eternal bliss! And Thou, O Mother of God, from whose hands Simeon received the Saviour, be Thou to me at that moment the Mother of light! Amen.

* * * *

ST. MATTHIAS, APOSTLE

(February 24; in leap years, February 25)

The INTROIT is the same as on the feast of St. Andrew.

GRADUAL ((Ps. 138: 17, 18)

1. *Nimis honorati sunt amici tui Deus*: 2. *nimis confortatus est principatus eorum.* ℣. 1. *Dinumerabo eos*: 2. *et super arenam multiplicabuntur.*

1. *Thy friends, O God, are exceedingly honorable*: 2. *Their principality is exceedingly strengthened.* ℣. 1. *I will number them*: 2. *and they shall be multiplied above the sand.*

The melody was explained on the first Sunday of Lent. In the original Hebrew version these verses are referred to the mysterious counsels of God and to the power by which they are realized. Who is there to number them, who can fathom their depths, or who can fully appreciate them for the blessings they bring? Certainly no one was so thoroughly imbued with their spirit as the Apostles to whom the Saviour revealed all that He had received from His Father (John 15: 15).

He shared with them His rights of sovereignity. They became founders of holy catholic Church, whose children are as numerous as the sands on the sea.

TRACT (Ps. 20: 3, 4)

1. *Desiderium animae ejus tribuisti ei*: † *et voluntate labiorum ejus non fraudasti eum.* 2. *Quoniam praevenisti eum in benedictionibus dulcedinis.* 3. *Posuisti in capite ejus* † *coronam de lapide pretioso.*

1. *Thou hast given him his soul's desire*: † *and hast not withholden from him the will of his lips.* 2. *For thou hast prevented him with blessings of sweetness.* 3. *Thou hast set on his head* † *a crown of precious stones.*

The present melody should be compared with that of the Tract on the feast of St. Joseph. Several formulas are repeated: *Tribuísti e-(i)* in the first verse is identical with *in benedictió-(ne)* of the second verse,

-rum ejus in the first verse with *corónam* of the third verse; *eum* in the first verse is similar to *-óne* of the second verse.

We might conjecture that St. Matthias, on the morning when Christ chose His Apostles, entertained a secret desire to become an intimate friend of the Master and be numbered among the twelve. Our Lord tendered him a cordial invitation, and by selecting him to supplant Judas, placed on his head a crown of precious stones.

The OFFERTORY is the same as that on the feast of the Apostles SS. Peter and Paul (q.v.).

COMMUNION (Matt. 19: 28)

1. *Vos, qui secuti estis me, sede-bitis super sedes,* 2. *judicantes duodecim tribus Israel.*

1. *You who have followed me shall sit on seats,* 2. *judging the twelve tribes of Israel.*

The melody places special stress on the word *vos*. You, My faithful Apostles, in company with Me shall one day judge the world. The melody over *tri-(bus)* is extended over *super*—possibly a matter of tone-painting, as in the Gradual of the third Sunday of Advent over the same word. The climax of the entire melody is realized over *sedes*, where there is question of the thrones of the Apostles. The word-accents over *judicántes* and *duódecim* are well defined. Preceded by a *pressus* the melody descends twice to low *c*, followed both times by an interval of a fourth. This cadence is very effective wherever an independent thought is brought to a close. This is not the case here, however, especially over the word *duódecim*. With the special prominence given the dominant *f* we should expect the second mode rather than the first. This melody is not found in manuscripts 339 of St. Gall's, 121 of Einsiedeln, or H. 159 of Montpellier.

The text, with an additional *dicit Dóminus*: "saith the Lord," forms the Communion for the feast of St. Bartholomew. The melody there, in the second mode, is very simple and almost entirely syllabic; nevertheless it accentuates the words *super sedes*, and particularly the important word *judicántes* (by means of recitation on high *g*).

Christ is speaking to His faithful Apostles. He to whom the Father hath given all judgment (John 5: 22), could not bestow a greater distinction than to assign them thrones next to His own seat of judgment, thus making them participants in His judicial power. He who has said: "Who heareth you, heareth Me," promises by the mouth of His Apostles eternal salvation to all who hear and observe their teaching, and eternal damnation to all who despise it, because in so doing they despise Christ.

*   *   *   *

ST. JOSEPH, SPOUSE OF THE BLESSED VIRGIN MARY, CONFESSOR

(March 19)

INTROIT (Ps. 91: 13, 14)

1. *Justus ut palma florebit: sicut cedrus Libani multiplicabitur:* 2. *plantatus in domo Domini, in atriis domus Dei nostri.* Ps. *Bonum est confiteri Domino:* * *et psallere nomini tuo, Altissime.*

1. *The just shall flourish like the palm tree: he shall grow up like the cedar of Libanus:* 2. *planted in the house of the Lord, in the courts of the house of our God.* Ps. *It is good to give praise to the Lord:* * *and to sing to Thy name, O most High.*

St. Joseph is the ideal just man. Already the Gospel calls him just, thereby proclaiming his saintliness. His soul reflects the Sun of justice. He is like the palm tree, modest, deriving next to nothing from the earth, rising from comparatively barren soil, but growing heavenwards and absorbing the light of the sun. In childlike simplicity he gave himself entirely to God. Fond of silence, not a single word of his is recorded. Like a flower which blossoms forth and displays its beauty in silence, so his life unfolded itself in its accomplishments in all quietness. Like the cedar which spreads its branches far and wide in protection, his life was characterized by faithfulness and firmness of character.

The second phrase indicates the fountainhead from which such a life can draw its great beauty and power; it is none other than the temple of God, the union with God and His holy will, the life in heaven. How wonderfully the holiness of Joseph developed when Providence transplanted him into God's garden at Nazareth, into the most intimate union with Jesus and Mary. He was privileged to pray, to speak, to associate and to labor with them for many years. That was the court of heaven, the house of God on earth *(domus Dei nostri).*

There, in company with Jesus and Mary, Joseph celebrated liturgy and glorified the name of the most High. Certainly if any prayer was ever good and perfect, it was that of the Holy Family.

Transplanted into heaven, this saint has all the more become like the palm tree which refreshes us with its luscious fruit. There he is become like the cedar under whose spreading branches the great family of the Church is well protected.

Both phrases contain parallelisms quite characteristic of Hebrew poetry. The word *palma* corresponds to *cedrus, florébit* to *multiplicábitur, domo* to *átriis*. Both phrases have practically also the same divisions. The first part of the first phrase rests on *f*, the second part on *a*. In the second phrase *f* is again predominant, *g* occurring occasionally.

Peace and serenity, which are the prerogatives of the just man, pervade the entire antiphon. *Justus* fashions a motive of its own and forms the grammatical as well as the spiritual subject of the Introit. The melody of this Introit must not be rendered in a heavy manner but rather airily and at the same time with great delicacy. The strophici over *florébit* should be sung *decrescendo*. The motive over *ut palma* is amplified over *cedrus Líbani*; *c d f f* becomes *c d f g a a*. The tarrying on the dominant *a* might suggest the idea of multiplicity, extension, and expansion of branches. The first syllable of *multiplicábitur* forms a rhythmic upbeat followed by several groups of two notes: *áa, ác, áa, ǵa, ǵg, fg, fg*.

The second phrase is characterized by serene quiet and firmness. The melody over *domo (Dómini)* is echoed over *domus (Dei)*, while that of the reverential *Dei* is repeated over *nostri*.

In the old manuscripts this melody occurs on the feast of St. Stephen, Pope. It will be instructive to compare the first phrase with the Offertory of the feast of St. John the Apostle.

GRADUAL (Ps. 20: 4-5)

1. *Domine, praevenisti eum in benedictionibus dulcedinis*: 2. *posuisti in capite ejus coronam de lapide pretioso.* ℣. 1. *Vitam petiit a te*, 2. *et tribuisti ei longitudinem dierum in saeculum saeculi.*

1. *O Lord, thou hast prevented him with blessings of sweetness*: 2. *Thou hast set on his head a crown of precious stones.* ℣. 1. *He asked life of thee*, 2. *and thou hast given him length of days forever and ever.*

St. Joseph was privileged to see and to hear the divine Saviour. Many kings, however, as an indulgenced prayer mentions, looked in vain for Him whom they so ardently desired to hear but were not permitted to hear. St. Joseph, moreover, was not only privileged to see and hear Him, but also to carry Him in his arms, to kiss Him, to clothe and protect Him—indeed, a singular blessing. Beyond doubt, his life was not devoid of sacrifice and suffering. He experienced great anxiety the night he fled with the Child to evade the evil eye of Herod. Herod lost his crown, but St. Joseph now wears a crown of precious stones the like of which has never been worn by an earthly king. In union with Jesus and Mary he enjoys a bliss which is eternal and indestructible.

In manuscript 339 of St. Gall's this Gradual is assigned to the feast of St. Adrian. Later it was embodied in the Common of holy Abbots.

The first phrase of the *corpus* ascends majestically when telling of the blessing which surpasses all understanding. The distribution of notes over *benedictiónibus* is striking. Principal as well as secondary accents have each only one note, whereas in each case the syllable following has 2, 5, and 5 notes respectively. The motive over *(praeve)-nísti eum* is repeated in practically the same form over *pretióso* and in accordantly extended form over *-bus dulcédinis* and *ejus corónam*. Over *-(tú)-dinem* in the verse, this motive assumes the form *fdec c*. In place of the descending fourth *g–d*, *posuísti* and *Vitam* have the fourth *a–e*. The melody over *posuísti* repeats itself over *lápide*. The last three groups of neums over *-(ó)-so* form the *jubilus* in the typical Alleluia of the fourth mode which is sung, for example, on the third Sunday of Advent. The *pressus*, however, is missing here before the last note.

The high *c* over *vitam* should be sustained rather than abbreviated. The tempo is gradually accelerated; the last three notes, however, are retarded. The Alleluia of the Tuesday after Easter greets the risen Saviour *(Surréxit)* with the same melisma. The melody over *et tribuísti ei* recurs over *diérum in saéculum*. An attempt at tone-painting reveals itself in the retarded notes over *(longi)-túdinem*. The Gradual of the twenty-second Sunday after Pentecost, and with minor variations the Alleluia-verse of the fourth Sunday of Advent and the twentieth Sunday after Pentecost, close with the melody over *saéculum*. This verse is written in the first mode, which also prevails in the *corpus*. The final comes somewhat as a surprise.

TRACT (Ps. 111: 1–3)

1. *Beatus vir, qui timet Dominum:* † *in mandatis ejus cupit nimis.* 2. *Potens in terra erit semen ejus: generatio rectorum benedicetur.* 3. *Gloria et divitiae in domo ejus: et justitia ejus manet in saeculum saeculi.*

1. *Blessed is the man that feareth the Lord:* † *he shall delight exceedingly in his commandments.* 2. *His seed shall be mighty upon earth: the generation of the righteous shall be blessed.* 3. *Glory and wealth shall be in his house: and his justice remaineth forever and ever.*

In its second half each verse has the same formula which, descending to the tonic, sets in one syllable before the word-accent: *-tis ejus, rec-tórum, -a éjus*. The first and second verse have the same final cadence, a change from *b* to *b♭* being introduced. The melodies of the second and third verse are identical up to the florid close over *saéculum saéculi*.

Happy St. Joseph, who in the fear of the Lord, even at the cost of great sacrifice, promptly and joyfully carried out every commandment of God. Can we find another house or home possessing the fame and spiritual wealth of the house of Nazareth? What great and innumerable blessings have been bestowed upon the entire world by this house!

The old manuscripts assign this composition to the feast of Pope Gregory the Great.

OFFERTORY (Ps. 88: 25)

1. *Veritas mea et misericordia mea cum ipso*: 2. *et in nomine meo exaltabitur cornu ejus.*

1. *My truth and my mercy are with him*: 2. *and in my name his horn shall be exalted.*

This piece marks the only place in the Gradule where the Fa clef is on the fourth line. This would indicate that the melody has a strong tendency to descend. The first half of the first phrase with a range of but five note moves in intervals of seconds and thirds (repercussion); the second half has one interval of a third, with the other intervals seconds. Over the word *ipso* the melody modulates to a full step below the tonic —a turn much favored by the second mode. The second phrase has a range of an octave and comparatively large intervals; there are, however, fewer neums on individual syllables than in the first phrase. The melody over *-córdia* recurs over m*ea*, and in an abbreviated form over *ejus.*

The melody is solemn and well sustained, which is all the more fitting particularly when the word of God is quoted.

God redeemed His promises in the mystery of the Incarnation and thereby exemplified His fidelity and mercy. St. Joseph was chosen the guardian of this mystery. The text, however, may also bear a particular application to the saint. He possesses the Truth of that God who said: "I am the Truth." With him are the merciful Heart of Jesus and she whom we greet as the Mother of mercy. He was privileged to spend years in the most intimate companionship of Jesus and Mary. God ordained him (Preface of feast) to be the Spouse of the Virgin Mother of God and placed him, his faithful and prudent servant, at the head of the family, that he might be the foster father of the Only-Begotten, conceived of the Holy Ghost. The eternal decrees provided for the exaltation of this humble and hidden Saint of God, and determined him the protector of the universal Church. Such is the providence of God, portrayed by the triumphant ring of the melody with its major chord over *nómine meo.*

The old manuscripts assign this number to the feast of Pope St. Marcellus.

COMMUNION (Matt. 1: 20)

1. *Joseph, fili David, noli timere accipere Mariam conjugem tuam:* 2. *quod enim in ea natum est, de Spiritu Sancto est.*

1. *Joseph, son of David, fear not to take unto thee Mary thy wife:* 2. *for that which is born in her is of the Holy Ghost.*

Both phrases have similar divisions. The first phrase begins on *g–c*, tarries on *d* and *g*, and concludes on the tonic. The second phrase begins on *g–d*, makes a half-pause on *d* and with a florid melisma closes on the tonic. The significant words *María* and *Spíritu* are well emphasized in both phrases. The melodic distinction given to *est* at the end of the two half-phrases is conspicuous and provocative of thought. The original is embodied in the Communion *Erubéscant* of the Monday of Holy Week. The first phrase develops freely in its first half. After that there is an apparent correspondence between various members of today's Communion and the Communion *Erubescant: accípere Ma-(ríam)* and *gratulántur ma-(lis), (cón)-jugem tuam* and *(ma)-lis meis, in ea natum* and *(indu)-ántur pudóre, est* and *(-ti) -a. Spíritu* is again treated more freely, while *Sancto est* corresponds to *(ad)-vérsum est*.

Indeed, the Communion text holds glad tidings for St. Joseph, following as they do the painful anxieties and doubts and fear he experienced. Now he will not need to separate himself from her whom he regarded as the purest of Virgins and whom he loved with the chastest love. The close relation with the supernatural and miraculous paralyzed his soul, St. Bernard says. (Oberhammer, II, 247). He has been initiated by the Angel into the mystery of the Incarnation, into the miraculous operation of the Holy Ghost in the womb of his Spouse—the Holy Ghost ever co-operates at the celebration of the Holy Eucharist. May He also prepare our hearts that they become worthy to receive the Son of the purest of Virgins!

* * * *

THE ANNUNCIATION OF THE BLESSED VIRGIN MARY

(March 25)

This is one of the most ancient feasts of the Church and can be traced back to the fifth century. Its chants are contained in the oldest manuscripts, while the Mass as such is post-Gregorian.

INTROIT (Ps. 44: 13, 15, 16)

1. *Vultum tuum deprecabuntur omnes divites plebis:* 2. *adducentur regi virgines post eam; proximae ejus adducentur tibi in laetitia et exsultatione.* Ps. *Eructavit cor meum verbum bonum: * dico ego opera mea regi.*

1. *All the rich among the people shall entreat thy countenance:* 2. *after her shall virgins be brought to the King: her neighbors shall be brought to thee in gladness and rejoicing.* Ps. *My heart hath uttered a good word: * I speak my works to the King.*

The words of the psalm-verse are heard frequently during the course of the ecclesiastical year, bur scarcely ever are they so full of meaning as today. Most ardently heaven and earth awaited the word which the Virgin of Nazareth was to utter! And today it is spoken, a good word, a word which drew down from heaven the Son of God and gave us in Mary a loving Mother; a word, which imparts to her soul a new beauty. And when the Word was made flesh, Mary became the Mother of God. Truly sublime in her dignity of motherhood, she is almost more noble when uttering the simple words: *Ancílla Dómini*—"I am the handmaid of the Lord." She is not only prepared to give the Word of God a human body, human life, but also ready to share with Him poverty, persecution, insults, and suffering.

Heaven and earth vie with one another in paying her homage. While the mighty of heaven salute her in the Archangel Gabriel, the kings of earth prostrate themselves before her, offer their crowns at her shrine, and implore her blessing.

As if in deferential obeisance, the melody descends gracefully and ascends in a similar manner. The whole is characterized by a suppressed affection, a holding of one's breath, as it were, in the presence of the majesty of Him whom Mary carries in her womb: *super quem Reges continébunt os suum.*

The second phrase introduces a new line of thought. The angel declares unto Mary, but she avows that she knows no man. What an ideal of perfect virginity to strive for! Following in her footsteps *(post eam),* countless virgins *(vírgines)* have given their hearts and their undivided love to the King of Kings. The accented syllable here, as is frequently the case, has but one note while the syllable following has several. The same holds good with regard to the secondary accent on *deprecabúntur* and *adducéntur.* The melody moves in simple fashion within the tetrachord *d–g.* The first half of the third phrase likewise confines itself to a tetrachord *(c–f).* The interval of a fourth over *adducéntur* harks back to *(di)-vites* of the first phrase. Over *laetítia* a bright joy characterizes the melody and depicts for us the serene happiness that the chaste soul of the Mother of God experiences when immersed in the contemplation of the Deity.

In the oldest manuscripts this Introit is assigned to the first of January, and bears the superscription *Statio ad Sanctam Mariam*; it is likewise assigned to today's feast, to the feast of the Assumption of the Blessed Virgin, and, as if by way of illustrating the second and third phrases, to the feasts of St. Agnes (January 21) and St. Euphemia (September 16). It forms the Introit of the second Mass in the Common of a Virgin at the present time.

GRADUAL (Ps. 44: 3, 5)

1. *Diffusa est gratia in labiis tuis*: 2. *propterea benedixit te Deus in aeternum. V̆. 1. Propter veritatem, et mansuetudinem, et justitiam*: 2. *et deducet te mirabiliter dextera tua.*

1. *Grace is poured abroad in thy lips*; 2. *therefore hath God blessed thee forever. V̆. 1. Because of truth and meekness, and justice*; 2. *and thy right hand shall conduct thee wonderfully.*

The words of the Gradual refer in the first place to the Messias; a part of them is thus sung on the Sunday within the octave of the Nativity. Considering the close relation which exists between Child and Mother, however, the Liturgy refers them to the Mother also.

Mary has on this day proffered a wonderful word which has won for her a further blessing, yea, the plenitude of all blessings. The eternal Son of God will become her Child.

> Her word a blessing to the world imparts;
> Mankind it saves from Satan's fiery darts.
> —*G. Dreves*

The text of the corpus forms the Offertory for the feast of the Purification, the Alleluia-verse for the feast of St. Lucy (December 13), and the Communion for the feast of St. Anne (July 26). The first phrase rises to unwonted heights. A particularly happy coincidence is the fact that just today the words *lábiis tuis* are sung with such intensity of expression. The tonal as well as the harmonic foundation of the second half of the second phrase is formed by *f*, and the high point of the melody which heretofore was *b*, now becomes *b♭*.

The text of today's verse introduces also the Gradual on the feast of the Assumption and forms likewise the Alleluia-verse for the Mass of a Virgin not a Martyr. The introductory is known to us from the verse of the second Sunday of Lent. The melody forms a splendid climax over the final syllable of *mansuetúdinem*, then returns deftly to the tonic. The *et justítiam* is reminiscent of Epiphany; that which follows, of the feast of the Assumption; the conclusion, of the second Mass of Christmas.

TRACT (Ps. 44, 11—13, 10, 15, 16)

1. *Audi, filia et vide, et inclina aurem tuam:* † *quia concupivit rex* (—) *speciem tuam.* 2. *Vultum tuum deprecabuntur omnes* † *divites plebis:* † *filiae regum in honore tuo.* 3. *Adducentur regi virgines post eam:* † *proximae ejus* (—) *afferentur tibi.* 4. *Adducentur in laetitia, et exsultatione:* † *adducentur in templum regis.*

1. *Hearken, O daughter, and see and incline thy ear:* † *for the king hath greatly desired* (—) *thy beauty.* 2. *Thy countenance entreat shall all* † *the rich among the people:* † *the daughters of kings in the honor.* 3. *After her shall virgins be brought to the king:* † *her neighbors* (—) *shall be brought to thee.* 4. *They shall be brought with gladness and rejoicing:* † *they shall be brought into the temple of the king.*

The first verse is identical with the verse of the Gradual on the feast of the Assumption. The last three verses are practically the same as the text of the Introit.

As usual, the middle cadence precedes the sign (†), while the caesura precedes the sign (—).

DURING PASCHAL TIME

FIRST ALLELUIA VERSE (Luke 1: 28)

1. *Ave Maria, gratia plena, Dominus tecum:* 2. *benedicta tu in mulieribus. Alleluia.*

1. *Hail, Mary, full of grace: the Lord is with thee:* 2. *Blessed art thou among women. Alleluia.*

This text with its melody is already found in Codex 121 of Einsiedeln. Most likely it was original to the ninth Sunday after Pentecost.

SECOND ALLELUIA VERSE (Num. 17: 8)

1. *Virga Jesse floruit:* 2. *Virgo Deum et hominem genuit:* 3. *pacem Deus reddidit, in se reconcilians ima summis. Alleluia.*

1. *The rod of Jesse hath blossomed:* 2. *a virgin hath brought forth God and man:* 3. *God hath given peace, reconciling the lowest with the highest in himself. Alleluia.*

The text as such forms a beautiful panegyric, and, coupled with its sweet melody, is like a bouquet of fragrant blossoms which becomes a genuine delight to the singer. *Allelúia* with its *jubilus* forms the theme, and is repeated with variations in the verse. The introductory resembles the Alleluia *Dulce lignum* on May 3. The first half of the melody over -*lú*- is repeated over *virga*, is developed over *se reconcíli-(ans)*, and simplified over *(réddi)-dit*. The second half of the same melody terminates phrases and half-phrases no less than five times, and yet this repetition is ever delightful; in most cases these phrases have a varied introduction. The first part of the *jubilus* has an interval of a fifth; the concluding part has the same range. This interval reappears over *Jesse* and over *pacem*. All combine and effectively depict for us how God alone can grant the inestimable treasure of peace. The second part of the *jubilus* produces an after-effect at *(Vir)-go*.

Today, in the womb of the purest Virgin, abject human nature is espoused to the Word of the Most High, and thus, "reconciling the lowest with the highest in Himself, God hath given peace" to the disturbed world.

OFFERTORY—COMMUNION

Both of these chants are identical with those of the fourth Sunday of Advent: *Ave María* and *Ecce Virgo*. At Mass the priest introduces the *Pater noster* with the words: "Taught by the precepts of salvation, and following the divine commandment, we make bold to say: Our Father ...." Instructed by a like divine command the Archangel Gabriel approaches Mary with the salutation *Ave*. Filled with reverence for the Virgin he dares pronounce these words only as God's messenger. We likewise should pray and sing these words imbued with the sentiments of the Archangel.

Today is realized the first part of the Communion text, for on this day the Angel declared unto Mary and she conceived of the Holy Ghost. Today the Word was made flesh, became our Emmanuel, God with us, and dwells among us. This union of Divinity and humanity in the person of the divine Word is indissoluble. The soul indeed separates from the body on Golgotha, but Divinity and humanity can never be separated in Christ. Thus has human nature been elevated to a place of singular dignity and blessing. And in Holy Communion this same Christ comes into our hearts with His Divinity and with His humanity.

*   *   *   *

ST. MARK, EVANGELIST
(April 25)

The Introit opens with the word *Protexísti*. In it the Evangelist gives expression to his gratitude to God for the protection which he has been given against his enemies and persecutors (particularly at his martyrdom). The melody repeats identical and similar forms and requires lively rendition. The tonic of the seventh mode is found only at the beginning and at the end of the antiphon.

The first ALLELUIA VERSE and the OFFERTORY are the same as those on the feast of the Apostles Philip and James (May 1).

The second ALLELUIA VERSE *Posuísti* describes in a beautiful and tuneful melody how God has placed on the head of the saint a crown of precious stones. The verse repeats the motives of *Allelúia* and its *jubilus*: a b c d. *Posuísti* corresponds to a, *Dómine* to b c and the first part of a; *ejus* is an extended form of c, a free repetition of which is given over *corónam*; *de lápide pretióso* repeats the entire melody of *allelúia* and the *jubilus*.

The melody dates back to the twelfth century.

The COMMUNION *Laetábitur justus* belongs to the most effective and worth-while chants of the Graduale. It rouses to the height of enthusiasm. The introductory motive *f gga gf* becomes *fa ag cc a cg* over *in Dó-(mino)*, and *fac $e^1d^1c^1$* over *et sperábit*. Such is the song of a faith that knows neither enemy nor difficulty. After a quiet, contrasting melodic descent, the jubilant *Allelúia* with its *fac^1 $d^1f^1e^1c^1e^1d^1c^1$* brings the piece to a close. Even as the beginning of the members of each phrase depict exuberant joy, so the final groups with their rhymes *-mino, corde, -lúia* and the sequences *recti* and *-lúia* with *cab♭éb♭ ga ♭ba g fg ágf* breathe the peace of a soul united to God.

Revue, 20, 138.

*   *   *   *

SS. PHILIP AND JAMES THE YOUNGER, APOSTLES
(May 1)

It was on this day during the pontificate of John III (661–674) that the Church of the Twelve Apostles at Rome, which possessed relics of the two Apostles Philip and James, was dedicated. The same date commemorated the deliverance of Rome by Narses from the Gothic king Totila. The resulting joy of the populace is clearly expressed in the Introit.

INTROIT (Neh. 9: 27)

1. *Clamaverunt ad te, Domine, in tempore afflictionis,* 2. *et tu de caelo exaudisti eos, alleluia, alleluia.* Ps. *Exsultate justi in Domino:* * *rectos decet collaudatio.*

1. *They cried to thee, O Lord, in the time of their tribulation,* 2. *and thou heardest them from heaven, alleluia, alleluia.* Ps. *Rejoice in the Lord, ye just:* * *praise becometh the upright.*

These words of the Introit we can readily apply to the Apostles. Philip willingly heeded the call of the Lord: Do thou follow me! In fact, whosoever would follow Jesus, and particularly he who is called to the apostolate, must walk the way of the cross and be prepared for sacrifice and suffering. The Lord and Master clearly predicted this for the Apostles. In their own country they were driven out of the synagogues, scourged, and dragged to civil courts; in foreign countries where Providence assigned them fields of labor, they were subjected to poverty, privation, and persecution. The first phrase recounts how often these same Apostles cried to the Lord for help, while the second phrase notes that their prayers were heard. The assurance of the Lord that He would be with them all days never failed them, even in that supreme moment when they climaxed their life with a martyr's death. Death, however gruesome, brought the fulfillment of their only wish, union with their divine Master. Hence, the psalm-verse breaks forth into jubilation.

After the solemn intonation and the effective emphasizing of *Dómine* we should expect further development. The melody continues modestly, however, and moves quite regularly within the range of the D plagal mode. The two *allelúia* are those which usually conclude the Introits of the second mode. The modulation over *eos* into a full step below the dominant is quite in place.

FIRST ALLELUIA VERSE—OFFERTORY (Ps. 88: 6)

1. *Confitebuntur caeli mirabilia tua, Domine:* 2. *etenim veritatem tuam in ecclesia sanctorum.*

1. *The heavens shall confess thy wonders, O Lord:* 2. *and thy truth in the church of the saints.*

Who, we might ask, are the heavens and who the community of the saints? In first order we might place the starry firmament, proclaiming as it does by its beauty and its harmonic laws, the glory and the fidelity and the power of God. Pope St. Gregory, commenting on the words of the psalm: "The heavens are confirmed by the word of the Lord," tells us that by the term "heavens" we are here to understand the Apostles. They derive their power from the divine Spirit; failing this, they could never have dared to oppose the powers of the world. The community of saints, according to the favorite interpretation of St. Paul, are the (first) Christian communities. It was to them that the Apostles first proclaimed the wonderful deeds of the Lord. They were made to share particularly the miracle of His divine incarnation, the wonders of His goodness, humility, meekness, and compassionate, never-tiring, unselfish love. The Apostles carried the truth of Christ to the ends of the world and taught that He alone is the truth which makes us free and happy, that He remained faithful even unto death.

In heaven, the saints without ceasing proclaim the operations of God's miraculous power and fidelity in them. True, they had to suffer persecution for justice' sake—the Epistle of the day indicates this—but now they are in heaven, "are numbered among the children of God, and their lot is among the saints" (Epistle).

The Offertory has the same text as the Alleluia-verse with the exception of the word *étenim*; the latter is compensated for by two *allelúia* at the end of the piece. Both compositions are in the seventh mode, have the same structure and similar melodies over *mirabília*; both emphasize the word *caeli*, the Offertory particularly, with a view toward word-painting.

The *jubilus* has the form a a^1 b. The melody over *allelúia* recurs over *Confitebúntur*, while that over *mirabília* recurs in fine symmetry over *veritátem tuam*. The first phrase is constructed in psalmodic form, having intonation, middle cadence on the dominant, and final cadence on the tonic. The *étenim* repeats its melisma. The fact that the second syllable of this word has neums may be ascribed to the pronunciation of the vulgar Latin which separated compound words into their component parts, thus: *et—énim*.

The Offertory surpasses the Alleluia in boldness of movement and display of enthusiasm. The melody is characterized by the fiery zeal with which the Apostles spoke of the wonderful deeds of God and with which they inflamed others. It depicts the influence of Apostolic teaching spread to the very confines of the world. The intervals of a fourth especially are effective. The second phrase, which begins with the same motive as the first, is more quiet. The *c d c c g c c* over *(sanc)-tórum* is extended to *cc dcd éc g a ccc* over the first *allelúia* and to *ede éc g a ccc* over the second *allelúia*.

SECOND ALLELUIA VERSE (John 14: 9)

1. *Tanto tempore vobiscum sum et non cognivistis me?* 2. *Philippe, qui videt me, videt et Patrem meum.*

1. *So long a time have I been with you, and have you not known me?* 2. *Philip, he that seeth me, seeth my Father also.*

The melody was explained on the vigil of Christmas.

These words of the Saviour, filled with loving complaint, call to mind the prayer of St. Augustine: *Nóverim Te*—would that I knew Thee, and knew the Father in Thee! Every day that I am granted to serve and dwell in Thy house let me grow in knowledge and love of Thee, so that my song and prayer may become ever purer, deeper, and more perfect.

COMMUNION (John 14: 9, 10)

1. *Tanto tempore vobiscum sum, et non cognovistis me?* 2. *Philippe, qui videt me, videt et Patrem meum, alleluia:* 3. *non credis, quia ego in Patre, et Pater in me est? alleluia, alleluia.*

1. *So long a time have I been with you, and have you not known me?* 2. *Philip, he that seeth me, seeth my Father also, alleluia:* 3. *believest thou not that I am in the Father, and the Father in me? alleluia, alleluia.*

The first two phrases of the Communion, which form the text of the Alleluia-verse, as well as the third phrase, are taken from the Gospel. The first part is tinged with the sadness which the Saviour must have felt when speaking these words. The melodic figure over *témpore* recurs over *Philíppe* and that over *cognovístis me* again over *(Pa)-trem, alle-(lúia)*.

The above selection serves also as a Responsory at Matins. This is at times mirrored in the responsorial character of the melody. According to Wagner (III, 338 f.) the piece has three musical periods, the first of which closes with the word *credis*. The second, which has an energetic upward tendency, begins with *quia ego* on low *d*. The preceding musical period should then, if we consider the need and rules for contrast when combining phrases, close with *e f*. This is actually the case in the present instance with *credis*. The same reason might explain the notation over *est* which immediately precedes the first word of the third musical period. In this case, however, the interrogatory form of the sentence which closes with an upward inflection, should also be given due consideration. The two *allelúia* which form the third musical period in many Responsories include the most important motives. The ascent of the melody in the third phrase is similar to that of the Communion on the Sunday after the Ascension, and reminds us of the Ascension of our Lord to His heavenly Father. Taken as a whole, there is something about the melody that demands respect and reverence, at the same time filling us with holy astonishment.

To know our Saviour is to imitate Him. How well, then, can we apply to ourselves the gentle reproof and urgent exhortation to a more faithful imitation, as the first phrase of the Communion indicates! In Holy Communion the Saviour gives us a new and deeper understanding of His essence and of His intimate union with the Father. Together with the Father and the Holy Ghost He comes into our heart, and imparts to us the necessary strength to follow in His footsteps without faltering.

*   *   *   *

THE FINDING OF THE HOLY CROSS

(May 3)

The Mass is post-Gregorian. The Introit and the Offertory are the same as those on Maundy Thursday. But what on that day was still prophecy is now become reality. The Crucified has shown Himself to be our salvation, our life, and our resurrection. He who was exalted on the cross is now elevated to the glory of the Father. He will die no more, for He is now in possession of the eternal life of glory. A complete transfiguration was effected with the dawn of an Easter morn, with the jubilant ring of an Alleluia.

FIRST ALLELUIA VERSE (Ps. 95: 10)

1. *Dicite in gentibus,* 2. *quia Dominus regnavit a ligno.*

1. *Say ye among the gentiles,* 2. *that the Lord hath reigned from the wood.*

During the Christmas season the words: "The Lord hath reigned," in conjunction with the phrase: "He is clothed with beauty," were of frequent occurrence. Today, however, in place of the second phrase, we supply the following: "The Lord hath reigned from the wood." During the first Christian centuries it was generally believed that these words had been quoted from the Psalter. The Jews had even been accused of deleting them from the Psalter. The fact of the matter is that they form a later addition, albeit, full of deep meaning. The inscription on the cross bore witness that the Lord is King. The Saviour Himself, in fact, called the day of His crucifixion the day of His exaltation and triumph. For Him the cross is the royal throne whence He draws all things unto Himself, the throne of grace which all may approach with confidence. The early Middle Ages delighted in making the cross of precious metals studded with gems, and placing a golden crown on the head of the Crucified.

The melody is sung with the same text on Friday of Easter Week, and again on Saturday of Pentecost Week with the text: "It is the spirit that quickeneth, but the flesh profiteth nothing." The *allelúia* has the form a b b[1]. The first phrase, which has the mode-rate range of a fourth, moves about the tonic. The second phrase has a more extended range. The *ĉ d c g á g f* over *-(lú)-ia* becomes *b̂ c b g á b a* over *-te*, and *f̂ g f e f̂ e d* over *Dó-*. *Regnávit* is an extension of b and closes with the final cadence of the Alleluia of Holy Saturday.

SECOND ALLELUIA VERSE

1. *Dulce lignum, dulces clavos dulcia ferens pondera*: 2. *quae sola fuisti digna sustinere Regem caelorum, et Dominum.*

1. *Sweet wood, sweet nails, bearing a sweet weight*: 2. *which alone wast worthy to bear the King of heaven, and the Lord.*

The first phrase is like a solemn echo of the refrain which is inserted after every second stanza of the hymn sung during the Adoration of the Cross on Good Friday. The full import of the phrase for today's feast is indicated by the words *Flecte ramos* of that hymn. There the cross is besought to relax its native tension and rigidness and become a soft and quiet place of rest for the King of heaven; the cruel nails are entreated not to inflict pain, but to consider the sweet burden it is their privilege to bear.

The touching melody, the first phrase of which especially should be rendered delicately, is characterized by tenderness and fervor. The melody over *allelúia* recurs over *dulce lignum*. It likewise introduces the *Lauda Sion* on the feast of Corpus Christi. The second part of the first phrase bears some similarity to the first Alleluia-verse. The second phrase emphasizes the thought that the cross alone was worthy to bear the King of heaven. The melody over *sustinére* is similar to that of the first member of the *jubilus*.

This cross of our Saviour has sweetened the bitter trials of this life and made them bearable, it has lightened the many heavy burdens under which mankind labors, it has reconciled souls with the hard lot which has been made their portion. Therefore: Hail to thee, thou sweet Cross!

COMMUNION

1. *Per signum Crucis de inimicis nostris* 2. *libera nos, Deus noster, (alleluia).*

1. *By the sign of the cross, from our enemies,* 2. *deliver us, O thou our God, (alleluia).*

The circumstances of the times and the fear of the Lombard invasions into Roman territory very likely occasioned this prayer, the content of which was already expressed in the Secret. In the Old Testament the destroying angel passed the houses of those whose doorposts were sprinkled with the blood of the sacrificial lamb. The cross of Christ, crimson with the blood of the true Paschal Lamb, is a source of terror to all the enemies of Christ and of our soul. We will be safe against all attacks of the enemy if we place ourselves under its protecting arms, if we look confidently to the Crucified and model our life on His life of obedience unto death.

In Holy Communion our souls are sprinkled with the blood of the same Christ, thus protecting us from all spiritual harm.

On the Monday after the fourth Sunday in Lent this melody is sung to the text: "From my secret sins cleanse me, O Lord: and from those of others spare Thy servant." Today's petition for deliverance, *libera nos*—"deliver us"—is made particularly impressive by its interval of a fifth, and by emphasizing and accentuating high *e* with a double *pressus*. The beginning of this second phrase, then, implies a lively gradation of melody in comparison with that over *de inimicis nostris*, where *c* predominates. The word *noster* also receives special prominence, and, like the three preceding parts, has the same florid melody with a double *pressus*. The *a gagf* over *Crucis* seems to recur as *e decb* over *-ra nos*.

This melody is also sung on the feast of the Most Pure Heart of Mary. Its origin is most likely to be found in the Communion *Dilexisti*, which is now in the Common of a Holy Woman not a Martyr; in the old manuscripts it is given on the feast of the Assumption. *Per signum Crucis* is identical with *Dilexisti*, and *-cis nostris* with *-titiam*; *-ra nos* resembles *-disti nos*, while *Deus no-* resembles *iniquitá-(tem).*

* * * *

SOLEMNITY OF ST. JOSEPH
(Spouse of the Blessed Virgin Mary, Confessor, and Patron of the Universal Church.)
AFTER EASTER

Today's feast dates back to the year 1847. Since the time of Pius X it has been celebrated on the Wednesday of the second week after

Easter. In some places it is celebrated on the third Sunday after Easter.

The feast was formerly known as the *Patrocinium*—the Patronage of St. Joseph. The same thought persists in the liturgy of the Mass for today, which celebrates him as the patron of the universal Church. It is in this sense that the word *Protéctor* in the Introit and the first Alleluia-verse and the word *Patrocínium* in the second Alleluia-verse is to be taken. The Offertory, moreover, is a hymn of thanks for the blessing and protection which the saint has imparted to the Church. God gave him the sublime office of protector of the divine Child, that he might guard Him against all dangers and enemies, and might nourish and foster Him. The small house of Nazareth, however, has now grown to be the universal Church, and the love which St. Joseph centered on the divine Child now embraces all those who belong to the mystical body of Christ.

INTROIT (Ps. 32: 20, 21)

1. *Adjutor et protector noster est Dominus*: 2. *in eo laetabitur cor nostrum*, 3. *et in nomine sancto eius speravimus*. 4. *Alleluia, alleluia*, Ps. *Qui regis Israel, intende*: * *qui deducis velut ovem, Joseph.*

1. *The Lord is our helper and protector*: 2. *in him our heart shall rejoice*, 3. *and in his holy name we have trusted*. 4. *Alleluia, alleluia*. Ps. *Give ear, O thou that rulest Israel*: * *thou that leadest Joseph like a sheep.*

The Introit *Salve sancta parens* for various feasts of the Blessed Virgin takes its melody from the feast of the Epiphany. In like manner the melody of the second and third phrases of the Introit for today is taken from the Introit of the third Christmas Mass. With the latter melody we greet on this occasion the royal Child with His Mother, and on another the Child with His divinely appointed foster father.

The first phrase sings the praises of God for the help and protection he has deigned to grant us through the mediation of St. Joseph. The word *protéctor* is given prominence melodically. The emotional *laetábitur*, the vigorous *cor*, and the trusting *sperávimus* of the second and third phrases have such well-adapted melodies, that we might be led to suppose an original composition. Through an association of ideas *nómine sancto eius* recalls *vocábitur nomen eius* of the Christmas Mass. The first *allelúia* repeats the melody of *laetábitur*, while the second has the same close as the Christmas Introit.

The verse reminds us of the loving guidance with which God led the Israelites, especially the patriarch Jacob and the Egyptian Joseph, who is the prototype of St. Joseph. With still greater love God guides and directs St. Joseph and all who are entrusted to his care.

FIRST ALLELUIA VERSE

1. *De quacumque tribulatione clamaverint ad me, exaudiam eos,* 2. *et ero protector eorum semper.*

1. *In whatever tribulation they shall cry to me, I will hear them,* 2. *and be their protector always.*

The melody makes frequent use of the intervals *c–e–g* with pauses mostly on *g* and *e*. It might thus be assigned to the ancient C mode, which, like the *Pópule meus*, closes on *d* (cf. Jeannin, *Mélodies syriennes et chaldéenes*, Leroux, Paris, p. 124). As early as the eleventh century it was sung in honor of the Cross, to the text beginning with *Nos autem*. The three *pressus* serve as so many pillars for the buoyant melody of the *jubilus*. The melody over *De quacúmque* is repeated over *clamáverint*, while that over *exáudiam* is similar to *(pro)-téctor eorum* (*Revue*, 3, 163). A peculiar joy should characterize our rendition of the two phrases in which St. Joseph speaks to us in a reassuring manner and we, in turn, gratefully acknowledge his loving protection.

SECOND ALLELUIA VERSE

1. *Fac nos innocuam, Joseph, decurrere vitam*: 2. *sitque tuo semper tuta patriocnio.*

1. *Obtain for us, O Joseph, to lead an innocent life*; 2. *and may it ever be safe through thy patronage.*

The text forms a distich. The melody, however, is not influenced by its metrical form.

The original melody dates from the eleventh century. A feeling of earnest entreaty and of lofty aspiration pervades the melody, depicting, as it were, anticipation of an ascension to heaven. Well adapted to the pleading character of the text is the soaring melody at the close.

Faultless and pure was the life of St. Joseph to whose care God entrusted the Virgin of Virgins and the Christ Child, who was innocence itself. The melodies over *Fac nos* and *Joseph* show similarity. The florid melisma over *tu-(ta)* has the form a b c. Part a has rhymelike consonance to which b with its descending line forms a contrast; c is made up of *semper tu-(ta)* and *vitam*.

Being mindful of our own helplessness, we should sing this melody with great fervor. When entreating St. Joseph to be our protector at all times, let us not forget the great need we shall have of his protection in the hour of death. An atmosphere of glad and trusting hope in the faithful, and often proven, love of St. Joseph will then pervade our chant.

Revue, 9, 131 ff.

OFFERTORY (Ps. 147: 12, 13)

1. *Lauda, Jerusalem, Dominum*: 2. *quoniam confortavit seras portarum tuarum*: 3. *benedixit filiis tuis in te*. 4. *Alleluia, alleluia*.

1. *Praise the Lord, O Jerusalem*: 2. *because he hath strengthened the bolts of thy gates*: 3. *He hath blessed thy children within thee*. 4. *Alleluia, alleluia*.

The phrasing of the text is both clear and distinct. The first phrase is an exhortation to Jerusalem to render praise to God, the second and third phrases give the reasons for this exhortation, while the fourth phrase comprises a joyous Alleluia. *Lauda* is not so much a call to an energetic awakening as to sober reflection: Jerusalem, city of peace, reflect and realize, how according to the implication of your very name, you have every reason to praise your God. God has so strengthened the bolts of your gates that enemies shall storm against them in vain. He has given you a powerful protector in St. Joseph. The melody over the accented syllable of *confortávit* is invigorating and triumphant. The musical turn *c bc ac ga a* immediately preceding and introducing this word is very charming. St. Joseph not only protects the Church from external enemies, but mediates for her inner life and well-being *(in te)* rich graces and blessings from which all her children may draw. The veins through which these graces and blessings flow to the individual are the Sacraments of the Church. The melody now becomes more quiet, more simple, one might say more intimate The second part of each of these phrases shows various similarities:

gc	ag	gf	gag		
Dó-	mi-	num			
abca	ag	g		gfag	g
se-	ras	por-		tá-	rum
gc	ag	g		gfag	g
fi-	li-	is		tu-	is.

The first *Allelúia* is an earnest, almost timid cry of joy, following which the melody develops brilliantly and joyfully. The *pressus*, which are each preceded by four-note groups, form the points of support for the rich melisma. These four-note groups invariably set in a third higher than their preceding note. There is also a group over -*ia* similar to the one at the close of the first phrase.

COMMUNION (Matt. 1: 16)

1. *Jacob autem genuit Joseph, virum Mariae*, 2. *de qua natus est*

1. *Now Jacob begat Joseph, the husband of Mary*, 3. *of whom was*

Jesus, qui vocatur Christus. Alleluia, alleluia.

born Jesus, who is called Christ. Alleluia, alleluia.

The above enumeration brings to completion the genealogy of Christ. Although Jesus is called the Son of David, the Gospels refer to St. Joseph as the son of David also, thus indicating his royal lineage. Over and above this, he stands in closest relationship to our Lord by reason of his inner disposition, and by the fact that he was the worthy consort of the Mother of God.

The melody is taken from the Communion on the vigil of St. Andrew. The dramatic, sparkling vivacity of the original, its feeling of exultation and joy in the cry: "We have found the Messias," obviously cannot be developed with the present modest text. Where the original has: *Invénimus Messíam, qui dícitur Christus,* today's text has: *natus est Jesus, qui vocátur Christus.* This close textual relationship may have occasioned the choice of the melody. Unhappily there is an interval of only a fourth over *Jesus,* while the corresponding word in the original has a fifth. In three instances only does the melody here extend beyond the dominant of the eighth mode, while it becomes the mainstay for the fuller developed second phrase. Low *f* over the second *Allelúia* forms the antithesis to high *f* over *natus.*

The holy names of Jesus, Mary, and Joseph, in whatever sequence they may appear when combined in one sentence, should always be precious and dear to us.

*   *   *   *

THE NATIVITY OF ST. JOHN THE BAPTIST

(June 24)

INTROIT (Isa. 49: 1, 2.)

1. *De ventre matris meae vocavit me Dominus nomine meo,* 2. *et posuit os meum ut gladium acutum;* 3. *sub tegumento manus suae protexit me,* 4. *et posuit me quasi sagittam electam.* Ps. *Bonum est confiteri Domino,* * *et psallere nomini tuo, Altissime.*

1. The Lord hath called me by my name from the womb of my mother, 2. and he hath made my mouth like a sharp sword; 3. in the shadow of his hand he hath protected me, 4. and hath made me as a chosen arrow. Ps. It is good to give praise to the Lord. * and to sing to thy name, O most High.

In the Introit St. John tells of the wonderful things that God has wrought in him. His is the voice of one crying in the wilderness—austere, earnest, solemn. This is graphically depicted by the melody which is devoid of drama, rather restrained, has no noticeable gradations, and employs only few, albeit artistic, forms. The melody, moreover, must be sung in a low pitch, since the verse with its high dominant precludes any transposition upward. A feeling of gratitude is nevertheless apparent, and the whole is pervaded by a joyous ring like an echo of the joyous and bright *Magníficat* which the Mother of God sang in the house of St. John's parents. Our rendition, especially of the numerous bistrophas and tristrophas should not be slow and cumbersome. Rhythmical manuscripts indicate no less than nine *celeriter* (rapidly), and seldom employ sustained neums.

The motive over *(nómi)-ne meo* recurs over *(proté)-xit me* and *(pósu)-it me*. *Acútum* and *manus suae* correspond imitatively to *(pósu)-it os meum*. The second *pósuit* is identical with *protéxit*. The *porrectus* over these two words are resolved into three single notes over *teguménto*. The endings over *meum*, *(a)-cútum* and *suae* have rhythmic similarity.

The melody is assigned to the first mode. As a matter of fact, the actual dominant is that of the second mode, *f*, not *a* of the first mode. There is, moreover, the tone range from low *a* to high *b♭*, and the descent to low *a* which is characteristic of the second mode. These considerations indicate not the first mode but the plagal form, the second mode. If in spite of this the melody is nevertheless assigned to and sung in the first mode, this is evidently done in consideration of the fact that the introduction of the Introit employs a form typical of the first mode. (Cf. *Púeri Hebraeórum*, p. 151). But even then, a rule formerly observed directed that the final cadence of the psalmody should adapt itself to the beginning of the antiphon.

The earnestness and sobriety of the present melody become more apparent if we consider the great joy radiated in the text and melody of the Introit *Ne tímeas* of yesterday's vigil. We should naturally expect an intensification of this joy in the Mass of the feast. This seeming paradox vanishes, however, if we advert to the fact that the Introit of the vigil depicted an angel from heaven as speaking, while today it is St. John, entering upon an austere and sacrificial life which will end in martyrdom, who speaks. And St. John's one wish is to diminish, that Christ may increase.

The text is taken from the prophet Isaias and refers primarily to the coming Messias. When "the angel declared unto Mary"—therefore, before the actual birth of Christ *(De ventre matris meae)*—the name of Jesus was given Him for the first time. God endowed Him with all that was necessary to carry out His vocation. His preaching *(os meum)* carried with it irresistible authority which struck His enemies near by like a "sharp sword," and those at a distance like a "chosen arrow." This sword, however, is sheathed and the arrow is in the quiver and will be used only when and how God wills; but then they will strike true and without fail.

These words of Isaias the Church applies to St. John; today he makes them his own. Like our Saviour, St. John was also called by name while still in the womb of his mother. After he had been conceived an angel addressed him with the name John—"God has shown His mercy." It was this mercy of God that freed him from original sin already in the womb of his mother and filled him with the Holy Ghost. Even before the Sun of Justice has risen, It penetrates with Its sanctifying rays the soul of St. John and makes it holy. In the course of time God leads him into solitude where great souls are prepared and matured for their vocation. The penitential austerity he practiced throughout his life fitted him well for preaching and demanding penance of others. His words smote like a "sharp sword" and "a chosen arrow" all that was unclean and vulgar. He carried out the will of God with the abandon and lightning speed of an arrow. This is the picture of St. John who today sings the earnest words of the Introit.

In contrast with the antiphon, the verse is joyous and jubilant. In it the Church gives expression to that happiness which the Angel prophesied would mark the birth of St. John, and sings the praises of the Lord for all the miracles of grace wrought upon our saint.

Musica sacra, 45, 125 ff., *Caecilia,* 31, 85 ff.

GRADUAL (Jer. 1: 5, 9)

In the *corpus* of the Gradual the person of God is portrayed as speaking; in the verse, the person of the prophet Jeremias, whose words are allotted to St. John. With the Introit taken from Isaias and the Gradual from Jeremias we have the two greatest prophets of the Old Testament represented on the feast of St. John, who "is more than a prophet." Like the Introit, the Gradual describes the operations of God's grace and love in preparing St. John for his sublime vocation and sanctifying him *(sanctificávi te)* "in his mother's womb." Introit and Gradual have thus many points in common.

The *corpus* exhibits textual parallelism.

1. *Priusquam te formarem in utero, novi te:* 2. *et antequam exires de ventre, sanctificavi te.*

1. *Before I formed thee in the bowels of thy mother, I knew thee:* 2. *and before thou camest forth out of the womb, I sanctified thee.*

The second phrase, in repeating the thought of the first, explains and develops it further. Just because God "knew" St. John, He also "sanctified" him *(sanctificávi te)*. The principal thought: "I have sanctified thee," is brought into plastic relief by the melody. In the first phrase the melody moves about the tonic *f* and is consequently low-pitched; in the second it rises to the dominant of the mode. This latter is given special emphasis over *sanctificávi* and *te*. The intonation *Priúsquam* corresponds to the melody over *ántequam exíres*, which is a fifth higher. The fact that the accented syllable of *Priúsquam* has only one note, while the other two syllables have several notes, is probably due to the fact that vulgar Latin was wont to pronounce compounded words as separate words. According to the rules of grammar the words should be accented *priúsquam, étenim, circúmdate*; chant, however, accents them *príus-quam, et-énim, circum-dáte*.

The text of the verse reads as follows:

1. *Misit Dominus manum suam.* 2. *et tetigit os meum,* 3. *et dixit mihi.*

1. *The Lord put forth his hand,* 2. *and touched my mouth,* 3. *and said to me.*

At the end of the third phrase we are prompted to ask the question: What did God say? A colon was formerly placed after the words "said to me," and the Alleluia with its verse was then considered their logical continuation. The fact is, however, that Gradual and Alleluia do not combine to form one whole; they are each assigned to a different mode, at least in the present case. Moreover, the words of Zachary as contained in the Alleluia-verse could hardly be ascribed to our Lord to whom the words of the Gradual refer. The term "Gradual responsory" implies what the answer to the above question will embody. After *dixit mihi*, the text *Priúsquam...sanctificávi te* of the Gradual should be repeated. Needless to say, this sequence was alien to the mind of the prophet Jeremias.

The melody sets in brightly on the dominant, about which it weaves a pleasing melody, and should be sung with a lively tempo. After the graceful descent and ascent over *suam*, the arsis comes to a sharply accented close on the dominant. The thesis, which introduces a relaxation, begins with *et tétigit*. The close over *dixit mihi* is quite common (cf. the Gradual of Epiphany).

ALLELUIA VERSE (Luke 1: 76)

1. *Tu, puer, Propheta Altissimi vocaberis:* 2. *praeibis ante Dominum parare vias eius.*

1. *Thou, child, shalt be called the Prophet of the Highest;* 2. *thou shalt go before the Lord to prepare his ways.*

Here the father of St. John depicts in prophetic vision the honor and dignity which will accrue to his God-given child and the pre-eminence it will be accorded over all other prophets. These latter beheld the Messias only in the distant future; St. John, however, can point with his finger to "the Lamb of God who takes away the sins of the world." He is privileged to prepare the way upon which the Messias will enter when seeking to find that which was lost.

There is something intimate and homely about the melody. It has a Christmas spirit about it, such as we frequently heard in the Alleluia from the third Christmas Mass up to Epiphany. This fact also indicates the intimate relation which exists between the birth of Christ and the birth of St. John. The twofold division *Tu puer* and *praeíbis, prophéta* and *Dóminum* is well known to us.

There can be no thought of an original composition here. All other Alleluia melodies of this type have the melismas that are here over *prophéta*, either at the end of a phrase or at least at the end of a member of a phrase. The caesura after *prophéta* (immediately preceding *Altíssimi* with which it is intimately connected), however, is somewhat disturbing. Melodic considerations most likely occasioned the change of text. The composer did not choose the wording of the Benedictus-verse: *Tu Puer ...praeíbis ante fáciem Dómini* as found in all, even the oldest, translations of the Bible, but a shorter one. A close study of this type of Alleluia will show precisely that our melody can be employed only with a sentence structure which has six word-accents of two or three syllables each. The usual wording of the Benedictus-verse has an additional accent. And hence the composer, in order not to mutilate the musical form or to detract from its effectiveness, arranged the text in favor of musical form—a procedure of comparatively frequent occurrence in the old chant. The present Alleluia did not exist before the eleventh century. Prior to that a different text was used.

OFFERTORY (Ps. 91: 13)

1. *Justus ut palma florebit*: 2. *sicut cedrus quae in Libano est, multiplicabitur.*

1. *The just man shall flourish like the palm-tree*: 2. *he shall grow up like the cedar of Libanus.*

The melody depicts the palm and cedar of Libanus in such a clear and perceptible manner that we can readily visualize them as standing before us, pointing upward, elevated above all that is earthly, and completely immersed in a warm flood of sunlight. In a similar manner we might speak of the saints of God. Since their habitation is in heaven, they have no further need of anything earthly. Among such is St. John, the beloved disciple of Christ, to whose feast the oldest manuscripts assign our present melody. St. John the Baptist also grew like the palm in a lonely, barren desert, and like the cedar developed strength in preparation for his difficult vocation. In this he persevered bravely and vigorously until his life was crowned with a martyr's death.

For further explanation, see the feast of St. John the Evangelist.

COMMUNION (Luke 1: 76)

1. *Tu, puer, Propheta Altissimi vocaberis*: 2. *praeibis enim ante faciem Domini parare vias eius.*

1. *Thou, child, shalt be called the Prophet of the Highest*: 2. *for thou shalt go before the face of the Lord to prepare his ways.*

The Communion has the same text as the Alleluia, and to a great extent the same melody. In regard to the latter we need but make the following comparison:

Communion		Alleluia
Tu puer	=	*Tu puer*
paráre	=	*Altís-(simi)*
vias eius	=	*-simi vocáberis*

We might be inclined to think that, since Alleluia and Communion have the same text, the melody of the former had some influence on that of the latter. The fact of the matter is, however, that in the oldest manuscripts the Alleluia has a different text and melody. From an artistic standpoint, the Communion melody is rated higher than that of the Alleluia. The word *prophéta* is impressive—annotated manuscripts have a broad *podatus* over the accented syllable—while the melody, with its high *a*, depicts wonderment over the honor and dignity of this child of grace. A holy admiration has overtaken the father of St. John; at the same time a proud paternal joy vibrates through the melody. This joy is especially apparent over *praeíbis* for, among all prophets, St. John alone was permitted to be a contemporary of the Messias. He was permitted to go before the Saviour and prepare His ways. The low descent over *paráre* with its *pressus* recalls to us the difficulties and trials St. John experienced in preparing the way for the Lord.

Codex 121 of Einsiedeln assigns this Communion to the first (authentic) mode, probably because in the same mode was sung the verse which continues the text of our Communion: *ad dandam sciéntiam*—"to give knowledge of salvation to his people, unto the remission of their sins."

If this hymn should be for us a true Communion prayer, we shall also enter into its sentiments and beg St. John to prepare the way for the Lord into our heart and to invest our being with that humility which at one time prompted him to exclaim: "I ought to be baptized by Thee, and comest Thou to me?" (Matt. 3, 4) and by which he adjudged himself unworthy to loose the latchets of the shoes of Christ.

* * * *

SS. PETER AND PAUL, APOSTLES
(June 29)

This feast, as indicated by its Collect, has always celebrated both Apostles simultaneously. Indeed, both had, as Pope St. Leo indicates (Migne, *P. L.*, 54, 427 f.), the same calling, the same labors, and the same end. It is their combined feast, a feast of the papacy and of the Church, commemorating the victory of the cross over heathendom and paganism.

The dramatic sense of the Church is well demonstrated in the construction of the Mass formulary. First of all are cited the words of St. Peter in the Introit of the Mass. Then in the *corpus* of the Graudal and in the Offertory it is we who, filled with holy wonder over the dignity accorded the Apostles, address ourselves to almighty God. The verse of the Gradual offers our felicitations to the Church on the Aposles and the unbroken line of Popes which God has given her. In the Alleluia and Communion we finally hear Christ Himself speaking to Peter. All of these texts are characterized by a direct approach, devoid of any preparatory remarks.

INTROIT (Acts 12: 11)

1. *Nunc scio vere quia misit Dominus Angelum suum*; 2. *et eripuit me de manu Herodis*, 3. *et de omni expectatione plebis Judaeorum*. Ps. *Domine probasti me, et cognovisti me*: * *tu cognovisti sessionem meam et resurrectionem meam*.

1. *Now I know in very deed that the Lord hath sent his angel*, 2. *and hath delivered me out of the hand of Herod*, 3. *and from all the expectation of the people of the Jews*. Ps. *Lord, thou hast proved me, and known me*: * *thou hast known my sitting down and my rising up*.

With the words of the Introit St. Peter makes public the experiences of his soul at the time he was miraculously liberated from prison. The text and thought serve nicely as a prelude to the clear text of the Epistle which follows, and which is likewise taken from the Acts of the Apostles. Peter is in prison, the universal Church the meanwhile praying for his deliverance. God then intervenes miraculously, but only at the last moment, for the beheading of St. Peter was to have taken place on the following morning. Divine intervention often comes only when, humanly speaking, every other resource has been exhausted. Peter, ever trusting, is not perturbed; he removes his sandals, takes off his mantle and lays himself down to sleep. An angel enters his cell, loosens the chains that bind him, and bids him put on sandals and cloak. Together they pass by the iron gate which opens of itself. St. Peter, however, does not realize the meaning of these happenings; to him they seem unreal and dreamlike. It is only after the angel has accompanied him for some distance and then vanishes that he comprehends the situation and knows that he has been saved.

The melody over *nunc* is somewhat dreamlike. Very quickly, however, the soul of the Apostle grasps the reality of the situation. "In very truth the Lord has sent His angel and He has liberated me." The melody begins *piano*, grows rapidly, and over *quia misit* breaks forth like a radiant sun which has triumphantly pierced a persistent fog. Manuscript 121 of Einsiedeln places an emphatic "t" (*tenere*, hold) over the *virga* of *quia*. In the main, however, the tempo should be lively, and the tendency to lag, especially in several passages, must be avoided. If we make the joy of the Apostle our own, we will sing his hymn with a thankful and rejoicing heart. All three phrases begin with *f*; the close of the second and third have some similarity with that of the first. The repetition over *de (omni)* of the initial motive over *Nunc* is the more noticeable in manuscript 121 of Einsideln, since there we have in both cases a bistropha and a *porrectus*. The four intervals of a fourth which follow—alternately ascending and descending—have an effect like irony on the eagerness of the Jews, who feel certain of their prey. Their well-laid plans are now become like a torn spider's web. All three phrases, be it once more mentioned, should be rendered fresh and lively. The construction of the melody may possibly have been influenced by the use of the tetrachords *d–g* over *Nunc* and *et de, g–c* over *scio vere* and *expectatióne, e–a* over *de manu Heródis* and *Judaeórum*.

In the psalm-verse the Apostle expresses gratitude for the guidance of divine Providence. While he lay bound in prison he was not forgotten; his liberation was effected and with it went the grant of a new life. The text of the verse, taken from Psalm 138 and well adapted to the feasts of the Apostles, reminds us of the Easter Introit. In fact, the deliverance of St. Peter is effected by none other than the risen, transfigured Christ. Numerous popes might have reiterated these same words of St. Peter. Death and affliction threatened them also, but the Lord protected His representative even to the extent of miraculous intervention (Kramp

Messliturgie und Gottesreich, III, 294). With subtle reserve St. Luke remarks that St. Peter, having been liberated from his prison in Jerusalem,
went into another land *(in álium locum).* Divine Providence led him to
Rome. The Lesson from the Acts which follows is like an attestation, a
record of the birth of the Church in Rome, the mother and teacher of
all Churches. (Schuster IV, 301).

GRADUAL (Ps. 44: 17, 18)

1. *Constitues eos principes super
omnem terram:* 2. *memores erunt
nominis tui, Domini.* ℣. 1. *Pro
patribus tuis nati sunt tibi filii:*
2. *propterea populi confitebuntur
tibi.*

1. *Thou shalt make them princes
over all the earth;* 2. *they shall remember thy name, O Lord.* ℣. 1. *Instead of thy fathers, sons are born
to thee:* 2. *therefore shall people
praise thee.*

Reverentially the melody announces a wonderful work of God, a
great distinction that God has conferred upon His Apostles: He has
created them princes. With awe the melody bows low before such great
dignity. The mora over *f, d, e,* and *c* should be given due attention. The
Apostles are to conquer the world. The inception of a fifth, the stressing
of the dominant *c,* the ascending fifth *g–d,* the descending *c–f* depict for
us this Apostolic conquest which embraces all lands and all peoples.
The melody is withal peaceable and reassuring, for He who chose and
commissioned the Apostles, came into this world to preach the Gospel
to the poor, "to heal the contrite of heart" (Luke 4: 18). In this selfsame spirit the Apostles should subdue and bring peace to the world.
They know and recognize the Prince of peace, know His name and understand the real nature of His being. His likeness is too deeply engraven
on their souls that they should ever forget it. And that His holy name
might be made known to the limits of the earth and be praised and rever-
enced by all nations, they pledged themselves even to the shedding of
their life's blood. Today, when the universal Church renders praise and
homage to these Apostle-princes, she does so with the consciousness
that she is giving praise to the holy name, that Peter is moved by the
same spirit which prompted Paul to say: "By the grace of God I am
what I am."

The motive over *nóminis tu-(i)* is repeated over *Dómine,* after which
the bistropha of *(tu)-i* is pleasantly developed. Following *tui* a breath
will evidently be necessary. By observing the *mora* on *a* which follows
the pause in the melody over *Dómine,* quiet two-note groups will be
effected. The close of *Dómine* recalls that of *príncipes* and *terram.* The
latter two, however, are more closely related: *fga gg f* rises to *gac bb a.*

In holy wonderment the singer now contemplates the Church and pours forth his praise of her wonderful fruitfulness in saints, apostles and confessors. Special emphasis might well mark the word *filii*—designating the Apostle-princes—as also the word *confitebúntur*; technique of composition calls for florid melismas at the beginning of the verse, resulting in the extended melody over *pátribus tuis*. The bistropha on *a* divides the first member of this melody into two groups which, however, are not in harmony with one another. The energetic *c b a c b g á* corresponds to the more soft *b♭ a g á g f g*.

The melismas after the second pause enhance one another and reach their high point on *f*, which is twice extended. The *nati* following should be sung broadly, while *filii* should be given especial warmth even though the melody is not very effective. Manuscripts 339 of St. Gaul and 121 of Einsiedeln seem to have sensed this and give the first eight notes over *filii* the broad form. To be sure, this typical form is always found in Graduals of the fifth mode. To illustrate we might refer to *preces* in the Gradual *Protéctor noster* of the fifth Sunday after Pentecost, although there the melody really belongs to a significant word. The *c a b g g a c d c* over *proptérea* answers the *c a b♭ g f g a c* over *(ti)-bi*. In the first case *b* is qualified by the following *c*; in the second *b♭* by the following *f*.

The melody of the present Gradual is also sung on the feast of the Blessed Trinity. Where today we have a definite break in the melody after *terram*—demanded by textual punctuation—the Gradual of Trinity Sunday continues without interruption in its first phrase the melody over *mémores*. A similar continuation over *Chérubim* in the same Gradual is somewhat unpleasant. A happier result was achieved in the verse. The melody of today's verse has been adapted almost perfectly to the verse on the feast of the Immaculate Conception.

Rassegna, 2, 241 ff.; *Revue*, 7, 206 ff.

ALLELUIA VERSE (Matt. 16: 18)

1. *Tu es Petrus, et super hanc petram* 2. *aedificabo Ecclesiam meam.*

1. *Thou art Peter, and upon this rock* 2. *I will build my Church.*

The adaptation of this Christmas melody for use during the summer cycle was already noted on the feast of the Nativity of St. John. This may explain the fact that in some churches the present feast was celebrated on December 27 or 28.

In the Gospel, the text of which combines intimately with that of the Alleluia, Peter professes his faith in our Lord with the following words: "Thou art Christ, the Son of the living God." And as a reward for this profession of faith, Christ answers him: "Thou art Peter, and upon this rock I will build My Church." To these words of Christ the text of the Alleluia acts as a prelude. The inception on the dominant and the development over *Tu es Petrus* produces a truly festal ring. The series of *pressus* over *aedificábo* might depict a structure firmly built of well-fitting granite stones, which like the melody over *Ecclésiam meam*, proudly and triumphantly raises itself on high. With a joyful heart we conclude the whole by a repetition of *Allelúia*.

OFFERTORY (Ps. 44: 17, 18)

1. *Constitues eos principes super omnem terram:* 2. *memores erunt nominis tui, Domine, in omni progenie et generatione.*

1. *Thou shalt make them princes over all the earth:* 2. *they shall remember thy name, O Lord, throughout all generations.*

The Offertory text adds to the *corpus* of the Gradual the words *in omni progénie et generatióne*, which form the closing verse of the psalm in question. If in the Gradual the word *mémores* makes the assertion that the Apostles will ever remember the holy name of our Lord, in the Offertory it gives assurance that every tribe and generation will sing the praises of this same holy name. Universal praise, however, was made possible only by the fact that the Apostles carried this name to the ends of the earth, thereby making all people happy, for God alone is the salvation of the world.

This solemn, royal hymn should not be sung too fast, yet it must be enlivened by festal joy. The numerous fourths especially should be emphasized. The initial motive *dg acb cdc c* over *super omnem* becomes *efg ga cbc* and *efg gabc* over *-ratió-(ne)*. *Tui* in the middle of the piece has a closing cadence; hence we must distinguish three phrases of practically equal length. The three consecutive groups of three notes over *constítues*, over the closely related *in omni* at the beginning of the third phrase, and over *omnem* enliven the entire piece. As in the Gradual, the composer here also gave special prominence to *príncipes* and *omnem terram*. The entire first phrase with its effective close on *f* inspires a conviction that this kingdom founded by God need fear neither revolution nor overthrow. It stands immovable because it was established by One who is eternal. A spirit of recollection characterizes the beginning of the second phrase. Presently, however, the melody waxes bright and joyful at the thought of the divine name; the repetition of the same motive over *nóminis* is descriptive rather of the trepidation this name inspires. Finally the soft melody over *tui* gives us a foretaste of the sweetness of the Lord. The *f́ d ǵ b a g* over *mé-(mores)* corresponds to the *f̂ d f̂ a g e* over *erunt*. The consciousness of the universality of the Church induces word-painting by means of large intervals over *in omni progénie*. After *omni* there may be need for a pause. The intervals of a fourth should be sung broadly; likewise, according to the annotated manuscripts, the *rhombus* over *(progé)-ni-(e)* and *(generatió)-ne*.

COMMUNION (Matt. 16: 18)

Tu es Petrus, et super hanc pe-   Thou art Peter: and upon this
tram aedificabo Ecclesiam meam.   rock I will build my church.

This same melody is sung on the feast of the Holy Trinity; the phrasing, however, differs somewhat. Four phrases were formed from the three of today and various minor divisions introduced that are not altogether satisfactory. The close over *terram* constitutes the middle member of *Unigenitúsque*. The impulsive onward movement over *mémores* is there halted by a major pause after *fílius*. The closing cadence over *tui* furthermore has lost its significance. In the former feast this cadence—together with the melody over *in omni* which follows it—forms a continuous melody over the words *quoque spíritus*. Finally the repetition of the melody of *Benedíctus* and *Spíritus* over *nobíscum* is rather tiring. The adaptation of the present melody to the feast of the Trinity is found already in manuscript 339 of St. Gall's.

The text brings us once more the words of Christ: *Tu es Petrus*. Through the worthy reception of Holy Communion we also become an integral part of the Church, we pulsate with her innermost life, and are bound to her in a most intimate manner. Today we can only thank God for this grace which he has vouchsafed to us, as well as for all the graces which He bestowed on St. Peter, His vicar on earth, and on all the sovereign Pontiffs.

The melody is very simple. The one major interval is that of a fourth over *Petrus*; beyond this there are only minor thirds and seconds. The motives over *(aedificá)-bo* and *Ecclé-(siam)* are antithetical. Would that the entire body of the faithful might be congregated as one unit to sing this hymn; each individual could then realize the more fully how he forms an element in that *one*, holy, catholic and aspostolic Church of which Christ said: This is My Church.

In past centuries the Communions of the vigil and the feast were interchanged. The gripping melody of the Communion of the vigil would set off the Mass liturgy of today's feast very effectively.

*   *   *   *

THE MOST PRECIOUS BLOOD OF OUR LORD JESUS CHRIST

(July 1)

This feast was first prescribed for the universal Church in 1849, and its present date determined by Pius X. Formerly it was commemorated on Passion Sunday.

INTROIT (Apoc. 5: 9, 10)

1. *Redemisti nos, Domine, in sanguine tuo, ex omni tribu, et lingua, et natione:* 2. *et fecisti nos Deo nostro regnum.* Ps. *Misericordias Domini in aeternum cantabo:* * *in generationem et generationem annuntiabo veritatem tuam in ore meo.*

1. *Thou hast redeemed us, O Lord, in thy blood, out of every tribe, and tongue, and people, and nation,* 2. *and hast made us to our kingdom.* Ps. *The mercies of the Lord I will sing forever:* * *I will show forth thy truth with my mouth to generation and generation.*

This, as the Apocalypse indicates, is the song of the saints in heaven, the song that continues to resound for all eternity. And only an eternity will suffice to render gratitude for our redemption through the Blood of Christ, for our gracious vocation to be members of the kingdom of Christ. This song has celebrated the advent of every human soul into the midst of the saints, and has been re-echoed by such out of every tribe, tongue, people, and nation as have attained the heavenly Jerusalem. Ineffective and feeble though our chant and our gratitude on earth may be, it is consoling to know that this selfsame song is rendered with the fullest perfection by the saints in heaven. Our goal should be to strive for the ideal of this choir of heavenly singers; to become as faithful and persevering subjects of the heavenly king as they are.

The beginning of the melody recalls that of the Introit *Cognóvi* which is sung on the feast of a Holy Woman neither Virgin nor Martyr, and in the old manuscripts is assigned to the feast of St. Sabina (August 29). The beginning of the Introit of May 12 also bears some similarity to the present melody. In each case the word *Dómine* marks the high point, and today especially emphasizes the fact that God alone through the shedding of His precious Blood effected our deliverance from sin and death. The only and somewhat soft $b\flat$ is found over *tuo*. The classical age of choral composition would, without any further ado, have sung here the closing cadence of the fourth psalm tone: $a\ b\ g\ e$. Nevertheless, the combination with $b\flat$ is already found in the Introit of SS. Peter and

Paul over *suum*. In the second phrase, of the words *tribu, língua, pópulo, natióne,* the first and third form the arsis while the second and fourth form the thesis. In imitation of the passage *caeléstium, terréstrium et infernórum* of the Introit *In nómine Dómini* of Wednesday in Holy Week, we should have expected a gradation here. The close over *natióne* nevertheless is very effective and permits a greater modulation in the three phrases, all of which have the same range. A lively and joyful melody begins with *et fecísti. Torculus* and bistropha should be sung over *(pópu)lo.* The third phrase predominates over the other two, its melody attaining melismatic richness. Some similarity exists between *et fecísti nos Deo* of today's Introit and *et fac nobíscum secúndum* of the Introit of the twentieth Sunday after Pentecost; also between *nostro regnum,* and the close of the Introit of the fifth Sunday after Easter and the tenth Sunday after Pentecost.

The tempo can be taken quite lively. In the psalm-verse the major accents should be given prominence. Softer secondary accents on *generatiónem* and *annuntiábo* will give the melody a nice, even flow.

GRADUAL (1 John 5: 6, 7, 8)

1. *Hic est qui venit per aquam et sanguinem, Jesus Christus:* 2. *non in aqua solum, sed in aqua et sanguine.* ℣. 1. *Tres sunt qui testimonium dant in caelo:* 2. *Pater, Verbum, et Spiritus Sanctus,* 3. *et hi tres unum sunt.* 4. *et tres sunt qui testimonium dant in terra:* 5. *spiritus, aqua, et sanguis,* 6. *et hi tres unum sunt.*

1. *This is he that came by water and blood, Jesus Christ:* 2. *not by water only, but by water and blood.* ℣. 1. *There are three who give testimony in heaven;* 2. *the Father, the Word, and the Holy Ghost;* 3. *and these three are one.* 4. *and there are three who give testimony on earth:* 5. *the Spirit, the water, and the blood;* 6. *and these three are one.*

The first two phrases of the above text are wanting in all of the old Greek manuscripts and in the best manuscripts of the Vulgate. They are a later explanatory addition (Comma Johanneum).

The melody is the same as that of the Gradual for the Sunday within the octave of Christmas (q.v.). Corresponding passages of the two Graduals are grouped in the following scheme:

1. *Hic est qui venit (per aquam) et sánguinem*
2. *Speciósus for-ma prae fíliis.*

1. *Jesus Christus: non in aqua solum, sed in*
2. *hóminum: diffú-sa est grátia, in*

1. *aqua et sánguine. ℣. Tres sunt, qui*
2. *lábiis tuis. ℣. Eructávit cor*

1. *Testimónium dant in caelo: Pater Verbum*
2. *meum [audívimus: patres nostri*

1. *est Spíritus Sanctus: et hi tres unum sunt.*
2. *annuntiavérunt nobis] dico ego*

1. *Et tres sunt, qui testimónium dant in terra*
   =above: *Tres sunt, qui testimónium dant in caelo*

1. *Spíritus, Aqua, et Sanguis: et hi tres unum sunt.*
2. *ópera mea regi:...velóciter scribéntis.*

The melody over *per aquam*, in parentheses above, cannot be substantiated in the Gradual of the Sunday within the octave. The melody from *caelo* to *sanctus* is taken from the Gradual verse of the Tuesday after the fourth Sunday in Lent; the corresponding text above is enclosed in brackets. The same melodical treatment accorded the two *Tres sunt...* is in no wise wearisome. In fact, the present arrangement is much more effective than had the melody over *lingua mea cálamus scribae* been adapted to *Tres sunt*. In this case, the composer happily chose identity of melody for an identical text.

At the baptism of Christ in the waters of the Jordan, the Father and the Holy Ghost proclaimed Him the Son of God. His own claims that He was our Lord and Saviour He attested by shedding His blood for us. The water and the blood that flowed from His pierced side—of which we read in the Gospel—bore witness that He offered Himself for us as a sacrifice of propitiation. To these supernatural, invisible witnesses of His divine mission, we add the earthly, visible testimony of the operations of the Holy Ghost through grace, the waters of Baptism, and the bloody death of Christ on the cross. The testimony which these three witnesses bear is all in accord.

ALLELUIA VERSE (1 John 5: 9)

1. *Si testimonium hominum accipimus,* 2. *testimonium Dei majus est.*

1. *If we receive the testimony of men,* 2. *the testimony of God is greater.*

The melody is taken from the twelfth Sunday after Pentecost (q.v.). It differs from the latter in the close over *(accípi)-mus*—where the present text has a dactyl, the original has two trochees. In the original, moreover, the first phrase is rightly given melodic superiority, while today, in accordance with its import, the second phrase is given prominence. The manner of rendition will aid to proper interpretation.

The text is a continuation of the Gradual text, as if to indicate that Alleluia and Gradual were to form one composite whole.—St. John here adduces proof that Christ was already conceived and born as the Son of God; He did not become such through His Baptism.

OFFERTORY (1 Cor. 10: 16)

1. *Calix benedictionis, cui bene-dicimus, nonne communicatio san-guinis Christi est?* 2. *et panis quem frangimus, nonne participatio cor-poris Domini est?*

1. *The chalice of benediction which we bless, is it not the communion of the blood of Christ?* 2. *and the bread which we break, is it not the par-taking of the body of the Lord?*

The priest raises the chalice a first time at the Offertory. Soon after he raises it again, but higher and in a more solemn manner. He has blessed the chalice, spoken over it the words of transubstantiation, and it now contains the blood of Christ. At the tinkling of the small bell the assembled congregation bends its knee in profound adoration. And wonderful to contemplate, we mortals are permitted to unite most in-timately, with this blood, and by partaking of it can in very truth be-come blood-relations of Christ. O truly precious blood that imparts such nobility and dignity! And the consecrated host which is broken, "is it not the partaking of the body of the Lord?" The interrogatory form with its double *nonne* is for us the expression of our deepest conviction that we believe this word spoken by the Son of God, than which nothing can be more true.

This conviction is reflected also in the melody, the phrasing of which is determined by the text. The first phrase with a range of a ninth is especially well developed melodically, due perhaps to the fact that it refers to the blood of Christ. The second phrase which is more quiet and lower-pitched has a range of a sixth. The second *nonne* corresponds to the first, but is a fifth lower. Just why the former has not the *porrectus* toward its close like the latter is difficult to see. In the rendition, the conclusion of each *nonne* should be extended, or even a short breathing space inserted. The gradual growth of the melody in the first phrase: *Calix*: c–g; *benedictiónis*: c–a; *cui benedícimus*: d–$b\flat$; *nonne*…*est*: d–d^1 is very effective. The melodic flourish over the last syllable of *communi-cátio* is pitched a third lower over the corresponding *participátio*. A simi-lar condition obtains with *est* at the close of the first and second phrases.

This ascending close at the end of a selection is rarely found. It occurs with the Alleluia *Tóllite jugum* of the new Sacred Heart feast, *Opportébat* of the third Sunday after Easter, *Post partum* of the votive Mass of the Blessed Virgin, and occasionally with the *Amen* of the third and fourth mode. The interrogatory form may have influenced the melodic construction. Otherwise the general rule for the conclusion of readings and lessons obtains, that is, when no *Tu autem, Dómine* follows, the usual closing form of a declarative sentence is used, and not that of a question.

COMMUNION (Heb. 9: 28)

1. *Christus semel oblatus est ad multorum exhaurienda peccata*; 2. *secundo sine peccato apparebit expectantibus se, in salutem.*

1. *Christ was offered once to exhaust the sins of many*; 2. *the second time he shall appear without sin to them that expect him unto salvation.*

The first phrase is similar to the *Hoc corpus* of Passion Sunday (q.v.). As a kind of leitmotif, the intimate connection between the sacrifice of the cross and the Eucharistic Sacrifice is stressed melodically. Over *oblátus est* the melody of the original might have been assumed without change; the major third was most likely introduced to give prominence to the word-accent. Seemingly motives from the Communions *Justórum ánimae* (June 21) and *Primum quaérite* (fourteenth Sunday after Pentecost) were adapted to the second phrase.

In Holy Communion Christ enters our souls. His love for sinners prompted Him to veil His majesty under the ordinary form of bread and wine. When He shall come again, however, when He "shall appear a second time," it will radiate splendor and power. And this splendor and power He will share with those who expect Him, and who have become one with Him in Holy Communion; He will be to them a source of eternal happiness and salvation. The gradation, apparent in the text, is easily recognizable and actualized in the melody. In place of the suppressed dominant *b* of the first phrase, the second phrase has the brighter *c*.

* * * *

THE VISITATION OF THE BLESSED VIRGIN MARY

(July 2)

The Franciscan Order celebrated this feast already in 1263. The Council of Basle made it obligatory for the universal Church.

Several texts of the Mass are not taken from Holy Scripture. Formerly the Introit *Vultum tuum* and other chants of the Annunciation were sung on this feast. The Gradual and Alleluia have been taken over from the Greek Liturgy[1].

INTROIT

1. *Salve, sancta Parens, enixa puerpera Regem*: 2. *qui caelum terramque regit in saecula saeculorum.* Ps. *Eructavit cor meum verbum bonum*; * *dico ego opera mea Regi.*

1. *Hail, O holy Mother, who gavest birth to the King* 2. *who governeth heaven' and earth for ever and ever.* Ps. *My heart hath uttered a good word*; * *I speak my works to the King.*

Today was sung the most beautiful song ever conceived by man; it proceeded from a heart burning with the fire of purest love. Never has mankind heard a more perfect or elegant hymn of praise than the *Magnificat*, the song with which the Mother of God today greeted Elizabeth. Her self-abandon in God and her fervor of heart ought to be the ideals toward which we should strive in our singing. The activities of her entire life, as the words *ópera mea Regi* in the verse indicate, were centered on the heavenly King. Only when our own lives are likewise dedicated to almighty God will our offering of song approach the inner reality and perfection of the ideal set for us today by the Blessed Virgin. The more important element of the Introit is not the verse, which represents Mary as speaking, but the antiphon in which we direct our praises and salutations to the Virgin, as the Mother of "the King who governeth heaven and earth for ever and ever." These sentiments of respect and awe for the dignity of the divine motherhood should characterize our rendition of *Salve*. This same *Salve* should also be an expression of heartfelt gratitude for the many visitations of divine grace which, due to Mary's intercession and solicitude, our soul has experienced.

For an explanation of the melody see the Introit of Epiphany.

The text is taken from the Easter hymn of Sedulius (Book II, verses 63, 64). The second hexameter, which originally closed with *tenet per sáecula cujus*, was changed, and in place of *tenet* we have *regit*. This is the only Introit which has metrical form.

Wagner, I, 69; *Revue gr.*, 23, 167 ff.; *C.O.* 47, 129 ff.

GRADUAL

1. *Benedicta et venerabilis es, Virgo Maria,* 2. *quae sine tactu*

1. *Thou art blessed and venerable, O Virgin Mary*; 2. *who, without*

---

[1] Schuster IV, 317.

pudoris, inventa es Mater Salva-
toris. ℣. 1. *Virgo Dei Genitrix,*
quem totus non capit orbis, 2. *in*
tua se clausit viscera factus homo.

*any violation of purity, wert found
the mother of our Saviour.* ℣. 1. *O
Virgin Mother of God, he whom the
whole world is unable to contain,*
2. *being made man, enclosed himself in thy womb.*

The melody (cf. March 19) is very expressive and well adapted to
this text. The *corpus* is dominated by the stirring melody over *María,*
while the verse has its fervent *Virgo*—a wondrous hymn of praise to the
Virgin Mother of God. We begin the first phrase in a suppressed tone
but lively tempo, and then continue *Virgo María* with bright and sunny
warmth. If possible, *sine tactu pudóris* should be sung without pause for
breath; the delicacy of its text calls for fine tonal shading. The same
melody—more rounded out, however—recurs over *Mater Salvatóris.*
After the tender and extended melody over *virgo,* care must be taken
that the important words *Dei Génitrix* be not stunted. The development
of the melody over *quem totus non capit orbis* differs somewhat from the
original. Keeping the above remarks in mind, we might now compare
-rábilis es and *Salvató-, sine tactu* and *-venta es, pudóris* and *mater, Génitrix, quem totus* and *tua se clausit víscera.* The melody over *orbis* suggests word-painting; that over *homo,* the abasement of the Son of God in
His Incarnation.

The melody is not influenced by the fact that the verse is a distich.

ALLELUIA VERSE

1. *Felix es, sacra Virgo Maria,*
2. *et omni laude dignissima;* 3. *quia
ex te ortus est sol justitiae, Christus
Deus noster.*

1. *Thou art happy, O holy Virgin
Mary,* 2. *and most worthy of all
praise:* 3. *because from thee arose
the sun of justice, Christ our God.*

"And blessed art thou that has believed." These are the words
with which Elizabeth addresses the Mother of God. *Allelúia* preludes
this thought with melodies of holy jubilation and triumph in God the
Saviour, who has poured out streams of light and grace upon the soul
of Mary. From her arose "the Sun of justice." The celebration and
import of today's feast conjures up in our minds a picture of the glorious morning sun rising to the accompaniment of myriad choirs of birds
and transmuting by the touch of its magic ray the prosaic, ragged moun-
taintops into peaks of gold.

When Elizabeth had heard the salutation of Mary, the infant rejoiced in her womb, and, filled with the Holy Ghost, she extolled the

Mother of God. Would that our chant were likewise inspired by the
Holy Ghost, so that it might be rendered in a manner worthy of her
high dignity. The gradual intensification of the melody, especially through
the *pressus a c d*, should be brought out in the rendition. Over *(alle)-*
lú-(ia) two-note groups *(ac ac)* should be sung before the *pressus*. The
c which is merely sounded here, receives a compensation in the first
member of the *jubilus*, where it is especially accented and extended.
The appended *climacus* should be given prominence; the following
neums will then form the thesis. The *pressus d* with its energetic fifth
then comes to the fore; this is followed, in turn, by a relaxing thesis.
The third member is also introduced by means of a *pressus*. The ensuing
joyful passage should not be forced. After the two groups of two over
(sa)-cra, e d c should be rendered in a full and satisfying manner. The
second phrase has practically the same melody as *allelúia* with its *ju-*
bilus. The third phrase, over against the ascending movement of the
two previous phrases, takes a pleasant turn downward. After all, how
mysterious is the birth of the eternal Sun from the "holy Virgin Mary."
The first four notes over *ortus* should be taken as a preparation for the
two following groups: *g a ć a g* and *e f ǵ f e*. The intonation of a fifth over
sol gives the word merited prominence.

The melody can be traced to the eleventh century.

OFFERTORY

1. *Beata es, Virgo Maria, quae*
omnium portasti Creatorem: 2.
genuisti qui te fecit, 3. *et in aeter-*
num permanes Virgo.

1. *Blessed art thou, O Virgin*
Mary, who didst bear the Creator of
all: 2. *Thou didst bring forth him*
who made thee, 3. *and thou remain-*
est a Virgin forever.

The Offertory continues with new melodies the salutation of Elizabeth to the "Mother of God." Mary bore the Creator of the world; she
brought forth Him who had created her. These two thoughts are emphasized by giving melodic prominence to *Creatórem* and *fecit*. Another
thought, however, dominates the spirit of the Offertory as a whole. It
is the inspiring and wondrous beauty of the Virgin Mother, who alone
of all creatures was privileged to combine the dignity of motherhood
with the radiant luster of virginity. Virgin *(Virgo)* thou art and virgin
thou wilt remain *(pérmanes)* in eternity. These considerations induce us
to sing her praises in holy wonderment.

The above interpretation we should like to apply to the present
Offertory. The study of original sources, however, shows that this
melody has been borrowed, and is therefore not original. In the old manu-

scripts we find it on the feast of St. Gorgonius (September 9) and on Easter Monday. On the former feast it forms the melody over the words *Magna est*...of the third verse for the Offertory *Posuísti*, while on the latter it is found over the words *Jesus stetit*...of the third verse for the Offertory *Angelus Dómini*. The Easter Monday composition is probably the original one. The final *allelúia*, which is sung only in the votive Masses of the Blessed Virgin during Paschal time, has a melisma truly festal and triumphant in character.

In its general mood and atmosphere the present Offertory is much akin to the *Magna est* of the above mentioned feast. In each case the melody depicts amazement at the wonderful things God has wrought in a human soul and admiration for its consequent worth and beauty. A rare instance of recitation in monotone is exemplified in this Offertory over *quae ómnium por-(tásti)*. The same holds true for the above *Magna est* over the words *in salutári*.

The melody over *Beáta es* not only forms the introduction for the above verses, but for the Offertory of Easter Monday and of the feasts of St. Gorgonius and the Assumption. The high *d* over *Virgo* should be slightly retarded; the interval of a fourth will in this way be made more effective. In the final member of *Virgo* the descending fourth *g–d* forms a contrast to the ascending fourth *a–d* in the two foregoing members. *María* should be sung with warmth and fervor, and the two final clives somewhat retarded. The monotone recitation of *quae ómnium portá-(sti)* should be measured rather than rapid. The melody over *creatórem* is found also in the Offertories *Angelus Dómini*, *Posuísti*, and *Assúmpta est*. Its two bistropha, which are to be slightly retarded, should combine the well-defined groups of four notes. The melody depicts for us the greatness of Mary who bore in her womb and in her arms Him who not only created but also sustains the world. The interval *c–g*, which is to be retarded, divides the melismas over *fecit* into two unequal parts, the second of which can be considered an extension of the first. Mary, although a mother, remains a Virgin for all eternity; this is the theme of the final phrase with its large intervals. *Pérmanes* should be phrased like the final *Allelúia* of the Offertory on Easter Monday.

COMMUNION

1. *Beata viscera Mariae Virginis,*
2. *quae portaverunt aeterni Patris Filium.*

1. *Blessed is the womb of the Virgin Mary,* 2. *which bore the Son of the eternal Father.*

All of today's chants, the majority of which are characterized by direct approach, begin by glorifying the Virgin Mary. They not only breathe a joyous love for her beauty and greatness, but a reverent awe for her great and singular privilege as well. These sentiments also pervade the Communion. Mary bore "the Son of the eternal Father." The melody over *aetérni*—extending beyond the entire tone line—begins significantly with a fifth, while the following word begins a fifth lower, as if to say: the Son of Mary surpasses the limits of time and space and is beyond that which is earthly and human.

Virginis marks the climax of the first phrase. The notes *f, f g, g a* over the accented syllables of the preceding words lead gradually to the melodic climax at *a bb*. These accents become more plastic and the melodic line more enlivened as the melody, following the individual accents, descends. Care should be taken not to accent the *bb*, but to give the preceding *a* somewhat of an accent; this will produce the effect of two *torculus*. The phrase closes on the dominant. The second phrase is not so happily constructed. The cadence over *portavérunt*, for instance, is absolutely final. According to the import of the text, however, only a slight pause is permissible here. The first phrase was characteristically ethereal and light. The second phrase begins more quietly, in an almost depressed manner, and yet Mary bore in her most pure womb the sweetest burden, bore it while sunk in contemplation. The first phrase speaks of our love for the childlike trust in Mary; the second, of our adoration and reverence for the eternal Son of God, who became her Child. The partial cadences over *(ví)-scera, (porta)-vérunt* and *(Fí)-lium* are similar.

This Communion is of later composition, dating from the eleventh century.[1]

The text of the Communion forms part of the closing prayer recited at the end of the hours of the Divine Office. Today's feast affords possibly the only instance where none of the Mass texts are taken from Holy Scripture, although some of them remind us of scriptural passages. The present Communion, for instance, might remind us of the woman in the Gospel who extolled the womb that bore Christ (Luke 11: 27).

Holy Communion, whereby we receive into our hearts the Son of the eternal Father, will then become a source of inner joy *(Beáta)* to us, if we follow the example of the Mother of God and are numbered among those who not only hear but also preserve the Word of God in their hearts. Then will our soul also experience a blessed and holy visitation.

---

[1] *Revue,* 24, 6 ff; *Analyses,* 5, 16 ff.

*   *   *   *

ST. JAMES THE ELDER, APOSTLE

(July 25)

The INTROIT is the same as that on the feast of St. Andrew, while the GRADUAL is that of the feast of SS. Peter and Paul (q.v.).

ALLELUIA VERSE (John 15: 16)

1. *Ego vos elegi de mundo, ut eatis et fructum afferatis,* 2. *et fructus vester maneat.*

1. *I have chosen you out of the world, that you should go, and should bring forth fruit,* 2. *and your fruit should remain.*

The text of the Alleluia is taken from the words of our Lord at the Last Supper. Christ there reminds His Apostles of that morning when, after having spent the entire preceding night in prayer, He chose them as His disciples. By His teaching He freed them from the spirit of the world and instilled into them a burning love for immortal souls. He commissioned them to go out into the world and sow there the seed of the word of God that should bring forth fruit in due season. They responded and in their own time showed themselves to be a fruit well-ripened by much prayer and many sufferings. The world was not only to hear their words, but also to see realized that which the Gospel had worked and brought to maturity in their own persons; and precisely for this reason have their preaching and labors and sufferings been of lasting worth. There is every reason then to sing this Alleluia with a grateful heart.

In the oldest available manuscripts today's melody is written with the text *Justi epuléntur*. It is there found among the melodies *per circulum anni*, from which the chanter might choose at pleasure. In the modern Graduale it finds its place in the Mass *Sapiéntiam* (Common of many Martyrs). The melody was also adapted to the text *Ego dilécto* for the feast of the Most Pure Heart of Mary.

Allelúia with its *jubilus* has the form a and b, a¹, a², c, d. The final member, however, with its *fff gag ef éed* is rhythmically in close relation to the preceding member c. There is also great similarity between *Ego* and member a. The present text is well adapted to the original melody. *Elégi* is duly emphasized; *mundo,* which modulates to a full step below the tonic, combines the two half-phrases. A similar melody, but devoid of the concluding *pressus,* recurs over *fructum.* The double command, expressed by the words *eátis* and *afferátis,* has melodies much akin to one another. The melody over *fructus* is like an admiring look upward to the harvest of gathered fruits. In the original the latter word is replaced by *delecténtur*—"let them rejoice." Its florid melisma, reminiscent of the Gradual verse *Vitam* on the feast of St. Joseph, has three members, the beginnings of the first two of which are similar. The third member with its three *pressus* carries the major accent, and extends to a fifth above the preceding and following member.

OFFERTORY (Ps. 18: 5)

1. *In omnem terram exivit sonus eorum*: 2. *et in fines orbis terrae verba eorum*.

1. *Their sound hath gone forth into all the earth*; 2. *and their words unto the ends of the world*.

The text in the original does not refer to vocal sounds but rather to the light waves which, emanating from the heavenly bodies, sweep the whole world. The Gospel, which the Apostles carried to the ends of the earth, is like this brightening, warming, healing, and life-giving light. According to legend St. James brought its doctrines to far-away Spain, at that time considered the edge of the world. During the Middle Ages crowds of pilgrims journeyed to his tomb and considered this visit as sacred and solemn as a pilgrimage to the Holy Land, to the places sanctified by the sufferings and death of our Lord.

The melody was explained on the third Sunday after Epiphany. Comparison might also be made with that of the Offertory of Maundy Thursday.

The COMMUNION is the same as that on the feast of St. Matthias.

*   *   *   *

ST. ANNE, MOTHER OF THE BLESSED VIRGIN MARY

(July 26)

This feast was introduced into the Roman liturgy under Gregory XIII, in the year 1584. All of its chants are taken from older feasts. The Introit *Gaudeámus* (cf. the Assumption) naturally inserts the name of St. Anne. Codex 339 of St. Gall's assigns today's Gradual, Alleluia, and Communion to the feast of St. Lucy (December 13). The latter feast has at present a different Communion. The Offertory is taken from the feast of St. Prisca (January 18).

GRADUAL (Ps. 44: 8)

1. *Dilexisti justitiam, et odisti iniquitatem. ℣. Propterea unxit te Deus, Deus tuus, oleo laetitiae.*

1. *Thou hast loved justice, and hated iniquity. ℣. Therefore, God, thy God, hath anointed thee with the oil of gladness.*

Here, as also in the Alleluia, the text is directed to the saint of the day. Not only does the Church accord praise, but Christ Himself glorifies her. Simple though the life of St. Anne may have been, she nevertheless accomplished the work of self-sanctification and had the courage and resoluteness to employ all those means necessary "to love justice," and out of love to practice this justice at all times. She was a worthy mother to that child whom we extol as the Mirror of Justice and as the Mother of fair love. God, therefore, annointed her with the oil of gladness. She could become just and holy, however, only with that help of God's grace given to her as a reward for her faithful love. But her soul must have experienced a very special gladness when she was privileged to become the mother of the Mother of God. We also were anointed with God's grace in holy Baptism and in Confirmation so that we might likewise love justice and hate iniquity. And he who co-operates with this grace, will in the end be anointed with the oil of everlasting, imperishable gladness.

The melody has a wonderful gradation: *Dilexísti c–g, justítiam c–c¹, odísti f–d¹, proptérea f–e¹*. The introductory melody reminds us of *Dirigátur* from the nineteenth Sunday after Pentecost. The melody over *-tátem* recurs over *Deus*, that of *proptérea* over *laetítia*. The close is identical with the *jubilus* of the Alleluia which follows. An intervening quiet undulation about the tonic *g* is reminiscent of the peace of God.

ALLELUIA VERSE—COMMUNION (Ps. 44: 3)

1. *Diffusa est gratia in labiis tuis: 2. propterea benedixit te Deus in aeternum.*

1. *Grace is poured abroad in thy lips: 2. Therefore hath God blessed thee forever.*

With true southern naivete, Schuster (IV. 378) comments on this text: "The grace which St. Anne brought the world is none other than the Virgin Mary. Grace was poured abroad in her lips insofar as she was often permitted to kiss the Virgin Mother and the Christ Child. In order to describe the intimate relations of SS. Joachim and Anne with the Saviour, the Greeks apply to her the endearing epithet of 'Grandmother of God'."

The Alleluia employs the typical melody of the eighth mode (cf. the first Sunday of Advent). The intonation of the second phrase is followed by a lengthy recitation on the dominant *c*.

The Communion begins like a Gradual of the fifth mode. We might compare it with the beginning of the Communion of the fourth Sunday after Pentecost. The word *proptérea* here, as well as in the Gradual, receives special prominence. The close over *aetérnum* resembles passages in the sixth mode, well known especially from the Introit *Réquiem*. Its final member rhymes with *tuis*.

Grace and harmony are poured abroad also in the melody.

OFFERTORY (Ps. 44: 10)

1. *Filiae regum in honore tuo*: 2. *astitit regina a dextris tuis in vestitu deaurato*, 3. *circumdata varietate*.

1. *The daughters of kings in thy glory*: 2. *the queen stood on thy right in gilded clothing*, 3. *surrounded with variety.*

The faithful bear their offering to the altar at least spiritually. Among these there is many a royal soul that joyfully offers and dedicates itself to the heavenly King. But at the altar Christ has a still more stately escort of honor. For, previous to the consecration, the prayers of the Canon mention the names of holy men, to which the names of holy virgins and women ennobled by their martyrdom are added after the consecration. In the first place *(In primis)*, however, is mentioned the name of "the glorious and ever-virgin Mary, Mother of our Lord and God Jesus Christ" (Canon of the Mass). The Offertory describes her as the queen "in gilded clothing, surrounded with variety." Glittering gold symbolizes that purest love glowing in her heart, while the graces and privileges she received from God and the virtues she nurtured, clothe her with charming variety. This queen is the child of St. Anne, and all the honor which is bestowed on the child accrues to the honor of the happy mother. She shows herself today a royal daughter, and heaven and earth pay her homage.

In the first phrase both *torculus* should be discreetly emphasized, and after the second, the clives; bistropha and *porrectus* are then sung. In this manner the oft-repeated *d* in the *torculus* receives its proper value. Similar, but a step higher, is the development over *tuo*. The *climacus* with its *e* here indicates the climax: "The daughters of kings in thy glory." The vibrant bistropha of the second phrase call attention to the appearance of the queen. Here *b*, which so far had been avoided, occurs for the first time; it recurs over *varietáte*. Quiet, solemn groups of two notes are sung, followed by a somewhat more rapid rendition of *a dextris.* The motive over *regina* is abbreviated over *in vestítu,* and developed over *circúmdata.* The ornate *deauráto* might depict for us a heavy gold brocade. The melody here attains its greatest range. Like the first phrase, the second closes on the dominant *c* which, as a matter of fact, plays an important role throughout the melody. The third phrase repeats the formula *b¹ c a g c¹* and continues it immediately. The tonic *e* of the third mode, to which this melody is ascribed, appears only as a final note. The lowest note of the third phrase then is *e,* of the second *f,* and of the first *g.*

This is one of the sublimest Offertories in plain chant, characterized, as it were, by the festive splendor of an Eastern sun.

* * * *

THE TRANSFIGURATION OF OUR LORD JESUS CHRIST

(August 6)

In the Occident this feast can be traced to the seventh century while in the Orient it was celebrated on various days since the eighth century. The present date was assigned to it by Callixtus III in 1458 in the victory that St. John Capistran and George Hunyadi won over the Turks at Belgrade (Keller, *Heortologie,* p. 81).

INTROIT (Ps. 76: 19)

1. *Illuxerunt coruscationes tuae orbi terrae;* 2. *commota est et contremuit terra.* Ps. (88, 2) *Quam dilecta tabernacula tua, Domine virtutum.* * *Concupiscit, et deficit anima mea in atria Domini.*

1. *Thy lightnings enlightened the world:* 2. *the earth shook and trembled.* Ps. (88, 2) *How lovely are thy tabernacles, O Lord of hosts.* * *My soul longeth and fainteth for the courts of the Lord.*

For the older feasts it was a general rule that when the antiphon was taken from the Psalter, the verse was taken from the same psalm. Later feasts, as that of today, seemingly ignore this rule.

The flood of light which enveloped our Lord on Tabor, or rather, which emanating from His divinity had transfigured His human nature, in all likelihood occasioned the choice of the first psalm-verse. The effect of this unusual but happy spectacle caused St. Peter to exclaim: "Lord, it is good for us to be here...Let us make here three tabernacles." The second psalm-verse again calls this happiness to mind. As a matter of fact, God does occasionally impart to us His illuminations and consolations. But they should serve to show the more clearly that our lasting home is not on this earth; they should enkindle in us a yearning and desire for an eternal transfiguration in heaven, the true home of our soul. To be sure, in order to attain this we must walk the same path that Christ has walked: suffer, and so enter into glory.

The shaking and trembling of the earth mentioned in the second verse of the antiphon should induce us to look beyond Tabor to the end of time when Christ will come again in great power and glory. At that moment not only Moses and Elias and the three Apostles, but all mankind just risen from the grave, will see Him in His glory and offer Him homage. The ardent longing of all the just is centered on that great day when "the body of our lowness will be made like to the body of His glory" (Philipp. 3, 21), on that transfiguration at their entrance into the courts of heaven.

The Introit for the feast of St. Lawrence seems to have served as a model for this Introit; compare for instance *Illuxérunt* and *Conféssio, corrusca-(tiónes)* and *pulchritúdo, (corrusca)-tiónes tuae* and *conspéctu eius, contrémuit terra* and *(sanctificati)-óne eius.* In the original melody the first phrase closes by tarrying quietly on the dominant, while here it is supplemented with the words *orbi terrae,* whose melody is evidently modeled on that over *terra.* These two words must be sung somewhat more broadly. The melody over *commóta est* is energetic and forceful.

GRADUAL

Text and melody were explained on the Sunday within the octave of Christmas. We can scarcely picture to ourselves the Christ Child in the manger without giving thought also to the transfigured glory of His divinity. On Christmas we consider above all else His human charm and entrancing beauty. Today, however, we contemplate the divine element which transfigures the Son of Man. Never before did a human form radiate such supernatural beauty as did Christ's on Tabor. He who would sing praises of this King of glory must needs do so with the feelings of deepest emotion and reverential enthusiasm.

ALLELUIA VERSE (Wisd. 7: 26)

1. *Candor est lucis aeternae,* 2. *speculum sine macula,* 3. *et imago bonitatis illius.*

1. *He is the brightness of eternal light,* 2. *the unspotted mirror,* 3. *and the image of his goodness.*

The shining countenance and the transfigured appearance of Jesus on Tabor were irradiations of the divinity which dwelt in Him. This divinity, in turn, was naught but the reflected splendor of the eternal light of the Father. The Father sees in the Son the reflection of His own Being, the brightness of His own eternal light, His own overflowing goodness and endless perfections which suffer neither diminution nor decrease. And then, as if in recognition, He exclaims: "This is My beloved Son in whom I am well pleased." These same words are in a certain sense also directed to us, for by them, as the Collect of the day indicates, we are assured of our perfect adoption as sons. Would that we might show ourselves worthy of this distinction and become spotless children of light, true images of divine goodness!

The melody, although not proper to the text (cf. Corpus Christi), is well adapted and gives it a lucid and joyful signification.

OFFERTORY (Ps. 111: 3)

1. *Gloria et divitiae in domo eius:* 2. *et justitia eius manet in saeculum saeculi. Alleluia.*

1. *Glory and wealth shall be in his house:* 2. *and his justice remaineth forever and ever. Alleluia.*

The divine Saviour was very fond of speaking about His Father's house. The treasures and riches of this heavenly mansion and the grandeur of His own glory are celebrated today, especially by St. Peter in the Epistle: "We were eye-witnesses of His majesty. For He received from God the Father honor and glory; this voice coming down to Him from the excellent glory: This is My beloved Son in whom I am well pleased, hear ye Him" (2 Pet. 1: 16–19). With these words the heavenly Father spoke His solemn approbation and canonization of the Son of man and of the works He would perform. In the display of His zeal for justice and for the honor of His Father, Christ will even suffer death and thus merit for His human nature endless riches and glory. And those who tread with Him the path of justice will, as the Collect says, become His co-heirs and the sharers of His glory.

The melody of the first phrase is simple, giving prominence to the word-accents only. The second phrase is more developed and utilizes the florid melismas taken from the Offertory *Desidérium* over the words *corónam*.... The latter Offertory is found in the Common for holy Abbots. In the old manuscripts it is assigned to the feast of St. Eusebius.

COMMUNION (Matt. 17: 9)

Visionem quam vidistis, nemini dixeritis, donec a mortuis resurgat Filius hominis.

Tell the vision you have seen to no man till the Son of man be risen from the dead.

So that the glory of His majesty might be revealed only at the opportune time, Jesus forbade His disciples to tell of this vision. The dis-

ciples could hardly expect that the publication of such a miraculous
event would obtain credence; without doubt they would be scoffed at as
visionaries and dreamers. Our Lord could not permit the manifestation
of His holiness to become a subject of ridicule. After He had risen from
the dead, however, and had thus proved Himself to be the Son of God,
then the knowledge of His transfiguration would no longer cause surprise. The fact that He had predicted not only His death but also His
glorious resurrection would then serve to confirm and corroborate His
divine dignity (J. B. Hirscher, *Betrachtungen ueber die sonntaeglichen
Evangelien*, p. 170.).

The event on Mount Tabor, however, was only a type of the beauty
which the transfigured Saviour displayed on Easter morning, which
henceforth needs to be kept secret no longer. Easter morn has come,
and today we make public the experience of our Lord on Tabor. Holy
Comunion, which gives us a foretaste of the happiness of Tabor, is the
seed of our own transfiguration and the pledge of our glorious resurrection at the end of time.

The melody is practically syllabic throughout and duplicates the
Magnificat antiphon of the first and second Vespers for the second Sunday of Lent. The only difference lies in the *pes* over *(hó)-mi-(nis)*; the
antiphon in a somewhat monotonous manner signs all three syllables of
the word on the tonic *d*.

* * * *

ST. LAWRENCE, DEACON AND MARTYR
(August 10)

All of today's chants, with the exception of the Alleluia, are found
in the oldest manuscripts.

INTROIT (Ps. 95: 6)

1. *Confessio et pulchritudo in conspectu eius*: 2. *sanctitas et magnificentia in sanctificatione eius.* Ps. *Cantate Domino canticum novum*: * *cantate Domino omnis terra.*

1. *Praise and beauty are before him*: 2. *holiness and majesty in His sanctuary.* Ps. *Sing ye to the Lord a new canticle*: * *sing to the Lord, all the earth.*

Sung in the vast and beautiful basilica which houses the tomb of
St. Lawrence, this chant undoubtedly creates a lasting impression. As a
matter of fact, the above text may quite possibly have been chosen with
special reference to this beautiful structure, which was designated a

basilica *speciosior* by Pelagius II (578–590). During the past century Pius IX effected many restorations on it and, after his death, was buried according to his express desire next to the relics of the holy archdeacon. Beautiful though the basilica may be, the soul of the saint is yet more noble and more precious. His life, his charitable undertakings, and above all his martyrdom, were a public avowal of his love for Christ, and will ever continue to be a song of praise of wondrous beauty. His soul shone forth in all the beauty of its purity, sanctity and sacrifice. Radiating the splendor and sublime magnificence of divine grace, it became a source of joy to God Himself. Hence all creation is invited to sing "to the Lord a new canticle."

In the melody youthful freshness vies with dignified solemnity. With the former there is an upward tendency over *conféssio e d g a c c,* over in *conspéc-(tu) e f g c c,* over *magnificén-(tia) f g a c c,* and over *(sanc-tifi)-catió-(ne) e f a c c.* It thus employs variations of one motive only, meanwhile emphasizing high *c,* the dominant of the mode. On the other hand, the quiet seconds over *(magnificénti)-a* and the reverential half-steps over *sanctifi-(catióne)* bespeak solemnity. *In conspéctu eius,* text and melody, is also found in the Introit of the Saturday before the second Sunday of Lent.

Care must be taken that high *c* is not made to predominate, but that the preparatory and following notes form the melody proper.

GRADUAL .(Ps. 16: 3)

1. *Probasti, Domine, cor meum,* 2. *et visitasti nocte.* ℣. 1. *Igne me examinasti,* 2. *et non est inventa in me iniquitas.*

1. *Thou hast proved my heart, O Lord,* 2. *and visited it by night.* ℣. 1. *Thou hast tried me by fire.* 2. *and iniquity hath not been found in me.*

The Benedictus antiphon of the morning Office is composed of a part of St. Lawrence's prayer: "On the gridiron I have not denied Thee, O Christ." The text of the Gradual continues this prayer. In truth, it was not an insignificant test that he underwent when he was scourged and tortured and subjected to a slow and extremely painful death on the glowing gridiron. Many others subjected to the same test failed to prove themselves, and after the dark night of pain there came for them the darker night of apostasy. The heart of St. Lawrence, however, burned with love for Christ; it rejoiced to suffer and give its all for Him. The saint's night knew no darkness, but radiated instead a wondrous light.

Today the saint looks back upon his martyrdom and is moved to sing this hymn to God. The *corpus,* with its lower pitch and range of c–c^1, according to some interpreters would first depict for us the saint's feeling of melancholy over his tortures, and later the feeling of joy over his triumph. Neither text nor melody, however, give occasion for this interpretation, although it is true and very obvious that in contrast to the *corpus*, the verse portrays a noticeable gradation of melody. The melody over *cor meum* recurs on the feast of the Assumption over *justitiam*, while that over *visitásti* seems to be entirely original. In the verse *Igne* is given effective emphasis. The florid melismas over the accented syllables of *examinásti* and *invénta* show the following close relationship: *bag agf acc* and *fdb cag abcc*. The melody reaches its climax over *et'non est invénta*, where, in an assured, we might almost say conscious, manner it rises stepwise to a height not frequently found in Graduals. By means of large intervals it then descends. Indeed, the soul of St. Lawrence was that purest gold which is tried by fire.

The same text recurs in the Introit on the octave of the feast, due attention being given to the rules of style proper for Introits. The use of the same melody for both Gradual and Introit—once in the seventh and a second time the eighth mode—was accomplished by the editors of the Medicean Gradual.

ALLELUIA VERSE

1. *Levita Laurentius, bonum opus operatus est,* 2. *qui per signum crucis caecos illuminavit.*

1. *The levite Lawrence wrought a good work,* 2. *who by the sign of the cross gave sight to the blind.*

Impelled by his ardent love of God St. Lawrence manifested sincere love for the poor and suffering. Of his many charitable works this verse only mentions that he gave sight to the blind, not indeed by his own power, but by the sign of the cross. Would that we might color our rendition of this chant with the sentiments which those who were healed must have experienced. Let us also ask a blessing of the saint, so that, with hearts enlightened, we may better comprehend and meditate the words of the Gospel which is about to be sung.

OFFERTORY

The Offertory has the same text, the same phrasing, with a major pause before the dominant of the respective mode, the same tonal range, and the same close on *e* as the Introit. The two chants differ in character, however. High *c*, which permeates the Introit with is bright ring, occurs but once in the Offertory. In its place we have bistrophas and tristrophas on low *f*. In fact the entire piece is more deliberate, more reserved, more solemn. Similar sequences are repeated at *(pulchritú)-do* and *(e)-jus*, over the close of the first *eius* and the first half of the second *eius,* over *(sáncti)-tas* and *(magnifi)-cén-(tia).* Rhythmical groups are likewise repeated. Thus, for instance, we find four groups of two and three over *magnificénti-(a),* and three groups of two and two with an emphasis on the *pes* over *sanctificati-(óne).* The *pes* forms the arsis, while the *clivis* forms the thesis. This arrangement brings about a threefold undulatory movement, and serves as a preparation for the brilliant word-accent to which three neums give prominence.

The inner spiritual reality that transpires in the Eucharistic Sacrifice, which is directly introduced by the offering of the oblation, makes itself felt from the very outset. Thus the words of the Offertory tell us: the Eucharistic Sacrifice is the noblest hymn of praise and beauty *(conféssio et pulchritúdo)* that can be rendered to the Most High. According to the words of the Canon of the Mass, it renders to the Blessed Trinity all honor and glory. In this sacrifice the pure, holy *(sánctitas),* spotless sacrificial Lamb offers Himself. To the Church it represents the fountainhead of all the wonderful splendor *(magnificéntia)* which she possesses in her saints, for from it they drew their "every heavenly blessing and grace" (Canon of the Mass).

COMMUNION (John 12: 26)

1. *Qui mihi ministrat, me sequatur:* 2. *et ubi ego sum, illic et minister meus erit.*

1. *If any man minister to me, let him follow me:* 2. *and where I am, there also shall my minister be.*

This Communion is now assigned to the Common of a Martyr not a Bishop; it originated, however, with the feast of St. Lawrence. The text repeats the words of our Lord in today's Gospel.

St. Lawrence was filled with a burning desire to imitate and follow his divine Saviour even unto death. As his bishop, St. Xystus, was being led to martyrdom, he was filled with an intense longing to make the supreme sacrifice with him whom he had so often served at the offering of the Eucharistic Sacrifice. Only then was he satisfied when told that after three days he should follow *(me sequátur)* in the footsteps of the martyred bishop. He went to his death and his heart rejoiced: "Now is my joy full," he said, "because I am become a martyr *(hóstia)* for Christ's sake."

The melody of the first phrase is filled with sweet harmony, as if Christ were speaking invitingly to the saint: Behold, I am with you; through self-denial and suffering you will come closer to Me. The second phrase might be an explanation of the first in the sense that the disciple who shares the lot of his master must be prepared to endure also suffering and persecution. *Ego* rises in a solemn manner. Annotated manuscripts give the first four and the last two notes of this word the broad form, thereby knitting the melodic line more closely together. The pronounced upward tendency of the melody would depict for us Christ as enthroned above the clouds, elevated above all pain, sorrow, and persecution; and he who ministers to Him shall attain to these same heights. As if in joyful longing for that happiness, *illic* is given a comparatively rich melody. The low pitch of *minister*, however, reminds us that only humble service will realize this longing in us.

*   *   *   *

THE ASSUMPTION OF THE BLESSED VIRGIN MARY

(August 15)

The present Mass formulary of the feast is post-Gregorian, the Gradual alone being found in the oldest manuscripts. Formerly the Introit *Vultum tuum* (now sung on the vigil), the Offertory *Offeréntur* of the feast of St. Agatha (today *Afferéntur*), and the Communion *Dilexísti* of the Common of Holy Women were sung. This entire older Mass formula is found as late as 1511 in a Graduale printed by Pforzheim at Basle.[1]

The Introit, Alleluia, and Offertory have this characteristic, that they hold out the angels to us as models whom we may imitate in praising the Mother of God. We can easily imagine the feelings of joy with which they greet their queen today and lead her triumphantly into the heavenly courts. United in spirit with these angels we also rejoice in honoring and felicitating the Blessed Virgin upon the distinction and honor which is accorded her on this feast. Fundamental to the beauty and grandeur of today's celebration is the consoling conviction that this same queen of heaven ever remains to us a Mother of mercy.

INTROIT

1. *Gaudeamus omnes in Domino, diem festum celebrantes sub honore beatae Mariae Virginis:* 2. *de cuius Assumptione gaudent Angeli et*

1. *Let us all rejoice in the Lord, celebrating a festival day in honor of the blessed Virgin Mary;* 2. *for whose Assumption the angels re-*

---

[1] R. Molitor, *Choralwiegendrucker*, p. 62.

collaudent filium Dei. Ps. *Eructavit cor meum verbum bonum:* * *dico ego opera mea regi.*

joice and give praise to the Son of God. Ps. *My heart hath uttered a good word:* * *I speak my works to the king.*

"A bright, clear and inspiring melody, distinguished not so much by its deep and mystical appeal or its tender fervor as by its joyous, festal character. It displays a brilliant development, a uniformly simple —we might say naive—construction, and a clear and calm assurance of victory in its every phrase. Like the beautiful morning sun which rises without effort above the mountain peaks and floods the earth with its golden rays, this hymn of joy springs from the depths of loving souls to sing the triumphs of the Blessed Mother."[1]

Originally the melody was composed for a Greek text on the feast of St. Agatha. It soon attained popular favor and was sung on a number of feasts.

Text and melody have two phrases. The first phrase summons the entire Church militant to rejoice in the Lord, for "it is a festival day in honor of the blessed Virgin Mary." The second phrase depicts the joy of the Church triumphant in the victory of Mary over death, "for whose Assumption the Angels give praise to the Son of God." Each phrase has two members, each of which in turn has two sub-members. Both major members of the first phrase close on a high pitch: *Dómino, Vírginis.* The second phrase repeats over *Assumptióne* and *collaúdent* the ascending musical line of the first part. The melody here develops according to the declamatory accents that intelligent rendition would demand. The development and division of the piece might be pictured graphically as follows:

> *Gaudeámus omnes in   Dómino,*
> *Diem f. c. s. honóre Maríae Vírginis:*
> *d. c. Assumptióne gaudent Angeli,*
> *et collaúdant Fílium Dei.*

We might take note at once of the two motives that run through the entire Introit. The first occurs over *sub honóre, Assumptióne,* and with a variation, over *collaúdant* and *in Dómino.* It begins with the interval *f–g* and ascends by means of a lively *torculus* (once by means of a *pes subbipunctis*) to *c,* thus recalling *Gaudeámus.* The second motive with its quiet seconds occurs over *Dei,* again a full tone higher over *(An)-geli,* and finally a fourth higher over *(Dó)-mino.*

---

[1] *C. O.*, 50, 147.

"Let us rejoice—in the Lord." The high points of the melody are not reserved to the accented syllables alone. The significant *in Dómino* —"in the Lord"—for instance, is very prominent, and rightly so, since even the most solemn feast of the Blessed Virgin is a feast of our Lord also. It is this very thought, in fact, that forms the burden of the invitatory prayer at Matins: "Come, let us adore the King of Kings, whose virgin Mother was today bodily assumed into heaven." The same thought recurs once more in the second phrase of the Introit—the angels glorify God because He has honored, crownèd, and transfigured His Blessed Mother.

The first phrase begins solemn and festal in character, the stress of voice increasing gradually up to the word *Dómino* over which *a* and *b* are given special emphasis. Soft accents mark the words *di-(em) fe-(stum) ce-(le)-brán-(tes)*, the thrice recurring double *f* especially being sung very lightly. This entire member should be rendered fluently. The member following is characterized by a progressive ascent and a gradual swell of the melody up to *Vírginis*, which has a refreshing *b*. The double *c* over *(Mari)-ae*, the only mention of the name of Mary in the entire piece, should be rendered with warmth rather than with volume.

In the second phrase, a minor accent is placed over the second syllable of *(As)-sump-(tióne)*. The *porrectus* over *Ange-(li)* carry the melody and should be somewhat emphasized. The dynamic high point of the phrase centers over *collaúdant*. A further secondary accent stresses the third note over *Fí-(lium)*.

In the verse Mary casts a retrospective glance over her earthly existence. The *Fiat*—"Behold the handmaid of the Lord"—which she spoke on the day of the Annunciation was indeed a good, a happy word. This sentiment pervaded her entire life and she knew not to speak any other word than: "My works to the King"—and to Him alone.

Analyses, 7, 13 ff.; *Revue* 7, 232 ff.

GRADUAL (Ps. 44: 5, 11, 12.)

1. *Propter veritatem et mansue-tudinem et justitiam*: 2. *Et deducet te mirabiliter dextera tua.* ℣. 1. *Audi, filia, et vide,* 2. *Et inclina aurem tuam*: 3. *quia concupivit rex speciem tuam.*

1. *Because of truth, and meekness, and justice*: 2. *and thy right hand shall conduct thee wonderfully.* ℣. 1. *Hearken, O daughter, and see,* 2. *and incline thy ear,* 3. *for the king hath greatly desired thy beauty.*

The Gradual employs numerous typical formulas. The melisma over *justítiam* was recently heard on the feast of St. Lawrence over *cor meum*. The melody of the verse up to the first *tuam* is the same as that of the second phrase, while the first half of the third phrase repeats that of the Gradual verse for the second Sunday of Lent. The melody for these first two phrases of the verse as also the close over *spéciem tuam* is common to other Graduals. The satisfaction and joy which the rendition which this piece affords should not, however, suffer on that account. Taken as a whole, it is really a masterpiece of musical composition and a jewel in the setting of today's feast. It prepares and carries out its various musical gradations carefully and methodically, and reaches an artistic climax in the first phrase of the verse.

The first four words have a range of the major third *f–a*, and should be sung *piano*, almost *pianissimo*. Over *et justitiam* there is at first the range of a fourth, later that of a fifth; the melody as such, however, maintains itself on the newly found *b♭*. This melody should be given a *crescendo* which gradually diminishes toward the close until the five last notes become next to aspirates. After the *f* of the third syllable most singers will find need for a pause.

The second phrase has in the main a range of *f–c*, although after the astonishing descent at *déx-(tera)* the melody ascends to high *d*, a range of a seventh. Fluent rendition will be facilitated by giving the second note before the syllable *-ra* a light secondary accent. The motive over *-(bí)-liter* is repeated and strengthened over *-ra*. In case of necessity a pause might be made after the second bistropha over *dex-*; here the *corpus* attains its greatest range, that of an octave *d–d¹*.

The verse begins with a resolved major triad and immediately ascends to high *d* which is accented emphatically. The thrice descending *d¹ a f* has as complement the twice ascending *f a c d¹*. We might here picture to ourselves the angels coming down to the Mother of God on earth and, having paid their court and invited her to the heavenly kingdom, returning thither and mustering other choirs of angels to prepare for her reception. Relying on authoritative manuscripts, some of the Graduals have the eleventh note *(c)* over *fi-* prolonged and thus effect a fine proportion. On the tristropha the melody seems to seek strength necessary for the bold ascent to high *e*. Progressively the melody expands in a brilliant manner until it reaches high *f* over *inclína*. These various high points of the melody, however, should not be overemphasized as such; rather should an entire group or a complete *torculus* be developed as an integral part of the whole melody. *Aurem* begins *piano*. This is followed by a large crescendo over *tuam*, where the modulation to a fifth above the tonic, which was only indicated over *fília*, is evident. The motive over *inclína* is repeated over *concupívit*; it has ascending fourths in place of the descending fourths over *fília*. After the preparatory notes over *(tu)-am* have been sung, the group beginning with *g* should be emphasized, then the group beginning with *a*, and finally the double *c*.

Regarding the application of rhythmic motives in this Gradual, cf. *N. Sch.*, 240 f.

The beauty of the virtues of Mary are described in a series of pictures in the Epistle. She is likened to "a cedar, a cypress tree, a palm tree, a rose plant, an olive tree, a plane tree." She resembles "a sweet-smelling cinnamon and aromatical balm." Among her many virtues, the Gradual calls especial attention to the following three: her truth—she is the realization of the divine dispensation of God; her meekness—she is the clement, pious, and sweet Virgin; her justice —she is the mirror of divine justice. And therefore now, with a choir of angels as an escort, she is assumed into heaven in a miraculous manner.

In the verse the angels call out to her: *Audi, filia*—"Hearken, O daughter." During her earthly life there were hard and bitter words which cut deep into the innocent soul of the Blessed Mother; every word that grieved her divine Son wounded her heart likewise. Many were the heart-rending sights she had to experience: the abject poverty of the stable at Bethlehem, her Son dying on the cross and finally dead in her arms. But the bleak winter of this life has passed—and all suffering is ended; a perpetual balmy spring has come. Now she hearkens to heavenly hymns, contemplates the heavenly bliss, and receives the heavenly crown to adorn her head. The King greatly desires her beauty. All the beauty and sublimity of her soul is now displayed in heaven, and the Almighty has bestowed upon her body the brilliance of His own transfiguration.

ALLELUIA VERSE

1. *Assumpta est Maria in caelum*:   1. *Mary is assumed into heaven:*
2. *gaudet exercitus Angelorum.*   2. *the angel hosts rejoice.*

Following as it does an artistic Gradual, the Alleluia, although rich in neums, might pass as a popular hymn. It soon becomes a favorite with singers, especially youthful singers. A song of bright jubilation emulating that of the angels, it sounds modern in its major tonality and close on *c*. It is nevertheless one of the oldest chant melodies we have. Originally it was sung to the text *Te gloriósus Apostolórum chorus* (cf. the Alleluia on the feast of St. Bartholomew, Apostle, and St. Matthew, Evangelist), and was finally adapted for use on the Dedication of a Church during Paschal time. Its adaptation to the text on the feast of the Assumption is so happy that we might judge it to be an original composition.

The melody over *Allelúia*, exclusive of its *jubilus*, has two sections, the first of which reaches its climax on the *pressus* and recurs in the second member of the *jubilus*. In chant practice the two sections should be taken successively as shown in the following scheme:

cd   efgáag   g

All-   e   lú...and

cd   efgáag   g

a--------------

The second section is further developed in the first member of the *jubilus*, which in turn has two members that are well rounded off by the *climacus*. The second member of the *jubilus* is an abbreviated form of all which precedes.

The tone material for the first part of the verse as well as the energetic accents over *est* and *Ma-(ría)* are taken from the melody of the first part of *Allelúia*. This first phrase moves quietly, is almost narrative. Groups of two notes should be sung over *est* and *-ría in*. The melody here has a strong cadencing tendency and is more effective than in the original. Beginning with *gaudet*, the exuberant joy of the angel choirs again makes itself felt. The melodic figure over *exércitus* is identical with that over *Allelúia*; its arrangement differs somewhat, since, on account of the "i" in the latter word, a liquescent *climacus* is placed between the two vowels. The choir will experience some difficulty setting in with *Angelórum*. The *jubilus* of *Allelúia* recurs over *-ló-*. A little discrepancy arises here. According to a so-called "golden rule" it is neither allowed to retard nor to pause before the various syllables of the same word, consequently neither before *-rum*. On the last note of the corresponding *torculus resupinus* in the *jubilus* of the *Allelúia*, however, a *mora vocis* was made. In order to reconcile both renditions, *Revue* (24, 149 ff.) suggests that this retarding in the *jubilus* be made light and short (cf. also *Revue*, 11, 165 ff.).

Although the Alleluia *Angelus Dómini* of Easter Monday and *Verbo Dómini* of the Wednesday of Pentecost Week are quite similar to the present melody, they are nevertheless assigned to the eighth mode because of their close on *g*. They really belong to the fifth mode, as does the Alleluia of today.

OFFERTORY

1. *Assumpta est Maria in caelum:*
2. *gaudent Angeli,* 3. *collaudantes benedicunt Dominum.*

1. *Mary hath been taken up into heaven:* 2. *the Angels rejoice,* 3. *and blessing God, praise him with one voice.*

This text, like that of the Introit and the Alleluia, is non-scriptural. For an Offertory this is rather singular. It occurs four other times on feasts of the Blessed Virgin: *Beáta es*, on the feast of the Visitation; *Recordáre*, on the feasts of Mount Carmel and the Seven Dolors; and *Felix namque*, in the votive Mass of the Blessed Virgin during the Christmas season. To these four should be added the Offertory *Prótege* on the feast of the Exaltation of the Cross, and *Dómine Jesu Christe* of the Requiem Mass.

The melody was explained on Easter Monday. It was quite probably adapted to this text in the eleventh century.[1] The intonation bears some resemblance to the melody over *collaúdant* in the Introit; this is only fortuitous, however. The whole rivals by its warmth and vivacity the Gradual and the Alleluia.

The Gospel narrates the meeting of Jesus with Mary and Martha, the sisters of Lazarus. The blessed Virgin was both Martha and Mary to our Lord. As a Martha she served Him with a tireless love and carried out all such duties which the needs of a child might demand of its mother. As a Mary she sat at His feet hearkening to His every word and absorbing the divine truths that fell from His lips. She chose the better part which was not taken away from her. What constituted this better part forms the theme of the Offertory: she was assumed into heaven, angels the while rejoicing and praising the Lord. Would that we could realize in our person the voice and spirit of the angels in singing the praises and celebrating the triumph of the Mother of God!

COMMUNION (Luke 10: 42)

1. *Optimam partem elegit sibi Maria, 2. quae non auferetur ab ea in aeternum.*

1. *Mary hath chosen for herself the best part: 2. which shall not be taken from her forever.*

The Communion refers back to the Gospel and points out to us its significance for the present feast. To the original text the composer here added the words *in aetérnum* at the end. The melody was explained on the feast of the Annunciation.

Eternal happiness is the only true happiness. Such eternal happiness is the reward which God bestows upon Mary today. True, He made her the recipient of numerous graces; it was only by cooperating faithfully with every grace, however, that Mary finally attained the blessings of eternal salvation.

---

[1] *Revue*, 4, 163; *Rassegna*, 2, 341 ff.

The highest good which we can choose on earth is Holy Communion: therein is contained heaven with its eternal happiness. "He that eateth this bread shall live forever."

*   *   *   *

ST. JOACHIM, FATHER OF THE BLESSED VIRGIN MARY, CONFESSOR
(August 16)

This feast, introduced into the Roman liturgy under Julius II (1503–13), is now invariably celebrated on the day following the Assumption. Thus also in the liturgy, father and child stand in close relationship to one another.

INTROIT (Ps. 111: 9)

1. *Dispersit, dedit pauperibus*: 2. *justitia eius manet in saeculum saeculi*: 3. *cornu eius exaltabitur in gloria.* Ps. *Beatus vir qui timet Dominum*:* *in mandatis eius cupit nimis.*

1. *He hath distributed, he hath given to the poor*: 2. *his justice remaineth forever and ever*: 3. *his horn shall be exalted in glory.* Ps. *Blessed is the man that feareth the Lord*: * *he shall delight exceedingly in his commandments.*

The Introit is taken from the vigil of St. Lawrence, where the text is descriptive of the great exertions of that saint, of his self-sacrificing service to others, and of his paternal devotion to the poor of Rome. While tradition also extols the tender and self-sacrificing love of St. Joachim, we can readily picture to ourselves the contemporaneous poverty in which he lived. Without doubt, he sheltered in the person of the Virgin Mother the greatest riches this world possessed; in fact, he himself was a model of justice (Introit). On the other hand, the home he provided was evidently poor in the goods of this world, as is evidenced by the poverty which accompanied Mary and Joseph to Bethlethem on the first Christmas. St. Joachim was therefore always solicitous to provide by the labor of his hands the necessaries of life for his own, these truly poor in Christ. Now he is exalted in glory, and his justice endures as a shining model for us.

The melody has a brisk and joyful swing; this is already exemplified in the use of numerous fourths. Each phrase also gives melodic prominence to high *e*. Beyond this, however, the phrases do not vary greatly.

In the first phrase, *g* has a predominating influence; in the second, *f* is effective in relation to *bb*; in the third, *b* is stressed while *c g e* are the most conspicuous notes. Although every phrase of the text terminates with a dactyl, the melody nevertheless gives neums to the second last syllable of each. *Cornu* sets in a fourth higher than the close of its preceding phrase. There can be no thought of word-painting, however, since we find the same figure over *(magnifi-)céntia* in the Introit of the feast of St. Lawrence. *Dispérsit* is sung *ǵca ǵcc*; *(paupé-)ri-(bus)*, on the other hand, has three quiet groups of two notes.

GRADUAL (Ps. 111: 9, 2)

1. *Dispersit, dedit pauperibus:* 2. *justitia eius manet in saeculum saeculi.* ℣. *Potens in terra* 2. *erit semen eius:* 3. *generatio rectorum* 4. *benedicetur.*

1. *He hath distributed, he hath given to the poor:* 2. *his justice remaineth forever and ever.* ℣. 1. *Mighty upon earth* 2. *shall be his seed* 3. *the generation of the righteous* 4. *shall be blessed.*

The *corpus* is identical with the first two phrases of the Introit. The text of the verse has an especially bright ring. How mighty has the child of St. Joachim become as the queen of heaven and mistress of earth, the terror of evil spirits and the joy of the just. The very King of Kings humbles Himself before her and becomes subject to her; generations will ever sing her praise and never cease to cry: "Blessed art thou among women and blessed *(Benedicétur)* is the fruit of thy womb, Jesus."

The melody is of the type explained on the first Sunday of Lent. Both text and melody are taken from the vigil of St. Lawrence.

ALLELUIA VERSE

1. *O Joachim sancte, coniux Annae, pater almae Virginis,* 2. *hic famulis ferto salutis opem.*

1. *O holy Joachim, spouse of Anne, father of the glorious Virgin,* 2. *assist now thy servants unto salvation.*

In the eleventh century this melody was sung to the text *O quam metuéndus est* (Dedication of a Church). The beginning of the verse repeats the motive over *-le*. This same motive with its *torculus* is repeated a fifth higher over *coniux*, and with a slight variation over *almae*. The first member of the *jubilus* is echoed over *sanctae*.

The Vatican Gradual, both textually and melodically (typica figure *dc fga*), combines *sancte* with *Jóachim*; according to the Missal however, it belongs to *Annae (sanctae)*.

The verse adduces various reasons for confiding in the intercession of St. Joachim. He is a saint, the spouse of St. Anne, and the father of the Blessed Virgin Mary. His intercession on our behalf will merit the sympathetic support of the Mother of God. And he himself, moved by the petitions which his servants present to him, will implore from God the grace of our salvation.

OFFERTORY (Ps. 8: 6, 7)

1. *Gloria et-honore coronasti eum:* 2. *et constituisti eum super opera manuum tuarum, Domine.*

1. *Thou hast crowned him with glory and honor:* 2. *and hast set him over the works of thy hands, O God.*

Florid neums give especial prominence to *honóre* and *Dómine*. These two words, in fact, summarize the content of the entire Offertory: Honored by God. The melody as such is very effective, especially in its rise to and frequent use of high *c*. The song is like an act of solemn homage to the saint. The introductory motive over *-nó-(re)* is repeated immediately, then once more over *-(i)-sti* and *má(-nuum)*, and, with a slight variation over *(-ná)-sti eum*. The first half of the first phrase closes on *g*, since the following intonation begins on *f*; in a similar manner, its second half closes on *f* since the following intonation begins on the higher *a* (rule of adaptation of phrases). While the first phrase has a range of a fifth, that of the second is much more extensive. The second phrase, which begins with the high-pitched and strongly accented motive *a cc da* over *et constituísti*, comes to a close a fifth lower with *d ff fgd* over *-mine*. The low-pitched melody over *super ópera* stands out in strong contrast to its two adjoining high-pitched melodies.

In old manuscripts this Offertory is assigned to the vigil of the Apostle St. John, when it was sung in the early morn of the feast itself.

During his lifetime St. Joachim was made custodian of God's most beautiful handiwork. As a reward for his faithful service, the Lord has bestowed upon him immortal glory.

COMMUNION (Luke 11: 41)

1. *Fidelis servus et prudens, quem constituit Dominus super familiam suam;* 2. *ut det illis in tempore tritici mensuram.*

1. *O faithful and wise steward, whom his Lord setteth over his family;* 2. *to give them their measure of wheat in due season.*

Older manuscripts assign this melody to the feast of St. Gregory the Great. Prior to this, however, it was already sung on the feast of Popes Urban and Sixtus.

The melody grows systematically, *ǵa b́g ác c* becoming *ćb ćd d* and finally *d́c d́e d́cc*; following this, *c* becomes the actual dominant. The rhyme at the end of the first and second phrases is also very effective, *ćd ćb gg* becoming *ćd ćb ǵag g*. Both phrases have three divisions. The second phrase has a richer development than we ordinarily find in a Communion. Over *trítici* the Vatican Gradual calls for a slight retarding after *c* and *a*, thus resulting in three groups, of which the first and third form the arsis.

If ever a household deserved the name of Family of God surely it was the one over which St. Joachim presided. God himself appointed Joachim its head, and insofar as its sole aim was the greater glory of God, it was truly God's family *(familiam suam)*. The needs of this family, imposed upon St. Joachim by divine decree, were served by him with such thoughtfulness and fidelity that he has become a model for us and an object of universal admiration.

Christ has also united Himself with us under the form of bread *(trítici)*. According to His human nature He came to us from the most pure womb of Mary. Mary, however, was the child of St. Joachim and St. Anne. May their intercession procure for us (Postcommunion) in the present life the graces of God, so that in the life to come we may be sharers in eternal glory.

* * * *

ST. BARTHOLOMEW, APOSTLE

(August 26)

INTROIT, GRADUAL and OFFERTORY are the same as those on the feast of St. Andrew.

ALLELUIA VERSE

1. *Gloriosus Apostolorum chorus*
2. *te laudat, Domine.*

1. *The glorious choir of Apostles,*
2. *praises thee, O Lord.*

The text is taken from the *Te Deum*. In the words of the Collect God "has given us a reverent and holy joy in this day's festival." The Alleluia, which refers to the glorious and venerable choir of Apostles, gives lively expression to this joy. In the Gospel we are told that our Lord devoted to prayer the entire night which preceded the election of His Apostles. During the years in which these Apostles were associated with Him, He imparted to them a wealth of truth and of power. They in turn served Him in holiness and justice, even though—as in the case of today's saint—a martyr's crown awaited them at the end of their laborious lives. Glorious indeed is the choir of the Apostles.

The melody was heard only recently on the feast of the Assumption. The second last and last syllables of the first word should not be retarded. The brevity of the text did not permit after *laudat* the usual repetition of the melody over *allelúia*.

The COMMUNION was explained on the feast of St. Matthias.

* * * *

THE NATIVITY OF THE BLESSED VIRGIN MARY
(September 8)

In Rome this feast dates back to the pontificate of Sergius I (687–701); it was celebrated by the universal Church only some time after the ninth century. The chants are identical with those of the feast of the Visitation.

How noble was the vocation of the Virgin Mother! Her body and soul had been made a worthy habitation for the Saviour by almighty God Himself. Beautiful and pure, stainless and perfect she came from the master-hand of God. Happy and content in her inner perfections, she brought supernatural happiness to a poor deluded world. Her birthday is made the occasion of solemn rejoicings. In the Introit she is greeted with *Salve*, in the Gradual with *Benedícta es tu*, in the Alleluia with *Felix es*, and in the Offertory and Communion with *Beáta*.

THE EXALTATION OF THE HOLY CROSS
(September 14)

In the Orient today's feast was celebrated as early as the fourth century. In the Occident it became known in the eighth century, and then only gradually.

The INTROIT and the GRADUAL are taken from the Mass of Maundy Thursday. The ALLELUIA-VERSE is the second from the feast of the Finding of the Holy Cross (May 3), from which feast the COMMUNION also has been taken. Something akin to the spirit of autumn pervades this feast, an expectation of that great day when the cross will appear in the clouds of heaven as the sign of the "Son of man."

OFFERTORY

1. *Protege, Domine, plebem tuam, per signum sanctae Crucis, ab omnibus insidiis inimicorum omnium:* 2. *ut tibi gratam exhibeamus servitutem,* 3. *et acceptabile fiat sacrificium nostrum, alleluia.*

1. *Protect thy people, O Lord, by the sign of the holy Cross, from the wiles of all their enemies:* 2. *that we may render a service pleasing unto thee,* 3. *and that our sacrifice may be acceptable in thy sight, alleluia.*

The sentiment of the Offertory is similar to that of the Communion, but places greater stress upon the protection from the enemies of the soul. These enemies must not hinder us from the service of God, must not disturb our interior peace, must not rob us of the joy in God's service, must not delude us with the enticements and seeming joys of the world, must not induce us to desert our recognized duty and become unfaithful. Against all these dangers may the holy cross protect us and strengthen us in perseverance and fidelity in the service of God. If in this manner our service becomes pleasing to the Lord, then our worship and the union of our sacrifice with the Eucharistic Sacrifice will also become pleasing to Him.

Something akin to melancholy pervades the melody. It has a very modest development. Despite its length, its greatest interval is a third. The first and second phrases begin with the same descending motive. Abstracting from this, the first half of the first phrase confines itself to the range of a fourth, the second half to a fifth, as does also the third phrase. The second phrase alone has a range of a sixth. Over *exhibeámus servitútem* the melody of *per signum sanctae Crucis* is extended and developed, while that of *sacrificium* is simplified. Only the first syllable of this word receives any special accent. *Omnibus insídiis* resembles *acceptábile fiat*. An enlivening effect is produced by the *pressus*, particularly over *signum Crucis* and the corresponding passages.

The whole should be rendered as a fervent prayer, without strong accents. It should breathe the conviction of a soul conscious of its own weakness in the face of the evil one, but firmly reliant on the power of Christ's cross. In sentiment it is closely allied to the Offertory *Dómine Jesu Christe* of the Mass for the Dead, which likewise belongs to the second mode.

Revue, 16, 114.

*　　*　　*　　*

THE SEVEN SORROWS OF THE BLESSED VIRGIN MARY
(September 15)
INTROIT (John 19: 25)

1. *Stabant juxta crucem Jesu mater ejus, et soror matris ejus Maria Cleophae, 2. et Salome, et Maria Magdalene. ℣. Mulier, ecce filius tuus, dixit Jesus; * ad discipulum autem: Ecce mater tua.*

1. *There stood by the cross of Jesus, his mother, and his mother's sister Mary of Cleophas, 2. and Salome, and Mary Magdalen. ℣. Woman, behold thy son, said Jesus; * to the disciple, however: Behold thy mother.*

The peculiar style of this text makes it unsuitable for composition. At the beginning of the first phrase we have the predicate, whereupon follows a fourfold subject. True enough, the Mother of Jesus is given first place. For it is she alone who on this day deserves our attention, our love, and our sympathy. She is deserving of first mention. Rightly, also, do the words *Mater ejus* dominate the melodic line of the first-phrase. But beyond this the piece can really no longer develop, or rather, it shows development where we least expect it, namely, over *María Cléophae*. There is, however, a melodic reason for this. The Introit *Státuit* for the feast of a Martyr and Bishop and of a Confessor and Bishop, served as a model for this Introit. *Stabant=Státuit, mater ejus= ut sit illi, María Cléophae=sacerdótii dígnitas, (Ma)-gdaléne=aetérnum.* The leading thought of the original is *sacerdótii dígnitas*—"the dignity of the priesthood." Here the melody moves along solemnly in a recitative tone, a third above the dominant, and flows into a festal cadence. Thus the tone-sequences occur above *María Cléophae*, which certainly is not the textual apex of the present Introit. Perhaps the identical initial syllable *Stá-(tuit)=Stá-(bant)* brought about this association of melodies. Nor would this be an isolated instance. Some of the newer feasts borrow their melodies from older feasts with which they are closely related in the liturgical year.

In spite of this, however, we should not overlook the fact that to-day's Introit contains much that is delicate and beautiful. The melody over *juxta crucem Jesu* is noble and tender; over *mater ejus*, almost pathetic. This passage should be made emphatic with a slow, but not dragging, tempo; it must create the correct atmosphere for today's feast. It ought to express a tender sympathy with the Mother of sorrows, for Mary must witness the death of her only Son on the wood of the cross. Many a mother may well say of her child: My one and all! But Mary alone has the right to speak these words in their fullest sense. Her Child dies, dies in unspeakable agony, while she must stand by, unable to offer any help! Her sorrow and pain but increase the desolation of her divine Son. Mary, however, desires to stand there, to remain there, desires to participate most intimately in the great sacrifice which her Son is offering for the salvation of the world.

The second half of the first phrase is free composition at the beginning, like *et Salóme* in the second phrase. The first phrase closes on on the dominant *a*, and uses this as a base from which to ascend higher. The second phrase never extends beyond *a*. Similarly *et Salóme* and *María* introduce and stress the word-accent. The low pitch of the second half of the latter phrase may suggest the picture of Mary Magdalen kneeling at the foot of the cross.

The verse is not taken from the psalms, as is customary with other Introits, but from the Gospel. The dying Saviour is speaking directly. He appoints His mother the mother of St. John and of us all. What feeling and sentiment is contained in this simple, typical melody!

GRADUAL

1. *Dolorosa et lacrimabilis es, Virgo Maria,* 2. *stans juxta crucem Domini Jesu Filii tui Redemptoris.* ℣. 1. *Virgo Dei Genitrix, quem totus non capit orbis,* 2. *hoc crucis fert supplicium, auctor vitae factus homo.*

1. *Thou art sorrowful and worthy of tears, O virgin Mary,* 2. *standing near the cross of the Lord Jesus, thy son, our Redeemer.* ℣. 1. *O virgin mother of God, he whom the whole world doth not contain,* 2. *beareth this punishment of the cross, the author of life, made man.*

The melody was explained on July 2 and is admirably suited to this text.

To be blunt of feeling, St. Paul remarks, is a mark of paganism. This was not the case with the heart of Mary, St. Bernard says, neither should it be with her servants. How we are to participate in her sorrow who was "worthy of tears" (the first meaning of the Latin *lacrimábilis*), is told us in the Sequence.

Oh, the bitter irony of it! He whom the heavens and earth can not contain is nailed to the cross. In the Lamentations He complains: "He hath built against Me round about, that I may not get out: he hath made My fetters heavy;" and: "The author of life is fallen a victim to death." And His mother weeps.

ALLELUIA VERSE

1. *Stabat sancta Maria, caeli Regina, et mundi Domina,* 2. *juxta crucem Domini nostri Jesu Christi dolorosa.*

1. *Holy Mary, the queen of heaven, and mistress of the world,* 2. *stood by the cross of our Lord Jesus Christ, full of sadness.*

The melody dates from the eleventh century and was originally sung to the text *Stabunt justi.* Here again the identical initial syllable of *Stabunt* and *Stabat* may have influenced the selection of the melody. With the *climacus* of the *jubilus*, the first three notes should be taken together, the fourth should receive a slight secondary accent; the same holds true of the notes of the *climacus* in the verse, made striking both by their prolongation and their melody. Compare, also, the delicate structure of a similar formula in the second Alleluia of Pentecost over *amóris*. First *Stabat sancta* is simplified, then expanded over *caeli Regina*. In contrast to the high *b♭*, the second phrase has a low *a*.

Who would believe that this weeping woman—together with her Son an object of ridicule—is the queen of heaven and the mistress of the world? And yet the world has seen nothing more noble than this woman—how she bears her pain and *stands* beneath the cross. Gradual, Alleluia, and Sequence stress this point: *stans* and *stabat.* Truly, she deserved to become the queen of heaven and mistress of the world.

Revue, 6, 160.

SEQUENCE

Jacopone da Todi (✠ c. 1306) was long credited with the authorship of this sequence. Cogent reasons, however, point to St. Bonaventure (✠ 1274). The melody owes its origin to the Benedictine, Dom Jausions (✠ 1868). It strikes a note of heartfelt sympathy without becoming sentimental. It possesses a beauty all its own, but does not attain the artistic height of the text, the communicative warmth of its feelings, the delicate swelling and contraction of its mood, and the pleasantness of its rhythm. The melody, no doubt, would have been enhanced had it followed the text more faithfully. The strophes show too little individualism, even though they avoid lengthy repetitions. Every choirmaster will experience that, although sung frequently, the Sequence never attains its full possibilities.

The text has two major divisions and a short conclusion. These, however, have had no influence on the formation of the melody. The first part comprises the first four double strophes and considers the Mother of sorrows beneath the cross of her Son. Melodically, it surpasses the second part.

From the first to the fourth double strophe, the melody has increasingly greater intervals (fifth, sixth, seventh, octave). The quint at the beginning of the second double strophe is especially happy. Likewise the descent to *c bb a* in the third double strophe.

FIRST PART

1a. *Stabat Mater dolorosa*
Juxta crucem lacrimosa
Dum pendebat Filius.

1a. *At the Cross her station keeping,*
Stood the mournful Mother weeping
Close to Jesus to the last.

1b. *Cujus animam gementem,*
Contristatam, et dolentem,
Pertransivit gladius.

1b. *Through her heart, His sorrow sharing,*
All His bitter anguish bearing,
Now at length the sword had passed.

2a. *O quam tristis et afflicta*
Fuit illa benedicta
Mater Unigeniti!

2a. *Oh, how sad and sore distressed*
Was that Mother, highly blest
Of the sole-begotten One!

2b. *Quae moerebat et dolebat,*
Pia Mater dum videbat
Nati poenas inclyti.

2b. *Christ above in torment hangs;*
She beneath beholds the pangs
Of her dying glorious Son.

3a. *Quis est homo qui non fleret,*
Matrem Christi si videret
In tanto supplicio?

3a. *Is there one who would not weep*
Whelmed in miseries so deep
Christ's dear Mother to behold?

3b. *Quis non posset contristari,*
Christi Matrem contemplari
Dolentem cum Filio?

3b. *Can the human heart refrain*
From partaking in her pain,
In that Mother's pain untold?

4a. *Pro peccatis suae gentis*
Vidit Jesum in tormentis,
Et flagellis subditum.

4a. *Bruised, derided, cursed, defiled,*
She beheld her tender Child:
All with bloody scourges rent.

4b. *Vidit suum dulcem natum*
Moriendo desolatum
Dum emisit spiritum.

4b. *For the sins of His own nation*
Saw Him hang in desolation,
Till His Spirit forth He sent.

SECOND PART

In this part all the strophes have a range of a sixth. Melodically related are the second verses of the seventh and eighth double strophes, the third verses of the seventh and tenth strophes, the first verse of the eighth strophe and the second of the tenth strophe. The eighth strophe forms its third verse like that of the fourth strophe. Strophe 6b has the internal rhyme: *Tui nati vúlnerati, tam dignáti pro me pati*; similarly strophe 8b: *Fac ut portem Christi mortem, Pássionis fac consórtem*. The frequently recurring *fac* ("Obtain for me this grace!") gives the text a childlike and prayerful aspect. It receives special fervor and intimacy through the various appellations with which Mary is addressed: "Mother, fount of love," "Holy Mother, Virgin of all virgins, Virgin."

5a. *Eia Mater, fons amoris,*
Me sentire vim doloris
Fac, ut tecum lugeam.

5a. O Thou Mother, fount of love!
Touch my spirit from above;
Make my heart with thine accord.

5b. *Fac ut ardeat cor meum,*
In amando Christum Deum,
Ut sibi complaceam.

5b. Make me feel as thou hast felt;
Make my soul to glow and melt
With the love of Christ my Lord.

6a. *Sancta Mater, istud agas,*
Crucifixi fige plagas
Cordi meo valide.

6a. Holy Mother! pierce me through;
In my heart each wound renew
Of my Saviour crucified.

6b. *Tui nati vulnerati,*
Tam dignati pro me pati,
Poenas mecum divide.

6b. Let me share with thee His pain,
Who for all my sins was slain,
Who for me in torments died.

7a. *Fac me tecum pie flere,*
Crucifixo condolere,
Donec ego vixero.

7a. Let me mingle tears with thee,
Mourning Him who mourned for me,
All the days that I may live.

7b. *Juxta crucem tecum stare,*
Et me tibi sociare
In planctu desidero.

7b. By the Cross with thee to stay,
There with thee to weep and pray,
Is all I ask of thee to give.

8a. *Virgo virginum praeclara,*
Mihi jam non sis amara:
Fac me tecum plangere.

8a. Virgin of all virgins best!
Listen to my fond request:
Let me share thy grief divine.

8b. *Fac ut portem Christi mortem,*
    Passionis fac consortem,
    Et plagas recolere.

8b. *Let me, to my latest breath,*
    In my body bear the death
    Of that dying Son of thine.

9a. *Fac me plagis vulnerari,*
    Fac me cruce inebriari,
    Et cruore Filii.

9a. *Wounded with His every wound,*
    Steep my soul till it hath swooned
    In His very Blood away.

9b. *Flammis ne urar succensus,*
    Per te, Virgo, sim defensus
    In die judicii.

9b. *Be to me, O Virgin, nigh,*
    Lest in flames I burn and die,
    In that awful Judgment Day.

THIRD PART

In the conclusion we pray to Christ crucified for a happy death in the name of His Sorrowful Mother:

10a. *Christe, cum sit hinc exire,*
    Da per Matrem me venire
    Ad palmam victoriae.

10a. *Christ, when Thou shalt call me hence,*
    Be Thy Mother my defense,
    Be Thy Cross my victory.

10b. *Quando corpus morietur,*
    Fac ut animae donetur
    Paradisi gloria.
    Amen. Alleluia
    C. O., 50, 153 ff.

10b. *While my body here decays,*
    May my soul Thy goodness praise,
    Safe in paradise with Thee.
    Amen. Alleluia

OFFERTORY (Jer. 18: 20)

1. *Recordare, Virgo Mater, in conspectu Dei,* 2. *ut loquaris pro nobis bona,* 3. *et ut avertat indignationem suam a nobis.*

1. *Remember, O Virgin Mother, of God,* 2. *to intercede on our behalf,* 3. *and to turn away His anger from us.*

In the Offertory we address to the Mother of God the words which the sorely tried prophet Jeremias speaks to the Lord in behalf of his ungrateful people. She stood beneath the cross of Jesus and looked into His glazing eyes. She heard Him pray: "Father, forgive them!" And she prayed with Him. She intercedes for us, for us who are the cause of those unspeakable sorrows her motherly heart had to bear. She bears us no ill will, but with the solicitous heart of a mother she implores God to avert His just anger from us.

As once she prayed beneath the cross, so now she prays in heaven for us, *in conspéctu Dei*, before the face of Him who suffers no more, but has entered into His glory. Even today during the sacred Mysteries she will intercede for us, and when the bell at the consecration announces that He has once more become present among us, then Mary implores abundant graces on our behalf. So long as there is a human heart that is sighing and struggling and suffering, Mary does not weary of interceding for it, until the time when she will bring us all into the blissful presence of her divine Son.

In a few of the ancient manuscripts the present text and melody are found as the second verse of the Offertory for the twenty-second Sunday after Pentecost. In Codex H. 159 of Montpellier this composition was inserted later. This melody exhibits the technique of thematic execution as few others do. Over the word *Recordáre* the small note *e* forms the connecting link between two motives, the first of which we shall call a, the second b. Over *bistropha* and *pressus*, which should be kept well separated in the rendition, motive a has an upward movement to the dominant, after which the melody descends a third. Motive b exhibits a downward movement and then ascends. Over *Virgo Mater* the same two motives are repeated. *Bona* follows motive b; the three preceding notes re-echo a part of motive a, as do also the notes over *et ut avér-(tat)*. *Indignatiónem suam* with the descending minor third *c–a* repeats motive a in an amplified manner. If we include the preceding third we have in that which follows a middle cadence of the fifth mode. Of the greatest artistic value is the employment of the two motives in the florid vocalization over *a*. Before *f* is attained, the melody descends in a fifth to the tonic *d*. Motive b sets in on high *c* and ends with an ascent of a third. In a brilliant rise, motive a is now attached a fifth higher and then leads over to motive b, which sets in on *c*. This trope realizes to the full the beauty inherent in the melody.[1]

The melody is characteristic of fervent petition. With *ut loquáris* it becomes still more appealing. *Indignatiónem suam* sounds the outcry of a heart tortured by the weight of divine wrath. But the confident melody of *Recordáre* returns, swells to victorious height and power, and dies away with the expression of quiet resignation.

Musica sacra, 48, 36 ff.

---

[1] Cf. *Revue*, 4, 161 ff., and Wagner, III, 507 f.

COMMUNION

1. *Felices sensus beatae Mariae Virginis,* 2. *qui sine morte meruerunt martyrii palmam sub cruce Domini.*

1. *Happy the senses of the blessed Virgin Mary,* 2. *which without death obtained the palm of martyrdom beside the cross of the Saviour.*

With striking fidelity the melody follows the textual development and reveals a wonderful brilliancy in the words *martyrii palmam.* They begin a fifth higher than the preceding words, while the subsequent words set in a fifth lower. If we add to this the prominence given to the dominant *a,* we have a strikingly original effect. Nevertheless we have also here a part adaptation of a melody which is sung on the feast of the Visitation (July 2) and on many other feasts of the Blessed Virgin. The insertion of the word *beátae* hinders somewhat the easy flow of the original. Less disturbing is the abbreviated repetition of *Maríae Vírginis* over *sine morte.*

At the foot of the cross Mary is the queen of martyrs. Although she did not taste death there, yet so great, so deep was her pain, that no martyr ever suffered like her. Rightly, therefore, is she awarded the palm of martyrdom. Interwoven with this palm is the virginal lily. For a *Virgin* has suffered, in whose heart there was never the least disorder or shadow of sin and who is so exalted, so noble in her suffering precisely because she bears all this innocently. The strength to do this she found in gazing upon her dying Son, *sub cruce Dómini.*

Let us also stand at the foot of the cross of Jesus together with Mary, His Mother. Then we shall be victorious in all our struggles and, should our life become a martyrdom, then we also shall obtain the palm of victory. This sorrowful Mother prays for us always. And during to-day's celebration of the sacred Mysteries Christ again makes available for us the fruits of His Passion. Christ's sufferings are for us a source of strength.

*   *   *   *

ST. MATTHEW, APOSTLE AND EVANGELIST

(September 21)

INTROIT (Ps. 36: 30, 31)

1. *Os justi meditabitur sapientiam,* 2. *et lingua ejus loquetur ju-*

1. *The mouth of the just shall meditate wisdom,* 2. *and his tongu*

dicium: 3. *lex Dei ejus in corde ipsius.* Ps. *Noli aemulari in malignantibus*: * *neque zelaveris facientes iniquitatem.*

shall speak judgment: 3. *the law of his God is in his heart.* Ps. *Be not emulous of evildoers*: * *nor envy them that work iniquity.*

Matthew did not consider himself one of the righteous. He was a publican and the friend of those who were regarded as sinners. But He who is Justice itself, justified him, healed his soul (cf. Gospel of the feast), and called him to be an Apostle and an Evangelist. Thereafter he wrote and taught what he had heard from the lips of eternal Wisdom. He was privileged to announce the glad tidings of a saving Gospel. From him we learn of the judgment, of the judgment of his people and of every soul that resists grace; above all, the judgment at the end of the world. His writings and teachings were to him life and truth. The law of God was in his heart, and as the blood flows from the heart into the veins, so the law of God was the force that enlivened all his actions. Would that we might gaze into the heart of this saint and observe how the grace of God changed it, ennobled it, and filled it with ardent love!

This saint calls to us from his celestial home: If in your daily lives you perceive many who lead a life of sin and nevertheless seem to prosper and be happy, do not lose courage. God's wisdom still governs all things; one day it will lay bare everything, and give victory to the just.

We immediately recognize the identical endings of the first and third phrases. Upon closer investigation we discover that the melody over *lex Dei ejus* at the beginning of the third phrase is a somewhat abbreviated form of that over *meditábitur sapi-(éntiam)*. This creates a parallelism between these two phrases, diverting attention from the textual parallelism existing between the first and second phrases. In fact, the second phrase with its range from high *b♭* (the only one found here) to low *c*, forms a certain contrast with the first and third phrases. The tonic of the sixth mode *(f)* plays an important role in all the phrases.

Over *sapiéntiam* the principal and the secondary accents are short, the following syllable in each instance having more notes. The groups over *(cor)-de ipsius* might be divided into two divisions of three notes each. The chords *g* and *a* would produce a more pronounced harmonic effect. The rhythm $2+2+2$, however, is more effective. Quiet, solemnity, clearness proper to "wisdom" characterize this song, filled as it is with the peace that comes from God.

GRADUAL (Ps. 111: 1, 2)

1. *Beatus vir, qui timet Dominum*: 2. *in mandatis ejus cupit nimis.*

1. *Blessed is the man that feareth the Lord*: 2. *he shall delight exceed-*

℣. 1. *Potens in terra erit semen ejus: 2. generatio rectorum benedicetur.*

ingly in his commandments. ℣. 1. His seed shall be mighty upon earth: 2. the generation of the righteous shall be blessed.

The melody has comparatively few typical forms. We are acquainted with the formula over *erit semen* from the Gradual of the Assumption over *(in)-clína aurem,* and with *benedicétur* from Epiphany over *orta est.* The very last group brings the *corpus* to a close. The resolved major chord *f a c,* much favored by the fifth mode, is used a number of times both in ascending and descending passages, brightening the entire melody. It seems that the ending over *Dóminum,* and particularly the cadence and the ascent over *in (mandátis) ejus* and *(semen) ejus* have been borrowed from the first mode, the fourths over *(cu)-pit nimis* from the third. For the rest, however, this Gradual has many characteristics of its own. At the beginning *g e f d* is repeated a second and a third time; only *d* had to be changed to *f,* since the second half of the phrase sets in on high *c.* Before the first *f* over *Dóminum* a pause for breathing will have to be made, as well as after *mandátis;* likewise after the sixth note of *nimis,* and in the verse after *generátio.* The cadence which closes *terra* appears in an extended form over *ejus,* the groups immediately preceding being repetitions of *semen e-(jus).*

The fear of God becomes a source of joy if it leads us to fulfill the command of God in a practical way and to bear His yoke gladly. For the Lord Himself has said: "My yoke is sweet and My burden is light" (Matt. 11, 30). In fact, it becomes a fountain of blessing for all mankind. What an immense spiritual family the Gospel of St. Matthew has gathered about itself, what a veritable fountain of blessings has it revealed! Through it numberless souls have become righteous *(recti),* have deserted the crooked path of sin, have become just men, good characters, and have thus merited God's blessing.

The ALLELUIA VERSE is the same as that on the feast of St. Bartholomew (August 24); cf. also that of the Assumption (August 15).

OFFERTORY (Ps. 20: 4, 5)

1. *Posuisti Domine in capite ejus coronam de lapide pretioso: 2. vitam petiit a te, et tribuisti ei, alleluia.*

1. *O Lord, thou hast set on his head a crown of precious stones: 2. he asked life of thee, and thou didst grant it to him, alleluia.*

Many have borne a precious crown, only to lose it later. And even if worn for many years, death finally snatched it from its owner. Whoever is crowned by Thee, O Lord, remains crowned for all eternity. And compared to Thy glory, all the gems of this world are but as dust. Thou hast crowned Thy saint with immortal glory.

"He asked life of Thee." When Thou didst stand before the revenue collector's desk and didst say to him: "Follow Me!" but one longing burned in his heart: Away with the life I have led until now; I shall follow Jesus! And Thou hast given him life, life with Thee; for many years he was privileged to be the witness of Thy teaching and of Thy miracles, and later, when he wrote his Gospel, all that he had seen and heard was re-enacted in his soul. And Thy word: "He that shall lose his life for My sake, shall find it" (Matt. 16: 25), gave him the incentive to shed his blood for Thee and thus to attain life eternal, alleluia!

The melody was explained on Easter Monday.

COMMUNION (Ps. 20: 6)

1. *Magna est gloria ejus in salutari tuo: 2. gloriam et magnum decorem impones super eum, Domine.*

1. *His glory is great in thy salvation: 2. glory and great beauty shalt thou lay upon him, O Lord.*

The song opens with a festal ring, expressing in its jubilation almost amazement over the glory prepared by God for His saint. In his mind's eye the singer sees all the churches of the Catholic world in which St. Matthew is venerated today. He beholds the solemnity with which the Gospel written by the saint is read at the divine services. He beholds in spirit all the sublime things that have been wrought in souls through meditation upon this Gospel. Transcending this world, he gazes upon the glory of heaven, and this forces him to cry out: *Magna est glória ejus!* But the Lord effected all this. This fact is stressed by the florid melody over *tuo*. The low *e* over *tuo* finds its antithesis in the high *c* over *glória*.

In the second phrase the jubilant ring is somewhat subdued; reverent admiration now dominates. The renown of the saint is one which never ceases, a glory which never wanes. "Thou, O Lord, layest it upon Him." What a tender preparation the accent over *impónes* receives! The honors of this world are but too often a burden. The glory of heaven is refreshment and sweetness and bliss in God.

The gentle close over *Dómine* seems to breathe the tender petition: Lord, in Holy Communion Thou hast again become my salvation—be Thou my eternal salvation, lead also me into Thy glory!

* * * *

THE DEDICATION OF ST. MICHAEL THE ARCHANGEL

(September 29)

Originally this feast commemorated the anniversary of the dedication of a basilica to St. Michael.

INTROIT (Ps. 102: 20)

1. *Benedicite Dominum omnes Angeli ejus: potentes virtute, qui facitis verbum ejus,* 2. *ad audiendam vocem sermonum ejus.* Ps. *Benedic anima mea Domino:* * *et omnia quae intra me sunt, nomini sancto ejus.*

1. *Bless the Lord, all ye his Angels: you that are mighty in strength, and execute his word,* 2. *hearkening to the voice of his orders.* Ps. *Bless the Lord, O my soul:* * *and let all that is within me bless his holy name.*

The Introit opens with the psalm-intonation of the third mode *g a c c,* and is repeated with variations over *poténtes virtú-(te), qui fácitis ad audi-(éndam),* either at the beginning of the phrase or part of the phrase. The interval of a fourth over *(Ange)-li* prepares us for the accent of *e-jus* and the important melodic structure over this word. For there is question here of *His* angels, those who have remained faithful to God. They possess marvelous strength and virtue, and all this strength, their entire being, they place in God's service. Lucifer, in his vain delusion, it is true, cried: "I will not serve;" the good angels, however, are like the stars. When God calls them, they answer: "We are here," and serve Him with gladness. For to be allowed to serve God is their glory. This they have learned from their intrepid leader, St. Michael. As soon as God manifests His will in any manner whatever, they obey without hesitation, without delay, without seeking the reasons. *Ad audiéndam vocem*: as soon as they know that God wills a thing, they carry the behest into execution.

We now entreat and exhort the angelic spirits to praise the Lord. And with one accord these countless legions render their hymn of praise with a melody powerful, pure, and inspiring.

With such excellent guidance we now dare to direct our song heavenward. The choir of angels sweeps us along with all that we have and are, and all the graces and blessings that God has implanted in our hearts impel us to join with them.

Over *fácitis verbum ejus,* as well as over *sermónum ejus,* quiet two-note groups are sung. Noteworthy, although not exceptional, is the fact that the principal and the secondary accents of *audiéndam* have only one note each, while the following syllable has several notes.

Festal joy characterizes the entire Introit.

GRADUAL (Ps. 102: 20, 1)

1. *Benedicite Dominum omnes Angeli ejus*: 2. *potentes virtute, qui facitis verbum ejus.* ℣. 1. *Benedic anima mea Dominum*, 2. *et omnia interiora mea nomen sanctum ejus.*

1. *Bless the Lord, all you his angels*: 2. *you that are mighty in strength, that do his will.* ℣. 1. *Bless the Lord, O my soul*: 2. *and all that is within me, bless his holy Name.*

With slight differences the Gradual has the same text as the Introit. Almost all the formulas of the melody are typical. The first half-phrase occurred on the third Sunday of Lent, as likewise the entire second phrase of the verse. *Corpus* and verse have the same florid closing cadence over *ejus*, and the same extensive cadence at the close of the first phrase over *ejus* and *(Dómi)-num*. In the *corpus*, *(Dómi)-num* and *(virtú)-te* have the same endings, while the subsequent phrase in each case begins with an interval of a fourth. In the verse *(Dómi)-num* and *(me)-a* have a similar ending. The interval of a fifth over *verbum* is peculiar to this Gradual.

ALLELUIA VERSE

1. *Sancte Michael Archangele, defende nos in praelio*: 2. *ut non pereamus in tremendo judicio.*

1. *Holy Archangel Michael, defend us in the battle*: 2. *that we may not perish in the dreadful judgment.*

In this Alleluia, assignable to the eleventh century, we discern a more clever motivation than that exhibited in the Alleluia-verse of Pentecost and the third Sunday after Pentecost. Here the form is a, b, b¹, b.

The song has a ring like that of the clashing of swords. Its initial motive begins with a sharp accent and then continues somewhat heavily. In the second member, *d ǵgf á* becomes *g áag ć*, in the third *a ́bba d*; and after a relaxation *g áag c* recurs. Over *práelio* we have the same form as over the third member. The address in apostrophe at the beginning shows gradual development, is then followed by an intrusting *defénde*. The singer then sees himself drawn into battle, and extreme distress forces from him the cry: *ut non pereámus*.

He who cannot vindicate himself in the final judgment is lost forever. Hence, O holy Michael, warrior of God and defender of souls, do thou stand by us! Help us to conquer in the battle against the devil and his host in this battle, which is daily, almost hourly, being waged against us! "Do thou, Prince of the heavenly host, by the power of God thrust down into hell Satan and all the wicked spirits who wander through the world seeking the ruin of souls!"

Sancte Míchael and *treméndo judício* have the same melody. Over *allelúia* it appears in a simplified form, no doubt, because the word has only four syllables. This melody is cleverly adapted to the Alleluia on the Commemoration of St. Paul (June 30); there it beseeches the Apostle of the gentiles for his powerful intercession.

The ancient manuscripts assign to today's feast a typical melody of the fourth mode with the text *Laudáte Deum omnes Angeli ejus.*

OFFERTORY (Apoc. 8: 3, 4)

1. *Stetit Angelus juxta aram templi,* 2. *habens thuribulum aureum in manu sua*: 3. *et data sunt ei incensa multa*: 4. *et ascendit fumus aromatum in conspectu Dei,* 5. *allelúia.*

1. *An Angel stood near the altar of the temple,* 2. *having a golden censer in his hand*: 3. *and there was given to him much incense*: 4. *and the smoke of the perfumes ascended before God,* 5. *alleluia.*

1. An angel is standing before the altar of God when in spirit we bring our gifts to the altar to add them to the sacrificial gifts of the priest. In a mute way our gifts say, as once said St. Michael: "Who is like God!" They acknowledge God's infinite perfection and our absolute dependence upon Him. Would that we might offer our gifts with the purity and devotion of the holy angels!

In the first phrase almost every word with any prolonged melody conveys something special to us, particularly the word *Angelus.*

2. The angel had a censer of great value. The gift we chanters bring, our compositions and their rendition, ought also to have artistic value. The diminished chord over *habens* receives its natural resolution in the subsequent *f*. In its first half *aúrem* resembles *templi*; in its second half, *aram* of the first phrase. The motive over *in manu sua,* which we hear again at the end of the third and fourth phrases, has a truly festive ring.

3. "There was given to him much incense." Surely it would be ignoble if we were to be niggardly with God. *Ei* is a condensed form of *templi.*

4. Practically at the same time that we are singing this phrase, clouds of incense are ascending at the altar during a solemn high Mass. Thus song and liturgical action are joined. The melody graphically describes how the sweet-smelling incense is wafted upward, how at the top of the canopy the clouds disperse and slowly settle, only to be borne aloft again by new clouds. From the angel's golden censer came rays of heat and the glow of fire. In a similar manner the soul of the creative or imitative artist must glow. That which proceeds from the soul must ascend upward to the presence of God, must seek to glorify Him. Only then will our chant lift the hearts of the faithful aloft to God. May the sentiment of the hymn for Terce be verified in us: *Flamméscat igne cáritas, accéndat ardor próximos*—"Let love light up our mortal frame, till others catch the living flame."

Over *ascéndit* the *pressus* on *c, c, f, a,* form the points between which the melody undulates. A *crescendo* should develop here which reaches its summit in the last group before *-dit*. The following are to be sung in two-note groups: *ég, ác, ác, áa, ga, f. Fumus* resembles *aram,* while *arómatum* is like *templi.*

5. The second group of *allelúia* reminds us of the motive over *templi.*

The fact that it has nine members ending on the tonic and not one on the dominant *(a)* detracts somewhat from the possibilities of the piece.

Today's Offertory gives the impression that it belongs to the second (plagal) mode.

This melody is also sung on the feast of All Saints to the text *Justórum ánimae,* and, with the same text, in the third Mass for several Martyrs; likewise in the Mass for Deliverance in Time of Pestilence to the text *Stetit póntifex,* and its first half on the feast of St. Peter's Chair at Rome (January 18) to the text *Tu es Petrus.* In some places it is sung on the feast of St. Vincent de Paul (July 19) to the text *Inclínet.*

The angel stood very near to the altar. Formerly that also was the place assigned to the singers. If in many instances they are now physically distant from the altar, they should strive the more to be very near it in spirit.

COMMUNION (Dan. 3: 58)

1. *Benedicite omnes Angeli Dominum: 2. hymnum dicite, et superexaltate eum in saecula.*

1. *All ye Angels of the Lord, bless the Lord: 2. sing a hymn, and exalt him above all forever.*

The Communion repeats the mode and content of the Introit and the Gradual. Again and again the choirs of angels are exhorted to the praise of God. A single summons does not suffice. The prophet is not content simply to say, "Praise the Lord," but he cries, "Sing a song and exalt him above all forever." Today this *superexaltáte* contains a special signification. Lucifer had cried, "I will ascend into heaven, I will exalt my throne above the stars of God" (Isa. 14: 13); but today the angels sing, "How art thou fallen, O Lucifer, who didst arise in the morning.... Thou wast brought down to hell, into the depth of the pit" (Isa. 14: 12, 15). And without ceasing they proclaim with Michael: "Who is like God!"

The melody, indeed, is not inspired by this thought; it manifests a dignified reserve. *Benedícite* begins with a reverential awe and descends to low *d* before the following interval of a fourth. The same occurred twice in the foregoing Gradual. After this, however, a greater energy manifests itself. *Hymnum dícite* repeats the melody of *omnes Angeli.* At the close, the significant *in saécula* is well accented and receives a melody florid as no other. It has, nevertheless, the same range, the same intervals, and above all the same solemn spirit as the beginning.

The fact that our Lord deigned to make us partakers of the Bread of Angels in Holy Communion, should impart special consolation to us when exhorting the angelic spirits to continue their never-ending *Sanctus, Sanctus!*

* * * *

THE HOLY GUARDIAN ANGELS
(October 2; in many churches on the Sunday nearest September 1)

This feast was extended to the universal Church in 1670.

The INTROIT and COMMUNION are identical with those of the feast of St. Michael; the GRADUAL, with that of the first Sunday in Lent.

ALLELUIA VERSE (Ps. 102: 21)

1. *Benedicite Domino omnes virtutes ejus:* 2. *ministri ejus,* 3. *qui facitis voluntatem ejus.*

1. *Bless the Lord, all ye his hosts:* 2. *you ministers of his* 3. *that do his will.*

In four different instances the angels are exhorted today to praise the Lord. The Alleluia-verse uses as its means the typical melody of the fourth mode, which we heard for the first time on the third Sunday of Advent.

In the text the angels are addressed as a heavenly host, as servants of God. But in His infinite goodness, God has appointed those who always serve Him to be our servants also, surely a signal honor and distinction. To each of us He addresses the words of today's Lesson: "I will send My Angel, who shall go before thee, and keep thee in thy journey, and bring thee into the place that I have prepared." In union with our guardian angels and all the choirs of angels, we join in offering a hymn of thanksgiving for this signal grace. With what alacrity they fulfill the *Benedícite Dómino* we address to them! And what solicitude they manifest to see that we arrive at that goal which God intended for us when he said: "I go to prepare a place for you." They make it their concern that we, like themselves, should become servants of God, prepared to carry out His every behest; that we, like themselves, should lead a spotless life, singing to God a pure song, so that one day we be allowed to join with them in an unending Alleluia. Their protection is our glory and our hope. For they belong to a victorious host *(virtútes)*, fighting the battles of God; against them all the forces of hell cannot prevail.

OFFERTORY (Ps. 102: 20, 21)

1. *Benedicite Dominum omnes Angeli ejus:* 2. *ministri ejus, qui facitis verbum ejus,* 3. *ad audiendam vocem sermonum ejus.*

1. *Bless the Lord, all ye his angels:* 2. *you ministers of his that execute his word,* 3. *hearkening to the voice of his orders.*

The Offertory has almost the same text as the Introit and the Alleluia-verse. The melody of the first two members is practically identical with that of the Offertory *Benedícam Dóminum* for Monday after the second Sunday in Lent. The rest, however, adheres faithfully to the Offertory of Passion Sunday; today's shorter text has been adapted to the original with extreme cleverness. The whole demands a lively, energetic rendition.

*   *   *   *

THE MOST HOLY ROSARY OF THE
BLESSED VIRGIN MARY
(October 7)

The INTROIT and the GRADUAL have been taken from the feast of the Assumption, except that in the Introit the word *Assumptióne* is replaced by *Solemnitáte*.

ALLELUIA VERSE

1. *Solemnitas gloriosae Virginis Mariae, ex semine Abrahae,* 2. *ortae de tribu Juda,* 3. *clara ex stirpe David.*

1. *This is the solemnity of the glorious Virgin Mary, of the race of Abraham,* 2. *of the tribe of Juda,* 3. *of the illustrious family of David.*

Here, in a most abbreviated form, is adduced the genealogy of the "Queen" of the Most Holy Rosary. Compare it with the Alleluia-verse for the feast of St. Joachim and the Communion for the solemnity of St. Joseph.

The energetic melody was explained on the feast of Corpus Christi. Used here, it can embellish the text, but not interpret it.

OFFERTORY (Ecclus. 24: 25, 38, 17)

1. *In me gratia omnis viae et veritatis,* 2. *in me omnis spes vitae et virtutis:* 3. *ego quasi rosa plantata super rivos aquarum fructificavi.*

1. *In me is all grace of the way and of truth,* 2. *in me is all hope of life and virtue:* 3. *as a rose planted by the water-brooks have I budded forth.*

The melody of the first and second phrases is taken from the feast of the Purification, due perhaps to the word *grátia*, which occurs in both Offertories. In content also the two texts are closely related. *Diffúsa est* seems to be the theme which is developed in the Offertory *In me*. It tells us wherein the plenitude of blessings which has been poured out upon Mary consists. The adaptation of the melody is extremely ingenious. Textually *omnis* in the first phrase belongs to the preceding *grátia*, just as in the second phrase we have *omnis spes*. The melody, however, would combine *omnis* and *viae*. Mary can indeed say of herself: In me is all grace of life; but also: In me is the grace of full, of entire life.

The third phrase has a construction proper to itself, even though it bears some resemblance to already existing melodies. The leading thought of the feast receives here a marvellous development. The Offertory of Palm Sunday with *dedérunt* and *acéto* served most probably as a model for the two final phrase-members.

Mary possesses "all grace." The mysteries of the Rosary further us on the "way of truth," the ideal of moral perfection, and offer us the means of realizing this ideal. We can, therefore, in truth say that Mary is "all hope of life and of virtue." Whoever imitates her, his soul will blossom like the rose and bear fruit for eternal life.

Musica sacra, 45, 213 ff.

COMMUNION (Ecclus. 39: 19)

1. *Florete flores quasi lilium, et date odorem, et frondete in gratiam:* 2. *collaudate canticum, et benedicite Dominum in operibus suis.*

1. *Send forth flowers, as the lily, and yield a smell, and bring forth leaves in grace*: 2. *and praise with canticles, and bless the Lord in his works.*

The melody is taken from the Communion *Confundántur supérbi* of the Mass *Loquebar* (for a Virgin Martyr); its phrasing, however, is not entirely happy. In the original, the first phrase treats of the godless ones who should be confounded and closes with the melody which we here have over *odórem*. *Injúste* (here *lílium*) expresses just anger over the wrong that has been perpetrated on the saint by her persecutors. Out of this dark and somber background rises the beautiful figure of a Virgin and Martyr with the words *Ego autem* (here *et frondéte*). In the ancient manuscripts the melody is assigned to the feast of St. Cecilia. The saint rises above all that is earthly, takes as it were her flight to heaven, and pledges immutable fidelity to the Lord's commandments. This magnificent line is interrupted on the feast of the Holy Rosary by a large pause after *grátiam*. The motive in the original stands over *in mandátis* but here begins a second phrase over *collaudáte*. This, as the *Gregoriusblatt* (44, 65) remarks, is obviously a mistake. Abstracting from this, the Offertory with its new text can be made extremely effective. The *clivis* and *torculus* over the closing syllables of *lílium, grátiam,* and *Dóminum* are as pleasing as flower-buds, while *collaudáte* is expressive of true joy.

By "flowers" *(flores)* we are, no doubt, to understand the mysteries of the Lord and His blessed Mother. In quiet meditation they will blossom forth, vivifying and invigorating our hearts. They will encourage us to praise the Lord, to glorify His works, and all that "the only-begotten Son by His life, death, and resurrection hath purchased for us" (cf. the Collect). They should glorify the deeds which the Lord has wrought upon His Mother, the victories of Lepanto and Temesvar, the marvels of grace in every individual soul, and not least, the work of redemption which He has renewed today in the Sacrifice and in the Eucharistic Banquet—for we are singing a Communion song.

Musica sacra, 45, 237 ff.

*   *   *   *

THE MATERNITY OF THE MOST BLESSED VIRGIN MARY

(October 11)

To counteract the false teaching of Nestorious, the Council of Ephesus in 431 declared and defined that Mary, of whom Jesus was born, is truly the Mother of God. As a fitting close to the fifteenth-centenary jubilee of this Council, Pius XI in 1933 extended the feast of the Maternity of the most Blessed Virgin Mary to the universal Church, thus according this article of faith solemn recognition in the liturgy also.

INTROIT (Is. 7: 14)

1. *Ecce, Virgo concipiet, et pariet filium et vocabitur nomen eius Emmanuel. Ps. Cantate Domino canticum novum, * quia mirabilia fecit.*

1. *Behold, a Virgin shall conceive, and bring forth a son, and his name shall be called Emmanuel. Ps. Sing ye to the Lord a new canticle: * for he hath done wonderful things.*

There are miracles which the omnipotence of God repeats now and then in the course of time. But the miracle He wrought in Mary, combining in her the dignity of virginity with that of maternal fecundity, was a thing so singular and exceptional that she alone was deemed worthy of it, and by it was exalted above all other creatures. As the heavenly Father offered His only-begotten Son for the world, so Mary presents to us in human form this only-begotten Son of God, the true Emmanuel —God with us. It is meet, therefore, that we sing a new canticle to the Lord.

The text of the antiphon forms the Communion for the fourth Sunday of Advent (q.v.). The psalm-verse is the same as that of the Introit for the third Mass on Christmas.

The melody employs various motives. Noticeable resemblance exists between *concípiet* and *cor meum* in the Introit *Tibi dixit* of the Tuesday after the second Sunday of Lent. *Fílium* and *et vocábitur* are practically the same as *Dómine* and *et sancti* of the Introit *Sacerdótes tui*. *Eius* resembles *mea* in the Introit *Ego clamávi* of Tuesday after the third Sunday of Lent, while *Emmánuel* corresponds to *prótege me* of the same Introit.

GRADUAL (Isa. 11: 1, 2)

1. *Egredietur virga de radice Jesse, 2. et flos de radice eius as-*

1. *There shall come forth a rod out of the root of Jesse, 2. and a*

cendet. ℣. Et requiescet super eum | *flower shall rise up out of this root.*
Spiritus Domini. | ℣. *And the Spirit of the Lord shall rest upon Him.*

"My memory is unto everlasting generations." These words, taken from the Lesson which precedes, are well ascribed to Mary since, according to today's Communion, she bore the Son of the eternal Father in her womb. Centuries and milleniums sought her and longed for her; she was the "rod" from which should blossom forth the most beautiful "flower." In another simile the Lesson refers to her as the "vine" which produces a "pleasant odor." The Spirit of God rests over the fruit of her womb. And in a solemn moment of some future day her Son will exclaim: "The Spirit of the Lord is upon Me. He hath sent Me to preach to the meek, to heal the contrite of heart." This Spirit of God rests over Him and remains in Him because the divine and human nature have been intimately combined in His person and will never be separated. This thought is suggested by the rich melody over *requiescet super eum.*

The melody is original to the Gradual of the nineteenth Sunday after Pentecost (q.v.). There the *corpus* has only one phrase, while the verse has two. Today, however, in accordance with the import of the text, the above division is reversed. A happy adaptation brings *flos* into pleasing prominence. The original, however, emphasizes the word-accent at the end of the *corpus* more effectively than is the case today. The initial motive over *eum* is first developed and its closing motive then abbreviated over *(Dómi)-ni.*

ALLELUIA VERSE

1. *Virgo Dei Genitrix, quem totus non capit orbis,* 2. *in tua se clausit viscera factus homo.* | 1. *O Virgin mother of God, he whom the whole world is unable to contain,* 2. *being made man, enclosed himself in thy womb.*

The Alleluia text is the same as that of the Gradual verse on the feast of the Assumption (q.v.). In the latter the word *Virgo* is given melodic prominence, while here the word *Génitrix* is characterized with particular splendor and reverential awe. The melody over *orbis in tua* of the Assumption corresponds to that over *totus non capit* of today. In reality, however, the complete melody for today is taken from the Alleluia *Leva in circúitu* for the feast of Mary, Mediatrix of all graces. The word-accents are very effective. The first member of each phrase is richly developed and strongly accents the third over the dominant, while the second member of each phrase is simpler and more quietly sustained. The melisma over *Géni-* is repeated over *-trix*. The latter also employs a much-used thesis of the first mode. The awe and amazement depicted over *Génitrix* continues to grow over *clausit*. So exalted, so inconceivable, and yet so sweet is the mystery that lies hidden in the soul of the Virgin Mother.

Allelúia with its joyful ascending movement is also sung on the feast of the Seven Holy Founders of the Order of Servites (Feb. 12). The *jubilus* has an arsis and a thesis in each of its members.

OFFERTORY (Matt. 1: 18)

1. *Cum esset desponsata Mater ejus Maria Joseph,* 2. *inventa est in utero habens de Spiritu Sancto.*

1. *When Mary, the Mother of Jesus was espoused to Joseph,* 2. *she was found with child of the Holy Ghost.*

Relative to their melodies, the following passages from today's Offertory and that of Quinquagesima Sunday should be compared: *desponsáta* and *Benedíctus es, María Joseph* and *(justificati)-ónes tuas, invénta est* and *in lábiis meis, in útero* and *judícia, Spí-(ritu)* and *(ó)-ris, Sancto* and *tui.* Thus the phrases whose melody is not founded on that of the Offertory of Quinquagesima Sunday are: *Cum esses, mater ejus,* and *habens.*

The adaptation of the melody is especially happy in this, that it emphasizes the dignity and honor accorded St. Joseph in becoming the spouse and protector of the Mother of God. St. Joseph also merits our gratitude for the faith, although severely tested, he had in the Blessed Virgin and for the love he bore her. According to the text, however, the second phrase which emphasizes the divine source of Mary's maternity should be stressed. "I am from on high," our blessed Lord says. And this applies not only to His divine nature but to His human nature as well, insofar as the genesis of the latter is due to the mysterious workings of the Holy Ghost. The dictum of St. Bede[1] nevertheless remains true: "Just as Christ is the Son of God and consubstantial with the Father, so is He also the Son of Mary and consubstantial with His Mother. Conceived in her virgin womb, He took upon Himself human flesh only from the body of His Mother."

COMMUNION

The Communion is the same as that on the feast of the Visitation. We have received the Son of the eternal Father into our hearts and

---

[1] *Commentary to Chapter II of St. Luke,* Book IV, Chapter 48.

so accepted the invitation of Mary in today's Lesson: "Come over to me, all ye that desire me, and be filled with my fruits." The same Lesson closes with the words: "They that explain me shall have life everlasting." This promise of the eternal Truth and—in the sense of the Liturgy—of the Mother of God should be a source of inspiration and consolation to all singers. The opportunities to sing the praises and virtues of Mary are abundant. Let us make use of them to show our ever-increasing awe and reverence for her exalted dignity as Mother of God, and to chant with ever-renewed love and gratitude the praises of her whom the Lesson calls "the Mother of fair love," who possesses "all grace of the way and of the truth...all hope of life and virtue."

*   *   *   *

ST. LUKE, EVANGELIST
(October 18)

The INTROIT and the OFFERTORY are the same as those on the feast of St. Andrew.

GRADUAL (Ps. 18: 5, 2)

1. *In omnem terram exivit sonus eorum: 2. et in fines orbis terrae verba eorum. ℣. 1. Caeli enarrant gloriam Dei: 2. et opera manuum ejus annuntiat firmamentum.*

1. *Their sound went forth into all the earth: 2. and their words to the ends of the world. ℣. 1. The heavens show forth the glory of God: 2. and the firmament declareth the work of his hands.*

This melody belongs to the type explained on the first Sunday of Lent. Its first phrase and first half of the second phrase are very closely related to the somewhat freer form found in the first and second phrases in the first Mass for Christmas. The text of the Offertory was explained on the feast of St. James.

The ALLELUIA VERSE is the same as that on the feast of St. James.

The COMMUNION is the same as that on the feast of St. Matthias.

*   *   *   *

SS. SIMON AND JUDE, APOSTLES

This feast, occurring on October 28, is not celebrated on a Sunday if it is only of the second class, since the feast of Christ the King falls upon the last Sunday of October.

The INTROIT is the same as that on the feast of St. Andrew; the GRADUAL as that on the feast of SS. Peter and Paul. The ALLELUIA VERSE has the typical melody of the eighth mode. The OFFERTORY is the same as that on the feast of St. James, the COMMUNION as that on the feast of St. Matthias.

*   *   *   *

KINGSHIP OF OUR LORD JESUS CHRIST
(Last Sunday in October)

Pope Pius XI brought the Jubilee Year of 1925 to a close with the introduction of this new feast. It was to be a continual reminder to the world of Christ's inalienable regal privileges, belonging to Him by virtue of His divine Sonship and His office as Redeemer. It was intended to bring about a subjection of all nations and individuals to the sweet yoke of Christ.

Old melodies were fitted to the texts of this new feast.

INTROIT (Apoc. 5: 12; 1: 6)

1. *Dignus est Agnus, qui occisus est, accipere virtutem, et divinitatem, et sapientiam, et fortitudinem, et honorem. 2. Ipsi gloria et imperium in saecula saeculorum.* Ps. *Deus, judicium tuum Regi da:* * *et justitiam Filio Regis.*

1. *The Lamb that was slain is worthy to receive power and divinity and wisdom and strength and honor. 2. To him be glory and empire forever and ever.* Ps. *Give to the King thy judgment, O God:* * *and thy justice unto the King's Son.*

Mankind has indeed witnessed numerous triumphs of the greatest solemnity. And although it seemed that their splendor could not be surpassed, yet other celebrations were held that eclipsed those that preceded. These also had their limitations, since they were earthly festivals. But when heaven celebrates its feasts, the feasts of its God, nothing is lacking, everything is perfect. There the homage of hearts entirely submissive becomes the homage of adoration and praise of an infinite Being and the glorification of a deed which God alone was able to perform. Of this homage, this adoration, this praise, the Apocalypse speaks in the twelfth verse of the fifth chapter and in the sixth verse of the first chapter. Ten thousand times ten thousand angels pay their respects, crying with a loud voice: "The Lamb that was slain is worthy to receive power and divinity and wisdom and strength and honor." *Because* Christ the Lamb was slain, He has earned this honor. No one has ever been so humiliated, no one has ever borne sorrow so great and

deep, as the Lamb of God in His voluntary sacrificial death. For all this
torture and pain, for all this derision and contempt, the hosts of heaven
now sing a pean of glory to the Lamb, and this song will resound unto
endless ages. It is directed to Him whom the Father has appointed absolute ruler, to the Son of the King, to the Son of God, to whom He has
intrusted all judgment.

Today, in the Introit of the Mass, the entire earth may also join in
this song. Today we are privileged to appear before the Lamb of God,
paying our homage and offering our adoration.

The vigorous text with its accents might have lent itself to a brilliant composition. Consider the marvelous effect produced by Handel
in his *Messias* with these words! If one were satisfied with the mere adaptation of an existing melody, a much more brilliant one might have been
found in the profuse wealth of the ancient chants. The melody chosen,
it is true, has a festal ring; but it is dominated by a guarded reverence,
at least in its first phrase, which prefers seconds and thirds. Only in the
second phrase, in which greater power is also discerned in the text, are
the intervals extended to a thrice-repeated fourth. Here the melody for
the first time becomes impressive. But he who is acquainted with plainsong, especially with the ferial chants of Lent, meets here many familiar
passages; he finds the original in the Introit *Dum sanctificátus fúero*,
sung on the Wednesday after the fourth Sunday in Lent, which announces to those to be baptized their cleansing through the pouring of
clean water and the gift of a new Spirit.

Small variations result from the different length, accent, and meaning of the text; thus the stressing of *Dignus* and *impérium*. The significant *occisus est* is fittingly brought to the fore; if *divinitátem* bears a
similar melody, this may serve to remind us that the Lamb of God receives these honors precisely because He has gone to a sacrificial death.
With *Ipsi glória* the rendition ought to be more lively and festal. The
original reaches its summit at *mundabímini*—"you shall be cleansed."
On account of today's short text, the melody of the final phrase of the
original—over *et dabo vobis spíritum novum*—is wanting; in place of it
we find over *saeculórum* the closing cadence of the Introit of the feast
of SS. Cyriacus, Largus, and Smaragdus (August 8).

GRADUAL (Ps. 71: 8, 11)

1. *Dominabitur a mari usque ad mare*, 2. *et a flumine usque ad terminos orbis terrarum.* ℣. 1. *Et adorabunt eum omnes reges terrae*: 2. *omnes Gentes servient ei.*

1. *He shall rule from sea to sea,* 2. *and from the river unto the ends of the earth.* ℣. 1. *And all kings of the earth shall adore him*: 2. *all nations shall do him service.*

Before the introduction of this special feast to commemorate the kingship of Christ, Epiphany was regarded as the feast of Christ the King. Since the chants were to be borrowed from other feasts, it was only natural to take them from Epiphany. This, beyond doubt, explains the fact that the Gradual of Epiphany has been carried over to the new feast, note for note. Another reason may be seen in this, that the text of the Gradual of the new feast and of the second half of the Offertory of Epiphany correspond exactly. But the adaptation evidences a delicate sense for rhythm and truth of expression.

Special attention ought to be given to the beginning and close of the verse. At Epiphany the melody begins immediately with an interval of a fifth. There the exhortation *Surge*—"Arise and be enlightened!"—wishes to be as impressive as possible. We find the word-accent on the very first syllable. Today it occurs only on the fourth syllable, being introduced by a series of low notes. This constitutes the only feature not borrowed immediately from the Gradual of Epiphany. At Epiphany *orta est* with its interval of a fourth might remind one of the flaring up of divine splendor. We do not find this interval over the text *(sérvient) ei*—"They shall do him service"—the reason perhaps being that instead of the dactyl *orta est*, the melody in the present instance has at its disposal only the spondee *ei*.

These may appear small matters. But he who possesses a sense for the beautiful flow of melody and, above all, for truth of expression, will appreciate them. Things such as these give the original its artistic value. Perhaps *aurum*, which begins with a fourth, and which in the original hints at the value of the gift, should have been slightly altered in the adaptation. No doubt the insignificant *et* is surprised at the prominence that has been given it.

One is tempted to ask whether the magnificently swelling melody, which over *illumináre* portrays the waxing of the light from the first ray of morning to the full glare of noonday, fits well with the quiet text *(et adorábunt) eum*.

But our song cannot be joyous enough, festal enough, if we think of those who gather from all the ends of the world in a mighty, invisible stream to do homage on their knees to Christ their King. They realize that the rule of this King concerns but their welfare, and that in themselves alone have the words of today's Lesson been verified. For it is God the Father "who hath made us worthy to be partakers of the lot of the saints in light: who hath delivered us from the power of darkness, and hath translated us into the kingdom of the Son of his love, in whom we have redemption through His blood, the remission of sins" (Coloss. 1, 12 f.).

In an extended form the initial motive of *Dominábitur* returns over *a mari usque*, and in its original form at the close of *terrárum*. The resolved descending major chord *c–a–f* over *términos* and *(terrá)-rum* gives the piece a bright ring. In the verse the descending *c a f* is twice extended to *d a f* over *eum*. This descent may be looked upon as a symbol of adoration.

ALLELUIA VERSE (Dan. 7: 14)

1. *Potestas ejus, potestas aeterna, quae non auferetur*: 2. *et regnum ejus, quod non corrumpetur.*

1. *His power is an everlasting power, that shall not be taken away*: 2. *and his kingdom that shall not be destroyed.*

The melody agrees exactly with that of the second Alleluia-verse for the fourth Sunday after Easter.

In the following schema we give in the first place the text of the Sunday just mentioned, and in the second that of the new feast, indicating how the latter agrees with the original melody:

1. *Christus resúrgens ex mórtuis=*
2. *Potéstas ejus potéstas aetérna,*

1. *jam non móritur:=2. quae non auferétur:*

1. *mors illi ultra non dominábitur=*
2. *et regnum ejus, quod non corrumpétur.*

Is it, perhaps, that the adaptation of *non móritur* and *non dominábitur* to *non auferétur* and *non corrumpétur* has led to the borrowing of the entire melody? For both verses have a related thought-content and portray similar sentiments. The one speaks of the fullness of life which has to fear death no more; the other of the plenitude of power which none can diminish, which can neither weaken nor collapse. And in the *Credo* we sing: *Cujus regni non erit finis*—"His kingdom shall have no end."

In the original the second phrase has a richly developed melisma over the word *mors*. Here it is placed over the insignificant *et*. This doubtless causes difficulties in some minds and suggests the question: Would it not have been possible, since it was a matter of choice, to select a different melody and thus have avoided this defect?

But, really, the matter is not so serious, for the melody exhibits remarkable phrasing. We see that even chants of the classical period do not shrink from embellishing a word like *et* with a florid melisma, for example the Alleluia for the fifth Sunday after Pentecost. Above all we are to grasp this thought: "Christ's power is invincible." This is made the easier, since the second phrase continues in a sort of parallelism the thought already clearly expressed in the first phrase. Hence this *et* should also be sung with the joy of victory. Like the original, the melody over *mors* is a song of triumph coming from the lips of the "the Prince of life." *Quod non corrumpétur* repeats *Allelúia* with its *jubilus*.

The TRACT has the typical form. During the Paschal season, the ALLELUIA is taken from the Mass for the feast of the Crown of Thorns, celebrated on the Friday after Ash Wednesday; in the thirteenth century it was sung to the text *Qui confídunt*.

OFFERTORY (Ps. 2: 8)

1. *Postula a me, et dabo tibi Gentes hereditatem tuam, 2. et possessionem tuam terminos terrae.*

1. *Ask of me, and I will give thee the gentiles for thine inheritance, 2. and the uttermost parts of the earth for thy possession.*

Coming from the lips of anyone else, these words would be presumptuous, a promise which no man could fulfill. And even when occasionally the then known world had to bow to a single sovereign, many years did not elapse before everything again fell into ruins. God alone has a right to speak these words, and God alone can bring their promise to completion. He will found a kingdom which, as we may infer from the preceding chants, will have limits neither of space nor of time.

Furthermore, Christ alone has the right to express such a desire *(Póstula)*. For He is the Son of God by essence, and the fidelity with which He fulfilled the work His Father gave Him to perform assures Him of an eternal reign.

The melody is reminiscent of chants we hear at Christmastide. Quite probably the beginning of the Offertory of the third Mass for Christmas, with its mystic obscurity and its reserve, in contrast to the powerful text: "Thine are the heavens, and Thine is the earth," served as a model for the first phrase. Here we call to mind the saying of Adalbert Stifter: "That which is truly great does not trumpet forth; it exists and thus exerts its influence." The two Offertory texts express related thoughts. Beginning with *haereditátem* we hear the melody from the Offertory of the Christmas Midnight Mass over the words *exsúltet terra*: "Let the earth be glad before the face of the Lord, because He cometh." Thus today's Offertory makes clear to us the words of the heavenly Father concerning Christmas joy; adding thereto with tender voice the message of that peace for which the subsequent Secret prays in particular. The most potent reason, however, for this universal reign of Christ is given in the Preface in these words: Thou "didst anoint with the oil of gladness Thine only-begotten Son, our Lord Jesus Christ, the eternal Priest and universal King."

After *Gentes* a half pause is indicated. Considering the text, one should prefer a greater pause after *a me*; thus the exhortation *Póstula* and the promise *dabo* would be more effectually separated. The melody of the original, however, demanded a different grouping. The fact that *haereditátem* recites on *e*, and not like the original on *f*, produces a pleasing effect. The notes over *Póstula*, which begin the Offertory for Sexagesima Sunday, are the only ones which do not have the sound of Christmas about them.

The whole should portray the dignity and solemnity of the words of the heavenly Father; dynamic climaxes should not be wanting, especially over *possessiónem tuam*.

COMMUNION (Ps. 28: 10, 11)

Sedebit Dominus Rex in aeternum; Dominus benedicat populo suo in pace.

The Lord shall sit king forever; the Lord will bless his people with peace.

In the Offertory we were reminded of the Christmas chants. With its melody the Communion carries us back to the preparation for that great feast. Its very first word repeats the melody of the Communion of Ember Saturday in Advent. The rest employs the melody of the Communion of Ember Friday in Advent from *sancti ejus* on with slight variations. Here again an inner relationship exists between the two texts. The Communion of Advent speaks of the Parousia, when the Lord will return in glory, bringing all His saints with Him. Today's Communion contemplates the Lord sitting upon His throne, which will never be shaken, which will stand forever. The word *aetérnum* receives melodic prominence. The Lord blesses His people. As the Preface says, He presents them with "a kingdom of truth and life, a kingdom of holiness and grace, a kingdom of justice, love, and peace." In the holy Sacrifice He has blessed His people with all heavenly blessings and graces; He has given Himself to His people in the Sacrificial Banquet. And every Communion acts as a preparation for eternal union with God, and gives an anticipatory taste of that eternal peace with which Christ the King will favor those who, as the Postcommunion says, have battled with Him and conquered with Him. He will fulfill His promise: "To him that shall overcome, I will give to sit with Me on My throne; as I have also overcome, and am set down with My Father on His throne" (Apoc. 3: 21).

Of all this the melody sings simply and modestly, without display, without agitation, without any great development. The plain, rhythmic torculi, which lift the middle note an interval of a second, strengthen this impression. It is the song of the King of peace.

The chants of this new feast betray throughout adaptations of older melodies. This should not, however, spoil our joy in singing them. Each of them is like a new stanza added to a beloved old song, awakening memories of the most beautiful seasons of the liturgical year.

*   *   *   *

ALL SAINTS DAY

(November 1)

"All Saints is a feast of exalted joy; a memorial day dedicated by the Church militant to the honor of its triumphant members in heaven, to its own welfare and consolation. It is a feast full of unrestrained jubilation and thanksgiving. Wide horizons unfold themselves before the meditating eye, presenting views similar to those seen by the inspired, heaven-rapt disciple on Patmos in the golden depths of eternity. Peoples, nations, tongues, innumerable hosts of men, all and each of them a thought of God, a picture of God, a world, a marvel of divine creative power, of divine redemptive love and wisdom. All perfect and transfigured, illumined by the sun of eternal bliss, surrounded by the rays of glory emanating from God's sublime majesty and from the throne of the Lamb. All joined in one immense family of God, members of one Body. The most sublime and glorious ideal realized in all of them: Christ in them, God in His Christ, God all in all" (C. O., 50, 147).

Only in the ninth century was this feast definitely introduced into the Church. Hence we ought not wonder if we find no references to it in the most ancient manuscripts of plainsong. The chants have been borrowed in part from older feasts;[1] some parts, like the Alleluia and the Communion, have been composed in the classical style of plainsong.

It is the feast of All Saints. Scarcely another feast brings out the truth so forcibly, that God is the Sun from which emanate all those rays we admire in the saints. Already in the Invitatory for Matins the Church sang: "Come, let us adore the King of kings, for He is the Crown of all the saints."

---

[1] C. O., 50, 147.

INTROIT

1. *Gaudeamus omnes in Domino, diem festum celebrantes sub honore Sanctorum omnium*: 2. *de quorum solemnitate gaudent Angeli, et collaudant Filium Dei.*

1. *Let us all rejoice in the Lord, celebrating a festival day in honor of all the saints*: 2. *at whose solemnity the angels rejoice and give praise to the Son of God.*

This Introit was explained on the feast of the Assumption.

In the antiphon *we* have been exhorted to rejoice; in the psalm-verse (Ps. 32: 1) we cry to the saints:

Exsultate justi in Domino: * *rectos decet collaudatio.*

Rejoice in the Lord, O ye just: * *praise becometh the upright.*

GRADUAL (Ps. 33: 10–11)

1. *Timete Dominum omnes sancti ejus*: 2. *quoniam nihil deest timentibus eum*, ℣. *Inquirentes autem Dominum non deficient omni bono.*

1. *Fear the Lord, all ye his saints*: 2. *for there is no want to them that fear him.* ℣. *But they that seek the Lord shall not be deprived of any good.*

The text exhibits parallelisms: *Inquiréntes...Dóminum* corresponds to *Timéte...ejus*; *non deficient...bono* corresponds to *quóniam nihil...eum*. Of this parallelism the melody takes notice insofar as the endings of these two parts agree: *eum—bono*. In the ancient plainsong manuscript we find this piece with the same text for the feast of St. Cyriacus.

In the middle and at the close the first phrase of the *corpus* has the same rhythm; in this feast we have already met related tone-sequences. *Quóniam* in the second phrase is like *omnes* in the first. *Nihil* predominates almost like a reminiscence of *nihil sollíciti sitis* in the Introit for the third Sunday of Advent.

After the fifth note over *(Inquirén)-tes* in the verse a brief pause for breathing will have to be made. It portrays an earnest seeking of and tending toward God. This is brought out by the ascending fifth and the rise to high *c*. Here, indeed, we meet tone-sequences with which we are acquainted from other sources; thus the groups immediately before and after the first pause in the Gradual for the twenty-second Sunday after Pentecost over *(unguén)-tum*, the group after the second pause on the first Sunday in Advent over *mihi*, the group after the third pause in the Gradual *Dómine* from the Mass of holy Abbots over *vitam*. The second half of the phrase sustains itself on *f*.

To whom are these words addressed? In accordance with St. Paul's mind, we may suppose *Sancti* to refer to all those who belong to the Church, through which they have been sanctified and called to personal holiness. Those speaking are the saints in heaven, just as the angel in the Apocalypse calls out with a loud voice: "Fear the Lord, and give Him honor." Today they look down lovingly upon us, filled with the desire that one day we also may be united with them. They indicate the way, admonishing us: Fear God, seek God! This fear of God must be such that it awakens the longing after God, the desire for Him; and Him alone, in our souls. The saints were true seekers of God. In all things and everywhere they looked for Him and found Him. The florid melody reminds us that in all the events of life, in all misfortunes and disillusionments, whatever their magnitude and number, the eyes and the hearts of the saints remained fixed on God. Others may have pursued pleasures and honors and wealth, but *(autem)* they sought God. In Him, where alone true joys are to be found, were their hearts firmly established.

But at the same time they tell us how God rewarded them for all their sufferings, labors, and privations. In the contemplation of God they feel no further need, for no good is wanting to them. They confirm this statement by their own experience. For they possess God, the highest good, and in Him they have all that the human heart can desire; and because God is eternal and immutable, their happiness can never diminish, can never be lost, or undergo change.

"This song echoes the admonition which the saints so often heard while following the Lord upon earth in the pilgrim's vesture of this sinful humanity. The gentle, humble song is wafted to them as from afar, from a distant past; not as a woeful sigh and a suppliant petition; but as a glorified remembrance, a greeting from remote well-known lands where once they lived, struggled, and conquered" (C. O., 50, 149).

ALLELUIA VERSE (Matt. 11: 28)

1. *Venite ad me, omnes qui laboratis, et onerati estis*: 2. *et ego reficiam vos.*

1. *Come to me, all you that labor and are burdened*: 2. *and I will refresh you.*

This Alleluia again is a prelude to the subsequent Gospel and its beatitudes. Its splendor, its solemnity, and its triumphant joy is spread over the melody like the light of a glorious dawn. It is one of the most valued chants in the Graduale, one which grips the singer spontaneously.

Indeed, there is mention of those who are afflicted and heavily burdened. But the Saviour invites them to Himself; and according to the interpretation of the composer of the plainsong melody, He has

placed in this invitation a fullness of consolation and refreshment, of
liberty and bliss. Although we must admit that the melisma over *laborátis* is considerably drawn out, yet there is nothing oppressive about
it, nothing that suggests pain or sore distress. It is a thorough Alleluia-
song, giving one the impression that all difficulties have been overcome,
just as the saints in heaven with joy and fervent thanksgiving to God
now cast a glance backward at their earthly existence.

The *jubilus* has the form $a + a^1$, b, c, c^1. We find that the melody
of *Allelúia* likewise begins the verse *Veníte*. The b-member of the *jubilus* has exerted an influence on the melody over *omnes*. "If in the beginning with *Veníte ad me* the melody was tender and mild, almost in-
gratiating, with *omnes* it rises wide and high, as if Christ were opening
His arms to embrace the many thousands" (*C. O.*, 50, 150).

The melisma over *laborátis* with its fifty-two notes clearly reveals
the structure: a b b a; a is repeated immediately after the third pause,
contracting the individual notes over *qui laborátis* into a *torculus*. Here
the motives ascend forcefully upward. Contrasting with this, we find
between these motives the descending motives c and c^1 of the *jubilus*.
"Scarcely has the word *refíciam* been uttered, than the entire choir
joins in. The melody of *allelúia* rises to the lips. For they have experienced a hundred and a thousand times the meaning of this *refíciam*.
They can only thank, praise, and rejoice, and in their hearts and on their
lips the grateful response to the promise of Christ finds expression in
the melody of the *jubilus*, until it once more brings this gripping, highly
dramatic picture to a close" (*C. O.*, 50, 150).

In the subsequent Gospel we are shown how God comforts His
people. He will console and give them their fill, will show them mercy,
and will lead them to the contemplation of Himself; they will be called
and truly be children of God: He will give them His heaven. Would
that we might think of this oftener in this our earthly exile!

Today the Saviour has again invited to Himself all who have come
to the house of God. In the sacred Mysteries He will be our strength,
and through them He will prepare us for that eternal Alleluia with
which the streets of the heavenly Jerusalem forever resound.

OFFERTORY (Wisd. 3: 1, 2, 3)

1. *Justorum animae in manu
Dei sunt,* 2. *et non tanget illos tor-
mentum malitiae*: 3. *visi sunt oculis
insipientium mori*: 4. *illi autem
sunt in pace,* 5. *alleluia.*

1. *The souls of the just are in
the hand of God,* 2. *and the torment
of malice shall not touch them*: 3. *in
the sight of the unwise they seemed
to die,* 4. *but they are in peace,* 5.
alleluia.

Our souls come from the hand of God, and by His grace they are justified; in God's hand they will rest secure as long as their will is in accord with God's will. God will then protect His faithful ones as the apple of His eye. Man's malice may try to subvert them in every possible way, may try to entice and seduce and conquer them by threats and violence, by chains and prisons, but all efforts will prove fruitless. It is true, the lives of the saints were not free from temptation and storms, pain and worry and misfortunes. Nevertheless, already in this life God fulfilled in them the promise given by the mouth of the prophet: "Behold I will bring upon him as it were a river of peace, and as an overflowing torrent the glory" (Isa., 66: 12). Obviously the foolish man has no conception of this rich, ample, bright and blissful state. For him life is dreary and sad; it is a living death.

In the next world, how happy are the souls of the just in the hand of God! How secure from all assaults of evil! There is found peace, eternal peace in God.

Today during the celebration of the sacred Mysteries, we are privileged to taste again of this peace; we are allowed to rest in God's hand, to rest on His breast, and to drink of the fullness of His life.

The melody was explained on the feast of St. Michael. The happy adaptation of this text was accomplished in the twelfth century. We are tempted to ask why the small word *autem* was favored with such florid neums. In the original we find them over *ascéndit*, which easily lends itself to tone-painting. But we must take into consideration not so much the word as the entire thought. This part, with its jubilant melody, forms a magnificent contrast to *mori* ("to die") with its low pitch in the preceding phrase. Individually, the phrases, according to their text, are shorter than those of the original. This might explain the omission of the descent to the fourth below the tonic which we find there at the end of the second, third, and fourth phrases.

"The priest offers up pure sacrificial gifts in the sight of God. With these gifts also the earthly sufferings and heavenly joys of the saints ascend to the throne of God. A most mysterious and most intimate connection is thus forged between their lives and the life and death of Christ. Their lives are woven into His sacrifice, and together with the Eucharistic Sacrifice they are immolated to God. The singer recognizes this; he would also have his song ascend to heaven bright and clear as the clouds of incense which he sees rising from the altar" (*C. O.*, 50, 151).

COMMUNION (Matt. 5: 8–10)

1. *Beati mundo corde, quoniam ipsi Deum videbunt*: 2. *beati paci-*

1. *Blessed are the clean of heart, for they shall see God*: 2. *blessed are*

fici, quoniam filii Dei vocabuntur: 3. *beati qui persecutionem patiuntur propter justitiam,* 4. *quoniam ipsorum est regnum caelorum.*

the peacemakers, for they shall be called the children of God: 3. blessed are they that suffer persecution for justice' sake, 4. for theirs is the kingdom of heaven.

Our attention is once more called to three of the eight beatitudes which the Lord announced to us in today's Gospel and which are given to us, as it were, to take along into life. The first half of the first phrase mentions the beatitude, while the second half comprises its argument. In the third phrase the beatitude forms an independent melodic phrase, as does also its argument. Thus there result four musical phrases, the first and last of which have an identical musical rhythm, while the other two, written a third higher, have practically the same rhythm (*N. Sch.* 232). This melodic correspondence may serve to remind us that basically all the beatitudes are but the fulfillment of this word of God: "I am...thy reward exceeding great" (Gen. 15: 1).

Special attention should be given the threefold *beáti.* The first, as if sung by angels' voices, sets in on the dominant of the mode, transcending the misery of sin. The descending movement which follows brings, as it were, the purity of heaven down to earth. The beatitude embraces here the range of a fourth. Peace and simplicity characterize the second phrase, which ranges within a minor third. To be a harbinger of peace is the quiet yet blessed work of the "children of God." The third *beáti* has an entirely different ring. It proclaims that even when you must undergo persecution, when you must bring sacrifice to be just and to uphold what is right, when you must suffer to protect and defend the Church, then also are you blessed, for the kingdom of heaven awaits you. This third *beáti* the Church wishes to be deeply engraven on the soul. No persecution, however vehement, can drown its triumphant ring. It seems to encourage us with the words of Tertullian: "One Christian is greater than the whole world." Even though *ć a, ć g, á g, á g* over *persecutiónem patiúntur* may sound like the strokes of a scourge, like the striking of stone against stone, still the heart of the martyr is hopeful and happy as he sings: *beáti!*

In Holy Communion we were allowed to contemplate God, we were privileged to receive the King of peace into our hearts, and with Him the kingdom of heaven: He it is who gives us strength for sacrifice and for persecution. And He will remain with us until He can endow us with His entire blessedness for all eternity, until, united with all the saints, we can render Him our thanks without ceasing.

*   *   *   *

ALL SOULS DAY
(November 2)

The commemoration of the souls of all the faithful departed originated with Abbot Odilo of Cluny (✚ 1048). In the very earliest plainsong manuscript, however, we already find an *Agenda Mortuorum*, a Mass liturgy for the deceased, with the same Introit and Gradual as in today's Mass.

Today's liturgy affords us a searching glance into the motherly heart of the Church. She is, as St. Augustine tells us on this day, the *pia mater communis*, the loving, solicitous mother of all. She forgets none of her children, even when they have passed from this life and their name is no longer remembered. She prays and offers the Sacrifice of atonement for all of them. And these sentiments the faithful make their own.

A supernatural quiet seems to hover over the prayers and chants of this day; they express unbounded confidence in God's merciful love. Over the liturgy of the dead of the first Christian centuries, one might inscribe the words: *quia pius es....* Thou, O God, art goodness, mildness, and mercy. This spirit pervades especially today's Introit, Gradual, (Tract), and Communion. The Middle Ages, however, have altered this spirit by stressing almost exclusively the idea of jugdment and punishment for sin—the leading thoughts of the Sequence *Dies Irae*. The liturgy knows nothing of this spirit which is dominated by a purely human sadness over the departure of a loved one, as if there were no eternal life. Such sentiments must by no means be allowed to influence the interpretation or the rendition of today's chants.

INTROIT

1. *Requiem aeternam dona eis Domine:* 2. *et lux perpetua luceat eis.* Ps. *Te decet hymnus Deus in Sion, et tibi reddetur votum in Jerusalem:* * *exaudi orationem meam, ad te omnis caro veniet.*

1. *Eternal rest give to them, O Lord:* 2. *and let perpetual light shine upon them.* Ps. *A hymn, O God, becometh thee in Sion, and a vow shall be paid to thee in Jerusalem:* * *hear my prayer, all flesh shall come to thee.*

The very first words of the Introit bring the devout petition and the leading thought of the day. We implore eternal rest for the faithful departed—the Church's prayer of predilection whenever she thinks of her beloved dead. She already prayed thus in the third century, for we can trace these words to an epitaph of that time.

The divine Saviour has said: "Take up My yoke and learn of Me . . . and you shall find rest for your souls." But we all know how easily human weakness betrays us. Man's life upon this earth is a warfare, and not a few fall in the battle. Under the trials, disappointments, and the enticements of this life, in bodily pain and distress of soul which often sadden and embitter the final moments of life, man's heart becomes vacillating and unstable. Hence we pray for those who have preceded us: Lord, grant unto them eternal rest, take them into Thy kingdom of eternal, immutable peace, draw them to Thy heart!

"And let perpetual light shine upon them!" Perhaps in the storms of life the supernatural light was often threatened with extinction. The departed may have for a time pursued illusory objects, or may have determined to be a light unto themselves and not always lived as children of light. In Thy goodness, O Lord, forgive them their folly. Now, when all other lights have been darkened, when the world with its attractions and seductions has disappeared, the only thing they long for, the only thing they desire is Thy eternal light. Thou art that immense Sun, toward which their entire being gravitates, the Sun that never sets, *lumen indeficiens*; every being that approaches Thee Thou dost enrich with a blissful eternity.

This, also, is the mute prayer of the many candles which, according to ancient custom, are lighted during the Mass for the Dead. Formerly candles were not only used to illumine the subterranean burial places, but were also a symbolic prayer for light.

Our most powerful intercessor, however, is Christ in the Sacrifice of the Mass. He is the Sun of justice; in His sea of light He can cleanse all the defects that mar the human soul, and with His infinite merits supply its needs and deficiency of love and make reparation for it.

Filled with confidence in the reparatory power of the holy Sacrifice, the psalm-verse begins joyfully: *Te decet laus*—"A hymn, O God, becometh Thee." How often have eternal rest and eternal light been asked of God, and how often has He granted the prayer! How many have attained Him, singing in a blissful spirit as they entered into heaven: *Te decet laus*!

"The psalm is a harvest song. At one time all Israel made a pilgrimage to God in Jerusalem and offered Him the first fruits of the harvest according as they had vowed. So we also, in order to sing a fitting hymn to God in Sion for His many blessings, bring to the Lord in the deceased member of our community the gift of a ripened spiritual harvest *(votum)*, that thus, being united in the closest manner to Christ's sacrifice, he may find eternal rest and eternal light. The world of this psalm portrays such a consoling picture of the soul that has departed in the Lord, that, as in bygone days, we should like to hear more: 'The words of the wicked have prevailed over us: and Thou wilt pardon our transgressions. Blessed is he whom Thou hast chosen and taken to Thee: he shall dwell in Thy courts. We shall be filled with the good things of Thy house; holy is Thy temple, wonderful Thy justice' " (*Betende Kirche*, p. 572 f.).

The melody of the antiphon is especially warm and pleasant. Something of the quiet of death, or better, of the peace of eternal life, or again of heartfelt sympathy with those who have been bereft of a loved one seems to hover about it. As soothing balsam it penetrates the afflicted heart. The parallelism of the text is reflected in the melody.

Each of the four half-phrases closes with a quiet *clivis*: $g\,f$ and $g\,f\,f$, and each phrase with the same rhythm. In the second phrase the cadence sets in on the fifth last syllable: *lúceat eis*. The first phrase closes with a dactylic word *(Dómine)*, over the first syllable of which, as is often done, a single note is set: *(do)-na eis (Dó)-mine*. In the first phrase the melody grows gradually: $f\,g$, $f\,ga$, $f\,g\,a\,c$, and then, as in the second phrase, come those serene closing notes: $g\,f$ and $g\,f\,f$. *Aetérnam* —only eternal rest can satisfy the human heart—receives prominence through its *pressus*. With *(e)-is* care must be taken that the high point of the melody be not neglected; nevertheless c must not be accented. In the first phrase each member began on the tonic f; in the second phrase they all set in on the dominant a. *Perpétua* has not the heavy *pressus* of *aetérnam*; here everything is lighter, one might almost say more spiritual, reminding us of a descending light. In the closing rhythm, the top notes of the melody give the following descending line: $c\,b\,a\,g\,f$.

This Introit has two psalm-verses. The first has a solemn intonation but is wanting in the solemn Introit-psalmody as noted in the most ancient manuscript. We have here the simple form, which Dom Pothier tries to justify in *Revue* (15, 153). We also note the mournful *mediatio correpta* over the Hebrew words *Sion* and *Jerúsalem*.

The text of the antiphon is closely related to a verse of the apocryphal fourth Book of Esdras (20: 34). Psalm 64, of which our verse in an excerpt, bears the inscription: "To the people of the captivity, when they began to go out." Even more than the captive Jews, the souls in Purgatory yearn for their fatherland, the heavenly Sion, where they shall glorify God for all eternity.

Revue, 21, 74 ff.; *Analyses*, 3, 23 ff.; *Gregoriusbote*, 42, 117 ff.; *Rottenburger Monatsschrift*, 6, 101 ff.; Merk, *Die Totenmesse mit dem Libera* (Stuttgart, Schloz, 1924).

At first the Kyrie with its quiet seconds preserves intact the spirit of the Introit. Then, however, it has as a new motive the descent below the tonic to *e* which the Introit always avoided, and as its highest point *b*, which must not be accented. It should be sung thus: *f g á b a a*. The final Kyrie, with its inception on a descending and ascending fifth and its rise to high *d*, sounds like the persistent knocking at the gate of heaven to ask mercy for the poor souls. The quietly descending seconds intimate that the prayer has been heard.

GRADUAL

The corpus has the same text as the Introit-antiphon.

℣. (Ps. 111, 7) 1. *In memoria aeterna* 2. *erit justus*: 3. *ab auditione mala* 4. *non timebit.*

℣. (Ps. 111, 7) 1. *In everlasting remembrance* 2. *shall be the just man*: 3. *of the evil hearing* 4. *he shall not fear.*

The melody was explained on the first Sunday of Lent, and is practically the same as that sung on Easter Sunday. For Christ's resurrection is the pledge of the resurrection of our beloved dead and of our own resurrection. In the Latin countries, the poor souls are frequently referred to as "holy souls," and with good reason, for they are possessed of sanctifying grace, which renders them "just" and assures them heaven, even though they have still to make atonement for some of their offenses. In God's courts they were given a favorable verdict. Although the world may be harsh and unjust in its judgments, they are now far removed and it can affect them no longer. And though they must suffer the effects of God's justice, yet they are fully conscious that God will be their final end. How pleasing and sublime is the effect of this verse in the liturgy of the dead!

TRACT

1. *Absolve, Domine, animas omnium fidelium defunctorum* † *ab omni vinculo delictorum.* 2. *Et gratia tua illis succurente,* † *mereantur evadere judicium ultionis.* 3. *Et lucis aeternae* † *beatitudine perfrui.*

1. *Absolve, O Lord, the souls of all the faithful departed* † *from every bond of sins.* 2. *And by the help of thy grace* † *may they be enabled to escape the judgment of punishment.* 3. *And enjoy the happiness of eternal light.*

Ordinarily the Tract is taken from one of the psalms. Here, however, we have an example of an oration from the best period of the liturgy. Verses one and three pray for the departed. The second verse pictures to us the decisive moment before the awful judgment, which is emphasized still more in the Offertory.

Except that the first verse has a florid intonation, the first half of all three verses is alike, having also the same middle cadence. The second half of the first and second verses shows the same descending formula, which sets in one syllable before the word-accent: -lictórum, -tiónis. The third verse has a florid closing melisma.

Here the chants, so far of a quiet character, take on a gloomier coloring, yet even now the petition for liberty and light, yes, eternal happiness, predominates above all else. The melody is not in the serious second mode, but in the lighter, brighter eighth mode.

SEQUENCE

The Franciscan Thomas of Celano (1200–1255?) is considered the composer of this Sequence, although we find his name attached to it only a century later. Not before the second half of the fourteenth century was this song included in the Requiem Mass, having been previously employed merely for private devotion. It was prescribed for universal adoption in the sixteenth century. It seems that the serious and solemn trochees were created particularly for the awful scene here described. "This monumental piece of poetry could make even a Goethe tremble. The reference to it in his *Faust* has been duly noted by the modern Christian and non-Christian world of *littérateurs*. And even today it serves to remind us that the poetical powers of the Middle Ages need fear nothing by comparison with the poetry of a later period, indeed, that the latter in great part shares in the heritage of the former" (A. Baumgartner, S.J., *Weltliteratur*, IV, 458).

Exclusive of the last six verses, there are three double strophes that repeat the same melody thrice. In the first strophe the second verse extends beyond the melodic peak of the first verse. In still greater measure the second double strophe predominates over the first and third. The text concerning the blasts of the trumpet may have influenced the composer. The third verse descends to low *a* once, the third double strophe does the same twice. The fact that every strophe, as well as every individual verse, closes on the tonic, heightens the force of this chant and has the effect of the somber tolling of bells. Berlioz, who employs all the possibilities of the modern orchestra in his *Requiem*, admits that in the unbounded wealth of musical art there is nothing to compare with the effect produced by this plainsong Sequence.

FIRST PART (STROPHES 1–6)

By its vivid portrayal of the end of the world and the final judgment, this part grips one's very being.

1a. *Dies irae, dies illa,*
     Solvet saeclum in favilla:
     Teste David cum Sibylla.

1a. *That day of wrath, that dread-*
     ful day,
     When heaven and earth shall
     pass away,
     Both David and Sibyl say.

1b. *Quantus tremor est futurus,*
     Quando Judex est venturus,
     Cuncta stricte discussurus!

1b. *What terror then shall us befall,*
     When lo, the Judge's steps
     appal,
     About to sift the deeds of all!

2a. *Tuba mirum spargens sonum*
     Per sepulchra regionum,
     Coget omnes ante thronum.

2a. *The mighty trumpet's marvel-*
     lous tone,
     Shall pierce through each
     sepulchral stone
     And summon all before the
     throne.

2b. *Mors stupebit, et natura,*
     Cum resurget creatura,
     Judicanti responsura.

2b. *Now death and Nature in*
     amaze
     Behold the Lord His creatures
     raise,
     To meet the Judge's awful gaze.

3a. *Liber scriptus proferetur,*
     In quo totum continetur,
     Unde mundus judicetur.

3a. *The books are opened, that the*
     dead
     May have their doom from
     what is read,
     The record of our conscience
     dread.

3b. *Judex ergo, cum sedebit,*
     Quidquid latet, apparebit:
     Nil inultum remanebit.

3b. *The Lord of judgment sits*
     Him down,
     And every secret thing makes
     known;
     No crime escapes His vengeful
     frown.

SECOND AND THIRD PARTS (STROPHES 7–17)

After consideration of the terrific drama enacted at the end of the world and at the final judgment, the consciousness of guilt rises before the mind. Forthwith the soul turns to prayer, hoping for forgiveness on the basis of Christ's redemptive work, and finding consolation in the

fact that even a Mary Magdalen and a thief on the cross found pardon.
An ardent petition goes forth to be numbered among the saved, among
those who will stand at the right hand of the Judge (Merk, *Die Totenmesse*, p. 72).

1a. *Quid sum, miser tunc dicturus*
     Quem patronum rogaturus?
     Cum vix justus sit securus?

1a. *Ah, how shall I that day en-
     dure:*
     *What patron's friendly voice
     secure,*
     *When scarce the just them-
     selves are sure?*

1b. *Rex tremendae majestatis,*
     Qui salvandos salvas gratis,
     Salva me fons pietatis.

1b. *O King of dreadful majesty,*
     *Who grantest grace and mercy
     free,*
     *Grant mercy now and grace to
     me.*

2a. *Recordare, Jesu pie,*
     Quod sum causa tuae viae:
     Ne me perdas illa die.

2a. *Good Lord, 'twas for my sin-
     ful sake,*
     *That Thou our suffering flesh
     didst take;*
     *Then do not now my soul for-
     sake.*

2b. *Quaerens me, sedisti lassus:*
     Redemisti crucem passus:
     Tantus labor non sit cassus.

2b. *In weariness Thy sheep was
     sought;*
     *Upon the cross His life was
     bought;*
     *Alas, if all in vain were
     wrought.*

3a. *Juste judex ultionis,*
     Donum fac remissionis
     Ante diem rationis.

3a. *O just avenging Judge, I pray,*
     For pity take my sins away,
     *Before the great accounting-
     day.*

3b. *Ingemisco tamquam reus:*
     Culpa rubet vultus meus:
     Supplicanti parce, Deus.

3b. *I groan beneath the guilt,
     which Thou*
     *Canst read upon my blushing
     brow;*
     *But spare, O God, Thy supli-
     ant now.*

THIRD PART

1a. *Qui Mariam absolvisti,*
Et latronem exaudisti,
Mihi quoque spem dedisti.

1a. *Thou who didst Mary's sins unbind,*
And mercy for the robber find,
Dost fill with hope my anxious mind.

1b. *Preces meae non sunt dignae:*
Sed tu bonus fac benigne,
Ne perenni cremer igne.

1b. *My feeble prayers can make no claim,*
Yet, gracious Lord, for Thy great Name,
Redeem me from the quenchless flame.

2a. *Inter oves locum praesta,*
Et ab haedis me sequestra,
Statuens in parte dextra.

2a. *At Thy right hand, give me a place*
Among Thy sheep, a child of grace,
Far from goats' accursed race.

2b. *Confutatis maledictis,*
Flammis acribus addictis:
Voca me cum benedictis.

2b. *Yea, when Thy justly kindled ire*
Shall sinners hurl to endless fire,
Oh, call me to Thy chosen choir.

3a. *Oro supplex et acclinis,*
Cor contritum quasi cinis:
Gere curam mei finis.

3a. *In suppliant prayer I prostrate bend*
My contrite heart like ashes rend,
Regard, O Lord, my latter end.

FOURTH PART

Here the verse-structure and the melody change. Three dimeters follow. No doubt, this close was added only after the whole had been adopted for liturgical use. Still we find it in some old manuscripts.

1. *Lacrimosa dies illa,*
Qua resurget ex favilla,

1. *Oh, on that day, that tearful day,*
When man to judgment wakes from clay,

2. *Judicandus homo reus.*
Huic ergo parce, Deus:

2. *Be Thou the trembling sinner's stay,*
And spare him, God, we humbly pray.

3. *Pie Jesu, Domine,*
   Dona eis requiem. Amen.

3. *Yea, grant to all, O Saviour*
   Blest,
   Who die in Thee, the saints'
   sweet rest. Amen.

The second half of the first and second verses has the same melody. *Judicándus* produces a marvelous effect. The subsequent *huic ergo* ought to be sung more softly, after which *Pie Jesu* should be rendered with the utmost devotion.

Although the double strophes of each of the first three parts have the same melody, still in every instance the text will give the cue for the rendition, without of course, introducing any sharp contrasts.

Formerly this Sequence was sung after the Mass for the Dead, as the procession made its way from the church to the cemetery. In some places it was sung in Advent as a preparation for the coming of the universal Judge.

Schulte, A., *Die Hymnen des Breviers nebst den Sequenzen des Missale* (Paderborn, Schoeningh), p. 200 ff.; *Stimmem aus Maria-Laach*, 42, 512 ff.; Kayser, H., *Beitraege zur Geschichte und Erklaerung der alten Kirchenhymnen* (Paderborn, Schoeningh); *Revue*, 16, 46 ff.; Dreves-Blume, *Ein Jahrtausend lateinischer Hymnendichtung*; Gihr, *Dies Irae*.

OFFERTORY

1. *Domine Jesu Christe, Rex gloriae, libera animas omnium fidelium defunctorum de poenis inferni, et de profundo lacu:* 2. *libera eas de ore leonis, ne absorbeat eas tartarus, ne cadant in obscurum:* 3. *sed signifer sanctus Michael repraesentet eas in lucem sanctam:* 4. *Quam olim Abrahae promisisti, et semini ejus.* ℣. 1. *Hostias et preces tibi Domine laudis offerimus:* 2. *tu suscipe pro animabus illis, quarum hodie memoriam facimus:* 3. *fac eas, Domine, de morte transire ad vitam,* * *quam olim Abrahae promisisti, et semini ejus.*

1. *O Lord Jesus Christ, King of glory, deliver the souls of all the faithful departed from the pains of hell and from the deep pit:* 2. *deliver them from the mouth of the lion, that hell may not swallow them up, and they may not fall into darkness;* 3. *but may the holy standard-bearer Michael introduce them to the holy light:* 4. *which thou didst promise of old to Abraham and to his seed.* ℣. 1. *We offer to thee, O Lord, sacrifice of praise and prayers:* 2. *do thou receive them in behalf of those souls whom we commemorate this day:* 3. *grant them, O Lord, to pass from death to that life,* * *which thou didst promise of old to Abraham and to his seed.*

Great difficulties are experienced in the explanation of this text. Some would translate *defunctórum* not by "departed," but by "dying." Considered in this light, the prayer carries us to the moment of death, where it will be decided whether the soul will be condemned to eternal darkness or whether it will attain to perpetual light. We may pray thus for those who will die today, as well as for all men, whom, as today's Preface says, "the certainty of dying afflicteth;" we can also call to mind the approaching hour of our own dissolution. In the present instance, *líbera* does not signify "deliver," but rather "preserve from," just as the various invocations of the Litany of the Saints do not always presuppose that we have been afflicted with the evils there enumerated, but pray for protection against and preservation from them. Hence we here implore the King of glory to preserve the dying from the pains and the darkness of hell. This first part, with the twofold *líbera*, is the negative part.

The significant *sed* leads to the second, the positive part, with its petition for the "holy light." St. Michael the standard-bearer, was once victorious in the struggle against the evil spirits; may he lead also our souls to true peace. He is the angel who bears the gifts and the prayers of the faithful to heaven, letting them ascend like sweet-smelling incense (Offertory for his feast); may he bring our souls after that most important moment of death to the holy light, so that we also may become partakers of the promises made by God to Abraham. May God become our reward exceeding great.

This antiphon is perhaps native to Ireland. Originally the verse did not belong to it. In reality it is a Secret, a silent prayer for the deceased. Today's sacrifice, however, is also a sacrifice of praise, because it is the Sacrifice of Christ. It is Christ who imparts to it its efficacy. Hence we confidently hope that the departed, by virtue of this sacrifice, may pass from death to life. The verse harks back to the last phrase of the antiphon. The composer has treated the two parts as a whole.

The melody is not so tender as that of the Introit, nor so powerful as that of the *Líbera*. It is serene, serious, a prayer with restrained emotion. Frequently it recites on the tonic. Only in two passages does the melody become somewhat florid, first to give the words *Rex glóriae* prominence, and secondly with *sémini*, that by means of tone-painting it may cast a sweeping glance over the innumerable children of Abraham, entrusted to him by virtue of God's promise. The passage $\acute{d} f e \acute{d} e c$ corresponds to $\acute{d} f e \acute{f} g e$. *Christe* rhymes with *(glóri)-ae*, and the two *líbera* have similar introductions. Alternately the melody over *defunctórum* is expanded and contracted over *de profúndo lacu, ne absórbeat eas tártarus, Abrahae promisísti, (a)-nimábus illis, (me)-móriam fácimus.* Related to it is the motive over *Hóstias*, which opens the verse. This motive, recurring several times, makes the petition here expressed more appealing. *De ore leónis* with its fourth and accented *g̣* is especially powerful, making one almost see the hellish lion with its distended jaws. *Repraeséntet eas* has practically the same formula; the energetic fourth, however, is wanting. It is sung gently and brightly, similar to the third and fourth phrases, in accordance with their lucid text.

The petition of the verse is more fervent. Its first phrase confines itself to the range of a fourth. The second phrase gives prominence to the words *tu, quarum hódie*, and *transíre*, and demands a rendition of special warmth. Thou wilt graciously accept the offerings we bring for those whom we particularly commemorate today, and we trust and know that Thou wilt bring them to eternal life.

In more than thirty instances, the accented syllable has a higher pitch than the following syllable, and is also frequently higher than the preceding syllable.

If any chant deserves to be sung prayerfully, with serene confidence in God's goodness and with inner emotion, it is today's Offertory.

Revue gr., 6, 165 ff. and 205 ff.; *Rassegna*, 2, 488 ff.

The SANCTUS begins with the closing note of the Preface, whose natural continuation it is. Hence the celebrant's pitch is to be taken in this manner: *dicéntes: Sanctus. Glória tua* and *nómine Dómini* (each having a cadence with two accents) remind us of *Dignum et justum est* while the second *Hosánna* reminds us of *Per ómnia saécula*.

The AGNUS DEI is the same as that at the end of the Litany of the Saints. The petition *dona eis* should be sung impressively, but without harshness. *Sempitérnam* and *réquiem* are sung without an intervening pause.

COMMUNION

1. *Lux aeterna luceat eis, Domine*: * 2. *Cum sanctis tuis in aeternum, quia pius es.* Ꝟ. 1. *Requiem aeternam dona eis Domine, et lux perpetua luceat eis*: * *Cum sanctis tuis in aeternum, quia pius es.*

1. *May light eternal shine upon them, O Lord*: * 2. *With the saints for ever, because thou art merciful.* Ꝟ. 1. *Eternal rest give to them, O Lord, and let perpetual light shine upon them*: * *With thy saints for ever, because thou art merciful.*

The Communion harks back to the thoughts of the Introit, setting them forth in brighter light. It is a song of triumph, a song of victory. Such were the sentiments of the early Christians when, singing, they bore to the tomb the remains of those who were privileged to become a sacrifice to Christ through martyrdom. The antiphon *Iste Sanctus*, sung at the *Magnificat* on the feast of a martyr, begins and closes with the same melody as the Communion. We hear expressed today the conviction that the sacrifice of the Mass just completed has poured out the fullness of blessings over Purgatory, and that through its efficacy many souls have entered into the kingdom of comfort, of light, and of peace. They are now joined with the army of the saints *(cum sanctis)*, are themselves saints, entirely immersed in the blissful light of God. All that was obscure and confusing, that troubled them so frequently in their lives, has vanished. One truth alone shines out brightly before them: "All the ways of God are mercy and truth."

This Communion plays a very important part in the history of the liturgy, precisely because it alone preserves the old custom of having a verse follow the antiphon. Today this custom is retained in the Introit only. The psalmody is not of the simplest. Before the accent of the cadence a preparatory *d* is inserted, as we find in the solemn Introit-psalmody of the fifth mode; moreover, the second half of the verse has at its beginning a decorative *a*. In the antiphon, *Cum sanctis tuis* corresponds to *lúceat eis*. Something like the light of resurrection and the mild splendor of God's goodness ought to characterize the rendition: *quia pius es....*

RESPONSORY Libera

1. *Libera me, Domine, de morte aeterna, in die illa tremenda*: * 2. *Quando caeli movendi sunt et terra*: 3. *Dum veneris judicare saeculum per ignem.* ℣. *Tremens factus sum ego, et timeo, dum discussio venerit, atque ventura ira.* * *Quando caeli movendi sunt et terra.* ℣. *Dies illa, dies irae, calamitatis et miseriae, dies magna et amara valde. Dum veneris judicare saeculum per ignem.* ℣. *Requiem aeternam dona eis Domine: et lux perpetua luceat eis.* —*Libera me* [usque ad ℣.].

1. *Deliver me, O Lord, from everlasting death in that dreadful day*: * 2. *When heaven and earth shall quake*: 3. *when thou shalt come to judge the world by fire.* ℣. *I tremble and am sore afraid, for the judgment and the wrath to come.* * *When heaven and earth shall quake.* ℣. *O that day! that day of wrath, of woe and of tribulation! a great day and exceeding bitter. When thou shalt come to judge the world by fire.* ℣. *Eternal rest give unto them, O Lord, and let perpetual light shine upon them.*—*Deliver me* [to the ℣.].

In this responsory we no longer hear the expressions of peace, rest, and confident hope that characterized the prayers of the early Christians regarding death. Rather we find the fear and anguish that had laid hold of the mind of the Middle Ages, anticipating the impending destruction of the world. It is an impetuous appeal to the universal Judge. *Judicáre* dominates the entire piece, sounding almost like a shrill piercing cry. Only over this word does the melody ascend to high *c*. This phrase has indeed the greatest range, the largest intervals (fifth and fourths), and the richest, well-prepared development. The first three words have the range *c—f*, the subsequent three, *d—g*. In the second half of the first phrase, with the range *c—g*, the words *die illa* are accentuated by means of a higher pitch and also by means of the *pressus*, which had already served to strengthen *aetérna*. The second phrase points to the catastrophe that will shake both heaven and earth. The third phrase begins immediately a fifth higher than the closing note of the preceding; similarly *judicáre*. Rarely in plainsong are the accents which dominate members and phrases given such plastic prominence as here: *me, morte, die illa, movéndi, judicáre*, and rarely do we see such a carefully planned gradation. All this must be brought out in the rendition.

In a certain sense, the quiet, reserved character of the verses forms a contrast to the agitated *corpus*. They are almost syllabic and avoid large intervals, never going beyond *a*. Both in text and melody, the second verse without doubt formed the nucleus for the later Sequence *Dies Irae*; there also *judicáre* finds an echo in *tuba mirum spargens*. Originally the *Dies irae* served as a trope to *Líbera*; then it became a Sequence. Cf. *C. O.*, 49, 55 ff.

After the first verse the second phrase is repeated, after the second verse the third phrase, after the third verse, which exhibits special warmth with *Dómine* and gives impressiveness to the word *lux*, the entire *Líbera* up to *ignem* is sung again. The form here reminds us of the rondo. The melody in the Vatican Gradual can be traced back to the end of the tenth century.

These same chants are employed at the burial, on the third, seventh, and thirtieth day after death, and on the anniversary.

*   *   *   *

THE DEDICATION OF A CHURCH

In the most ancient manuscripts the chants of this Mass are found before the feast of Christ's Ascension. For at Rome the dedication of the Pantheon as a Christian Church *(Sancta Maria ad Martyres)*, in the year 607, that is, three years after the death of St. Gregory the Great, was celebrated on May 13.

The Mass formulary was considered the crown of the church's dedication, and in it each year we re-experience that which was consum-

mated at the time when our parish church and our mother church
(metropolis), the cathedral of our diocese, received its solemn consecration at the hands of the bishop. In this way every church is again intimately united in a special manner to the "Mother and Mistress of all
churches throughout the world," the cathedral church of the Pope, St.
John Lateran in Rome. Hence it is that the entire Catholic world com-
memorates the consecration of this church on November 9. On November 18 our thoughts again travel to Rome when the consecration of the
churches of SS. Peter and Paul is solemnly commemorated.

INTROIT (Gen. 28: 17)

1. *Terribilis est locus iste:* 2. *hic
domus Dei est, et porta caeli:* 3. *et
vocabitur aula Dei.* Ps. *Quam dilecta
tabernacula tua, Domine virtutem!
* concupiscit, et deficit anima mea
in atria Domini.*

1. *Terrible is the place:* 2. *it is
the house of God, and the gate of
heaven:* 3. *and it shall be called the
court of God.* Ps. *How lovely are
thy tabernacles, O Lord of hosts! *
my soul longeth and fainteth for the
courts of the Lord.*

The first word of the Introit today again determines the attitude
of the soul. Deep reverence grips man when God approaches. The Patriarch Jacob was overcome with awe when in a dream he saw the
ladder reaching up to heaven. The same feeling fills the faithful soul
when it enters the church, for this is the house of God. "That Thou, O
God, wilt deign to visit this place, we beseech Thee, hear us!"—this
was the underlying spirit of the prayers at the consecration of the
church. The soul knows that prayer here has not been in vain. With a
ring of conviction it sings: "This is the house of God." And in the *tre-
mendum Mysterium* of the Mass, Christ appears among us in His divinity and His transfigured humanity. Then the church becomes the
gate through which heaven, yea, the Lord of heaven comes to us; it
becomes the courtyard of heaven, bringing to us an anticipation and
taste of the joys that await us there; it consecrates and sanctifies our
souls so that one day they may inhabit the heavenly mansions.

Precisely for this reason the holy reverence which overshadows the
soul is not something oppressive of which we would wish to rid ourselves,
but a reverence blended with an inner happiness. Exceeding lovely is
the tabernacle of God among men; for the souls of men yearn and lan-
guish.

The first phrase sets in as if bowing profoundly before the holiness
of the place, and has the effect of an A minor. The second phrase begins
and closes with C major and has a much brighter ring. Its close *fg ff*

éde bears some rhythmic similarity to *iste* in the first phrase with its
fgff éd. At the same time there is a tendency toward a cadence, which
in other melodies of the second mode, for example, in the Introit for the
first Mass of Christmas over *meus es tu*, is made to stand out in sharper
relief by means of *e*, which has the quality of a leading note. With its
ecac cdf the third phrase reminds us of *terríbilis est* of the first phrase,
while at the same time it has a *pressus* in common with the second
phrase. Thus the words *domus Dei* and *aula Dei* are given prominence.

Is the whole to be sung with gentle modulations, or should the accents be strong, almost violent? The former interpretation has the
greater appeal. The twofold tristropha would then graphically describe
the singer's trembling and awe for the mysteries of the Catholic house
of prayer.[1]

GRADUAL

1. *Locus iste a Deo factus est,
inaestimabile sacramentum,* 2. *irre-
prehensibilis est.* ℣. 1. *Deus, cui
adstat Angelorum chorus,* 2. *exaudi preces servorum tuorum.*

1. *This place has been made by
God; it is a mystery beyond measure,*
2. *it is free from all stain.* ℣. 1. *O
God, before whom the choir of angels
stands,* 2. *give ear to the prayers of
thy servants.*

God has traced the plans of the Catholic Church; He has created
its atmosphere and given it that supernatural strength from which its
faithful can so liberally draw. These attributes are as true and real as
they are mysterious; their consequences we see realized in the lives of
the saints. Each church is a mystery, a *Sacraméntum*; in it most of the
sacraments are also administered. No one can rightly define it nor rightly
estimate its value. In its very essence it shows forth the universal Church,
the Communion of Saints, the city of God in heaven, the Bride of Christ
for whom He has sacrificed Himself, that she might be glorious, without
spot or wrinkle *(irreprehensíbilis)*.

The "mystery beyond measure" which makes up the Church, has
been unveiled to some extent in the Epistle. The Church is a holy city;
she has come as a heavenly bride celebrating her espousals with Christ,
the Bridegroom, in the mystery of the Mass. There God comes to us
and takes up His abode among us; He becomes our God.

As mysterious as it is real, the entire drama is but an anticipation
and preparation for the eternal wedding feast in heaven. Then God shall
wipe away all tears and in His everlasting kingdom make all things new.

---

[1] *K. K.*, 23, 116 ff.

The *corpus* is quiet and serene. Actually it has a range of only a fifth. Once the melody goes below the tonic, and once it ascends above the dominant. *Inaestimábile* is modeled on *admirábile* of the ninth Sunday after Pentecost. Over *sacraméntum fgágfg* becomes *gaƀaga*. The resolved descending major chord occurs three times.

The verse exhibits great development. Its florid melisma over *(cho)-rus* is easily recognized; suffice it to mention only Maundy Thursday. The entire second phrase, text and melody, is taken from the second Gradual for the Ember Saturday of Lent.

God appears surrounded by His celestial court. In some churches the mural decorations depicted the choirs of angels. The thousands and tens of thousands of angels pay Him homage and are happy in His presence, all their desires being fully realized. We, on the contrary, have many things to ask for and to lament over: we must cry: *exáudi*—"hear our petitions!" And no matter how many or how great they may be, we may bring them all. Today, however, we will above all—*Imprimis*—pray for the Church, that God may protect, unite, govern, and preserve her in peace over the entire earth. We will pray that our souls also, created and redeemed by God, and sanctified through the sacraments, may ever retain their dignity as temples of God and ever strive after greater holiness. Only then can we hope that our prayers will be acceptable to God and worthy of being heard. Here it will be opportune to ask ourselves: What must be my attitude in choir so that I may measure up to the standard of the choirs of angels?

ALLELUIA VERSE (Ps. 137: 2)

1. *Adorabo ad templum sanctum tuum*: 2. *et confitebor nomini tuo.*

1. *I will worship towards thy holy temple,* 2. *and I will give glory to thy name.*

The beginning of this Alleluia shows some resemblance to that of the nineteenth Sunday after Pentecost. On the syllable *-ia* a *torculus* and then a *pressus* should be sung. The close of the verse has only the *torculus* of the second member and the last eight notes of the *jubilus*. According to Wagner[1] this Alleluia marks approximately the division between the archaic (Gregorian) and the classic (post-Gregorian) type of Alleluia. Indeed, he says that there is only wanting "the agreement of the coda of the verse with the jubilus and its symmetrical construction and brilliant melody," but that it shows a great step forward in comparison with the type portrayed in the three Christmas Masses.

---

[1] III, 402 f.

The first phrase portrays reverence, an awe-inspired reverence in the "holy temple" of God. The second phrase is a jubilant song of praise. Over *confitébor* the melisma with the form a a b is, according to Wagner,[1] "one of the most beautiful musical inspirations of the Middle Ages." To the solemn ascent to high *f* there is a corresponding recollected descent. Care must be taken not to sing the ascending notes too rapidly. The annotated manuscripts here give all the notes the broad form. The motive $f^1 f^1 c d$ is repeated delicately over *ccga*, followed by a repetition of the entire melisma. It would seem that we are listening to the fifth mode, were it not that *abc* leads us back to the seventh mode. This formula was already sung over the close of *(Ado)-rá-(bo)*. The group over *tu-(um)* is enhanced over *(tu)-o*.

Who prays thus? In Codex 339 of St. Gall's this Alleluia, text and melody, is assigned to the feast of the Purification. It is, therefore, really Christ Himself, who, in every church, at every Mass, adores the Father in spirit and in truth, who glorifies and praises Him in the measure that His infinite Being demands. Let us rejoice that we have one who can offer an adequate adoration, a worthy song of praise, and let us strive to render this song in a manner truly divine.

During the Paschal season the verse *Bene fundáta* is sung according to the melody which was explained on the feast of the Assumption. After Septuagesima the Tract *Qui confídunt* is sung as on the fourth Sunday in Lent.

Revue, 15, 34 ff.

OFFERTORY (1 Par. 29, 17–18)

1. *Domine Deus, in simplicitate cordis mei laetus obtuli universa: 2. et populum tuum, qui repertus est, vidi cum ingenti gaudio: 3. Deus Israel, custodi hanc voluntatem.*

1. *O Lord God, in the simplicity of my heart, I have joyfully offered all these things: 2, and I have seen with great joy thy people, which are present: 3. O God of Israel, keep this will.*

Simplicity and joy add a special odor of sweetness to the sacrifice that we offer to almighty God. There is no desire of retrenching in His sacrifice, nor do we feel ourselves to be a sacrificial lamb; we are conscious only of the happiness we experience in being allowed to offer God our gift. The first phrase of the Offertory sings of this simplicity and joy. Simplicity here seems to have derived its bright melody from joy—and the joy is entirely simple and unadorned. *Laetus óbtuli* could scarce be

---

[1] *l. c.*

sung with more modesty or with greater simplicity. The twofold bistropha must be sung lightly and must not be held longer than four
beats. *Univérsa* can be sung with a slight *crescendo*. The final groups
remind us of *Deus*.

The Gospel recounted with what readiness Zachaeus made sacrifice:
"Behold, Lord, the half of my goods I give to the poor, and if I have
wronged any man of anything, I restore him fourfold," and how pleased
the Saviour was with these words!

The second phrase is characterized by the "great joy" which here
seeks full expression; it should be sung with a great *crescendo*. The heart
of King David leaps with joy when he sees his people—yea, God's people
—enthusiastic to bring sacrifices. *Pópulum tuum* bears some resemblance
to the beginning of today's Gradual.

After the second phrase a large pause is to be made, for here a new
thought, a prayer is introduced: "Keep this will!" This phrase begins
with a soft, humble tone, expressing the wholehearted longing for God's
helping grace, while the following *custódi* is given some prominence. On
the closing syllable of *voluntátem* the joy of the first two phrases is once
more felt. Here two motives are interwoven: *ác ǵfg* and *gf ácf*, and in
both of them we find an echo of *fǵ ácff* over *óbtuli*. *Dómine Deus* possesses the simplicity and modesty of the first phrase.

It would be difficult to conceive of a more beautiful Offertory song.
Permeated with its spirit, the Secret continues: "Grant that all we...
by full and perfect devotion, be acceptable to Thee both in body and
soul; that we who now lay our votive gifts before Thee, may by Thy
help be found worthy to win Thine everlasting rewards."

As a pledge for this we hear these words from the lips of the Lord:
"This day I must abide in thy house." It is in Holy Communion that
He deigns to come into "our house" to sit at meat with us; and then we
experience that salvation has entered into our house, into our heart.

COMMUNION (Matt. 21: 13)

1. *Domus mea, domus orationis
vocabitur, dicit Dominus: 2. in ea
omnis qui petit, accipit: et qui
quaerit, invenit; et pulsanti, aperietur.*

1. *My house shall be called the
house of prayer, saith the Lord: 2.
every one that asks therein, receives:
and he who seeks, finds: and to him
who knocks, it shall be opened.*

This house is a house of prayer. The first two members of this
Communion would, as it were, engrave these words in large letters over
the entrance of the church; hence the many large intervals. The accented second *domus* sets in with a fourth; the fifth *c–f*, and the fourths

c–g and *b♭–f* occur at varying intervals. The third member with its sequence-like passages is then a quiet thesis after the great arsis. Its closing cadence was heard a pitch higher over *mea*. This unusual inception for a piece of the fifth mode demands clever manipulation on the part of the organist.

The second phrase has only seconds and thirds; its last member has the sole fourth. Throughout a preference is shown for the ascending and descending major chord *f–a–c*: *qui petit, (quae)-rit, ínve-(nit), (a)-perié-(tur). Omnis*—"every one" rightly receives a special accent. In the rendition a slight pause might separate the petition from its fulfillment, thus: *qui petit—áccipit*, etc. The second phrase, therefore, explains why the church is a house of prayer; it is there, namely, that our prayers are heard. Would that all the churches of the Catholic world might relate how much consolation they have dispensed, how many tears they have dried! Today the words of this Communion have again been realized in holy Mass. The heavenly Father did not give us stones when we prayed for our daily bread. We sought mercy and peace and found them. We knocked, and the gates of heaven opened and rained manna. Indeed, in the ultimate analysis we were not the ones who asked and sought and knocked; Christ is our intercessor; He it is who prays for us continually.

This Communion song is at the same time a song of invitation, calling us to return soon and often to this place of intercession, so that we also may share in its blessings.

The dedication of the church! Our soul also celebrates the feast of its dedication which took place at Baptism; this is the secondary thought that permeates the prayers of the rite of consecration. Just as in the dedication of the church, so at Baptism the priest commanded the evil spirit to depart from us; and after the saving waters had been poured upon our heads, the Holy Ghost with the Father and the Son made our souls their sanctuaries. And the holy oil and chrism with which we, as also the church, were anointed, was the pledge of our participation in the riches of God's infinite grace. We can, therefore, predicate of our soul the words: This is the house of God. If we make these truths a part of our everyday life, then our prayers and song will resound with a pure, full ring in the house of the Lord!

ASPERGES ME and VIDI AQUAM

Singers should make it a duty to consider also these chants as something sacred. Hence they will not make their appearance in choir during the time that holy water is being sprinkled or even afterward. Rather they will be there without exception from the very beginning, and assist wholeheartedly throughout the ceremony. These chants form a sort of overture to the sacrifice of the Mass. No orchestra, for instance, which takes any pride in its art and which values its reputation, will tolerate the presentation of its overtures by indispensable instruments only; it will demand that the entire ensemble be present for the whole program. These songs, however, play a much more important role, especially the *Asperges*.

ASPERGES ME (Ps. 50: 9)

1. *Asperges me, Domine, hyssopo, et mundabor*: 2. *lavabis me et super nivem dealbabor.* Ps. *Miserere mei, Deus*: * *secundum magnam misericordiam tuam.*

1. *Thou shalt sprinkle me with hyssop, O Lord, and I shall be cleansed*: 2. *thou shalt wash me and I shall be made whiter than snow.* Ps. *Have mercy on me, O God*, * *according to thy great mercy.*

Hyssop is a wild, bushy plant, which was employed in many ritual sprinklings of the Old Law. This sprinkling with hyssop symbolizes interior purification. Even the pagan Greeks and Romans used water in their various cults to symbolize the cleansing of the soul. In the Christian cult the use of holy water can be traced back as early as A. D. 200. In monasteries it was customary to sprinkle the various apartments with holy water every Sunday. Gradually this practice was adopted by the universal Church.

God is holiness itself; and when man appears before Him, the prayer of the publican forces itself to his lips: "God, be merciful to me a sinner!" If we consider the obligation we assumed when the waters of Baptism made us children of God—Sunday reminds us of this—and how often we have been unfaithful, then the *Aspérges* and the *Miserére* will well up from the innermost recesses of our souls. Furthermore, we have gathered to celebrate, in union with the priest, the sacrifice of the Mass, that awful Mystery, at sight of which even the angel choir of Powers trembles in reverence. With what sentiments of profound humility and contrition ought we to approach the altar!

But as sinners we have special duties. Before the priest sings the Gospel, he prays, bowing profoundly: "Cleanse my heart and my lips, O God almighty, who didst cleanse the lips of the prophet Isaias with a live coal: vouchsafe, of Thy gracious mercy, so to cleanse me, that I may worthily proclaim Thy holy Gospel." We singers also are messengers of God, announcing the divine word, and by our singing we can become the mediators of grace. This requires that our hearts be clean. Thus the *Aspérges* is to us what the *Munda cor* is to the priest. If a Cecilia prayed to the Lord: "Let my heart be spotless," how much more becoming is such a prayer to our own lips!

The text of the antiphon exhibits a pronounced parallelism, which is perfectly portrayed in the melody. *Aspérges me—lavábis me, (hyssó)-po et mundábor—(ni)-vem dealbábor.* Hence, we find rhythms not only at the ends of the phrases but also—a rare occurrence—at the beginning. The text shows a gradation of thought in the second phrase. In the first phrase, however, the melody treats the word *Dómine* with distinction, and this with good reason. For only the Lord in His great mercy can cleanse our soul, and thus make it worthy to take part in the celebration of the sacred Mysteries.

In the psalm-verse care should be taken that *magnam* and *misericórdiam* be sung without an intervening pause; similarly *sáecula* and *saeculórum.*

The first melody given in the Graduale can be traced to the thirteenth century. It is an expanded form of that which is found among the *Cantus ad libitum* (I), which dates from the tenth century. That marked II dates from the twelfth century. Its *lavábis me* is similar to that of the other two; it also has rhythms at the close of the first and second phrases; *d e* leads over to *c d.* We find in it expressions of more devout and suppliant feelings than in the other two. The psalm-verse with the harsh *b a g f e* is an admirable expression of a contrite heart. While the first two melodies employ the solemn Introit-psalmody, the third employs the simple psalmody.

Gregoriusbote, 23, 89 f. and 24, 3 f.—*Caecilia*, 23, 22 ff.

VIDI AQUAM (Ezech. 47: 2)

1. *Vidi aquam egredientem de templo a latere dextro, alleluia: 2. et omnes ad quos pervenit aqua ista salvi facti sunt, et dicent: alleluia, alleluia. Ps. Confitemini Domino quoniam bonus: * quoniam in saeculum misericordia ejus.*

1. *I saw water flowing from the right side of the temple, alleluia: 2. and all to whom that water came were saved, and they shall say: alleluia, alleluia. Ps. Praise the Lord, for he is good: * for his mercy endureth for ever.*

In vision the prophet Ezechiel sees the new Temple and the new worship that will replace the Mosaic. The mysterious waters flowing from the sanctuary remind us of the spring which was inside the old Temple to the right side—south for the Hebrews—which flowed into the valley of the Cedron and thence into the Dead Sea. These waters are an image of Baptism, of that Baptism which flows over the entire earth like a stream of water, freeing souls from original sin and some of its evil effects, giving new life and bestowing the strength to fully recuperate and attain the eternal salvation to which this Sacrament has given us a claim.

The water flowing from the right side of the sanctuary may serve as an allusion to the commixture of water and blood which flowed from the pierced heart of the Saviour, and as an indication that the baptismal water derives its supernatural power from the death of Jesus.

Psalm 117, which follows the antiphon, is the great Easter psalm, the psalm of the resurrection and the triumph of Christ. The present verse is sung in the Gradual for Easter Sunday.

In Christian antiquity the *Vidi aquam* was sung during the procession which, after the Vespers of Easter, led the neophytes back to the baptismal font. There they gave thanks with this song for the graces they had received. We can easily imagine with what fervor they sang *salvi facti sunt*, which marks the climax and which has an admirable melodic construction, and how enthusiastically all must have joined in the *allelúia!* The preceding *et omnes* shows affinity to a well-known form of Tract melody (cf. the passages *sitívit* and *fuérunt* in the Tract *Sicut cervus* for Holy Saturday). With the recitation of *pervénit* in a somewhat low pitch, *aqua* is brought to the fore so much the more prominently. The melodic descent over *ista* might remind us of a fine drizzling rain. This descent to the tonic is also a means of giving *salvi facti* a brilliant, victorious character. In this manner the second phrase is made to excel the first. We can speak here of the predominance of a rhythmic motive: *áf ág ǵ éb ba ć, áb ǵa ǵ, ďa ág á ǵa fǵ ǵ.* The melody over *-re dextro* is repeated over *et dicent*, each time before the inception of *allelúia.*

The whole piece demands an extremely energetic rendition, animated by the joy of Easter.

Since about the twelfth century *Vidi aquam* has been sung in place of *Aspérges* at the sprinkling of holy water during the Paschal season.

Caecilia, 24, 17 ff.—*La vie et les arts liturgique* (Liguge, Aubin), 9, 251 ff.

*   *   *   *

A LAST WORD

The celestial choir, with which the Preface of the Mass unites us, should be the ideal of our prayer and song. There the angels laud God's majesty: *Majestátem tuam laudant.* Every thought of self-praise and self-exaltation is foreign to them; they know naught else than the glorification of God. They look into the depths of His perfections and tremble in holy reverence. Before themselves they see the infinite expanse of God's holiness and beauty, and are urged to thank Him for His own great glory and for the glory into which He has deigned to elevate them. We should make our own that reverence which they experience before God's majesty. Like them we should have but this one object in mind: to glorify God, the immortal, eternal God. Then also something immortal, eternal will enter into our song. Then our song becomes endowed with an acoustic which ennobles everything it reaches, tempering that which is rough and hard, resounding unto eternity.

In heaven they sing *sócia exsultatióne*—"with common joy, in unison," for from the heart of the one God wells forth a stream of joy and bliss, encircling all the heavenly city. Little wonder that there all the streets resound with the cry of Alleluia. We, on the other hand, realize only too frequently that we have not yet reached our goal, that we are not yet in our true fatherland. We feel the difficulties and trials of our vocation. In like manner we know that polyphonic music is appreciated much more at a high Mass than plainsong, no matter how much effort is spent in its preparation and rendition. Hardly ever is there a word of praise or a mark of distinction for the singers of Gregorian chant; perhaps it will even be a matter of suffering persecution for the sake of justice and for that which the Church loves and desires. If this be the case, then the heavenly choir and its singing should be our model; then will we immerse our heart in this atmosphere of joy and relieve it, set it free, and revivify it. If the celestial choir exults and triumphs, then surely we will not consider the performance of our duty a matter of strict obligation. Rather will we mutually help and encourage one another that we also may realize a *sócia exsultátio*, a common happiness, a united joy. How happily this will materialize in plain chant! For plain chant can and does produce joy and happiness and jubilation, as these pages have shown more than once.

In heaven there is unceasing praise: *non cessant clamáre: Sanctus*— "They do not cease to cry out: *Sanctus*." In heaven every day—if we may designate time there—brings new knowledge, new marvels, new joy, and therefore a new song. This never-ending progress should be an ideal for us also. The more deeply we penetrate into the mysteries of the liturgy, the fuller will be our joy, and the more ardent our love for the liturgical chant. Polyphony, it is true, is in no way to be ousted from its rightful place; on the other hand, plainsong does not everywhere hold the position it deserves, nor does it receive the attention it demands in churches where it is sung. Let us formulate our resolve and once more draw our inspiration from the zeal of the heavenly choir, and with prudent, but unflagging application work for the realization of the program of Pope Pius X. Assuredly our work will not be in vain. We shall prepare our soul for a fervent concelebration of the Eucharistic Sacrifice—and the Lord will one day grant the petition of the Preface, and unite our voices to those of the heavenly choir.

```
                    B
                    E
                    N
                    E
          B E N E D I C A T
                    I
                    C
                    T
                    U
                    S
```

INDEX

(Abbreviations: A—Alleluia, C—Communion, G—Gradual,
I—Introit, O—Offertory, T—Tract, S—Sunday).

A

Accent, Influence on melody 62, 79 f., 107, 230, 298, 351
Adam of St. Victor 237
Adaptation of melodies 56, 346
Adducentur A. 38
Adorna 364
Advent: 1. S., 13 ff., I. and O. 5; 2. S. 20 ff., O. 4; 3. S. 27 ff., A., 374, I. 4, 241; 4. S. 34 ff..
Agatha 425
Agios O Theos 171
Agnus Dei (Requiem) 482
Alleluia 7 f.; archaic form 8, 18, 54; of Christmastide 59
All Saints 466 ff.
  Litany of 175 f.
All Souls 472 ff.
Amavit eum A. 272, 339
Amen 351
Andrew 353 ff.
Angelus O. 39
Anna 414 ff.
Arsis 242
Art, religious 10 f.
Ascension of Our Lord 211 ff.
  Sunday after 215 ff., A. 349
Ash Wednesday 111 ff.
Asperges me 490 ff.
Assumpta est O. 186

B

Bartholomew 434 f.
Beata es O. 39
Beethoven 108
B flat (*bb*) 134, 330, 348
Blood, Most Precious 403 ff.

C

Cadence, middle and final 2 ff., 14, 113
Caesura, with Tract 8 f.; with Gradual 95
Candlemas 362 ff., A. 354
Candor est A. 236
Caro mea A. 236
Chants, artistic whole 2
Chorus of ancient tragedy 81
Christmas, Vigil 41 ff., O. 5, G. 47; Feast: 1. Mass 45 ff., A. 8, G. 122 f., O. 87; 3. Mass 50 ff., A. 310, 395, C. 87, G. 280, O. 464
  Sunday after 69 ff.
Christmas carols 45 f.
Circumcision of our Lord 74 f.
Clamaverunt G. 301
C—mode 186
Communion 6
Concussum est A. 236
Confessor 89, 170
Contrast 4, 6
Corpus 6
Corpus Christi 232 ff.
  Sunday after 240 ff.
Cross: Finding of 385 ff., A. 237; Unveiling 170; Exaltation 435 ff.; Adoration 170 ff.
Crucem tuam 172

D

Dactyls 80, 87
Dante 175
Development of melody 7 f.
Dedication of Church 484 ff., 322, A. 310, 329